An Introduction to Object-Oriented Analysis

Objects and UML in Plain English

An Introduction to Object-Oriented Analysis

Objects and UML in Plain English

Second Edition

David William Brown
Northern Alberta Institute of Technology

John Wiley & Sons, Inc.

New York   Chichester   Weinheim   Brisbane   Singapore   Toronto

ACQUISITIONS EDITOR   Beth Golub

MARKETING MANAGER   Jessica Garcia

COVER DESIGNER   Karin Kincheloe

This book was set in 10/12 Century Schoolbook by the author and printed and bound by Malloy Lithographing. The cover was printed by Phoenix Color Corporation.

This book is printed on acid free paper.

ISBN 0-471-37137-8

Printed in the United States of America

10 9 8 7 6 5 4 3 2

To Nieves

Preface

· ·

Object-oriented methods, techniques, and technologies are now in place all over the computer world. Since the first edition of this book went to press, much has changed. New languages – Java and XML in particular – have made inroads into areas that used to be the domain of COBOL and other procedural programming languages. UML arose to become *the* way to document analysis and design results – and has been enshrined as a formal world standard.

This book brings objects down to earth and explains them in a way readily absorbed by systems developers, business users, and students alike. This second edition brings it up to date, the largest change being the addition of UML, its notation and its terminology. Details of these changes are in the final section of this preface.

CONCEPT AND PURPOSE.

· ·

This is a book written for students to learn from. It presents object-oriented concepts and object-oriented analysis techniques in straightforward and understandable language, using real-world, business-related examples. Explanations begin with concrete examples, leading to abstract principles, the natural way. Object concepts are first introduced in a familiar, concrete context, and later generalized.

This is a book that *actually delivers on* these promises. The conceptual level of the material is kept suitably high, while being made accessible to the students by the detailed explanations, the **plain English**, and examples that are much like situations the students will encounter after graduation. The case studies further illuminate the concepts and methods, since most are presented in narrative form, simulating the way real-world systems analysts and users go about the business of Systems Analysis.

An Introduction to Object-Oriented Analysis, Objects and UML in Plain English focuses on front-end *business area analysis,* with some overlap into the systems design area. It does not cover the entire field of object-oriented technology (OOT), but provides in-depth *theory and skills* for practical application of object-oriented methods at the analysis phase of the *system development life cycle* (SDLC). This is now often referred to as the *object-oriented development life cycle* (OODLC or ODLC).

There is, of course, considerable discussion of the effect this has on later phases in the development cycle, and how these later phases benefit from object-oriented methods. The book has a strong *business bias*, since that's the area least well served by the existing books. There is some discussion of object-oriented programming languages (OOPLs), Databases (OODBMSs or ODBMSs), and systems development tools and environments at an overview level.

This is intended to be the first object-oriented analysis book written in *plain, everyday English*, with all the pedagogical devices and learning apparatus that one would expect to find in a true textbook. This is a book intentionally written to be *understood*, and from which students can truly learn better, both more effectively and more efficiently.

MY REASON FOR WRITING THIS BOOK.

My teaching career has been a constant search for books that my students could learn from. Over the years, a number of incidents have illumined and spurred that search.

For some years in the 1970s, the Northern Alberta Institute of Technology (NAIT) where I was teaching, tested all its entrants each year, all of them Grade 12 diploma graduates. One unexpected finding was a surprisingly *low average reading level.*

Ten years or so later, the University of Alberta, across the river from NAIT, ran into similar problems. As reported in the local papers, they attempted to upgrade the reading levels of their incoming students by testing and insisting on an adequate reading level for acceptance. They were swamped. With so many students requiring remedial reading courses, they allowed them to proceed on the understanding that they must qualify before being allowed into second year.

You can imagine the uproar when they tried to enforce that one! A year later, they were faced with hundreds of irate students who had passed all their first-year courses, but were being barred from second year because they had neglected to take the remedial reading classes. We at NAIT sympathized, of course, and shook our heads wisely.

But back to the 1970s. In one of the years tested, I had an awakening, a real "Aha!" experience. We were teaching programming in IBM Assembly Language, a language I had not used before. We had what I considered to be an excellent text, from which I learned the language myself. *But I was beginning to feel a little superfluous*. I began to think that I should just be giving reading assignments, the book seemed to be that good.

And then Bob voiced a complaint one day in the middle of a discussion. "That book's just written to impress!" he avowed. "It's so full of big words!" I was really quite taken aback. And then I realized what was going on. The book was written at about *Grade 12* reading level, and the hotshots in the class were all reading well above that level. If Bob was an *average* reader for that year's intake, then the book must have been *several grades above his ability!* Hence his frustration. If students cannot read it, they cannot possibly learn from it. It's as simple as that.

Other Books

There have been dozens of books published in the field of object-oriented analysis. Almost without exception they have been written by academics and high-level consultants who are advancing the state of knowledge and the state of the art, and this is reflected in the style, organization and language used in these books.

In this writer's view, these books have not been aimed at the average systems analyst. By that I mean the busy, hardworking, overworked developer, who needs to be able to work through a book and immediately apply the ideas in the real world of systems development. Nor do these books appear to cater to the needs of undergraduate students, those struggling to make sense of the entire field of systems development, and OOA as the primary tool with which it is done.

The landmark works of these writers have made significant contributions to the state of the art, and contain material and ideas of immense value. Their books, however, are written at a very high level, both conceptually and in terms of language and reading level.

However, one author, Grady Booch, has an inspired sense of humor, and I have often used his cartoons to liven up classes. You will find a number of cartoons in *"An Introduction to Object-Oriented Analysis, Objects in Plain English"* and I freely admit to being inspired by Booch in this. I hope they will contribute to your understanding, while at the same time perhaps increasing your enjoyment of the learning process.

This book is the first in the field written with the primary objective that the reader should *learn and understand.* It is the first written with heavy emphasis on pedagogical issues and devices. Some of the features included were inspired by my work in educational psychology and in instructional design; others have been influenced by authors and books in numerous fields, and by the classroom and industrial experience of myself and colleagues. Much that is relevant may be found in a book by Joyce and Weil (1986), who provide a concise survey of a vast number of teaching and learning principles and techniques.

One of the key points about this book is its *reading level.* I have paid careful attention to readability, while preserving the necessary rigor and conceptual level of the material. There has been virtually no sacrifice of *academic* rigor. This has been kept up to an appropriate level for undergraduate students, while the English syntax, style, and vocabulary have been maintained at a point where more students can read and understand the content. The simplified syntax may sometimes lead to sentences which, when taken in isolation, may appear a little imprecise, but when taken in context their meaning is quite clear.

I cannot over-emphasize the importance of this simplification for the purpose of enhancing the students' learning and comprehension.

Over the past two or three decades there has been a marked decline in the level of reading ability in high school graduates. The simple fact is that

If students cannot *read* the material they clearly cannot *learn* it!

It is necessary that a textbook be presented at the student's own level. It is not the place, the function, or the purpose of this book to stretch and advance the reading level of the student. That's another course and another book. No, a book such as this must take the student as (s)he is. The book must treat that delicate raw material as it needs to be treated, in order to produce a satisfactory and qualified end-product – a knowledgeable and capable graduate.

Who Should Use This Book

This book is aimed at the following:

- University students in undergraduate *computing science, management information systems (MIS)*, or *business* programs.

- *MBA* students (those with a non-business bachelor's degree.)

- Students in *two-year college* or *technical-school* programs in these same areas

- *Systems development practitioners*; programmers and systems analysts, who need to upgrade to object-oriented methods.

- *Users*, typically business professionals (engineers, accountants, and other professionals), administrative staff, and line managers. Some of these people will be working alongside systems analysts during development projects, and all of them will be making use of the system that is eventually built from the results of the analysis.

"An Introduction to Object-Oriented Analysis, Objects and UML in Plain English" is intended specifically for three groups. There is a recommended portion of the book that each of these three groups should read:

1.   Undergraduate college and university students.

This book is primarily intended as the basis of a long-term (i.e., semester-based) course for students planning to work in MIS after graduation. Many of the basics of systems analysis (as opposed to object-oriented analysis in particular) have been included for the benefit of students with computer knowledge (i.e., programming) but without industrial experience.

This book will fit at the university level for first- to third-year students in undergraduate programs, and also in two-year college diploma programs. Suitable programs would include:

- MIS programs
- Programs aimed at producing programmer/analysts
- Business programs with a major or minor in computing or in information systems
- Computing Science programs with a concentration on business
- All programming or computing science students could also benefit from the explanations of objects. The business point of view could lead to a useful broadening of perspective.

An Introduction to Object-Oriented Analysis, Objects in Plain English provides an introduction to concepts and techniques, and students would expect to read one or more of the senior texts, or "guru books," in object-oriented analysis either as part of a senior or graduate course and/or after they begin working.

The techniques presented are applicable not only in business computing but also in engineering applications, and for such things as embedded software and process-control software. Most books in the OOA field concentrate on these nonbusiness applications, and it is my goal to provide the business concentration that is missing from some of these others. However, this book could be used for students in the various engineering disciplines, since the techniques are aimed at establishing the true needs and requirements, whatever they may be, of the actual real-world users, whoever they may be.

The book has also been written with an eye to self-study, correspondence, and distance learning, both for newcomers to the field and for experienced practitioners.

2.   Practitioners.

In addition to college courses, this book is suitable as a basis for short, intensive upgrading courses and seminars to introduce MIS and other professionals to object methods. After this book, however, MIS professionals will need a more thorough grounding in whatever method, style, or methodology is adopted. So they too should follow up afterwards with some of the other books in the field that treat their chosen method, and with books that give in-depth information on UML. It is my intention to produce a comprehensive set of detailed UML books by the year 2003.

These practitioners are the thousands of systems professionals – programmers, developers, and systems analysts – working in systems development in all branches of industry, commerce and government. Over the *next 3 to 5 years*, virtually *all* of them will need to upgrade to object-oriented methods. (See discussion of "Early and Late Adopters of a New Technology" in Chapter 16.) Here are some guidelines for the two main groups:

• Systems Managers.

These busy people should read Chapters 2 – 5. They will thus learn about objects, but avoid the details of how it is done. If they want more detail, Chapters 7 and 8 would be appropriate. If they become involved in the day-to-day management of a project, then they should join the next group in reading the entire book.

• Systems Professionals.

Experienced programmers, analysts, data administrators, database administrators, and the like will need the whole book. If they have already had some exposure to the ideas, this will be helpful, of course. They will then find sections throughout the book that are review for them, but there isn't really any complete chapter that they should skip.

3. Line Managers and End Users.

This third group is somewhat smaller but nonetheless important. These are the *end users*, the operational, clerical, and professional personnel, and the line managers, who must live with the system that is eventually built from the analysis exercise. Some of these people will need to be deeply involved in its development.

- Users Working with MIS.

Some users, those who will be working directly with the MIS personnel during a systems development project, will need a thorough understanding of object-oriented methods. To this end, they should plan on reading the entire book, and perhaps taking a course based on it. After that, the more technically inclined among them may wish to follow the MIS people into the more senior works in the field, UML books and "guru books" as mentioned earlier.

- Senior Managers (Operational; Non-MIS; CIO; CEO).

Busy senior nontechnical (i.e., non-MIS) executives and vice-presidents should read Chapters 2 – 4. They should then keep the book around for reference, and, of course, in case something sparks their interest as the projects progress. Since their need is to be informed with as little investment of time as possible, the systems person advising them may wish to suggest they skip the Introduction chapter and go straight into Chapter 2. Also, as you'll see from my later comments under "Pedagogical Devices," the design of the index will make it very effective and helpful for these nontechnical people.

At this point, a wide variety of people need an introduction to objects and object-oriented analysis. In a few years' time, when everybody is learning object-oriented analysis in school, and all the existing professionals have had time to adjust, this will no longer be true to the same extent. By that time, the audience for a book like this one will be almost entirely students, along with a few users and managers.

All of that, then, is background to what comes next. Now that you have some idea of the groups of people who go through the process, you can tell where you fit. You may then choose what parts of the book are for you.

PEDAGOGICAL DEVICES AND FEATURES

A rich set of tools is included in this book to ensure that the necessary *associations* and *review* occur to ensure a high level of *learning, understanding and retention*. The features and innovations that make *An Introduction to Object-Oriented Analysis, Objects in Plain English* stand out from others in its field are listed below, with comments where appropriate:

- **Introduction.**

There is an introductory chapter including a short "how to use this book" section, which is numbered in such a way as to dictate that the reader should *start here*. This introduction explains how to make the best use of all the things built into the book, that are intended to maximize your learning and retention.

- **Chapter Prerequisites.**

Each chapter is preceded by a brief list of topics, prior knowledge of which is deemed necessary for complete understanding of the chapter. These are supported by references both to previous chapters and to other relevant works.

- **Objectives.**

There is a statement of learning objectives for each chapter, in "performance" or "behavioral" format. That is, they state what a reader should be capable of *doing* as a result of reading the chapter.

- **Topic Overview.**

The objectives are supported by a brief statement of the topics to be covered in the chapter, outlined in the sequence they appear in the chapter.

- **Advance Organizers.**

Advance organizers are a device for enhancing the relevance and meaning of verbal material, in order to bring about improved understanding and retention. Ausubel (1963) defines ***advance organizers* as topics introduced ahead of the target material, and he stresses that they must be more general, encompassing, or overview concepts compared with the ones they precede.** That is, they should be at a higher level of *abstraction* and *inclusion* than the topics in the target material. Joyce and Weil (1986) give a brief but excellent description.

- **Narrative Scenarios.**

Continuing throughout the book is a case study in narrative form, reading like a novel with dialogue. This depicts a team of users and analysts involved in the business of system development. Whitten et al. (1999) and Joyce and Weil (1986) both make excellent use of this technique. It is particularly effective for introducing advance organizers. The final chapter consists of another case, complete within the chapter, similarly presented with dialogue.

- **Thought Questions.**

To further direct the reader's associations, essential for retention of the material, each narrative episode is followed by a set of "Thought Questions," the purpose of which is to provoke *critical questioning and analysis*. These will foster long-term retention by encouraging the reader to *actively process information* relating to their own real world, to the topics, and to the advance organizer concepts.

- **Inductive Sequencing (Specific to General, Concrete to Abstract)**

This is an important one! As infants, each of us was faced with the need to make sense of the complex world around us. Indeed, it took some little time before we were able to ascertain that what initially appeared no more than random sensory inputs, did in fact emanate from a "world around us."

The method we all used, and continue to use, for understanding such complexity is to *observe*, note patterns and commonalities, and infer a *rule, principle,* or *concept* that binds together the isolated observations. One of the first such inferences, of course, is that the child postulates the existence of *"objects"* in this "world around me."

This reasoning is *inductive* in nature, that is, reasoning *from* specific examples or occurrences (usually concrete) to a *general rule* or *principle* (frequently abstract). This approach is so natural that all of us continue to use it, and is so effective that we have institutionalized it and called it the *scientific method*.

Unfortunately, there is a conflict with what appears to be the more natural way to *explain* things. For those of us who already understand the subject, it seems more natural to begin with a statement of the general principle, and then explain and perhaps support it with examples. In books, scientific treatises, classrooms, and everyday conversations we repeatedly take this approach, ***to the detriment of our audience's understanding.***

This book presents most of its material in an inductive style, by starting with one or two examples, drawing the *concept from the examples*, and then completing the explanation with further examples and discussion.

As an aside, I should point out that, like the newborn child, the systems analyst frequently ventures into an unfamiliar world, in this case the business area inhabited by users. The analyst is faced with the need to understand a complex, bewildering, and very foreign environment that appears at first sight to have no organization to it, no rhyme or reason. Like the world encountered by the newborn, it is an apparently random reality, out of which (s)he is required to make sense.

Learning to understand it takes skill and patience. Like the newborn, the analyst investigates this strange and fascinating world by identifying and studying the *objects* that populate it. Object modeling techniques bear a remarkable similarity to the set of methods used naturally by newborns (i.e., all of us). Part of the power of object methods lies in the fact that they are based upon techniques that are natural to us as human beings, and that we have already been using all our lives.

- **Accessible Reading Level.**

This has been explained at length above. I should describe the book as being at an "accessible" reading level, which really means that it can be read easily by anyone with typical Grade 12 reading ability.

- **Explanatory Diagrams.**

Clear and carefully designed diagrams are essential as an aid to understanding. It is important to have diagrams that *adequately* relate to and support the textual explanations.

An Introduction to Object-Oriented Analysis, Objects and UML in Plain English includes many diagrams and illustrations. The diagrams are not merely referenced within the text, but are *explained in detail*. The explanation in most cases takes the reader *step by step* through the diagram, to ensure complete understanding.

The now-world-standard UML notation is used throughout, except where other notations are being discussed. David Taylor, (1995) for example, has developed a particularly effective style of diagraming for objects and classes (two of the central constructs of OOA) that clearly indicates the way objects encapsulate both data and program code. His notation is introduced early in the book.

- **Cartoons (inspired by Booch).**

Only a few authors have attempted to use significant amounts of humor to reduce boredom and enhance learning, notably Coad and Yourdon, and Grady Booch. Booch's delightful cartoons introduce a lighter note, while at the same time serving to illustrate his points. A young brother-and-sister team, Haydee and Jay Viardo, helped me to provide a considerable number of cartoon designs. I have worked closely with them on the design of the drawings, to ensure that the humor and explanatory value are appropriate and properly coordinated with the textual material.

- **Definition of Terms.**

I am always disturbed when I see authors use new and complex or abstract terms either before defining them or without defining them at all. I have emulated

Meigs, Meigs and Lam (1990) who have made excellent use of colored ink in this regard. In the body of the book, I have adhered rigorously to the following pattern:

- When a new term is encountered it is highlighted in a ***bold font***.

- The definition follows immediately, usually in the very same sentence, also in a **bold font**.

- The term and its definition also appear in the Chapter Glossary at the end of the chapter.

- In the index at the back of the book, the page references to the definition page and the chapter glossary will be **bolded.** See also under "Index" below.

- **Lead-On (Bridge) Sentences.**

Many textbooks, but as far as this writer has seen, no OOA books, have adopted the simple but effective practice of finishing each section or topic with a sentence that relates it to the one immediately following. When a paragraph or section devoted to one topic suddenly terminates, and the next paragraph takes off on a radically different topic, the resulting discontinuity in the flow of the reader's thoughts can interfere markedly with the learning process.

The *lead-on sentence* or *bridge sentence* can be very simple, and the relationship can be relatively superficial, yet it will still have the desired effect. Removal of discontinuities in the topic matter has a number of subtle but significant effects, many of them *affective* in the sense that they influence the reader's *feelings* and *attitude* toward the book and the subject matter.

Discontinuities can cause feelings of frustration, anger, and most importantly, *inadequacy*, in the sense that a reader who is already struggling to understand the topic may become very discouraged. Obviously, any of these negative feelings can have disastrous effects on the amount and quality of learning taking place, not to mention unnecessary escalation of stress levels. (We are all well acquainted with the effects of excessive stress on performance, health, and quality of life.)

- **Main Point Summary Lists.**

Bouldin (1989) has made excellent use of bulleted summary lists of main points throughout her very practical and effective book. Such lists are sprinkled liberally throughout *An Introduction to Object-Oriented Analysis, Objects in Plain English.* They provide a very necessary intermediate level of review, supported by the end-of-chapter summaries.

- **Class Exercises and Problems.**
- **Individual Exercises and Problems.**
- **Class and Individual Projects and Cases.**

In this book there is an ample set of problems, exercises, group exercises, cases, and work projects at the end of each chapter. Earlier comments on learning styles and other issues of course apply. The exercises are presented in a roughly graduated order of complexity and difficulty.

You will find the exercises and questions at the end of each chapter are somewhat arbitrarily arranged into two collections:

- Those I have found to work better as group exercises

- Those better done individually

However, these groupings are not to be considered sacrosanct. Any of the exercises and problems may be attempted by or assigned to individuals, groups, or a class as a whole. I have intended that in a school or seminar setting the group exercises would be done in teams of about four to six people, so that the results may be compared and contrasted afterwards. Even in a class as small as four, I will sometimes use two groups of two to achieve this.

- **Chapter Summaries.**

There are end-of-chapter summaries *suitable for effective reviewing*. The most important thing about end-of-chapter summaries is *that they are there*. But secondly, they must have some *real meat* to them; that is, they must actually précis the material covered under each topic, rather than just give a list of topics covered. Sentences of the form "... we covered X and we considered Y..." are simply not adequate. I have gone to some length to provide comprehensive, "meaty" summaries to enhance the students' reviewing.

- **Chapter Glossaries.**

Glossaries are important and very necessary. Glossaries organized by chapter have a number of advantages from the point of view of convenience, and I firmly believe that busy, highly-stressed students and professionals will only make proper use of such facilities if they are **perceived** as both *convenient* and *beneficial*. For example:

- The glossaries are physically located close to the relevant reading material, making reference to them easy while reading.
- They may be wholly or partly assigned as study or review material, with assured relevance to the current area of study. Similarly, for instructors they become a ready and convenient source of test material.
- The glossaries are located with the summaries and other back matter for the chapter, thus being readily available as part of the student's review processes.

- **Self-Test Questions**

A variety of questions are provided, along with directions for their effective utilization. There are multiple-choice, fill-in-the-blanks, matching and short-answer questions to provide the reader with an in-depth evaluation of her/his learning.

You may note that some of the multiple-choice questions have way more choices than is usually recommended in the design of this type of question. This practice is acceptable – and effective – here, since these are not quiz questions, but are for *self-evaluation*.

• **Design for Varying Learning Styles**

Most of us in the computer profession possess an ability to learn from lectures and books. Any computer professional who has made it into the industry, or any student who has made it through high school and into college-level computer courses, has already demonstrated this ability, overwhelmingly. Nonetheless, these are only two out of a much larger number of "learning styles" or "learning channels" that we are all capable of utilizing.

Learning styles or channels, also called ***learning modalities,*** **are *methods* or *channels* for accepting information into the human memory.** Though available and usable for any learner, each channel is favored by certain people as their *preferred* way to learn. Each of us has our own hierarchy of preferred learning styles, and for the lucky ones, lectures and books are at or near the top of their list. For some, however, these particular channels are well down the hierarchy of preference. Success in this field is even more of an achievement for such students!

The verbal and visual learning channels are the ones needed for books and lectures. But students who score high on these two can still learn more effectively when additional channels are engaged. To this end, as well as to benefit those students who may be primarily spatial, tactile, or kinesthetic learners, I have included a number of exercises and projects that involve the students in a variety of activities, including some that are nonverbal and nonvisual.

A work such as *An Introduction to Object-Oriented Analysis, Objects and UML in Plain English* is a ***book***. As such, its overwhelming concentration is necessarily on only the verbal and visual channels, out of the eight learning styles identified by McCarthy (1987). She has developed a lesson-planning methodology that is marketed as teacher-training seminars under the trade name "4-MAT" The core of her methodology is a system for developing class materials and exercises so as to provide learning experiences appropriate to students with a variety of identified learning styles. The seminars, of course, include considerable material on the research and theory behind the method, all of which is in her book.

To enable learning for readers with other dominant learning styles, we need activities that are active, experiential, and nontextual. Exercises are included in this book, and also on the Wiley web site, constructed so as to use alternative learning modalities. For an example, you may wish to check Exercise 8.2, "The Object-Oriented Treasure Hunt (OOTHunt)."

CHANGES FOR SECOND EDITION

The continued rapid evolution of the field, and in particular the emergence of UML and Java, have necessitated that the book be updated.

Key Points

UML

In light of the eventual (and fully expected) publication of UML, its (fully expected) rise to prominence, and its laudable, albeit rather *un*expected, adoption by OMG as part of the CORBA standard, the need arose for some fairly extensive modification to most of the book to accommodate the changes. Much of the terminology has been updated, and many concepts are now explained following the style and usage prevalent in UML.

Notation

All object diagrams in the book have been redrawn in UML notation, except of course for those few where the purpose is to illustrate another notation. The majority of the diagrams from Chapter 4 on have been redrawn for UML.

Instructors Manual CD

An updated version of the test-bank is provided, in both .txt and .pdf formats.

Additional exercises and questions were generated, particularly on UML.

Wiley Web Site

The publisher is planning to host additional student and instructor materials on its Web site at www.wiley.com for this book and for others.

End-of-Chapter Questions and Exercises

Additional exercises and self-test questions have been provided.

Also, the *self-test* questions are included on the Instructors Manual CD, but in a separate file. These are of a different structure from the quiz/exam test bank, sometimes using six or seven distractors, or frequently distractors such as "a and d," or "None of the above." Since they are intended as a (formative) self-evaluation rather than for (summative) use for grading, these aberrations from standard design are acceptable. These questions are intended as a learning tool for the student's own use, and not for the purpose of judging her/him.

However, I have found that the occasional use of one or two of these questions, perhaps with reduced number of distractors, serves as a nice little reward for those students who bothered to use the questions as intended.

Changes in the Text of the Book

The first few chapters are concerned with history and basic definitions, such as "What an object is," so UML makes a multitude of minor differences to the text, but does not alter the basic organization or content. Most of the changes were detail wording changes. Changes to ensure UML compatibility were mostly a sentence or two at a time, or a paragraph or two, although there were many such changes that involved only a few words each. Others involved pages at a time, or whole new sections.

There are many detail changes to the wording, for a variety of reasons:

- For improvements to explanations.

- For improvements to readability – shorter sentences and paragraphs, replacement of polysyllabic words. The use of contractions with apostrophes, such as *isn't, don't, you'll,* etc., makes for a more colloquial attitude, an easier reading level, and therefore, most importantly, a higher rate of understanding, learning, and retention.

- For adaptations for UML.

- To update numerous references to more up-to-date works and recent editions

- To accommodate many definitions now referencing the 1998 *New Oxford* and the 1999 *Random House Webster Unabridged* dictionaries. In many cases, I added to or replaced the older dictionary definitions, but sometimes the old ones fit better for the current purpose.

Changes in Topic Areas

- Chapter 6 includes a new section on feasibility analysis. While this is not strictly an object-oriented topic, it is a critically important systems analysis topic, especially for students with little or no experience of the harsh financial realities of the business world.

- Chapter 10 has been reworded into UML terminology and concepts, and all diagrams have been redrawn. Specifically, *Exit Actions* and *Transition Actions* have been included for UML, in addition to the existing Entry Actions.

- Chapter 11 has been retitled: "Following the Trail: Examining Execution Sequences" to reflect the fact that it now includes *Sequence Diagrams* as well as CRC cards for tracing events and execution. Because several reviewers requested that Chapter 11 not be shortened, I have added a second half with Sequence Diagrams (a.k.a. *Interaction Diagrams* or *Event Trace Diagrams*) since these are widely used in UML.

- Chapter 12 has had a discussion of UML Packages added.

- Chapter 16 has been preserved in response to popular demand. However, I did trim out the section and exercises on reading improvement by visualization. This will reappear in a more appropriate place, in a later series of self-improvement books (2003 timeframe).

Acknowledgements

I am indebted to numerous people, without whom this book would, as they say, never have seen the light of day. My ever-patient editor, Beth Golub, was assisted by Jennifer Battista, with Ken Santor on the technical side.

The very necessary review process invoved a considerable number of people, whose feedback enabled me to correct my numerous errors, some small, many large. In alphabetical order, they are:

Donald R. Chand, Bentley College
Rick Gee, Okanagan University College
Robert H. Grenier, St. Ambrose University
Harvey Hayashi, Loyalist College of Applied Arts and Technology
Patrick Jaska, University of Texas at Arlington
Jean-Pierre Kuilboer, University of Massachusetts--Boston
Alan Graham Peace, Duquesne University
Keng Siau, University of Nebraska--Lincoln
Sandra Slaughter, Carnegie Mellon University
Craig W. Slinkman, University of Texas at Arlington
Anna Wachholz, Sheridan College
Steven Walczak, University of Colorado at Denver
Randy S. Weinberg, Carnegie Mellon University
Eli J. Weissman, DeVry Institute of Technology
Vincent C. Yen, Wright State University

• •

CHAPTER GLOSSARY.

Learning Styles, also called ***Learning Modalities***, or sometimes ***Learning Channels.*** Each of these is a method or channel for accepting information into the human memory. Though available and usable for any learner, each channel is favored by certain people as their preferred way to learn.

advance organizers Topics introduced ahead of the target material, that must be more general, encompassing, or overview concepts compared with the ones they precede. That is, they should be at a higher level of abstraction and inclusion than the topics in the target material.

David William Brown

David Brown has spent half of the last 30 years or so *doing* systems analysis, and half of them *teaching* it. His technical specialty is object-oriented analysis, and his life's mission is education.

Having taught at the Northern Alberta Institute of Technology, he is dedicated to developing educational styles, techniques, materials, and technologies. His goal is to enhance and *ensure* learning in the domain of computers and information systems.

After beginning his career in Wellington, New Zealand in 1965, David moved to Edmonton, Alberta, Canada in 1970, and spent a couple of years on various systems projects. In 1971, he made the switch to teaching, and discovered his vocation. After 10 years at NAIT in the Computer Systems program, which graduates business-trained programmer/analysts, David went back into the industry for eight years, at the City of Edmonton.

Then, after realizing that teaching is really what he wanted to devote his life to, he returned to NAIT. At the NAIT Microcomputer Institute, he taught everything from "What is a Computer?" and "Intro Windows," to upgrading courses for software developers and systems analysts. These included such things as Oracle, data modelling, prototyping, database design, and, of course, object-oriented analysis and object-oriented programming.

David is a member of DPMA and holds a CCP designation.

Contents

CHAPTER FOUR
. . . .

Data-Oriented Models 59

CHAPTER NINE
Finding Objects and Classes in the Real World   278

Chapter Ten

Object States and the Statechart Diagram 342

CHAPTER SEVENTEEN

"The Royal Korona Yacht Club" Membership System   582

Chapter One

· ·

An Introduction to the Book

START HERE

Welcome to my book. My name is David, and my sincere wish is that this book will be a tool that you'll use to explore the world of objects. Everything in this book has been done with an eye to making it a learning device for you, my readers. In this introductory chapter, you'll discover some of the features built into the book and how to use them to your own advantage.

Most authors would put these elements in the preface. I've placed them here because nobody reads the preface (except teachers), and I want *you* to be aware of these things so that you can make the best use of them. What is my goal? That you'll finish this book knowledgeable and capable in object-oriented analysis (OOA), and that you'll *retain* that knowledge and skill in the long term.

To that end, each chapter has been carefully laid out to help make learning happen for the reader. Don't skip any of the parts, especially not at the front and back of each chapter.

WHAT YOU WILL LEARN IN THIS CHAPTER

This is where I state the objectives for each chapter. They'll give you a map of where the chapter is taking you, so you'll know when you've arrived. You can be satisfied that you understand the material in this chapter when you can:

- Explain all or most methods used in this book to enhance learning.

- Follow the directions given for effective study, making use of the "pedagogical devices," that is, all the things built into the book to help you learn.

- Read the book and make use of these devices to learn about objects, with improved comprehension and retention.

WHAT YOU SHOULD KNOW TO START THIS CHAPTER

Starting this introductory chapter really means starting the book itself. So instead of listing the facts you need to know to get started, for this chapter only, this section describes the readers I expect to address.

However, I've left the section heading unchanged since you'll be seeing it in other chapters throughout the book. Those of you who must read the chapters out of sequence (for whatever reason) will need to check this section carefully at the front of each chapter, because it details the prerequisite knowledge for that chapter.

For the book as a whole, however, here is my picture of who you are, my readers. Whoever you may be, I expect you'll probably fall into one or more of these groups:

- Students in graduate or undergraduate computing science programs

- Students in graduate or undergraduate management information systems (MIS) or computer systems technology (CST) programs

- Students in MBA or undergraduate business programs

- Students in two-year college or technical-school programs in these areas

- Systems development practitioners – programmers, software developers, systems analysts, and business analysts – who have been working in the field for a number of years and who need to upgrade to object-oriented methods

- Users – typically business professionals, operational staff, or clerical staff – who are to be involved in a systems project. These people will be end users of the object-oriented systems, and will be working alongside the systems analysts during development. The preface to this book explains which groups of readers should read which sections of the book.

CHAPTER OVERVIEW

This chapter first introduces *The Outhouse Saga* and then takes you on a guided tour of the sections that make up the following chapters. As I explain the structure and purpose of each section, you'll see where it fits in its chapter. Then the body of this chapter talks about why I wrote this book and describes other books in the field. After a few comments about the style of this book, you'll find descriptions of some of the *pedagogical devices* that are included to enhance your learning. The chapter closes with a description of the sections that form the "backmatter" in the chapters.

Now the chapter continues by introducing you to Nancy Forsyth, a consultant beginning a contract with a new client.

"THE OUTHOUSE BATHROOM BOUTIQUE" SALES REPORTING SYSTEM – EPISODE 1

Nancy Forsyth stepped into the cool of the store. It was a medium-sized place, full of interesting bathroom paraphernalia. The store was larger and the range of stock seemed more extensive than in the two other stores she had visited. Nancy made a mental note to return when she had time to browse. She headed toward the back and soon found the Administrative Offices sign by the stairs.

At the top of the stairs, she was greeted by a receptionist behind a small desk. "You must be Ms Forsyth. Mr Buchanan is expecting you," she said. "He told me if you came early to send you right in." She pressed a button that produced a muffled "Yeah?" and responded, "Tim, Ms Forsyth is here. I'll send her in."

Tim Buchanan was seated behind a large, messy desk with a sign declaring him to be "President." Middle-aged and slightly graying, he greeted her with a pleasant, not-too-formal smile. "Hi," he said, proffering his hand. "You don't realize just how glad we are to have you on board. We are definitely in need of some help with our computerized systems, and John has given you quite a buildup."

Nancy smiled confidently, although with somewhat more confidence than she actually felt. She hoped her dress and manner were sufficiently businesslike and professional."Well, we'll have to see if I can live up to my reputation." She sat in the chair that Tim indicated, picked up her leather clipboard portfolio, and unzipped it, ready to take notes. Tim seated himself behind the desk, and Nancy turned the conversation to a more serious note.

"Well," she began, "I've done some research on your company. Partly it consisted of browsing a couple of your stores and trying not to buy anything too expensive. You certainly have some nice stuff! And then I read the shareholders' annual report that you gave John, and I looked at the various reports that you currently receive from your computer. They look fairly reasonable, but John tells me you've found you need something different. Why don't you start by telling me about the old reports and how you presently make use of your computers, but describe the problems as you come to them."

The story that Tim told to Nancy is one that properly belongs in Chapter 2, "Systems Development and the Software Crisis," so we'll rejoin them when we reach that point.

THOUGHT QUESTIONS

While this introductory episode of *The Outhouse Saga* hardly warrants any deep and serious "thought questions," you'll find them in the remaining chapters. In each chapter, the "thought questions" that follow The Outhouse episode are intended to emphasize the points brought out in the story. The story is an attempt to give a realistic simulation of the kind of projects you can expect to meet in the real world of business systems development. The situations and problems it depicts are like those you'll actually meet.

For those of you who are practicing systems professionals, no doubt you've met problems like these already. For the students among you, I've tried to bring you real people going about the business of systems development, for three main purposes:

- To show you where the techniques and ideas that you're learning will fit into the real world out there.

- To show you how to use these ideas in practice in the real world.

- To focus your awareness on the issues raised in the narrative. In this way the narrative comes closer to being an ***advance organizer,*** **setting a context for information that is to follow, for more effective learning.**

The thought questions are best attempted in groups of three to six people, with lots of thoughtful discussion, and the answers brought to the full class for comparison and further discussion. However, even lone readers can benefit. Pause a few moments, think through the questions posed, and write down your responses.

Writing them forces you to clarify the thoughts inside your head, and this action alone gives them more emphasis. Thus they're firmly planted in your head to act as "keys" or "pegs" to hang the information on as you progress through the chapter. This is a most important learning tool – don't skip it!

Now that you've seen the "frontmatter," it's time for the *body* of Chapter 1.

1.1 WHY THIS BOOK?

My teaching career has been spent searching for books that my students could learn from. Some of my students read at third- and fourth-year university level or better, and some do not. Most OOA books are written by those who are leaders in the field, and are bringing about changes that will affect us all. Their books form the mainstream of the object-oriented world, and you and I must read them and learn from them.

For the geniuses among you, the conceptual level and the reading level of the books by leading thinkers present no problem. For the rest of us, if we can't read it, we simply can't learn it. So I've set out to write a book that my students and my peers can learn from. My goal is that after reading this book you'll be able to

- Begin building information systems using object-oriented methods

- Learn effectively from the writings of the leaders in the object-oriented field (that is, from the "guru books")

I discuss these issues in more detail in the preface to this book. If you skipped it, you may wish to go back and read it.

1.2   WHY OBJECT-ORIENTED ANALYSIS?

The technique of object-oriented analysis (OOA) has really emerged only in the last eight or nine years. Object-oriented methods organize both the information, and the processing that manipulates that information, according to the real-world objects that the information describes. Despite its newness, OOA has become established as the new direction for the information systems industry. OOA is now well beyond the experimental stage and has entered the mainstream of information systems development. This move has been accelerated by two factors:

- The success and rapid spread of object-oriented programming

- Recognition that object-oriented methods produce more effective, efficient, flexible, and stable information systems

We'll discuss these points throughout the book.

At the time of writing (Fall 2000), many universities are offering courses in object-oriented analysis (and often design as well). However, OOA & D is widely and increasingly being used in systems analysis courses at the undergraduate and two-year diploma level. Many undergraduate courses are appearing with "object-oriented analysis and design" in the course title.

Many schools are teaching object-oriented programming. I expect that soon *everybody* will be learning object-oriented techniques in systems analysis and programming courses. And within a very few years almost everybody out in industry will be programming in Java and other OO languages.

Then there are the practitioners, the graduates, and others "in the trenches" building information systems on a daily basis. New object-oriented tools, languages, methodologies, and development environments are hitting the market every month. There is pressure for these people to learn the new methods. But then, could this be just another bandwagon for all of us to jump on? Is it really no more than just the latest fad and buzzword?

Yet Another Paradigm?

In Chapter 4 we'll define the terms *paradigm* and *paradigm shift*. For now, let's simply say that a ***paradigm*** **is a way of viewing things and thinking about things.** In the last two decades we've seen process modeling with data flow diagrams, then data modeling (a.k.a.[1] information modeling) with entity-relationship diagrams, and now object-oriented modeling. (Chapters 3 and 4 describe all of these in detail.)

Each has come along appearing to be "the answer." The first two took us giant leaps ahead but didn't solve everything. Should we now hope that objects will? I doubt it! Objects have evolved from entities, and have already given our productivity a significant boost. They're now firmly established as the new direction for Information Technology (IT) and the software industry, but they won't be the "final solution."

Over the next few years, objects will have many and unforeseen effects upon our industry, our lives, and ourselves. At this point I have no idea what will come next, but you can bet something will. It will be as exciting then as objects are now for those of us who like to be on the leading edge. But does being on the leading edge mean that each of us has to come up with a new way of doing things, a new methodology?

1.3 YET ANOTHER METHODOLOGY?

Emphatically "No!" As you'll see in the next section, many of the leading thinkers and writers in the object-oriented field have done just this. And some, such as Rumbaugh, Booch, and Jacobson have joined forces, merging their companies and their methodologies. It is not my objective to confound my readers with yet another one, but instead to explain the concepts underlying the ones that exist already.

In particular, we'll be working with the UML notation developed by Booch, Rumbaugh and Jacobson, who are sometimes referred to as *"The Three Amigos"* after the film of that name. UML was destined to become a de facto world standard, simply because of the number of followers these three had. But more than that, it has now been adopted by the Object Management Group (whom you'll meet in later pages) as the *official world standard* object notation.

1.4 OTHER BOOKS IN THE FIELD

So far perhaps fifty books have been published about object-oriented analysis. Almost without exception they have been written by brilliant academics and high-level consultants who are advancing the state of the art. This is reflected in the style, organization, and language used in these books.

In my estimation, these books have *not* been aimed at the average, busy, hardworking, and overworked systems analyst or programmer. This person needs to be able to read a book and then immediately turn the ideas to practical use in the real world of systems development.

Nor do these "guru books" seem to cater to the needs of undergraduate students, wqho are struggling to make sense of the software development process, and of OOA as the primary tool with which it is done. Rather, each book has been a statement of the techniques, notation, and methodology developed by that author or team.

This is indeed true of the likes of Rumbaugh et al. (1991; 1999), Wirfs-Brock et al. (1990), Booch (1995), Booch et al.(1999), Jacobson et al. (1992; 1999), Coad and Yourdon (1991), and Shlaer and Mellor (1988). The landmark works of these and other writers are major contributions to the state of the art, and contain material and ideas of immense value. Their books, however, are written at a very high level, both conceptually and in terms of language and reading level.

My goal is that you should be able to read this book and understand it right away. You should not be spending valuable time and effort on the language used. Instead, you should be using that energy for understanding and using the subject matter.

In the preface I explain in more detail how and why I settled on a reading level for this book. Those of you who read above that level will find this book a breeze to read and learn from. Those who read at or close to the average level for college entrants will, I hope, find this to be a book you can learn from effectively. (I should point out that the average reading level for college students has been measured by numerous studies over the decades. See the preface for more.)

1.5   WHAT THIS BOOK CAN DO FOR YOU

These are some of the concerns that motivated me to write this book. I hope you'll see that my primary goals involve your learning, your software development abilities, and your eventual success.

A Bang for Your Buck

Whatever price you paid for your copy of this book, you're entitled to your money's worth. I've spent much time and energy on a number of things that are intended to make that happen.

Writing Style

This book is written in an informal style and at an accessible reading level. In the preface I explain the reasons and how the super-readers among you will still benefit from using this book. Use all the summaries, exercises, and the like, as I recommend, and don't shortchange yourself. This way your investment of time, money, and energy will pay increased dividends.

The Objectives of the Book

- You will learn object-oriented analysis in the most efficient and effective manner possible.

- You will learn from this book and enter the workplace better prepared to make software development happen *right*, and *right on time*.

Systems Development Methodologies

As I indicated earlier, you won't find a "methodology" presented in these pages. You'll find overviews of methodologies and parts of methodologies from some of the well-known leaders in the field of object-oriented development. In this new edition, it is all expressed in the now world-standard Unified Modeling Language notation, UML.

While there's certainly enough in this book for you to study object-oriented analysis and then begin doing it, you'll still benefit greatly from further reading. This book will prepare you well to understand the books from the leaders in the field.

For some of you, a methodology will have been chosen by your professor, or in industry by your client or employer. It may be from one of these well-known authors, or it may be a proprietary methodology bought from a consulting firm. Either way, you may expect the writing to be at a fairly high level, and this book will give you a good head start toward understanding and learning it.

Pedagogical Devices (Things to Help You Learn)

In this section I outline some of the features in this book, things I did for the purpose of making it easier and more effective for you to learn from. Some have already been mentioned at the front of this chapter, that is, in the position where you'll find them in each chapter.

The most important point I can make about this, however, is that none of them can possibly work for you unless you *read them* and *use them!* Use them as I suggest here, and most of you will find that the learning sticks significantly better. Read all the front and back matter for each chapter, and do the problems.

The place to begin each chapter is the "Objectives," which tell you why I wrote that chapter. You will notice that there are "bleeds," or shading, on the upper corners of the pages to mark the beginning of each chapter, and on the lower corners of the pages to mark the ends, to help you find your way around.

CHAPTER OBJECTIVES

At the beginning of each chapter, you'll find a statement of the objectives for the chapter, under the title "What You Will Learn in This Chapter." Notice that they don't say we'll "cover" this topic and "examine" that one. Rather, they state *what new things you'll be capable of doing* when you understand the contents of the chapter. This does a number of things:

- You know from the objectives exactly what you're expected to learn.

- You know how to tell when you've learned these things.

- Your instructor has a guideline for an evaluation to see how well you've learned them.

- You can use the objectives as a study guide, knowing they'll match up with the tests your instructor has planned.

TOPIC OVERVIEW

The objectives are supported by a brief statement of the topics to be covered in the chapter. This gives a further level of preparation to ensure good learning and retention. The objectives and topic overview together serve to alert you to the main points of the discussion, so that you'll notice them more (and thus retain them better) as you read through the body of the chapter.

KEY CONCEPTS

This list of terms to be introduced and explained in the chapter is intended to titillate and catch your attention. Scan this list and you'll recognize many of the terms already. Terms you've never seen before will also lodge in your awareness.

Each time you see the term, it will be embedded in your mind, and this focuses your attention and learning on it when you finally meet it in the text. Through the principle of *association*, this will automatically enhance your learning and retention.

AUTHOR'S ADDRESS

I've included my e-mail address at the front of the book (and here) both to gain feedback for future revisions and, equally important, as a service to you, my readers. Please feel free to contact me with questions and comments, objections and errors, and suggestions for rewrites, additions, or even for new books.

E-mail: flykiwi@home.com

CHAPTER PREREQUISITES

This is entitled "What You Should Know to Start This Chapter." Each chapter is preceded by a brief list of topics, prior knowledge of which I consider necessary for complete understanding of the chapter. These are supported by references both to previous chapters and to other relevant works.

DEFINITION OF TERMS

Definitions for new words are highlighted in a boldface type, with the new term underlined, at the place where they're first introduced, and then they're repeated in the glossary at the end of the chapter.

CHAPTER GLOSSARIES

You'll find all the definitions from each chapter collected into a glossary at the chapter's end, so you can find them quickly and easily while reading. Occasionally, a term is repeated from earlier chapters when I felt it would help you.

These are the terms defined in the text in boldface type, and both the glossary entry and the original definition in the text are highlighted in the index by setting the page number reference in boldface. The shaded areas on the lower corners of the pages, known in pubkishing as *bleeds*, are to mark the ends of the chapters, to help you find the glossaries as you read.

MAIN POINT SUMMARY LISTS

Liberally sprinkled throughout this book, you'll find summary lists. These provide a very important level of immediate review and reinforcement, and are supported by the main summary at the end of each chapter.

END-OF-CHAPTER SUMMARIES

Consolidated summaries are provided at the end of each chapter for reviewing. To make your reviewing more effective, I've ensured that they have some "real meat" to them. You need summaries that actually give a précis of what you learned about each topic, so you can read through the summary and review all the main points of what you learned. And since this is what *I* demand from a book, why would I give my own readers anything less?

STUDY METHODS

Here is a study hint, using the summaries, that could make a significant difference to your learning as you read this book (or any other):

1. Begin each chapter by reading through the following:
   - The Objectives ("What You Will Learn in This Chapter")
   - The "Chapter Overview
   - The Key Concepts
   - The *Outhouse* episode
   - The End-of-Chapter Summary
   - The Glossary
2. Whenever you put the book down and then pick it up again later:
   - Reread the objectives, overview, key concepts, summary, and glossary.
   - *Then*, and only then, go back into the chapter where you left off.
3. Finish the chapter by reviewing everything mentioned above, including the *Outhouse* episode and the glossary.

When you read this way, you'll find that picking up the book after you leave off is like walking into a room with the lights on instead of in darkness. All the material you were studying yesterday is floating around on the top surface of your mind, ready for you to continue adding to what you know about it. You'll also find that all the points you haven't yet got to are primed in your head, so you'll recognize them when you read about them, and this *association* helps make them stick.

END-OF-CHAPTER EXERCISES

Effective study methods always include questions and exercises. You'll find exercises and questions at the end of each chapter. They're somewhat arbitrarily grouped into those that I've found work better as group exercises and those best done individually. However, these groupings are not to be considered sacrosanct.

Any of the exercises and problems may be assigned to individuals or groups or a class as a whole. I have intended that, in a school or seminar setting, the group exercises would be done in teams of about four to six people so that the results may be compared and contrasted afterward. Even in a class as small as four students, I'll sometimes use two groups of two to achieve this. Groups larger than six or seven tend to bog down in too much discussion.

The exercises are grouped as follows:
- Class exercises and problems
- Individual exercises and problems
- Class and individual projects and cases

The best learning sequence is to do the class or group problems first. This exposes you to the process, with the mutual support of your group ("I get by with a little help from my friends" – The Beatles). Once this is done, you should be ready to fly on your own with the individual exercises. The purpose of all this is twofold:
- To consolidate the learning of the current topic
- To find deficiencies that need to be relearned.

To Consolidate the Learning of the Current Topic

No matter how well some of us may learn from lectures or from books, we all learn better by *doing*. Exercises force us to think through hypothetical problems and to reason through (hopefully) realistic simulations of real-world projects. In doing so, we all have insights that fill in the gaps in our learning or cast further light on matters that we understood only dimly.

To Find Deficiencies That Need to be Relearned

It's important that the student or reader – and in a classroom setting, the instructor as well – should become aware of concepts that were missed the first time through. The best way to do this is to try the knowledge out in a real-world situation, or in a simulation as realistic as we can manage. It's also important to share the knowledge and insights gained so that others may benefit from our mistakes and discoveries.

So, to achieve these goals I've included exercises that are then followed by projects and case studies. Each exercise concentrates on one or a few points, but a case study takes the process through from beginning to end. One project that carries through from chapter to chapter in this book is to go out to a small business and develop a small system for them, for real.

In each section the exercises are presented in a graduated order of complexity and difficulty. You should attempt them (or your instructor assign them) roughly in the order shown. You may, of course, be selective, although time permitting I would recommend you do them all.

SELF-TEST QUESTIONS

Following the exercises and projects, each chapter has a series of self-test questions, both multiple-choice and fill-in-the-blanks. These are sufficient to give you a quick evaluation of how well you've learned that chapter.

Answer these questions each time you read through the chapter, on a separate sheet of paper, and look up in the chapter any that you don't get right. Read the chapter again, answer the questions again, and look up again. By the second or fourth time through, you'll have the questions nailed and you'll know the chapter thoroughly. And when looking up the corrections, you'll be able to make effective use of the index.

THE INDEX

The index has been carefully built to help you use the book effectively, both as a text and as a reference on the job. Here's a summary of what's built into the index:

- The index is large enough to contain a worthwhile number of entries.

- The page numbers where the term is defined or explained are boldfaced. The "incidental mentions" are included in standard type for completeness.

- Subheadings are clearly indicated by indenting.

- Where an indented sublist extends onto another page, the main heading is repeated, and subheadings continue on the indentation.

- Indented sublists have been limited in length.

- Entries are repeated and cross-referenced under every alternative title that my reviewers and I could think of.

The Outhouse Bathroom Boutique
Sales Reporting System

The Outhouse Saga continues throughout the book, with a very definite purpose. It's there to organize the material in the reader's mind, in a way that greatly improves learning, as I explain in detail in the preface, under "Advance Organizers."

Now we've reached the end of the chapter body. From here you'll notice that the format is the same in every chapter, beginning with "Deliverables."

• •

Deliverables

Most modern software development methodologies focus on the **documentation or other products that are produced at the end of each phase and subphase of the project; these are referred to as *deliverables*.** The advantage of this approach? The methodology focuses on *what* is produced and leave the developers more freedom to determine *how* it's produced. At each chapter end, you'll find brief descriptions of deliverables that typically go with the activities you've just read about.

In this way, you can use the contents of this book as a methodology if need be, although it's not my intent to generate "yet another methodology." This book is intended to be more or less methodology-free, and my wish has been to focus on concepts and techniques that can be applied in any development environment.

Further Reading

Following "Deliverables" in each chapter is a list of places to go for more on the topics discussed in the chapter. These will point you to chapters, and sometimes to page numbers, in what I sometimes refer to as the "senior" books in the field.

By this I mean that they're written by the leaders in the field, the Original Thinkers who have developed the ideas and techniques of object-oriented analysis. These are the geniuses who have created their methodologies and written some very significant books describing them. One of the major objectives of my book is to present these ideas in a palatable and digestible form, to prime you for understanding the higher-level language of these other books.

Note that not every citation in the chapter necessarily warrants mention here. I have included only the ones where I think you would benefit from following up. The others can be found in the bibliography.

Chapter Summary

- The objectives for this book are that you will be able to:
  - Begin building information systems using object-oriented methods.
  - Learn effectively from the writings of the leaders in the object-oriented field
- The move to object-oriented analysis and design has been accelerated by:
  - The success and rapid spread of object-oriented programming.
  - Recognition that object-oriented methods produce information systems that are more effective, efficient, flexible, and stable

- Most books on OOA are written by academics and senior consultants. This book is written in a style intended to give you a decent bang for your buck, educationally that is. It has an accessible reading level for efficient learning.
- The objectives in doing all this are so that:
  - You will learn effectively about object-oriented analysis
  - You will learn from this book and go into the workplace better prepared to make things happen right, and right on time
- This book is not a methodology. It is mainly a book about concepts. It includes overviews of methodologies and parts of methodologies from some of the leaders in the field. It's enough to get started doing OOA.

CHAPTER GLOSSARY

Here, at the end of each chapter, is where you'll find a glossary consisting of all terms that were encountered and defined in that chapter, as described under "Pedagogical Devices." Here are a few that arise from this chapter:

advance organizer A section of text setting a context for the information that is to follow, to make for more effective learning.

deliverables The documentation or other products that are produced at the end of each phase and subphase of the project.

object-oriented method Organizes both the information, and the processing that manipulates that information, according to the real-world objects that the information describes.

paradigm A way of viewing things and thinking about them.

WHAT COMES NEXT

This practice was first suggested to me by a friend, an elementary school teacher who found it in one of her university texts. When I saw it, I noticed immediately how well it gave continuity to the work, and further examination confirmed this first impression. So after summarizing the chapter and reviewing its glossary, we're ready for a preview of what will follow. A paragraph or two is all that is necessary to alert you and increase the level of receptiveness, all of which serves to enhance your learning.

Then there are these last four sections:

- "Class/Group Exercises and Problems"
- "Individual Exercises and Problems"
- "Projects and Cases"

These have been described under "Pedagogical Devices" in the preface, and you see them here just to show where they will appear at the end of each chapter. And they bring us to the end of this introduction, so now we're ready to dive into the body of the book. We'll begin with a brief look at the current and historical state of software development, and some of its problems. Note how the next chapter follows the structure you saw outlined above.

Chapter Two
. . . .

Systems Development and the Software Crisis

What You Will Learn in This Chapter

This chapter will introduce you to the problems that have arisen in systems development over the last few decades, and why this has given rise to a need for object-oriented methods. You can feel comfortable that you understand the material in this chapter when you can:

1. Explain why output-oriented and process-oriented methods fell short of the goals of rapid and effective design, and of producing stable, resilient systems.
2. List three or more serious problems caused by poorly designed databases.
3. List three benefits and two costs of moving to object-oriented methods.

What You Should Know to Start This Chapter

What is really needed here is that you have personally encountered some of the problems that have plagued systems developers for a long time. Those of you who are already working in the field will, I'm sure, have met some of them already. For the neophytes among you, Episode 2 of *The Outhouse Saga* shows just this kind of thing. But I do wish you could see it happening for real.

Chapter Overview

After viewing the sad state of affairs in the *Outhouse* episode, we take a very brief historical look at how software maintenance and system request backlogs became such a problem. We see how this brought about the search for new ways of developing systems, and a little of why object-oriented methods are so effective. Finally, we check the downside, what it costs to move to object-oriented working.

Key Concepts

- Systems analysis
- Maintenance
- Finding errors sooner
- Backlogs: visible and invisible

- End-user computing
- System stability
- Maintainability
- Reusable components
- Reality-based systems
- Data accessibility
- User involvement and ownership
- Costs of object-oriented techniques: installed base, retraining
- Object-oriented: A whole new way of thinking; a different mind-set

"THE OUTHOUSE BATHROOM BOUTIQUE" SALES REPORTING SYSTEM – EPISODE 2

When Nancy Forsyth invited Tim Buchanan to describe his present information systems, she found that he was anxious to talk about the old reports and the problems with them. "When we got our first computer back in 1982, we really had no idea where to start," he began. "So I asked our company accountant for help in setting it up. He already had one, and he was about the only person I knew back then who seemed to know anything at all about computers."

"Yes, I understand," commented Nancy. "It has always seemed to me that for most small businesses the nearest thing they have to a business adviser is their accountant."

"Well that's right," Tim continued, "so he and I sat down and figured out what should be on my sales reports, and then he set up a bunch of reports in Lotus. I was interested to note that he started out by asking me what reports I needed to have to run my operation. In other words, he said, he wanted to know what did I want to see come *out* of the computer. These reports worked great for three or four years. Every few months we would want an extra column on one of them or change the way we calculated a total or something, and he would come and make the changes for us.

"Then after a while, we ran into some things that he said were caused by shortcomings of a spreadsheet program. Some things we needed he couldn't do with a spreadsheet, and some reports took too long to run. Not Lotus's fault, he said, just that a spreadsheet was not the right tool to use for the kind of things we wanted. He suggested we needed a database to do it properly, but said that was out of his range and we should hire a programmer to do it for us. As it happened, I had a friend who had taken some university computer courses in his engineering degree. He had written lots of programs in FORTRAN and C and had just finished teaching himself dBASE. So he set up a dBASE database that gave us all the old stuff plus the new things we wanted."

"So then you figured you were in pretty good shape," said Nancy.

"Yes, we thought so," Tim went on," and it was great for a time. But again we found we were always needing changes. My friend was able to keep up with the changes for a couple of years, but then we hit a rough spot when his company transferred him to Seattle. We had a number of people make changes for us after that, and it seemed to be much more difficult for them than it had been for him. They all spent way more time on the changes, and then they didn't always work too well! Finally we found a woman who used to be a programmer, and she was able to make some sense of what the others had all been trying to do.

"But by then we were in a position where the computerized system just wasn't adequate any more. Over the years we had changed a lot of things about the way we do business, and all my supervisors and administrative staff were asking for things from the computer. So we sat down with the programmer and had a couple of long meetings where we described what we needed. She seemed to think she could do what we wanted with about five or six months work, so we said to go ahead."

Tim stretched back in his chair, shaking his head. "And that's when it all started to fall apart. She worked long hours, and she was always pounding away on the keyboard, but she just didn't seem to be able to give us the reports we wanted. And I really don't understand why not! We had been keying stuff into the database for six years or so, plus all the information from the old Lotus reports had been transferred over. We knew the information was in there because we could still get all the old reports. I kept asking her, 'Why can't I get the information I need to run the company? It's all in the computer, so why can't I see it the way I need to?'"[1]

The problems Tim described are common to many businesses, but solutions exist, as we'll shortly see. For now, we'll leave Tim and Nancy and pick up with them again in Chapter 3, where Nancy will explain the causes and solutions for Tim's troubles.

THOUGHT QUESTIONS

Discuss these briefly in your small groups. Then (again briefly) present your answers to the class.

1. Awareness exercise: Assuming The Outhouse consists of a dozen smallish stores, try to put a dollar figure on Tim's *MIS* adventures with his computer system. Now extend that by estimating how many companies in your city might be this size and then estimate the total dollar cost. Next come up with a cost for all businesses in your city, regardless of size. Compare these figures with other groups' answers. Tabulate all results on the board.

2. In the mid-1980s when Tim's problems began, what steps or precautions could he have taken to avoid this costly scenario? How different is it in today's business world? These days, how should a business go about computerizing? Put your thoughts on a flip-chart sheet and compare with the other groups. Keep this to check at the end of the coure.

2.1 A BRIEF HISTORICAL PERSPECTIVE

As you'll see in detail in Chapter 3, systems analysis as practiced in the 1960s was done very much by the seat-of-the-pants method. It was much like flying an airplane with no instruments; we had no tools, and no one had developed any methods for us to follow. All we could do was simply interview our users and hope we had a good enough idea of their problems and enough information to develop a solution. We were very good at programming and building solutions in those days, but we were weaker in the important early steps of analysis and problem definition.

Through the next three decades, we developed methods and techniques and were doing a much better job. However, it was still not good enough. Perhaps the two biggest issues were changes (that is, maintenance), and backlogs, and the two are not unrelated. What follows is a discussion of these and some of the other problems that we ran into in those days, and are still trying to remedy.

Maintenance

In Chapters 3 and 4, we'll see why maintenance changes in software became so difficult and so fraught with errors in the early days of computing. And it seems not much has changed! Actually, a lot has changed. Software in the new millennium

---

[1]This is the "plaintive cry of the CEO" discussed in Chapter 4 (where you'll find the definition of CEO).

still has about as many problems with bugs as it did in the 1950s and 1960s, but this is an improvement since software today is several orders of magnitude larger and more complex.

A large business application in the 1960s might have had a few thousand lines of code, no more than, say, ten or fifteen thousand. Today a "large" project consists of many millions of lines of code. In addition, today's software must interact, intercommunicate, and even interoperate with possibly hundreds of other software products. The complexity is mind-boggling, and the probability of errors becomes a certainty. I have a lot more to say about complexity, and how object-oriented methods help us handle it, in later chapters.

The term *error* as I'm using it here needs to be broadened a little. Besides what we commonly call "software bugs," my comments apply equally to errors at the initial stages of a project. In Chapter 3, we'll see how modeling-based methods not only help us avoid errors but also allow us to *find* our errors sooner. We'll see later just why this is so critically important.

Since under these conditions errors have become a certainty, software maintenance continues to be a part of the lives of software developers. Fixing bugs is one part, but adding things that we missed, or that the users forgot to tell us, takes another huge slice of our time. All these changes, corrections, and adjustments then must queue up for their turn at the systems development resources (i.e., *us*, you and me), along with all the new requests for systems. This combined demand on the resources (us) has led to an impossible backlog situation.

Backlogs

At any time in the last thirty years, a review of the systems development industry would have shown about a five-year backlog. Despite the new tools and techniques that came along and the increased understanding of our own processes, our users' needs expanded apace. We've now reached a far better comprehension of what we do and how we should do it, but we haven't been able to eliminate this backlog millstone hung about our collective neck.

But that's only the first part. Besides this visible backlog, there's another that we can't see. The ***invisible backlog* consists of all requests that our users didn't bother to make because of the visible backlog!** These requests will surface only when users perceive that the visible backlog is beginning to dwindle (more about this in Chapter 3).

In the meantime, this combination of the two backlogs has led to the following two major effects:

1   A move toward ***end-user computing*, where users do many of the smaller, less complex tasks themselves, such as reports, screens, and downloading to spreadsheets.** Some of these end users may end up developing complete systems or subsystems, usually on a smaller scale. Modern systems development tools such as screen forms designers and report generators have further fueled this move. Spreadsheets have been used extensively, but they've been a bit of a mixed blessing in this context.

2   A constant search for a better way to develop systems.

Reliability

The excessive maintenance was responsible, of course, for the backlogs. What caused the maintenance? Besides the errors in design described above, poor design of information systems historically has led to a number of problems that have made maintenance more difficult, more time-consuming, and more costly, thus driving up the backlogs.

These consisted mostly of a *lack* of these three things:

- *Flexibility:*   The ability of a system to handle unusual or unforeseen transactions and events.

- *Resilience:*   The ability of a system to adapt and withstand the changes during maintenance, without a host of additional problems arising whenever any little change is made.

- *Quality:*   Good old-fashioned do-it-right and do-it-well; take the time to do it right first time; go the extra mile; build a system that does its job correctly and reliably, without a lot of exasperating crashes and reliability problems; one that users find predictable, so they're not afraid to use it. Later we'll define quality more formally.

2.2   THE NEED FOR A NEW APPROACH TO SYSTEMS DEVELOPMENT

Many businesses large and small have had experiences similar to those of Tim Buchanan in *The Outhouse Saga*. With perfectly understandable naiveté, they have hired people who represented themselves as competent to build their information systems. Sometimes they do an adequate job, sometimes even better. Often they run into the very same problems that have dogged mainframe programmers throughout the short history of systems development. Then projects fail, data is lost, or frightening discrepancies destroy the credibility of the computerized reports.

Only then do business owners and managers begin to realize that there's more to this development stuff than they first thought. There is a body of theory that needs to be understood and followed. There are good ways and bad ways, right ways and wrong ways, of doing this. Good systems consultants are expensive because *that's how much they're worth* in terms of effectiveness, reduced headaches, and ultimately in return on investment (ROI). *You* can learn these techniques and become very valuable to an employer or client. *That* is the purpose of this book.

As we'll see in more detail in Chapter 3, a succession of modeling-based methods has been developed, each taking us a little closer to the goal of simple, effective, and efficient systems development. This has led us to object-oriented methods, which are by far the best yet. However, I would hesitate to tout them as being the last word. Something else will come along in a few years that's even better. I've no idea what it'll be, but we'll all be thrown once more into an exciting learning and experimental role when it happens.

2.3 BENEFITS OF OBJECT-ORIENTED TECHNIQUES

Any new technique, method, or system will be adopted only if it promises worthwhile benefits. It will survive beyond the initial adoption only if it delivers on these promises, and provided the people who use it on a daily basis *see it as a benefit*. In other words, it must not be something forced upon the systems developers, but they must perceive it as improving their lives in some way. They'll continue to use it if they see it as improving their performance, making their users happier, or in some other way smoothing out the stresses of their busy lives.

There's an important caveat, however. There is a delay from switching to using objects and seeing the major benefits. In Chapter 15, "Moving to Object-Oriented Techniques," we'll discuss in detail how objects are not just a new trick to add to what you do now, but an entirely new way of viewing and doing systems development. Objects are a new and different way of thinking about the world and the information it contains.

Because of this, we have a double learning curve to deal with. First, we must learn the new languages and databases and development environments – we're used to that in our industry. And then, in addition, we must learn this *new way of thinking*, which is totally different this time around.

On top of all that, while objects promise major reuse of program code and of analysis and design results, this doesn't normally bear fruit in reduced errors and development time until the third or fourth project. It takes that long to build up a class library of reusable components.

The following are a few of the many benefits that have been found with object-oriented methods. Some of these benefits came first with entity-relationship diagrams (ERDs) or from process modeling with data flow diagrams (DFDs). Those stayed with us when ERDs replaced DFDs, and then as objects evolved from entities.

System Stability

The phrase used is "resilience to change." By this I mean that a program or information system, once installed and running, can be modified to handle the inevitable changes in the users' needs over the years. It is *resilient to change* if these changes can be made without major disruption, with minimal time and effort, and with little fear of disturbing something else in the system, which will then need to be fixed and debugged.

This stability and resilience happen with objects because the system is truly designed to manage and support the users' business, and is based on a fundamental understanding of the data needs of the business, rather than on the ad hoc needs of a few output reports.

Maintainability

Earlier methods tended to base the system design on the needs of the currently known set of reports. These tend to change continually, so changing the software to keep up becomes difficult, to say the least. Object-Oriented methods produce systems that can be maintained and enhanced more readily. This is discussed in detail in Chapters 3 and 4.

Reusable Components

One of the biggest benefits from objects is the reuse of program code and analysis results. While code reuse has always been an objective, it has taken until now for the reuse of analysis results to become truly feasible. Object-oriented features such as inheritance and polymorphism, which are explained in Chapter 8, lead to smoother, more efficient reuse, in ways that programmers never dreamed of before.

This has led to the development of libraries of reusable object classes, such as JavaBeans.

Reality-Based Systems

The techniques used with object-oriented methods give a far more accurate picture of the users' business operation and its information needs. This means that the final system as delivered is closer to the one the users actually need to run their business. Earlier methods tended to allow programmers and analysts to get away with a relatively cursory problem analysis, so we could start coding sooner. (After all, coding programs is what we techies are good at!)

Data Accessibility

It's one thing to file data, but it can be quite another to retrieve data when needed! The *design* of a database is what sets a good one apart from a bad one. The design of a database depends on a thorough understanding of the users' data and the relationships among the data items. The entity-relationship model took us a giant leap ahead in this regard, and the object-oriented techniques take us even further, as you'll see in the coming chapters.

User Involvement and Ownership

This is one of those intangible things that are so hard to measure but can sometimes be worth all the other benefits put together. Historically, the relationship between information technology (IT) personnel and our users has been one of significant distrust. Users often feel inadequate and "blinded by science" around us. Sometimes they'll passively resist by simply keeping quiet in meetings, or refusing to participate in the systems development exercise.

Often they're afraid of looking bad in front of their peers and bosses if they don't catch on quickly enough. This is a very understandable fear, given that they're stepping into *our* world, a world some of them fear and don't understand. All this fear has a habit of coming out either as anger or as withdrawal.

With object-oriented techniques, it's rather easier to get the users fully involved in the systems project. We've learned that we must make the process comfortable for them if we're to get our own job done effectively. The end result is that users develop a sense of ownership in the system, and this often brings about a level of cooperation that wasn't seen as much in the old days.

IBM introduced the term JAD (Joint Application Design), which others have called FTS (Facilitated Team Sessions), where a group of users and developers meet to explore the requirements, under the leadership of an experienced facilitator.[2]

---

[2]You'll note that IBM, along with numerous others in this field, have a habit of using TLAs. In fact, they *are* one – TLA is a Three-Letter Acronym for "Three-Letter Acronym."

Even though JAD / FTS did encourage users to participate more freely, the use of older methods sometimes limited this. With objects, properly handled, there can be a vast improvement in user ownership and participation in the software development process.

But as with anything in this life, there's a cost. All these benefits are great, but there has to be a downside. This is what accountants call cost-benefit analysis.

2.4   COSTS OF OBJECT-ORIENTED TECHNIQUES

Once object-oriented methods are established in an organization, there should be no additional costs. As with any major change, however, there are costs involved in making the change. There are two major sources of costs in moving to object-oriented methods, the installed base and retraining.

Installed Base

Any large organization already has a huge collection of functioning systems and programs designed the old way and coded in standard procedural languages. COBOL won't go away just because we all learn Java, C++, or Smalltalk. There are literally billions upon billions of lines of installed code around the world.

At one time, perhaps 80% or so of it was in COBOL, though that number has now reduced considerably, more like 60% or thereabouts, and much of the rest is in FORTRAN or Pascal. These languages are being used less and less as the years go by, but all that old code must be replaced eventually. No business can afford to just throw it out and start over. (Remember the visible and invisible backlogs we talked about earlier?)

Some of these old systems will need to be converted to object-oriented designs, *at a cost*. Others will need to interface to the new object-oriented systems, *at a cost*. The design of the new systems will need to adjust to accommodate the needs of these ***legacy systems,*** **that is, older systems that already exist and must continue to exist for the foreseeable future.** These adjustments must, of necessity, render our new systems something less than optimal, but we simply can't afford to rebuild all the old systems (yet!)

Retraining

Along with the old systems and languages go the Old Programmers. At the time of writing (Fall 2000), many programmers have not learned the new OO languages and techniques. These people are likely soon to have a very painful encounter with change.

However, we not only have to deal with the prospect of learning a new language, but also something very different, even for those who are accustomed to learning new languages. Object-oriented working requires more than just a change of syntax rules – it requires a whole new way of thinking.

This is easy to say in a short little sentence, but I think you'll see, as we progress through this book, just how different the mind-set needs to be when we work with objects. The danger in using hybrid object-oriented languages such as C++, Object COBOL, or Object Pascal, is that the programmers may simply use the new and powerful tool to do all the old things.

A language such as Java, Eiffel or Smalltalk, on the other hand, will force developers to use object-oriented methods because there's just no other way in those languages. But in this case, we're faced with putting our entire staff through a learning curve in a totally unfamiliar language, much like the poor old-fashioned logger learning the chain saw (see story in Chapter 15).

This brings us to the backmatter of this chapter, beginning with a rather thin "Deliverables" section.

DELIVERABLES

Because we have not yet begun to discuss object-oriented methods, this chapter has no deliverables to mention.

FURTHER READING

Unlike following chapters, this one doesn't have any academic citations because most of it is drawn from general reading and my own personal observations and experience. However, Whitten et al., (1989) have some important things to say. In their second edition, on page 223 as the introduction to Chapter 8, they tell the story of Precious Jewels, who have a story worth telling. Unfortunately, they saw fit to drop this little story from their otherwise excellent later edition (Whitten et al., 1994, 2000).

CHAPTER SUMMARY

- Systems analysis in the 1960s was often done by seat-of-the-pants methods. The two biggest issues are backlogs and changes (that is, maintenance). Besides the *visible* backlog, the *invisible* backlog is all the requests the users didn't make because of the visible one.

- A large application in the 1960s was a few thousand lines of code; today a large project has millions of lines. Today's software must interact, intercommunicate, and interoperate with other software products. We need object-oriented methods to handle the higher probability of errors.

- Modeling-based methods help avoid errors and assist in finding errors sooner, which is critically important.

- Systems development problems have had two major effects:
  - A move toward end-user computing, where the users do many of the smaller jobs, and
  - A constant search for a better way to develop systems.

- Modeling-based methods have been developed, taking us closer to the goal of effective and efficient development. At this time, we have object-oriented methods, but who knows what will come next?

- The benefits of object-oriented working are many:

- **System stability** – that is, resilience to change – happens with objects because the system design is based on a fundamental understanding of the data needs of the business, rather than on the ad hoc needs of a few output reports.

- **Reusable components** such as JavaBeans are based on object-oriented features such as inheritance and polymorphism.

- **Reality-based systems** deliver closer to what the users actually need: data accessibility and user involvement and ownership. With object-oriented techniques, users are fully involved in the project.

- Costs of object-oriented techniques:

  - **Installed base:** A large organization has functioning systems and programs in COBOL, for example, with billions of lines of installed code around the world. The new object-oriented systems will need to adjust to these legacy systems.

  - **Retraining:** Object-Oriented working is more than a change of syntax rules; it requires a whole new way of thinking.

- The danger in hybrid object-oriented languages such as C++ or Object Pascal is that programmers may use the new tool to do old things.

- A language such as Java, Eiffel or Smalltalk forces programmers to use object-oriented methods because there's no other way. However, then we must put our entire staff through a learning curve in a totally unfamiliar language.

CHAPTER GLOSSARY

end-user computing Where users do many of the smaller, less complex systems development tasks for themselves, such as reports, screens, and downloading to spreadsheets.

invisible backlog All requests that users don't bother to make because of the visible backlog.

legacy system An older system that already exists and must continue to exist for now.

resilient to change A system is resilient to change if changes can be made without major disruption, with minimal time and effort, and without disturbing something else in the system.

WHAT COMES NEXT

Chapter 3 gives a brief description of output-oriented and process-oriented methods. Chapter 4 takes us through data-oriented methods and entity-relationship diagrams, and then moves on to an introduction to objects, which are explored in depth in the following chapters.

CLASS/GROUP AND INDIVIDUAL EXERCISES AND PROBLEMS

Since this is an introductory chapter, not much opportunity has arisen for worthwhile exercises. (Expect exercises with real meat to them in the next chapter!) However, one or two things are worth doing to strengthen and review what was said in the chapter. Somewhat arbitrarily, I've placed the one and only exercise for this chapter under "Projects and Cases."

PROJECTS AND CASES

P2.1   Find someone who has been in business systems development / MIS / IT for a long time – at least twenty years, preferably many more. Interview him or her about these topics:

(a) How was systems analysis done when he or she started?

(b) What changes to systems analysis did he or she see take place over the years and decades?

(c) Ask for his or her perspective on each of the four "oriented" styles of systems analysis that are mentioned in the chapter.

(d) Ask for his or her perspective on the problems of backlogs and maintenance over the decades.

(e) Ask him or her whether any of the earlier methods were seen as the solution to most of the problems the industry was having, that is, were they viewed as a "silver bullet"? Does he or she still think that of those methods? How does he or she now see objects in this regard?

SELF-TEST QUESTIONS

Note: The Appendix has answers to the Self-Test Questions.

Q 2.1   The major cost(s) in moving to object-oriented methods is(are):

(a) The installed base of C++, Ada, and Smalltalk programs.

(b) The cost of retraining people in COBOL.

(c) The cost of retraining people in Java, C++, Ada, and/or Smalltalk.

(d) The installed base of COBOL programs.

(e) (a) and (b)

(f) (a) and (c)

(g) (b) and (c)

(h) (b) and (d)

(i) (c) and (d)

(j) None of the above

(k) All of the above

Q 2.2   Among the benefits of object-oriented techniques, we find:

(a) System stability

(b) Resilience to change

(c) Reusable code

(d) Data accessibility

(e) User involvement and ownership

(f) All of the above

(g) None of the above

Chapter Three

. . . .

Models and Modeling

WHAT YOU WILL LEARN IN THIS CHAPTER

In this chapter, you'll learn about models and their use in systems analysis. You will also learn how earlier methods for systems analysis arose and how they led to the development of model-based methods. You can be confident that you understand models when you can:

- Define *model* and explain why models are important in systems development

- Produce a small model depicting a simple business scenario

- Briefly describe the history of systems analysis and development methods, in particular the progression through modeling-based methods

- List and describe the phases in the traditional systems development life cycle (SDLC)

WHAT YOU SHOULD KNOW TO START THIS CHAPTER

This chapter assumes that you've written computer programs before and that you understand what a database is. Although not essential, it would help if you've ever been involved in an information systems (IS) or software development project. Some understanding of businesses and how they operate would also be helpful.

CHAPTER OVERVIEW

To talk about object-oriented analysis and object-oriented models, we first need to establish just what it is that we mean by the terms *analysis, object*, and *model*, and we'll need a little bit about *oriented* as well. In this chapter, we define systems analysis and discuss models. We'll discuss what models are and how and why we use them in various ways, particularly in systems development. (In Chapter 4, we discuss object models in particular and why object-oriented techniques are so effective for the various phases of the systems development life cycle.)

This chapter begins with the formal definition of a model and discusses why it's a form of *abstraction*. You'll see how humans constantly use models to understand the world around them and, particularly in the field of systems analysis, to understand the users' problems.

We define the systems development life cycle (SDLC) and present a brief history of systems analysis to show how modeling-based techniques arose. These earlier modeling methods are examined to show how object-oriented methods were developed. We'll look at the various stages in the history of systems analysis in the following order:

Chapter 3 (i.e., this chapter)
- Unsystematic early approaches, 1950s to the early 1960s
- "Output-oriented" methods, late 1960s
- Process-oriented methods, 1970s; data flow diagrams (DFDs)

Chapter 4
- Data-oriented methods, 1980s; entity-relationship diagrams (ERDs)
- Object-oriented methods, 1990s

KEY CONCEPTS

- Model, abstraction
- Random sensory inputs
- Object, attribute, behavior, message
- Systems development life cycle (SDLC)
- Analysis, design, construction, implementation, maintenance
- Parallel run
- Methodology
- Listening and people skills
- Business processes
- Requirements definition
- Effect of error expands with time; need to get it right the first time
- Functional decomposition
- Analysis
- Structured Design
- Process models, data flow diagrams (DFDs), leveled set
- Data, data flow, data store, external entity
- Medium (plural media)
- Physical/logical data flow diagrams, "implementation-independent" models
- Modularity
- Deliverables

THE OUTHOUSE BATHROOM BOUTIQUE
SALES REPORTING SYSTEM – EPISODE 3

In our last episode Tim had just finished describing all the troubles his company had had with computers and how he knew the data was in there, but he couldn't get at it. "I guess that was very frustrating," commented Nancy.

"You're not kidding!" Tim responded, somewhat agitated. "How can it happen this way? I see it, but I just don't understand why!"

"Actually, I think I can shed some light on that," Nancy ventured. "It's not an uncommon problem at all. Mostly it seems to be a matter of inexperience and lack of training. There are a lot of people out there who are very good programmers, but lack skills and knowledge in two very important areas. One of these is knowing how to look at a business in terms of its information needs. We need to go much deeper than just the output reports. We need to look at how the people in your company use information at each step of their jobs and what data they generate as they work. Some very powerful techniques are available nowadays for doing this analysis."

"But," interjected Tim, "shouldn't my accountant or the programmer have known about these methods?"

"Not necessarily," answered Nancy. "You see, your accountant, although he thoroughly understands businesses in general and yours in particular, was not specifically trained in modern systems analysis methods. His knowledge of Windows and computers was probably good, and most accountants are highly skilled with spreadsheets, but his understanding of how information is used by your organization was likely not deep enough. Your engineer friend and your programmer may both have been competent at programming, but probably neither would have been aware of these methods.

"Engineers, accountants, and other noncomputer professionals don't learn these things in school. If they ever get to learn them, it's usually not until they are working in their profession. And then only if they're involved with systems analysts in a systems project in their own business area. And my guess is that your programmer probably graduated well before these techniques were being taught in the colleges. A lot of IS professionals are having to upgrade these days to these new methods."

"Uh, 'IS' means . . .?" Tim looked puzzled.

"Oh, 'Information Systems.' Just jargon," apologized Nancy. "And people often use 'IT' for 'Information Technology' as a synonym, although it's not quite the same thing."

"Right. Well how would I know who to trust?" queried Tim. "Do you people have anything like the CA or CPA[1] designation that accountants have?"

"As a matter of fact we do," replied Nancy. "You may have noticed the initials CCP on my business card. CCP stands for Certified Computing Professional. This is a worldwide designation administered by the Institute for the Certification of Computing Professionals, or ICCP, a body made up of about forty professional associations from countries all around the world.[2]

Their goal is to have the CCP designation recognized the way the CA and CPA are for accountants. There are others in various countries around the world. Canada, for instance, has the ISP, or Information Systems Professional. It's administered by CIPS, the Canadian Information Processing Society. They're one of the constituent bodies of the ICCP, and the ISP is held in high regard in many countries. There are reciprocal agreements among many of these bodies to recognize each other's designations.

"I find it interesting, though," she chided him gently, "that while you wouldn't dream of having your books set up by anyone less than a specialist accountant, you seem to have picked a bunch of amateurs to do your computer work!"

"And I'm living to regret it, too!" Tim said with a wry grin. "So what difference do these fancy new-fangled techniques make? Can you give me some idea what they're about, in a dozen words or less?"

"Not really," Nancy laughed. "But I can give you an example of the kind of problem they help avoid. You see, when nonprofessionals develop an information system (non-IS professionals, that is), of course, like anybody else they want to do a good job. So they try to find some logical way to go about it. What they usually come up with is to ask: 'What do you want to see come *out* of this?'"

"Sounds reasonable to me," commented Tim. "That's where my accountant started."

"Yes," said Nancy, "it's reasonable all right, but it's not enough. Both your accountant and your engineer started out this way, and the unexpected result for both of them was this: They built a system that was *custom tailored to the set of reports that they knew about*, and didn't have the flexibility to adapt as your business changed over the years.

---

[1]CA: Certified Accountant (Canada); CPA: Certifed Public Accountant (USA).

This is why your programmer had so much trouble trying to extend their work!"

"Yes," said Tim, "it took her almost a year to get something going. That's twice the time she estimated. We weren't very happy with her by the time she left, and she wasn't very happy with us either! That was just over a year ago now, and since then we've been struggling along with the few reports she was able to come up with."

"Well I'm confident we can do something far better," smiled Nancy. "What I'm proposing is that we start with a meeting of your key people, and I'll use these new methods to pick their brains for what I need. From that we'll build a model that's really a set of diagrams that describe how your company uses information and creates data. It will show flows of data between parts of your company and what data need to be kept in the disk files. From the model, we can build you a system that will give your people exactly what they need, and it will continue to do that for a considerable number of years as well."

"Sounds good," said Tim a trifle dubiously, "but after what we've already been through around here, I'm sure you'll pardon me if I reserve judgment until I see what you can do for us."

"Fair enough!" rejoined Nancy. "How would Tuesday morning do for about three hours? And let's talk about who you think should be there. Oh, and could you have someone pick up a few copies of a book for me. It explains the new methods really well. It's called *An Introduction to Object-Oriented Analysis*. Most bookstores will have it. It's by David Brown, a close friend of mine, who is also a CCP."

Thought Questions

These questions are intended for a large class broken into discussion groups, but they are also important for individual readers who may be reading this book without taking any classes. Individual readers should think through each question and make notes of their thoughts on the issues raised. Readers in a classroom environment should discuss them briefly in small groups, then (again briefly) present their answers to the class:

1. In your group, list as many reasons as you can why a business would bother hiring someone with a professional designation (i.e., a designated professional) to do their systems development, when there are many skilled people around who can do the job for less. If time permits, you may wish to research this by getting some brochures from one of the IS professional associations. You may be able to find them in your phone book, your instructor may be able to help, or you may need to ask a programmer or systems analyst who belongs to one.

2. In your group, discuss a system or project one of you has encountered, that was designed for the known set of outputs but lacked the flexibility to change as the users' and clients' needs changed over time. Discuss the problems this caused and the effects these problems had on the business, the users, and the clients of the business. This may be a computerized system or any other kind of system that you've met. You may have been involved in any way, perhaps as a system builder or as a user, client, taxpayer, or just as an onlooker.

3. What do you think caused people to begin by looking at the output as the basis of a system design, when it turns out that the data is actually a better place to start?

4. In your group, think about and discuss a time when you encountered a
    system that you know or suspect had a history of development problems
    much like Tim's. You may have been the user (like Tim), or perhaps the
    customer, or an interested third party like Nancy. Or (heaven forbid!), you
    may have been the analyst or programmer. Be honest, now!

Now, let's start at the very beginning, with a discussion of some basic points that
the entire concept of object-oriented modeling rests upon.

3.1   DEFINITIONS

Data and Information

I think it's appropriate to explain how I use these two words since they are what
this book and the whole object-oriented thing are all about. You'll find my
definitions consistent with, but not identical to, those of most authors. I think you'll
find these definitions make a lot of sense.

Data:

The word is actually the plural of the Latin *datum*, which means "fact." I like
to think of __*data*__ as **"*raw facts*," in the sense that they're unprocessed in any
way. They're just facts, and they just exist.**

This I find to be a very workable definition, although you need to keep in mind
that it does involve some simplification. For example, if your name is misspelled in
a computer file, it's still *data*, but it's not exactly a fact. With that little warning in
mind, then, let's check how information is different from data.

Information:

The key word here is *useful*. __*Information*__ **is data that has in some way been
made *useful* to someone.**

Useful for what? Why, for making decisions. To make *data* into useful
information, we must *process* it in some way. We may organize it, calculate
averages and indices, put it in columns side-by-side, and so on. This is what gives
rise to the older term *data processing*.

Model

You may wonder why we need to be so formal about defining a word like *model*.
After all, it's a word you've used all your life. I get a variety of answers when I ask
my classes this question: "What comes to mind when you hear the word *model*?"
They'll say it's smaller than the real thing, it looks the same, it looks different,
made of different stuff, a representation, it does some of the same things, it's for
understanding something, and so on. Each answer is correct, of course, at least to
some extent.

So let's begin by taking a look at some applications of models. Did you notice in
recent years that cars got rounder in shape? The reason was to improve the
streamlining. Ford was the first, which led to some controversy at NASCAR stock
car races – it seems that, at speeds of over 200 miles per hour, the Fords were
gaining an extra 10 mph or so! (This was resolved two years later when General
Motors also rounded off their sharp edges.) For the rest of us, it meant improved gas
mileage and reduced emissions at highway speeds.

So how did they do it? How did the car companies resolve the compromise of wind resistance, weight, interior space (yes, we need room for people), and a number of other important variables? They put it in a wind tunnel!

Right. But exactly *what* did they put in a wind tunnel? It was not a succession of real cars – that would be way too expensive. It was a series of *models*. These models were not full size; the usual size is one-third scale. They were not steel; they were in fact made of clay. The models had no wheels, no engine, and no room for people, but they had *everything they needed for the problem at hand*. And they were simpler, cheaper, and quicker to build.

The mannequins in a clothing store have all they need to do a fine job of marketing the clothes they wear, but they lack many of the attributes of real people. Similarly, the form that a dressmaker adjusts to the size and shape of her client is perfect for sewing clothes that fit, but I'm sure you'll agree it lacks certain important features of a real woman.

Plans and blueprints are an essential representation of the finished product, even though they look only vaguely like the actual product. Electrical schematics and program flowcharts tell us much about the actual thing but look nothing like it at all. A map is essential for navigating, even though it only shows shapes and relative sizes; if it has colors, they're probably coded for something, and they're not the actual colors you might see from an airplane. What is it, then, that all these have in common?

An important factor links all these examples together. Every one of them in some way *represents* something that exists or is planned in the *real world* and that in some way is too *complex* or large for us to *understand it* as it stands. So each is in some way *simplified*, or reduced in size, scope, or scale. Thus, a **_model_ is a simplified representation of a complex reality, usually for the purpose of understanding that reality, and having all the features of that reality necessary for the current task or problem.**

Abstraction

Modeling is actually a form of **_abstraction_, the process of focusing on those features that are essential for the task at hand and ignoring those that are not.** The distinction is that with models we actually *build* something. It may be physical, like the clay car, or it may be drawings on paper such as an organization chart. It may be textual such as a report summarizing a survey, or it may be conceptual like a mathematical model full of equations or like the "picture" you carry in your head of the world around you.

One way or another, we build a *representation* of some part of the real world. It's also possible to abstract without having to build something, but in this book we'll focus on *modeling*. You'll learn how to build and use models to help you understand some very complex realities – in particular that foreign and complex part of the real world that belongs to our users. This you and I need to understand if we're going to do a decent job of software development.

3.2 MODELS AS AN AID TO UNDERSTANDING

In Section 3.1 above, we stated that models are "usually for the purpose of understanding"; and yes, for all you builders of model "Trains and Boats and Planes" (with apologies to Roger Miller) and for all you fashion models, there are exceptions.

Any equation that describes something in the real world is a model. It helps us understand and perhaps control some part of our reality. Increase the complexity, and you have the mathematical models that have proved so useful in all branches of science and technology.

From these we have computer simulations, where thousands of equations describing an industrial process or a natural phenomenon must be solved simultaneously to arrive at an answer. Any simulation, including video games, is a model. The space shuttle flew thousands of missions on the computer before it orbited for real. So also the Boeing 777, and the Dodge Prowler. These are all ways of using models for understanding. And actually, this is something we've all done since the moment of birth (or perhaps even earlier).

A Child's First Model

One of the strengths of the object-oriented way of looking at things is that each of us has been using objects implicitly all our lives. Right from birth and before, a child is bombarded with what must at first seem to be just random sensory inputs. Through those early hours and weeks, the child begins to perceive patterns and to relate patterns arriving from different input systems: sight and sound, for example, or sight and taste.

After a while, the child begins, as the psychologists put it, to "perceive objects" in the world about her. Actually, the child goes through a process that's so effective we've formalized it and named it the "scientific method." That is, the child observes what is going on and comes up with rules that connect the patterns and allow her to predict what might happen next. Then the child forms a concept (or theory) to explain what she has observed and to allow further, more complex predictions.

The concept of objects appears to be part of the core of our experience, since it's one theory that's used by all of us. A child notes certain repeating patterns in her environment and associates *attributes* with them. These attributes might be things like color, size, shape, taste, and "how it feels to be held by this object, on a score of 1 to 10."

The child also observes that these objects exhibit certain *behaviors*, sometimes spontaneously and sometimes in response to messages from the child. She soon discovers that if she opens her mouth and yells, someone will put something soft, comforting, and pleasant-tasting in it.

She also realizes that there are different kinds of objects and that they fall naturally into groups or *classes* based on having similar attributes. This may mean, for example, that they're all the same color, or it may mean that they belong together simply because they all *have* a color.

And she learns to expect similar behavior from objects within a class. Then she learns that the objects within a class can be divided into smaller groups, or subclasses, based on a wide variety of criteria. A food object might be meat, or it

A child perceives objects in the world around her

might be vegetable, or it might be a drink. People may be divided into men and women, or into "Mother," "Father," and "Others."

Initially, a baby will smile at any football-shaped object above the crib. Later, this object must have a face drawn on it to get any reaction. Then it must be a real head with a face, and eventually it must be *Mother's* face. This progressive differentiation leads to the concept of *subclasses*, which depends on recognizing *kinds of* objects within a class.

Finally, the child completes her study of objects (for now) with one last realization. Have you ever noticed that when a young child is watching something and it passes out of her field of view, she forgets about it and turns her attention to something new? This is not a problem with attention span but arises from the fact that she's unaware of something you and I take for granted. She is unaware that the object still exists even though she can't see it. Later you'll find that when you remove it from her view, she will turn and look for it. By then, she has "achieved *object persistence*," as the psychologists put it.

Note the italicized words in this discussion of an infant's learning. These ideas are fundamental to the way human beings handle complexity and make sense of the world around them. These words and their meanings have been borrowed directly from human experience and used unchanged in object-oriented methods. We'll be revisiting all these ideas in great detail in later chapters, and we'll see just how powerfully they relate to systems development, specifically in terms of developing *the right system* and developing it *right*.

For now, let's look at the evolutionary history of systems development, beginning before models were even considered, to see how and why modeling and object-oriented modeling in particular is so important. We'll begin with the early methods that were used before we learned about models.

3.3 EARLY (PRE-MODELING) SYSTEMS DEVELOPMENT METHODS

We will look at the following stages in the history of systems analysis, in this order. This list just gives the sequence for these topics, not the entire contents; other topics will be interspersed.

In This Chapter

- Unsystematic early approaches, 1950s to the early 1960s

- "Output-oriented" methods, late 1960s

- Process-oriented methods, 1970s; data flow diagrams

In Chapter 4

- Data-oriented methods, 1980s; entity-relationship diagrams

- Object-oriented methods, 1990s

You can see from this list that a major change occurred in the approach to the business of systems development in each decade. These changes were in fact deep enough and significant enough to qualify for the label *paradigm shift*, which is explained in detail in Chapter 4.

Unsystematic Early Approaches:

1950s to the Early 1960s

When I began my career in 1965, although the terms *systems analysis* and *systems analyst* had been coined, most of us had only a vague idea of what they really meant. Certainly, we knew very little about how to actually *do* systems analysis. In the late 1960s, the members of our profession realized that we needed to introduce more rigor and logic into the way we went about finding a solution to our users' problems.

Notice how I phrased that "finding a solution." Our focus was on the solution, and we were really quite good at finding and building solutions. What we didn't realize was that the core of our difficulty lay in understanding the user's problem in the first place, before we ever went looking for a solution.[2]

Peter Drucker, a well-known management consultant and author, has said that "*efficiency* is doing the job right, and *effectiveness* is doing the right job." That about describes where systems analysts were in the 1960s (and only too often, some still are today!).

---

[2] I have distinct philosophical problem with vendors who insist on marketing "solutions" and who never use the word *product* when they can call it a "*solution*." I always feel they want to mold my problem to fit their "solution," a process often described as *solution-oriented thinking*, when I believe what we really need is *problem-oriented thinking*. We must *understand the problem*, before we go looking for a solution.

We needed ways to investigate and understand our users' business and the problems they were having so that we could produce the right solution *to the right problem*. Our first attempts at formalizing the way we went about our job were, of course, far less effective than today's methods, but they were a definite improvement over what went before.

The Systems Development Life Cycle

One idea that surfaced around 1970 was that the steps we go through in developing an information system follow a recognizable pattern. The systems development life cycle (SDLC) consists of a number of steps or phases that are all necessary if the system is to do what the users need, and do it well. The basic SDLC is outlined below. Some writers prefer to break down some of the steps into smaller ones, but for now we'll do it this way:

Analysis

In this phase, we study the users' business and their problems in order to discover *what* the users need the system to do, so it can help them to do their job better. We specifically do *not* consider *how* it will be done, nor with what hardware or software.

Design

In this phase, we produce a plan or design showing *how* we intend that the system will do the functions identified in the analysis phase. Here we consider such things as the hardware/software platform, choice of language, operating system, and database software (DBMS). We design the databases, programs, screens, and reports. We produce program specifications (specs), which are to be passed on to the programmers in the next phase.

Construction

Here the programs are written and the databases are built. Then the whole system is tested and debugged, first by the programmers, and then by the users and the development team together.

Implementation

The system is installed in production, the users are trained. Sometimes **the new system and the old (which may be automated or manual) are both run side-by-side for a period, typically a month. This procedure is known as a *parallel run*.**

Maintenance

Once the system is installed and running, you can expect a steady stream of corrections. Some of these will be bugs (program errors), some will be design errors, and some will be things the users forgot. There will also be a steady stream of improvements to the system (usually termed "enhancements") requested by the users throughout the life of the system.

Keeping this pattern in mind, we'll now take a look at the history of how systems analysis evolved, to arrive finally at object-oriented methods.

Unsystematic Early Approaches:

"Output-Oriented" Methods of the Late 1960s

The earliest procedures we tried started with the reports and screens that the users needed the system to produce (Figure 3-1). Users and programmers didn't have too much trouble with this since it's relatively easy to visualize. The users, being experts in their own jobs, usually have little trouble suggesting some of the reports and screens they want to see at each step of their job, what details should appear on these reports, and how the figures should be calculated.

The next step was to work backward from these outputs to see what data needed to be calculated and what needed to be stored, when and for how long. Finally, from there we would work back to see what we needed to enter into the system and where it could be found. In this way, the design of the reports drove most of the decisions made during the system development (Figure 3-2).

As a matter of fact, in 1969 I was using a paper-and-pencil systems development methodology that did exactly that. A ***methodology*** (Random House Webster 1998) **is a set or system of methods, principles and rules, for regulating a certain discipline [in this case, the discipline of information systems (IS) development, or management information systems (MIS).]** This early and somewhat primitive methodology is illustrated in Figure 3-2.

The process began with a Report-Design form ruled in squares, something like an overgrown sheet of graph paper. I'm sure some of you have seen this kind of thing, often called a *printer spacing chart*. What was different about this one was the cross-referencing section off to the right, as shown in Figure 3-2. Under each data element diagrammed in the body of the report, we entered a number that matched up with one in the cross-reference table.

Beside that number in the cross-reference table was a form type, form number, and field number, linking this data element to one on another form. The other form could be a calculation, record-layout or input form.

A record-layout form allowed us to design a layout for a data file record. And each field in the record was similarly referenced to calculation or input or to another record-layout form. The calculation forms did the same, referencing each data element back to an input form, a record-layout form, or another calculation form. In this way, we built a chain that went all the way from output back to input.

One big advantage of this system was that it gave us a *completeness check*. That is, we could ensure that everything we designed onto our outputs was in fact entered somewhere, and that a path existed for it to follow through the system to end up on the appropriate output(s). Also, the method helped enormously just by giving us a structure to organize our work and a consistent notation with which to represent it.

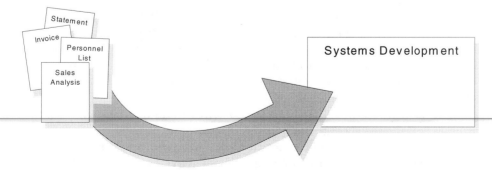

Figure 3-1 "Output-oriented" Methods: The reports drive all decisions during system development

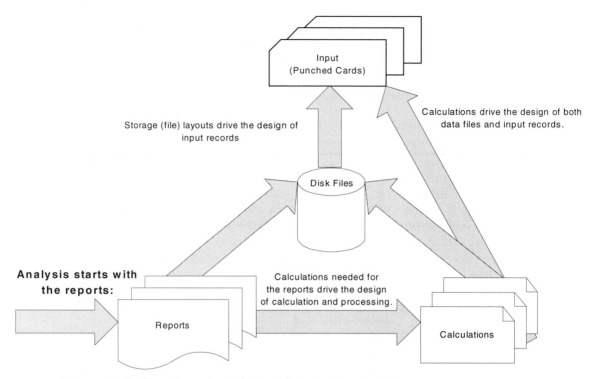

Figure 3-2 Overview of an "Output-Oriented" methodology

However, systems designed this way suffered a serious drawback that didn't show up until some time after each system was designed.

We in the Information Systems (IS) industry didn't recognize until the late 1970s why we had a maintenance problem. We noticed that some changes, which to our users appeared quite small, often required weeks or months of work on our part. We seemed to spend most of our time doing maintenance on existing systems and programs, rather than developing new ones. This was due to our "output-oriented" design methodology.

The systems we were building were turning out to be customized for the set of reports that we based our design on. In reality, however, users' reporting needs kept on changing. This is natural because, as we now realize, there's no such thing as a stable business – they're all either growing or dying.

Thus, whenever a manager needed a new figure or column or a new report, we would find we had to deal with a massive cascade of changes. These would extend from the reports back through all our files, calculations, and inputs. The consequent changes were sometimes scattered all throughout our system, often affecting practically every part of it.

Eventually, we did figure out better ways to do our analysis, leading to the model-based methods described in the next section. But I've recently observed an interesting phenomenon in the desktop computer world, where many people seem to be repeating the mistakes we in information systems made so long ago.

In my college, we used to offer a 2-day course called "Introduction to Systems Analysis for Microcomputer Users." The major objective was to steer people away from the kind of experience you read about in Episodes 2 and 3 of *The Outhouse Saga*.

Time and again, I hear the same tale from accountants, small-business operators, and clerical staff when they take this course (or sometimes a database course). Their boss will say to them, "Go take an Oracle (or Access or Paradox) course from Dave and then come back and build us a database for this problem we're having." Or a business owner will turn to his accountant, usually the only business advisor or management consultant he has, and say, "You understand these computers. Help me set this up to do what I need."

To their credit, these clerks and accountants, suddenly thrust into the role of management consultant cum systems analyst, will realize that they need to be systematic in their approach to the boss or client's problem. So in trying to hit upon a logical approach, can you guess what they so often end up trying?

You got it! "What information would you like to see come *out* of this thing?" they say. And off they go, earnestly repeating the mistakes that we in the mainframe world made so long ago. This is rather sad, especially when we consider that the newer techniques, especially OOA, are so much better, and these days so readily available to specialists and nonspecialists alike.

All they need is a course like the one you're taking right now, and a book like the one you have in your hand!

Back then, we were all basically untrained, even the so-called information specialists. As we progressed in our search for effectiveness, we came to the important realization that our first step must be to *understand the users' world*. We began to adapt the principles of modeling to the world of information.

Ed Yourdon (Yourdon and Constantine, 1976) and others in the 1970s came up with the first modeling-based methodologies, under the rubric of *Structured Analysis*. In the next section, we look at how modeling-based techniques fit into IS development. Then, in the following sections, we'll examine some of these earlier kinds of models that eventually led us to OOA.

3.4 MODELS IN SYSTEMS DEVELOPMENT

"God gave us two ears and one mouth!"

This anonymous quote accurately describes the attitude required of a systems analyst. In analysis we're here to listen and learn. As information experts,[3] it behooves us to *listen*, although you may not think so when you hear some of us talk. One major problem in systems analysis has been a tendency for us to believe that we fully understand the users' problem, when in fact we have only half the story. It's only in recent years that systems analysts have seriously addressed this problem.

The first hurdle was to admit, even to ourselves, that the problem existed. Now that modeling-based techniques are in widespread use, finally we've learned just how important it is to recognize our own ignorance of our users' business. In the past, we were blithely unaware of how much we didn't know; we didn't even know we were ignorant!

---

[3] *"Expert:"* An "ex" is a has-been, and a "spert" (spurt) is a drip under pressure! So be careful how you apply this term.

Nowadays, it's widely recognized that systems analysis is a *people-oriented* profession. Technical competence is, of course, a requirement of a good analyst, but by itself not enough. In addition, we need business knowledge and training, to help us understand the users and their problems, and above all the analyst needs *people skills*.

It's primarily through interacting with the *people* and observing the *people* that we come to an understanding of the world our users live and work in, and the difficulties they have with parts of that world.

Users who are feeling intimidated by us techies or by their own management won't freely admit to problems and deficiencies, so of course they can't discuss solutions. You simply can't solve a problem if you won't admit that it exists. The unfortunate result is that we analysts may easily miss a number of important details, and that can often make a noticeable difference to the success and usability of the final system.

To understand the users' world adequately then, we need three things:

- **Modeling *notations*** to document and communicate all that we learn from our users

- **Modeling *techniques*** that ensure we use these notation tools properly to produce an accurate picture of the users' business

- ***People sensitivity,*** and interviewing and listening skills, to ensure that we gather all relevant information, so that our models form a complete and accurate picture of the users' business

Our understanding, to be complete, should not only cover the business the users are in and their own operation in particular, but also include the various environments in which they must function. We must check what effect their technical, commercial, and political environments might have on the problems we're addressing. We must consider also the social aspects of their workplace, their interactions with clients or other outsiders, and how this affects their operation.

In Chapters 7 and 9, when we address object-modeling techniques, and further in Chapter 16, on people skills, you'll learn specific strategies for involving your users in the analysis process. You'll discover ways to draw out the quiet and fearful ones, to make sure everyone's ideas are heard and considered. As your users move with you through this process, you may find them very interested and even excited about some new perspectives they may gain on their own operation.

Information Aspects New to the Users!

Your users have probably never considered their own business from the point of view of the data and information that it uses and must have to continue functioning. In a sense, we can say the business is "driven by" its data, or we can view it as being "supported by a pool of data."

Either way, it's a fairly safe bet that all or most of your users will never have examined their business in terms of objects, data to be stored about those objects, and the functions that manipulate or use this data. This is the essence of object orientation.

Even if your users have been involved in systems projects in the past, they probably have not been exposed to formal modeling techniques. If they have, it was most likely some form of process modeling where they would consider what they *do* in their jobs, rather than the *data* and the *objects* that they do it *with*.

This is an important distinction. Earlier forms of modeling (and the premodeling methods), tended to focus on **_business processes_, what people do in order to make their organization run. To put it another way, _business processes_ are all the things that must happen and activities that must be performed in the course of the organization doing its business.**

As you'll see in the later chapters, object modeling takes a totally different approach. Object modeling first considers the data, the things people must know to run the organization. But object modeling, like its immediate ancestor data modeling, begins even further back than the data. It starts with the *objects*, things people need to know *about*, that is, the real-world objects that they need to keep data about. Only later does the object modeler consider the processes that use this data for the benefit of the users and their operation.

If you're really lucky, your users have read this book already and are raring to go building object-oriented models. But modeling with any style of model does bring its own set of problems. One of these, which can at the same time be both a blessing and a curse, is the fact that more work must be done *early in the project*, before we start showing any tangible results for our efforts.

Development Effort Moved Up Front

All the various modeling techniques that systems analysts have used over the last two or three decades have had one thing in common: Analysis modeling forces us to spend time with the users up front. As we progressed over this period from the earlier functional decomposition models and data flow diagrams, to the later entity- and object-based models, we became more aware of this factor.

Now we recognize it and even use it to our benefit (ours and the users'). The major benefit is that we gain a more thorough and complete understanding of the problem. Not perfect, of course, but way ahead of the older methods.

I cannot overemphasize the importance of this understanding, of the need to identify clearly and accurately just _what the problem is_ that we will attempt to solve, before we even _begin_ to conjure up a solution.

As the earlier quote from Peter Drucker would suggest, it doesn't matter how good the eventual solution may be, *a solution to the wrong problem won't put us far ahead!* It may easily turn out to be counterproductive and put us several steps behind. We'll encounter some of these situations in the scenarios later on in this book.

This leads me to another comment, this time about information professionals. Since most of us systems analysts began our careers as programmers, we feel comfortable writing programs. We love to get our hands dirty writing code. We simply are not comfortable with all this people stuff and all the up-front time spent modeling. For so many of us, *plan* is a four-letter word. So we ask a few questions, and when we think we have a handle on the problem, we dive in and get started on the "real work" of *coding*.

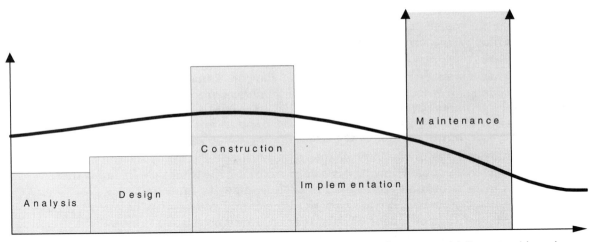

Figure 3-3 Time-effort distribution for systems development: old (bar graph) and new (line graph)

The difference between the older and newer ways is shown in Figure 3-3. The bar graph shows clearly how we used to (and many of us still do) skim through the analysis phase, do a bit more in design, and spend our time on our first love, programming. We regarded implementation, installing the system, and training the users, as something of a necessary evil ("This'd be a great job if there weren't any users"). Then we wondered why every system we built required so much maintenance!

In contrast, the line curve in Figure 3-3 for the modeling-based methods shows much more time spent on Analysis. This leads to a far more accurate *__requirements definition,__* **the document that spells out what the eventual system must do, the information it must produce, and when and where,** ***without*** **dictating** ***how*** **it will be done.** (We'll look at requirements definitions in more detail later in the book.) There's less time spent on programming, for a variety of reasons. With object-oriented programming, the level of code reuse is so high (after the initial adoption period) that the coding effort is still further reduced compared with the earlier kinds of models.

The time and resources spent on maintenance are sharply reduced by getting it right (or close) in the first place. Of all the modeling styles available, object-oriented modeling has shown the greatest reductions in both maintenance and initial coding. The cost, of course, is the extra time spent in analysis. The overall result is not only a system of higher quality, but also reduced total cost because errors tend to be detected earlier.

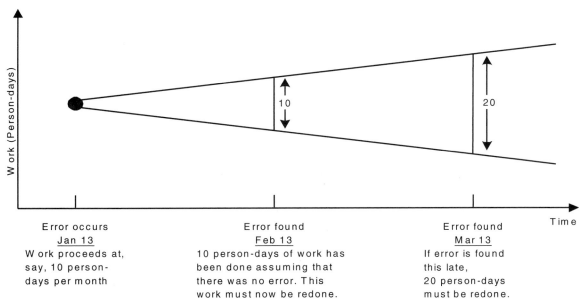

Figure 3-4 The effect of an error, and the cost of fixing it, grow with time.

Need for Early Detection of Errors

The reductions in programming and maintenance effort are in large part owing to the early detection of errors. The statistics are that of all the errors made in constructing information systems, 56% occur in the initial determination of the users' requirements. Not only that, but in terms of the effort and expense required to correct errors, 81% is spent on these early requirements definition errors. Why is such a huge proportion spent on errors that are made early in the project?

By way of analogy, consider an assembly line, building desktop computers. Each person adds a component and passes the assembly on to the next person in line. One assembles the frame, another mounts the power supply, and another the motherboard; after that, the RAM DIMMS, the video board, the hard disk, the floppy disk, the disc controller board, and, finally, the case. The last person packs it in a box, and it's done.

But what if the motherboard person installed the wrong motherboard? No problem, just take it out and replace it. But what if the error was discovered by the person putting on the case? Just look how much stuff went in *after* the incorrect motherboard and now has to come out!

So you see, the farther down the line the error is discovered, the more work has to be undone and then redone to correct it. This applies equally in any field of endeavor and is certainly true in systems development. As you can see from Figure 3-4, when an error is made in the early stages of a project, as time goes by more and more work is done on the assumption that there is no error.

Thus, the earlier the error occurs and the later it's discovered, the more expensive and time-consuming (read *delaying*) it is to fix. And, of course, the more difficult and frustrating your job becomes as an analyst, and there's less chance of a successful project and a satisfied user community.

All of which simply highlights the need to *get it right the first time*. This is where the modeling techniques have helped, each one an improvement over what went before it.

All is not a bed of roses, however; there is a difficulty with moving the effort up front to the analysis phase. Management is always hungry for results. They want to see screens and output reports to show that you and I are producing something with all the time we, and their staff, and our staff are spending on this project.

Generally speaking, many managers don't fully understand the systems development process, and this too adds to their fears. They quite naturally don't feel comfortable with assurances that "the analysis is proceeding according to plan." They wish to see some tangible results, something they can see and touch, and perhaps understand, coming out of all the meetings and interviews.

Unfortunately, it's not until the design phase of our project that we start producing report and screen designs and file- and database-layout diagrams. But we're still OK because of the concept of *deliverables*, which are described in the section later in this chapter labeled, appropriately enough, "Deliverables."

Quality

A widespread movement is afoot in industry in general, to improve the quality of what we produce. We've all seen "Quality Is Job One!" and "The Quality Goes In Before the Name Goes On!" Corporations, government, and educational institutions alike have been establishing quality initiatives, Total Quality Management (TQM), and Continuous Quality Improvement (CQI).

As a result, many organizations have experienced marked improvement in both the functioning of their operation and the quality of their output. One of the central themes of these efforts has been a redefinition of the term *Quality* to equate it with *client satisfaction*. Viewed from that angle, it's easy to see that no matter how well a product functions and how long it lasts, if it *doesn't do the job* the client needs the way she needs it, the product is not worth building.

This directly applies to the building of information systems. We must produce a system that *does the job*, does it well, and does it for an adequate length of time, and with enough flexibility to handle the inevitable changes. Above all, it must *do the right job*, and do it *the way the users need it*. The succession of modeling methods has been a constant evolution of new and better ways to approach this problem, each one building on what went before.

The current state of the art is object-oriented modeling. I would not presume to predict what will come next, but, as I said before, I'm quite sure something new, better, and even more exciting will appear before too long. The next section describes the earlier techniques and shows how each improved upon the state of the art in systems development.

3.5 EARLIER MODELS

A number of techniques and notations have been developed over the years to represent a problem area graphically, and to allow us to bring structure to complex and poorly structured problems. Some of the more successful ones are discussed in the rest of this chapter.

Functional Decomposition

One of the most intuitive ways to analyze a business process is to break it down into smaller, more manageable steps or subprocesses. After all, this is implied in the definition of the term analysis:

*   *Analysis:* **the resolution of something into its simple elements.** (Oxford, 1985).

*   *Analysis:* **The separating of any . . . entity into its constituent elements . . . as a method of studying (it).** (Random House Webster, 1998)

For this reason, one of the earliest approaches to understanding a business operation was to break it down into smaller and smaller chunks, until they were of a size and complexity such that they could easily be understood. This was formalized and notations were developed in the early 1970s.

Notable workers in this area included DeMarco, Yourdon and Constantine, Jackson, Page-Jones, and Warnier and Orr. Known also as *Structured Design* or *Structured Systems Design*, its major application was for designing computer programs, but it was found to have value for analysis as well.

Compared with more modern methodologies, however, this usefulness was somewhat limited. The focus tended to be on program design, which is really just one step in the total process of system development. The technique was of little help with such things as business analysis, file design, database design, user interface design, and input/output design, to name only a few.

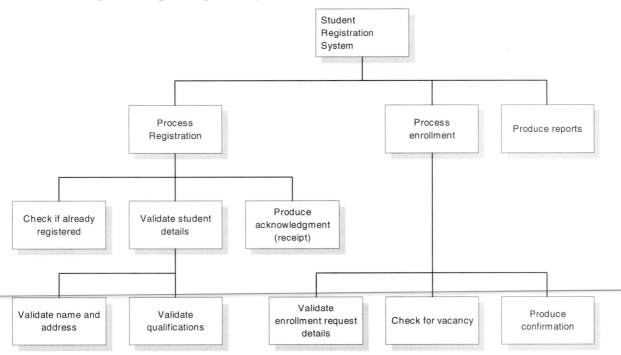

Figure 3-5 Functional decomposition: a student registration system (compare with Figures 3-6 to 3-12)

In the analysis phase, functional decomposition can be used as a way to understand the user's business. As the name implies, the technique involves breaking down (decomposing) the business processes (functions). Figure 3-5 shows how it works. We begin with a box to represent the entire project, system, or business area that we wish to model. We then expand this box on the next level of the diagram into the major subsystems or subprocesses that make up the project or business area.

Each box at this level is then further subdivided into subprocesses, functions, or steps and so on. At some stage in this process (and there has been continual argument among practitioners about exactly where), we begin to call them *functions* to indicate that they have become significantly simpler and easier to understand. At the lowest level, we end up with ***unit functions* that each represent a single operation or step.** (One rule of thumb that has been suggested for this: A ***unit function* should be small enough to document in a page or less of English.**)

You may have noticed that the diagram as shown in Figure 3-5 bears a strong resemblance to an organization chart, and this is not a coincidence. Organizations are usually organized into groups that perform one function or a set of related functions. That is, they're organized "along functional lines."

However, the mapping from the org chart to the functional decomposition diagram is seldom one-to-one. Some organizational units perform several functions, and some functions are spread over a number of organizational units. Still, many analysts like to begin with the organization chart (and perhaps the corporate phone directory!) to gain an overview of the operation and as a starting point for a more detailed and rigorous analysis.

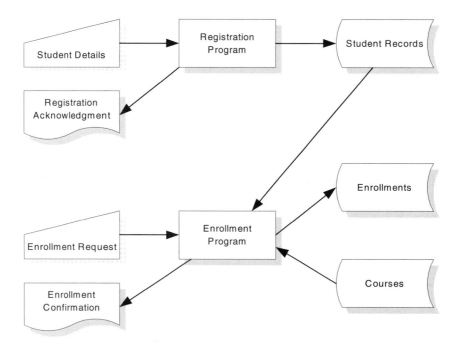

Figure 3-6 System flowchart: a student registration system.

As an analysis tool, functional decomposition is of some assistance, albeit somewhat limited. Where it's very useful with more modern methods is as a first step in producing data flow diagrams (DFDs), which we describe in detail in the next section. Functional decomposition actually forms the core of the DFD, with a lot more information added and a different system of notation.

Process Models: Data Flow Diagrams

Consider a simple, manual (paper-and-pencil) student registration system. The student provides his personal information to a registrations clerk, who enters it in a file of some kind. The student is then directed to the enrollments clerk, who records the student's selection of courses and dates. A schedule of courses and dates is also given to the student. Figure 3-6 is one possible way of diagramming this procedure, but Figure 3-7 is a better way.

Notice that, instead of including the two clerks in the diagram, in Figure 3-7 we show the *functions* that each clerk performs. Observe that the student *does* however appear in the diagram. The arrows show where information was passed from the student to the first clerk, and then from one clerk (i.e., one process) to another, and where data is stored in or retrieved from the files. Although functional decomposition was an advance over what went before, it could not show nearly as much information as you see on this DFD.

More important than simply the breakdown of business processes into smaller ones is the relationships among the processes. The kind of connection we're concerned with in this case is where data is passed from one process to another. We need to know what data is required to perform a process, and where it come from. We must establish what data the process generates or creates, and what happens to that data next.

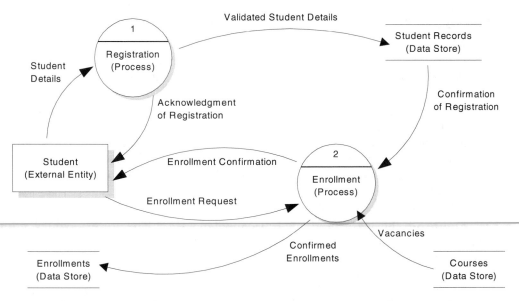

Figure 3-7 Data flow diagram: a student registration system.

In some cases, we'll find processes that occur sequentially one right after the other, so data produced by the one is used immediately by the next. In other cases, we'll find there's a need to save some of the data at the time it's created, so that a later process may have access to it. Figures 3-7– 3-12 show all of these things, and because they're all linked by data pathways, it's known as a *data flow diagram* (DFD).

DFDs are one of the best ways ever developed to model the activities, functions, and processes that make up the users' business. The diagram carries a lot more information than a functional decomposition diagram, which makes it a more complete representation of the users' world. It also provides a stepping stone to program design. However, in the object paradigm it has been replaced by other and better diagrams (see Chapter 10).

For each process that a user will end up doing, we now know what information they'll need to see on reports and screens, and what data they'll want to key into the programs. For each process that ends up being performed by a computer program, we'll be able to tell what data must be available to it and what data it will generate.

In the days of Structured Systems Analysis, which was totally based on DFDs, analysis would consist of building DFDs and then proceeding to the design and coding of programs. Later methodologies in the 1980s and 1990s used DFDs in conjunction with *entity-relationship diagrams* (ERDs) a.k.a. *data models*, which are described in Chapter 4.

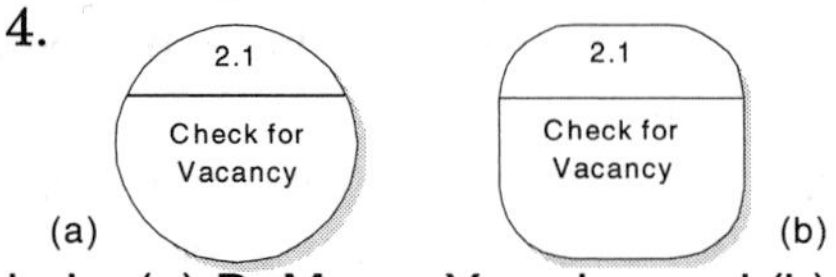

Figure 3-8 Process symbols: (a) DeMarco-Yourdon and (b) Gane-Sarson.

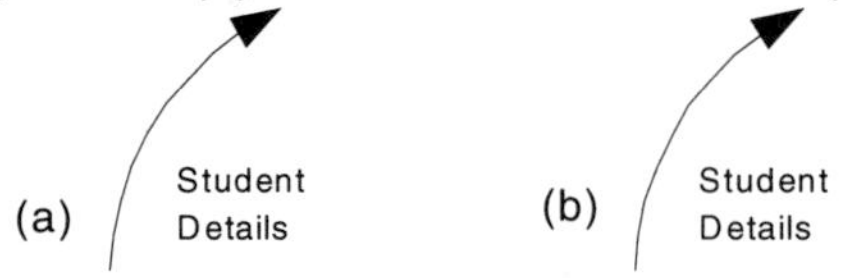

Figure 3-9 Data flow symbols: (a) DeMarco-Yourdon and (b) Gane-Sarson.

Two sets of symbols are used in DFDs, either of which will work. The Gane–Sarson symbols look good and are supported by many CASE[4] tools, but the DeMarco–Yourdon set of symbols work equally well and are a little easier to draw by hand. Use the one that you and your users will be most comfortable with.

Four symbols are used in DFDs, for processes, data flows, data stores, and external entities. Figures 3-8(a) – 3-11(a) show DeMarco–Yourdon symbols, and Figures 3-8(b) – 3-11(b) show Gane–Sarson symbols. Explanations of how to use each symbol are in the paragraphs that follow. Both symbol sets are widely used and easy to understand, so you should use whichever you or your instructor/boss/ client prefers.

I find the circles easier to draw by hand, so I mostly use the DeMarco–Yourdon set. Figure 3-8 shows the fundamental symbol in a DFD: The process symbol, often referred to as a "bubble," depicts a function or activity or process that transforms data in some way.

---

[4] *CASE:* Computer-{Assisted | Aided} {Software | Systems} Engineering.

CASE tool: A software product for use by systems analysts, designers, and programmers to help in systems development, such as Popkin System Architect, ObjectTeam, GDPro, or Oracle Designer. Many object-oriented languages and databases come in the form of development environments that typically

(a) Student
     Records

(b) Student
     Records

Figure 3-10 Data store symbols: (a) DeMarco-Yourdon and (b) Gane-Sarson

These processes may be physically performed by people or machines. They'll always have data flowing out of them, and there will almost always be some flowing in as well. A data flow always begins and/or ends at a process bubble; it must have a bubble at one end or the other, or both. Process is what people *do*; data is what they do it *with* or *to*.

Data inputs and outputs, represented by arrows, are referred to as *data flows* (Figure 3-9). **A *data flow* is a named arrow showing where data passes from one process to another or to or from a data store or external entity.** Physically, data flows can be any form of communication. They could be verbal messages, live or by phone, or documents passed back and forth. They could also be remote data links or any other mechanism that can transfer data.

(a) Student

(b) Student

Figure 3-11 External entity symbols: (a) DeMarco-Yourdon and (b) Gane-Sarson

Sometimes one process will create or cause a data output, but the next process won't be ready for it yet, perhaps not for a few seconds, perhaps not for a few hours, weeks, or years. In these cases, the data is shown on the DFD as being passed to a *data store* (Figure 3-10). **A *data store* is a place where data is held until needed, when it's passed via a data flow to the process(es) that need it.** These stores may be paper files, computer databases, or even a spike file or desk drawer.

External entities, on the other hand, are sources and "sinks" of data (Figure 3-11). ***External entities*, sometimes referred to as *external agents*, are people, organizations, systems, and other things outside our system that either provide data to the system or draw data from it.** They're often clients, governments, or other systems, manual or computerized.

Development of a DFD typically begins with a *context diagram*, which shows our system in relation to the world outside itself. A context diagram shows the system as a single large box, with arrows showing data flows to and from external entities, represented by smaller rectangular boxes. We'll discuss these in more detail in Chapters 6 and 7.

DFDs have one more special feature: they can be constructed in levels of increasing detail. This allows you, when reading a DFD, to begin with an overview of the whole project or business area and then work "top-down." Thus, you can first gain a broad understanding of the operation and then focus, in progressively more detail, on ever-smaller sections of the whole. This is called "top-down working" and is discussed in more detail below and in Chapter 9.

In this way, you can avoid the masses of detail that would otherwise cloud your initial attempts to learn about what your users do. This process is illustrated in Figure 3-12, where you'll see that the student registration system is shown first as a single bubble. Every data flow to or from this bubble must also appear on the next level, as a flow into or out of the diagram, but vice versa is not necessary. Checking to see that this has been done correctly is called "balancing" the DFD.

include a number of CASE functions and sometimes complete CASE functionality. Many of the proprietary object-oriented methodologies include a customized CASE product.

(a) Context diagram

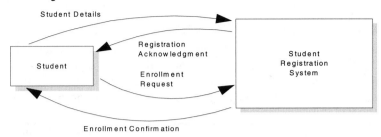

(b) Data flow diagram (same as Figure 3-7)

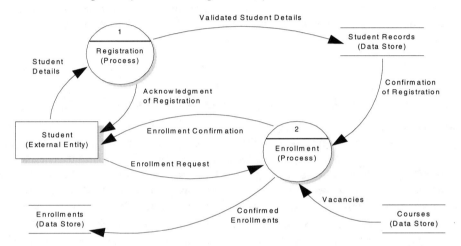

(c) Process 1: Registration

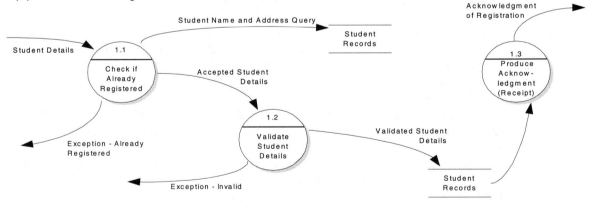

Figure 3-12 A levelled set of DFDs   *(continued)*

DFDs historically have been used for analysis in two styles of methodology. The Yourdon–Constantine methodology was entirely DFD-based, as were a number of its contemporaries. Other methodologies have been published based on Martin and Finkelstein's (1981) Information Engineering concepts. These use DFDs, and also the entity-relationship data models developed initially by Chen (1976, 1981).

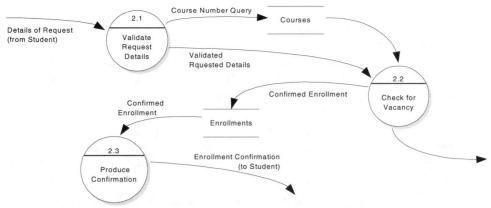

Figure 3-12 (continued)

Let's first examine Structured Systems Analysis to see how DFDs formed the central core around which the methodology was constructed. We'll discuss entity-relationship data models in Chapter 4.

Structured Systems Analysis

This methodology was developed and promoted by Yourdon and Constantine (1976), DeMarco (1978), and Gane and Sarson (1978). Popular in the 1970s and 1980s, it was eventually replaced by methodologies based on entity-relationship diagrams (ERDs), and now by objects. Yourdon proposed four main steps:

1. Prepare a physical DFD model of the existing system. This will indicate which person or program will perform each process. It'll show precisely how data is passed from one process to the next, whether on paper or as an electronic signal or whatever medium. It will also show what medium each data store is recorded on. The *Random House Webster* (1998) defines a **_medium_ to be an agency, means or instrument by which something (in this case data) is conveyed, or a channel of communication.**

   For us then, a **_medium_ (plural _media_) is the thing, substance, or device that is used to carry or to store data.** Newspapers, TV, and radio are examples of news media. Each one is a news medium. Disk, CD-ROMs, paper ledgers, and RAM are all examples of data-storage media. Finally, optical fiber, satellites, co-ax, television cable, twisted-pair, and local area networks are examples of data transmission media.

   A physical data flow diagram shows

   ° The actual physical form that each item on the diagram will take when the system is built and implemented and

   ° The media for the data stores and data flows. A physical DFD is usually built with only one level, that is, the most detailed level.

2. Convert these to the implied logical data flow diagrams, which display the essence of the processes and the flow of data throughout the system, showing only what processes must be performed and what data must be passed and stored, with no reference to how it's passed or stored in the physical system. The phrase used to describe any logical model (not just logical DFDs) is *implementation-independent*.

The difference between the two kinds of model will become clearer when we talk about the analysis and design phases of the systems development life cycle in a later chapter. For now, suffice it to say that a logical model, saying *what* must be done by the system, is an analysis tool. A physical model, because it describes *how* these things will be done, is properly a tool of the Design phase.

3. After that, develop logical DFDs for the new system, referred to as the *target system*, based on a study of the users' current requirements. These DFDs will be in a number of levels, each level exploding into the next, with all the data flows appropriately balanced.

4. Then make implementation decisions about such physical details as which person, group, or program will perform each process, and how each data flow and data store will be built in the real system. As these implementation options are being considered and the decisions made, we convert the logical DFDs of the current requirements to physical DFDs of the new system.

This outline of the process of Structured Analysis is brief and somewhat incomplete, but it serves to introduce the ideas. It has also provided us with a context for introducing some critically important definitions, such as DFDs and logical and physical models. In Chapter 4, you'll learn how Information Engineering marries the DFD to a very different and somewhat more fundamental tool, the entity-relationship diagram (ERD), or data model. This gave rise to a kind of methodology that turned out to be the immediate ancestor of object-oriented methods.

3.6 SHORTCOMINGS OF OUTPUT-BASED AND PROCESS-BASED METHODS

Process-based systems development methodologies such as those based on DFDs were indeed a major advance over the output-based ones that went before. However, as they were used on more and more projects and those systems went into production, some problems were discovered. These problems were rather subtle since they had to do with the ability of the system to change, and to handle changes in the way the users do their business. You saw some of this in the *Outhouse* episode at the beginning of this chapter.

The problem had been present since the beginning of systems analysis, of course, but had not been recognized because of more immediate problems. The more urgent problems were to get a system built, that provided users with what they *currently* needed.

Thus, the focus of the developers was to understand the users' business, and produce the reports and screens they needed to see. The DFD certainly improved our understanding and was a great help in doing this. What turned out to be less urgent, but in the long run perhaps more important, was the ability to *make changes* to the system when the users' needs changed.

Remember, there's no such thing as a stable business; all are either growing or dying. As the months and years go by, everybody's job changes, and with it their needs for information change too. Once an information system is in place and functioning, the users will see new things it could do for them, and a string of change requests will begin. Add to this the inevitable adjustments and corrections expected with anything new and complex, and you have even more changes. This is an ongoing process, with a constant parade of changes and enhancements throughout the life of the system.

There's a further complication to this process. For programmers and analysts, it's a fact of life that a seemingly simple change to the output is likely to cause a cascade of changes to all parts of the program or system. Many of these changes will turn out to have obscure and unexpected side effects on distant parts of the program or system, necessitating further changing, and more testing and debugging.

These two factors, the inevitability of change and the ramifications of change, historically have combined to cause an ongoing problem of maintenance. From the 1960s to the 1990s, we in the systems industry have struggled with the problem of system maintenance. By the 1970s, we had figured out that something wasn't being done right.

The first solution became known as the "freeze-the-specs mentality." And there are those who still think that this is the way it should be done. But it's really nothing more than an attempt to make the problem go away. When the users' requirements had been more or less established, they would be asked to sign them off, and the developers would then go away to design and build the system.

Months, sometimes years, later they would be back with the finished system, only to be told by the users, "Sorry, but our needs have changed. That's no longer what we want." With the introduction of structured programming, and later when Yourdon and others introduced the DFD, matters improved significantly.

The use of DFDs ensured that the requirements definitions were more accurate. In other words, they gave a truer picture of what the user actually needed. Both techniques (DFDs and structured programming) made the systems and programs more ***modular*, that is, organized into more or less independent units.** The independence of these units helped reduce the ripple effects of changes. This modularity was an early form of encapsulation, an important property of object-oriented methods, and one that we'll explore in Chapter 5.

The net effect was to produce better systems, but the maintenance problem still was not completely solved. As we entered the 1980s, there still were five-year backlogs of requests from users, for new systems and system enhancements, along with the five years' worth of hidden backlog, all requests that the users never made because of the visible backlog. Obviously, something more was needed. And the first part of that something was provided by Peter Chen (1976) (1981) in his landmark 1976 paper, when he proposed the entity-relationship data model. We'll begin Chapter 4 with a discussion of Chen's models.

• •

DELIVERABLES

Deliverables **from each phase are the documents and other products generated during the phases and subphases of the project, and whose production marks the completion of each phase.**

Since the methods described in this chapter were used in the early stages of the Analysis Phase, the final deliverable was a Requirements Definition. This will be described in more detail in Chapter 7.

FURTHER READING

Virtually every book that has "systems analysis" in its title gives an introduction to the older methods, unless it specifically mentions data analysis, data (or information) modeling, entities, or objects. Books on the newer methods usually say so specifically in their titles. Books by Yourdon (without Coad), Jackson, DeMarco, and their contemporaries from the 1970s would fall into the Structured Analysis/DFD group.

For an excellent concise explanation of data flow diagrams, I recommend Chapter 9 of Whitten, et al. *Systems Analysis and Design Methods*, fifth edition (2000)

For a more in-depth study of DFDs, try Tom DeMarco, *Structured Analysis and System Specification* (1978). This book is the classic in the field, for DFDs and Structured Analysis. Also a classic, and perhaps a little easier to read, is *Structured Systems Analysis: Tools and Techniques* by Chris Gane and Trish Sarson (1978).

CHAPTER SUMMARY

- A model is a *simplified representation* of a *complex reality*, usually for the purpose of *understanding* that reality, and having all the features of that reality necessary for *the current task or problem*. Modeling is actually a form of *abstraction*.

- The strength of the object-oriented modeling methods is that objects are one of the fundamental ways that humans organize their experience.

- The *systems development life cycle* consists of a number of steps or phases:

  - In the *analysis phase,* we study the users' business and their problems to discover what the users need the system to do. It produces a requirements definition that spells out what the system must do and the information it must produce, without dictating *how*.

  - In the *design phase*, we produce a plan or design showing how the system will do the functions identified in analysis. Here, we consider hardware-software platform, choice of language, operating system, and database management software (DBMS). We design the databases, programs, screens, and reports. We produce program specs that are passed on to the programmers in the next phase.

  - In the *construction phase,* we write the programs are written and build the databases. Then the whole system is tested and debugged, first by the programmers and then by the users and the development team together.

  - During the *implementation phase* we install the system, train the users, and do a parallel run.

  - In the *maintenance phase,* we handle program bugs, design errors, and things the users forgot. Enhancements come throughout the life of the system.

- **The history of systems analysis is:**

  - Unsystematic early approaches, 1960s

  - "Output-oriented" methods, late 1960s

- Process-oriented methods, 1970s; data flow diagrams
- Data-oriented methods, 1980s; entity-relationship diagrams
- Object-oriented methods, 1990s and the New Millennium
- Earlier methodologies focused on business processes. Object modeling first considers the data in terms of objects, things people need to know about – that is, the real-world objects that they need to keep data *about*.
- Analysis modeling forces us to spend time with the users up front. There is a need to identify the problem before we look for a solution. A brilliant solution to the wrong problem will not do.
- With object-oriented methods, there is much reuse of program code (after the initial adoption period). The resources spent on maintenance are sharply reduced by *getting it right the first time*.
- Object-oriented modeling has shown the greatest reductions in both initial coding and maintenance. The cost is the extra time spent in analysis. The overall result is higher quality and reduced total cost since errors are detected earlier. Here are two important definitions from this chapter:
  - **Functional decomposition:** Breaking a business process into smaller functions Helpful for analysis, more useful for programming
  - **Data flow diagram:** A process model diagram showing *business processes* and the *data* that they use and pass among themselves. Also shows *data stores* and *external entities*. Makes use of functional decomposition to produce *leveled sets* of DFDs.

CHAPTER GLOSSARY

abstraction   The process of focusing on those features of something that are essential for the task at hand and ignoring those that are not.

analysis   The resolution (breaking down) of something into its simple elements. (*Oxford*, 1975)

analysis   The separating of any . . . entity into its constituent elements . . . as a method of studying (it). (*Random House Webster*, 1998)

business processes   What people do in order to make their organization run. To put it another way, business processes are all the things that must happen, and activities that must be performed, in the course of the organization going about its business.

CASE   Computer-{Assisted | Aided} {Software | Systems} Engineering.

CASE tool   A software product for use by systems analysts, designers, and programmers to help in systems development, such as Popkin System Architect, ObjectTeam, GDPro, Rational Rose, or Oracle Designer.

context diagram   A diagram that shows the system as a single large box, with arrows showing data flows to and from External Entities, represented by smaller rectangular boxes.

data   The plural of the Latin *datum*, meaning "facts," or "raw facts," in that they're unprocessed. In the computer business, *data* is usually considered to be a collective noun like *information* is, so it's used in the singular form rather than the plural.

data flow A named arrow showing where data passes from one process to another, or between a process and a data store or external entity.

data flow diagram (DFD) A process model, a diagram showing business processes and the data they use and pass among themselves; also shows data stores and external entities. Makes use of functional decomposition to produce leveled sets of DFDs.

data store A place where data is held until needed, when it's passed via a data flow to the process(es) that need it. These stores may be paper files, computer databases, or even a spike file or desk drawer.

deliverables The documents and other products from each phase that are generated during the phases and subphases of the project and whose production marks the completion of the phase.

external entities (external agents) The people, organizations, systems, and other things outside our system that either provide data to the system or draw data from it. They are sources and "sinks" of data.

functional decomposition Breaking down a business process into progressively smaller functions.

information Data that has in some way been made useful to someone.

logical data fow diagram A diagram that shows the essence of the processes and the flow of data throughout the system, displaying only what processes must be performed and what data must be passed and stored, with no reference to how it's passed or stored in the physical system. The phrase used to describe any logical model (not just logical DFDs) is *implementation-independent*.

medium (pl. media) An agency, means or instrument by which something (in this case data) is conveyed, or a channel of communication. (*Random House Webster*, 1998)

medium The substance or device that is used to carry or store data.

methodology (*Random House Webster*, 1998)   A set or system of methods, principles, and rules for regulating a certain discipline [in this case, the discipline of information systems (IS) development, or management information systems (MIS).]

model A simplified representation *of a* complex reality, *usually for the purpose of* understanding *that reality, and having all the features of that reality necessary for* the current task or problem.

modular Organized into more or less independent units.

objects **Things** people need to know about, that is, the real-world objects that they need to keep data about.

parallel run The process of running both the new system and the old (which may be automated or manual) side by side for a period of time, typically a month.

physical data flow diagram A diagram that shows (1) the actual physical form that each item on the diagram will take when the system is built and implemented and (2) the media for the data stores and data flows.

process symbol In a data flow diagram, depicts a function, activity, or process that transforms data in some way. These processes may be physically performed by people or machines. They'll always have data flowing out of them, and there will almost always be some flowing in as well. A data flow always begins and/or ends at a process bubble.

requirements definition The document that spells out what the eventual system must do, the information it must produce, and when and where, without dictating how it will be done.

unit function Represents a single operation or step, the smallest division of a process, small enough to document in a page or less of English.

WHAT COMES NEXT

Now that we've examined models and their use in systems development, Chapter 4 will show entity-relationship models in detail and then move on to object-oriented models. In Chapter 4, we'll learn what objects are and discover some of their basic pro perties. In Chapter 5, we'll look at objects and classes of objects and how to relate real-world objects to data objects.

CLASS/GROUP EXERCISES AND PROBLEMS

Ex 3.1 Draw a logical data flow diagram for doing your homework. Remember, this is not a sequential step-by-step how-to; that would be a flowchart. This shows all functions – things that must be done – and the data that each requires and/or generates. It must show where each data item comes from so that a process can use it, or goes to when a process generates it. Since it's a logical DFD, don't mention how or where each data item is stored.

Ex 3.2 Now take each process in your DFD from Exercise 3.1, and explode it on another sheet of paper into several subprocesses. Repeat the explosion to further levels where necessary, so you end up with a 'leveled set' of DFDs.

Ex 3.3 Now take all the lowest-level (i.e., the most detailed) DFDs you produced for Exercise 3.2, and redraw them as physical DFDs, with the media identified for all data stores. Also show the media for all the data flows and indicate who or what will perform each process.

Ex 3.4 Each group should choose a process that one member was involved in recently. It may be when someone registered for a course, applied for a marriage (or other) license, or whatever. Develop a DFD for this process. Draw upon this person's experience of what went right and what went wrong, as well as other people's knowledge, to produce a DFD that can handle all the necessary exceptions.

INDIVIDUAL EXERCISES AND PROBLEMS

Ex 3.5 Choose an activity or project from one of your favorite hobbies or interests and draw a logical data flow diagram showing how it should be done. Design the DFD so that a total novice who has no prior knowledge could follow it and do the job adequately. Explode it if necessary into a leveled set of DFDs. Redraw the DFD as a physical DFD, showing all the media and the actors.

PROJECTS AND CASES

P 3.1   Find a business or organization that has a process or organizational problem of some kind. It could be a friend's small business or an office of a large organization. It might be a club, church, condominium association, or some other group that you or a friend belong to. Along with some of the people who are familiar with the problem, develop a physical DFD of the problem area. From this, develop a logical DFD, if necessary as a leveled set.

Now examine these two models to see if you can find a solution to the original problem. Can you also see some ways in which other functions in this area could be smoothed or improved? Draw a modified logical DFD showing the changes that you've recommended. Then from it, draw a physical DFD for the new way of doing things.

SELF-TEST QUESTIONS

Note: The Appendix has answers to the Self-Test Questions.

Q 3.1   Models are important in systems development to:

(a) Ensure a better understanding of the modeling process

(b) Develop a complex version of a simple reality

(c) Ensure that the users don't see the real thing

(d) Simplify the development of a complex reality

(e) Ensure that the staff are insulated from complexity

(f) Simplify things and help us understand them

Q 3.2 The five phases of the traditional systems development life cycle (SDLC) are:

(a) Analysis, design, construction, implementation, and maintenance

(b) Analysis, design, implementation, and maintenance

(c) Design, construction, testing, implementation, and maintenance

(d) Design, construction, implementation, maintenance, and enhancement

(e) Analysis, construction, implementation, maintenance, and enhancement

(f) Analysis, construction, testing, implementation, and maintenance

Q 3.3   The "orientation" of the historical development methods went from:

(a) Process to data to behavior to objects

(b) Data to output to process to objects

(c) Process to data to output to objects

(d) Output to process to data to objects

(e) Abstraction to process to data to objects

(f) Process to abstraction to output to objects

Q 3.4 Which of the following is true?

(a) Modeling methods move the effort to the front end of the project.

(b) Models function as a vehicle for communication with the users.

(c) Most users have never examined their own operation from the point of view of the data it handles and stores to do its job.

(d) DFDs and ERDs are good, but objects are way better.

(e) All of the above are true.

(f) Some of the above are true.

Q 3.5 Which of the following is true?

(a) A model is really a form of abstraction.

(b) People skills and listening skills are as important as technical skills.

(c) A logical model says only what will happen.

(d) A data store keeps data until it's needed.

(e) All of the above are true.

(f) None of the above are true.

Q 3.6 Abstraction is:

(a) Writing a précis for the technical documentation.

(b) Ignoring everything that is not part of the DFD.

(c) Cutting a piece out of something else.

(d) Ignoring what is not important for the job at hand.

(e) None of the above.

Q 3.7 A model is a _____ _____ of a _____ reality, usually for the purpose of _____ that reality, and having all the _____ of that reality necessary for the _____ task or _____ . Modeling is actually a form of _____ .

Q 3.8 The _____ of the object-oriented modeling methods is that objects are one of the _____ ways that humans _____ their _____ .

Q 3.9 The systems _____ life _____ consists of a number of _____ or _____ .

Q 3.10 In the _____ phase, we study the users' business and their _____ , to discover what the users _____ the _____ to do. It produces a _____ _____ that spells out what the system must do and the _____ it must produce, without dictating _____ .

Q 3.11 In the design phase, we produce a _____ or _____ showing how the system will do the _____ identified in _____ . Here, we consider hardware–software platform, choice of _____ , operating system, and _____ _____ _____ (DBMS).

Q 3.12 In the _____ phase, the _____ are written and the _____ are built. Then the whole system is _____ and _____ .

Q 3.13 The implementation phase is where the system is _____ , the users are _____ , and a _____ run is performed.

Q 3.14 In the _____ phase, we handle _____ _____ , design errors, and things the users _____ . _____ come throughout the life of the system.

Q 3.15 Earlier methodologies focused on business _____ . Object modeling first considers the data in terms of objects, things people need to _____ _____ – that is, the _____-_____ objects that they need to keep _____ about.

Q 3.16 Analysis modeling forces us to _____ _____ with the users _____ _____ . There is a need to _____ the _____ before we look for a _____ . A brilliant _____ to the wrong _____ will not do.

Q 3.17 With object-oriented methods, there is much _____ of program code. The resources spent on _____ are sharply _____ by _____ it _____ the _____ time.

Q 3.18 _____ decomposition: Breaking a business _____ into _____ functions.

Q 3.19 _____ flow diagram: A _____ model diagram showing business _____ and the _____ that they use and pass among themselves. Also shows _____ _____ and external _____ .

Chapter Four

Data-Oriented Models

WHAT YOU WILL LEARN IN THIS CHAPTER

In this chapter, you'll learn about entity-relationship models and their use in systems analysis. You'll also learn about objects and the object-oriented model. You'll see how the object-oriented model differs from those that preceded it, and some of its advantages. You can feel confident that you understand entity-relationship diagrams (ERDs) and object-oriented models when you can:

- Distinguish between logical and physical models.
- Describe the various constructs used in entity-relationship models.
- Build a small ERD from a simple business scenario.
- Define object, class, and instance.
- Explain how object-oriented models differ from previous styles of model, and describe some of their advantages.

WHAT YOU SHOULD KNOW TO START THIS CHAPTER

If you skipped Chapter 3, you should still have no problems with this chapter as long as you're familiar with the use of models in systems development and you understand the systems development life cycle (SDLC).

CHAPTER OVERVIEW

You'll meet the two modern modeling methods, both based on the *data* found in the users' world. We'll introduce the Entity-Relationship Diagram (ERD) and show how radically different it was from earlier methods. In defining the term *paradigm shift*, you'll see that these new methods are different enough to qualify truly for that much overused name. Next, we'll investigate the ERD in depth and the major reasons for its success as a systems development tool. This part will end with a mention of some methodologies that are based on ERDs among them, Information Engineering.

In the latter part of the chapter, we'll begin our study of objects by defining what they are and discussing some of their basic properties. After a section on object-oriented versus object-based programming languages, we'll consider the three levels of abstraction: conceptual, logical, and physical models. Then we'll finish with a discussion of models as a tool for communication.

Key Concepts

- Paradigm, paradigm shift
- Data entity, entity type, and entity occurrence
- Attribute
- Candidate key, primary key
- Relationship, association
- Entity-relationship models for database design
- Each entity becomes a file or table.
- Attributes become fields/columns.
- Association becomes access pathway.
- Foreign key
- Data entities stable over time
- Stability reduces costs and delays
- Significance of the data of an enterprise
- Data is the center of the universe
- Data as a corporate asset
- Multiplicity / Cardinality
- Object-based vs object-oriented
- Classes, subclasses
- Inheritance
- Instance, occurrence
- Transient and persistent objects
- Conceptual, Logical and Physical models
- Exclusive access to data
- Models as communication tools

The Outhouse Bathroom Boutique
Sales Reporting System – Episode 4

As Nancy approached the door of The Outhouse, she noticed Tim waving to her from the sidewalk by the coffee shop next door. "Even as a kid on the farm," he said straight faced as she walked up to him, "I didn't think much of drinking coffee in the outhouse."

Nancy groaned. "Your puns are as bad as that author, David Brown," she said. "I heard him speak last month, and his whole speech was full of them, all just as bad as that one. I should have guessed it when I first saw the name of your company!" Tim chuckled and guided her to a seat by the window. When they had ordered, he began, "I've put together the list of people for the meeting on Tuesday."

He handed her a sheet with seven names on it. Nancy scanned the list. "This looks OK. And I'll bring along a *recording analyst* to take notes."

"Oh, we could use my secretary for that, couldn't we?" asked Tim.

Nancy smiled. "I'm afraid not. The recorder needs to be someone thoroughly familiar with systems and modeling. I'll bring Deanna. She's a programmer/analyst and she's done a lot of this sort of thing. In fact, I'm in the process of grooming her to lead modeling sessions, so she'll also be able to fill in for me if necessary. I always like to have backup."

Tim looked impressed. "You guys are thorough. Always prepared for everything. And something else," he went on. "Ever since our conversation yesterday, I've been thinking about the things you said. It just makes so much sense that I should have brought in someone who was properly qualified, who could do the job and do it right. But I just had no idea it was that complicated or that critical!"

Nancy smiled again. "That's quite an admission," she observed. "But you're not alone. Most of the users and businesspeople I've worked with didn't seem to be fully aware of just how important *information* can be to their business. Nor do they realize that dealing with it is a whole separate discipline, just like Accounting, or Human Resources. Or any other resource management specialty. Data is, in fact, a resource just like any of those and it needs to be managed as a resource. In large organizations, the specialists in that area are called Data Resource Management. Their job is to manage data and information the way accountants manage budgets and finance."

"So I guess that makes you kind of a 'Data CA,'" Tim grinned.[1]

"Right. I like that!" Nancy smiled in return. "And it's not all that complicated, really, but it certainly is critical. The modeling techniques I mentioned are really quite straightforward, although they're going to seem pretty weird to start with. It's just that it's not at all intuitive to begin with the data. The output is a much more natural place for most people. But we just go through a set of procedures step by step, and after a lot of hard work we come out the other end with what we need. It's not exactly like a recipe, but there's a standard way to approach these things."

"Well, I do hope it works out the way you predict. Just talking to you these couple of times, I've been relieved to find that we're normal! And the confidence you seem to have that we can fix it makes me feel a whole lot better already," admitted Tim.

Then he went on seriously. "And I've got a few more troubles to add to the pile that I laid on you yesterday," he said. "Over the last few months, we began to notice some really strange things happening. We've sometimes found sales or purchase records, but we have no corresponding record in the inventory showing the stock we were supposed to have sold or bought. And a couple of times we found inventory records for stock with no record of our ever having purchased it!"

"And although these have been pretty rare cases, the scary thing is that we never know when it might happen next. Or whether the next one might be for thousands of dollars worth. And they do seem to be happening a bit more often as time goes by. And" Tim was beginning to warm up "sometimes I get different figures for the same thing on two reports! How can that be? Surely, once the computer has the figures, the answers must always come out the same. And then again, sometimes I'll see something on a list that I know was supposed to be deleted weeks or months before!"

"Does sound pretty scary!" agreed Nancy.

"Darn right! I'm starting to get really scared. I feel like I'm losing control. I mean, you can't run a business like this! Have you seen stuff like this before? Is it another problem of poorly designed programs?" Tim was beginning to look very anxious.

"I have, and it is. And," she reassured him, "we can stop it right there before it gets any worse. By the time we've finished the new system, I may not be able to solve all the mysteries you've already found, but I'll unravel a bunch of them. I *can* promise that no more new ones will happen.

"The symptoms you're describing usually mean that the database was not correctly designed. Yesterday we talked about how you can't locate data that you know is in there. That's usually because the data items are not correctly linked together. Or some of them may not be linked at all, or the wrong things are linked together. These problems you just mentioned, like the same total coming out different on two different reports, all have similar explanations. That particular one usually results from redundant data. When you have the same number stored twice in two different places in the database, Murphy's Law says you must *expect* them to get out of step!"

---

[1]CA: Chartered Accountant

"Murphy's Law?" Tim had his puzzled look on again.

"Yes, the principle that everything that possibly *can* go wrong eventually *will* go wrong," Nancy explained. "Hadn't you noticed that life is like that?"

"Well, now you mention it, I suppose it is."

"Right," said Nancy, "and in cases like this you can bet on it! And the way around it is like this: The modeling methods will enable us to understand your data properly. Then the models we draw up will give us a template so that we can design you a database that properly suits your needs, now and into the future."

"Well, it sounds OK at first glance," said Tim doubtfully, unaware of his mixed metaphor. "But what if I can't get the hang of all your technical lingo and complicated ideas? I have the feeling I'm going to end up being blinded by science here."

Once again, Nancy's voice was reassuring. "Actually, I would expect you'll get the hang of it pretty quickly. And once we have the models, you'll find they help a lot in our discussions. They really do become a communication aid, a way for each of us to visualize what the other is trying to explain. I find that by the time the modeling is finished, most of my users are all gung-ho about the methods as well as about their system. And the other thing is, they end up calling it 'their system,' and not referring to it as 'Nancy's system.'"

At this point, Nancy was ready to introduce Tim to the concept of objects, so at the beginning of Chapter 5 we shall rejoin the story on that topic.

THOUGHT QUESTIONS

Consider the following in your groups (or individually if necessary) and present and compare your results. In a large class, each group should do one question, and each question should be assigned to several groups. This way you can still compare ideas on each issue.

1. Can you suggest some reasons why it has taken so long for data to be recognized as a "resource"?

2. Suggest some of the functions required in asset management in general and discuss how each one might apply to the management of data and information.

3. List some businesses, organizations, operations, and functions where anomalies like the ones Tim described could be a problem. Briefly describe the anomalies and list them in four groups:

   ° Those where such anomalies would be disastrous or fatal for the organization

   ° Those that would be merely difficult

   ° Some where the anomalies would not cause a problem at all

   ° Some where the anomalies might be fatal for the client

4. Discuss an actual situation from the past or present of one of your group members, where you believe the difficulties experienced may have resulted from the kind of problems Tim was describing. It may be a system where you were the end user, or perhaps you were a client of the unfortunate user. Or (heaven forbid once again!) it could be a system that you helped build or design (and again, be honest now.) Discuss how your actual experiences were caused by such things as redundant data or incorrectly linked data.

4.1 DATA MODELS: THE ENTITY-RELATIONSHIP DIAGRAM

When Peter Chen published his seminal paper proposing the ERD as a data model (Chen, 1976), databases were just coming into widespread use. Much research was being devoted to finding ways to model the data in an organization, and then use that model as a template for a database design. A number of notations had been proposed and tried. In his celebrated paper, Chen made two significant contributions to the state of the art:

1. The entity-relationship principle

2. The entity-relationship notation

Closely related to the first of these are three other issues that have been investigated by Chen and others:

3. E-R models for database design

4. The significance of the data of an enterprise

5. The stability of the data of an enterprise

Before looking at these issues in detail, let's pause for a moment to consider what a profound change these methods made in the way we do systems analysis.

4.2 PARADIGM SHIFT

These factors were responsible for a dramatic change in the way people developed systems, a change sufficiently radical that it qualified to be described as a *paradigm shift*. True paradigm shifts are rare, and I refer you to the book by that name (Brooks, 1972). There was, for example, a paradigm shift in astronomy caused by Galileo's observations that the planets revolved around the sun and not, as the Inquisition insisted, the other way around.

Another paradigm shift was from Newton to Einstein. For 300 years, Newtonian mechanics was the paradigm that enabled the sciences to progress and flourish. Then Einstein's Theory of Relativity changed everything. Scientists had to think in a totally new way. In the field of biology, Darwin was another who caused a paradigm shift in the way we understand our world.

In our context then, a *__paradigm__* **is a pattern or mode of thinking and believing that serves to organize the way we approach knowledge, learning, and understanding.** Thus, a *__paradigm shift__* **occurs when we adopt a radically different way of organizing all or part of our worldview.**

In the last decade or so, the IT industry has experienced two major shifts. The first was from process-based methods to data-oriented, and the second was to object-oriented methods. It's interesting that, though the first was a somewhat abrupt change, it didn't really qualify to be called a paradigm shift.

On the other hand, the move from data-oriented to object-oriented methods was *evolutionary* in nature, achieved by adding the processes to the data entities to give objects. Yet the change had such a profound effect on the computer world that it surely qualifies as a genuine paradigm shift. In the following sections, we'll study the data-oriented methods, beginning with Chen's principles.

4.3 ENTITY-RELATIONSHIP MODELING

We will now discuss Chen's ideas in the following order:

- The entity-relationship principle
- Entity-relationship models for database design
- The stability of the data of an enterprise
- The significance of data
- Data as a corporate asset
- Entity-relationship notation

The Entity-Relationship Principle

A few years ago, I was involved in the development of a number of systems for the Edmonton Transit System (ETS) in Edmonton, Alberta. ETS operates a fleet of buses just like that in any major North American city. To begin the analysis of a system for ETS, we needed to focus on the things the users needed to know about in order to get their jobs done. Notice that I said "know *about*" – not the things they need to know. The things they need to know are also important, obviously, but the starting point has to be the things to know *about*.

These are things such as *buses, drivers, routes,* and *passengers.* What do the users need to know about buses, drivers, routes, and passengers? They need to know things like bus number, make, year, and model. These are things to know about a *bus.* The *bus* is the *thing* they need to know *about.* They need to know the driver's employee number, name, address, age, sex, and phone number, among other things.

These are what they need to record *about a driver,* and the *driver* is the thing they need to know about.

According to *Oxford* (1998), an ***entity*** is **"a thing with distinct and independent existence."** For our purposes and Chen's, we'll consider a ***data entity*** **to be something that has separate and distinct existence in the world of the users, and is of interest to the users in that they need to record data about it.** By this definition, then, the entities of interest to Edmonton Transit System are – you guessed it – bus, driver, route, and passenger.

For another example, consider an accounts receivable system. The entities in such a system would include *Account, Customer, Sale,* and *Journal Entry.* These are the *things* an accounts receivable clerk would need to know *about* in order to do his or her job. In a college registration system, the entities might be *Student, Course, Subject Area, Room, Instructor,* and *Enrollment.*

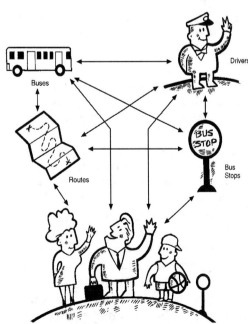

Buses, drivers, routes, bus stops, and passengers.

Combined for Candidate Key		Not Suitable as Candidate Keys			
Last Name	First Name	Address	Age	Sex	Phone No.
Smith	Mary	Here	22	F	555-1313
Smith	Joe	There	24	M	555-1414
Forsyth	Nancy	There	24	F	555-1414

Figure 4-1 Candidates for candidate keys.

Notice that I'm using singular words rather than plural; this is intentional. What we're describing here is really the *type* of entity. The name "Student" is really intended to stand for "the kind of thing described by the word student."

We capitalize this name and say that an ***entity type*** **is a grouping or classification of entities that are all the same kind of thing. Thus, an entity type is a *classification* or *category* expressing the common properties that allow a number of entities to be treated similarly.** An entity type describes the important features of every entity of that type, important to our project, that is, and so it can be called an *abstraction* of these entities, to a very high level of abstraction.

We refer to an individual student as an *occurrence* of the entity type Student. An ***occurrence*** **of an entity type is a specific, individual thing of the kind described by the entity type.** But what about the Student ID, Name, Address, Age, Sex, and Phone Number? These are the *attributes* of the entity-type Student. ***Attributes*** **are data elements carried by an entity that describe it and record its state** – that is, ***attributes*** **are the things we need to know *about* an entity.**

It's also important in an information system to be able to tell one occurrence from another. For this we designate *key attributes*, such as employee number for bus drivers, bus number for buses, or purchase order number in a purchasing system. *Key attributes* are as follows: **Any attribute or group of attributes is considered to be a *candidate key* for an entity type if each entity occurrence has a different (that is, unique) value in that attribute (or in that group of attributes taken as a whole).**

Let me give an example of what I mean by "taken as a whole." To identify people, let's say that first name and last name together are good enough. If we take the two attributes first name and last name as a group, then Joe + Smith and Mary + Smith would be considered as two distinct values (Figure 4-1).

We then choose one of the candidate keys to be the one we use most often. The ***primary key*** **is whichever candidate key is chosen to be the main or most important key.** The choice of primary key will depend on the relative importance to the users of the various candidate keys.

Lastly, we need to check out what happens when entities interact. When I bought my Jeep (I loved my new toy, but no room to put anything), the dealership had to create some kind of a record of that event. That record involves data that's held in several different entities. It'll involve customer data, product data, salesperson data, and sale data (yes, Sale turns out to be an entity type, too).

Many of the operations, processes, or events that happen in a business as it operates from day to day involve data. Usually, an operation or process needs data from more than one entity type. To be able to match the right customer with the right product on the right day, for example, we need to look at actions where one entity *does something* to another. All actions and events that make up the day-to-day functioning of the business need to be recorded. Many of these involve *inter*actions between entities: "Customer *buys* Product," for example.

For another example, consider Edmonton Transit. Here we have a sizable operation with 800 buses, 1200 bus drivers, thousands of bus stops, and hundreds of thousands of passengers – which is nice, but we still don't have a business! There is no business until somebody *does* something; until a driver *drives* a bus, a bus *carries* a passenger, a bus *follows* a route, and a bus *stops at* a bus stop.

Similarly, a college is not functioning until a student *enrolls in* a course, the course *is held in* a room, and a teacher *teaches* the course. A sales operation is worth keeping around only if someone is selling something and someone is paying for it. That is, a customer *buys* a product, a salesperson *sells* a product, a sale *appears on* an invoice, a customer *pays* an invoice, and a payment *is credited to* a receivables account.

Any business or other operation of any kind can be analyzed this way. What we've done is to focus on the *actions* that connect entities, in other words, their *inter*actions. Each interaction is represented by an *action word*, that is, a verb or verb phrase.

Or it can be represented by one or two nouns that state what *role* each entity plays in the life of the other. A customer would have a *purchaser* role in his relationship with a product. A room would have a *location* role in connection with a course.

Each time a business action occurs, it must be recorded by changing the values of some of the attributes, and sometimes by creating new entity occurrences (e.g., new buses in the Bus file). So, in the E-R paradigm, we say an **_association_ is the interaction of two entities and is represented by a verb, a verb phrase, or by roles.**

The purpose of associations is to provide access paths for the data. As we record the details of a sale, we'll need to select a customer and a salesperson and connect them both for the moment to a product. Later, when we need to produce a sales report, we may need to select each product in turn and connect to it all the sales for the past month (that were of that particular product).

These interactions among the entities show us the pathways we need to follow through the database to access the data. In data modeling we call these interactions *relationships*, hence the term *entity-relationship (E-R) model* or *entity-relationship diagram* (ERD). In the object paradigm we call them associations. As I'll demonstrate in Chapter 7, we must identify a role name(s) and/or verb(s) for each and every association as we do this analysis. This ensures that we've found *all* the relationships that matter, and *only* the ones that matter.

Note that if we can't come up with a role name or a verb (or verb phrase) to describe a relationship that we think exists, then it probably is not there after all. Also, we should note that in object modeling and UML the term *relationship* is given a more general definition, and the term *association* is used for what we have just discussed. You'll see more about this later in this chapter and in Chapter 5.

Let's recap what we've said about the constructs used in E-R analysis:

- An *entity* is a *thing* the users need to know (i.e., need to record) something about.

- An *entity type* is a group or class of entities that are all the same kind of thing.

- An *occurrence* of an entity type is a specific, individual thing of the kind described by the entity type.

- *Attributes* are the things we need to know *about* an entity.

- Any attribute or group of attributes is considered to be a *candidate key* for an entity type if each occurrence has a different (i.e., unique) value in that attribute (or in that group of attributes taken as a whole).

- A *primary key* is whichever candidate key is chosen to be the main or most important key.

- A *relationship* or *association* is the *inter*action of two entities and is represented by a verb.

- These *inter*actions among the entities – that is, these *relationships* – show us the pathways we need to follow through a database to access the data.

Why would we want to go to all this trouble? There's a very significant reason why entities, attributes, and relationships are so fundamentally important.

Entity-Relationship Models for Database Design

The original search for data-modeling methods was motivated by the need for a database design strategy. In the 1970s as the database concept spread and database management system (DBMS) software became more widely used, it became apparent that there were good and bad ways to design databases. Many methods and notations were proposed in research papers, and some were tried in the real world.

When Chen published his ERD notation, however, the others were promptly abandoned. Although it was originally proposed for database design, the ERD quickly caught on as a way for systems analysts to get a very important view of a business. Thus, it soon became an analysis tool as well as a database design tool, but the database design function was not lost.

After using ERDs to examine the business problem (we'll see how this is done in Chapter 9), developers then use it as a template for the design of the database in the following way:

- Each *entity* in the model becomes a file or *table* in the database (see Figure 4-2). Later, in Figure 4-4, we'll see that the data model is in the real world, not the computer world. The database is its *analog* in the computer world.

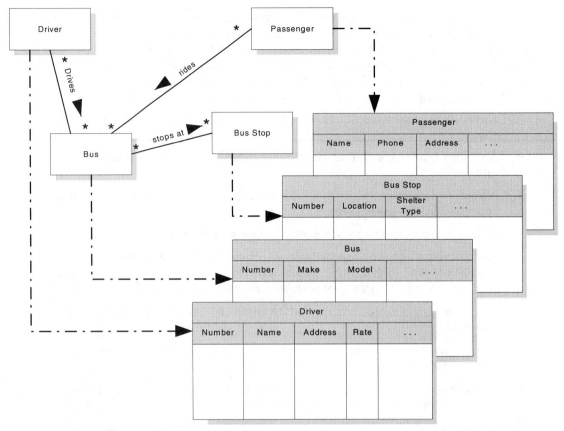

Figure 4-2   The connection between entity types and relational tables.

- The *attributes* then become the fields (that is, the *columns* in a relational database).

- Each *relationship (association)* in the model becomes an access pathway in the database

In an old-fashioned network database (and in some of the new object-oriented databases), each access pathway would be a set of pointers. In a relational database, it would be a foreign key. A ***foreign key*** **is a column (or a group of columns) that appears in one table as the primary key and in another table as a nonkey column.** Its purpose is to allow records (rows) in the two tables to be related – for example, by forming a relational join.

As an illustration, the Customer Number, which is the primary key in the Customer file, can be used to find all rows in the Sales table that belong to a given customer, as in Figure 4-3. Note that the Customer Number is *not* the primary key in the Sales table. In some designs that might be Order Number, and in Figure 4-3 it's Customer No. + Product No.

The final test of a database design is to enact a business process, task, transaction, or function. You'll turn it into a scenario and "run" it against the model. By following the access pathways, you'll be able to tell whether your database can properly support that business function.

Primary Key =
Customer No.

Linked by
Customer No.

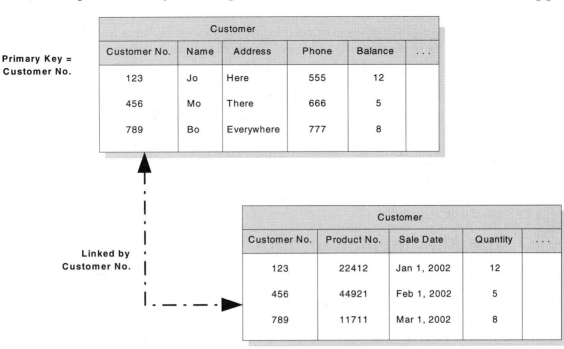

Figure 4-3 Foreign keys.

What about changes in the way these business functions are handled by the users over the years? What about totally new functions, and what I like to call **"_unanticipated queries_?" These are the queries that we were unable to foresee at system design time** and that traditionally have been the cause of much of the maintenance backlog.

You saw some of that happening in *The Outhouse Saga* at the beginning of this chapter. Can our ERD-based database handle all of this? In the next section, you'll discover that, for ERD-based databases, the answer is a resounding "Yes!"

The Stability of Data

This year, Edmonton Transit is concerned with the entity types Bus, Driver, Route, and Passenger; but as we saw earlier, businesses are always changing. Ten years from now, there will have been a colossal number of changes in the way that ETS does its business, and corresponding changes in the ways its people do their jobs. And ten years ago it was different again.

But some things never change. ETS will still be concerned with buses, drivers, routes, and passengers! And when those passengers sign up for a course at our college, we'll still have to deal with entity types called Student, Course, Subject Area, Room, and Enrollment, just as we did before.

What this tells us is that *data entities are stable over time*. When we organize our data around the entities we find in the real world of the users, those entities are stable. They are, however, neither static nor stagnant. Over time, there may be an occasional new entity, but as long as we remain in the same business there is very little activity adding new entities.

On the other hand, we may need to add attributes, perhaps Hourly Rate to our Driver entity or Average Grade to our Student entity. In fact, we can expect that there will often be a need for new attributes, but it'll be a relatively minor change, especially with modern databases. This stability contributes greatly to reducing the costs and delays of system maintenance.

I should, however, add a note of warning. Edmonton Transit didn't stay in the same business. When it entered the railway business (light rail transit, or LRT), of course, we had a whole new data-modeling effort and many new entities. Be prepared to find that mergers, acquisitions, takeovers, and diversification can all have this effect.

Which now brings us to the proper place that data occupies in the overall scheme of things.

The Significance of Data

Figure 4-4 is a data modeler's view of the universe. As you can see, the universe is divided into two hemispheres, the western one being data and the eastern one process. By *process*, I mean functions or activities that must be performed in the course of running a business, as we saw in Chapter 3.

We also divide the universe into northern and southern hemispheres. North represents the real world and south the computer world. (And I have news for all you techies out there – contrary to what you may have thought, the computer world is *not* the real world!) The circle in the center is the boundary of our project or business area. Everything inside the circle is part of our concern, and everything outside represents the rest of the universe.

There is a "path of logic" wending its way from the northwest quadrant, through the southwest and southeast to the northeast quadrant. This can be considered in either direction, so let's begin at the northeast and follow it back.

This northeast quadrant represents all real-world processes that are performed in the universe. Inside the circle are the ones that matter to us. These are the functions and processes our users must do each day in order to run their business.

To support these processes, our users must have access to certain information at each step of their job. They'll also generate data as they do their work, and our system must provide for that new data to be captured as it occurs. To achieve this then, we must provide computer programs that present suitable screens at each step of the user's work.

These programs we find represented in the southeast quadrant (bottom right) of Figure 4-4. The programs, however, need stored data and a place to store data, which are provided by the databases shown in the southwest quadrant (bottom left). The databases, in order to perform properly, provide the right data, and keep it in an accessible format, must be based on the *real-world entities of the users*. These entities are depicted in the northwest quadrant (top left), *within* the circle.

To recap, let's start from the other end and summarize. Beginning in the northwest quadrant (top left):

• Out of the universe of all the real-world data that exists, our system is concerned only with the subset in the northwest (top left) part of the circle, that is, the data in the business area we're studying. The ERD is the tool we use to understand and document this data.

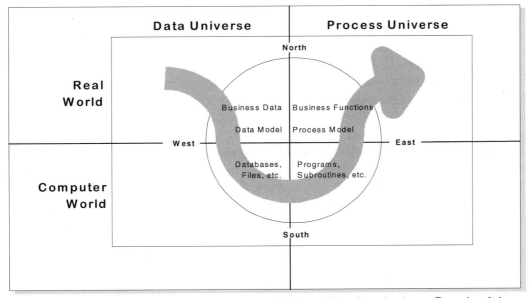

Figure 4-4 Diagram of "Life, The Universe and Everything," apologies to Douglas Adams

- Below, in the southwest quadrant (the *computer part* of the *data half* of the universe), we have the databases that must store that data, that is, that subset of the universe of all data.

- The databases drive the design of the programs, which are in the southeast quadrant (bottom right).

- The programs in turn support the users' operation, represented by the northeast part of the circle.

Data as a Corporate Asset

Now you can see that the entire operation of the users' business *rests upon a pool of data*. Viewed from the other direction, we can say that, in a sense, the organization's data drives its operations. Either way, it becomes clear that data can be regarded as an asset, with a value to the organization.

Like any corporate asset, however, it also costs money to acquire, organize, store, and keep it safe from harm or deterioration. This view of data as a corporate asset leads to the two related and relatively new disciplines of *data administration* (DA) and *data resource management* (DRM). The focus of these functions in any company is to manage data as any other corporate asset would be managed. The data model, and in particular the ERD, is the tool used to understand and document this pool of corporate data.

Whether for purposes of DRM or for specific systems development projects, Chen's ERD turned out to be the best way yet to understand the users' data. Also, at the systems project level, it gives a template for the database design, and has provided the first viable solution to the "plaintive cry of the CEO"[2] that we saw in *The Outhouse Saga* episode at the beginning of this chapter.

---

[2] CEO (Chief Executive Officer) is the senior salaried executive in an organization, reporting directly to the owners, who are usually represented by a board of directors or by a politician. The CEO usually has a title such as President, General Manager, Director, or in government, Deputy Minister, Director-General, Secretary of State, or in the military, Chief-of-Staff.

All these benefits stayed with us, of course, when we evolved from entities to objects, since an object can be viewed as "an entity with behavior." Both entity modeling and object modeling have given rise to a variety of notations, but all are based to some extent on Chen's original notation.

In the next section, we'll take a look at an evolved and somewhat simplified version of Chen's notation, and the principles of this notation will carry on into our study of object models. This is the *Unified Modeling Language*, or UML.

Entity-Relationship Notation

The various notations available all work just fine. Each has its champions and its detractors. However, in the words of the mathematician Maxwell, "It is *notions,* not *notations,* that are important." The object world also has spawned a multitude of notations, with UML finally emerging as the universal standard. However, once you become comfortable with the principles behind the notations, you should have very little trouble switching from one to another if necessary.

ENTITIES

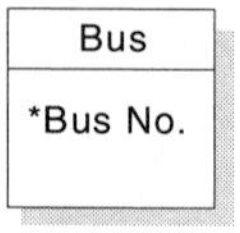

Figure 4-5

We represent an entity with a square or rectangular box, as Figure 4-5 shows. A line near the top divides the box in two, and above the line we place the name of the entity. This name is singular, because the box is actually representing the entity type, or class. That is, the entity type Bus stands for the set of all things that are of type Bus. Even though Edmonton Transit (ETS) has many individual buses (that is, occurrences of the entity type Bus), the entity type Bus is only one type and is thus singular.

ATTRIBUTES

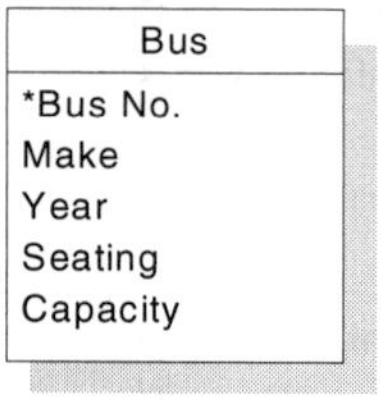

Figure 4-6

Attributes can be shown in a number of ways. If there are not too many, they may be shown in the bottom part of the box, with the primary key attribute first, optionally marked with an asterisk, as in Figure 4-6. If there are too many for this, then only the primary key should be shown in the box, as in Figure 4-5. The others must then be documented in the accompanying write-up.

RELATIONSHIPS (ALSO CALLED ASSOCIATIONS)

A line joining two boxes on the diagram will indicate that a relationship (association) exists between those two entity types. If you have a verb or verb phrase that describes the association, it should be written above the line, with an arrowhead to show which direction to read it. If you use one or two role names (nouns) to describe the association, with or without the verb, they should go below the line. In the first example in Figure 4-7, the association is depicted by the sentence "Driver *drives* Bus," with the role name "Driver."

In the second example, the association is "Customer *purchases* Product." Then we have "Student *enrolls in* Course" and "Teacher *teaches* Course." In each case, we have a simple sentence made up of "subject *verb* object." (Here, of course, we're using *object* in the grammatical sense, not the object-oriented sense.) The subject and object nouns are the entities (strictly, the entity *types*), and the verb or verb phrase expresses the relationship or association between them.

In Figure 4-7 notice that the association reads as a pair of sentences:

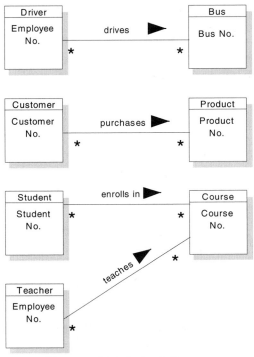

Figure 4-7 Associations

- Driver *drives* Bus
- Bus *is driven by* Driver.

But there's still one more thing to tell about relationships on the ERD, and that is *how many* of each entity are involved.

MULTIPLICITY (SOMETIMES CALLED CARDINALITY)

When a driver *drives* a bus, how many buses does she drive? The answer to this little riddle is "Only one, usually." The answer might be different in some environments. (For example, perhaps, consider those little piggy-backed trains of semi-tractors, each running on its rear wheels only, with its front end sitting on the back of the truck in front. We see them being delivered all around the North American continent, and this arrangement allows one driver to "drive" several trucks at once.)

At Edmonton Transit, and this is usually the case, a Driver *drives* many Buses *over time*. Similarly, a Bus *is driven by* one Driver at a time, but by many Drivers over time. We don't need to know exactly how many are involved, as long as we know whether it's *one* or whether it's *many*. Later, we'll see how to add more information to this part of the diagrams, but the most important thing is the distinction between "one" and "many."

This is the *multiplicity*, a.k.a. *cardinality*, of the association. *Random House Webster* (1998) defines **cardinality** **as the number of members in a set.** For our purposes, we say that **multiplicity (cardinality) is the number of occurrences of each entity type that are or can be involved in an association.**

We now need to take each of the simple sentences we've generated to describe relationships and add a symbol at each end of the line representing the multiplicity. There are a number of notations to choose from, and you'll need to pick one that works for you. Chen's notation uses a single arrowhead for the "one" end of a association line (if there is a "one" end) and a double arrowhead at each "many" end.

A Driver *drives* many Buses

At the many end (or ends), we'll use the UML symbols. These are little numbers or a star (asterisk or " * ") at each end of the line, as in Figure 4-7. You can easily draw these with pen and paper, and also on a whiteboard in front of a group. We'll leave the *one* end of a association as a simple line, with the number "1" optional, and place the star below the many end. A lot more information can be placed on the diagram, but for now we'll leave it as it is. Figure 4-7 shows the diagram with everything on it that we've discussed so far.

Here is a summary about entities and UML:

- There are many ERD notations. This book uses UML notation.
- An entity is a square box, with a *singular* name above a horizontal line.
- The key attribute is below the line with a star (" * "), and other attributes are either listed below it or documented separately.
- A relationship (association) is a line joining two entities. The verb is written above the line with an arrowhead, the role names may go beneath it. Entity–*verb*–entity should make a sentence.
- The cardinality is one (digit "1") or many (star " * ") at each end of the line, usually below the line.

There's an unexpected side benefit to E-R modeling, a true serendipity, that has also been inherited by the object methods. When I first began using this technique, I found that it gave me a far better understanding of the users' business than any method I had used previously. Peter Coad and Ed Yourdon (1991), in the introduction to their book, describe the same finding. We end up with a document (the model) that serves these four important functions:

- Allows us to understand the users' business
- Documents the information needs of that business
- Provides the Data Administrator with the tool needed for understanding, documenting, and ultimately *controlling* the data
- Forms a template, or pattern, for database and software design

The ERD data model is highly effective for all these functions. Object-oriented models are too, because everything about entities is also true about objects. A number of systems development methodologies have been developed around ERDs, the best-known being Information Engineering (IE) from James Martin (1982). Now let's see how the ERD evolved to become the OOA model.

4.4 OBJECT-ORIENTED MODELS

In effect, object-oriented modeling grew out of E-R modeling. In 1985 when I first encountered ERDs, we at the ETS group used to describe ourselves as being on the "bleeding edge" that is, we were so far out on the leading edge it hurt! As I mentioned earlier, those who had been there before me had had the courage and vision to stumble around with the principles of ERDs until they developed a technique that worked.

An object participates in relationships with other objects

They were thoroughly vindicated, of course, a few years later when the ERD became the direction the information systems (IS) industry was headed. Mind you, as I write this chapter in fall 2000, only perhaps half of the IS industry has ever used them. This is more than enough, however, for ERDs to have been the "state of the art." And so just where, on this continuum from bleeding edge through leading edge to state of the art, would I place object-oriented analysis?

Object-oriented programming (OOP) is a relatively mature discipline compared to object-oriented analysis (OOA). OOP still has enormous potential for development, of course. So far only a minority of programmers are using object-oriented programming languages (OOPLs). They are a significant minority, however, with their numbers growing daily, and more so with the advent of Java.

There is no doubt that at this time OOP can rightly be considered state of the art. Its maturity is partly because it was used early in graphics applications, for drawing and drafting and so on, and also caught on in engineering and real-time applications. This growth was further fueled by the arrival of Java, which took objects to the Web, and then into mainstream IS development.

Thus, objects were already well explored and understood by the time they were borrowed by business systems analysts. In 1992, when I moved into OOA, I once again had that bleeding-edge experience. Right now, I believe that OOA and its companion object-oriented design (OOD) have migrated from the bleeding edge to the slightly more comfortable but still very stimulating leading edge. But the current progress is rapid, and by the time you read this, it will surely be true that OOA is the way things are done in this business.

Object-oriented database management systems (ODBMSs) are another matter. Of the three parts of object-oriented technology that I've mentioned, ODBMSs are the least mature. They also have recently come in from the bleeding edge to the leading edge. Much work has been done, and a number of products are on the market and in use in production environments.

The work of the Object Management Group (OMG) and the Object Data Management Group (ODMG, formerly the Object Data*base* Management Group) has hastened the ODBMSs along the path to maturity (see Chapters 13 and 14). We'll look at some of them in Chapter 14, along with some OOPLs and some object-oriented development environments (OODENVs).

It is significant that Oracle, the most widely-used industrial-strength database in the world, is a member of the OMG, and Oracle is on its way to being object oriented (more in Chapter 14.)

Object-oriented development environments (OODENVs) are also new and exciting. The ones that are on the market so far are not pure object oriented, however. Most are hybrids that have true object-oriented features only for the graphical user interface (GUI, pronounced "gooey"). They have some important object-oriented features for screen objects such as windows and buttons.

These features include true inheritance and polymorphism, where subclasses inherit both attributes and behavior from their superclasses. (We'll study inheritance in detail in Chapter 7.) But the database behind it all is usually relational. Many OODENVs function as front ends to popular relational databases such as ORACLE and SYBASE. Some also have their own built-in relational databases. They don't have a database with user objects and classes, such as Employee, Account, Sale, or Bus. Very soon, however, we can expect more and more of these front-end products to start working with true ODBMSs.

The situation, then, is like this:

- Object modeling grew out of ERD modeling.

- It has become the state of the art, and it's the way of the future.

- OOP is the most mature part of object-oriented technology (OOT).

- As of the time of writing, OOA is now the IS industry's direction, the state of the art since by now a large number of analysts are using it (though they're still a minority, but a significant one.)

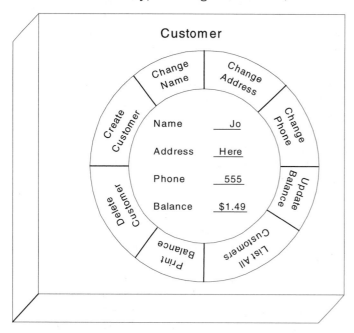

- ODBMSs are out of their infancy. Though some are in production use, they're still in a state of rapid development.

- OODENVs are so far mostly object-oriented front ends to relational databases, but that's changing even as I write.

I am writing this book as an invitation. It is an invitation to you to accompany OOA and me on the journey to industry acceptance. Now let's begin our journey by discussing some of the basics of objects.

Figure 4-8 A David Taylor donut diagram

4.5 AN INTRODUCTION TO OBJECTS

In this section, you'll get a quick tour to give you an overview of objects. In Chapters 5 to 7, you'll have an in-depth exposure to them with all the details explained. So for now, relax and marvel at what I have to show you about these wonderful new objects. To repeat, according to Oxford (1998), an **_entity_ is "a thing with distinct and independent existence."** So for our purposes, we shall say that a **_data entity_ is a thing with distinct and independent existence in the world of the users, and is of interest to the users in that they need to record data about it.**

It is technically correct to view an **_object_ as being an "entity with behavior."** (We'll give a more formal definition early in Chapter 5.) Like an entity, an object is described by a *noun*, has *attributes* to carry data, and participates in *associations* with other objects, but it has more, much more. In addition to the data, an object also includes the program code *that uses or changes that data*.

If I were to choose one principle that represents the core of the object-oriented paradigm, it would be this:

> The *only way* that a program can read or change the data carried by an object, or *access the data in any way at all*, is by invoking one of the pieces of program code that the object also carries within itself.

This is shown in Figure 4-8 using a notation popularized by David Taylor (1992). The "pieces of program code" are in fact functions or subroutines. They are actually program code, stored in the database somehow alongside the data. The name we give them in the object-oriented paradigm is *methods*. They're also sometimes called *functions, services* or *operations*, especially in OOA since there we are describing the real world rather than a programming detail.

In object-oriented programming languages (OOPLs) and object-oriented database management systems (ODBMSs), they're almost always called *methods*. Thus, in the words of Coad and Yourdon (1991), we may say that an object *encapsulates* both the "data and the exclusive functions on that data." By "exclusive functions on the data," we mean program code that accesses and manipulates the data exclusively – that is, no other code can do so. We'll have more about *encapsulation* in Chapter 5.

So our task as analysts, then, is to identify these operations (or services, functions, or methods). Our mission (. . . *should we choose to accept it* . . .) is to investigate our users' business, looking for the objects, their attributes, and the operations that can be performed on, to, with, or by the objects.

Then we need to consider how each operation will use or affect the data attributes. In the design phase of the project, we produce specifications for each operation. In the construction phase, these specs enable us to write the operations as methods in whatever OOPL we've chosen.

OOPLs and ODBMSs actually do store the program code for each function (method) along with the data entity or object that the method manipulates. There are a number of ways this is done in the various products, each with its advantages and disadvantages. The whole idea is to write small pieces of program code that each provide a single service or operation.

All objects of type Customer, for example, will need an operation called UpdateAddress and a piece of code (a method) to carry it out. The method is stored in the database attached in some way to the Customer file. (Later you'll see some of the ways that program code for the methods is handled, in the section on OOPLs and ODBMSs in Chapter 14.)

Note that the phrasing is *"data and functions for it."* It's no accident that I mention data before process. Throughout the 1980s as the ERD ushered in the era of data-oriented methods, there was a continual debate as to whether *data* or *process* was more central and fundamental to software development.

The "data-oriented" methodologies published during this period attempted to give equal weight to these two aspects of the systems development process. They all espoused doing data models as well as process models. However, there were many who, as I did, firmly believed that the data half of the equation was the more significant.

With the advent of object-oriented modeling, I feel we data specialists have been vindicated since, as I love to put it, what we've done is to "slice up the process model and tape the pieces to the entities, to make objects." What I'm saying is that data comes first, then come the functions, important only in that they manipulate the data. So you can see that I still believe in the Data Modeler's Creed: "Data is the center of the universe." We'll examine this in more detail in Chapter 5.

There's another interesting thing about objects that's currently the source of much research, and that's the topic of *object persistence*. In most OOPLs, when an object is created, it's built in the RAM, where its data is updated and used during the program or session. Finally, it's deleted from RAM, or just disappears when you turn off the machine.

Such objects are termed ***transient* or *transitory objects* because they do NOT survive beyond the current session.** These are fine for real-time and graphics applications, but for business systems we need them to stick around a little longer. The problem for designers of ODBMSs is to devise an effective way to provide ***persistent objects* that *DO* survive beyond the current session.**

What we've discovered so far about objects, then, is as follows:

- Objects are entities (things that carry data) with behavior (operations) added.

- These operations exclusively access and manipulate the data carried by an object – that is, no other program code can touch the data.

- The operations are coded in an OOPL as *methods* (which are really just functions or subroutines).

- The program code for the methods is stored in the database along with the data for the object.

- Any program, function, or method that wants data from this object can only get at it by calling one of these methods defined on this object.

- Transient objects are created by OOPLs in the RAM of the computer and *do not* survive beyond the current session.
- Persistent objects are stored by a database (ODBMS) and *do* survive beyond the current session.

From this, we can develop a definition to take us a step further than the definition of real-world objects. **A *data object* is a place to store data to record the state of its real-world counterpart, along with the operations (program code), for the exclusive access to that data.**

Now that we've talked a little about the objects themselves, we need to highlight two different ways that programming languages can handle them.

4.6 OBJECT-ORIENTED VERSUS OBJECT-BASED LANGUAGES

In the introduction to this chapter, I promised to discuss a little about the "oriented" part of the term *object-oriented*. Since it's the latest buzz word, there are many products out there claiming to be "object-oriented." Some are, some are not, and some are more than others. Fortunately, the industry has by now advanced to where there's a fairly clear consensus on just what does constitute *object-oriented*. But at the same time, marketing hype can still be misleading as to how much a particular product actually is object-oriented, or which parts of it are and which are not.

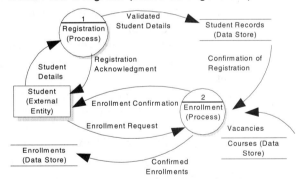

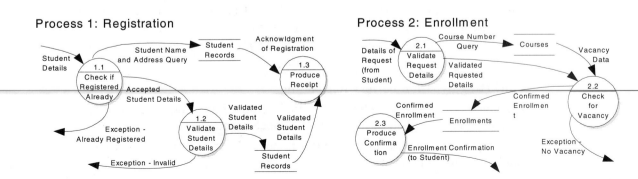

Figure 4-9(a) Data flow diagrams at different levels of abstraction: a logical DFD

Some programming languages do have objects but cannot properly be called object-oriented. VisualBasic is one such. The original version of Ada was another one. Ada-85 had what it termed "packets," which satisfied the requirements for objects, but lacked two very important features that must be present to earn the label *object-oriented*. These are *inheritance* and *polymorphism*, and they're both present in the newer Ada-95.

These two features (described in detail in Chapter 8) give object-oriented technology (OOT) so much of its power compared with older languages. Inheritance and polymorphism provide the vast potential for reuse of program code, as well as analysis results. This is something that has long been promised by OOT, and is loudly claimed by fans of objects, and many people have become somewhat jaded by the advertising hype that has centered on it.

Nonetheless, both code and analysis results are being reused on object-oriented projects. However, because of the learning curve for the new development tools and the new paradigm, not usually until the third or fourth project (Love, 1993). (Remember, the new paradigm implies learning a whole new way of thinking, in addition to some new languages and software products.) We'll look at this process in detail in the section on *pilot projects* in Chapter 15.for student registration

And what about a product where parts of it are object-oriented and parts are not? Where we see a lot of this occurring is in so-called object-oriented development environments (OODENVs) that are actually just an object-oriented front end. They provide an object-oriented environment, with full inheritance and polymorphism, for building a user interface.

This interface is typically a graphical user interface (GUI), either Windows-based or else windowing in some other way, such as in UNIX or on the Mac. The environment is object-oriented for developing the GUI, but then all the processing behind the GUI in the eventual system is conventional, and not object-oriented.

The environment has either a back-end relational database of its own, or a back-end interface to a regular relational product such as Access, Oracle or Sybase. The objects involved are things such as "window," "button," "radio button," and "scroll region." There are no objects like Customer, Product, Sale, Account, or Employee. This data, the central data to the enterprise and to the project, is held in an old-fashioned relational database.

However, for the majority of these products, the windowing front end is truly object-oriented, with all the properties and benefits thereof, including inheritance, polymorphism, and the promised reuse. True OODENVs are somewhere just around the corner, when the current ones get connected to ODBMSs.

Here, then, is a summary of object-oriented state of the art:

• Some products are more object-oriented than others and some not at all. Marketing hype can be very misleading.

• Languages such as Ada-85 have objects, but they have neither inheritance nor polymorphism, and so they're termed object-based.

• Inheritance and polymorphism make it possible to reuse program code, and analysis results as well.

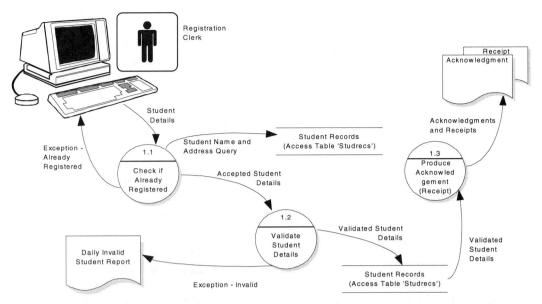

Figure 4-9(b) A physical DFD for student registration, showing a design using a MS Access database on a desktop computer (Compare with Figures 4-9(a) and 3-12)

- Because of the learning curve for object-oriented thinking, as well as the new languages, the reuse benefits don't become significant until about the third or fourth object-oriented project.

- Object-oriented development environments are mostly OOGUI front ends that attach to traditional relational databases.

Now that you've had a brief guided tour of objects, it's time to consider the four kinds, or levels, of models that we can build, and then finish this discussion of models and modeling with a section on the use of models as communication tools.

4.7 CONCEPTUAL, LOGICAL, AND PHYSICAL MODELS

Whatever kind of model we're building for our system, be it a data flow diagram (DFD), an entity-relationship diagram (ERD), object model, or whatever, we can do it in a number of ways. Think for a moment about a DFD. It will have process bubbles, data stores, and so on. We have a choice, however, about how much detail we put in the model.

Say we have a DFD for a personnel system, and it shows a process called "Update Hourly Rate." We can go all the way with this, and we can document who (i.e., which person, position, or computer program) will actually perform this operation in the real business world of the users, once the system is in production. This we call a *physical DFD*.

Or, we could simply state that it needs to be done, without specifying by what or by whom. In this case, we would consider it to be a *logical DFD*. (Recall that logical and physical DFDs were introduced in Chapter 3.) The key thing to remember about logical models is that they're *implementation-independent*. That is, they carry no information relating to how the system will be built, or on what hardware or software platform, or any other factor relating to the final physical implementation of the system.

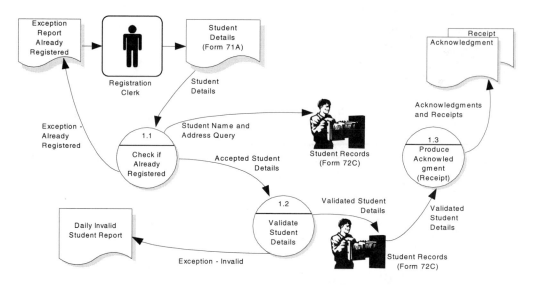

Figure 4-9(c) A physical DFD for student registration, showing a design using paper processing and filing.

With ERDs we can make a similar distinction. A logical ERD shows what data is needed and the associations that exist. It shows entities, attributes, and associations, but it doesn't show how each is implemented or built in the eventual database. For data, the physical model is considered to be the database itself – the files on the disk, as created with the DBMS software ready for programs to be run against it.

For DFDs, we typically have a leveled set of diagrams starting with the Context Diagram, with each lower level having more and more detail. Figure 4-9(a) shows a logical DFD model consisting of all levels, right down to the lowest and most detailed, but still showing only what needs to be done, not who or what will do it. For the physical DFD model, the lowest and most detailed level is repeated with implementation details added, as in Figure 4-9(b) and (c).

This diagram now tells what person, machine, program, or business unit will be performing each process. It will also show whether a data store consists of paper, a filing cabinet, computer files, databases, or whatever. In other words, it shows what *medium* the data stores will be kept on when the system is built. Each data flow will also show its medium – that is, whether it's a piece of paper (identified by form number or name if possible) or a verbal or electronic message. (Recall that we defined the term *medium* in Chapter 3.)

So, what we have seen is that a ***logical model*** **shows what a system must do or have, without regard for how it is to be done, built, or represented.** This, is truly an analysis model, according to our definition of systems analysis in Chapter 3. On the other hand, a ***physical model*** **is either the actual implemented system (or part of it) or else is the final design document showing how things will be done or built and depicting all platform details, and data storage and transmission media.** Thus, it is the *result of the design activity* and possibly of the construction activity as well.

There's more. For data models especially, more levels of abstraction are available than just logical and physical models. When we first begin working with our users to produce system models, we're documenting what the users tell us about their operation. Our model closely reflects the way the users perceive their own operation. As we document the users' view of their world, we draw diagrams to match it.

One significant feature of the users' world that appears on this level of ERD or Object Model is relationships (associations) with a many-to-many (M:M) multiplicity. Users tend to view their business in terms of many-to many associations. For example, "Customer *buys* many Products" and "Product *is sold to* many Customers" (or at least we would hope so!). Or again, "Student *enrolls in* many Courses" and "Course *has* many Students."

There's an important principle here that must always be applied. Every many-to-many relationship (association) breaks apart into three components: a ***new entity*** and a ***pair of one-to-many*** (1:M) associations.

In Chapter 9, we'll explore further just how and why this happens. For now it suffices to note that, since users tend to think of their world in terms of many-to-many relationships, such a model is close to *the users' conception* of their world. For this reason, it's called a ***conceptual model*, a representation of the users' business in terms of their conception of how it operates.** This means it includes many-to-many associations.

Some methodologies also include functional models, which are like conceptual models, except they show more detail. A ***functional model* shows everything the users are aware of about their operation, including things that would normally be hidden from all or some of them.** Figure 4-9 shows the relationship of the logical and physical models.

Now let's quickly review:

- A *conceptual model* is the users' concept of their operation. For ERDs and object models, this includes the many-to-many relationships (associations).

- A *logical model* shows what a system must do or have, without regard for how. A logical model is implementation-independent.

- A *physical model* is a plan of how the system will be built to make the things happen.

- The three models are built in that order.

These three levels of abstraction – the conceptual, logical, and physical models – are typically built in that order. This is a *top-down* sequence since it begins with a high-level, conceptual overview and then moves to progressively more detail. The sequence is *from abstract to concrete* since the conceptual model is the one that's *least* like the reality being modeled. This makes it the *highest* level of abstraction, in keeping with our earlier definition.

The physical model, on the other hand, most closely resembles the physical reality of the users' world and is thus the *lowest* level of abstraction. As with the leveled set of DFDs we discussed earlier, the purpose of the progression is to allow you, or anyone reading your document, to begin by learning about the whole business operation at an overview level. You may then refine your understanding step by step as you work to more detail.

As part of that learning, you'll need to discuss the business and the models with a variety of people. These models do in fact provide an excellent way of communicating among the various people involved.

4.8 MODELS AS COMMUNICATION TOOLS

Coad and Yourdon, in the introduction to their 1991 book *Object-Oriented Analysis,* have some stories to tell about the importance of understanding the data in the users' world, when designing an information system. My own experience exactly parallels theirs.

During my time at the City of Edmonton, I discovered the power of the entity-relationship model as a tool for communicating with my users, colleagues, and staff. As I moved into object-oriented modeling, I found that to be even better. By involving the users in the modeling process, we were able to build better, more accurate, more useful models. Also, once our users learned the modeling notation, we could talk with them in a language both groups could understand.

This had many benefits. We were much better able to understand their business and their problems. They were better able to express their problems and contributions and no longer felt that we were speaking a foreign language. When working with users new to these methods, we would find that at a certain point in the process (around step 4 of the Seven Steps in Chapter 9), they began to regard the system as *their own,* and not something that we the systems people owned, and were forcing upon them.

With earlier methods, it was rare to find users feeling this level of ownership in the project. With object-oriented methods, we found they came to view the system as "theirs" rather than "ours." So often I've listened to users among my students, or to users from other companies, complain about the "computer people who never listen" or "never do what we were asking for."

Or I hear that they "gave us way more than we needed." These are all problems that can and should be rectified, and the secret is communication. These modeling methods are great for forcing us to listen and helping us to be "user-driven" in our analysis and design work.

One of the keys to reaching a point where the users see such relevance to their own world is that *they feel we're listening* to them, especially when the definitions for classes are built around *their* contributions. Often, we find this is something many users have never before experienced with computer people. And remember, what we're doing with our object-oriented techniques is *documenting* **their** *business.*

In fact, an object-oriented model gives such a good picture of the business operation, that the techniques are now being used by management consultants. They first do an object-oriented model to learn about the business and all its functions and processes. Then, armed with this understanding, they redesign the way the clients do their business. This is often referred to as *business process re-engineering,* or BPR.[3]

---

[3]Or, as some of the analysts among my students put it, "business process *engineering,*" since these businesses were never "engineered" in the first place! And it's true. Most businesses have just "grow'd like Topsy," without much thought given to planning for an efficient and effective structure.

Our completed model has descriptions of their data, their processes, and even their jargon. Their jargon is actually the core of their corporate culture, in the same way that any human language enshrines the essence of its culture. To do this effectively, we must listen to them much more than we talk and much more than we have in the past. Our motto has to be (with thanks to Dr A. K. Kapur):

"Discover, Don't Invent"

To this end, I have no hesitation in recommending all kinds of interpersonal communications courses, and particularly courses on effective listening techniques, for those of us who are or will be "object-oriented systems analysts." In Chapter 9, I'll talk about brainstorming and similar methods, suitable for various parts of user-driven model development efforts, including a recent one called the Delphi method.

In Chapter 16, you'll find more people-oriented issues, along with some listening techniques and other interpersonal strategies that are particularly useful for this kind of modeling.

These models are, of course, equally suitable for communication among the technical members of the team. Many times I've sat over coffee with Anil (the same Dr Kapur), with the two of us arguing over something by drawing boxes and lines on the table napkins. To this day, I still draw object models on table napkins, much to the mystification of waitresses.

These diagrams and models are highly effective for discussions between teams and within teams, among all the players in the project. You'll find technical people using them to argue and discuss. Your analysts, designers, data administrators, database administrators (DBAs), programmers, and even some of the users will work the terminology and concepts into their conversation.

You'll even find the models useful for discussions with government departments and with regulating agencies. Reports required by these outside agencies must be considered at the Analysis phase to ensure the necessary data is available in the final system. (Mostly this will mean a few extra attributes and some methods to handle them.) Consultants and their clients have both contractual issues and day-to-day operational issues to discuss at all levels I've mentioned. They too will find these models helpful as tools for talking.

Senior managers need to get involved in the project and will find they too can learn the object-oriented notation and vocabulary. User management, systems management, and even senior executives will be able to make contributions and understand what is going on, more effectively than with the old ways.

With management, there's another need that your object-oriented models will help address. You will recall in Section 3.4 that we discussed the need to convince management that we're actually achieving something with all the time and money spent on analysis and modeling. One of the most important ways that model-based analysis methods can help us with this is the concept of *deliverables*.

. . . .

DELIVERABLES

There are a number of published methodologies in the world of systems development. These fall roughly into three groups:

- *__Proprietary Methodologies__* **Each has been developed, copyrighted, and marketed as a product, supported with extra-cost training and consulting.** They're often from large consulting firms such as *MacroScope* from the DMR Group, and *Method One* from Arthur Anderson.

- *__In-House Methodologies__* **developed by large corporations for their own internal use.**

- *__Authors' Methodologies__* **or** *__Guru Methodologies__* **are from the literature, such as** *__The Unified Software Development Process__* **from Jacobson, Booch, and Rumbaugh.** Some of these "guru authors" are actively marketing their methodologies, often with associated CASE software. In other cases, such as *The Unified Software Development Process*, a number of companies are marketing CASE tools to support the methodology.

Methodologies abound in the literature, though. Of the books published so far in the field of OOA, the majority have been statements of various methodologies developed by the author(s). A few are finding rather widespread acceptance, and some are now being formalized and packaged as a product for sale.

There are, however, a number of object-oriented development CASE tools and environments available, each of which, in effect, dictates a methodology or else is based on one of the "authors methodologies" from the literature, such as *The Unified Software Development Process*. Some of these "guru authors" are marketing their methodologies, often with associated CASE software.

One of the hallmarks of the "packaged" methodologies, which has continued from the ERD paradigm into the object world, has been their approach to documentation. They needed to accommodate a wide variety of conditions and circumstances in the many companies where they'll be used. As a result, most of these methodologies focus on the output documents from each phase of the system development, that is, the *deliverables*.

Rather than telling you how to go about the development step by step, they concentrate on *what* you should produce. They provide formats, examples, and templates for the documents required at the end of each phase and subphase of your project. In this way, they guide you as to *what* you should produce, and leave you plenty of freedom to decide *how* you'll produce it.

Importantly, some of these outputs are documents in a format suitable for passing up to senior management. It's necessary that those with the ultimate responsibility for the project and its funding should receive some concrete assurance that it's proceeding as planned.

Otherwise, they'll quite naturally begin getting anxious about all the time and money being spent with no apparent return. Other documents are in a quite different format and are intended as the input to the next phase. This more technical documentation will be in a more rigorous format and language, suitable for those doing the actual design and development work.

Yet another set of outputs from some of the phases will not be documents at all. They'll be the parts of the physical system itself. There will be such features as databases, programs, and operating procedures. These will be the actual functioning databases and programs. There will be a set of them in a "training environment" for the users to learn and practice on. Then there will be a separate copy set up on the computers for use as the "production environment."

All of these are referred to as the ***deliverables*, the documents and other products generated during each phase and subphase of the project and whose production marks the completion of the phase.** Throughout the rest of this book, you'll find at the end of each chapter a section detailing the deliverables for the activities described in that chapter.

Let's review these last few sections:

- Object models are a powerful tool for communication among developers, management, and users.

- The object-modeling process gives users opportunity for input and helps them generate a feeling of ownership in the project.

- People skills are essential for modelers, especially listening skills.

- Deliverables from each phase are the documents and other products generated during the phases and subphases of the project and whose production marks the completion of the phase.

FURTHER READING

For more about ERDs, I recommend Chapter 8 of Whitten et al., (2000) *Systems Analysis and Design Methods*. G. Lawrence Sanders (1995) gives a good explanation in his small volume (146 pages) called, appropriately enough, *Data Modeling*. For a more technical view, try Martin Modell (1992) *Data Analysis, Data Modeling, and Classification*, or some of the many books by James Martin, the "guru" of data modeling and certainly its most prolific author; try *Computer Data Base Organization* (1982), if you like mathematical derivations.

You will find much more detailed explanations about objects in the following chapters, and then if you feel you'd like more, here are some suggestions. For a good overview of OOT and methods read David Taylor's two books, *Object-Oriented Technology: A Manager's Guide* (1990) and/or *Object-Oriented Information Systems: Planning and Implementation* (1992).

More up-to-date with UML and a detailed case study in Java is *Understanding UML: The Developer's Guide* by Paul Harmon and Mark Watson (1998).

CHAPTER SUMMARY

- A paradigm shift occurs when we adopt a radically different way of organizing all or part of our worldview.

- Entity-relationship diagrams (ERDs) are data models. An ERD shows (1) the entities (things, nouns) in the users' world about which they need to store information, and (2) the structure of the users' data in terms of the associations (actions, verbs) that link the entity types.

- Object-oriented model: By taking an entity type and adding to it the exclusive processes that manipulate the data in that entity, we create an object. Besides all the benefits of data and process modeling, object modeling gives us powerful new features such as encapsulation, inheritance, and polymorphism.

- Out of the universe of all real-world data, our system is concerned with a subset, the data in the business area we're studying. The ERD is a tool to understand and document this data. The ERD also is a template for designing the databases, which drive the programs, which then support the users' operation.

- There are many ERD notations. For ERDs, this book uses a subset of UML notation. An entity (type) is a square box, with a singular noun name. The key attribute is below the line with a star, along with other attributes.

- An association is a line joining two entities; the verb goes above or beside the line with an arrowhead, and/or role names go below the line. Entity–verb–entity should make a sentence. Multiplicity (cardinality) is shown as digit (usually "1") and/or a star for many at each end of the line.

- The ERD allows us to understand the users' business, documents the information needs of the business, and provides the data administrator with a tool for understanding, documenting, and ultimately controling the data.

- Object modeling grew out of ERD modeling, and object-oriented programming (OOP) is currently the most mature part of object-oriented technology (OOT). Object-oriented analysis (OOA) is now the information systems (IS) industry's direction, leading-edge but not yet state-of-the-art.

- Object-oriented database management systems (ODBMSs) are still in their infancy. Though some are in production use, they're still in a state of rapid development.

- The Object Management Group (OMG) and Object Data Management Group (ODMG) are doing valuable work on compatibility standards. Object-Oriented development environments (OODENVs) are so far only object-oriented front ends to relational databases, but that should soon change.

- Objects are entities (things that carry data) with behavior (operations) added. These operations exclusively access and manipulate the data carried by an object – that is, no other program code can touch the data.

- The operations are coded in an object-oriented programming language (OOPL) as methods. The program code for the methods is stored in the database along with the data for the object. Any program, function, or method that wants data from this object can only get at it by calling one of these methods defined on this object.

- The only way that a program can read or change the data carried by an object or access it in any way at all, is by invoking one of the pieces of program code that the object also carries within itself.

- *Transient objects* are created by OOPLs in RAM and do **not** survive beyond the current session. *Persistent objects* are stored by a database (ODBMS) and *do* survive beyond the current session.

- Some products are "more object-oriented" than others, and some not at all. Marketing hype can be misleading. Languages such as Ada-85 have objects, but not inheritance nor polymorphism, and are termed object-based. Inheritance and polymorphism make it possible to reuse program code and analysis results. Ada-95 has these both and is truly object-oriented.

- Because of the learning curve for object-oriented thinking, as well as new languages and things, the reuse benefits only become significant on about the third or fourth object-oriented project.

- OODENVs are mostly graphical user interface (GUI) front ends that attach to relational databases. True OODENVs with ODBMSs are imminent.

- There are four styles of models: conceptual, functional, logical, and physical. They're developed in that order, from the conceptual model to the physical model.

- A *conceptual model* is a representation of the users' business in terms of their conception of how it operates. It's an overview of the business operation at a high level of abstraction.

- A *functional model* shows all parts and aspects of the users' operation that they're aware of, including some that are hidden from them.

- A *logical model* shows *what* a system must do or have, without regard for *how* it is to be done, built, or represented.

- A *physical model* is the final design document, a plan showing *how* things will be done or built.

- Object models are a powerful tool for communication. The object modeling process gives users opportunity for input and helps them generate a feeling of ownership in the project. People skills are essential for modelers, especially listening skills.

- Deliverables from each phase are the documents and other products generated during each phase and subphase of the project and whose production marks the completion of the phase.

Chapter Glossary

attributes The things we need to know *about* an entity.

attributes The data elements carried by an entity, that describe it and record its state.

author's methodology or *guru methodology* A methodology from the literature.

bleeding edge So far out on the leading edge it hurts!

candidate key Any attribute or group of attributes of an entity type where each entity occurrence has a different (that is, unique) value in that attribute (or in that group of attributes taken as a whole).

cardinality The number of members in a set.

conceptual model A representation of the users' business in terms of their conception of how it operates. This means it includes many-to-many associations.

data entity A thing with distinct and independent existence in the world of the users, and of interest to the users in that they need to record data about it.

data object A place to store data to record the state of its real-world counterpart, along with the operations (program code) for the exclusive access to that data.

deliverables The documents and other products generated during each phase and subphase of the project and whose production marks the completion of the phase.

entity A thing with distinct and independent existence. (Oxford 1998) (See also ***data entity***)

entity type A classification, grouping, or category that expresses the common properties that allow a number of entities to be treated similarly.

foreign key A column (or a group of columns) that appears in one table as the primary key and in another table as a nonkey column. Its purpose is to allow records (rows) in the two tables to be related, for example, by forming a relational join.

guru methodology or ***author's methodology*** A methodology from the literature.

in-house methodology A methodology developed by a large corporation for their own internal use.

logical model Shows what a system must do or have, without regard for how. A logical model is implementation-independent.

multiplicity (also ***cardinality***) The number of occurrences of each entity type that are or can be involved in an association.

object An "entity with behavior."

occurrence *(of an entity type)* A specific individual thing of the kind described by the *entity type*.

paradigm A pattern or mode of thinking and believing that serves to organize the way we approach knowledge, learning, and understanding.

paradigm shift Occurs when we adopt a radically different way of organizing all or part of our worldview, i.e., we adopt a new *paradigm*.

persistent object An object that survives beyond the current session.

physical model Either the implemented system (or part of it) or the final design document showing how things will be done or built and depicting all platform details, data storage media, and data transmission media.

primary key The candidate key chosen to be the main or most important key.

proprietary methodology A methodology that has been developed, copyrighted, and marketed as a product, supported with extra-cost training and consulting.

relationship The interaction between two entities, represented by a verb, a verb phrase, or by roles.

transient object or ***transitory object*** An object that does *not* survive beyond the current session.

unanticipated queries Queries we were unable to foresee at system design time.

This next one is not a definition, but it's such an important principle that I'm including it in the glossary anyway, for review:

> The *only way* that a program can read or change the data carried by an object, or *access the data in any way at all*, is by invoking one of the pieces of program code that the object also carries within itself.

WHAT COMES NEXT

In Chapter 5, we'll look at some of the properties of real-world objects and examine how object models help us in managing the complexity of the users' world. Then we'll discuss the mapping from the real-world objects and their properties to the data objects that represent them.

CLASS/GROUP EXERCISES AND PROBLEMS

Note: These exercises are intended to illustrate for you and to introduce you to the process of finding classes (entities) and attributes. You'll find some serious modeling exercises at the end of Chapter 9, which is all about how to find the classes in a real-world problem. After studying Chapter 9 you'll have the skills necessary to develop accurate object class diagrams.

Ex 4.1 In your group, gather together a collection of business forms from a business or a business area. You might, for example, gather all forms connected with registrations at your college, or all the forms used by a small business where you work or deal, or all the forms for listing, making an offer on, and buying real estate. Any collection of related forms all to do with a single business function will do. You'll need a minimum of two or three forms, and probably no more than eight or nine. If you have too many, reduce the scope of your collection and focus on a narrower set of business functions.

Examine the data fields on these forms. Do you have a cluster of fields (perhaps from several forms) that all describe the same kind of thing? Perhaps a cluster that describes one of the following:

a client , a student , an account, a customer, a sale, a course , a product, an employee, a property, a vendor , a purchaser, a registration

Or something of this nature. In this way, identify as many clusters as you can, and for each cluster name the class (entity type) it describes.

Ex 4.2 Now draw boxes to represent these entity types and label them as you saw in the chapter. Then join them with lines to show all the associations you can think of. To do this, ask yourself," What does one of these do to one of those?" to come up with a verb. Check each association you've discovered to see whether it's one-to-many (1:M) or many-to-many (M:M).

INDIVIDUAL EXERCISES AND PROBLEMS

Ex 4.3 Given the following lists of data elements (attributes), give a suitable name for the class (entity type) that each list describes:

Amount	Name	ID No.	Date	ID No.
Payee	Account No.	Mother ID No.	ID No.	Vet No.
Check No.	Address	Father ID No.	Weight of Feed	Date
	Phone No.	Species	Type of Feed	Procedure
Date	Balance	Breed		Cost $
	Overdraft Y/N	Birth Weight		
	YTD Deposits	Date of Birth		

Ex. 4.4 For the five classes (entity types) you've identified in Exercise 4.3, take all possible pairs of these classes and ask:

(a)   Is there an association between these two?

(b)   What does one of these *do* to one of those?

From the answers to these two questions, determine whether there is an association, and if so, what are the two verbs that describe it? (One verb in each direction.)

Ex 4.5 Now draw two ERDs for the two groups of classes (entities) in Exercise 4.3 and 4.4. Show the classes, associations, and the multiplicity of each association.

PROJECTS AND CASES

P 4.1 Develop a class diagram for keeping track of your CDs, audio tapes, videotapes, DVDs, and even maybe some old vinyl records. Remember that you can have more than one song on a disc or tape, and a song can appear on many tapes or disks, by a variety of performers. The same is true for a movie recorded on more than one videotape or a videotape containing more than one movie. Also keep track of who you've lent them to and when they're returned.

SELF-TEST QUESTIONS

Note: The Appendix has answers to the Self-Test Questions.

Q 4.1 A many-to-many association:
(a) Is the only way two entities can interact

(b) Does not exist in nature

(c) Is legal only in certain countries

(d) Exists to consolidate a transaction

(e) None of the above

(f) All of the above

Q 4.2 In general in real life, the student–teacher association, and the parent–child association, are, respectively:
(a) 1:M and M:M

(b) M:M and M:M

(c) M:M and 1:M

(d) 1:1 and 1:M

(e) M:M and 1:M

(f) M:M and 1:1

Q 4.3 The verbs that describe the student–teacher association and the parent–child association are, respectively:

(a) Teaches/Teaches	and	Fathers/Has
(b) Punishes/Teaches	and	Has/Learns-From
(c) Teaches/Teaches-to	and	Has/Daughters
(d) Teaches/Fathers	and	Has/Siblings
(e) Teaches/Teaches	and	Mothers/Daughters
(f) Teaches/Learns-From	and	Has/Has

Q 4.4 Which of the following is a true statement?
(a) Data is the center of the universe.

(b) Data entities are stable over time.

(c) An occurrence is a specific thing described by an entity type.

(d) An instance is a specific thing described by a class.

(e) The answer to life, the universe and everything is 42.

(f) All of the above.

(g) None of the above.

Q 4.5   Which of the following is false?

(a) Data has no financial value.

(b) This book uses the standard ERD notation.

(c) Persistent objects are a nuisance in a class.

(d) Objects are fundamentally different from entities.

(e) All of the above.

(f) None of the above.

Q 4.6   To be classed as object-oriented, a language must have:

(a) Objects and classes

(b) Objects, classes, and inheritance

(c) Objects, polymorphism, and classes

(d) Objects, classes, instances, and polymorphism

(e) Objects, classes, inheritance, and polymorphism

(f) None of the above.

Q 4.7   Which of the following is true?

(a) Logical models are more abstract than physical models.

(b) Process models can be conceptual, logical, or physical.

(c) The ERD is one kind of data model.

(d) The DFD is one kind of process model.

(e) Data models can be physical, logical, or conceptual.

(f) All of the above.

(g) None of the above.

Q 4.8   Which of the following is false?

(a) A logical model shows what the system must do.

(b) A physical model shows how the system will do it.

(c) Models are useful for communicating with the users.

(d) The modeler must listen carefully to all the users have to say.

(e) All of the above.

(f) None of the above.

Q 4.9   A paradigm _____ occurs when we adopt a _____ _____ way of organizing all or part of our world _____ .

Q 4.10 Entity- _____ diagrams (ERDs) are _____ models. An ERD shows:

- The _____ (things, _____) in the users' _____ about which they need to store _____ , and

- The _____ of the users' data in terms of the _____ (actions, _____) that link the _____ types.

Q 4.11 Object-oriented model: By taking an _____ type and adding to it the exclusive _____ that _____ the data in that entity, we create an object. Besides all the benefits of _____ and _____ modeling, object modeling gives us powerful new _____ such as _____, inheritance, and _____ .

Q 4.12 Out of the _____ of all real-world data, our system is concerned with a _____ , the data in the _____ _____ we're studying. The ERD is a tool to _____ and _____ this data. The ERD also is a _____ for designing the _____ .

Q 4.13 An association is a line joining two _____ ; the verb goes _____ or beside the line with an arrowhead, and/or _____ names go _____ the line. _____–_____–_____ should make a sentence. Multiplicity (cardinality) is shown as digit (usually "1") and/or a _____ for many at each end of the _____ .

Q 4.14 The Object _____ Group (OMG) and Object _____ Group (ODMG) are doing valuable work on compatibility _____ .

Q 4.15 Objects are _____ (things that carry _____) with _____ (_____) added. These _____ exclusively _____ and _____ the data _____ by an object – that is, _____ _____ _____ _____ can touch the data.

Q 4.16 The only way that a _____ can read or _____ the _____ carried by an object or _____ it in any way at all, is by invoking one of the _____ _____ _____ _____ that the object also carries within itself.

Q 4.17 Transient objects are created by OOPLs in _____ and _____ _____ _____ beyond the _____ _____ . _____ objects are stored by a _____ (ODBMS) and _____ _____ beyond the _____ _____ .

Q 4.18 Because of the _____ curve for object-oriented _____ , as well as new languages and things, the _____ _____ only become significant on about the _____ or _____ object-oriented project.

Q 4.19 There are four styles of models: conceptual, functional, _____ , and _____

Q 4.20 A _____ model is a representation of the users' business in terms of their _____ of how it operates. It's an _____ of the business operation at a high level of _____ .

Q 4.21 A _____ model shows all parts and aspects of the _____ _____ that they're aware of, including some that are _____ from them.

Q 4.22 A logical model shows what a system must _____ or have, without regard for _____ it is to be _____ , built, or represented.

Q 4.23 A _____ model is the final _____ document, a _____ showing _____ things will be _____ or built.

Q 4.24 Deliverables from each phase are the _____ and other products generated during each _____ and _____ of the project and whose production marks the _____ of the phase.

Chapter Five

. . . .

Objects and Classes

WHAT YOU WILL LEARN IN THIS CHAPTER

In this chapter, you'll briefly encounter some of the more important properties of objects. You'll be introduced to a number of topics that are needed for the later, "meatier" chapters, where you'll use these ideas to study the users' business and produce models to document it.

You can be confident you understand objects and classes when you can:

- Define object, class, and instance, and describe how these relate from the real world to the data world.

- Distinguish between various kinds of objects, such as *entity, interface,* and *control objects*; physical, conceptual, state, and event objects; and transient and persistent objects.

- Explain why attributes and behavior are of central importance to object-oriented working.

- Define and discuss object properties such as identity, encapsulation, inheritance, and polymorphism.

- Define *abstract class* and explain how these classes are used to enhance code reuse.

WHAT YOU SHOULD KNOW TO START THIS CHAPTER

This chapter follows on directly from the material in Chapter 4. You'll need to know the definition of an object and understand the use of various kinds of models in systems analysis.

CHAPTER OVERVIEW

In this chapter, we'll compare and contrast real-world objects and their data-world counterparts in considering each of the main points in the chapter.

First, you'll revisit the definition of just what an object is, as well as attributes and behavior. Then you'll examine identity and encapsulation in detail and the use of the Statechart Diagram for understanding the transitions an object makes from one state to another throughout its life cycle.

Next you'll see how useful the concept of class is for organizing data and managing complexity. You'll be introduced to subclasses, along with *inheritance*, one of the most powerful features of the object-oriented paradigm. We always need additional object classes beyond the ones found in the users' world, and you'll discover several kinds.

We'll look at the differences between transient and persistent objects and at associations between objects. Finally, you'll receive a little advice about how some authors use the term *object*, and you'll be exposed to a very useful technique for clarifying difficult problems by imagining the objects as actors, or by having people actually play the roles of the objects involved in a scenario or transaction.

KEY CONCEPTS

- Object, instance, class, abstraction
- Object = entity + behavior
- Systems Development Life Cycle (SDLC)
- Object-Oriented Development Life Cycle (OODLC)
- Seamless transitions in the life cycle
- Early binding, static binding; late binding, dynamic binding
- Entity, interface, and control objects
- Concrete, conceptual, state and event objects
- Attributes and behavior
- Identity, *o*bject *id*entifier (OID)
- Encapsulation, inheritance, and polymorphism
- Resilience to change
- Narrow published interface, crisp boundary
- Object states, state transitions
- Subclass, superclass
- Subclasses: kinds of, isakinda, canbea
- Abstract class
- Transient and persistent objects
- Event, relationship, association
- Anthropomorphism
- Association: what one object *does* to another
- Kinesthetic, auditory, visual, and symbolic learners

"THE OUTHOUSE BATHROOM BOUTIQUE" SALES REPORTING SYSTEM – EPISODE 5

When we left them at lunch, Nancy was about to explain to Tim the advantages of object-oriented models over earlier ones.

"Our big problem," she began, "is that the users, that's your people, know their own business thoroughly, but they can't tell us about it." Tim looked a little doubtful. Nancy went on, "They know what to do every step of their jobs, and they make good decisions dozens of times a day. But ask them to write down everything they do and everything they need to know to do it, and you'll have perhaps twenty percent of the story. The problem is that they learned most of it on the job, often by watching someone, and never actually read the step-by-steps in any kind of a manual. It's kind of like trying to explain grammar to a kid, or to someone who is learning English."

"Oh, I know what you mean there," said Tim. "I tried to learn the Thai language once. I was dating a Thai girl back then, and I had a guy from Thailand working for me as a supervisor. I wanted him to teach me some Thai so I could impress her, but he found it really difficult to explain the grammar and stuff to me. It wasn't his English. He spoke excellent English, had a business degree from Cal State, and had to discuss complicated issues in meetings every day. It seemed to be a problem understanding how his own language worked. I quietly dropped the idea, but it always puzzled me."

"Right," said Nancy, delighted with his example. "And if you tried to explain English to someone who doesn't know it, you'd be even worse than he was! English is about the worst language there is to try and learn. We all learn our own language sort of by osmosis, just soaking it up as little kids. We never really study its grammar and syntax in much detail. We just sort of *know* what's the right way to say something, without being able to explain in words *why* that's the correct way to say it.

"And the same thing applies to systems analysis," she went on. "We're dealing with experts in their own field, masters of their own jobs, and we need them to explain in detail what they do, how, and why. And above all, what information do they need, and what do they generate, at each step of their job."

"Yeah," said Tim, "I've seen them having difficulty explaining their jobs when they're training new people, but I hadn't connected that with my experience trying to learn a new language. I can just imagine how tough it's going to be for all of us, trying to figure out this information use and information-generating stuff. If we can't even explain to you what we do, we'll never get the information part right! Is this where your new techniques come in?"

Nancy smiled. "Of course. I knew you'd pick up on that. This is exactly what these object-oriented methods do. They provide a structure and framework, almost a recipe. They give us a reliable way of enquiring, so that we can pull out of your people's heads the stuff we need to know, and they don't even know they know! It's really rather exciting. I get a real kick out of seeing how much these people learn about their own jobs, just by looking at them from a new and unfamiliar angle.

"But we have a lot of hard work to do to get to that stage. Some of the ideas connected with objects are pretty strange, until you get used to them. And there's quite a bit to learn about objects before we start, so you can all make the best use of the methods. I'll be coaching you all along each step of the way."

THOUGHT QUESTIONS

Consider the following in your groups and present and compare your results:

1. Discuss an actual time in the past when one of your group members was trying to explain something she knew well but just couldn't explain what it was. This could be on-the-job duties or a foreign language, as in the story. Or it could be a concept in one of your classes, in a hobby or interest group or club, in a class you taught, or anything else. It should be a concept that you were very comfortable with, but for which you had difficulty putting together an explanation for someone to whom it was a brand new idea.

    How did this happen? What did you do about it? What might you do differently next time in the light of what you've read about Tim's experiences and Nancy's interpretation of them?

2. Discuss an actual time in the past when one of your group members was involved in a project where the people ended up with a totally new view of what they had been doing all along. It may have been a systems development project, or it may have been some other kind of project. It may have been

something right outside the area of work, in a sport or hobby, for instance. The new viewpoint may have been that of data, as in the story, or it may have been something entirely different.

What surprises did the participants encounter? What "Aha!" experiences did they have? What differences, if any, did this make to the way they approached their jobs afterward? How did it affect their attitude? What other differences did it make? What might you do differently in a similar situation in the future, to capitalize on these kinds of discoveries?

5.1 REAL-WORLD OBJECTS VERSUS DATA OBJECTS

As systems analysts, we spend a lot of time flitting back and forth between the real world and the computer world. Our users live in the real world, and our first task is to understand and document their part of the real world. Then we are to create a product in the computer world that will assist the users with their work in the real world. To be effective as a systems analyst, you need to make sure that the things you create in the computer world accurately reflect the things your users work with in their real world.

This is actually the whole reason behind object-oriented analysis (OOA). When the data in the databases is organized the same way as the real-world objects it describes, we end up with the maximum flexibility. That is, we'll be able to answer virtually any questions that the users might need to ask of the database.

Because this is such an important factor, I want to spend this chapter examining various things about objects and classes of objects. I want to show you how real-world and computer-world objects differ and ways that they're alike. So let's begin with a discussion of just what an object is in these two very different worlds.

An object is something that is capable of being seen, touched, or otherwise sensed.

What an Object Is

According to *Webster* (1975), an **object** is "some *thing* [my italics, everywhere you see the word *thing*] that is, or is capable of being, seen, touched or otherwise sensed." Or alternatively, it is "some *thing* physical or mental of which a subject is cognitively aware." That is, a person is aware of it with his thoughts (cognitive), not with his feelings (that would be described as *affective*). Random House Webster Unabridged (1998) says the same thing in different words; it is "any *thing* that may be apprehended intellectually."

The Oxford Dictionary (1979) describes an **object** as a "*thing* placed before the eyes or presented to the senses; a material *thing*; a *thing* observed with an optical instrument or a *thing* represented in a picture."

Figure 5-1 The world is full of *things* . . .

As you may already have guessed, I'm focusing on the fact that *an **object is a thing**.*[1] The dictionaries, of course, are mostly concerned with objects as they're found in the real world, so we'll begin with that kind of ***thing***.

WHAT AN OBJECT IS IN THE REAL WORLD

To quote Sally Shlaer and Stephen Mellor (1988, page 9), "The world is full of *things*." (My italics) Figure 5-1 shows one version of a world full of things. Only certain ones are important for any given business area or project that we may be working on, as Figure 5-2 shows.

Figure 5-2 Things involved in a personnel system

---

[1]The *New Oxford* (1998) has an interesting subsidiary meaning for *object*. In computer jargon, they tell us, an object is "a data construct that provides a description of virtually anything known to a computer (such as a processor, a peripheral, a document, or a piece of code) and defines its status, its method of operation, and how it interacts with other objects." You'll notice that I did not highlight this definition in the usual way. I'm quite sure it could not have been written by an aware programmer. This is nothing at all to do with "object-oriented." Both *Webster* and *Oxford* have totally neglected the object-oriented sense of the term. Rather, it would appear they mean *object* as the term is used within, say, a graphics program, or a word processor, a CASE tool, or a relational database. In Oracle, for instance, tables, views, indexes, constraints, and so on are all considered to be "database objects." However, the list of examples given in this dictionary is woefully inadequate, and would appear to have been generated by an operating system programmer, or perhaps a compiler-writer. Both of these groups are extremely small (though, of course, very necessary) subsets of real-world programmers.

For the ones that do matter, only certain things concern us about each of those. Does this sound a little like our earlier definition of abstraction? In Chapter 3, you'll remember, we defined ***abstraction* to be the process of focusing on those features of something that are essential for the task at hand and ignoring those that are not.** For a *personnel* system, we would be interested only in *people* objects, and then only those people objects that are employed by the company. You'll notice in Figure 5-2 that trucks and Lamborghinis, weigh-lifters and dancers, are not included.

An object in the real world can be any person or thing that you interact with in any way. Usually, however, we'll need to be a little selective and choose, from the millions of objects around us, only those that are relevant to our systems project. Then we'll group them into classes – in this case, the class of Employee objects. In doing this, we're focusing first on those attributes and behaviors that are characteristic of people. This defines the class of People for us.

Out of these people, we select a subclass of Employee objects. (Subclasses are defined and their power explored later in this chapter and again in Chapter 8.) In this way, we consider all the different objects and types of objects *that are significant to our project*. These will then be included in the object model. Just how we go about selecting the right ones, and making sure we don't miss any, is described in detail in the KRB Seven-Step Method in Chapter 9.

We should at this point remind ourselves that an object is an "entity with behavior," so everything that's true for entities is also true for objects. This includes issues of stability and other things that we discussed in Chapter 4. Also, if you've already been data modeling with entity-relationship diagrams (ERDs), then all the techniques you employed for working with users to discover the relevant real-world entities are still valid and useful for finding object classes.

And what do we do with them when we've found them? We take the object model we've built from the real world, and we design our databases and our programs from it. In this way, the objects we have in the data world are a mirror of those in the users' real world. This is important for building a system that's stable or, in other words, is resilient to changes in the users' requirements.

In Chapter 4, we defined an entity, and then we defined an object. Both of these we considered in the real world, so now let's see what they look like when translated into the data world.

WHAT AN OBJECT IS IN THE DATA WORLD

In general, a data object is a *representation* of a real-world object. It carries data describing the real-world object. And since it carries only the data we need for the job at hand, it is in this sense a model of its real-world counterpart (and thus an abstraction of it, too). So, we can formally define an ***object* as an abstraction of some *thing* in the real world, that carries both the data describing the real-world object (its real-world analog) and the operations (that is, program code) that have the only allowable access to that data.**

It's important to note that as we progress through the systems development life cycle from analysis through design to construction and maintenance, the objects we deal with are basically the same ones throughout. As I'll show you in Section 6.1, in the discussion of the variation that I like to call the object-oriented development life cycle (OODLC), this leads to two important benefits:

- "Seamless" transitions from one phase to the next, without losing any of the information in the model through changes of notation (this is examined in detail in "Seamless Transitions," Section 6.7)

- Enhanced *traceability*, allowing us to track features or changes from an object in one model to the corresponding object in another model, earlier or later in the OODLC (see Section 6.8)

As we move from phase to phase of the OODLC, each object or class will be defined more clearly. We make such decisions such as how to organize them on the disks, or how to organize them into hierarchies (see "Subclasses" in Section 5.2). In the Design phase, we'll even create some hierarchies just to take advantage of the powerful features of object-oriented technology (OOT), such as inheritance and polymorphism.

This will allow us to reuse large quantities of program code, as well as parts of our analysis and design results, in this and future projects. The results of our decisions are recorded as part of the model. Thus, the model grows more complex and more detailed as we go from analysis through design to construction. But just what is the actual physical form of these objects at each stage?

In the analysis and design phases, our model is a paper one. (It may be enshrined within a software product such as a CASE repository, but we'll call it a "paper" one anyway.) The design model has enough information on it for us to begin work with the programming language and database software. It's important to note, however, that the objects will have different physical forms when manipulated by these two kinds of software.

In an object-oriented programming language, objects physically are pieces of memory (RAM) set aside for the purpose. Each has an area of memory for the data, broken up into individual fields or data elements (in some OOPLs called *instance variables*). Each field corresponds to an attribute on the analysis and design models. When we write the program code or otherwise define the fields, we take the name, size, data type, and so on directly from the design model.

But so far, you may be excused for saying, this is really no different from the Struct in C or the Record in Pascal. And you would be right. What is added in all OOPLs is a *class* construct that extends this idea by providing a way to store program code as well as data. Precisely how this is done varies widely from one OOPL to another.

In an ODBMS, the objects may be implemented in a variety of different ways. All, however, similarly provide storage for *both data and program code*. One of the major differences between OOPLs and ODBMSs is that of persistence. In a database, we need persistent objects that will remain in the database for minutes, months, or years. In databases there are a number of ways to make this happen.

In some ODBMSs, described as _extended relational_, the instances are stored as rows in a table. This is just like a relational database, except the concept has been modified to handle behavior as well as data, and also to handle complex data types like lists, graphics, sound and video clips, BLOBs (*b*inary *l*arge *ob*jects, defined in Section 14.5), and others that are allowed by the modern databases.

A number of other formats are also used by various ODBMSs. Introduced in Chapter 8, and further discussed in Chapter 15, you'll read about how **some database products store the methods as partially compiled code, which is then linked into the program at compile time. This is referred to as** *early binding* **or** *static binding.*

Some ODBMSs, on the other hand, store the methods as binary executable code in the database, which at run time is executed directly from the database. This is called *late binding* **or** *dynamic binding*. Each has its pros and cons and, of course, its promoters and detractors. We'll discuss them in detail in Chapters 8 and 14.

I must now confess that, in defining data objects as being tied to real-world objects, I've been guilty of oversimplification. I feel that this is acceptable, however, since now I've admitted it and I'm about to correct my little bit of misinformation.

The truth is that there are two places in the OODLC where we'll find it necessary to create some object classes that are data-world only. One place is the design phase, where we'll often introduce additional classes in order to create hierarchies that will allow us to capitalize on some inheritance and polymorphism. The other covers both the analysis and design phases, where we can benefit by considering our objects and classes to be grouped into three types.

Jacobson's Three Types

In his book *Systemantics* (1988), John Gall bases his entire tongue-in-cheek yet thought-provoking theory of the failure behavior of large systems on the fundamental premise that "things have been going too smoothly around here lately!" Ivar Jacobson echoes this sentiment with the comment, "The basic assumption is that all systems will change" (Jacobson et al., 1992; page 135).

In the interests of building a system that's *resilient to change* – that is, less likely to fail when the inevitable changes come along – Jacobson classifies objects into these three types:

- Entity objects
- Interface objects
- Control objects

Beings	**Land and Buildings**	**Equipment**	**Goods**
Person	Store	Car	Tire
Employee	Rental unit	Computer	Book
Customer	Lot	Hammer	Boots
Student	Parking lot	Telephone	Snowboard
Citizen	Street	Grader	Chair
Tenant	Neighborhood	Press	Paper
Animal	Farm	CAT scanner	Coffee

Figure 5-3   Some concrete objects

Things have been going too *smoothly* around here lately!

The entity objects are so named because they're actually the same ones as the entities from ERDs, and the other two are added to provide functions that ERDs simply couldn't address.

ENTITY OBJECTS

These are the kind of objects we've been discussing all along. ***Entity objects*** **are the ones that mirror the objects in the users' real world and carry the data the users are primarily interested in.** They're so named because they're a direct outgrowth from the ERD.

Entity objects are the fundamental objects and classes that we discover in analysis by scanning the users' business, exactly as we always used to do for ERD models. All behavior directly associated with the real-world object is modeled by the methods (that is, program code) that will be carried by these entity objects (when we eventually build the system.)

The entity objects fall into a number of categories, based on the real-world objects that they represent. Here are three kinds of entity objects that you'll see in any information system.

- Entity objects:
  - ° Concrete objects
  - ° Conceptual objects
  - ° Event and state objects

These are explained below, with examples. Remember them; you'll need them for the discussion in Chapter 9 on how to find (i.e., how to *identify*) objects and classes during the modeling. These examples will help your understanding of the process and the accuracy of your models.

Concrete Objects

These are solid, tangible kinds of objects, things you can grab hold of (but be careful how you do that part with people objects!). Concrete objects are easily understood by both analysts and users. Figure 5-3 shows some examples.

Conceptual Objects

These are intangible and often far more difficult to grasp or understand. Conceptual objects are typically defined in terms of other classes of objects, often as a result of breaking out a many-to-many association into a pair of one-to-many. (You'll learn how to do that in Chapter 9.) Figure 5-4 shows some examples.

These are all conceptual in the sense that a lease or a contract is *not* a piece of paper. It is, rather, an *agreement*, that comes into existence the moment the two parties decide to do it and say so. It is then *documented* by signing a piece of paper, to help if it needs to be enforced. An undocumented agreement or contract still exists and theoretically is enforceable, but you may have problems enforcing it if you don't have signatures or witnesses.

Organizations	Abstractions	Agreements
Corporation	Strategy	Lease
Church	Plan	Mortgage
Regiment	Blueprint	Contract
Sports Club	Layout	Covenant
Government department	Proposal	Loan guarantee
Professional association	Map	Warranty

Figure 5-4   Some conceptual objects

Consider also a church or a regiment. It continues to exist and maintains its identity even if all of its members change. A plan or proposal also exists independently of the paper it's documented on, and the ink (or blood) it's written in. So we refer to all of these as *conceptual objects* since they're nonphysical in nature.

Event and State Objects

These are also highly abstract in nature. They're related in that typically, when an *event* of any significance occurs, some one or more objects will switch to a different *state*. They're thus interchangeable to some extent; some events might be considered as states, and vice versa. Whenever an event occurs in an organization, it is documented, and that's a *fact* that we must record – that is, it's *data*. A state, on the other hand, can be regarded as a condition or a situation (see also Chapter 10). Figure 5-5 shows a few of these.

INTERFACE OBJECTS

Interface objects **are used to handle communication between our system and external entities such as users, operators, or other systems.** In other words, communication with any external entities such as those you see in the context diagrams in Figures 3.12, 7.5, and 7.6. "Other systems" would refer to such things as other computerized MIS systems, manual information systems, real-time process control systems, embedded microchips, or real-world systems controlled by our system (such as an industrial process).

Events		States	
Purchase	Deposit	Ownership	Enrollment
Sale	Loan	Employment	Assignment
Negotiation	Return	Birth	Termination
Arival	Hire	Status	Immigrant
Departuure	Rental	Registration	License
Transaction	Delivery	In transit	Suspension

Figure 5-5   Some event and state objects

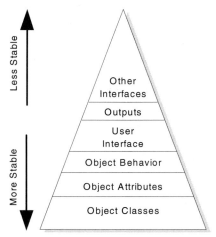

Figure 5-6 Stability of various aspects of a system

Some of the user/operator interface objects will be things like windows, buttons, radio buttons, and scroll bars. That is, they can be any of the features you see on a graphical user interface (GUI). Other interfaces the system has to deal with will be represented with various objects and classes, which we'll talk about in Chapter 7.

There's another advantage to handling these interfaces this way. As you can see in Figure 5-6, the least stable aspect of a system is its interfaces to other systems. This is because we have little or no control over what those other developers may do with their systems. So, it's to our advantage to be able to encapsulate these interface monsters within a class of objects. This allows us to make changes to the interface without affecting anything else in our system, and vice versa. (Encapsulation, and how it reduces the ripple effects of change, is discussed in more detail later in this chapter.)

And what if the communication to the other system is completely changed? It may be that we switch the medium from "sneakernet" to a modem/telephone connection, or from that to a LAN or an intranet. Or we may switch to a totally different system, perhaps drawing on-line data from an alternative source. In either case, the interface objects serve to hide these details from the rest of our system. This minimizes the impact of these changes, thus enhancing the stability and resilience of our system.

We may wish to write software that interfaces to a variety of external systems of a similar type. This could be various styles of one type of equipment or similar equipment from several manufacturers. Printer drivers for software products are a good example of this. In this case, we're able to create a new instance in the appropriate interface class for each variation. Again, encapsulation is simplifying our maintenance and enhancements for us.

CONTROL OBJECTS

**Control objects** **are created during analysis to give us somewhere to put behavior (that is, methods) that doesn't easily fit into the interface objects or entity objects that you already have.** These methods typically carry out tasks involving data from many different classes of objects.

If we attempted to build our model without these control classes, we would run into a problem. We're certain to find a number of operations that need to be performed, each using data from many objects. Usually with this kind of thing, we would end up splitting the operation into a number of methods, defined on several different objects and classes, and invoking one another in a complex pattern.

The problem, as usual, is changes. That way, almost any change we might want to make to this operation will mean changing methods in several classes. At the very least, it'll mean scanning all these classes to check which ones will have methods that need to be changed, and further checks when we're done to ensure we didn't miss any. We've complicated what should have been a simple problem.

We can simplify things by creating instead a single method with all (or almost all) of the program code for this operation. But then we're faced with the problem of which object to attach it to, since it may read and update data in several different classes of objects (by calling the locally available basic methods). The solution is to create an object of a type that's just for this purpose. These object classes are then referred to as *control objects*.

Since control objects exist solely to carry these methods, they typically carry very little data. In other words, they don't usually have many attributes. They often just have a few for results and partial results of calculations. Most of the data they need for their work is to be found in other objects. Because of this, it can only be accessed by calling up one of the methods defined on the class where it lives.

So our complex method will issue many calls to methods in other classes, but its major functionality will be coded within itself. All of this can give some significant advantages, which are outlined next.

Benefits of the Interface/Entity/Control Split

Many OOA methodologies don't bother with these three object types. Some, however, have reported significant advantage from doing so (e.g., Scharenberg and Dunsmore, 1991, as quoted in Jacobson et al., 1992). The technique can be grafted onto the front end of virtually any OOA method, however, and it does lead to a number of benefits:

- Simplifying system maintenance, leading to reduced time, effort, and errors and thus reduced cost.

- Stability, in the sense that the system is less sensitive to changes in the users' needs. This occurs because when we create a control class we bring together, or localize, in a single class, all the things that are likely to be affected by any change to this rather complex method.

  This is considerably more stable than having pieces of the method spread out over a whole bunch of classes, where we'll have trouble finding them or will be sure to miss some, when it's time for the inevitable change. In fact, what we've done is to increase the level of *encapsulation*, an important property of objects, which we'll examine later in this chapter.

- The use of interface objects further increases the level of encapsulation by separating out all methods and data concerned with the interfaces, both the user interface and the interfaces to other systems. In this way, we've ensured that changes in the interfaces are less likely to affect the core processing and data of our system, and vice versa.

  This also makes it so much easier to reuse interface objects from other projects or from purchased third-party object class libraries (e.g., GUIs). And again, it helps maintain consistency in the interfaces from one program to another and from one system or project to another.

Here is a summary of the properties of objects that we've discussed so far:
- An object in the real world is a *thing*, and data about it is carried by its corresponding data object. An object is an "entity with behavior."

- It gives stability to our system when the data is organized around the objects it truly describes.

- A data object is thus an abstraction of a real-world object, carrying the data describing it and the program code that is the only allowable access to that data.

- Using objects gives seamless transitions from one phase of the OODLC to the next, with no loss of data owing to changes of notation. Objects give *traceability*, allowing us to follow a feature or problem from an object in one stage of the OODLC to the same object in another stage.

- Entity objects are the ones matching the real-world objects. Interface objects handle data exchanged with users or with other systems, and control objects are created to handle complex operations that don't naturally fit with any one object or class.

- The entity/interface/control split simplifies maintenance and enhances system stability by increasing the level of encapsulation.

Having now established what an object is, we next need to look at some of the things it carries within itself, beginning with the data and the operations on that data.

Attributes

ATTRIBUTES IN THE REAL WORLD

In Chapter 3, we discussed how a child postulates the existence of objects. The child soon comes to the conclusion that there are objects out there, and he observes things about these objects. The child will notice that some objects are blue and some are red, that some are soft and some are hard. In other words, the child *gathers data* about these objects.

Each data item we'll call an attribute, and these attributes do in fact fit the definition we gave in Chapter 4. It's these attributes that describe the object for us and allow us to communicate our view of it to other people. They also make the object unique for us so we can tell it from other similar objects (that is, others in its class).

What a child actually does is to build a "mental model" in his head of the world around him. You can think of this as a "head-resident database," where a person records information. By now, it should hardly shock you to realize that this is an object-oriented database, or perhaps we should refer to it as an "object-oriented mental model (OOMM)."

A few years ago, in a cognitive psychology course, I encountered the Network Model of Cognition. This is the current model that psychologists are using to understand our thinking processes, that is, our *cognitive* processes. The instructor mentioned that it arose as the doctoral thesis of a psychologist who had begun life in computing science. I took one look at it and realized it was an ERD data model, but drawn with entity *occurrences* instead of entity *types*.

Imagine my surprise to discover later that this was indeed the doctoral thesis of one David Taylor, now a world-renowned author, management consultant, and

Object-Oriented Guru, whom I've cited frequently in these pages. As the artificial intelligence community has done already, we can learn a lot about the best ways to organize computerized data by studying the way it's set up in the human brain. It works best in both media (brain and hard disc) if you organize your data into *objects* and *attributes*.

At any instant, there is a certain set of values that are possessed by the attributes of an object. In some other moment, the object may be described by a different set of values. The object is still the same object, but there's definitely something that has changed. We say that the object now exists in a different *state*.

In this sense, then, the **_state_ of an object is defined by the set of values currently held by its attributes.** Note that this definition is actually an abstraction of the term *state*, in that it focuses solely on what is important *for systems analysis*. Under "Object States" later in this chapter, we'll look at some rather more general definitions of the term, and you'll find the full explanation in Chapter 10.

So from childhood, we all continue this process throughout life, using the concepts of objects and attributes to make sense of an increasingly complex world as we grow to maturity. Eventually, we arrive at the adult world of business and systems analysis. At this point, the objects that matter to us are things like accounts, employees, and customers. The attributes that concern us are account number and name, employee name and pay rate, customer address and balance, and so on.

This is quite a change from the attributes we began with in infancy, but the principle remains the same. The major challenge for us as adult systems analysts in the business world is to find a way to discover all of the object classes and attributes that are important for our project, and make sure we don't miss any. We'll be looking at techniques for this in Chapters 7 and 9.

An object responds to a message by performing the behavior that goes with that message

ATTRIBUTES IN THE DATA WORLD

In a database, each object instance carries a set of attribute values. These attributes represent all the data items that any user might ever need to know about the object. In a noncomputerized manual system, these would all be written down somewhere. This paper-and-pencil database would need to be well organized, maybe in a filing cabinet, but you would 't need any constraints on things like data type or field size.

In a computerized database, on the other hand, we need strict controls on data type and size, but fortunately not for each instance separately – that would be far too much work. What we do instead is to define these things once for each object class. Of course, we've always done just that with regular relational databases and even flat files. The reason I mention it here is that now, in the object paradigm, we also do very similar things with behavior and program code, as you'll see a few paragraphs ahead.

A few comments are in order here about how attributes are represented in a database. Since the state of the art is the relational database, and since many ODBMSs are using the extended relational model, I'll base my comments on relational ideas.

In relational terms, each object class will be implemented as a *table* or *relation*. The term *relation* comes from the theoretical foundation of relational databases, which is based in set theory. It actually has nothing to do with the ability to relate columns of data from different tables. That is certainly something we do, however, and it's one of the more powerful features of relational databases.

But the name *relational* comes not from relating, but from the table itself, which is actually a *relation*, as the term *relation* is defined in mathematical set theory. Each object instance will be represented by a *row* in the table, called a *tuple* in relational terms.

Each attribute value (that is, each element of the tuple) is a value drawn from the set of all possible values for that column, known as the *domain* for that column. We stay away from the term "range of values" since that means something different to a mathematician discussing functions and functional dependencies, and so we say the ___domain___ **is the set of all permissible values for an attribute (i.e., for a column).**

Now let's examine how object-oriented methods handle the other half of the equation.

Behavior

Objects carry more than just their state and the data that describe it. Entities can do that much. Objects also exhibit behavior in the real world, which, just like the data, must also be accommodated in their data-world representation.

BEHAVIOR IN THE REAL WORLD

To continue with the illustration, as we noted earlier, a child makes two kinds of observations about objects in the world around her. One kind refers to attributes, and the other is to notice that the objects *do things*. Not only that, but she discovers that she can influence the behavior of these objects by sending them messages.

A new father soon learns to distinguish his baby's different kinds of crying, and what she wants with each different cry. One cry means she's wet, and another means she's hungry. The father responds accordingly. *An object (in this case the father) responds to the child's message by performing the behavior that goes with that particular message* and in the process performs some service that the child wanted.

Again, throughout life we continue with this mode of manipulating the objects in the world around us, until by adulthood we have it pretty well figured out (some of us better than others!). In the adult world of work and life, we issue commands and requests to a variety of people, computers, cars, and other objects, and some of the time we end up getting the services or results we need.

There is a certain part of the real world that is inhabited by people who are likely to become your users. There you'll find a number of behaviors that you would expect to deal with. For example, graphic objects can be displayed or rotated; journal entries can be posted; loans can be paid down or paid off; employees can be hired, fired, or promoted; and invoices can be printed, and perhaps even paid.

Note that in this last case, in order to print itself, the invoice will have some work to do itself, and some messages to send to other objects, to ensure that each line item will get itself printed. In other words, our users employ this send-a-message/receive-a-service approach to practically everything they do, too.

BEHAVIOR IN THE DATA WORLD

All this means that for us, in general there are three kinds of behavior our system must provide for our users:

- One is what we call ***overt behavior*, where we actually instruct an object to make something happen.** For example, "graphic object display thyself!" or "graphic object rotate thyself!" or "journal entry, post thyself!" In English grammar this is the *imperative mood*, that is, issuing commands to something to do something. (Why the Elizabethan grammar? Somehow it just seemed more imperative to me that way. Or perhaps more *imperious* would describe it better.)

- The next kind is really just record keeping. ***Passive behavior* is the recording of the data generated by some action or event in the real world.** This time, rather than *make* something happen, we're simply providing a mechanism to record the effects of some occurrence, when somebody else caused it to happen.

- Third, ***responsive behavior* is providing information (i.e., attribute values) in response to a message requesting it.**

In the actual program code, the message is nothing more nor less than a function call. All three kinds of behavior are handled this way. In the first kind, the function (method) may generate significant visible input/output activity. In the second and third kinds, it merely queries or updates a database record. In all three kinds, the data-world object can alter its data to record a real-world event and the resulting change of state of the real-world object.

With graphic objects, it's more obvious that the state of the object changes. You can see the object rotate, appear, disappear, or change color on the screen. With other kinds of behavior, the change of state is less obvious, but nonetheless real. The state of the object is recorded in its data – in effect, the state *is* the data.

These changes are effected then by a message – that is, a function call – that carries the necessary parameters, as does any normal function call. Each object carries within it a set of routines (functions, or *methods*) that will cause the necessary behaviors to happen. And, as you'll remember from Chapter 4, these functions are the *only* way that any data within the object can be accessed or changed.

There's another thing I should mention here. Some will already be asking, "But how will we store all that program code with each and every object instance? Won't that lead to a lot of redundant storage of program code?" This is a very good question, and the answer is that you needn't worry. This is one of the convenient and powerful things about *classes*.

What we actually do in all OOPLs and ODBMSs is define the methods (functions) *once per class* and define them to be available to *each and every instance* of the class. One of the conditions of object orientation is that any method (behavior) is available to *every* object in the class. Just how the different OOPLs and ODBMSs do this is discussed in Chapter 14. You'll also remember that I promised that there will be a discussion of late and early (dynamic and static) binding in Chapter 8.

To summarize:

- The attributes are the data values carried by the objects.
- The set of values for its attributes form a tuple and define the state of an object.
- Each attribute value is drawn from the domain of all permissible values for that attribute
- Objects in the real world often exhibit certain behaviors in response to specific messages.
- Objects in the data world exhibit *overt behavior* where they do something observable in response to a message, *passive behavior* where they record information, and *responsive behavior* where they provide information in answer to a query
- The *messages* that data objects respond to are just function calls, carrying parameters or arguments. Data may be returned from the object either as the value of the function and/or in the parameters.
- In an OOPL or ODBMS, the program code for the methods (functions) is stored in the database attached in some way to the data. The code is stored once per class.

When we send a message to an object to elicit a desired behavior, we need to make sure we send it to the right one. Telling objects apart is a matter of *identity*.

Identity

We should start this section with a couple of definitions. The *New Oxford Dictionary* (1998) says ***identity*** is **"the fact of being who or what a person or thing is."** *Oxford* (1979) says ***identity*** is **"the condition or fact that a person or thing is itself and is not something else."** My preferred way to say this would be that ***identity*** **is the property that says two things are different, they're not both the same thing.**

Identity is pretty well common sense. You may wonder why we would need to examine something that simple. Well, consider that not only is common sense all too *un*common, but it's usually a matter of *unexamined assumptions*. And always, any unexamined assumptions we encounter anywhere *need to be examined*, just so we can be satisfied they're safe to continue using.

IDENTITY IN THE REAL WORLD

If we consider two ball bearings, then as far as we can tell they would appear to be identical – ame size, same color, same weight, same alloy. Everything would seem to be the same about them, yet they're not both the same ball bearing – they're two different ones. There they are in front of you, one on the left and one on the right. Swap them left for right, and there are still two of them, both the same, but not both the same one.

Pick any two ants off an anthill. They look pretty much identical, but they're two different ants. Even so-called identical twins are not both the same person. (I still haven't figured out whether they have the same fingerprints. This could be very confusing in court. Perhaps some of you twins out there in the real world would care to enlighten me.)

Any object has identity simply because it exists. In this sense, identity is said to be an *inherent* property of an object. The *New Oxford* (1998) defines ***inherent*** **as "Existing in something as a permanent, essential or characteristic attribute."** *Webster* (1975) defines ***inherent*** **as "involved in the essential character of something."** We don't have to assign it an identity; it has identity the moment it comes into existence.

Nor does identity rely on identifiers. A newborn infant has no name until one is assigned, but she does have identity right from birth or before. People who use aliases or pseudonyms are proof that a name does not *confer* identity but merely *recognizes* it. Change the name, but you still have the same person. Identifiers, such as names or numbers, are a convenient invention of humankind to be used as *evidence* of identity.

IDENTITY IN THE DATA WORLD

Data objects have identity, as do real-world objects. Like their real-world counterparts, this identity is inherent. It doesn't need to be conferred. But, as I'm sure many of you have already found out, it's very easy to confuse the identity of data-world objects. In the OOPL or database, we need some way to tell objects apart.

The first and most obvious solution is to use the real-world identifiers. I think we're all familiar with the reasons why names, addresses, and such are unsuitable for use as identifiers in computerized systems. Punctuation, spelling, capitalization, and spacing can all cause problems.

About 200 years ago, accountants began the process of using numbers to keep track of accounts, orders, purchase orders, customers, vendors, employees, invoices, and a host of other kinds of objects. These are in fact *artificial convenience identifiers*, but from our point of view they're part of the real-world, since the users invented them and are using them even outside the computer system.

And being real-world means that their uniqueness is automatically suspect. In my college, we have a steady trickle of exceptions where a student has registered several times over the years and been issued several student numbers. Our registrar's solution was to ask people for something every working Canadian has, their Social Insurance Number (SIN). That fixed most of the problems.

But I've been unable to ascertain whether the SIN is truly unique. It may seem reasonable that something allocated by a first-world government for the purpose of identifying its citizens could safely be assumed to be unique. Yet I'm assured that U.S. Social Security Numbers used to be reissued some years after their original holders died! So who can you trust? The point is that we can never absolutely trust a real-world identifier to be unique. If we do choose to assume that it is, we must be aware that we're taking some level of risk.

Many OOPLs and ODBMSs deal with this problem by automatically assigning an **_object identifier,_ or _OID,_ to each object instance when it's created. The system software guarantees it to be unique and never recycled,** so the problem goes away. (While some would pronounce this "oh-aye-dee," I prefer to call it an "oyd.")

Encapsulation

In dealing with complexity and huge amounts of data, humans resort to a number of devices to simplify what has to be understood. One such device is to take a few pieces of the world around us and form them into a kind of bundle. The idea is to make use of the "bundle" just by knowing how to use it, without having to understand how it was put together or how it works.

In a sense, there's a "shell" formed around the "bundle." This shell is built up from the appearance of the bundle and the rules or directions for making it work. Here are some real-world examples of what I mean.

Encapsulation in the Real World

Let me introduce this topic with a story. In my early twenties, an older friend asked me to teach his nineteen-year-old daughter to drive. He (rightly) believed that fathers should not teach their offspring (or wives) how to drive. She was exceptionally pretty, so of course I readily agreed.

Now, in those somewhat far-distant days, most cars were standard shift. So I began explaining to Katrina how the clutch was there to separate the engine from the wheels, so that the engine could be running while the car was stationary; how the clutch pedal was connected to the spinning plates that come together when you release the pedal and progressively feed the power to the back wheels . . . .

Her rather explosive reaction was to exclaim: "Don't tell me how it works! Just tell me what to do with it to make the damn thing go!" *Oops!* This was my introduction to an important fact: There are people in this world who think differently from the way I do. That day I discovered there are people who just want to get on with the job and get it done, not sit around trying to figure out what makes it tick.

What Katrina needed was to be shown the *published user interface* to a complex system that she needed to use. To make this system (the car) function properly, she needed to know what buttons and levers to push, when, and how hard. She needed to view the car as a "black box," a mystery device that would somehow do what she wanted if she gave it the right commands. She didn't want to be concerned with its inner workings. That could be left to the experts (the mechanics) and the curious (me). This *encapsulation* of the properties of the car is illustrated in Figure 5-7.

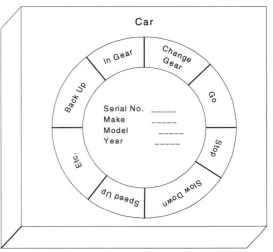

Figure 5-7 Attributes and behavior

An interesting thing happens when we take the black-box view of an object. What if Katrina's dad took the car for a tuneup? Or perhaps replaced the engine with one twice as powerful? Would Katrina need to know about that? Apart from a few safety considerations, basically *no*. She would just get to where she was going in a much shorter time! We would not need to change either the users of the object (that is, of the car), nor the uses to which they put it, just because we changed or optimized something within the object (car).

Conversely, what if we changed not the object, but its environment? Say, the family sold the car. As long as the car's new users understood the published interface (the pedals and steering wheel), they could use it for their own needs, which might be radically different from the uses to which Katrina and her dad had been putting it. We would not need to change the object to accommodate changes in its environment, specifically its users and its uses. Obviously, the published interface is one of the keys to this process.

Now try this one. Do you play golf? Do you know what's inside a golf ball? Do you care? No! You just need to know how to hit it right. (You're probably a lot better at this than I am.)

If you or I sniff at a gourmet soup in a fancy restaurant, we Ooh! and Aah! over it and maybe identify one or perhaps two ingredients. If your dog smelled it (and could talk), his sense of smell is so sensitive that he would be able to identify every single ingredient. But only the chef needs to know that. All we need is the published interface (in this case, the menu description and the price and which spoon to use) so we can do with it all the things one should do to a good soup.

It's important to have *consistency in the published interface* among the instances of a class of objects. For obvious reasons, we need to have the same pedal arrangement in all cars. While Katrina eventually became a very competent driver in spite of my efforts, she (or you or I) would be in trouble the moment we climbed into a Model T Ford. The clutch is between the brake and accelerator pedals! We could turn out to be really dangerous, tripping over our own feet as an accident approaches.

The QWERTY keyboard I'm using as I write this is fine as long as everybody has one, and in particular as long as all *my* computers have one.[2] It's not the most effective keyboard layout, but as long as we're consistent, we can all move around from machine to machine without hassle.

In the 1960s, I used to marvel at the ability of motorcycle mechanics to ride with various gearshift and brake-pedal layouts. Japanese bikes had the gears on the left foot, English bikes on the right foot. The English Triumph and Norton brands had the gearshift patterns upside down relative to each other.

When I borrowed a friend's Triumph while my Yamaha was in the shop, I kept shifting up when I intended to brake! The mechanics all seemed to have become used to this and could switch from bike to bike with no apparent problems. Nowadays, fortunately, motorcycles the world over use the left-foot gearshift (not uncoincidentally, the Japanese system), with first gear a step down and the rest up.

This kind of *encapsulation* with consistent user interfaces is indeed necessary because we simply could not function if we needed to know *everything* about *everything* just so we could use things. It's a method of compartmentalizing, or modularizing, a complex situation so that we can understand it and deal with it effectively. The same is true in the data world.

ENCAPSULATION IN THE DATA WORLD

Encapsulation is one of the major secrets of object-oriented methods. By hiding both data and program code within the object, we achieve a level of encapsulation that no earlier methods could approach. The twin results are *stability* and *portability*.

Stability is improved in the sense that once a class of objects has been studied, understood, and defined, future changes to the system will reuse those same classes, basically unchanged. These objects will be reusable with relatively few changes of any kind and especially with fewer changes of a major disruptive nature.

Increased portability arises from the ability to reuse a class in a new project or even on a new platform. At each reuse, we may add some new attributes or a few new methods. These incremental additions to the objects over time will serve to make them more and more reusable.

There is the published interface, which must be preserved as much as possible. Changes to this interface should be extremely rare, but they'll only be that way *provided we do our initial analysis correctly*. The techniques and methods that you'll see in later chapters will help ensure that this is so. The methods I describe are aimed at making sure the object carries the *right* data and the *right* methods inside it.

The object should have the data (attributes) that truly describe this object. In the "Olden Days" (i.e., before object orientation), we would often find records that might have Customer data and Sale data mixed in one record. Or we would see Employee data, Position data, and Position Assignment data all in one Personnel record. That is, they contained combinations of attributes that described related but different objects.

What they had was data in one record that should have been in several objects. We must ensure that each object carries attributes that do in fact describe this object, and only those attributes. It must not carry any attributes that describe something else.

---

[2] QWERTY, by the way, is designed to slow people down, because on early typewriters the arms would jam if you typed too fast. The Dvorak keyboard is much faster with the most common letters in the middle row, the next ones in the top row, and the least common in the bottom row. But what a learning curve if I go out and buy one right now!

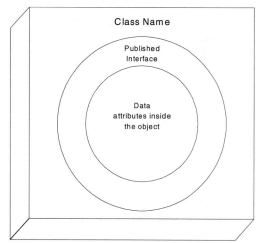

Figure 5-8 A David Taylor donut diagram

We must also make certain that it carries *all* the attributes that describe that object. Actually, what we're talking about here and in the previous two paragraphs is called *normalization*, which is described in detail in Chapter 9.

When our object classes are properly normalized, it has the effect of making quite clear just what parts of the world (i.e., which parts of the system) are *inside* the object and what parts are *outside* it. The object then has what Coad and Yourdon (1991) describe as a "crisp boundary." The net effect is to limit and constrain the ways that information can cross this crisp boundary. We say the object has a *narrow published interface.*

The published messages are the only ones an object will respond to and are the only way to access the data. The format of the message consists of the function call and its parameter formats. This is documented as part of the object, as is the meaning or purpose of the method – its effect or what it does (i.e., its semantics).

And so too are the details of the value(s) it returns. These published messages are the only way that information can cross the boundary from what is inside the object to what is outside it. What we've now described is a very "narrow" information highway, consisting of just these designated lanes. This encapsulation is illustrated in Figure 5-8.

The combination of a clearly defined "crisp" boundary and a narrow interface across it is what gives the high level of encapsulation. This clear and firm separation of the inside from the outside of the object is like having a breakwater at the mouth of a harbor. A breakwater also leaves a narrow "highway" for access from inside to outside, and limits (but doesn't totally eliminate) the effects that waves on one side will have on the calm water on the other side.

Since we've encapsulated all the behavior of our system within the object classes, we reduce the "ripple effect" of changes this way. Even if the saving in effort is small for each class of objects, remember that the number of interaction paths between objects goes up exponentially with the number of classes. So in a large system, this kind of encapsulation makes a huge difference.

VIOLATING ENCAPSULATION IN THE REAL WORLD

Making bread is an art that my mother could do well, that my wife, Nina, does superbly, and that I've never been the least bit motivated to learn. (I excel at the quality-control/surplus-disposal functions on the finished product. I love fresh, still-warm whole-grain bread!)

A lot has changed with the invention of the automatic bread maker. Now this mystical, black culinary art has been enshrined within the ROM programming of a microchip. Now we simply send it a message (via the "Start" button) with parameters (the ingredients and the time data) in classic object-oriented fashion, and a fabulous loaf of sweet bread results. Even *I* can do that much.

Strange behaviors and unguessed-at data values (such as temperature and stirring time) are encapsulated within the BreadMaker object. Even Nina the expert chef doesn't bother to guess at these data values. It's all stuff that she understands, but most of the time there's just no need to get involved.

But what if we wanted to help it along a bit? One of the simplest ways we might interfere with the process is to shut it down early. Perhaps we're in a hurry and can't wait for the cycle to finish. Now, if I did this, we would surely end up with a half-baked mess. Nina, on the other hand, is qualified and skilled enough to make an informed guess as to the earliest moment that it can safely be shut off and still give a good loaf of bread.

Or maybe we need to cook longer than the program allows for, when we use some exotic imported mountain grain flour or whatever. Again, I'm likely to screw it up completely. An expert like Nina would be able to set the timer manually and get perfect or near-perfect results on the first or second try.

She can also vary the recipes or even invent her own. But if her recipes or her variations require changes to the cooking program, they become difficult or impossible to port to another platform. Someone else trying one of Nina's recipes will also need to change the programming on his machine and may or may not have the skills and confidence to do this reliably.

What we have here is a series of lessons to be learned about violating encapsulation:

- Violating encapsulation can be dangerous. If, like me, you don't fully under-stand what you're doing, a mess may result that takes forever to clean up.

- Violating encapsulation can sometimes be beneficial, allowing us to optimize a process or to take advantage of something unforeseen or unusual. But it has to be done by an expert to be safe, reliable, and effective.

- Even then, violating encapsulation may limit or reduce the reusability and portability of the product or process.

Violating Encapsulation in the Data World

I'm sure you've already seen what I'm driving at. These lessons are equally applicable to violating the encapsulation of software objects. One of the beauties of pure object-oriented languages such as Eiffel, Java, and Smalltalk is that they simply don't permit such things.

Hybrid (C++, OO Pascal) and extended (Objective-C) languages *do* allow such tampering and are thus somewhat more dangerous. These languages allow inexpert or subexpert programmers to violate all the object-oriented rules, sometimes with disastrous results. They do allow the experts a chance to optimize, but still that can easily interfere with portability.

Now let's summarize what we've said about identity and encapsulation:

- Identity is what says that something is itself and not something else.

- Two things that are identical are still two different things; they're not both the same thing even if absolutely everything about them is the same.

- Identity doesn't rely on identifiers. It's an *inherent* property of objects. Identifiers are merely an aid to telling objects apart. In general, real-world identifiers cannot be trusted to be unique.

- Many OOPLs and ODBMSs assign OIDs to every object to guarantee uniqueness.

- Encapsulation is the forming of a "crisp" boundary or shell, with a "narrow interface" to allow communication across it.

- Encapsulation reduces complexity and increases stability by reducing the ripple effects of changes, much like a breakwater at the entrance to a harbor.

- Encapsulation allows us to use an object by understanding the published interface. We don't need to know its inner workings in order to use it effectively.

- We must communicate with the object by sending it messages in the format required by the published interface.

- Encapsulation, the "crisp boundary," and the narrow, controlled published interface allow us to make changes within the object (for example, optimizing some of its methods) without affecting any of the programs or functions that use it. We've localized the effects of change.

- Similarly, we can make changes outside the object, and we can change the ways we use it or use it in new places, without needing to change the object itself.

- Violating encapsulation can occasionally be beneficial but is fraught with danger.

All this assumes something. We're assuming that we'll be able to discover all the behavior within the system and assign each behavior to the correct class of objects. One of the keys to this process is to understand the life cycle of each object as it's created and disposed of and as it goes through various states in between.

Object States

We need to check the dictionaries again. The *New Oxford* (1998) defines **_state_** as a **"The particular condition that someone or something is in at a specific time."** The earlier *Oxford* (1975) says a **_state_** is a **"condition; manner or way of existence as determined by circumstances."** According to *Webster* (1975), a **_state_** is **"a mode or condition of being"** or **"a condition or stage in the physical being of something."** Let's see what all that really means.

STATES IN THE REAL WORLD

Most things in this world are temporary. You may think this is a funny kind of way to introduce a subject, but just think for a moment. Apart from a few anomalies such as mountains and stars, all the things around you came into being at some finite point in time. (Of course, this is also true of mountains and stars, but on a different time scale.)

You and I celebrate our birthdays in remembrance of these (to us) important events, when we came into the world. You and I and all the other people in this world grow and go through *stages* as we develop. Each person goes through developmental stages, and in parallel goes through career stages – school, college, working, and retired. At the same time, we also go through some personal stages. One pattern (with many possible variations) might be single, dating, engaged, married, DINKs, parenthood, DIKCs, and empty nest.[3]

---

[3] DINKs: *D*ouble *I*ncome, *N*o *K*ids; DIKCs: *D*ouble *I*ncome, *K*ids in *C*ollege

Other kinds of objects also go through stages, including inanimate objects. When you buy a car, you step into the middle of its life. It was made in a factory, sold to a dealer, then bought by you, possibly sold by you to another owner, and finally either retired to a junkyard for parts, or crushed and melted down for recycling. (That sounds kind of sad!)

Notice that in this little scenario, the life of a car has two possible endings. In the one possibility, it's kept around "out of sight and out of mind" in case it's ever needed for something. For purposes of transportation, it has ceased to exist, even if not physically. In the other case, it does actually cease to exist when no longer needed. It's crushed into an amorphous lump of metal, which is then melted down and blended and merged with many others, so it totally loses its identity.

Many other classes of objects can come to either of these two endings, after a lifetime similarly marked by stages of existence. In Canada, payroll records are required by law to be kept for seven years. So although the employee has "ceased to exist" for our purposes (i.e., has left the company), she's kept around for a while in the form of archived records.

At the other extreme, I saw a system for grading lumber boards as they came out of a sawmill. Four or five video cameras and an infrared scanner created billions of bits of data as each board went by at 50 km/h (30 mph). A bank of digital signal processor (DSP) chips analyzed this to find flaws, knotholes and such. The data was reduced to eight or nine numbers per second, which another processor used to make a decision. This one then sent signals to the machinery to set the gates and direct the board to the appropriate stack.

What happened to the billions of bits of original data? No longer needed, they were simply erased to make room in memory for the next board a few milliseconds later. Each Board object went through states Entering, Scanning, Waiting-for-Processing, In-the-Gates, and Stacked. Then it ceased to exist as far as the system was concerned, although the physical board was left sitting in one stack or another, awaiting sale or trimming.

Business documents such as purchase orders have a lifetime marked by a similar sequence of stages, as we'll see in detail below. Most of the objects that we'll be dealing with are born and then live and die in this way. In everyday English, we generally refer to the steps in these processes as stages, but the more technically correct term is *states*.

An object can exist in certain states. A light bulb can be off or on. A bit can be 0 or 1. A library book can be in but unshelved, shelved, reserved, or out. Any of the stages mentioned qualify to be called states, as you can readily see from the definitions above.

As each of these objects lives its life, the changes from one state to another are referred to as *ransitions*. So we can define a **_state transition_** **as the act or experience of changing from one state to another.** In Chapter 10 we'll look at some other definitions as well.

To illustrate further, let's take a look at a typical business document and follow it as it progresses from state to state through its life cycle.

A PURCHASE ORDER

In any bureaucracy – be it government, collegiate or private sector – *purchasing* is a complicated business. Far too many signatures and authorizations are needed to get a purchase order through the system and finally out to the vendor.

In a typical organization, a purchase comes into existence in the form of a PO request (Figure 5-9.) A document is filled out and routed to a person authorized to approve it. Its state at this point could perhaps be described as "initiated." (Each organization will have its own rules and its own jargon for describing these events. What we're describing is a typical case with names that you might find in some real organizations.)

After this person signs it, the PO request goes one or more levels up the chain of command, gathering more signatures, until according to the rules of the house it's deemed worthy of some action. As it does so, each signature *event* moves it to another *state* of existence. Something about the PO request changes at each step, so by our definition that means it has transitioned to another state. Eventually it arrives on the desk of the purchasing agent.

In many paper-based systems, the next step is for the purchasing agent to fill out yet another piece of paper. This one is the *purchase order proper*, a copy of which will eventually go to the vendor. Other copies will be sent to the originator and other interested parties. At least one copy will be filed. The purchase order must, of course, have a vendor assigned. The PO request may have a recommended vendor, which the purchasing agent may confirm or override.

In many organizations, the PO request and the purchase order proper are considered to be two different transactions. But from the point of view of information processing, they can be viewed as merely two states of the one object.

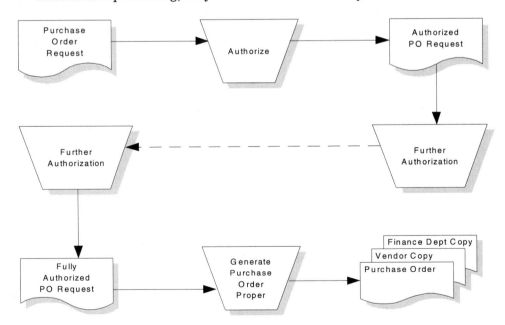

Figure 5-9 The routing of a PO Request

As we've just seen, this Purchase Order object was created with a state of Initiated, and then transited through a number of states representing various levels of authorizing. Then it transitioned to the state of being a Purchase Order proper and finally to the state of having been Sent (to the vendor). After that it can start to get complicated as we reconcile the orders placed with the shipments, partial shipments and back-orders from the vendor.

What we've just been following can be termed the *life cycle* of an object. An ***object life cycle*** **consists of the various *states* that an object may transition through, the set of permissible *transitions*, and the *sequencing* of those states and transitions, as it progresses from its initial creation to its eventual disposal.**

STATES IN THE DATA WORLD

As I mentioned above, within our system the only things we know about an object are the data values recorded on the matching data-world object. We use these data values to keep track of the changes of state that the real-world object goes through. The values of the data attributes then reflect the state of the real-world object.

In fact, we can go so far as to say that the attribute values *are* the state, at least of the data-world object. Or at the very least, we can say that they *represent* its state. The main implication of this view is that any change in the value of an attribute therefore causes a change of state for the object. Some classes of objects may even have a status attribute specifically for the purpose of recording the relevant states of the real-world object as it transitions through its life cycle.

In Chapter 10 you'll be introduced to the statechart diagram. This is a tool used to model and document object life cycles so that we can provide the necessary methods in each object class to handle all the expected transitions.

This is what we've said so far about states and transitions:

- At any moment in time, an object exists in a certain manner or condition, which we say is its *state*.

- If anything at all about the object changes, we say it has undergone a *transition* into a new state.

- The various permissible states and the permissible transitions among them form the life cycle of the object, as it is "born" (created), "lives" (exists), and eventually "dies" (is deleted or otherwise appropriately disposed of).

- For all intents and purposes, the values of its attributes are, or at least represent, the state of the object.

- The statechart diagram is a powerful tool used to model object life cycles.

5.2. CLASSES AND CLASSIFICATION

Here we go back to the dictionaries again! The *Oxford* (1979) tells us a ***class*** **is "a number of individuals having a character or feature in common."** *Webster* gives us a couple of choices. Their *New Collegiate Dictionary* (1975) defines ***class*** **as "a group, set or kind sharing common attributes."** A later edition, *Random House Webster Unabridged* (1998), describes a ***class*** **as "a number of persons or things regarded as forming a group by reason of of common attributes, characteristics, qualities or traits. Synonyms: kind of, sort of."**

We need to go a little further, however, and talk about:
- Attributes
- Behavior
- Associations
- Semantics (meanings of words)

Classes in the Real World

The young child gains understanding of his surroundings by grouping together objects with similar attributes and behavior and designating them to be a class. We continue to handle complexity with this method throughout our lives. Figure 5-10 shows some samples of object classes that we're likely to encounter in the everyday life of a busy systems analyst.

The classes used by children and adults alike can be defined in a number of ways. We can group objects by any or all of the following criteria:

- Those that have similar values for one or more attributes: for example, all red apples; all objects that are colored red; all programmers; all women; all union employees over age 30.

- Those whose values for some attribute are within a required range: for example, everyone earning from $20,000 to $40,000; all companies with 25 or fewer employees; all accounts more than 30 days in arrears; all accounts in credit; everyone from age 20 to 29.

- Those that all have the same attribute(s): for example, all employees who have a project code; everyone who paid taxes last year.

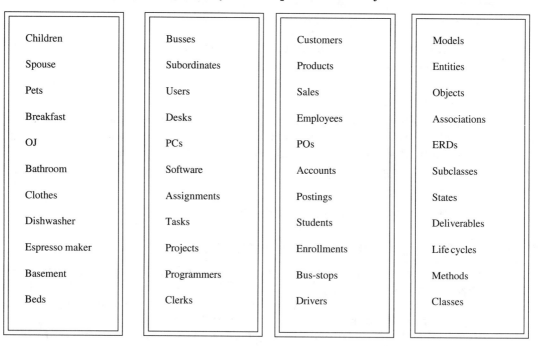

Children	Busses	Customers	Models
Spouse	Subordinates	Products	Entities
Pets	Users	Sales	Objects
Breakfast	Desks	Employees	Associations
OJ	PCs	POs	ERDs
Bathroom	Software	Accounts	Subclasses
Clothes	Assignments	Postings	States
Dishwasher	Tasks	Students	Deliverables
Espresso maker	Projects	Enrollments	Life cycles
Basement	Programmers	Bus-stops	Methods
Beds	Clerks	Drivers	Classes

Figure 5-10   Classes encountered every day by a systems analyst

• Those that display similar behavior (e.g., everybody who snores, everybody who buys from The Outhouse Bathroom Boutique, all drivers, all bingo players, all graduates from a given program.)

Sometimes a child (or even another adult) will group some objects together into a class that to you or me would seem completely unrelated. *But the grouping makes sense to them.* When this person is our user, then we must expect that very often *this* is the grouping that must be used, regardless of any difficulty you and I may have in understanding it.

Most times, the criterion for the grouping can be expressed as some combination of the criteria listed above. Usually our confusion arises from our own lack of understanding of our users' business. This lack of familiarity on our part is a problem that we must take responsibility for and work hard to correct.

Besides observing the attributes, the child learns to expect similar behavior from the objects in a class. This is true even when the grouping is based on attributes rather than behavior. Once she groups the objects together and views them as a class, she may then enunciate a membership rule or condition. The rule may not ever actually be verbalized. A very young preverbal child would of course be totally unable to verbalize it.

Even adults use a large number of these rules without ever explicitly verbalizing them. We mentally perceive objects as belonging to a class and treat them that way without ever actually stating the rule that unites them.

Either way, objects that satisfy the rule are predicted or expected to share the defined attributes and behaviors, as a minimum. They may well have others, perhaps as a result of belonging to some other class in addition to this one. Or perhaps the other attributes and behavior are inherited from a different ancestor class (see the discussion on multiple inheritance in Chapter 8).

A class is a group of objects with similar properties and common behavior

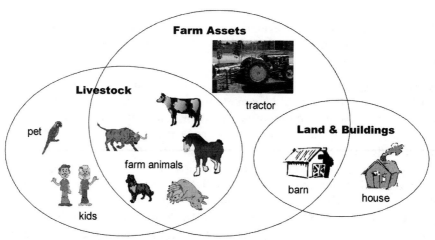

Figure 5-11 Cows, barns, and semantics

There are still some more points to consider. James Rumbaugh et al. (1991) in *Object-Oriented Modeling and Design* define a ***class*** **to be "a group of objects with similar properties (attributes), common behavior (operations), common associations to other objects, and common semantics (that is, meaning)."**

Allow me to expand on the term *semantics*. If we were developing software for a farming application, would we treat a cow and a barn as being in the same class? That is, would we consider both to be the same kind of object? It simply doesn't seem reasonable, does it? But what if we were developing an *accounting* system for a farmer? Then are they different?

If we abstract the features (attributes and behavior) that are needed for accounting, then that implies we should ignore everything that's not relevant for accounting. Viewed this way, the cow and the barn are just assets. They both have attributes such as Purchase Date, Purchase Price, and Book Value. They both have behaviors such as Purchase, Depreciate, DisposeOf, Mortgage, AdjustValuation, and so on. These are just the kind of attributes and operations we would expect to see in an Asset class in an accounting system.

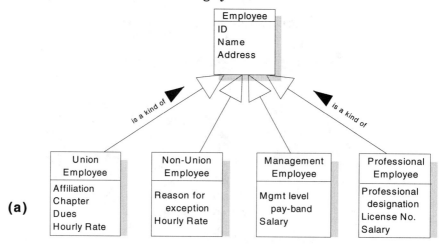

Figure 5-12(a) Class diagram showing subclasses of Employee

In other words, for accounting purposes they have the same attributes, operations and associations, and both words have the same kind of meaning. Both *cow* and *barn* boil down to mean *asset*. But if instead we were to produce a genealogical system (a breeding history and pedigree system) for our farmer friend, things would look very different. The cow would be a livestock item, related to its offspring and its parents. It would have attributes concerned with milk production, weight gain, and food consumption.

The barn would of course have none of these. It would have attributes such as Area, Height, Location, Address, and Structural Material. It would have very few behaviors, but it would be related to all the livestock, feed, and equipment stored in it. Thus, in the context of a breeding system, the barn would have a radically different set of attributes, operations, associations, and semantics from the cow.

But why would we go to all this trouble, first of all to define what classes are, and then to find ways to search out the classes in the users' business world? By organizing our databases as a reflection of the real world they serve, we gain all the benefits I've already described from a stable system. This is in addition to the massive benefits from the reuse of program code and the greatly enhanced understanding and communication that we gain, both within our team and with our users.

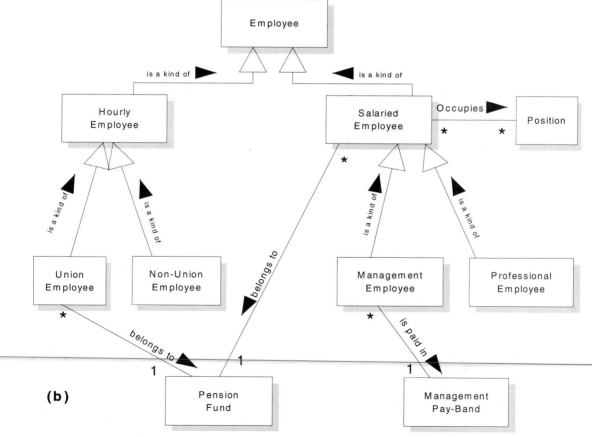

Figure 5-12(b) Class diagram showing various relationships

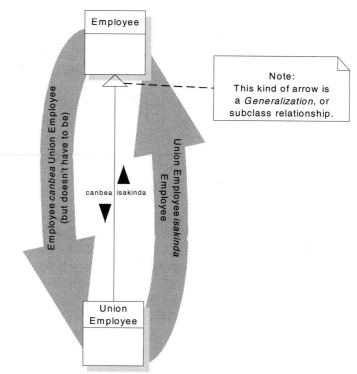

Figure 5-13 Verbs for subclass relationships

According to Coad and Yourdon (1991, page 53), "The primary motivation for identifying classes. . . is to match the technical representation of a system to the conceptual view of the real world." As we identify classes in the users' world, we'll encounter several special relationships.

One of these is the *subclass* relationship, which gives rise to inheritance and polymorphism.

Subclasses in the Real World

In a typical company, there are several *kinds of* employees. We may have Union and Non-Union, both groups being paid by hourly wages. Then we might have Management and Professional people, who receive annual salaries. Or we may divide them up according to full-time or part-time status. Or again we may separate temporary and permanent employees. We may even combine several of these ways of separating out different *kinds of* employees.

In each case, we'll find that we need to keep different information about each group [Figure 5-12(a)]. For the union employees, we'll need attributes for union affiliation, chapter, annual fees, and so on. These won't be needed for nonunion or management employees.

For professional employees, we might need to keep data about professional designations, the date of qualifying in their profession, their status with regard to requalifying, and so on. And then, for *all* employees, we'll need to keep the basic data such as employee number, name, address, age, sex, phone number, and the taxation identifier appropriate to the country (such as Social Insurance Number for Canada or Social Security Number for the United States).

We may also have differing associations for these different kinds of Employees. Figure 5-12(b) shows another possible arrangement that we might discover in some companies. This diagram shows some associations that only concern certain *kinds of* Employees, that is, certain *subclasses*. Perhaps management employees are paid according to a system of "pay bands," quite different from the simpler structure used for professionals and the hourly structure used for union and non-union employees.

This would mean that, for payroll purposes, Management objects would be related to certain classes of objects (including, for example, Pay Bands), and Wage Employees would be related to a different but overlapping set of classes. Again, perhaps Non-union Employees don't belong to a pension fund. This would dictate that we build our model in such a way that only Union, Professional, and Management Employee objects could participate in a "*belongs to*" association with a Pension Fund object.

What we have in this example is a class of objects – Employees – that can be divided into several *subclasses*. The key term here is *kind of*. A union employee *is a kind of* employee, as a Non-union Employee *is a kind of* employee. The same goes for management and professionals. A **_subclass_ is a class made up of selected instances from another class, referred to as the "parent class" or "superclass."** Conversely, a **_superclass_ is a class that includes *all* the instances of the subclass, plus possibly some more.**

You'll note from these definitions that a subclass *is a class*, and a superclass is also. And that sometimes the superclass and subclass both can have exactly the same set of instances. This may be either a temporary or permanent state of affairs. Even when it's permanent – for reasons of logic convenience, or readability – we still might want to keep the superclass–subclass relationship, rather than collapse the two classes into one. Or we might perhaps keep them separate in the analysis models and then collapse them for efficiency at design time.

The verbs we use to describe this relationship are shown in Figure 5-13. (Remember, all associations are described by verbs.) Reading along the downward arrow in Figure 5-13, we go from the Employee box down the left side of the line through the word "*canbea*" to the Union Employee box. We say that:

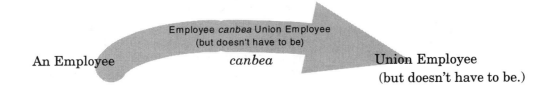

Employee *canbea* Union Employee
(but doesn't have to be)

An Employee   *canbea*   Union Employee
(but doesn't have to be.)

That is,

A superclass instance   *canbea*   subclass instance
(but doesn't have to be.)

In the other direction, going up the upward arrow, we start at the Union Employee box and go up the right-hand side of the line through the word "*isakinda*." This time the sentence reads:

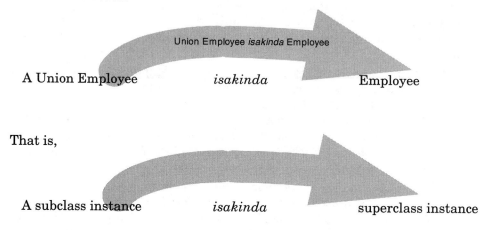

Union Employee *isakinda* Employee

A Union Employee   *isakinda*   Employee

That is,

A subclass instance   *isakinda*   superclass instance

Figure 5-14 *Isakinda* verb for subclass relationships

It's important to realize that this subclass relationship *isa* relationship just like any other, with a few additional features. James Martin has popularized the verb *isa* for this relationship, in both directions, but it doesn't always work.

A dog *isa* animal – yes, that works, since a dog *isakinda* animal. But Rover *isa* dog – this also is true, but it's not a subclass relationship. In this case, "isa" means "is an instance of." It's too ambiguous – *isa* could mean *isakinda*, or it could mean "is an instance of."

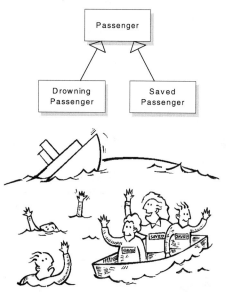

A subclass is selected instances from a larger class

So, I've found the verbs *"isakinda"* and *"canbea but doesn't have to be"* are more illustrative when explaining all this to students and users. You'll notice that the multiplicity of the subclass relationship is always one-to-one (1:1) since one Dog can only be one Animal, and one Employee can only be one Union Employee. Otherwise, he could be collecting multiple paychecks, which would be fraud.

There is an important property of subclasses that we should examine here. An accountant working for this company would qualify as a professional employee, and so would have attributes of Designation, Qualification Date, and Requalification Status. He would have these attributes just by virtue of being an instance of the class Professional Employee. The question is, Would this accountant have a name? Would he have an Employee Number, Address, Age, Sex, Phone Number, and Taxation Identifier (Social Security Number/Social Insurance Number)?

Obviously, the answer is *yes* because our accountant, by virtue of being a Professional Employee, is also an Employee. What we're saying is that he's *simultaneously* a member of *both classes*. So, by being a Professional Employee, he has one set of attributes. And since all Professional Employees *also* qualify as Employees, he also has the set of attributes defined for the Employee class.

We say that the subclass Professional Employees *inherits* all the attributes defined for the superclass, that is, the class of Employees. This idea of subclasses is used to great advantage in the object-oriented paradigm, and we'll discuss subclasses and inheritance in greater depth in Chapter 8.

Classes in the Data World

According to the generally accepted definition that we saw in Chapter 4, true object-oriented languages and databases are those that support classes, inheritance, and polymorphism. Support for inheritance, of course, implies support also for subclasses.

Classes perform functions such as

- **Creating instances.** The operation of creating an instance is a little different from other operations. An operation like updating a field must operate on a particular instance of the class, but for the Create operation this is not possible since the instance doesn't yet exist at least not until after the operation is complete. So in many OOPLs and ODBMSs, the Create-an-Instance operation is considered to be defined on the class, rather than on its instances.

- Classes provide a **place to put the program code**, the code that causes or implements the behavior of the instances. The program code for the methods, and the definitions and data types for the attributes, are stored once for the entire class and need not be repeated for each object instance.

  Obviously, it makes more sense to define these things once for the class, and then they can apply to all instances. In fact, it's one of the fundamental premises of object orientation that any instance must have a value for every attribute defined on the class and be capable of executing every method defined for the class.

- Classes serve as the **point-of-contact** for any associations. Most object-oriented methodologies view associations as connecting classes since, once it's defined for the class, the association applies to all qualifying instances. I say "qualifying" because some associations turn out to be optional, so only certain instances will participate in them.

Here is a summary about class membership:

- Objects are grouped into classes based on similar attributes, behavior, associations, and semantics (remember the cow and the barn).

- We use classes so that the internal structure of the system will closely match the structure of the users' world.

- The object instances that make up a class can be grouped within the class into subclasses.

- An instance that belongs to a subclass automatically and simultaneously belongs also to the superclass. It is at one and the same time a member of both classes.

- An instance of the subclass by definition has all the attributes and behaviors (methods) that are defined for that subclass. Because it is at the same time a member of the superclass, it also has all the attributes and methods that are defined for the superclass.

- Part of the definition of *object-oriented* is that an OOPL or an ODBMS supports classes, subclasses, inheritance and polymorphism.

- In an OOPL or an ODBMS, the class often carries operations that don't logically belong with any particular instance, such as the Instance Create operation or Instance Count. These are considered to be *class operations*.

- The class also carries the program code for all the methods since these methods must apply to all qualifying instances (or to the class as a whole).

- Associations are normally expressed as being *to the class* since any or all instances potentially could participate.

Managing Complexity

The world around us is incredibly complex. Most of us only ever make sense of a small subset of the total knowledge available to humankind.

MANAGING COMPLEXITY IN THE REAL WORLD

We introduced a Child's First Model in Chapter 3. We described how modeling allows the child to make sense of the world around her and to manage its complexities. What the child actually does is to construct a mental Object Model that she still has when grown up.

We adults use the same method to handle the huge amounts of data that we encounter every day. To visualize just how complex your own world is, imagine designing a robot to replace yourself at work while you go fishing . . . or even a robot that can fish like you do . . . or do anything at all the way you do it. You'll soon see that when you analyze your own existence, it sure is complicated!

There's a parallel here to the business world where most of your users live. Their reason for needing to manage complexity is the same as the child's: *to get the job done.* The child's job is to learn and understand and grow. Your users have a somewhat different task, but it overlaps considerably.

Whatever line of work your users may be in, they need to be constantly learning more and more about it. They are continually extending their mental models that they each carry in their heads.

Unsurprisingly, this mental model turns out to be object-oriented. Since this mental model has objects that reflect the real-world objects, the mental objects also have data attributes and behaviors. We simply carry all of this over with us into the data world.

MANAGING COMPLEXITY IN THE DATA WORLD

A database exists to help the users get their jobs done. It exists to help them to manage the masses of data they need and the data they create in the course of doing their jobs. Since its purpose is to manage information about the users' business, it really should be built as a computer-world image of the mental model that they have of their own world, or at least the business portion of it.

It would therefore seem logical that for best results the database, like the mental model, should be object-oriented, and in fact this is the case. Organizing the data this way gives us stability, resilience to change, ease of maintenance and change, and unprecedented levels of code reuse. We have hundreds or thousands of data values to keep track of and do things to (process), so we achieve best results by organizing them around the objects that they describe, just as they are both in the real world and in our mental model of the real world.

And now that we've stated how we believe that data should be arranged, how would we go about making that happen?

Mapping Classes

This is where we demonstrate the art of modeling for systems analysis. Like all forms of art, there's an underlying technology, but in the final breakdown, modeling for systems analysis is definitely an *art*.

FROM THE REAL WORLD

The process of finding the real-world classes is really the core of OOA. In Chapter 9, you'll read about ways to find and document real-world classes in order to build a matching set of data classes. This is the foundation of OOA, upon which the rest of the system is built. I'll go into great detail in Chapter 9 on just how to interview your users to find the object classes that matter to your system.

Sally Shlaer and Stephen Mellor (1988) considered this part of the process sufficiently important to devote a separate volume to it. The process is really just an update of data modeling, and Whitten, Bentley, and Barlow (1994) do a fine job of explaining data modeling in Chapter 8 of their third edition.

TO THE DATA WORLD

So what we produce is the class diagram, which is very close to the data model. In the ERD days, the two terms *data model* and *information model* were used interchangeably by many people, including many authors. However, according to our definitions of *data* as raw facts and *information* as something useful, it should really have been called a *data* model.

The name we'll choose to call it in this book is *class diagram*. This is the first step in the analysis process – but only the first. Once we've identified the real-world classes that are significant to the users, and their attributes and behavior, we still have some other classes that we need to identify and document.

Additional Data-World Classes

We'll find we need a number of classes in addition to those we discovered in the users' real world, especially during the Design Phase of the OODLC. Earlier in this chapter you were introduced to Jacobson's three types of objects. The real-world classes we've been discussing are his *entity objects*. Jacobson's other two types are *interface objects* and *control objects*.

INTERFACE CLASSES

As we saw earlier, interface classes are made up of two groups. There are classes that make up the user interface (in many cases, a GUI), plus classes that look after conversions and transmission of data to and from other systems. Some of these will need to be created anew for our project, but in the interests of consistency we'll need to reuse interface classes from earlier projects as much as possible.

This will, for example, give the users a consistent look-and-feel across all the various systems they use. We may even buy some of our interface classes as class libraries, perhaps in the form of a user interface management system (UIMS). This is a package of prewritten classes with attributes and methods that we can use to create a GUI for our system.

Interfaces to other systems can often be achieved by using classes already defined within those systems. Standard network and data communication protocols will be encapsulated within some of our interface classes.

CONTROL CLASSES

Control classes are sometimes discovered during analysis and sometimes at design time. They're added to the model when we become aware of a process or function or transaction that the system must perform, but which involves data and methods from a variety of classes. Since this operation doesn't naturally or neatly fit within any one entity class, we create a class just to carry it. Since the class exists just for this one operation, or perhaps for a few related ones, it most likely will have very few attributes and probably no other methods.

ABSTRACT CLASSES

Often we'll add classes just to take advantage of opportunities for inheritance of a common attribute or operation and for polymorphism (see Chapter 8). Sometimes we'll take classes that are not connected in the model and make them subclasses of an artificial superclass that we'll invent just for that purpose, as in Figure 5-15.

The new superclass is a little different in that it has no instances, except for the ones that are provided for it by its subclasses. That is, we say it has no *direct instances*. Such a class we refer to as an abstract class. We'll examine *abstract classes* in more detail in Chapter 8.

Our reasons for doing this are to improve the performance of the machine, the programmers, and the analysts. These classes will increase the level of code reuse and reduce programming effort, thus reducing both the amount of time spent, and the number of errors (bugs). Easing the programmer's job always results in reduced debugging and lowered costs. Inventing these classes will sometimes allow us to improve machine efficiency, reducing response times, or simplify a database design.

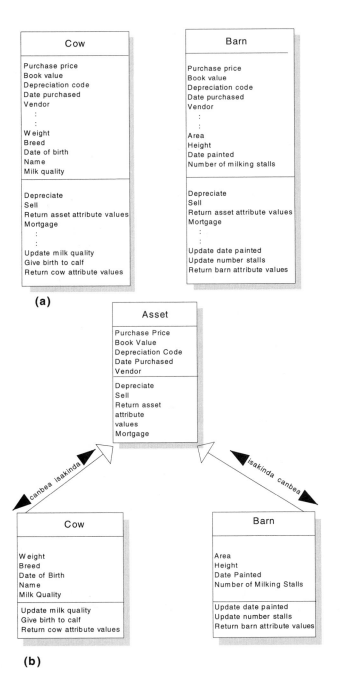

(a)

(b)

Figure 5-15 (a) The analysis model showing unrelated classes, (b) the design model with the absract class added to take advbantage of inheritance.

In summary:

• People make sense of their complex environment by constructing object-oriented mental models of it in their heads.

• In our databases, we need to organize the data values (attributes) around the objects they describe, as they're organized both in the real world and in our mental models of the real world.

• The foundation of object-oriented development is to find the significant classes in the real world. This is the first step of OOA and the most basic one.

• Once we've produced the class diagram in this way, we'll need to add some extra classes that are only in the data world and are not found in the real world.

• Interface classes look after data flows with the users and with other systems. They model things like the GUI and the data communication protocols. Reuse of these classes will ensure consistency within and across projects.

• Entity classes are the ones we found in the real world and incorporated in the class diagram.

• Control classes model behavior that doesn't fit in any existing class.

• Abstract classes, which have no direct instances, are often introduced to exploit inheritance and polymorphism.

These then are the various classes we'll be needing. Now, for all of these classes, we need to consider two kinds of objects in terms of the length of time they stick around.

5.3   Transient and Persistent Objects

In the real world, some objects last longer than others. A house or car is more or less permanent. A bus, an airplane, a customer, product, contract, or employee are all things that have a lifetime of significant length. A *trip* on a bus or airplane, on the other hand, is not very permanent, nor is a *sale* of a product to a customer. Any event exists for real only for the short time while it's happening. After that, it exists solely as a memory, that is, as recorded information.

For data objects, we arbitrarily consider *transient* objects to be those that don't survive the end of the session, as we defined in Chapter 4. This means that when you turn off your computer all transient objects will simply be lost. Physically, this is because the program creates them in its volatile memory (RAM).

But in business applications (and many others), we have a need for permanent records, so we need persistent objects that will survive after the power is turned off. We need object classes that will survive until the next session and beyond that is, we need *persistent* objects. Physically, this means they must be recorded on the disks, and not merely created in RAM.

So we're going to need some transient and some persistent classes for each project. And sometimes we'll come across a class where some instances are transient and some are persistent. And some will be more persistent than others. Which brings us to a consideration of the way some authors use the terms object, class, and instance.

5.4   Objects: Classes or Instances?

Given the way we've defined the term *object*, it should be fairly clear that I'm using the term to refer to an *individual object instance*. But not all authors perceive things the way I do. Many use the term *object* to refer to a class rather than to an instance. This can get very confusing, so one of the first things you'll need to do when beginning a book in this area is to check out which meaning the author is giving to the word *object*.

In this book, I try much of the time to use the words *instance* and *class* so that it's quite clear exactly which one I'm talking about.

Much to their credit, The Three Amigos (Rumbaugh, Booch and Jacobson) have done it *right*. In UML they talk of *classes of objects*, and only occasionally find it necessary to resort to using the term *instance* when they need to clarify a point. Quite correctly, they use *class* to mean *class*, and *object* to mean *instance*.

5.5   Associations

An object is the same thing as an entity. The difference is that an object has behavior, which can't be shown on an ERD. This means that everything I've said about associations among entities also applies to objects. Associations represent (i.e., they *abstract*) actions that involve two or more objects, that is, the *interactions* of the objects.

Associations are modeled by the association name, *verbs* that express what one kind of object *does to* another kind. In UML, associations may also be given *role names* (nouns) which express the *role* that one object plays in the life of the other. We'll visit associations in more detail in Chapter 8, where we'll discuss properties of objects and classes, and in Chapter 9, where we'll discuss how to go about finding the classes and associations in the real world of the users.

5.6 ANTHROPOMORPHISM

It's commonplace in children's literature and cartoons for trees and houses, trains and mouses, to grow hands and faces, to walk and run, and to hold conversations in English, French, or Tagalog. This process of giving human qualities and abilities to nonhuman objects is called *anthropomorphism* (anthro = people; morph = shape). The Oxford (1979) defines *anthropomorphism* as **the "ascription . . . of human attributes to something irrational or impersonal."**

It's less commonplace but considerably more enlightening to do the same thing to the objects we deal with in our object-oriented modeling. I've alluded to this earlier. This personalizing began with graphic programming, with things like "Object, draw thyself," "Object, rotate thyself," and so forth.

What happens here is that by giving an object a piece of program code that makes the object appear on the screen, we've given it a *behavior*, namely, the ability to draw itself on the screen. It *exhibits* that behavior in response to a message sent by another object or by a user of the system. The *result* of the behavior (the "answer") is returned to whoever sent the message.

When explaining things or trying to understand things during Analysis, we can simulate this pattern. We can role-play the behavior of the system by verbally issuing messages such as "Transaction, post thyself" or "Employee, assign thyself to a Project." This can be done on paper across a desk or on a whiteboard in any meeting or discussion.[4] I've even had people stand up in front of a meeting and role-play the objects involved, communicating by these kinds of messages.

Very often, the effect is to clarify our understanding of a complex interaction by tracing it through step by step in this manner. We'll revisit role playing at the end of Chapter 11, when we look at Rebecca Wirfs-Brock's Responsibility-Driven Design (RDD).

This now leads us into a discussion about the various different ways that people learn.

5.7 USERS' LEARNING STYLES

Role playing can frequently be very useful for users (or analysts or students, for that matter) who are primarily kinesthetic or auditory learners, rather than visual or symbolic learners.

Most of you who are studying in this area are already very good at manipulating symbols mentally (conceptual learning), and you're also effective as visual or textual learners, but *some of your users may learn better in other modes.* Each person has their favorite way of learning(see Chapter 16.)

I mention this here because it is essential that you communicate with your users in ways that they are comfortable with and best able to handle. *These may be modes that you and I are not used to,* or we're less comfortable with. So the onus is on us, as the supposed experts, to make sure these things happen in a suitable mode and manner.

It may help to visualize objects as if they were robots that *know* certain things and can *do* things when you send them a message.

You will find that some of your users are visual or auditory learners, and some learn best by feeling and handling something physical (tactile or kinesthetic learners.) Some want to watch you do it first, and others just want you to leave them to stumble and try things on their own. All of us learn best when the material is presented to us through *more than one* of these "channels" at once.

In your day-to-day work, this means you will often get better results by using *more than just words* to communicate. Pictures and diagrams are great, and very necessary. Physical objects and physical movement can sometimes help people to grasp an idea (see Exercise 8.2). Even better is for you to observe your users and colleagues, and note each person's learning style. This will give you insights into how best to present ideas and concepts to each person.

You'll find more on role playing as an analysis tool in Chapter 11. Also, Exercise 8.2, the "Object-Oriented Treasure Hunt," is designed to exploit various learning modes in the students using this book.

Another idea you and your users may find helpful is to visualize objects as little robots, especially when you're puzzling alone over how your model should work. Each robot is capable of doing certain functions for you. They communicate by sending messages to each other, and they can receive messages from you, as you simulate the users of the system.

Behavior is initiated by messages from the users. Each robot is also capable of knowing certain things (i.e., data) and has behaviors available to provide that information to you, or to update it from information you send in a message.

· ·

DELIVERABLES

This is one chapter that really has no deliverables since it just discusses the nature of objects and classes. However, each diagram in the chapter indicates how that kind of structure should be drawn in your models, when you do produce deliverables for the other chapters.

FURTHER READING

Probably the best explanation of the nature of objects is by David Taylor (1992), he of the network theory of cognition. His donut notation (Figure 5-8) neatly demonstrates the encapsulation of data within an object, and shows it surrounded and protected by a ring of exclusive methods. His text is possibly the most readable in the field so far. All the object-oriented authors explain these concepts, but I think Taylor should be the first you read after this book.

Another brief but excellent explanation is in the first three chapters of Timothy Budd's book, entitled simply *Object-Oriented Programming* (1991). The rest of his book gets deeper into OOP per se and is still good reading both for object-oriented concepts and for OOP.

CHAPTER SUMMARY

- An object in the real world is a *thing*, and data about it is carried by its corresponding data object. An object is an entity with behavior. A data object is thus an *abstraction* of the real-world object, carrying the data describing it and the program code that is the *only allowable access* to that data.

- *Entity objects* are the basic objects and classes that we find during analysis of the users' business. *Interface objects* are used to handle communication between the system and the users or other systems. *Control objects* are created during Analysis to give us somewhere to put methods that don't easily fit into interface objects or entity objects. The entity/interface/control split improves maintenance and stability by giving greater encapsulation.

- Attributes are the data values carried by objects. We gain stability when the data is organized around the objects it truly describes (normalization).

- Using objects gives seamless transitions from one phase of the ODLC to the next, with no loss of data owing to changes of notation. Objects give traceability, allowing us to follow a feature from an object in one phase of the ODLC to the same object in the diagrams from another phase.

- The *state* of an object is defined by the set of values currently held by its attributes. The set of values for its attributes form a *tuple*. Each attribute value is drawn from the *domain* of all permissible values for that attribute.

- *Identity* is the property that says two things are different, that they're not both the same thing. Two things that are identical are not both the same thing even if everything about them is the same. Identifiers such as names, numbers, or OIDs are used as *evidence* of identity.

- Identity is an inherent property of objects. Identifiers are an *aid* to telling objects apart. In general, real-world identifiers cannot be trusted to be unique. Many OOPLs and ODBMSs assign OIDs to every object to guarantee uniqueness.

- Objects in the real world often exhibit certain behaviors in response to specific messages. *Overt behavior* is where we instruct an object to make something happen. *Passive behavior* is the recording of data. *Responsive behavior* is providing information on demand.

- Objects in the data world exhibit overt behavior where they do something observable in response to a message; they exhibit passive or responsive behavior when they simply record or provide information.

- The messages that data objects respond to are just function calls, carrying parameters or arguments. Data is returned to the calling object either as the value of the function or in the parameters.

- By giving an object a piece of program code that makes it do something (such as appear on the screen), we've given it a behavior. It *exhibits* that behavior in response to a message sent by another object or a user. The *result* of the behavior (the "answer") is returned. When modeling during our analysis, we can simulate this by role playing the behavior, verbally issuing messages such as "Transaction, post thyself." This can be done on paper or in person with a whiteboard. (See also Chapter 11.)

- In an OOPL or ODBMS, the program code for the methods (functions) is stored in the database attached in some way to the data.

- *Encapsulation* is the forming of a "crisp" boundary or shell with a "narrow interface" to allow communication across the boundary. Encapsulation reduces complexity, and increases system stability by reducing the ripple effects of changes, much like a breakwater at the entrance to a harbor. Encapsulation allows us to use an object by understanding the published interface. We don't need to know its inner workings in order to use it effectively.

- Encapsulation allows us to make changes within the object (for example, optimizing some of its methods) without affecting any of the programs or functions that use it. We've *localized the effects of change.* Similarly, we can make changes outside the object – that is, we can change the ways we use it, or use it in new places, without needing to change the object itself.

- We must communicate with the object by sending it messages in the format required by the published interface.

- Violating encapsulation can occasionally be beneficial but is fraught with danger.

- At any moment, an object exists in a certain manner or condition, which we say is its *state.* If the object changes, we say it has undergone a *transition* into a new state.

- An *object life cycle* consists of the various states that an object may transition through, the set of permissible transitions, and the sequencing of those states and transitions as it progresses from its initial creation to its eventual disposal. The *statechart diagram* is a powerful tool used to model object life cycles. (See Chapter 10 for a full explanation of statechart diagrams.)

- A *class* is a group of objects with similar *properties* (attributes), common *behavior* (operations), common *associations* to other objects, and common *semantics* (meaning).

- We use classes so that the internal structure of the system will closely match the structure of the users' world.

- The object instances that make up a class can be grouped within the class into subclasses. An instance that belongs to a subclass automatically and simultaneously belongs also to the superclass. An instance of the subclass has all the attributes and behaviors (methods) that are defined for that subclass. It also inherits all the attributes and methods that are defined for the superclass.

- The subclass relationship is defined by the *isakinda* and *canbea* verbs. A subclass instance *isakinda* superclass instance. Conversely, a superclass instance *canbea* subclass instance but is not required to be.

- Part of the definition of *object-oriented* is that an OOPL or an ODBMS supports classes, subclasses, inheritance, and polymorphism.

- The class often carries operations that don't logically belong with any particular instance, such as Create or Count. The class also carries the program code for all its methods since the methods apply to all qualifying instances.

- Associations are normally expressed as being "to the class," rather than "to the instance," since any or all instances potentially could participate.

- People make sense of their complex environment by constructing object-oriented mental models of it in their heads, so in our databases we organize the data attributes around the objects they describe, as they are both in the real world and in our mental models of it.

- The first step of object-oriented development is finding the significant classes in the real world. Then we add some extra classes that are only in the data world and are not found in the real world.

- *Interface classes* model data flows with the users and with other systems, such as the GUI and data communication protocols. Reuse of these classes ensures consistency within and across projects.

- *Entity classes* are the ones found in the real world and incorporated in the class diagram. *Control classes* model behavior that doesn't fit in any existing class.

- *Abstract classes*, which have *no direct instances*, are often introduced at design time to exploit inheritance and polymorphism.

- Many people use the term *object* incorrectly to refer to a class rather than to an instance. You must check out which meaning an author is giving to the word *object*. In UML, The Three Amigos have done it right, and use *object* to refer to an instance.

- Associations are modeled by *verbs* that express what one kind of object *does to* another kind. In UML, an association can also be described by a *role name*.

CHAPTER GLOSSARY

abstraction   The process of focusing on those features of something that are essential for the task at hand and ignoring those that are not.

anthropomorphism   The ascription of human attributes or behavior to something irrational or impersonal – for example, to an animal, or to a data object.

class   (1) A group of objects with similar *properties* (attributes), common *behavior* (operations), common *associations* to other objects, and common *semantics* (meaning) (Rumbaugh et al., 1991). (2)"A number of individuals having a character or feature in common." (Oxford, 1979). (3) "A number of persons or things regarded as forming a group by reason of of common attributes, characteristics, qualities or traits. Synonyms: kind, sort." (*Random House Webster Unabridged*, 1998). (4) "A group, set, or kind sharing common attributes" (*Webster*, 1975).

control object   An object that is created during analysis to give us somewhere to put behavior (i.e., methods) that doesn't easily fit into interface objects or entity objects.

data object (see also **object**)   An abstraction of some *thing* in the real world, that carries both the data describing the real-world object (its real-world analog) and the operations (i.e., program code) that have the only allowable access to that data.

__domain__ The set of all permissible values for an attribute.

__entity object__ The fundamental objects and classes that we discover in analysis by scanning the users' business.

__extended relational__   A type of ODBMS where the instances are stored as rows in a table. This is just like a relational database, except the concept has been modified to handle behavior as well as data, and also to handle complex data types.

__identity__   The property that says two things are different, that they're not both the same thing.

__identity__   "The fact of being who or what a person or thing is." *Oxford* (1998)

__identity__   "The condition or fact that a person or thing is itself and is not something else" (*Oxford*, (1979).

__inherent__ "Existing in something as a permanent, essential or characteristic attribute." (*Oxford*, 1998)

__inherent__ Involved in the essential character of something. (*Webster*, 1975)

__interface object__ An object used to handle communication between the system and external entities such as users, operators, or other systems.

__object__   "Any *thing* that may be apprehended intellectually." (*Oxford* 1998)

__object__   A *thing*.

__object__   An abstraction of some *thing* in the real world, that carries both the data describing the real-world object (its real-world analog) and the *operations* (*methods* – that is, program code) that have the *only allowable access* to that data.

__object identifier (OID)__ A unique number or other identifier automatically assigned to each object instance when it's created.

__object life cycle__ Consists of the various states that an object may transition through, the set of permissible transitions, and the sequencing of those states and transitions, as the object progresses from its initial creation to its eventual disposal.

__overt behavior__ Where we actually instruct an object to *do* something.

__passive behavior__ The recording of the data generated by some action or event in the real world.

__relation__ A table (in a relational database).

__relationship__ The interaction of two entities, represented by a verb.

__responsive behavior__ The providing of information (i.e., attribute values) in response to a message requesting it.

__state__ (1) The set of values currently held by the attributes of an object. (2) "The particular condition that someone or something is in at a specific time."(*Oxford*, 1989) (3) "Condition, manner, or way of existence as determined by circumstances" (*Oxford* 1979). (4) "A mode or condition of being" (*Webster*, 1975). (5) "A condition or stage in the physical being of something" (*Webster*, 1975).

state transition The act or experience of changing from one state to another.

subclass A class made up of selected instances from another class, referred to as the parent class or superclass.

superclass A class that includes all the instances of the subclass, plus possibly some more.

WHAT COMES NEXT

In the next three chapters, you'll begin the how-to of building the analysis models. You'll see the steps to follow to find the objects and classes and then to discover their attributes and behavior. These will be the more practical, step-by-step chapters, but still with a lot of leeway for individual customizing.

CLASS/GROUP EXERCISES AND PROBLEMS

Ex 5.1 For each of the following object classes, have your class or group come up with a suitable definition. Appoint the instructor or one of the students as the user, to make decisions anywhere you have a choice or run into a conflict or disagreement. The user always has the final say. Remember, you're modeling *his* reality, *his* world, not the world as *you* see it. Remember also that each word in the list is a noun:

Vehicle	Owner	Mechanic
Rental	Car	Bus
Tool	Driver	Service Event
Truck	Garage	Purchase

Ex 5.2 For each of the following object classes, have the class or group brainstorm a list of attributes.

(a) Customer: A person who buys from XYZ Inc.

(b) Vendor: A person or business from whom XYZ Inc. purchases products for resale.

(c) Employee: A person who works for or used to work for XYZ Inc.

(d) Product: An item inventoried by XYZ Inc. for resale.

Ex 5.3 For each of the object classes you defined in Exercise 5.1, have the class or group brainstorm a list of attributes.

INDIVIDUAL EXERCISES AND PROBLEMS

Ex 5.4 For each of the following lists, draw an object class model. Draw a conceptual model and then a logical model. For each class, show its name and the unique identifier. For each association, show the verb that defines it and/ or role name(s), and its multiplicity, as you see them. Note that each list has deliberately been assembled as a mixture of classes and instances, so you can expect two or more items in each list to collapse into a single class. File your models carefully for reuse in Exercises 6.6 and 7.2, and in other chapters beyond that.

(a) Apple, Baker, Charlie, Donut, Employee, Flour, Bakery, Biscuit, Bread, Cake, Cookie, Customer, Dough

(b) Tree; Flower; Weedkiller; Spruce; 2,4,D; Peonie; Fertilizer; Pansy; RoundUp; Killex

(c) Account, Shirt, Jeans, Customer, Vendor, Belt, Sock, Salesclerk, Sweater, Product

(d) Desk, File Cabinet, Chair, Office, Floor, Building, Employee

(e) Property, Kitchen, Owner, Garage, House, Listing, Street, Lot, Suite, Flat, Bedroom, Realtor, Purchaser

Ex 5.5 Figure 5-16 shows an object Class Diagram for a motor vehicle licensing system. Designate the instructor or a student to be the user, to make decisions wherever there appears to be several ways of interpreting the model.

(a) Generate a suitable definition for each class.

(b) Write a suitable verb *and* role names on each association line, to indicate what business activity this association relates to. Add appropriate multiplicity.

(c) Add the following attributes to the diagram, making sure that you attach each attribute to the class of objects that it truly describes. Some of these attributes will fit on more that one class   for example, *Name* belongs with both Owner and Clerk.

(d) Add an abstract class called *Person*. What attributes will it have?

(e) Categorize each class as a concrete, abstract, state or event class.

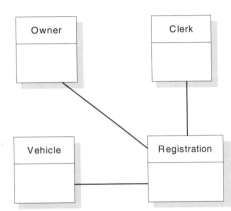

Figure 5-16 Conceptual Model for Motor Vehicle Registration.

PROJECTS AND CASES

P 5.1 Obtain the documentation for an existing database, or redo it from memory. It could be one that you or a group member have created, or one from a real-world project in the industry, or anywhere. Make sure it's not too large, so it's manageable.

Check this database out to see how well normalized it is, considering that a file, table, or set from an old-fashioned database corresponds to a class in OOT. Can you identify files/tables/sets that do or don't represent object classes, preferably real-world ones? Look for attributes that actually all describe the same class but are spread over several files/tables/sets. Write a brief critique of the design of this database, based on what you learned in this chapter.

SELF-TEST QUESTIONS

Note: The Appendix has answers to the Self-Test Questions.

Q 5.1   An instance is:

(a) A short period of time during which an object exhibits behavior.

(b) An individual object of the class in question.

(c) An example of the kind of thing under discussion.

(d) An object that has not yet been assigned to a class.

(e) A group of objects that all belong to the class in question.

Q 5.2   An entity class is a class that:

(a) Does not appear in the class diagram.

(b) Relates to the class diagram.

(c) Exists in the real world and in the class diagram.

(d) Exists in the real world but not in the class diagram.

(e) Exists in the data world but not in the real model.

Q 5.3   The state of an object is:

(a) Defined by the set of values of its attributes.

(b) A condition or stage in its physical existence.

(c) A stage in its life cycle.

(d) All of the above.

(e) None of the above.

(f) Some of the above.

Q 5.4   An abstract class has:

(a) No direct instances.

(b) Only direct instances.

(c) Some direct instances.

(d) No indirect instances.

(e) Some indirect instances.

Q 5.5   Describe how objects, instances, and classes relate from the real world to the data world.

Q 5.6   Distinguish among entity, interface, and control objects.

Q 5.7   Distinguish among concrete, conceptual, state and event objects.

Q 5.8   Distinguish between transient and persistent objects.

Q 5.9 Explain why attributes and behavior are of central importance to object-oriented working.

Q 5.10 Define identity, encapsulation, inheritance, and polymorphism.

Q 5.11 Mark each of the following objects as concrete (ct), conceptual (cl), event (ev), or state (st). Some may fit into more than one category. Compare and discuss your answers with a friend or with your group before looking them up in the appendix.

Vendor	Booking
Transaction	Product
Loan	Ownership
Registration	Shoe
Withdrawal	Department

Q 5.12 An object in the real world is a _____ , and data about it is carried by its corresponding _____ _____ . An object is an _____ with behavior. A _____ _____ is thus an _____ of the real-world object, carrying the _____ describing it and the program code that is the only _____ _____ to that data.

Q 5.13 Entity _____ are the basic _____ and classes that we find during _____ of the users' business. _____ objects are used to handle communication between the _____ and the _____ or other systems. _____ objects are created during Analysis to give us somewhere to put _____ that don't easily fit into _____ objects or _____ objects. The _____/_____ /control split improves maintenance and _____ by giving greater _____ .

Q 5.14 _____ are the data values carried by objects. We gain _____ when the data is organized around the objects it _____ _____ (normalization).

Q 5.15 Using objects gives _____ transitions from one phase of the _____ to the next, with no loss of data owing to changes of _____ . Objects give _____ , allowing us to follow a feature from an object in one _____ of the _____ to the same object in the diagrams from another _____ .

Q 5.16 Identity is the property that says two things are _____ , that they're not _____ _____ _____ _____ . Two things that are identical are not _____ _____ _____ _____ even if everything about them is the same. _____ such as names, _____ , or _____ are used as _____ of identity.

Q 5.17 By giving an object a piece of _____ _____ that makes it do something (such as _____ on the _____), we've given it a _____ . It exhibits that _____ in response to a message sent by another object or a _____ . The _____ of the _____ (the "answer") is returned.

Q 5.17 Encapsulation is the forming of a " _____ " _____ or shell with a "_____ interface" to allow communication across the _____ . Encapsulation reduces _____ , and increases system _____ by reducing the _____ effects of changes. Encapsulation allows us to use an object by understanding the _____ _____ . We don't need to know its _____ _____ in order to _____ it effectively.

Q 5.18 Encapsulation allows us to make changes _____ the object without affecting any of the _____ or functions that use it. We've _____ the effects of change. Similarly, we can make changes _____ the object – that is, we can change the _____ we use it, without needing to change the _____ _____ .

Q 5.20 Violating _____ can occasionally be _____ but is _____ with _____ .

Q 5.21 At any _____ , an object exists in a certain _____ or condition, which we say is its _____ . If the object _____ , we say it has undergone a _____ into a new _____ .

Q 5.22 A class is a _____ of objects with similar _____ (attributes), common behavior (_____), common _____ to other objects, and common _____ (meaning).

Q 5.23 We use classes so that the _____ _____ of the system will closely match the _____ of the users' _____ .

Q 5.24 An instance that belongs to a _____ automatically and _____ belongs also to the superclass. An instance of the _____ has all the _____ and _____ that are defined for that subclass. It also _____ all the attributes and methods that are defined for the _____ .

Q 5.25 Part of the definition of object-oriented is that an OOPL or an ODBMS supports classes, _____ , _____ , and _____ .

Q 5.26 The _____ step of object-oriented development is finding the significant _____ in the _____ _____ .

Q 5.27 _____ classes are the ones found in the _____ _____ and incorporated in the class diagram.

Q 5.28 Abstract classes, which have no _____ _____ , are often introduced at Design time to exploit _____ and _____ .

Q 5.29 Associations are modeled by _____ that express what one kind of object _____ to another kind. In UML, an association can also be described by a _____ _____ .

Chapter Six

. . . .

The Object-Oriented Development Life Cycle

WHAT YOU WILL LEARN IN THIS CHAPTER

In this chapter, you'll learn the major phases that make up the object-oriented development life cycle (OODLC or ODLC). You'll discover how to specify the system requirements with an appropriate model and then what models should be produced throughout the analysis phase of the OODLC. You can be confident that you understand the OODLC when you can:

1. List and describe the phases and activities of the OODLC.

2. List the components of the requirements model and briefly describe how to produce each one

3. List and describe the other models produced in the analysis phase.

WHAT YOU SHOULD KNOW TO START THIS CHAPTER

The material in Chapter 5 is a direct preparation for this chapter, and you'll need to know and understand it reasonably well. Check the overview at the front of Chapter 5 and the summary at the end.

CHAPTER OVERVIEW

We'll begin by defining the older systems development life cycle (SDLC), and then the OODLC. You'll then see the models that make up the deliverables for the Analysis Phase and how they're built and used. We'll continue with a brief discussion of the remaining phases in the OODLC, with some comments on the many activities of the Maintenance Phase.

KEY CONCEPTS

- OODLC
- Requirements model
- Project scope
- Feasibility analysis
- Context diagram
- Use case model

- Interface descriptions
- Object model, class diagram
- Entity classes, interface classes, control classes
- Statechart diagram
- Consistent notation, seamless transitions
- Traceability

"THE OUTHOUSE BATHROOM BOUTIQUE"
SALES REPORTING SYSTEM – EPISODE 6

We last saw Tim and Nancy in the coffee shop, talking about how difficult it can be to get the information needed for a good system design, from the users who know it but don't know that they know it. Nancy had just finished explaining to Tim how the object-oriented techniques were so effective for this, and now she branched onto another topic.

"Of course," she said, "there's a lot of planning needed for a project like this. And there's a whole series of steps that have to be done in the right order and done the right way. For instance, I read a recent article about a project where the users' senior manager would not allow the systems people to go directly to his own staff. He was worried they would take up too much of his people's time and keep them from their own work.

"He designated one of his supervisors as a contact, and just having a middleman totally screwed up the communication. The systems people struggled along as best they could, but they were isolated from their main source of information about the users' jobs, that is, the users themselves. It slowed everything down and delayed the project enormously, not to mention the extra time it took to find and correct all the errors in the system caused by the two-level communication. Like so many others, that system ended up late, poorly designed, and hideously overbudget!"

"Hideously, eh?" Tim said, grinning. "Well, I know in a bureaucracy, sometimes the politics can be fatal for a project like that. I don't think we can afford to have that happen with this one!"

"This is why I think you'll appreciate how useful the object models are as communication and discussion tools," Nancy explained. "As we build the models, we'll all learn a whole bunch about the operation, even those among us who are familiar with it already. And once they're built, we're certain to be using the models every day in meetings, discussions, and all kinds of places. Then, at the Construction stage of the life cycle, when the models are complete, we'll use them as templates to build the software. The data parts of the model will be used to design the database, and the operations in the Object Model will be used as a plan or design to write the programs.

"But I'm starting to use terms I haven't defined. Don't worry, I'll explain them all before we start, and they'll all make sense as we go through the modeling process." Nancy stood up.

"Well I'm starting to get excited myself," said Tim, signaling for the bill. "But I'm a little afraid to get my hopes up too high! I'll wait until I see all these ideas in action."

He helped her on with her coat. "So, we'll see you on Tuesday."

"Right," Nancy responded, "Tuesday at nine sharp."

THOUGHT QUESTIONS

Consider the following in your groups, and present and compare your results.

1. Discuss a time when one of your group members (or someone he knows) was involved in a project that ran afoul of organizational politics. If possible, use some kind of information-related or data processing related project; otherwise, any project will do.

Maybe it died because it "stepped on someone's toes." Perhaps because it ran contrary to the "hidden agenda" of somebody powerful in the organization. Or perhaps it offended someone's sensibilities or beliefs, or maybe it went against the prejudices of someone powerful. For instance, it might have been headed by a woman or a person from a minority group and thus run afoul of some powerful person's prejudices.

In what ways did the project run into trouble? How did it fail? How was the problem handled? What actions helped or hindered the project's attempts to succeed? What could have been done differently? (Be realistic. I know we would all like to simply remove this person, but in the real world it's not usually that easy.)

What additional precautions and preparations should we put in place in future projects to guard against or to handle such difficulties? Prepare an action plan or checklist to use on future projects.

2.   Prepare a half-page or so handout, aimed at the user personnel, justifying the use of object-modeling methods in their systems project. Consider carefully how they'll feel in reaction to your words. Will your words make them feel more like participating and cooperating? Will your words reduce their fears and make them feel good about the project?

Try your handout on other students and on some noncomputer people. Ask them to report their *feelings* back to you, as well as their opinion (i.e., *thoughts*) of your piece. These are two different things. Report to the class any discoveries or surprises you may have, as well as some suggested directions for further research. Review and revise this little handout when you've finished this chapter, in the light of your further learning. Then file it and keep it for possible use in your actual career projects.

6.1 THE LIFE CYCLE

The purpose of this chapter is to introduce you to the idea of an object-oriented development life cycle (OODLC). We'll briefly examine the various phases and subphases of it, in particular the analysis phase and its components.

Your primary goal must be to understand the cycle as a whole, and where all the pieces fit together. You must understand the sequence of events and why this particular sequence is important. The following chapters will explain each phase and step in detail and show you explicitly how to do each one.

The OODLC is really nothing more than the older systems development life cycle (SDLC) in a new guise, stressing the use of objects. The models are different in the new paradigm, but we still need to do much the same activities at each phase of the life cycle. These are shown in Table 6-1. The analysis phase is shown in more detail since it's the focus of this book.

In the various books and methodologies available, you'll find considerable variation in the detailed structure of the OODLC. I've attempted to summarize the current state of the art in Table 6-1 and to give you something that works, that you can take into your career and use right away.

My other objective is that, having learned the techniques involved, you'll be in a position to adapt to using whatever methodology you or your client or employer may choose. I also intend that you'll be able to do a better job of learning from the books published by the leaders of the object-oriented field once you've been prepared by reading *this* book.

In the rest of this chapter, we'll overview most of these phases, activities, and models, and then spend our time in Chapter 7 on a detailed step-by-step method for the very first part of your project, the requirements model.

6.2   THE OBJECT-ORIENTED ANALYSIS PHASE

In analysis we model the users' requirements for what the system must do. In the object-oriented version of the life cycle, the output of this process is a conceptual-level analysis model, consisting of these deliverables:

-   The requirements model

-   The object model

-   The statechart model

The Requirements Model

Most projects are initiated in response to a request, typically from the users themselves, written as a description of what the users perceive their needs are, and *written from the users' point of view*. There are of course many variations in the way this is done, but something like this is typical of many organizations.

Unless systems analysts or business analysts happened to be involved in its preparation, this document is not usually in the best format for developing a system from it. Nor is it usually complete. It's typically an outline of the major features the users would like to see, and it needs fleshing out with much more detail. There will also be many gaps where the users forgot things or were unaware that something would be needed.

Edmonton Transit

Memo to: John Donne

From: Mel Hutchings   Oct. 17

Re: Transit Operations and Dispatch

After talking to your consultant, Nancy Forsyth, last week, we figure we need a program that will keep track of buses and drivers, and give us statistics and reports for City Council and the other levels of government. Can we meet to discuss what we need and whether you think it can be done?

Figure 6-1   A "typical" systems request document

Table 6-1 Activities and phases of the OODLC

Phase	Activity	Models Produced	Components
Analysis	OOA	Requirements model	Project scope
			Feasibility study
			Context diagram
		Object model	Class diagram:
			Entity classes
			Interface classes
			Control classes
			Behavior diagrams:
			Statechart diagrams
			Collaborations & CRC cards
			Sequence diagrams
			Activity diagrams
Design	OOD	Design versions of the OO models	
Construction	OOP	Actual system	
Testing	O-O Testing	Working system	
Maintenance	All of the above	All of the above	

Figure 6-1 shows an example of a fairly typical (and seriously inadequate) systems request in the form of a memo, as it might be received from a user. Although you and I may feel it's somewhat inadequate from the point of view of systems development, we must bear in mind that it's the *user's perception* of the problem. As such, it needs work to become fully specified from the information point of view.

Because of the wide variation in size, detail, and format, it's difficult to suggest what a "typical" request would look like, but Figure 6-1 is something like you might see in many companies.

This is where the ***requirements model*** **fits in. Its purpose is to document the users' needs in full detail in a way that is both understandable for the users and usable by the developers as a starting point to develop a system.** When completed, the requirements model should become part of the formal contract or agreement between the users and the developers. It's ideal for this purpose since it's fully comprehended by the users (or should be), while at the same time it spells out the requirements in the way we the developers need to see them.

Booch (1996, page 241) makes a couple of important points when he exhorts us to "treat a requirements document not as a statement of objective, unchangeable fact but rather as a living contract between the users and developers of a system. As a contract, a requirements document infers obligations of both parties, and so it's open for negotiation."

Earlier methods used a huge textual requirements definition (often something that read like an old-fashioned novel), which was never easy to understand, let alone negotiate with. To enhance our ability to understand, communicate, and negotiate, we'll use a requirements model consisting of five closely related parts:

- Project scope
- Initial feasibility analysis
- Context diagram
- Use case script model
- Interface descriptions

PROJECT SCOPE

This is a statement of what the project is to produce. The project scope says in general terms what the system will do, what functions will be part of it, and which users it will service. It will also state what *will not* be part of the system.

INITIAL FEASIBILITY ANALYSIS

Feasibility analysis is an attempt to answer the question, "Should we really be doing this?" Users can ask for all kinds of things, and one of our frequent failings as programmers and developers is that we love to build software that tries to do absolutely everything.

It would be so nice to be able to build software with everything the users want, and every bell or whistle that you and I can imagine. But this would run us up against the fundamental principle of economics. That is, that while human wants are unlimited, human resources for satisfying those wants are strictly limited.

It's difficult enough to do a thorough requirements analysis, and come up with a clear picture of what the users need. It's another thing to actually be able to build it and get it right. But even if it's well within our abilities, we must first answer some tough questions.

These questions are about *can we* and *should we* build it? In other words, is the project *feasible*?

According to the Gage (1983) dictionary, ***feasible*** means **"capable of being done or carried out."** *Random House Webster* (1998) adds **"capable of being done, effected or accomplished."** *Oxford* (1998) tells us that ***feasible*** means **"possible to do easily or conveniently,"** and describes a ***feasibility study*** as **"an assessment of the practicality of a proposed plan or method."**

For us, feasibility is a matter of deciding on four things that will govern the success of the project. We should go ahead with the project only if we know it can be made to work, we have the technical resources, there is enough time, and it really is worth spending the money.

As part of the requirements analysis, we must evaluate the feasibility of the project from all these points of view. Then we and our clients the users can make an informed decision whether or not the project is worth doing at all in its proposed form.

As we progress through the OODLC, we need to stop at the end of each phase (and sometimes after major subphases) and take a new look at the project's feasibility. These points of decision are often referred to as "go / no-go" points. You'll find a detailed discussion of the four feasibility issues in the last section of this chapter (Section 6.9).

CONTEXT DIAGRAM

This was traditionally the starting point for a process model built with data flow diagrams (DFDs). The context diagram shows our system as a single box, surrounded by smaller boxes representing external entities, as shown in Figure 6-2. The arrows from the external entities in Figure 6-2 show how each one feeds data into our system or draws information from it. ***External Entities* are people, organizations, systems, and other things outside our system that either provide data to the system or draw data from it.**

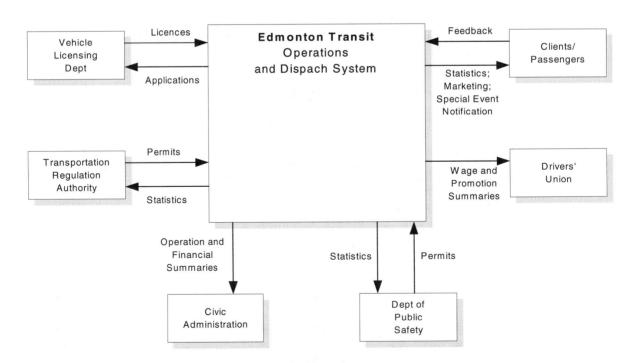

Figure 6-2   **A Context Diagram**

Use Cases

This model was developed by Ivar Jacobson[1] and his team at Objective Systems in Sweden (Jacobson et al., 1992). Jacobson calls it the "use case" approach. What it describes is a *case* of the *usage* of the system by "someone."

As you'll see in Chapter 7, the use case model documents the many ways that a user could make use of the system. A clerk could sit down at a terminal and spend the day posting entries to accounts. A corporate planner could use the system to prepare forecasts and "what-if" analyses.

That is, each ***use case*** **represents a script that "someone" could follow to make use of the system.** Each "someone" we'll call an ***actor:* a person, an organization, or another system that can initiate an instance of a use case, thus making use of one or more features of the system.**

In case you hadn't already guessed, the context diagram will be our starting point for finding the actors and the use cases. In Chapter 7, we'll look in detail at how to identify and document these.

Interface Descriptions

You'll need these for both user interfaces and interfaces to other systems. System interfaces typically will reduce to standard communication, hardware or network protocols, which will simply need to be specified by name and not described in detail. Person–machine interfaces, however, will need to involve the users extensively.

All this will be discussed in more depth in Chapter 7, *Building the Requirements Model*, along with ways to actually put it all together. Now let's take a look at the core of the analysis phase, and that's the *object model*.

The Object Model, or Class Diagram

This is often referred to (quite correctly) as the data model, or (perhaps somewhat less accurately) as the information model. As we saw in Chapter 5, the class diagram consists initially of the *entity classes*, that is, the classes found in the users' world. Then in the design phase, we add the necessary interface classes, control classes, and perhaps some abstract classes to round it out.

We may become aware of some of these extra design-phase classes during our analysis, and we may decide to include them in the model at the time we discover them during the analysis phase. This is a judgment call. My preference usually is to add such classes to the model at the time they're discovered, since they're within the users' conscious awareness at that time.

One guideline for this is to add them right away if you feel they'll add to the usefulness or clarity of the model. The alternative is to have the recording analyst make a note to go at the end of the session documentation, and add them later at design-phase time. In Chapter 9, we'll see how to go about finding the real-world classes that are important to our project.

---

[1]Ivar is Swedish, so it is *de rigeur* (i.e., *cool*) to pronounce his name correctly as "*Eevar Yah*cobson." As a matter of protocol (again, *cool*), it is simply *not done* in OO circles to anglicize his name.

The Statechart Diagram Model

In Chapter 10 we'll look at the statechart diagram as a tool for examining the life cycle of an object to discover what it does. An object moves from one stage or state to another as it lives its life cycle. We'll watch as it's created, as it goes through the steps of its various tasks, and as it's finally deleted, archived, or otherwise taken out of service.

The events that trigger these transitions from state to state, along with certain behaviors that go with each state, give us many important insights when searching to discover all the operations our objects need to be capable of.

6.3 THE OBJECT-ORIENTED DESIGN PHASE

In the object-oriented design (OOD) phase, we modify the analysis models to reflect decisions made about the environment that the system will function in. This includes hardware and software decisions, optimization issues such as response times, and so on.

There are three major factors in this process. First, the initial models produced during the analysis phase are at the logical level and will evolve progressively toward the physical level. The output deliverables from the design phase will mostly be *physical models*, that is, *plans* for how to build the system.

Second, they'll include a number of new objects and classes that don't directly model objects from the real world. You've already met one group of these, the control objects, in Chapter 5. As we'll see in the sections on abstract classes in Chapter 8, while some of these are added for machine efficiency, others are added for programming simplicity and code reuse. These last are two very important benefits from object-oriented technology (OOT), and we'll discuss them further as we go.

Thirdly, we'll decide all the other physical details, such as data types and sizes, screens and dialog boxes for handling errors and exceptions, and everything else that is needed for coding to begin. (More in Chapter 15.)

6.4 THE CONSTRUCTION PHASE

Eventually, at the construction phase, we build the databases and write the program source code. Both of these are in a sense also physical models, since they represent some part of the real world. Again, the objects and classes from the earlier models stay with us, especially if we're implementing our design in an object-oriented language or object-oriented database.

While it's not mandatory that you use an OOPL or ODBMS to build an object-oriented design, they do have many advantages over conventional programming languages. Not least among these is the smoothness of the transitions from analysis to design to construction to maintenance, which is discussed in Chapter 5 and also in Section 6.7.

Although conventional languages can be and often have been used to build object-oriented designs, in Chapter 15 you'll learn something of the difficulties involved in doing that. However, the current state of the world (as of Fall, 2000) is that many object-oriented systems are drawing some or most of their data from relational databases (see "Dealing with Legacy Systems," Chapter 15). Fortunately, the ODMG database standard has been extended to accommodate these. The standard allows for links via SQL and the Open Database Connectivity (ODBC) standard, and for Java, the JDBC.

6.5 THE OBJECT-ORIENTED TESTING PHASE

Many authors and published methodologies include testing activity in the construction phase, but I want to treat it separately here. My reason is that, in the object paradigm, we have a number of new testing techniques that were not available with earlier methods.

Also, the high levels of code reuse possible with objects means that testing must be more thorough and effective. Otherwise, reuse becomes fraught with problems. With high levels of reuse, each undetected bug has the potential of affecting a larger proportion of the system, of the company, or of its clients. In Sections 13.10 "Testing" and 15.9, "Testing and Quality Assurance," we'll look at some of these testing techniques, and at some issues around testing.

6.6 THE MAINTENANCE PHASE

To oversimplify just a little, we can say that the maintenance phase covers everything that happens after the system is "complete." When a system is built by a consultant, there is normally a definite contractual point where the purchaser signs off the project as complete, and then everything from that point on is considered to be maintenance.

Software development contracts typically have provision for so many months of maintenance as part of the contract price (a warranty period), and after that the client's in-house staff look after it, or else new contracts are negotiated. Often an ongoing maintenance contract will be on an hourly charge basis, but just as often it'll be a fixed annual or monthly charge, covering a list of services from a consultant.

Many in-house development teams have similar procedures for "completing" a system and providing maintenance. In some companies, the "client" signs for acceptance of the "completed" system, and then there may be formal procedures to request and/or charge for maintenance and enhancements. Other organizations are often less formal. For some, the process is almost totally casual and uncontrolled, but most are somewhere in the middle.

Notice that I have quotes around the references to the "completed" system. This is because systems are typically never completed to a stable and "finished" state. There are always things to do to the programs, databases, screens, and reports since the users' needs are constantly changing (as we saw in Chapter 4).

These activities can be grouped roughly as follows:
- Bug fixes

- Viruses

- Enhancements

- End-user computing

- Backups and restores

- Disaster preparedness and recovery

Object-oriented methods will have a significant impact on both bug fixes and enhancements. I discuss some of these in detail, and I include a few comments on the other activities just for completeness. Although these other activities are important, and indeed some are critical, they're not directly affected by the choice of object-oriented working. However, they're essential for a successful project.

Bug Fixes

Bug fixes are perhaps the most obvious component of maintenance. While most bugs should be caught during the testing phase, it's unavoidable that many will escape notice and need to be dealt with after the system is in production. There are a number of things about object-oriented methods that help to reduce the effort spent on debugging, both by improving the debugging process and by reducing the number of errors made in the first place.

The higher levels of encapsulation and of code reuse not only mean less code to write, but also a smaller percentage of errors in the code that does get written. Inheritance also reduces the amount of code to be written. Improved testing methods (some of which take advantage of inheritance, see Chapter 13) help find errors earlier, while they're quicker and easier (and cheaper) to correct.

Although it's quite normal to be finding, tracing, and correcting bugs during the early part of the production running, it can still be very disruptive to the users. Your users by this time are struggling with the normal everyday stress of their jobs plus a new computerized system that they don't yet fully understand. And for many, such a threatening monster can be so incomprehensible that they would still struggle even if it *was* working properly.

The programmers and analysts, on the other hand, are also under a great deal of pressure. Theoretically, the system should now be functioning smoothly, but this is never the case. Nonetheless, both user management and IT management by now expect everything to work, and all the user personnel to be fully up to speed.

What I'm trying to describe here is a situation that's often complex and difficult. Perhaps at risk of scaring you off your chosen career, I feel I must be both accurate and honest when explaining the organizational and social (people) environments you'll be working in.

Your technical skills are a given; these comments refer to the people skills and work ethic that make the difference between a good systems analyst and a great one.

The things I say in the paragraphs that follow are relevant to all of your systems development work, but I mention them here since this is one particular point in any project where these problems often flare up.

By the time a system goes into production, it's very often found to be overrated, overdue, and over budget (Brown, 1998). This sad but all too common state of affairs generates a number of problems and some short tempers. User management is under pressure from top management, and IT management is under pressure from both, to "just get it working!"

The user personnel experience pressure from their own management. The programmers and analysts get it from absolutely everybody: users, user management, top management, and their own IT management! Under these conditions, your ability to work under pressure and keep your cool will be thoroughly tested.

You also will need to work closely alongside your users through this period. With all these pressures, you may sometimes need to keep a rein on your own temper and deal with the anger, frustration, and other strong feelings that your users are likely to vent at times. You need to deal with their feelings and behavior, and your own as well, in such a way as to keep the work going forward.

Remember too that there's a fine line to tread sometimes between giving people the benefit of our technical knowledge, and telling them how they should do their job. (For some reason, they mostly seem to interpret things as being the latter.)

This requires a mature balance between assertiveness and sensitivity to the users (to "where they're at" or "where they're coming from"). And what's more, the balance is different with each user. We must, on the one hand, understand their fears of the new and unknown system. They're afraid of being "blinded by science" by us "techies," and of looking bad in front of their peers and bosses if they don't catch on quickly enough.

On the other hand, we still must get our job done. We must listen, and listen well, to their complaints, problems, and suggestions about the system. And when you do need to press your point of view, assertiveness is definitely appropriate.

All of this points to a very high need for *interpersonal skills* in a capable systems analyst. Chapter 16 has some important and effective techniques, and courses and seminars are available that you can make use of to develop your people skills and sensitivities. Meanwhile, let's take a look at another rather frustrating fact of modern life, and that's viruses.

Viruses

I mention viruses here because they may well find their way into your system. When they do, your users will simply report what is going wrong as they would for any bug, not realizing that this one is different. We need to be constantly on the alert for viruses, particularly in a production environment.

In a college lab or at home, viruses can be extremely inconvenient, even disastrous, but rarely fatal. In a business, they can cause loss of data potentially bad enough to *close down the business.*

As part of your system design, you should have in place virus protection software, reporting procedures, and procedures to scan and disinfect all floppy disks, Zip and Jaz disks, etc., that come into your shop from outside. There are many good books on how to protect yourself from viruses, such as Fites et al. (1993) and Fites (1999).

Enhancements

Another unavoidable fact of a systems analyst's life is expressed in the saying: "The users never know what they want until they see it." What this says is that no matter how good a job we do of our analysis and design, there will inevitably be things that we overlooked or that the users didn't think of. Once we turn the users loose on their new system, they can be expected to come up with all kinds of ideas for additions and improvements.

During the warranty period, these are usually handled along with the bug fixes, as long as they're reasonably small. Beyond that period, most organizations treat a major enhancement as a separate project. They may streamline the bureaucratic procedures for small ones, but the larger ones typically must go through the whole process of being justified and authorized, just as a new system would.

End-User Computing

One of the trends that began in the 1980s and has continued growing into the new millennium is that of end users creating some of their own programming. Mostly this consists of using report generator software, spreadsheets, and the like, although some users may also design screens or even do some actual programming in Visual Basic or some such language.

The report and screen generators available with today's object-oriented languages and development environments make this possible, and even easy, for any reasonably intelligent user. Indeed, it's now being done by clerks, accountants, engineers, managers, and research scientists. The advantage that they all appreciate is that they don't have to wait for us, the (overworked) developers, to do for them what they now can do for themselves.

There will be a continuing need for these people to be trained on the reporting tools. The amount of training required will depend on the number of people who wish to get involved, how involved they care to get, and how user-friendly the software is. There may be a steady trickle, or there may be a constant stream.

With a little luck, you may be able to delegate some or all of this training to a junior programmer or a particularly savvy user. I have at times had clerks on my staff who understood the reporting tools and had a bent for training, and they worked out very well. I think perhaps some of the users felt a little less threatened getting their training from such people as these, rather than technoids like us.

Backups and Restores

The primary responsibility for backups must rest with the users or the system or network administrators. However, as system designers we have a responsibility for setting the procedures in place and for training and motivating the users. (As far as backups are concerned, "motivation" consists mostly of scaring the wits out of your users with tales of real-world Murphy's law events.)[2] This will be the case for stand-alone microcomputers and some networks, where users must do their own backups.

---

[2] Murphy's law: Attributed by legend to a variety of Murphys, my favorite being "J. Edsel Murphy," though the historical Murphy who did in fact first promulgate the law, was a captain in the U.S. Air Force. This law states (as Nancy pointed out earlier) that "anything that possibly *can* go wrong, eventually *will*." Murphy (legendary, not Captain) is said to have formulated his law the day his girlfriend announced she

In many organizations, the mainframe operators or the network administrators look after backups across the network, so you'll simply coordinate with them to ensure the new system is included. The situation with restores is similar. Depending on the sophistication of the operators, network administrators, and other support personnel, you might simply need to set procedures in place and do some practice runs with them. In some other organizations, you may need to be available to do any restores and roll-forwards yourself, at least for the first few months that the system is in production.

While most organizations (although regrettably not all) *do* recognize the need for backups and give them suitable priority, unfortunately the next level of preparedness is rarely addressed adequately.

Disaster Preparedness and Recovery

Remember the World Trade Center bombing? You and I may feel it could never happen in our little town, but it could. Who could have anticipated the Oklahoma City Federal Building bombing? Does anyone really believe it would never happen again? (After I posed this question, during final editing of the first edition of this book, we had the Olympic Park bombing in Atlanta.)

My wife Nina and I were stranded for three days in the city of Baguio in the Philippines when the Richter 7.9 earthquake hit in 1990, killing 600 people. We've seen what happens when an entire city closes down, and hotels, hospitals, schools, and businesses are literally flattened. Many people in the Los Angeles area have seen something similar. There are earthquakes, fires, bombs, airplanes (one flew into the Empire State building in the 1930s), terrorists, epidemics, and computer viruses to worry about.

Numerous businesses in the World Trade Center suffered, and for many a big part of the hurt was *lost data*. Some, on the other hand, were well prepared. The *DPMA Journal* ran an article a few months later detailing how some businesses recovered quickly because they had well-thought-out disaster plans in place, while others suffered and some even died because they did not.

Disaster preparedness begins with backups and restores, but there's much more. You'll need to have plans in place for backup staffing, for finding replacement hardware and temporary premises, and so on. For large installations, some companies, who for a monthly fee, have "cold sites" and "hot sites" that are available in the event of a disaster.

---

was pregnant. There is also a corollary that says "When it *does* go wrong, it will do so at the worst possible moment." This law and its corollary are of critical relevance to two groups in particular: programmers and skydivers. And I wouldn't be at all surprised to discover someday that Murphy himself was stowed away on Apollo 13.

A *cold site* is a computer room with power and communications facilities, but you bring the hardware, either your original or a replacement hastily purchased from your supplier. A *hot site* has hardware as well, plus possibly your backup software ready to load and go. Some companies have trailers equipped with power, air conditioning, and hardware. They'll wheel into the parking lot alongside your burnt-out building, clamber down a manhole ("personhole"?) to hook up the communications, and you're back in business in a few hours.

Many manufacturers have a policy of providing hardware "next off the assembly line" to customers who have had a disaster. One insurance company in the World Trade Center reported that, with delivery of new terminals, they had 200 data-entry operators set up in three days, keying into another mainframe across the river in New Jersey. Of course, your plans must also include saving your people from the disaster, so there is someone to operate all this insurance hardware.

Even if these scenarios are beyond the realm of your current or foreseeable responsibilities, do take the time and trouble to set up what is needed to protect you and your part of the operation. Sometimes all you need is an uninterruptible power supply (UPS) to tide you over and/or to avoid data loss. It may be as simple as ensuring that one copy of your backups (including software) routinely goes off-site, preferably into fireproof storage.

It will certainly look good for your career if you're one of the few whose system or department was able to continue working after a disaster, all because of your efforts. And be sure you're properly prepared, trained, and practiced to ensure your own personal safety, so you can be around to bask in all that management approval afterward. The day *after* the bombing was not the time to go shopping for this stuff. *Do it now!* In disaster recovery planning, *procrastination can be fatal!* Literally.

Your backups must of course include software, both in-house and purchased. (It's perfectly legal to make copies of purchased software, as long as it's for backup purposes only.) You must also have backups for your people.

No one can afford to be irreplaceable. Required homework for our course on computer security is to rent and view the video of Jurassic Park and to count the number of safety and security flaws in their organization! This movie is a classic example of what happens when everything goes wrong at once and no precautions have been taken. The screenplay might well have been written by none other than J. Edsel Murphy himself.

If all is in order, your organization will have reasonable disaster-recovery plans already in place, and your new system will just be added to them. Otherwise, you and your users will need to evaluate how critical this system and its data are, and make your own independent plans for recovery, off-site storage, and so on. While the initial work will have been done in analysis and design, the plans need to be tried out (to the fullest extent that they can be) shortly after entering the maintenance phase.

You may also wish to check the *comp.risks* newsgroup for ideas.

Now that we've examined the various phases of the OODLC, there are some comments I wish to make about what happens as we move from one phase to the next.

6.7 CONSISTENT NOTATION THROUGHOUT THE OODLC

With the earlier development methodologies, there was always a problem moving from one phase to the next. Somewhat simplified, it went like this:

The requirements definition was typically a rather large textual document.

The analysis model, on the other hand, was developed in a totally different paradigm – that of data modeling with entity-relationship diagrams (ERDs), allied with process modeling using data flow diagrams (DFDs). Many of the design models were just physical versions of the ERDs and DFDs, which wasn't too bad.

But from design to construction and the actual programming, we had another major shift in language and notation. Old-style procedural programs are typically designed with flowcharts or top-down structure charts, neither of which bears much relationship to an ERD or DFD from the analysis and design phases.

One of the most useful and productive things about ERDs was that they did provide a direct path from the real-world data to the database structure and design. Unfortunately, DFDs were unable to do the same for the transition from process model to program module.

Seamless Transitions

The whole idea of these seamless transitions can perhaps best be grasped by considering a parallel situation with word processors. Any of you who have ever tried to pass a document between two unrelated word processors will have found that it rarely works smoothly. In any such conversion from one format to another, even if they're *supposed* to read each other's files, there's invariably some loss of data.

The same applies when we pass our system design from phase to phase of the system development life cycle (SDLC). (Yes, here I'm talking about the old one, the SDLC.) When each phase has its own language and notation, something is always lost or changed in the transition. Some of these losses can be fairly obvious, but many can be very subtle.

When the users and the analysts don't completely understand one another, then it follows that their decisions must be less than optimal. Any little block or impediment to communication during software development will cause unpredictable difficulties. Most will be minor, but a few may be very significant (read *time-consuming* and *expensive*).

One of the many blessings the object paradigm has brought us is a consistent notation for all phases of the OODLC, leading to smoother transitions and reduced information loss between phases. The enhanced communication brought about by object-oriented models definitely leads to better, cheaper, more accurate, and more effective systems, yet it's sometimes almost impossible to measure or quantify. It comes under the heading of *intangible benefits*.

6.8 TRACEABILITY

One other effect of staying in the object-oriented paradigm as we progress from phase to phase of the life cycle is to make it simpler and more reliable to move back and forth among the various models. *Traceability* is critically important since any system can expect to be modified a number of times over its lifetime. During development, we must have straightforward rules and procedures for transforming the analysis model to the design model to the source code.

Then in maintenance, if we're contemplating a change to our system, the idea for the change may originate in any of the models. Most times, the users will want a change, so it'll be discussed and decided using the analysis model.

But then we'll need to follow the effects of that change from the analysis models to the design models and finally into the program code. At each stage, we'll need to check what effects our proposed change will have on other parts of the system. Will a relatively simple-looking change turn out to cause extensive and costly changes throughout the system? Have we overlooked any details that will cause problems with the proposed change?

This process is far easier and less error-prone when we can trace things. We need to follow an analysis object or class, and its attributes and operations, to the matching object or class in the design models, and then into the program code.

In the object paradigm, we keep the same classes, attributes, and operations all the way through the object-oriented development life cycle (OODLC) and add new classes as we go. Even for the new ones added at the design stage, it's relatively easy to figure out where they came from. This level of traceability is simply not available in other systems analysis and design paradigms, although the level did increase as we progressed through the different methods over the years.

By way of illustration, Table 6-2 shows various analysis constructs mapped into their roughly equivalent C++ and Java structures.

Table 6-2   Traceability Table for C++ and Java
Adapted and extended from Jacobson et al., 1992

Analysis Model	C++ Source Code	Java Source Code
Analysis Class	One or more classes	One or more classes
Analysis Instance	Instance	Instance
Behavior in the object	Member function	Method
Attribute (Class)	Static variable	Static variable
Attribute (Instance)	Instance variable	Instance variable
Association	Reference to a (member) function	Reference to a (member) function
Interaction among objects	Call to a (member) function	Call to a (member) function
Use Case	A sequence of calls	A sequence of calls

6.9 FEASIBILITY ANALYSIS

Earlier in this chapter, in Section 6.2, we introduced the four issues that must be considered when deciding whether the project should be done, or whether the whole idea should be scrapped:

(a) Operational feasibility: Will the proposed system do the job being asked for and will it work in this company? (It may well have worked somewhere else, but will it work here?)

(b) Technical feasibility: Do we have the hardware, software and technical knowhow to do it?

(c) Schedule feasibility: Can it be done in the time allowed?

(d) Economic feasibility: Will it pay for itself?

Now let's explore each of these in detail. Remember, however, that not all of these questions can be answered satisfactorily at this point in the project. Feasibility is something that must be revisited after each phase of the project, and each time you'll improve your answers.

Then you must decide at each of these checks whether the project is still on track to a successful completion and should continue. If not, it may have to be reduced in scope, split into smaller projects, or perhaps scrapped altogether. One of the major rules in this business is never to throw good money after bad, unless you're absolutely certain (*with proof!*) that you can make it work.

Operational Feasibility

The first thing we need to check is that if we build the system, will it actually work in practice? We must answer these three questions:

(a) Will the proposed system do the job being asked for?

(b) Will it work in this company?

(c) Is it worth the effort to find a solution?

WILL THE PROPOSED SYSTEM DO THE JOB BEING ASKED FOR?

You'll find the first part of the answer to this one in the rest of the requirements analysis. Your concern there is to find out accurately what it is that the users need the system to do. Here we're more concerned with seeing whether it can be done properly, that is, will the system operate *in the way the users are going to need it*?

Here is a list of some of the things we'll need to check out:

(1) **Throughput and response time** I've seen a system where the update response time was initially acceptable – about 3 to 5 seconds. But as the database filled up over the months, it grew to minutes instead of seconds. Eventually it got to where the operators would key in a set of screens, press "Enter," and do something else for 15 minutes.

To avoid this kind of thing, you must have realistic estimates of the *capacity* of both the hardware and software parts of your system. Database tuning and a skilled DBA can be critical in meeting response time targets. So can **_stress-testing,_ testing with a realistically full database and authentic transaction loads.**

Acceptable response times will vary, but usually will be something like "1 sec, 80%" meaning that the user will get a response within one second on 80% of their mouse clicks or Enter key presses. Users may think this is overkill, but just put them in front of a slow PC for an hour or two, especially if they're working under pressure!

(2) **Quality data**. Will your system gather and store data, and produce reports and other information, that are:

- °   *Timely*   Neither late nor stale (out of date)
- °   *Pertinent*   Relevant – in other words, the *right* data, that the users will need to do their jobs
- °   *Accurate*
- °   *Usefully formatted*

(3) **Adequate security and controls** Your system must have enough checks and procedures to make sure it can keep on operating, and doing the job the users need of it. First, can it be protected against deliberate acts by employees and others:

- °   Fraud
- °   Embezzlement
- °   Hostile attacks:
  - - Hackers and vandals
  - - Competitors and industrial spies
  - - Real spies, if you happen to be in government or military
  - - Terrorists

Then your systems need to survive when things do go wrong, either deliberately or accidentally, as we discussed earlier in this chapter:

- °   Backup and recovery
- °   Disaster preparedness

(4) **Efficiency** Will your system make the best use of the people and other resources the users will have to expend in order to use it? Do the procedures (people procedures – the ones in the User Manual) minimize wasted time? Does the flow of paper forms, and other such functions, proceed smoothly, without undue waiting and delays?

(5) **Resilience to change** Your system must be flexible, so it can be expanded, fixed, or enhanced as the months and years go by, with as little hassle as possible. This is mostly a matter of good analysis and design using a suitable OO methodology, along with well-structured (and commented) code.

WILL IT WORK IN THIS COMPANY?

Political Acceptability

Here we're venturing into the world of corporate politics. The project needs to be supported by all the levels of managers. If senior management is forcing the project onto the lower levels, or the local user managers are forcing it on their staff, this could cause difficulties. This is the kind of thing that breeds "passive sabotage," which we discuss in the next chapter.

You also need to be aware of how the end-users *feel* about your new system. I mean the shop-floor people and sales and office workers who will use it, as well as their supervisors and any others.

In the 1960s my company had just computerized our auto parts inventory and invoicing. We were having a terrible time keeping the stock quantities in the computer in line with the quantities on the warehouse shelves. We gained considerable insight into the problem when one of the parts managers reported seeing a counter person make a sale, and do the form without bothering to fill in the boxes that were for the computer.

When the manager pointed out the error to the salesperson, the response was, "Oh, we don't have time to worry about that toy down there! We've got work to do!"

Now, this happened back at a time when no-one understood computers, except us weirdo programmers. This person had never seen one, and had no idea what it was there for, just that it *made more work for him*. It is important that the users, especially those more junior, should be aware of how the new system will benefit *them*, make *their* work easier, and make *them* look good. After all, the new system will be a big change for many of them.

Management of Change

Another part of this is that everyone is afraid of change, so it's important to look at how well the users are likely to handle the changeover to the new system, and what is being done to help them with that. You and the user management will need to look carefully at what changes are going to happen in the world of the ordinary user. You'll then need to assess how well you think the people will adjust to these changes.

Part of the implementation phase will involve training for the users. Older users and those not familiar with computers can be expected to have some difficulties. They will need orientation to the new system, as well as training. To allay their fears, *all* the users will need a steady flow of information to sell the project to them, throughout the development.

Change management is a whole area of study on its own. When the time comes, it may well be worth your while to do some reading or try and find courses in this area. There are times when it can make or break a project. Try Barbara Bouldin's (1989) little book, *Agents of Change*.

Scaleability

I know of a registration system that was purchased by a Canadian college on the recommendation of a U.S. college who were very satisfied with it. And then they wondered why they were spending vast amounts of time and money on maintenance and enhancements – including a permanent full-time person – but still never satisfying the users. This went on for years throughout the entire life of the software.

The problem was that the US college had about 3000 day students, and perhaps 4000 part-time. The other college had some 12,000 day and 40,000 part-time students! This poor little information system just could not keep up.

WordPerfect, with which I write this, is a marvelous product. It's just great for a one-page memo, or a 40-page report. But I wrote the first edition of this text, 700 pages, on a 486 computer with WP5.1 – and a 'control-end' command took *two minutes* to get me to the bottom of the document! Initially, I set the autosave feature to save every five minutes – but once the saves began to take three minutes, I had to change that!

Much of the problem was in the sequencing of the steps within the operation. Had WP been designed so that it gave me access to the screen while the operation completed in the background, half the problem would have been solved. MS Word, of course, had its own problems, and was similarly unsuited to such large documents.

What these stories demonstrate is that software (or hardware, or a manual process) that works well in one environment can often fall flat on it face when asked to handle vastly higher volumes of work. With a little care and forethought, it is possible to design *scaleability* into your work. It's very important to think about these issues when designing and coding objects, since they might be reused in projects that you can't even dream of. Wherever reasonably possible we must build *scaleable* objects.

IS IT WORTH THE EFFORT TO FIND A SOLUTION?

Are we confident we can really do this? Will the users actually use it? Or just ignore it? Will it have a positive impact on the working lives of the users? Will it improve working conditions and make them better at their jobs? Will it increase company revenue and/or cut costs? (These last two are discussed under "Economic Feasibility" below)

We'd better have some good answers to all these, otherwise it just doesn't make sense for the company to spend all this money on a new system, even if they're dying to have a flashy-looking computerized operation.

Technical Feasibility

DO WE HAVE THE HARDWARE, SOFTWARE, AND TECHNICAL KNOW-HOW?

If we don't, can we get it? Let's see

Hardware and Software

- **Capacity.** Do we have hardware and software capacity? Inadequate capacity will cause all kinds of problems. We already talked about throughput and response times above.

- **Availability.** Can we get what we don't have? Can we get enough, and can we get it in time? These questions have to be answered early in the project. We need enough lead time for the hardware and software to be acquired, so we don't have project personnel twiddling their thumbs waiting.

  To do this, you'll have to deal with the company politics (as we discussed above) and questions of economics (see below), but watch out for under-budgeting. There's always a fine line to walk between keeping the cost down, and ordering enough capacity to get the job done properly.

Technical Knowledge

- **Training.** Well, you may say, we can always send a few people to courses. And yes, you must do that. But there's a caveat here. For some things, like programming languages for instance, you can send an experienced person to a course, and they'll be productive in the new language soon after, and doing it well.

But other areas, such as OOA, have a longer learning curve after the initial training. For things like that, you need to gain experience working alongside an expert, *after* you take the course. The newly-trained person or the recent college graduate is not always ready to dive in and function at an expert level. (See Chapters 15 and 16.)

- **Consultants.** In Chapter 15 you'll see how consultants and others should be used as *mentors*. (In our context, a *mentor* **is a person with knowledge and experience, who is both willing and able to assist, advise, and nurture those who are beginning their work in this area.**) This is a most important part of the after-course apprenticeship, so that you can become a true expert. This leads to a process of knowledge transfer, where the skills of each individual can be shared around the group.

Schedule Feasibility

CAN IT BE DONE IN THE TIME ALLOWED?

Estimating for IT projects is not usually done well. As I pointed out in my Y2k book (Brown, 1998), the percentages in our industry are *bad*. Fully a quarter of all large software projects get canceled before completion. Another 50% come in late – typically a year late and 100% over budget. I kid you not! That leaves a miserable 25% that finish on time and on or under budget. Almost none finish early, and only a very few are actually under budget. (Yourdon, 1997, Jones, 1996).

So there's much to watch out for, and much to be learned, in the matter of timing a software project. Here are one or two points to watch for:

- Which deadlines are mandatory and which are desired?
- Late penalties

  ° What will happen if your project is late? You must check into all the consequences and ramifications of lateness, and of varying degrees of lateness

  ° Do you have penalty clauses in your contracts with consultants and vendors in case they're late?

It may well be better to deliver a system that works properly but is late, than one that is buggy, inadequate, and right on time.

Economic Feasibility

WILL IT PAY FOR ITSELF?

This is referred to as the ***cost-benefit analysis***, **since it must determine whether the lifetime benefits from building the system outweigh the lifetime costs of the system.**

But note that operational and economic issues often conflict. The "best" system may also be the most expensive, and thus it may not be possible to justify it on economic grounds.

The benefits are usually in some form of cost savings, or increase in profits. A few more forward-thinking companies have adopted the rule that unless a software system will actually increase sales by a measurable amount, it doesn't get built. They can then channel all that money into something else that will improve the profit picture, and that may be something other than a software project.

So you see that IT must compete with all the other departments in the company for scarce resources (read: for *money!*) Every department has projects and ideas that they figure will increase sales and/or reduce costs. So in the real world of business we must always be in a position where we can justify our projects to the managers who run the company.

Opportunity Cost

Let's say you've estimated that your $500,000 software project will save the company $60,000 a year. But the sales department figures it could spend the same amount of money to build a new showroom. They have estimated that this would increase profits by $20,000 a year.

Obviously, in this case *your* project will get the go-ahead from senior management. But wait a minute, says the Sales Manager. If we *don't* build the new showroom, we're missing out on that $20,000! And he's right. This is what we call an ***opportunity cost,*** **the unrealized benefit from a project that is denied, when choosing to invest in one project over another.**

While in this case your project would still get the go-ahead, you will only be saving the company a net amount of $40,000, so just don't go getting too cocky about it!

The Bottom Line

The bottom line is that the dollar value of the annual benefits (AB) from the system over the expected years of life of the system (L) must exceed the total of development costs (D) plus the annual operating costs (AOC) over the expected lifetime.

That is,

$$L * AB >= D + L * AOC$$

Where:

AB	is the annual benefits from the system
L	is the expected life of the system in years
D	is the total development costs
AOC	is the annual operating costs over the expected lifetime.

The annual benefits to the company from having the system in place will fall into two groups, which I'll explain for you below:

- Tangible benefits (TB)

- Intangible benefits (IB)

So since

$$AB = TB + IB$$

our little formula now looks about like this:

$$L * (TB + IB) >= D + L * AC$$

Otherwise we don't build it. It's as simple as that.

However, in the harsh world of reality out there, the user management may sometimes insist on building the project anyway. They may have other reasons for wanting the project, reasons that you and I may not entirely approve of. These may range from prestige, to a hidden agenda of a senior manager, political reasons (internal or external politics), empire building, and so on.

DEVELOPMENT COSTS

Some of these items cover more than just our project. Things like building expenses and office overheads are often shared with other parts of the company, so they must be prorated where necessary. Here's the basic list:

Wages and Other Personnel-related Costs

- Programmers/analysts/developers/testers
- DBAs and other specialist computer functions
- User personnel and managers, for the time that they devote to the project
- Project support staff:
  - ° Computer operators and system administrators
  - ° Secretaries, janitors, security
  - ° Help-desk staff
  - ° Trainers

Computer hardware resources

Have already/buy/lease/otherwise acquire:

- Mainframe
- Workstations
- Servers
  - Application
  - Database
  - Web
- Network
- Data communications

Computer Software Resources

Have already/buy/lease/otherwise acquire:

- Programming languages
- Development environments
- Configuration anagement/version management software
- CASE software
- Database software
    - ◦ DBA tools
    - ◦ Remote access/Internet access DBA software
- Network and communications software
- Internet access/remote access software for users

Training

- Developers
    - ◦ OOA&D
    - ◦ Languages
    - ◦ Development environments
    - ◦ Databases
    - ◦ CASE/repository
- Users
- More in Chapter 15

Office support costs

- Office equipment (desks, copiers)
- Supplies (paper, pencils)
- Phones

OPERATIONAL COSTS

Fixed:

- Leases and licences
- Salaries
    - ◦ Operators
    - ◦ Support – office, custodial, security
- Rent or other accommodation and building costs; offsite backup storage

Variable:

- Supplies (discs, tapes, preprinted forms, drums/toner, paper)
- Any computer and data communications costs that vary with the workload
- Prorated overheads (utilities, building rental, maintenance, telephone, etc.)

TANGIBLE BENEFITS

These can easily be quantified, so they're easy for users and developers to understand and believe in. Once you go through the exercise and put numbers on them, the users can be convinced that these will be real gains or savings.

- Saves time (and therefore wages) for users.

- Eliminates double work, such as keying in the same data twice. (In some companies you can find data being entered seven or eight times or more.)

- Eliminates manual filing.

- Improves response times.

- Reduces expenses.

- Improves credit checks on customers.

- Cuts bad debt losses.

- Reduces vehicle mileage through improved scheduling.

- Decreases customer waiting time.

- Gets more customers through per day.

- Sales or professional staff spend less time on record-keeping, more time on profitable work.

INTANGIBLE BENEFITS

These are not at all easy to quantify. There are estimating techniques that will allow you to place dollar values on them, and those are well worth while. You should find some in a book or course on cost accounting and estimating techniques.

- Customer goodwill

- Customer service

- Employee morale, commitment

- "Better" data

- Better decision-making

- Better corporate citizen

It really is difficult to say just how much money we'll make if the employees "feel better about their jobs and about themselves." Yet such things do have a significant effect on the financial picture. And it really is true that "Our people are our biggest asset."

Increased goodwill through improved customer service is similarly nebulous.

And what exactly is "better data," and "better decision-making?" Well, data that's more accurate, up to date, complete, better presented, and so on, leads to decisions that make the company run better, and in the end make more money.

So these things *do* have a value in dollars, it's just that it's terribly difficult to measure or estimate. But nevertheless the gains are real, and often significant. Your challenge is to get the managers and accountants to believe you!

The tool you convince them with is the *feasibility analysis* or *feasibility study*, along with the other deliverables for this phase.

. . . .

DELIVERABLES

The **requirements model** will be produced in its five component parts:

- The project scope says in general terms what the system will do, what functions will be part of it, which users it will service, and what will *not* be part of the system. It will be a paragraph or two in extent for many installations, and can be bigger for others. If your company or your clients have their own ideas about how big this document should be, do it their way!

- The feasibility analysis, to support the decision of whether we should go ahead with the project. This document will address the four feasibility issues, that is:
    - Operational feasibility
    - Technical feasibility
    - Schedule feasibility
    - Economic feasibility

    Expect this one to be quite a few pages even for a small system, and a whole volume if we're dealing with a team on a million-dollar project. Again, be guided by your boss or client's ideas, if any, on how detailed this should be. Otherwise, without going overboard, it's better to give a little too much on this one, rather than not enough detail. Especially on the economic issues.

- The **context diagram** will be a graphic showing our system as a single box, surrounded by smaller boxes representing external entities. There may be a page or two of supporting explanatory text.

- The **use case model** will describe *cases of the usage* of the system by the various Actors, as a detailed list of steps followed by each *Actor*.

- The **interface descriptions** for user interfaces and interfaces to other systems typically will reduce to GUIs or to standard communication, hardware, or network protocols. These may be specified by name and need not be described in detail. Person machine interfaces (GUIs) will need to be documented to whatever level of detail you may have taken them by this stage.

The **object model** will be documented in some detail. It will consist of

- The class diagram.
- The class definitions.
- Attribute lists and definitions.
- Notes and business rules.

Statechart Diagrams are dealt with in Chapter 10.

FURTHER READING

The requirements model is discussed by Jacobson et al. (1992) on page 132, although you may find the language somewhat quaint. The rest of his chapter outlines the remainder of the OODLC, in a slightly different sequence from what you've seen in this chapter. In his following chapter, from page 148, Jacobson gives a detailed description of requirements and analysis models and his ideas on how to go about building them.

He also has several relevant sections in "The Unified Software Development Process," (Jacobson, et al., 1999) which is his explanation of the composite methodology that has been produced by The Three Amigos.

Rumbaugh (1991) spends his page 146 discussing some of the impacts of object-oriented working on the development life cycle, and Wirfs-Brock (1990) compares her view of the OODLC and the SDLC on page 8.

Finally, Whitten and Bentley (1999) have an excellent, detailed description of the old SDLC. This is worth reading for the detail and thoroughness of their approach, even though they say very little about the object paradigm.

CHAPTER SUMMARY

- The object-oriented development life cycle consists of OOA, OOD, OOP, object-oriented testing, and maintenance. The maintenance phase is made up of all the previous activities.

- In the various books and methodologies available, you'll find considerable variation in the detailed structure of the OODLC. All involve repeated iteration through the cycle.

- In analysis we model the users' requirements for *what* the system must do. In the object-oriented version of the life cycle, the output of this process is a conceptual-level analysis model, consisting of these deliverables: the requirements model, the feasibility analysis, the object model, the statechart model.

- The systems request document, in whatever form it may be, is the user's perception of the problem and needs to be further specified from the information point of view.

- The requirements model should be part of the formal agreement between the users and the developers, since it is fully understood by the users, and yet it spells out the requirements the way developers need them.

- The requirements model consists of four closely related parts:

  - The *project scope* says in general terms what the system will do, what functions will be part of it, and which users it will service. It will also state what will *not* be part of the system.

  - The *context diagram* shows our system as a single box, surrounded by smaller boxes representing external entities, which are people, organizations, systems, and other things outside our system that either provide data to the system or draw data from it.

- Jacobson's *use case model* describes a *case of the usage* of the system by an *actor*. Each *use case* represents a script that an actor could follow to make use of the system.

  - There will be *interface descriptions* for user interfaces and interfaces to other systems.

- An *actor* is a person, organization, or another system that can initiate an instance of a Use Case, thus making use of one or more features of the system.

- *System interfaces* typically will reduce to communication, hardware, or network protocols, which will simply need to be specified by name and not described in detail. *Person–machine* interface design will need to involve the users extensively.

- The *object model*, or *class diagram*, is sometimes referred to as the data model or the information model. It consists of the *entity classes* – the classes found in the users' real world. Then in the design phase, we add the necessary interface classes and control classes.

- The *statechart diagram* is for examining the life cycle of an object to discover what it does. An object is created, goes through the steps of its various tasks, and is finally deleted or otherwise taken out of service. It moves from one *state* to another as it lives its life cycle.

- The events that trigger transitions from state to state, along with certain behavior that goes with each state and transition, help us to discover all the operations of a class.

- In the design phase, we modify the analysis models to reflect decisions made about the environment that the system will function in. This includes hardware and software decisions, optimization issues such as response times, and so on.

- The initial design models are at the *logical* level and evolve to the *physical* level.

- The design models include a number of new classes that don't directly model anything from the real world, such as control objects. Some of these are added for machine efficiency, others for programming simplicity and code reuse. These last are two very important benefits from object-oriented technology.

- In the construction phase, we build the databases and screens, and write the program code. The classes from earlier models stick around, and are traceable all the way to the OOPL or ODBMS.

- While it's not mandatory to use an OOPL or ODBMS to build an object-oriented design, they do have many advantages over conventional programming languages, not the least of which is the smoothness of the transitions from analysis to design to construction to maintenance.

- Most authors and methodologists include testing in the construction phase, but we treat it separately because the object paradigm has new testing techniques that were not available with earlier methods.

- The output of the testing phase is a "complete," functioning, tested system.

- The maintenance phase covers everything that happens after the system is "complete." There should be a definite contractual point where the user signs off the project as complete, and then everything from then on is considered to be maintenance.

- Software development contracts typically provide for so many months of maintenance as part of the contract price (a warranty period), and after that the client's in-house staff look after it. Often there'll be a continuing maintenance contract will be on an hourly charge basis, but just as often it will be a fixed annual or monthly charge.

- I say a "completed" system because systems are typically never completed to a stable and "finished" state. There are always things to do to the programs, databases, screens, and reports since the users' needs are constantly changing.

- In maintenance we're concerned with:
  - Bug fixes
  - Viruses
  - Enhancements
  - End-user computing
  - Backups and restores
  - Disaster preparedness and recovery

- One of the greatest but most subtle benefits of object orientation is a consistent notation throughout the OODLC, giving smoother transitions between phases, minimizing lost or reworked information.

- *Traceability* is also greatly improved and critically important since any system can expect to be modified a number of times over its lifetime.

- The *feasibility study* must look at the four criteria to decide whether we should go ahead and do (or finish) the project:

  - **Operational Feasibility:** The first thing we need to check is that if we build the system, will it actually work in practice? We must answer these three questions:
    - Will the proposed system do the job being asked for?
    - Will it work in this company?
    - Is it worth the effort to find a solution?

  - **Technical feasibility:** Do we have the hardware, the software and the technical know-how to do it?
  - **Schedule feasibility:** Can it be done in the time allowed?
  - **Economic feasibility:** Will it pay for itself?

- *Economic feasibility* is referred to as the *cost–benefit analysis*, since it must determine whether the lifetime benefits from building the system outweigh the lifetime costs of the system.

The bottom line is that the dollar value of the annual benefits from the system (AB = TB + IB) over the expected years of life of the system (L) must exceed the total of development costs (D) plus the annual operating costs (AOC) over the expected lifetime.

$$L * (TB + IB) \geq D + L * AOC$$

- *Tangible benefits* (TB) can easily be quantified.
- *Intangible benefits* (IB) are nebulous and not at all easy to quantify.

Note that AB = TB + IB

CHAPTER GLOSSARY

actor   A person, an organization, or another system that can initiate an instance of a Use Case, thus making use of one or more features of the system.

cost–benefit analysis   Determines whether the lifetime benefits from building the system outweigh the lifetime costs of the system.

external entities People, organizations, systems, and other things outside our system that either provide data to the system or draw data from it.

feasible   (1) "Capable of being done or carried out" (*Gage*, 1983). (2) "Capable of being dealt with successfully" (*Webster*, 1975). (3) "Capable of being done, effected or accomplished" (*Random House Webster*, 1998). (4) "Possible to do easily or conveniently" (*Oxford* 1998)

feasibility study   "An assessment of the practicality of a proposed plan or method." (*Oxford* 1998)

mentorA person with knowledge and experience, who is both willing and able to assist, advise, and nurture those who are beginning their work in the area.

opportunity cost The unrealized benefit from a project that is denied, when choosing one project over another.

requirements model The document that describes the users' needs in full detail in a way that is both understandable for the users and usable by the developers as a starting point to develop a system.

stress-testing   Testing with a realistically full database and authentic transaction loads.

use case A script that an actor could follow to make use of the system.

WHAT COMES NEXT

Now that we've examined the OODLC, it's time to start on the various steps and phases and learn in detail how to do each one. In Chapter 7, you'll learn to build a requirements model, in its several parts. Then in Chapter 8, there's some more theory about objects and classes and the structures that they can form. In Chapter 9, you'll discover how to approach the task of finding objects and classes in the real world of the users.

CLASS/GROUP EXERCISES AND PROBLEMS

Ex 6.1 Each group invents a fictitious client company and thinks up a different business problem or project for their client. Develop a system request document that might have come from the users. Do it in two forms:

- Once as you imagine it might come from the very worst possible users, full of holes and inadequacies.

- Then redo it in the perfect form that you would like it to come from the very best possible users.

  File these documents for use in Exercise 7.1 and beyond.

Ex 6.2 Members of the class provide instances from their past, or from friends, or from their reading, of cases where failures occurred and backups were needed (whether the backups existed or not). List all these events on the board, one line each. Then, depending on how many there are, select some or all for full explanation.

  Have the person(s) involved tell the story of each one. What went wrong to cause a problem? Were backups available? Was it a disaster? Was there a full disaster plan in place? What planning was done well? What was not? What additional planning was done afterward, or should be done in future? What other lessons are to be learned?

Ex 6.3 Have the class or group come up with two or three incidents from the past where a change in notation, language, file format, or software caused a partial or total breakdown in communication. If possible, relate it to a situation in systems development, but otherwise it's worth discussing any communication problem that resulted from a discontinuity of this nature.

  How could the discontinuity have been removed? Or at least how could the disruption have been minimized? Can you relate any of these incidents to the transitions between phases of the OODLC?

INDIVIDUAL EXERCISES AND PROBLEMS

Ex 6.4 For each class diagram you drew in Exercise 5.4, prepare a context diagram with all the external entities you can think of that might be appropriate. Compare your answer with others, or have all members of the group or class present their answers. Take particular note of additional external entities that the other students thought of.

PROJECTS AND CASES

P 6.1 Each group interviews one or more systems development practitioners to discover the format of the development life cycle that they're using. Be warned that they may not be consciously following a formal life cycle, so you may have to infer it from a general description of how they go about analyzing and developing systems.

Compare and contrast these life cycles with the SDLC and OODLC described in this chapter. Document your opinions and conclusions and present your results to the class. Add to your documentation the opinions expressed by the class.

SELF-TEST QUESTIONS

Note: The Appendix has answers to the Self-Test Questions.

Q 6.1 External entities are

(a) People

(b) Organizations

(c) Systems

(d) All of the above

(e) None of the above

Q 6.2 A requirements model includes a

(a) Project scope

(b) Statechart diagram

(c) Context diagram

(d) (a) and (b)

(e) (b) and (c)

(f) (a) and (c)

Q 6.3 Object-Oriented design moves us from the

(a) Physical model to the logical model

(b) Functional model to the physical model

c) Logical model to the physical model

(d) Logical model to the functional model

(e) Physical model to the functional model

Q 6.4 What do we call things outside our system that either provide data to the system or draw data from it?

Q 6.5 A use case represents a _____ that "someone" could follow to _____ the system.

Q 6.6 An actor is a person, an organization, or another system that can _____ a use case, thus making use of one or more _____ of the system.

Q 6.7 List all the phases and activities of the OODLC.

Q 6.8 List the components of the requirements model.

Q 6.9 List all the models produced in the analysis phase.

Q 6.10 In the object-oriented _____ (_____) phase, we modify the _____ models to reflect decisions made about the environment that the system will function in.

Q 6.11 The object paradigm has a consistent _____ for all phases of the OODLC, leading to _____ transitions and reduced _____ loss between phases.

Q 6.12 Match these definitions. Note that some will match more than once, and some are meaningless:

(a) Operational feasibility: (i)   Will it pay for itself?

(b) Management feasibility: (ii)   Can it be done in the time allowed?

(c) Schedule feasibility: (iii)   Will it do the job being asked for ?

(d) Economic feasibility: (iv)   Do we have the hardware and software?

(e) Technical feasibility   (v)   Will it work in this company?

(f) Organizational feasibility   (vi)   Have we the knowledge we need?

Q 6.13 Operational and _____ issues often conflict. The "_____" system may also be the most _____, and thus it may not be possible to justify it on _____ grounds.

Q 6.14 Opportunity _____ is the _____ benefit from a project that is _____, when choosing to _____ in one project over another.

Q 6.15 The object-oriented development life cycle consists of _____ , OOD, _____ , object-oriented testing, and _____ . The _____ phase is made up of all the previous activities.

Q 6.16 All methodologies involve repeated _____ through the cycle.

Q 6.17 In analysis we model the users' requirements for _____ the system must do. A conceptual _____ model, consists of these _____ : the requirements model, the _____ analysis, the object model, the _____ diagram model.

Q 6.18 The requirements model consists of four closely related _____ :

- The project _____ says in general terms what the system will _____ , what _____ will be part of it, and which users it will _____ . It will also state what _____ _____ be part of the system.

- The _____ diagram shows our system as a single box, surrounded by smaller boxes representing _____ _____ , which are people, _____ , _____ , and other things _____ our system that either _____ data to the system or _____ _____ from it.

- Jacobson's _____ _____ model describes a case of the usage of the system by an _____ . Each _____ _____ represents a _____ that an _____ could follow to make use of the system.

- There will be _____ _____ for user interfaces and interfaces to other _____ .

Q 6.19 An _____ is a person, organization, or another system that can _____ an instance of a _____ _____ , thus making _____ of one or more features of the system.

Q 6.20 The object model, or _____ diagram, is sometimes referred to as the _____ _____ or the _____ _____ . It consists of the _____ classes – i.e., the classes found in the users' _____ _____ .

Q 6.21 The statechart diagram is for examining the _____ _____ of an object to discover what it _____ . An object is _____ , goes through the steps of its various _____ , and is finally _____ . It moves from one _____ to another as it lives its _____ _____ .

Q 6.22 The _____ that trigger _____ from _____ to _____ , along with certain behavior that goes with each state and transition, help us to discover all the operations of a class.

Q 6.23 In the design phase, we modify the _____ models to reflect _____ made about the _____ that the system will function in. This includes _____ and _____ decisions, optimization issues such as _____ _____ , and so on.

Q 6.24 The _____ models include a number of new _____ that don't directly _____ anything from the real world, such as _____ _____ . Some of these are added for _____ efficiency, others for programming _____ and _____ _____ .

Q 6.25 In the construction phase, we build the _____ and screens, and write the _____ _____ . The _____ from _____ models stick around, and are _____ all the way to the _____ or ODBMS.

Q 6.26 The feasibility study must look at the four _____ to decide whether we should _____ _____ and do (or _____) the project:

Q 6.27 _____ feasibility: The first thing we need to check is that if we build the system, will it actually _____ _____ _____ ? We must answer these three questions:

- Will it do the _____ being asked for?

- Will it _____ in this _____ ?

- Is it _____ the effort to find a _____ ?

Q 6.28 Technical _____ : Do we have the _____ , the software and the _____ _____ - _____ to do it?

Q 6.29 _____ _____ : Can it be done in the _____ allowed?

Q 6.30 _____ _____ : Will it pay for itself?

Q 6.31 _____ feasibility is referred to as the cost– _____ analysis, since it must determine whether the _____ _____ from building the system outweigh the _____ _____ of the system.

Q 6.32 The _____ is that the dollar value of the _____ from the system (AB = TB + IB) over the _____ years of _____ of the system (L) must exceed the total of _____ _____ (D) plus the annual _____ _____ (AOC) over the expected _____ .

$$L * (TB + IB) >= D + L * AOC$$

Q 6.33 _____ benefits (TB) can easily be _____ .

Q 6.34 _____ benefits (IB) are nebulous and not at all easy to _____ .
Note that AB = TB + IB

Chapter Seven

Building the Requirements Model

WHAT YOU WILL LEARN IN THIS CHAPTER

In this chapter, you'll learn about a number of important considerations in setting up for the Analysis Phase of a systems development project. You'll also learn about the four models that make up the requirements model and how to work with the users to build them. You can feel confident that you understand how to build the requirements model when you can:

- Given a checklist of the eight factors to consider in preparing for FTS/JAD sessions for analysis, as discussed in the first part of the chapter, explain each consideration, its importance, and how it should be handled

- Explain the importance of the project scope and state the four points that need to be included in it.

- Describe the context diagram, define *external entity*, and produce a context diagram for a small project.

- Define *actor* and develop a few of the use cases for a small project.

- Describe the factors involved in the development of interface descriptions.

WHAT YOU SHOULD KNOW TO START THIS CHAPTER

For this chapter you won't need the depth of object-oriented understanding that's required for the later ones. You'll need to know the basic concepts of objects. You'll need to be familiar with the systems development life cycle (SDLC), or its later variant, the object-oriented development life cycle (OODLC). It's important that you know where the requirements model fits in the scheme of things before you try to build one.

CHAPTER OVERVIEW

In this chapter, we'll discuss how to go about the first part of the analysis phase, the requirements model, beginning with the preparations that need to take place before we start. We'll look at who should be present and other aspects of setting up the meetings. We'll go through the steps of developing each component of the requirements model, with particular emphasis on use cases, and finish by describing the interfaces to people and to other systems.

Key Concepts

- Passive sabotage
- Recording analyst
- Project scope
- Context diagram, external entity
- Use case
- Actor, primary actor, secondary actor
- Responsibility
- Interface descriptions

"The Outhouse Bathroom Boutique" Sales Reporting System – Episode 7A

This episode consists simply of the checklist prepared by Nancy for Tim. (You may wish to photocopy it when preparing for an actual modeling session. You'll need to adjust the meeting format under "Recommended.") Episode 7A will be followed later in the chapter by Episodes: 7B, 7C, and 7D. Each of these will follow after the subject matter it refers to and will show how a systems development team might go about developing the models.

Figure 7-1 shows the checklist for The Outhouse Bathroom Boutique.

Thought Questions

Where possible, these should be addressed in your groups.

1. Speculate on what difference it might make if we were to invite only one of the groups mentioned in the "Invite" part of the checklist. For each group mentioned, write down what you think the models, and thus the system, might be missing if this group were not invited.

2. Now write down what biases you might expect each of these groups to have that could interfere with the overall effectiveness of the final system.

7.1   Preparations to Begin Analysis

The classic situation, if perhaps a little exaggerated, is that we techies are faced with a group of users, some of whom are afraid of computers (cyberphobic) or technology in general (technophobic), and each group appears to the other to be speaking in a foreign tongue.

We're faced with the formidable task of learning to understand *their* world, *their* business, *their* technology, and *their* jargon, while not alienating them with too much of our own. Note that often we really are in much the same position as the newborn child we discussed in Chapter 3, trying to make sense of a totally foreign world that we've just been dumped into.

Our job is seriously complicated by the communication difficulties, the users' fears, and often our own ignorance of just what it is that they do. Too often in the past, our people (the techies), believing they understood the problem, would rush off and produce a solution that was at least partially inappropriate and inadequate.

Often the solution we produced this way turned out to be completely useless since it *solved the wrong problem*. It worked magnificently, but did nothing of any value to the users! *The cure for this problem lies in how we handle the relationship with our users.*

For systems analysis, we must of course have technical understanding and business knowledge. But what sets great analysts apart from merely good analysts is the level of their *people skills*. In this chapter, we'll examine the step-by- step details of how to approach our users and extract from them what we need.

My objective is that you should finish this book with all the necessary technical and interpersonal skills to perform as a *great* systems analyst, designing systems that will not only satisfy, but even *delight* your users. We begin the process in this chapter and continue through the following ones. Chapter 16 focuses on people skills and contains a number of important and useful techniques.

Modeling Session Wed, Feb 8, 2002

Invite:

- **Top managers.** At least for first session, even if too busy for later sessions. They have the broad view of the company and the directions it is likely to take

- **Middle managers.** Have a clear overview of daily operations.

- **Shop-floor personnel.** The workers and supervisors. They do the everyday work and know exactly what goes on.

- **Someone from each area** of the company that has anything to do with sales, such as Accounting, Marketing, Shipping and Receiving, etc.

Prepare:

- Isolated, neutral site

- Comfortable chairs

- Writing surface for recording analyst

- Room temperature (20^0 C / 68^0 F)

- Coffee, etc.

- Whiteboard and/or flipchart (self-printing whiteboard?)

- Message and phone facilities (access during breaks only!)

- Estimate and schedule enough time for enough meetings in advance

Recommended:

- Six meetings, three hours each, mornings, twice weekly.

Figure 7-1   The Outhouse: Checklist for systems modeling session

It would be all too easy to simply say that the users should take responsibility for passing on to us the information we need, to build them the best possible system, since they'll ultimately benefit from it. After all, the whole purpose of the system is to enable the users to do their jobs better and with less stress and hassle, to the benefit of both themselves and their clients. But that's begging the question; the world simply doesn't work that way.

Generally speaking – and I must hasten to say with notable exceptions – the users have very little idea what it is that we need to know. Typically, the users are very knowledgeable in their field, but have never examined their own discipline from the rather strange point of view that we require, that of information and data. So for us to be successful in this project, we need to approach the tasks with the attitude that we'll do *whatever is necessary* to carry out a successful analysis.

And that's just what I'm about to share with you. What follows is a distillation of the work and expertise of many. I didn't think it up or develop the techniques; I'm simply the chronicler bringing it to you, for you to learn and profit from.

As the "experts," we need to go to some pains to make our users feel comfortable participating in something that, to them, can sometimes be a pretty scary process. We may even have to go so far as to baby them along for a while, until they learn to trust us and feel comfortable opening up and telling us what they really think and feel.

Later in the process of analysis, you can expect them to take part in the project willingly and enthusiastically, but to begin with, their fear levels may well preclude it. This willing participation from the users is the only way we can guarantee to build that firm, straight foundation upon which the edifice of our system needs to stand. We start even before the first meeting, with some very necessary preparations.

There are a variety of ways to approach the analysis, and each has its strengths. I'll describe my favorite and comment on others as I go. You may adapt and adjust the method that I describe, as you find necessary, to fit any situation. You may wish, or be forced, to do it one-on-one, although these things work best in a facilitated team session (FTS), sometimes called a joint application development (JAD) session, as I describe in the following paragraphs.

With busy senior managers, you may only be able to get them together once or twice, or maybe not at all. In that case, you'll need to meet with each in turn, combine the results of the meetings, circulate them, and then meet with each one again to discuss and modify the model as a whole.

Whichever method you choose, the objective is that the model must reflect the *users'* views and viewpoints, and should document the *users'* knowledge of their business, and not what we the analysts may think. And it must include input from *all* of the users, especially the shy, timid, and reclusive.

My personal favorite is the FTS/JAD session. The users and analysts meet as a group for the required number of hours over several meetings. Here are some guidelines for putting this in place.

Attendees

You'll need a range of users, covering all levels and all parts of the business area you're modeling. You'll need to invite some management, as high as you can manage to get to your meeting, to give the weight of their influence and authority, and to give a broad perspective.

Their presence adds a lot of credibility in the minds of the more junior users. These are then encouraged to take the project rather more seriously than they otherwise might. Keep in mind that the typical user doesn't much understand just how important it is for their own job to have good information, and good information systems.

The presence of management is most important early in the project, to lend the weight of its authority to such things as the project scope. The users will tend to "push the scope" on you later in the project, trying to expand it beyond the size you intended. It's much more difficult for them to do this, when you can appeal to the authority of their own senior management to enforce the agreed boundaries of the project.

This is also why it's important, as I describe under "Project Scope" below, to specify both what is and *is not* part of the project. Of course, if you happen to be a consultant on a fixed-price contract, this can be a life-and-death matter!

At the other end of the scale, I always like to have someone from the "shop floor." The workers who actually make the company run often know about details or procedures that have been in place forever, but haven't filtered up to the awareness of the boss. (Or perhaps they were being deliberately hidden from the boss!). You and I must learn what *actually happens* in the users' world, not just what the boss or the company manual says should happen.

I remember a project where I had given Jim, then a junior programmer, total responsibility for a small system to track furniture movement within the company, and I was sitting in on his modeling sessions. We had two levels of supervisors present, along with Carl, the guy who drove the truck and wheeled the furniture around on dollies.

As it turned out, neither of the supervisors had sufficiently detailed knowledge of what went on, for our purposes. But Carl, an intelligent and verbal kind of person, helped us build a very successful model around his knowledge of the operation.

And there's one other aspect to worker-level participation. Their involvement will increase the sense of ownership that the workers feel toward the system. Too often, the people who do the job and make the company run end up feeling that the systems developers, and their own management, have conspired to *force* a new system upon them. Seeing little or no benefit to themselves in their daily grind, they're keenly aware of new procedures to learn and extra workload. This is allied to fears of looking bad if they have trouble adjusting to the new system, so they can be under a lot of stress.

A lack of cooperation is only the first response. Their resistance may progress to a level that can be described as "passive sabotage." This is such a subtle process that accusations and proofs become impossible and irrelevant. It takes the form of "accidentally" forgetting things, or "unintentionally" missing deadlines, and so on.

The cumulative effect of dozens or hundreds of such little "accidents" is that your system appears to be underperforming, or worse. The surest way to avoid such a "Cold War in a teacup" is to have them on your side, to enlist them on the team, and ensure that they have input into the entire development process.

Not only must they *have* input, but also they must see their input being sought, accepted, and *used*. (Much like "Justice must be *seen* to be done.") Once the workers realize they're being listened to, that they have some control over their own destiny, and that problems they voice actually get attended to, they're more likely to speak of "our" system, rather than calling it the "computer people's system."

The final group to invite is junior and middle management. These foremen, supervisors and managers are close enough to the operational level to have a clear idea of the day-to-day working of their staff. Yet they have a broader, more strategic view than their staff do. These are the detailed tactical planners, and their input is crucial to the success of your project.

Recording Analyst

You'll need a designated person to document the sessions and publish, not "minutes" per se, but documentation of the progress after each meeting. The important point, though, is that *this person must understand the process*. For this reason, I refer to him as a *recording analyst*, although a user experienced in systems projects and modeling methods would be fine. The main thing is not to allow someone to assign a stenographer or clerk; we need a "knowledgeable filter" for this function.

User Majority

The software developers and modelers should be in the minority to avoid overwhelming and intimidating the users. With more users than modelers, you'll find that the users are more willing to stand up and make their point, more willing to risk being heard. However, depending on the size of the group, it's usually best to have at least two modelers – the leader and the recording analyst.

Distractions

As a meeting leader, there's no way you can hope to compete against callers, salespersons, customers, bosses, angry bosses, children, or animals. Don't even try. If at all possible, set the meetings at your premises, where you can control the environment. Otherwise, use a neutral location, or even better, set up a retreat. All are preferable to meeting at the users' place, with phones and staff interfering. You need solid concentration and focus on the task at hand for whatever period has been set aside.

Background

Research the user group, its structure and function. Be aware of reporting relationships, so you know in advance who works for whom. You'll need advance study in their jargon, terminology, abbreviations, and so on, which you can get from such things as glossaries, training documents, introductory brochures, annual reports, and special reports. You may wish to read an introductory textbook in their specialty. *Do your homework!*

Environment

A whiteboard or chalkboard is a must, although flip charts will do at a pinch. A self-photocopying whiteboard is a marvelous idea, since it gives the recording analyst a snapshot of what the leader actually wrote, in addition to the organized version from her own notes. An overhead projector is also very helpful.

Be sure the temperature is low enough to keep everybody awake (20°C or 68°F works well, definitely not above 21°C or 70°F). The room should feel a little on the cool side. Better that one or two should have to wear sweaters or jackets, than to have some of them nodding off to sleep. For head work such as this, you need "a cool head and a warm body."

Encourage casual dress, especially if away from corporate eyes. It helps if user managers dress down, as it makes them a little less intimidating to their own staff. On the other hand, you as the modeler need to maintain a bit of an air of professionalism, so you should dress one level above what you expect the users will wear. A slightly dressier level of casual should be your aim.

Arrange for comfortable seating in an informal arrangement. Coffee, water, and juice *in the room* are very helpful, since they allow people an excuse to get up and move around from time to time, thus maintaining their alertness. Refreshments served *in the room* at breaks minimize the disruption from the break, and encourage on-topic discussion. This also reduces the number of people who visit their desks or the phone, and end up getting stuck there.

Smoking is a ticklish issue. It's far better not to allow smoking in the meetings, unless in an environment where a majority smoke and/or smoking is normally allowed (and expected) in meetings. Ask the user managers whether smoking should be allowed and do give frequent smoke breaks if needed.

Scheduling

The users *must* be made aware *in advance* what kind of time commitment will be expected from them. Schedule sufficient sessions in advance. Two to four hours per session is optimal, since (as my friend and mentor Dr Kapur is wont to put it) permanent brain damage tends to set in after that. Schedule half-day sessions in the mornings if possible; alertness is at its lowest after lunch. When you notice some eyelids drooping, call a three-minute break for everyone to get up and fetch a cup of coffee back to their seats.

Although we find half-days to be optimal, there will often be a need to do the modeling over several straight days. In that case the best you can do is take careful note of all I've said above, and just do the best you can.

Confirmation

Confirm the first session one day ahead of time, with a carefully nonconfronting approach. My personal favorite is to call and say, "Joe, did I tell you the time (or location) for tomorrow's meeting?" even if I'm fully aware that I did. This lets Joe off the hook should it happen that he forgot.

By deliberately putting myself on the defensive, I allow Joe to feel more positive and less threatened about the meeting and thus he's more likely to show up. If he did forget the time, or even forgot the meeting altogether, he can say "Ah, yeah, but just refresh me" and so save face while still getting the information he needs. This spares him any embarrassment or discomfort, making him more likely not only to make the effort to show up, but also to participate enthusiastically.

To recap – the eight factors in preparing for FTS/JAD sessions for analysis are:

- Attendees: All levels
- Recording analyst: Knowledgeable filter
- User majority: Avoid "blinding with science"
- Distractions: None allowed
- Background: Do your homework
- Environment: Your place or neutral
- Scheduling: Sufficient time, in advance
- Confirmation: Day before first meeting

7.2 DEVELOPING THE REQUIREMENTS MODEL: THE PROJECT SCOPE

We need to document two sets of objectives. We state the objectives of the business area first, and then we check to ensure that the objectives of the system fit in with them. If there's any conflict or discrepancy between the two sets of objectives, now is a good time to resolve it, *early!* **It is critically important that the system is built to support the objectives of the business area.**[1]

With luck, the users may already have done a strategic business plan, and we may be able to draw upon that for a statement of business objectives. The project scope will in effect be a statement of the system's objectives. We then state the purpose of the whole project, as in Figure 7-2.

Example Project Scope (simplified)

A system to track the location of furniture items. The system will produce annual and periodic inventory lists, and do searches by individual item or by type of item. It will *not* be concerned with valuation or any other financial factors.

Figure 7-2   An example of a project scope (simplified)

---

[1]This factor is discussed in depth in any course or text on *information strategic planning*. I would also mention a paper that appeared in *Communications of the ACM* several years ago, discussing why computerization of factories failed in the late Soviet Union. The article shows how the business objectives were to keep the factory going at all costs, and the managers were evaluated severely for any stoppages caused by running out of materials. In an economy of shortages, managers were thus motivated to overstock whenever materials were available, even if it meant excess inventory and occasional spoilage. The fancy new Moscow-developed computerized inventory system, on the other hand, attempted to minimize stocks consistent with a stated service level. This was done to reduce the capital tied up in stock. Since these two sets of objectives were diametrically opposed, something had to give. Here we had an example of passive sabotage, not from the shop floor, but from senior factory management! The result, naturally, was Managers 1, System 0.

The project scope is a statement of what the project is to produce. It says in a brief statement (a couple of paragraphs or a couple of pages) what it is we're gathered here to do. The project scope says in general terms:

- What the eventual system will do.
- What functions will be part of the system.
- Which users it will service.

Equally important, the project scope must also state:

- What will *not* **be part of the system.**

We must anticipate areas where the users might want to extend the scope and state clearly what will and what will not be part of our project.

The most important people who need to be present for this step are the senior user management. Their authority is needed here to set firm boundaries on the project, to keep it from growing beyond practical limits.

As the users (and sometimes the analysts) become aware of the possibilities of the system, they're likely to want to "push the scope" and add more and more functionality to the software. We'll want to be able to invoke the dictates of these senior user managers when we need to say "No!" to their staff.

"THE OUTHOUSE BATHROOM BOUTIQUE"
SALES REPORTING SYSTEM – EPISODE 7B: GETTING STARTED

Tim's accountant, Steve Jones, had his offices just a block or so from The Outhouse, so Nancy had arranged to borrow his conference room. "Important to avoid interruptions," she had assured Tim. Steve had asked to be allowed to sit in to learn about the new methods, and Nancy had said she would welcome his input.

Nancy mentally checked off her list as she approached the room. Deanna should be there to act as recording analyst and would have a dictionary and thesaurus, as well as her notepad computer. Tim had asked his secretary, Annie, to hold all calls for the people in the meeting, and he would call in for messages at breaks. Nancy had already checked out the room and the chairs and set the thermostat down to 19°C (66°F). She had whiteboard pens in her purse, and Annie had agreed to set up coffee and donuts, with juice for morning break. Nancy stepped into Steve's conference room, confident that all was ready.

"The Outhouse" Cast of Characters	
Tim Buchanan	CEO
Steve Jones	Accountant
Louise Murphy	Sales Manager
Allana Jenkins	Senior Buyer
Hartmut von Gaza	Warehouse Manager
Bill Petrie	Senior Salesclerk
Mary Voon	Accounts clerk
Deanna Dennis	Recording Analyst
Nancy Forsyth	Object modeler

Figure 7-3   "The Outhouse" cast of characters

Deanna was already there, chatting with Tim and some others. Tim introduced Nancy around, and Nancy made a point of giving her card to each person. Most offered a card in return. Nancy put these in her pocket to give to Deanna for the spelling of the names.

The Outhouse Sales Reporting System
Project Scope

A system to track product sales and purchases, inventory valuation, and stock on hand. It will produce sales reports at various periodic cycles, and will allow random and ad-hoc queries.

Figure 7-4   The Project Scope for "*The Outhouse*"

Within a few minutes, the rest had arrived, and Tim asked everyone to be seated. "Now you've all met Nancy," he began, "so I'll let her explain how this is going to work."

Nancy stood up and glanced around the room. Cast of characters, she thought to herself. Her mental review could be summarized as in Figure 7-3.

Nine of us, she thought, seven users and only two techies. Satisfied, she launched into a brief description of the analysis process, with a half-dozen overhead slides and a small handout. She finished by showing a slide Tim had prepared for her, summarizing the objectives of The Outhouse as they had been established at a strategic planning session a few months earlier.

Then Nancy started on the project scope. "What we need," she said, "is a paragraph or two, or up to a page or two, describing in general terms just what it is that you want this new system to do for you." A couple of people began talking in terms of the output reports they currently received and those they would like to see, and Nancy had to steer them gently toward a more general statement. Eventually, they came up with the scope you see in Figure 7-4.

"Now," said Nancy, "We have both a direction and a boundary for our project."

But before we observe Nancy doing the rest of the requirements model, we'll need to find out more about how it is done. We need to look at the people, organizations, and systems that will need to communicate with our system.

7.3 DEVELOPING THE REQUIREMENTS MODEL: THE CONTEXT DIAGRAM

The purpose of the context diagram – sometimes known as a *context data flow diagram*, a *context model*, or an *environment model* – is to show how our system relates to the world beyond itself. One part of this is to depict graphically the project scope that we developed in the last section. This gives a validation check on the scope to see if we got it right or where there may be some tuning needed.

The second part is to model the flows of data to and from the external entities that our system must interact with. Once we've identified these external entities, we'll use them as our "original cast" that is, our initial set of actors for identifying use cases in the next stage of the requirements modeling. In Chapter 3 in the discussion of data flow diagrams (DFDs), we defined **_external entities_** to be **people, organizations, systems, and other things outside our system that either provide data to the system or draw data from it.**

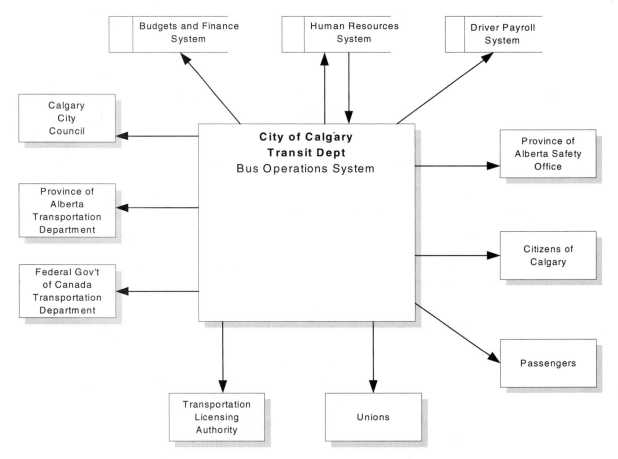

Figure 7-5 (a) A sample Context Diagram for Calgary Transit

In the context diagram, we show our system as a single box in the center of the page and use arrows to show data flowing into and out of it. This black-box approach allows us to concentrate on the external relationships our system has with the world outside itself. What happens inside the system will be considered in the next step with the use cases. Surrounding this box, we show the external entities as (regular square-cornered) rectangles.

These *external entities* may be people, such as Customers, Employees, Members, or Patients. They may be organizations, such as Government Departments, Regulating Authorities, or Subsidiaries or Parent Corporations. They may be systems within your company, such as Accounts Payable, Payroll/Personnel, Inventory, or Production Control. Or they may be systems external to your company such as those of vendors, customers, and banks.

Figure 7-5(b) Data store symbols used to represent other databases as External Entities. (i) DeMarco-Yourdon (ii) Gane-Sarson

External entities may consist of software embedded in a product or in a physical system, such as an oil refinery or some other automated industrial process. Another example of this would be the black boxes carried by aircraft (flight data recorders) or trucks and trains (hub data recorders). First, the recorder gathers data from the onboard systems of the vehicle, and then later data is taken from the recorder and passed to a PC-based system for analysis.

External entities, then, are sources and "sinks" of data. Figure 7-5(a) shows an example of a Context Diagram.   As you draw your context diagram, you're bound to find as well a bunch of things that provide or receive data but are *within* the business area. Keep a list of these as you go, because you'll need them as actors, too. These are likely to be operators, users, internal management, help desk personnel, network administrators, and so on.

Even though they don't belong on a traditional context diagram, it helps to show them on one that's intended to help find use cases. If they become too numerous and start cluttering your diagram, however, you may prefer to list them separately.

As on any DFD, the arrows show *direction of data flow* and are labeled to show *what data is passed* along this route. Related groups of data should be shown as a single arrow to keep the diagram simple and clear. The box in the center representing our system should have nothing in it except the name of the system; it should not show any "internal structure."

In the interviews or facilitated team sessions (FTS or JAD sessions), have your users list every business event or transaction they can think of involving "someone" outside their business area. Have them then list all the things the system must do or produce when each event or transaction occurs and also who (i.e., which external entity) receives that response.

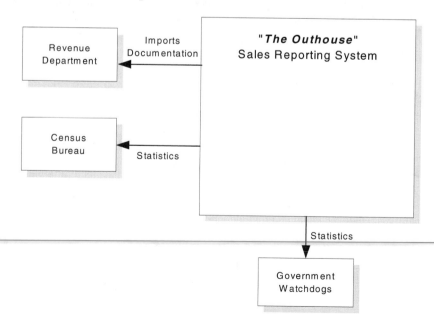

Figure 7-6   First cut of *"The Outhouse"* context diagram

You may also need to add computer files or databases that are outside your system but that your system will need to read or update. These we refer to as *external data stores*. They may be drawn using the DFD symbol for data stores, as shown in Figure 7-5(b).

These are files that you can access, but you can't change the structure by adding, changing, or deleting fields (at least, not without consultation and agreement with the system "owners" and the database administrators, or DBAs).

"THE OUTHOUSE BATHROOM BOUTIQUE"
SALES REPORTING SYSTEM – EPISODE 7C: THE CONTEXT DIAGRAM

"Well," said Nancy," it's time to do the context diagram. As I explained earlier, this large box I'm drawing represents our system. The little boxes all around it are the external entities. What I need to know from you is, What people, systems, or organizations give us information, or need to get information, from our system?" She paused. "Who do we need to send reports and information to, besides our own users?"

"Revenue!" Steve said quickly.

"Thank you, Mr Accountant," responded Nancy with a grin, writing "Revenue Dept." in one of the smaller boxes on the board. Then she asked, "What exactly does Revenue need from us?"

"They need all our international shipping documents and invoices for the duty paid," explained Allana, head of the Buying Department. She nodded her approval as Nancy wrote "Import Documentation" alongside the arrow she had just drawn.

"Census Bureau!" Hartmut called out.

"Right," said Nancy, writing. "They always need statistics. And there's lots of 'watchdog' departments in the government, too. Which ones monitor your kind of business?"

"There's Occupational Health and Safety, Corporate Affairs and Monopolies, the Human Rights Commission, the Ombudsman," cut in Tim. "I don't think they need too much from this particular system. Perhaps we could just put them all in a box marked 'Government Watchdogs.' We can work out the details later."

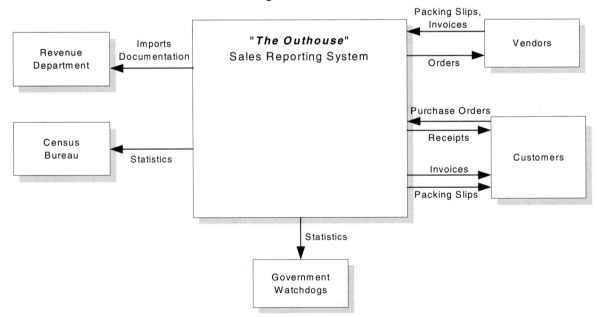

Figure 7-7   Second cut of "The Outhouse" context diagram

"Sure. That would work. Would the information they need come under 'Statistics'?" Nancy asked. Tim nodded, and she wrote some more. By now her board looked like Figure 7-6.

Allana continued the process. "There's vendors. They get orders from us and then send us the products . . . – Oh, but that's not data, is it? The data they send us would be packing slips and invoices, right?"

"Right, very good," approved Nancy. "But there's somebody very important that you all seem to have missed." They all looked puzzled. "What about the customers?""They're mine," said Louise, the sales manager. "I should have thought of them! Yes, they would send us purchase orders, and we would send them receipts and invoices and sometimes packing slips." Once Nancy had added this information to her diagram, it looked like Figure 7-7.

We'll leave them now to finish this part of the job without us, and from the context diagram we move on to the use cases. For the next few pages, there are some pieces of *The Outhouse Saga* embedded in the text. These are short quotes from the modeling sessions, each followed by the use case that was developed from it. You'll easily recognize them when you come across them in the chapter.

7.4 DEVELOPING THE REQUIREMENTS MODEL: THE USE CASE MODEL

The objective of the Use Case Model is to document what functions the system should offer to the users. The purpose is threefold:

- To construct the developers' view of what the users want

- To provide a starting point for discovering the object classes

- To provide a starting point for discovering the operations for each class

The developers need to understand what the users want. They need to understand it from a developer's point of view. The use case model, allied with the object model (see Chapters 8 and 9), gives just this kind of understanding. What guarantees the quality of the analyst's understanding is having the users work alongside the analysts in all these modeling efforts. In building the use case model, we also set ourselves up for the next stage, which is identifying the classes for the object class diagram.

In the use case model, we'll consider all the ways that the users make *use* of the system. From the detailed use case descriptions, we'll later extract the *nouns* to use either as candidate entity classes, or as a more-or-less complete list or to augment our brainstorming results, as described in Chapter 9.

And lastly, when we have the class diagram, we'll make use of the use cases, along with statechart diagrams for certain classes. These will show us what behavior is expected of each class of objects, as the users interact with the system while going about their jobs. Adding behavior takes us from a data model to an object model.

The use case method was developed by Jacobson ("Yahcobson") as part of his methodology, "*Objectory*, which has now evolved into the *Unified Software Development Process* (Jacobson et al., 1999). However, a rather strange thing occurred. Many analysts and developers, using various methodologies, found considerable benefit from adding Jacobson's use case method at the front end of whatever methodology they were using.

Then, several of the well-known methodologists in the OOA field, such as James Rumbaugh (1994), borrowed the method from Jacobson and added it officially to their products. The technique can also be used stand-alone and is

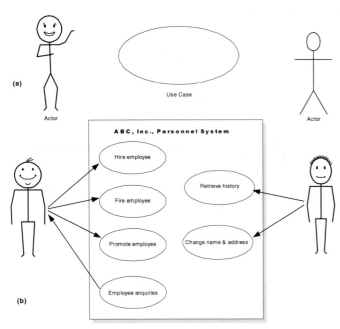

useful as a first phase in business process reengineering (BPR).[1] The technique is now enshrined in the UML. It's easy to use with naive users since it's free of unnecessary jargon and independent of any methodology or technology.

From the point of view of the users, all they'll see of the completed system will be the commands and data that they give it and the reports and responses they receive in return. To them, the system will appear as a black box into which they must feed certain things in order to get the results they want from it. In this sense then, the system can be viewed as consisting of nothing more than a collection of dialogues with its users.

If we were to document all the use case dialogues that could possibly take place, what we would

Figure 7-8 (a) Diagram symbols for an actor and a use case; (b and c) use case diagrams

have is actually a model of the system. It is in fact a model that completely describes the external behavior of the system.

As we noted earlier, a ***use case*** **is a script that some actor could follow to make use of the system.** So let's consider just what an *actor* is.

Actors

Each person, organization, system, user, or thing that interacts with our system we'll call an ***actor***, **a person, an organization, or another system that can initiate an instance of a use case, thus making *use* of one or more features of the system.** In case this sounds a little like the definition of an external entity, it is. External entities can sometimes turn out to be Actors as well.

Figure 7-8   (continued)

[1] See footnote p84 about "Business Process Engineering."

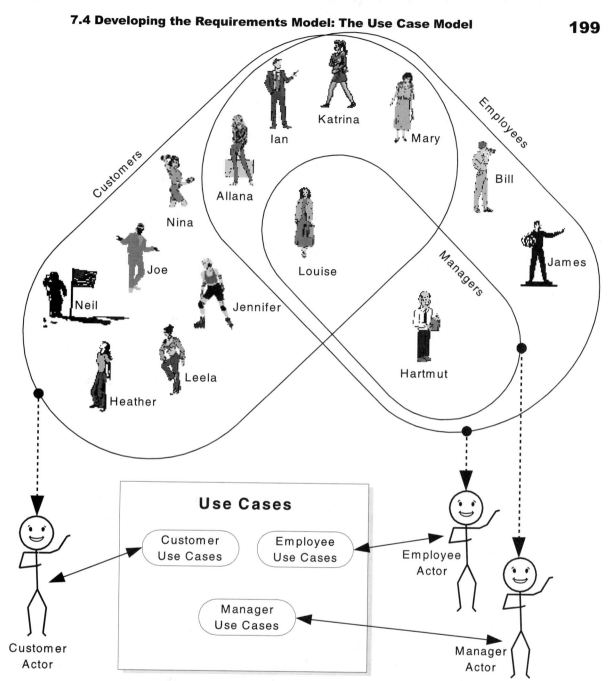

Figure 7-9   Users, roles, and actors: employees, managers, and customers

Jacobson (1992, pages 152, 153) likes to begin by identifying all (or at least most) of the actors. Others, such as Lenzi (1994), prefer to begin by looking at the ways the system is used, and discovering both actors and use cases as the analysis proceeds.

Either way, the idea is to describe *all* the ways that *all* the actors can interact with the system. By writing everything down in step-by-step form, we would end up describing the complete behavior of the system. From this model, we'll be able to identify both classes and operations for the object model.

The actors are usually diagrammed as stick figures [Figure 7-8(a)], with arrows joining them to the ovals or ellipses that represent the use cases, as in Figure 7-8(b) and (c). The ellipses are all within a rectangular box representing the system itself.

The arrows can be single or double-headed, showing the *net* or *main* flow of data between the actor and the use case. Double arrows indicate that there are major data flows in both directions, in and out of the system, for this use case. Don't allow yourself to get hung up on getting the arrows right initially; the immediate need is to *find* the actors and use cases, and to name and describe them.

From our context diagram, we can get a first pass at a list of actors. Each external entity may become an actor, although actors are more than just this. In discussing actors, I'll use the term *users* to include external entities that is, outside persons, organizations, or other systems as well as end users in the usual sense.

As you can see from Figure 7-9, Allana, Joe, Mary, Louise, and Heather are all customers, and Allana, Mary, and Louise are also employees, along with Bill and Hartmut. So the actors *customer* and *employee* (see the stick figures) each represent several physical people, and the two sets overlap (in set language, they *intersect*). Also, you'll see that Louise and Hartmut are managers.

Since every manager also *isa* employee (sound familiar?) the entire set of managers is within (that is, a subset of) the set of employees. So according to Figure 7-9, Louise is sometimes a manager actor, sometimes an employee actor, and sometimes a customer actor.

In other words, an actor can be a *role* played by *one or more users*; and an actor such as customer, employee, or manager may represent *several different persons* (or things). Thus, one user may use the system in several roles, and so be represented by several different actors. Louise is an example of one of these, since she's a manager, an employee, and a customer.

Actors tell us all the details of how the system is used. Everything the actor does that's of interest to us and to the system happens as part of a use case. So by checking out all the actions the actors are capable of, we'll eventually find all the use cases. We need to make sure we include all interfaces in the system, to people, systems, machines, and the like.

You'll find there's a lot of overlap. A user can be involved in a large number of use cases, or in only one or two. A use case may involve several actors, or perhaps only one. Either way, our objective is to model all the various roles that people and other external entities play in the operation of the system.

To find the actors, we start with the context diagram and add to it by asking the question, "Who is this system supposed to help?" The answer to this question may come in any of a number of forms. Someone may suggest a group or class of people, or a functional unit of the business. Or they may suggest one or more specific people by name, and this is okay too.

It often helps to begin by writing down the names of specific people and then generalizing to a valid actor title as we begin to understand that use case. Then, as we work at finding use cases we'll also find more actors.

It's also useful to divide the actors into two classes. Jacobson (1992, page 153) considers **users who are there to gain benefit from the system or to feed it data are *primary actors*.** Then there are people such as help desk operators or maintenance programmers and analysts. **Actors that exist in order to keep the system running or to deal with problems the Primary Actors may encounter, are known as _Secondary Actors_.**

In the case of embedded software, these may be service technicians; in applications such as vending or gambling machines or ATMs, they might be on-site attendants.[2] System administrators, network administrators, remote support services, data administrators, and database administrators can all fall into this category.

Now that we've decided what an actor *is*, let's have a look at what they do.

Use Cases

The focus of the use cases is on the *usage of the system*, rather than on the users themselves. The use cases provide an outside view of the system and what it must do, that is, the services and behaviors and responses it must provide.

The use cases don't give us any formal information about the internal structure of the system. They don't tell us *how* the system will do things internally, just *what* it will do. (Sound familiar? This is another example of encapsulation, this time at the level of a complete system rather than a single class or object.)

Since the use cases concentrate on the *what* rather than the *how*, this makes them a tool intended for analysis, more than for design, but there is of course some overlap. They also give us a good starting point for testing the system and give something concrete for the acceptance testing to refer to. In short, once built, the use cases will be exploited at all stages of the object-oriented development life cycle (OODLC).

To begin the process of finding the use case, ask your users to list everything they need the system to *do* for them. Write this on the board as a list of tasks, and beside each one write the actors who will be involved. These are actors whom you expect will either need information from the system or will provide data to it, as they work through the use case.

Where possible, I like to do this interactively in a facilitated team session (FTS/JAD) and draw them on the board as in Figure 7-10. This way, the people in the room feed off each other, with each suggestion stimulating others to come up with more ideas. Before we start, I have a sketch of the context diagram (on a flip chart), which is to help get the process rolling. As they think up tasks, we discover new actors, and new actors cause the people to think of more tasks.

(a)

Figure 7-10 Actors and use cases:
(a) for a payroll system and
(b) for a production control system

---

[2] ATM: automated teller machine. For some reason, it seems that 90 percent of books I've seen on OOA have used the ATM as an example. Can you explain it?

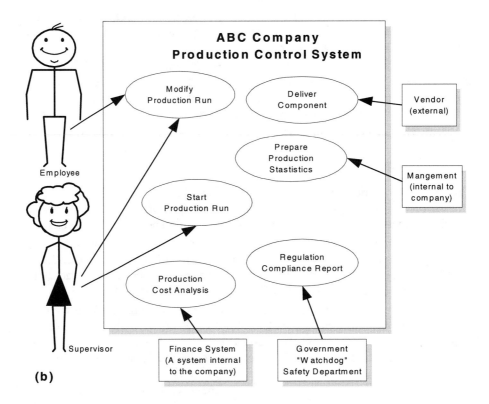

(b)

Figure 7-10   (continued)

What we're discovering at this stage can be viewed as the *responsibilities* of the system. Rebecca Wirfs-Brock, in her landmark book (Wirfs-Brock et al., 1990), page 61) defines the ***responsibilities*** **of an object to be all the services it must provide to users (Actors) or to other objects within the system.** Similarly, we can view the services our system provides to the users (actors) as the responsibilities of the system. We'll look at Wirfs-Brock's (1990) Responsibility-Driven Design (RDD) in detail in Chapter 11.

You might at this point be concerned that your list may not be complete. In fact, you should expect that during this stage you won't discover *all* the actors and use cases; it's just not possible in a large system. You must expect that, as you go through the rest of the analysis and design phases, you'll continue to find more. Each time you do, simply add them to the list, and iterate through the steps of naming and describing them.

When satisfied that your list is reasonably complete, or when the flow of suggestions slows to a halt, it's time to write a description for each use case. You and your users now go through the list of use cases, and do the following for each one:

- Validate the name.

- Write a narrative description.

VALIDATE THE NAME

"Posting" is not a very informative name for a use case. I would probably guess it means "Posting accounting transactions to ledgers", but in many parts of the English-speaking world someone might assume it means mailing a letter. Each use case must have a name that tells as much as possible about what it does. A descriptive name is needed not only for accuracy and communication but also as a trigger to start us thinking up a description.

And again, during this step you'll find that refining the name sometimes shows there are really two or three use cases where before you had seen only one. *Register Member* may well turn out to be *Register New Member* plus *Renew Existing Member*, if you realize later that the two processes are somewhat different. *Purchase* might resolve into *Retail Purchase, Trade Purchase, Dealer Purchase* and *Staff Purchase*.

So now you go through the list of Use Cases, and for each one you ask your users whether the name tells all it should. Does it tell the whole story? Are there exceptions? Special cases? Possible errors? Occasional variations? Does the name cover several related or similar processes, as in the previous paragraph? Can you think of a more informative or enlightening name? Then, once you have the best name you can come up with, you can move on to a full description of the use case as outlined below.

Use cases that simply request output with very little interaction between the system and the user need not be spelled out. You can simply keep lists of daily, weekly, monthly, annual, or other periodic reports. You may also want a list for ad hoc reports and one for queries.

WRITE A NARRATIVE DESCRIPTION

Jacobson describes a use case as a "course of events." It's a sequence of steps, or events, that a user will go through. So for each task, list out the basic course of events – the sequence that best explains or illustrates the task and the system (not necessarily the one that's most often executed.) Focus on this "main line" to begin with, until you have it well understood and documented. Then describe exceptions, options, and error processes.

> During *The Outhouse* modeling sessions, Louise contributed the following description of how she would like to do one of her tasks: "As sales manager, one of my main functions is daily monitoring of sales by store, by department, and by product category. Each day I want to view the sales summaries and then choose certain stores, categories, or individual products to get detailed figures.
>
> "Then I'll hit a key to mark any categories or products that need special attention, so they'll be added to the exception report. Once the exception report is sent to the store and department managers, they can call me to discuss any items that are a problem, and we'll both bring up the details on the screen while we're talking."

This little story gives rise to two use cases. The first one is for the initial analysis of the sales summaries, ending with the exception report being sent to the various sales supervisors. The second occurs when the supervisors call the sales manager to discuss items in the exception report. These are really two independent and distinct usages of the system, so they should be in separate use cases.

In the examples in Figure 7-11, I've added a few words in italics to indicate what "handle" I've used to call an actor by or to explain what the entry is about.

The Outhouse Sales Reporting System
Use Case #1: Daily Sales Reporting

0. System is showing Main menu *(initial state.)*

1. Sales Manager, Store Manager or Department Manager *(titles)* [i.e., Sales Supervisor *(actor)*] requests Sales Summary. Repeats as often as necessary for different summaries.

2. Sales Supervisor chooses a Store, Department, Category, or Product and requests detailed fugures.

3. Sales Supervisor marks any problems for inclusion in Exception Report.

4. Repeat Steps 2 and 3 as needed.

5. Sales Supervisor requests Exception Report to be distributed.

6. System reverts to Main Menu *(final state.)*

(a)

The Outhouse Sales Reporting System
Use Case #2: Discussing Sales Problems

0. System is showing Main menu *(initial state.)*

1. Sales Supervisor *(actor)* calls Sales Manager (a subclass of actor.)

2. Sales Supervisor (either of the above) requests Sales Summaries.

3. During discussion, Sales Supervior(s) scan Sales Summaries and request others (i.e., repeat Step 2) as needed.

4. At end of discussion, both exit.

5. System reverts to Main Menu *(final state.)*

(b)

Figure 7-11 Use cases: (a) Daily sales monitoring, and (b) Discussing sales problems

For each Use Case, write a narrative description. Have your users describe what they do or need to do. Just write down what they say as they go through the steps. It can be very helpful to watch them demonstrate or actually perform their work, either before or after you write down the first pass at the description.

When you need to mention people or actors, use the name of the actor if you're confident you know it. Otherwise it's okay to use the name, title, or position of the person involved and later figure out which actor that should be.

The actions should be described initially as a straight-line sequence, with no choices shown. These will be added next.

It may be tempting to write with abbreviations and fragments of sentences, since this at first appears more efficient. But in the interests of accuracy, you should use complete sentences. This reduces errors and misunderstandings and saves time, temper, and effort in the long run. Make sure you indicate clearly how the use case is initiated and halted by the actor, and what the initial and final actions and state of the system look like.

At *The Outhouse*, Bill, the Senior Salesclerk, told us how he would like the system to go about booking a room for a bathroom design consultation with a customer: "When I sit down to book a room for a customer consultation, I already know the date and time I want to book for, so I enter that. Then I can key in a Store ID, and it will display all the rooms free at that time. I choose the one I want, and it asks for a Customer Number and Consultant ID if I know them. When it's finished, I can check it over and make any changes I need to, then I confirm, and it prints a booking slip."

This little speech gives us the use case shown in Figure 7-12.

Note that although this sample use case has only one actor, in general they can involve more than one. This one is actually a little too detailed, particularly in the parts about dialog boxes disappearing and such, but it illustrates the main ideas. And with use cases, too much detail is usually better than too little.

But you will need to watch the level of detail. It's very easy to get carried away describing all the things that happen on the screen, when what we really need to document are simply the actions of the actors and the responses of the system.

Full detail is okay for those of you who are modeling something like a compiler or an operating system, but this kind of thing is rare for most of us. Too much detail can obscure important patterns and insights. On the other hand, there's a temptation to have use cases at the level of "Payroll," or perhaps "TV promotions," or "Purchasing." Labels like this are too vague and general and don't give a useful amount of information about what goes on.

The Outhouse Sales Reporting System
Use Case #3: Booking a Room

0. The Main menu is displayed on the screen (initial state) (Figure 7-13).

1. Salesperson or Customer (title) phones to book a room (initiation). Scheduling Clerk (actor) selects "Book a Room" from the Operations Menu and is presented with screen #11; the Book a Room screen (Figure 7-14).

2. Scheduling Clerk keys in Date and Time requested and Store ID and sees a pick list of rooms available at that date and time in that store.

3. Scheduling Clerk picks a room and sees the Customer/Consultant dialogue box (Figure 7-15).

4. Scheduling Clerk enters Customer ID and/or Consultant ID if known and clicks on the dialogue box OK button; dialogue box disappears.

5. Scheduling Clerk checks entire screen and makes any changes by clicking on any field.

6. Scheduling Clerk clicks on the main screen OK button. System prints a Booking Slip.

7. When printing is complete, screen 11 disappears and is replaced by the Main menu (final state).

Figure 7-12 Use case for Booking a room

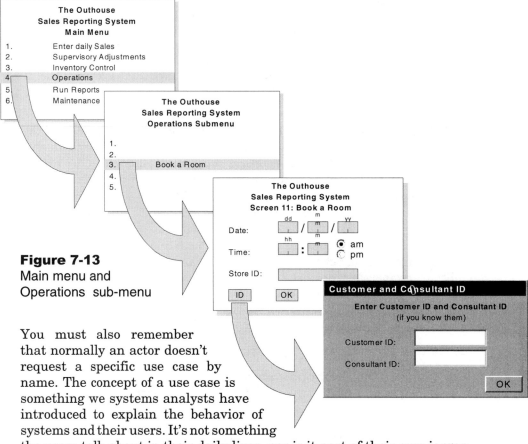

Figure 7-13
Main menu and
Operations sub-menu

You must also remember
that normally an actor doesn't
request a specific use case by
name. The concept of a use case is
something we systems analysts have
introduced to explain the behavior of
systems and their users. It's not something
the users talk about in their daily lives, nor is it part of their own jargon.

What actually happens is that an actor sits down at a terminal or sends a
message by whatever medium is appropriate for that actor. This initiates a course
of events that results in acting out a use case. In this sense, the result is an *instance
of a use case*. That is, any time a user (or other actor) actually performs work with
the system, the record of what the actor actually did describes an *instance* of the use
case that he or she invoked.

Note that there's a parallel relationship between people and actors; an actual
person (or other external entity) can be viewed as an *instance* of an actor. And
besides *instantiation* (what a ghastly word!), actors share other properties with
classes as well.

Inheritance Among Actors

In Figure 7-9 we met Allana and her friends, who are customers *and* employees.
The diagram also shows the set of managers (Louise and Hartmut) as a subset of
the set of employees. Since a Manager *isakinda* Employee, a manager should be
able to do anything an employee can do. So any use case that Allana, Mary, and Bill
can perform, Hartmut and Louise can also perform. In addition, Hartmut and
Louise can do a whole bunch more, that is, all the *Manager* use cases.

What I'm describing is exactly like the inheritance we discussed for classes, and we must be aware of it all the time while discovering the Use Cases. It helps us bring together use cases that are related, and like class inheritance, it helps avoid duplication.

That completes the how-to for the actors and use cases. Once they're found and documented, there's just one more piece required to complete the requirements model, and that's the interface model.

7.5 DEVELOPING THE REQUIREMENTS MODEL: INTERFACE DESCRIPTIONS

The interfaces to our system fall into two main categories:

- Human interfaces
- Interfaces to other systems

We'll look first at the human interfaces, which consist almost entirely of screens, and then at the way our system relates to others.

Human Interfaces

As we go through the exercise of finding the actors, and thus the use cases, each will involve one or more screens.

You should rough out the layout for each of these screens as you encounter it with your users. For this you may find it easiest to use pencil and paper, or you may prefer to use a screen painter tool or a CASE tool.

As you develop each use case, you'll find it helps to place the screen sketches or mockups in front of your users, and have them simulate the performance of the use case. Now, if this sounds a lot like user interface prototyping, that's no coincidence! In fact, requirements prototyping can be viewed as an early predecessor of use case analysis.

Each screen, partial screen, dialog box, pick list, submenu, and the like will need to be sketched, showing the data fields and their approximate placement, as shown in Figure 7-13. Details such as scroll bars and the like can be left until later, except for the odd one that you may think is significant. Check boxes, push buttons, and radio buttons actually represent data being entered, so they should be shown.

It's important that each screen should have a title and a screen number, an identifier unique within the system. You should limit your directions and procedures for the users to just the critical ones at this stage, and all other information on the screen should be kept to a minimum for clarity.

You may write any additional notes around the edge of the diagram, with lines connecting them to the screen items. Remember these are very much rough drafts at this stage, to be refined, corrected, and fleshed out later.

The *sequence* of the screens is important, however. This you'll get from the use cases, so make sure the screens are clearly identified there. Later, you may use the use cases, with the screens in the correct sequence, for your first pass at prototyping. Still later, after construction is complete, you'll use them as test scenarios.

Interfaces to Other Systems

Almost all systems of any size end up talking to (exchanging data with) other systems of some kind or other. These other systems fall into a number of types, and for each you'll need to specify how our system will request data from the other one and/or pass data to it. Just how you need to do this will vary from one interface to another.

OTHER SYSTEMS OR DATABASES WITHIN YOUR COMPANY

If the access to data in these is already documented, you may simply refer to that documentation, or if you think it necessary, include a copy in your own requirements model. Otherwise, you'll need to research it and write it up. Don't go into too much detail at this point if you have to do this. It can always be fleshed out later.

OTHER SYSTEMS OR DATABASES OUTSIDE YOUR COMPANY

Communications Systems

You'll need to research the published interfaces or protocols for these. Again, you can simply refer to the published source or include copies, as you feel is necessary.

Real-Time and Process-Control Systems

If your system is controlling a real-world system, such as a vending machine, medical equipment, or an industrial process, there should be documentation of the interfaces from the hardware design engineers. If, on the other hand, you're doing the entire project yourself and this is yet to be done, you'll need to draft at least a statement of the requirements for the interface.

Now that we've completed our discussion of the requirements model, let's see how Nancy does it.

"THE OUTHOUSE BATHROOM BOUTIQUE"
SALES REPORTING SYSTEM – EPISODE 7D: THE USE CASE MODEL

After the contributions from Louise and Bill, things started to roll. Everybody was anxious to tell their story of how they did their job. Nancy attempted to bring about some order. "Let's start with Bill," she said. "He can tell us how he goes about making a sale, since that's the business we're in."

"But before we do any more of that, we need to list all the functions you perform as part of your job. I need to know all the different things you do as you go through your day on the job. We can start with the file of job descriptions, and then you can each update me with any additional things you do that are not in the official description of your job. Tim, you promised to bring the job descriptions file."

"Right here," said Tim, passing a large binder to Nancy. She opened it at a marker that said "Sales Dept."

"According to this, Bill," she began, "your people in Sales are supposed to serve customers, write up sales, and sometimes assist with inventory."

"Right. And then we also have to record back orders, that is, customer requests for things we don't have in stock and requests for things we don't even carry. So we can keep statistics to see what new things we should add," Bill explained.

"That's five functions, then," said Nancy as she finished writing them all on the board. "Now, tell me how you would use the computerized system to help you when you're serving a customer."

The Outhouse Sales Reporting System
Use Case 4: Not Available

0. System is showing Main menu (*initial state*).

1. Salesclerk keys in stock number or scans it from tag. System returns stock on hand, back-order, and on-order quantities for this store, plus a menu with all the stores listed, including a line for "All."

2. Clerk chooses a store, or "All." System returns stock figures and a menu of actions.

3. Clerk chooses a store and an action.

4. Action: dial. System dials that store on a voice line for a verbal query or verification of stock.

5. Action: Reserve Stock. Clerk may enter a quantity; default is one. System places that quantity on hold at that store for customer pickup.

6. Action: Reserve From On-order. Clerk may enter a quantity; default is one. System places quantity on hold for when the stock on order arrives at that store. Sets a flag for customer to be phoned when stock arrives.

7. Action: Transfer From Stock. Clerk may enter a quantity; default is one. System initiates an order to transfer quantity from that store to this store.

8. Action: Transfer From On-Order. Clerk may enter a quantity; default is one.

Figure 7-14   A use case for serving customers

Bill was warming to his topic. "Well, I'd use it to look up the stock for an item a customer requested, first at our store, and then at all the others. It could be something they walked in and asked for, or it might be something they found, but we didn't have the color they wanted."

"OK," said Nancy. "Deanna, did you get all that? Good. Now Bill, what do you do if it's in stock at your store, what if another store has it, and what if it isn't in stock anywhere? Let's go through all of these one step at a time." By the time Bill had finished explaining all this, Nancy's whiteboard looked like Figure 7-14.

By the time they had spent a few meetings on this, our team accumulated more than 40 use cases. Each one described how someone on staff would use the final system, when it was built, to do a part of their job. They had also roughed out some 50 or so screens and were ready to move on to the next stage of the project. We'll catch up with them in the next chapter as they begin to identify classes for their object model.

• •

DELIVERABLES

The first is a somewhat minor deliverable: a checklist of the factors to be considered in setting up to begin the project, as detailed in The Outhouse Episode 7A at the beginning of the chapter.

Then, as you may have already guessed, there are four major deliverables from this chapter:

• The *project scope*. This will be a brief textual statement, although you may occasionally find a need to support it with some diagrams or some published literature. Remember to include some prenamed spaces for the necessary signatures from the user management (and possibly from your own management) to indicate that this document is to be the firm basis for the "contract" and can only be changed or extended with the agreement of these signatories.

- The *context diagram*. This should normally be a one-page diagram, often supported by a page or two (or more) of explanatory text. This text may include definitions or descriptions of the external entities.

- The *use case model*. This will be an extensive textual description in the form of detailed scripts. They'll probably resemble a cross between a script for a play and a detailed recipe. Remember they're not pseudocode, since they're not computer programs. They must be in English because they describe steps that are executed by *people*.

- The *interface descriptions*: For the people interfaces, these will be diagrams, such as screen layouts and the like, along with supporting documentation.

  For the interfaces to other systems, there is likely to be a wide variation in formats. Usually the best way is including the published documentation of the interface. However, if it's simply too big in volume, then you'll need to refer your reader to it instead. Where you're designing the interface yourself, but it's not done yet, draft a preliminary version in a likely format so that your readers can get some idea of how the interface will eventually function.

FURTHER READING

Any good textbook on Systems Analysis or Systems Analysis and Design, such as Whitten et al. (2000) will have sections scoping a project, on Context Diagrams, and on interfaces.

The core of this chapter is the section on use cases, based originally on Jacobson's (1992) work. While his language is sometimes quaint and not always easy to follow, his treatment of use cases is quite clear. Strangely enough, although they have become one of his major contributions to the art of systems analysis, Use Cases are not mentioned at all in Jacobson's table of contents. His index, however, gives a good number of references.

Jacobson first introduces Use Cases in his Chapter 6 (page 125) and discusses them in some detail in Section 6.4.1, "Actors and Use Cases" (page 128). After that, they become an integral part of his method, so they're mentioned frequently throughout the book.

You'll find use cases covered in significant depth in the later books from The Three Amigos: Booch et al. (1998) *The Unified modeling Language User Guide*, Jacobson et al. (1999) *The Unified Software Development Process*, and Rumbaugh et al. (1998) *The Unified Modeling Language Reference Manual*. In the *Reference Manual*, you'll find use cases on pages 26, 63, and 488, with Actors on page 433.

While these books are remarkably detailed and complete, they are very difficult to read. It is my intent to cover use cases in detail in my next book, *UML: The Developers' Plain English Guide*, due to be published in 2002.

CHAPTER SUMMARY

- To be successful in any project, we need to approach the tasks with the attitude that we'll do whatever is necessary to carry out a successful analysis. This includes much attention to the people side of systems analysis.

- The models must reflect the *users' views* and viewpoints and should document the users' knowledge of their business, and not what we the analysts may think. The models must include input from *all* users, especially the shy, timid, and reclusive.

- You need a range of users, covering all levels and all parts of the business area you're modeling. Invite some management, as senior as possible, to give credibility in the minds of the more junior users.

- Designate someone to document the sessions and publish "minutes." This person must understand the process; a recording analyst is the best choice, although an experienced user is okay. Do *not* use a stenographer; you need a knowledgeable scribe.

- Meet at *your* premises, where *you* control the environment, or at a neutral location or a retreat; all are preferable to meeting at the users' place. You need solid concentration to focus on the task at hand for whatever period has been set aside.

- Research the user group, its structure, function, and reporting relationships; research jargon, terminology, abbreviations, and the like, which you can get from glossaries, training documents, introductory brochures, and annual (and other) reports. Take courses, read books.

- State the *business objectives* of this business area first, and then check to ensure that the objectives of the system harmonize. Any conflict should be resolved *early!* It's critical that the system is built to *support the objectives of the business area*. If the users have a strategic business plan, it will include a statement of business objectives.

- The *project scope* will in effect be a statement of the system's objectives. The Project Scope is a statement of what the project is to produce. It says in general terms what the eventual system will do, what functions will be part of it, and which users it will service. The project scope must also state what will *not* be part of the system.

- The most important people for the scope are senior user management. Their authority is needed to set firm boundaries on the project, to keep the users from "pushing the scope."

- The *context diagram* also known as a *context data flow diagram*, a *context model*, or an *environment model* shows how the system relates to the world beyond itself. It graphically depicts the Project Scope to give a validation check. It models the flows of data to and from the *external entities* our system must interact with.

- *External entities* are people, organizations, systems, and other things outside our system that either provide data to the system or draw data from it.

- The objective of the use case model is to document what functions the system should offer to the users. The purpose is to construct the *developers' view* of what the users want and to provide a starting point for discovering the object classes and the operations for each class.

- Developers using various methodologies found benefit from adding Jacobson's use case method at the front of whatever methodology they were using. Several methodologists in the OOA field have borrowed the method from Jacobson and added it officially to their products. It is now officially enshrined in both UML and the Unified Software Development Process.

- A use case is a *script* that some actor could follow to make use of the system.

- *Actor*: a person, an organization, or another system that can initiate an instance of a use case, thus making *use* of one or more features of the system.

- Check *all* the ways that *all* the actors interact with the system to describe the complete behavior of the system. From this model, we'll identify both classes and operations for the object model.

- From our context diagram, we can get a first pass at a list of actors. Each external entity may become an actor, although actors are more than just this.

- Actors tell us details of how the system is used. Everything the actor does that's of interest happens as part of a use case. By checking all their actions, we'll find the use cases. We need to ensure that we include all interfaces to people, systems, and machines.

- Users who are there to gain benefit from the system or to feed it data are *primary actors*. *Secondary actors include* help-desk operators, maintenance programmers or analysts – actors that exist in order to keep the system running, or to deal with problems the primary actors may encounter.

- Ask your users to list everything they need the system to do for them. Write this as a list of tasks, and beside each one write the Actors who will be involved.

- Go through the list of use cases, and for each one validate the name and write a narrative description.

- There is inheritance among subclasses of actors, exactly like the inheritance we discussed for classes, which helps bring together use cases that are related, and like class inheritance, this helps avoid duplication.

- The interfaces to a system fall into two main categories: human interfaces and interfaces to other systems.

- As you develop use cases, place screen sketches or mockups in front of your users, and have them simulate the performance of the use case. This is the start of user interface prototyping.

- The sequence of the screens is important. This you'll get from the use cases, so make sure the screens are clearly identified there. Later, you may use the Use Cases for prototyping, with the screens in the correct sequence, and later still for testing.

- If the access to data in other systems or databases within your company is already documented, you may refer to that documentation or if necessary include a copy of it in your own requirements definition. Otherwise, you'll need to research it.

- For other systems, databases, or communications systems outside your company, you'll need to research the published interfaces or protocols. Again, you can simply refer to the published documentation or include copies, as you deem necessary.

- If your system is controlling a real-world system, there should be documentation of the interfaces from the hardware design engineers. If you're doing the entire project, including the controlled system, then you'll need at least a draft statement of the requirements for the interface.

CHAPTER GLOSSARY

actor Person, organization, system, or thing that interacts with our system.

external entities People, organizations, systems and other things outside our system that either provide data to the system or draw data from it.

primary actors Users who are there to gain benefit from the system or to feed it data.

responsibilities All the services an object must provide.

secondary actors Actors that exist in order to keep the system running or to deal with problems the Primary Actors may encounter.

use case A *script* that some Actor could follow to make *use* of the system.

WHAT COMES NEXT

Once we have a requirements model, agreed to and signed off by the users, we're ready to dive into the object business. But before we learn how to build object models, which we will in Chapter 9, we need to spend Chapter 8 discovering some of the more powerful properties of objects.

These are the things that give object-oriented methods their advantages over the methods that went before, and we need to understand them well before we can step out into the real world to begin the serious work of analysis.

CLASS/GROUP EXERCISES AND PROBLEMS

Ex 7.1 After referring to Exercise 6.1, each group should now take the complete set of system request documents and prepare a project scope for each one. That is, each group should do a scope for every project. Make sure your scope mentions everything you think may be important. Make sure it establishes boundaries to the project by stating what will not be part of the project.

Each group should now put their project scope on a flip chart and present it to the class. Present, compare, and discuss all the different scopes for the first project, then all the scopes for the second project, and so on. Each group takes a turn at being the first to present.

Ex 7.2 Now refer to Exercise 5.4. For each of the object class diagrams that you drew, and also for the one in Exercise 5.5, propose a Project Scope that would fit with the model as it has been drawn. Present and compare them as in Exercise 7.1. You'll also want to consult the context diagrams you drew for these projects in Exercise 6.4.

Ex 7.3 The class or group brainstorms each of the projects from Exercise 7.1, to list a few external entities for each project. In the first phase, there's no evaluation of the suggestions, just write them down. In the second phase, each suggestion is questioned to see whether it's really of interest and should be included. Then draw a context diagram for each project.

Ex 7.4 By now you hould have quite a collection of project documentation. So far, each project should now have a project scope, a system request, and a context diagram, and some have an object class diagram. Now in the larger group (that is, the whole class), identify some Use Cases. Brainstorm each project to come up with a short list of transactions that users or other Actors will need to be able to do with the system. Just list a name, the actor(s), ad a one-sentence description for each use case.

Ex 7.5 Now assign one or two projects to each group, and that group then expands all the transactions into detailed Use Cases. Present to the class and encourage feedback and comment.

INDIVIDUAL EXERCISES AND PROBLEMS

Ex 7.6 At this stage, some of the projects are missing some of the models and diagrams. Assign each student one or more of these incomplete projects to complete to the level of the others.

Ex 7.7 Each student adopts a Use Case, and roughs out a sequence of screens.

Ex 7.8 Each student develops a brief description of the external system interfaces for one of the projects.

PROJECTS AND CASES

P 7.1 Each group prepares a presentation for one of the projects from the preceding exercises. Present your context diagram to the class and discuss what information is to be exchanged with the external entities.

    The use cases can be your source for a description of what the system should do, and you should describe all the main features of the system. Prepare slides showing some of the more important initial screen designs (preliminary designs, but neatly drawn) and present them to the class and interested outsiders, as if you were the project manager presenting the proposed system to senior management. Wear your best business dress for this presentation.

P 7.2 Each group selects a small business that has expressed a problem or need. Working with these users, prepare a complete requirements model. Discuss with the business owner or manager the importance of selecting the right personnel from the business to assist with the project. Evaluate and choose these people carefully. Involve the owner or manager in the planning for the project, including the scheduling of sufficient meetings.

Document your model carefully and in a presentable format and copyright it in the joint names of the group and the client. Give the client at least one copy. By presentable format, I mean something the client will be proud to show off to peers, shareholders, and potential investors. In other words, do it with suitable text and graphics software and remember always that this document is marketing your client, yourselves, and your school.

Keep it simple, do it right, and make it look good.

Prepare a presentation as in Project 7.1 and present it to your class, clients, faculty, and other interested parties. Again, you must "dress for success" to present. Keep your documentation for Projects 8.1 and 9.1.

SELF-TEST QUESTIONS

Note: The Appendix has answers to the Self-Test Questions.

Q 7.1 The requirements model consists of four parts:

(a) use cases, interface descriptions, class diagram, project scope

(b) project scope, use cases, class diagram, context diagram

(c) Interface descriptions, data model, context diagram, class diagram

(d) project scope, use cases, interface descriptions, context diagram

(e) project scope, use cases, interface descriptions, class diagram

Q 7.2 An Actor:

(a) Requests a particular use case by name and executes it.

(g) Inherits a use case from a subclass and executes it.

(b) Executes a use case and then inherits it.

(c) Does all of the above.

(d) Does none of the above.

Q 7.3 List eight factors to consider in preparing for FTS/JAD sessions for analysis, as discussed in the first part of the chapter.

Q 7.4 Explain the importance of the project scope and state the four points that need to be included in it.

Q 7.5 Define the following:

(a) Context diagram

(b) External entity

(c) Actor

(d) Primary actor

(e) Secondary actor

(f) Use case

Chapter Eight

Properties of Objects and Classes

WHAT YOU WILL LEARN IN THIS CHAPTER

In this chapter, you'll learn the details of how subclass hierarchy structures and aggregation (whole part) structures work and the effects they can have on your models and your systems. You'll discover how subclass hierarchies lead to code reuse through inheritance, polymorphism, and overriding. You'll see how both kinds of structure can clarify the associations in your models by being more precise about just which classes are involved in certain associations.

You can feel confident that you understand classes, hierarchies, and aggregations when you can:

- Identify subclass hierarchies in the real world and document them in your models.

- Demonstrate the existence of inherited attributes and operations in the real world and show them in your models.

- Define *polymorphism* and find examples of polymorphic operations in the real world and in your models.

- Define static (early) and dynamic (late) binding.

- Describe how overriding takes place, and typical ways that object-oriented compilers resolve polymorphic methods.

- Define abstract and concrete classes, and abstract and concrete operations, and explain why a concrete class cannot have abstract operations.

- Describe the three kinds of aggregation, identify them in the real world, and document them in your models.

What You Should Know to Start This Chapter

You'll definitely need to be comfortable with data-oriented modeling methods as discussed in Chapter 4. The object-oriented ideas are fully explored in this chapter, but before you go into it you'll need a thorough understanding of objects, classes, and associations.

Chapter Overview

This chapter ventures deeper into the area of classes, subclasses, inheritance, and polymorphism. It takes you into static and dynamic binding, multiple inheritance, and other important aspects of subclassing. You'll see how these more advanced properties of objects can add a lot of information to your models, so that they better describe the real world. Then you'll discover the three kinds of whole–part relationships, or *aggregation*, and finish with a section to clarify the differences between subclassing and aggregation.

Key Concepts

- Class, instance, object
- Inheritance, overlapping sets of attributes
- Subclass, isakinda, canbea
- Supporting a feature
- Generalization and specialization
- Parent class, superclass
- Polymorphism
- Early binding = static binding
- Late binding = dynamic binding
- Overriding
- Multiorigin multiple inheritance, single-origin multiple inheritance
- Object class libraries
- Instantiate
- Direct instance, directly instantiable
- Abstract class, concrete class
- Abstract operation, concrete operation
- Aggregation, subassembly

"The Outhouse Bathroom Boutique"
Sales Reporting System – Episode 8

"But then, there's the products," mused Hartmut at the start of one of the later meetings.

Nancy's ears pricked up. "What about the products?" she asked with a carefully noncommittal air.

"Well," said Hartmut reflectively, "as warehouse manager, my job is all about the products. And since you talked about all that *isakinda* stuff last meeting, it's just been going round and round in my head all week." Nancy tried her best to look encouraging, and Hartmut went on. "We have three *kindsa* products. There's soft goods, like towels and such, and there's hardware, like bathroom furniture, soap-dishes, scales, and other stuff. And then there's paper goods, and I suppose we need a category called 'other,' like you said.

"And then, for the hardware, we have several *kindsa*. There's your basic stuff like the soap dish, which is just a single piece. It just sits there and doesn't have to *do* anything. Then there's mechanical items like toilets and showers and bathroom scales. They have moving parts, and they do things, and they need maintenance. And they need parts for maintenance. So they fit your assembly–component thing, don't they?

"And some of the soft goods come in *collections*. I don't know if it's going to be important for our system" – Nancy mentally noted that the phrase "our system" had unconsciously slipped into his speech – "but we have towels and things in the Regal Collection and the Waldorf Collection and so on. Wouldn't these fit the collection–member thing you were talking about?"

"Yes, I think they might," exclaimed Nancy, delighted that he had put so much thought into the problem even away from the meetings. In the rest of this chapter, you're going to discover just why Nancy was so delighted, as we explore subclasses, components, and collection–members in some depth.

THOUGHT QUESTIONS

1.   Look around at the people in your class or group. How many different *kinds of* people can you identify among them? How many different factors can you find that will allow you to divide them into *kinds of* people? That is, how many *discriminators* can you identify that would allow you to group the class of *People* into subclasses in different ways?

2.   Have each member of your group write down a story from their past, where they learned about something by taking it apart, or emptying it out, or some equivalent operation. Each story should describe what led up to this, how it actually happened, whether they got it back together, what the responses were from the people around them.

     Most important, what did they learn

     (a) About the thing they dismantled,

     (b) From the experience in general.

     Now have each person share their story with the group, and the group question them about it. Share the best ones with the entire class.

8.1 SUBCLASSES AND INHERITANCE

Now it's time to revisit the subclasses that we met in Chapter 5. Let's begin with a few more examples.

At The Outhouse Bathroom Boutique, we realized during the analysis that our customers and our employees are all *people*. We came to this somewhat astonishing conclusion after noticing that both our Customer file and our Employee file had fields for storing the name, address, phone, date of birth, sex, and so on. These are all data items that we need to know about any *kind of* person.

We need to know this basic data about any kind of person we deal with, which includes both customers and employees, and it could also include some who don't fall into either group. These are the people who might come under the heading of "other." (More about these "others" later.)

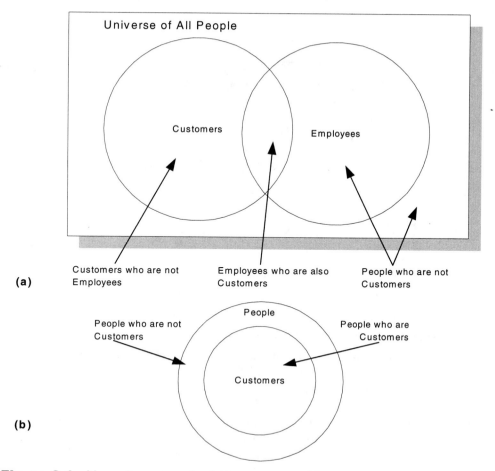

Figure 8-1 Venn diagrams of subclass membership

On the other hand, there are some things we need to know about customers that we do *not* need for other kinds of people. We need to track their balance owing; amounts overdue 30, 60, and 90 days; credit rating; date of last payment; and so on. All these are details related to the fact that this particular *person* is also a *customer*, *in addition* to being a *person*.

Then there are the employees. For them we need to know the tax identifier (Social Insurance/Security Number), marital status, number of dependants, date hired, wage rate, and so on. These details are related to the fact that this *person* is also an *employee*, *in addition* to being a *person*. These are things we don't need to know about a customer, only about an employee. Of course, there could quite possibly be someone who is both a customer and an employee, and for these we would need both sets of attributes.

The question we need to ask now is, Does a customer have a name? The rather obvious answer is "Yes, of course!" But *why* does a customer have a name? Because a *customer* is also a *person*, and all *persons* have names! Ignoring for the moment all the complications such as corporate customers and the like, we can see that in the real world this is very true and very obvious. It's a rule and an association that we use every day without even thinking about it. We use this one and hundreds of other rules like it, day in and day out our whole lives through.

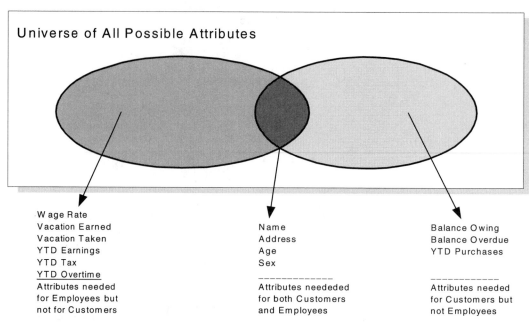

Universe of All Possible Attributes

Wage Rate		
Vacation Earned		
Vacation Taken	Name	Balance Owing
YTD Earnings	Address	Balance Overdue
YTD Tax	Age	YTD Purchases
YTD Overtime	Sex	
Attributes needed	Attributes needeed	Attributes needed
for Employees but	for both Customers	for Customers but
not for Customers	and Employees	not Employees

Figure 8-2 Venn diagram of subclass attributes

But for systems development, we need to carefully scrutinize many of these hitherto unexamined assumptions. What we're saying is that a customer, simply by virtue of being a customer, is also a person, and therefore has all the properties of a person, including a name. This customer-person thus also has an address, phone, date of birth, sex, and so on, because these are the attributes of a person.

So we say that a customer "*inherits*" these attributes or, more correctly, the subclass of Customers *inherits* all the attributes of its superclass, Persons.

There are various ways we can illustrate this situation with diagrams, so let's try a few. First, we can draw Venn diagrams, as in Figure 8-1. The first diagram shows the universe of all people, and the two circles represent the set of people who are customers and the set of people who are employees.

Each set, then, is a subset of the Universe of All People.

Repeating our definitions from Chapter 5, we see that a ***subclass* is made up of selected instances from another class, referred to as the *parent class* or *superclass*.** Conversely, we say that a ***superclass* includes all the instances of the subclass, plus possibly some more as well.**

Where the two circles overlap is the *intersection* of the two sets that is, the set of people who at the same time are both customers and employees.[1]

You'll notice, however, that in Figure 8-1(a) some people are outside the *customer* set. This is fine, since in the real world of *The Outhouse* there are many people who pass by the store without ever becoming customers. But then what if there were a portion of the customer circle that's outside the people circle?

Since for the moment we're not considering corporate customers, this can't happen. There are no Customers in this example who are not at the same time also People. Figure 8-1(b) tells it like it is (for this example).

---

[1]*Set intersection:* The *intersection* of two sets A and B is a set consisting of every element that is simultaneously a member of *both* set A *and* set B.

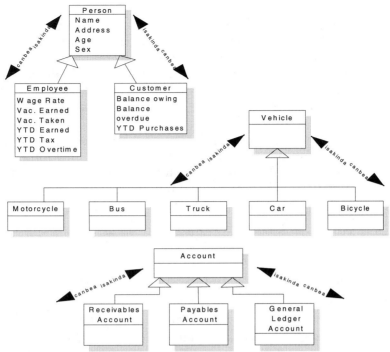

Figure 8-3 Subclass hierarchy diagrams

On the other hand, Figure 8-2 is not about people but about *attributes*. It shows the universe of all possible attributes, from which we've drawn three subsets of interest. The oval shaded area on the left represents all attributes we would need to keep about employees, such as wage rate, and so on. The oval shaded area on the right shows the attributes that we would need to keep about customers, such as balance owing, and the like.

The area in the center where the two shadings overlap – that is, the *intersection* of the two sets of attributes – is all the attributes we need that describe both customers and employees, such as name, address and so forth. These, of course, are the *people* attributes.

Finally, the *usual* way we diagram the subclass relationship is as a hierarchy, or a tree structure. In Figure 8-3, we show the superclass, or parent class, of Person at the top, that is, at the "root" of the tree. The subclasses, or child classes, are then shown as descended from it. Now we can say that the child class (Customer) *inherits* all the attributes of its parent class (Person), such as name and address. This is *in addition* to having its own attributes such as balance owing.

The other child class, Employee, also inherits all the attributes of its parent class Person, *in addition* to the ones that it provides for itself such as wage rate. So this means that an Employee is automatically also a Person, thus inheriting the name and address attributes and all the other things that go with being a Person. ***Inheritance*** **is when a subclass instance, in addition to the attributes and behavior it has by virtue of belonging to the subclass, also has all the attributes and behavior that instances of the superclass have.** On the Venn diagrams in Figures 8-1 and 8-2, the overlapping area indicates that this is a subclass relationship.

Now, a subclass relationship is actually very much like an *association* in the sense that we defined it in Chapter 5, so it requires a verb to define it (though we don't usually show this verb on our diagrams). In one direction, we could use a verb popularized by James Martin to say that this particular Person *"isa"* Customer. Martin liked the idea of the *"isa"* verb to describe this relationship in both directions, since it's perfectly true to say that "Customer *isa* Person" and "Person *isa* Customer."

But there's more information that we could show on our model to describe this relationship. While *isa* is always true one way, it may only sometimes be true the other way. In the other direction, we modify Martin's usage, and I prefer to say that a Customer *"isakinda"* Person. I prefer the word *"isakinda"* since it highlights the specialization involved, the fact that Customer is a special case of Person – that is, *isa special kinda* Person.

Reading the relationships on the diagram in Figure 8-3, following the arrows, we can add the "always" and read such things as:

Employee	*always isakinda*	Person
Customer	*always isakinda*	Person
Bus	*always isakinda*	Vehicle
Receivables A/C	*always isakinda*	Account

The *always* comes from the definition of a subclass, the fact that every instance of the subclass is simultaneously and automatically an instance of the superclass.

The other direction is not always true. While the list above shows that all Customers are People, in the real world only some people are customers. So the preferred way to state the case in this direction goes like this:

Customer	*isakinda*	Person
Person	*canbea*	Customer

The verb *canbea* (pronounced "can-be-a") is intended to show that the relationship in this direction is optional – that there can be Persons around who are *not* Customers.[2]

And there's more. In addition to inheriting all the *attributes* of a Person, a Customer also inherits all the *behaviors* of a Person. That is to say, anything a Person object can *do*, so a Customer object can do, because a Customer *isakinda* Person! Of course, there are also behaviors (as well as attributes) that a Customer has that other *kindsa* Persons are not capable of.

These include such actions as Make-a-Payment, Purchase, Adjust-Credit-Rating, and so on. These are operations defined on the Customer class, so they're only available to instances of that class. The Person superclass, or parent class, has other operations such as Change-Name-and-Address, Retrieve-Phone-Number, and Change-Sex (for error correction only, of course). A Customer, because he's also a Person, is capable of *all* of these behaviors.

---

[2] The verb *canbea* was suggested to me by a colleague, Jeff Davis, at the CIPS Edmonton 1995 conference.

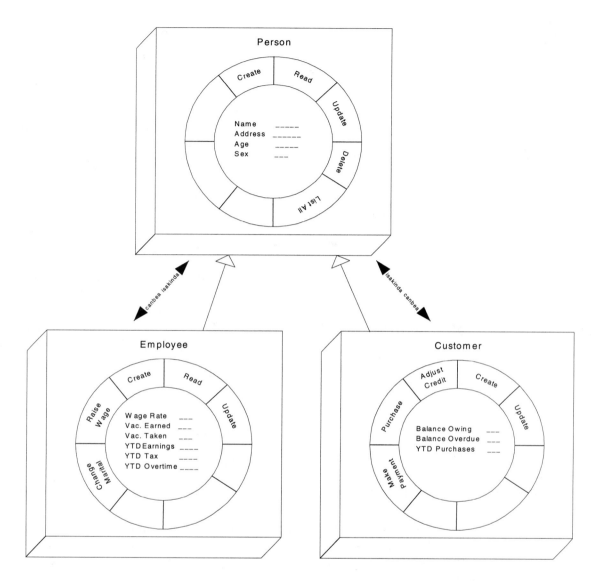

Figure 8-4 Persons, Customers, and Employees, hierarchically (using Taylor's donut notation)

An Employee has certain behaviors because she is an Employee – for example, Raise-Wage-Rate and Change-Marital-Status. Since an Employee, like a Customer, is at the same time a Person, she has all the Person behaviors too. So we can say that a child class, in addition to inheriting attributes, inherits all the behaviors (operations or methods) of the parent class.

This is also illustrated in Figure 8-4, using Taylor's donut notation. Figure 8-3 has some additional examples, showing subclasses of the Vehicle and Account classes.

Of course, an Employee who is also a Customer has all the attributes and all the behaviors from all three classes: Person, Customer, and Employee.

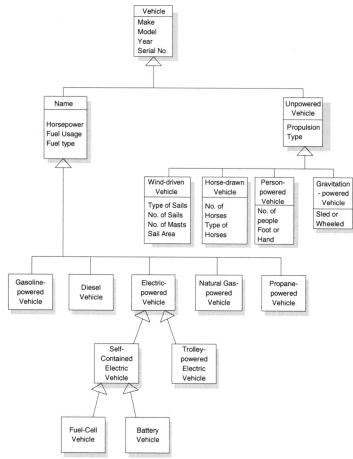

Figure 8-5 A vehicle subclass hierarchy

To summarize:

• A subclass instance *inherits* all the attributes of its superclass.

• The subclass relationship actually is very like an *association*. It requires a verb to define it. In one direction, we use *canbea* (a superclass instance *canbea* subclass instance). In the other direction, a subclass instance *isakinda* superclass instance.

• In addition to inheriting all *attributes* of the superclass, an object also inherits all *behaviors* of the superclass. Anything a Person object can do, so a Customer object can do, because a Customer *isakinda* Person.

• An object that happens to be an instance of two subclasses has all the attributes and all the behaviors from all three classes.

For another example, let's look at vehicles. Figure 8-5 shows there are two main kinds of vehicles, powered and unpowered. Among the *unpowered*, there are horse-drawn, person-driven, gravitational and wind-driven vehicles.

Among the powered ones, there are gasoline, diesel, propane, compressed natural gas (CNG) and electric. The electric vehicles can be centrally powered (as trolleybuses and streetcars are) or else self-contained, in which case they can be powered by battery or fuel cell.

So we can walk up the tree in Figure 8-5 from battery-powered vehicle, which *isakinda* self-contained electric vehicle, which in turn *isakinda* electric vehicle, which *isakinda* powered vehicle, which in its turn *isakinda* vehicle.

What we've just done is to follow a chain of superclasses up the hierarchy. The significant thing here is that any instance of the Battery-Powered Vehicle class is simultaneously an instance of the Self-Contained Vehicle class. It's also an instance of the Electric Vehicle class, the Powered Vehicle class, and the Vehicle class.

That is to say, an instance that belongs to a subclass automatically and simultaneously belongs also to the superclass. It is at one and the same time a member (instance) of *both* classes. It is thus an instance of *every one* of its ancestor classes, and the state of the object at any point in time includes a value for every attribute of every one of its chain of superclasses.

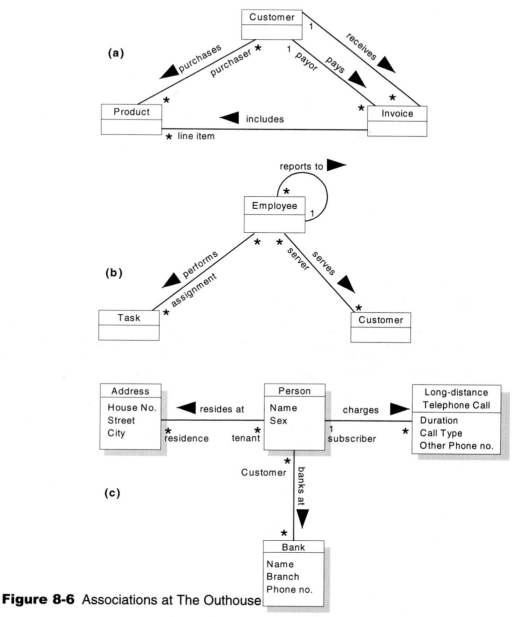

Figure 8-6 Associations at The Outhouse

An instance of a subclass by definition has all the attributes and behaviors (methods) that are defined for that subclass. *Because it is at the same time an instance of the superclass,* it also has all the attributes and methods that are defined for the superclass, and so on up the chain of superclasses.

The *isakinda* verb expresses an identity relationship, which is like equality only stronger. An Employee *isakinda* Person; a G/L Account *isakinda* Account. A subclass instance *isakinda* superclass instance (and thus also *isa* superclass instance). So the *isakinda* verb expresses that a powered vehicle is at the same time a vehicle. It's one of these, and it's also one of those, so it has the attributes and the behavior of both. (I wish to stress this point heavily, since this is totally different from the *whole–part* or *assembly–component* relationship we discuss later.)

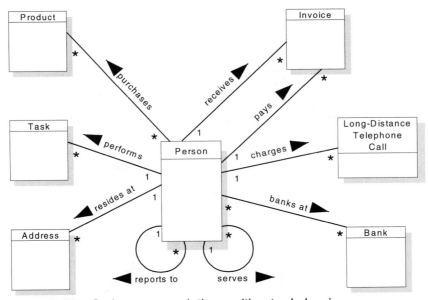

Figure 8-7 The Outhouse associations *without* subclassing

Part of the definition of object-oriented is that an OOPL or an ODBMS *supports* classes, subclasses, inheritance, and polymorphism. We say **a language _supports_ a feature if it contains constructs and mechanisms that make it easy and convenient for programmers to take advantage of the feature.** To be considered truly object-oriented then, a language or database should do more than merely *allow* subclassing and inheritance; it should actively *support* them both.

There are some other reasons for subclassing and consequences too. Next we'll talk about how to handle associations involving subclasses.

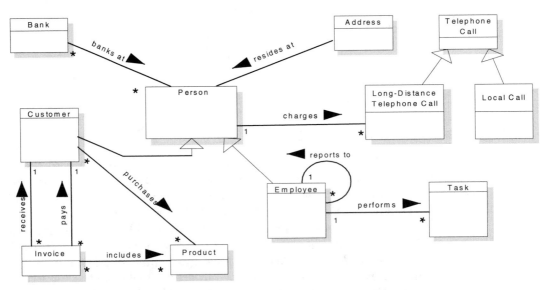

Figure 8-8 Combined Outhouse relationships *with* subclasses
(compare with Figures 8-6 and 8-7)

Associations and Subclasses

At *The Outhouse*, we find that the class of Customers takes part in a number of associations, as shown in Figure 8-6(a). These can be expressed as **Customer** *purchases* Product, **Customer** *is sent* Invoice, **Customer** *pays* Invoice, and so on.

Similarly, in Figure 8-6(b), you'll see the associations for the class of Employees. These are **Employee** *serves* Customer, **Employee** *reports to* Employee (i.e., to Supervisor, which *isakinda* Employee), **Employee** *performs* Task, and so on. In Figure 8-6(c), you'll find some associations that can involve any Persons (including, of course, Customers and Employees). These are **Person** *resides at* Address, **Person** *charges* Long-Distance Phone Call, **Person** *banks at* Bank.

As they're shown in Figure 8-6, the class diagrams showing the associations are fragmented and far from optimal. If subclassing and inheritance were not available to us, we might try to combine the three parts of Figure 8-6 as you see in Figure 8-7.

This solves the fragmenting problem, but it still leaves the diagram incomplete. The information that's missing is that only Customers *purchase* Products, and not Employees. Only Employees *perform* Tasks; while all *kindsa* Persons *bank at* a Bank. You can see this clearly in Figure 8-8. You'll also notice that phone calls can be subclassed into two *kindsa* calls, Local and Long-Distance. Assuming flat-rate local calls, only the Long-Distance Calls get charged.

So we can say that when an association involves only instances of the subclass and doesn't involve other instances, it should be shown on the diagram as a line to the *subclass* box. An association that involves any or all of the instances of the superclass (including instances of the subclass) should be shown as a line to the *superclass* box.

With the subclass structure, we're able to show more clearly just which objects are involved. We can position the associations on our models to reflect more accurately which kinds of objects actually take part in the association, and which do not.

Subclassing and inheritance are extremely important devices in object-oriented working, and there's much more yet for us to discover. In the next section, we discuss another view of subclassing and a couple of useful reasons for using inheritance.

8.2 MORE ABOUT INHERITANCE

Coad and Yourdon (1991) have used the term *generalization-specialization*, or gen-spec, for the inheritance subclassing hierarchy. Their rationale is that this name highlights two of the more important aspects of subclassing.

Generalization and Specialization

There are two directions from which we can approach the issue of subclassing. We can begin from the superclass, or parent class, and treat the subclasses as special cases. Alternatively, we can begin from the subclasses and find common attributes and behavior that indicate the need for a superclass.

Both approaches are valid and necessary, each presenting a different view of the situation. Both will need to be used at different places in the modeling process.

Table 8-1   Overlapping Sets of Attributes

Customer Attributes	Balance Owing Amount Overdue 30 Days Amount Overdue 60 Days Amount Overdue 90 Days Credit Rating Date of Last payment	
People Attributes	Name Address Phone Number Date of Birth Sex	Name Address Phone Number Date of Birth Sex
Employee Attributes		Tax Identifier Marital Status Numberof Dependants Date Hired Wage Rate

A Customer is a special case of a Person. What makes this *Person* different (i.e., specialized) is that he's also a *Customer*. In this sense, both the Customer and Employee subclasses may be viewed as *specializing* the Person class. A subclass is said to **_specialize_ its superclass(es) by including only certain of the superclass instances.** Alternatively, we can address the fact that an inherited attribute or behavior can be changed or redefined (i.e., *specialized*) in the inheriting subclass.

Conversely, we can say that a superclass **_generalizes_ its subclasses by including all those features that are "general" to all the subclasses.**

The subclass may inherit an attribute exactly as it is in the parent class or ancestor classes, or it may modify the attribute in some way. For example, the attribute may have the same name in both classes, but its permissible domain of values may be different or its size (length or width) or data type may be different. (There are some restrictions on just what differences are allowed, see below.)

Similarly, an inherited behavior may be inherited unchanged, or it may be totally different between the parent and child classes. This is *polymorphism* (more in the next section), and in the same way as for attributes, it allows us to *specialize* a behavior for a particular subclass.

For the opposite point of view, we can begin at the subclass. Let's say that during analysis we discovered the Customer and Employee classes at *The Outhouse*, but we've not yet found out about the Person class. The class of Customers, we find, has attributes of Balance Owing; Amounts Overdue 30, 60, and 90 Days; Credit Rating; Date of Last Payment; and so on.

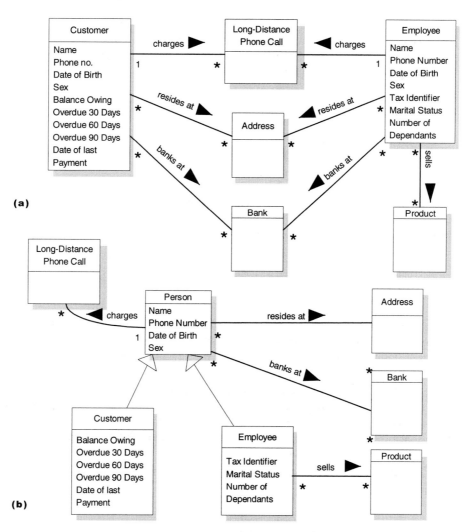

Figure 8-9 Associations (a) before and (b) after subclassing

You may also expect to find that it has Name, Address, Phone, Date of Birth, Sex, and so on. A check of the Employee class reveals that it also has Name, Address, Phone, Date of Birth, and Sex, in addition to Tax Identifier (Social Insurance/Security Number), Marital Status, Number of Dependants, Date Hired, Wage Rate, and so on. Table 8-1 shows this.

The large number of attributes common between these two classes suggests that you may benefit from creating a superclass to carry them. This becomes especially true when you observe that the set of attributes that they have in common actually does describe something identifiable – in this case, a Person. Thus, we can extract the common attributes and place them in a superclass called Persons, which we'll create for this very purpose.

Similarly, we'll find that the behaviors Change-Name-and-Address, Retrieve-Phone-Number and Change-Sex (for error-correction only, of course) appear in both the Customer and Employee classes, so they also can be extracted into the parent class, Persons. Again, we'll find the associations showing similar commonality. Figure 8-9(a) shows some of the associations from Figure 8-6, redrawn to emphasize that both Customers and Employees can take part in these associations:

Customer *resides at* Address.

Customer *charges* Long-Distance Call.

Customer *banks at* Bank.

Employee *resides at* Address.

Employee *charges* Long-Distance Call.

Employee *banks at* Bank.

These associations, then, may be treated the same as the attributes and behaviors were and become features of the Person class. We then have these associations, as shown in Figures 8-9 (a) and (b):

Person *resides at* Address.

Person *charges* Long-Distance Call.

Person *banks at* Bank.

Other associations such as Employee *sells* Product belong only with the Employee, and not with the Customer. Instead of the arrow going to the Person box on the diagram, these ones will go straight to the Employee box.

Thus, we're able to view the subclass/superclass relationship from either end. When we find a class that we later realize needs subclasses, **these subclasses are said to _specialize_ the parent class.** From the other point of view, when we find **classes that we recognize have some common attributes, behaviors, and/or associations, we can create a superclass, which is said to _generalize_ what have now become its subclasses.**

Figure 8-10 shows another example of a subclass hierarchy, with both class and instance diagrams.

In summary:

- An instance that belongs to a subclass automatically and simultaneously belongs also to the superclass. It is at one and the same time a member (instance) of *both* classes.

- An object is an instance of *every one* of its ancestor classes. Its state includes a value for every attribute of every one of its chain of superclasses.

- The *isakinda* verb expresses an identity relationship, which is like equality only stronger. A subclass instance *isakinda* superclass instance (and thus also *isa* superclass instance). Conversely, a superclass instance *canbea* subclass instance, but doesn't have to be.

- Part of the definition of *object-oriented* is that an OOPL or an ODBMS *supports* classes, subclasses, inheritance, and polymorphism. A language *supports* a feature if it contains constructs and mechanisms that make it *easy and convenient* for programmers to take advantage of the feature.

- To be considered truly object-oriented, it should not only *allow* subclassing and inheritance, but it should also actively *support* them.

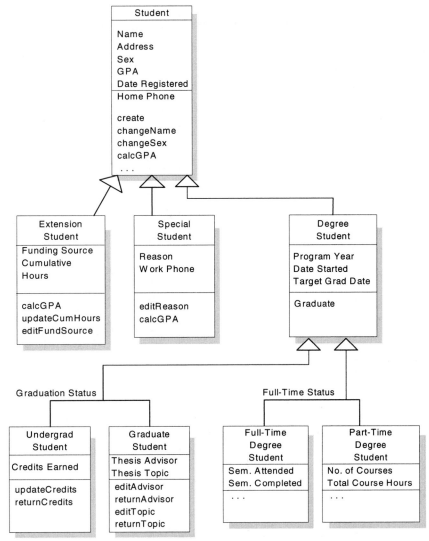

Figure 8-10 Multilevel inheritance with instances (a) Class Diagram and (b) Instance Diagram

- When an association involves only instances of the subclass, and not other instances, it's shown on the diagram as a line to the *subclass box*. An association that involves instances of the superclass (including instances of the subclass) should be shown as a line to the *superclass box*.

- We can begin from the superclass and treat the subclasses as *specialized* cases. Or we can begin at the subclasses and find common attributes and behavior to generalize by creating a superclass. Both approaches will be used at different places in the modeling process.

- When a class needs subclasses, they're said to specialize the parent class. When classes have some common attributes, behaviors and associations, we might create a superclass that *generalizes* them.

Student Attributes	Degree Student Attributes	Special Student Attributes	Full-Time Attributes	Part-Time Attributes	Undergrad Attributes	Grad Attributes
Name: Joe Address: 486 Lintel Way Sex: Male GPA: 2.4 Date Reg: Mar 6, 2001 Home Phone: 555-4213	Program: PhD Year: 2 Date Started: Mar 8, 2000		Semesters Attended: 8 Semesters Completed: 2			Thesis Advisor: Dr McLean Thesis Topic: Distributed Objects
Name: Alison Address: 11 Plaza Prado Sex: Female GPA: 2.6 Date Reg: Jan 11, 2000 Home Phone: 555-1140	Program: BEd Year: 2 Start Date: Sept 1, 2001			Number of Courses: 2 Course Hours: 70	Credits Earned: 0	
Name: Mary Address: 1399 Hal Place Sex: Female GPA: 3.5 Date Reg: Jan 13, 2000 Home Phone: 555-1401		Reason: Training required by employer. Work Phone: 555-4681				
Name: Jim Address: 1900 Icicle Dr Sex: Male GPA: 3.4 Date Reg: Jan 29, 2001 Home Phone: 511-7112	Program: BSc Year: 3 Start Date: Sept 2, 2001		Semesters Attended: 5 Semesters Complete: 4		Credits Earned: 18	

(b)

Figure 8-10 (continued)

One of the secrets of the power of inheritance is that attributes and behaviors are not always inherited in their original form. The next section tells how they're often altered to meet the needs of the subclass.

8.3 POLYMORPHISM AND OVERRIDING

Polymorphism

The word *polymorphism* refers to "many" (*poly*) "shapes" (*morph*). According to Webster (1975), *polymorphism* means **"occurring in various forms."** The *Random House Webster* (1998) gives us **"having, assuming or passing through many forms."** For our purposes, we're concerned with behaviors that have the same name and meaning, but are actually different behaviors depending on which class we mean. Following is a little scenario that introduces a problem that polymorphism solves very neatly.

At The Outhouse, we defined an operation Change-Address on the class of Persons. That is, we've found that all *Persons* (i.e., Customers, Employees, and Others) have need of a piece of program code (a method) that will allow their address attribute to be updated. However, upon questioning we discovered that the way The Outhouse does their business is a little complicated. For "historical reasons," The Outhouse has evolved a system of double-checking customers' names and addresses.

The same system was never applied to employees because these people were always readily accessible if any questions arose or errors needed correcting. Some customers, on the other hand, had in the past complained about not receiving their discount coupons. Since the coupons were time-limited, this gave rise to numerous cases of bad feelings.

And since the coupons were intended to be a promotion for the store, the bad feelings kind of defeated the purpose. As you'll see next, Customers and Employees needed different procedures and *different program code* to achieve what was essentially the same objective for both.

To avoid the problem, The Outhouse has instituted several levels of checking. When a new Customer is entered into the database, a card is printed on the spot for the customer to check and to take with her. Then, within a few days, a "Welcome to *The Outhouse*" letter is sent out, with some discount coupons and a ticket to be returned to go in a monthly draw. The envelope is covered with messages to the effect that "if this is *incorrectly* delivered to your address, please return it and you too will go in the draw."

In addition, the coupons and draw ticket, when used, are entered into the database as confirmation that the letter was correctly addressed. Although this may seem like quite a rigmarole, The Outhouse found that the reduced errors – and consequently fewer bad feelings – had a significant effect on the response to their promotions, and thus on sales.

It was never felt necessary to go to this much trouble with Employees. For them, it was simply a matter of keying in the information, and the Employees would report any errors if they appeared on paychecks and other outputs.

And this next statement is important for much of what follows: *The few* **Persons** *whom The Outhouse had in the database for various reasons, but who were* **neither Employees nor Customers**, *were* **treated the same way as Employees.** These we shall call *Others*.

From the point of view of designing an object-oriented database, this scenario tells us that we have two distinct procedures, and two separate pieces of program code, for handling this Change-Address operation. For Customers, we have a complicated procedure that's actually made up of several smaller procedures, and the program code that we eventually write for this must handle several additional outputs and accept some extra inputs.

For the Employees (and the Others), the procedures and the program code will be much simpler. But the name of the operation is the same in both cases, Change-Address.

And what is more, this name actually *means* the same thing in both cases. It means "please update the address value." In other words, the semantics are the same for these two forms of the operation. This means that they are in fact both the same operation, even though they're done differently, for different *kindsa* people.

Both methods, the complex one for Customers and the simpler one for Employees and Others, exist to update the value of the Address attribute of certain types of Persons, so the *semantics*, or *meaning*, of the operation are the same in both cases.

What this situation demands is something that's quite impossible in standard procedural programming languages. We're asking the language to allow us to write two completely different methods (i.e., subroutines) and give them both the *exact* same name! This is *polymorphism*. It can only be done in an object-oriented environment, and almost always in an inheritance (subclass) hierarchy.

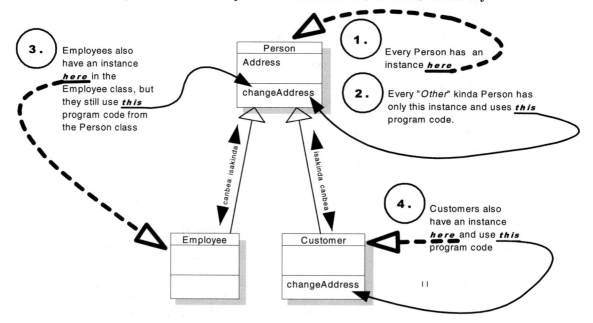

Figure 8-11 Location of method code within the subclass hierarchy

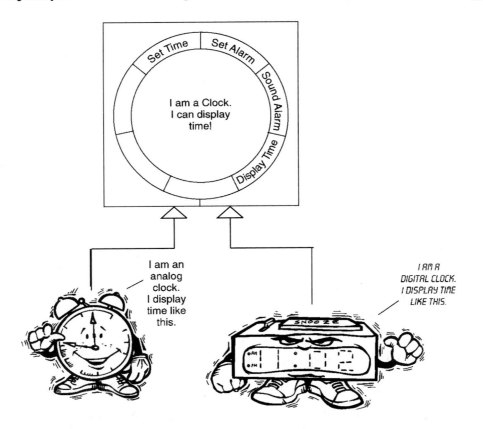

Polymorphism is the ability to write several versions of a method (function, subroutine) in different classes of a subclass hierarchy, and give them all exactly the same name, and rely on the object-oriented environment to establish which version should be executed, depending on the class of the target object when the method is invoked.

In this example, we would code the Employees-and-Others version of the method in the Persons class, where it would automatically be used for any Person who was not an instance of either subclass, that is, for the Others. Then we would code the Customer version of the method, but this time do it in the Customer subclass, as is shown in Figure 8-11.

This version would then automatically be used by any instance of the Customer class. The subclass version of an attribute or operation is said to **_override_ the version from the superclass, because it's used in preference to the superclass version.**

And what about the Employees? You'll no doubt have noticed that we didn't write any program code in the Employee class. What happens is this: When we go to change the address of an Employee, since this class has no method called Change-Address, it *inherits* the one from its parent class – in this case, the Persons class.

But this is the very same piece of program code that's also used for changing the address of Others, those who are instances of Persons but not of any subclass. And this is okay since, you may remember, a few paragraphs back we said that *the few **Persons** whom The Outhouse had in the database but who were **neither Employees nor Customers**, were* **treated the same way as Employees.**

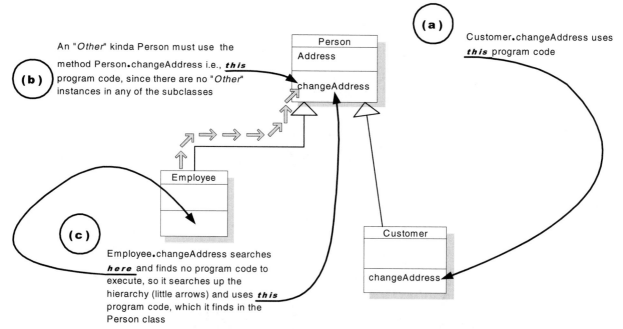

Figure 8-12 Resolving polymorphism

So far, then, this is what we've discovered about polymorphism:

- Polymorphism means "occurring in various forms." For our purposes, we're concerned with behaviors that have the same name and meaning but are actually different depending on which class we're talking about.

- Polymorphism means a behavior may be inherited unchanged, or it may be totally different between the parent and child classes; and, in the same way as for attributes, it allows us to specialize a behavior for particular subclasses.

- Polymorphism is possible only in object-oriented environments and is part of the definition of object-oriented.

- Abstract classes, which have no direct instances, are often introduced to exploit inheritance and polymorphism.

So what have we achieved? We've been able to write a generic version of an operation. Then we've arranged for it to be used for all classes in the hierarchy, except for the one subclass (Customers) where we coded a specialized (there's that word again, *specialized*) version of the method. The next section explains how an object-oriented compiler works this little piece of seemingly impossible magic.

Resolving Polymorphism

It's not such a terrible mystery, really. In principle it's actually quite simple. Object-oriented compilers are designed so that each object normally has access only to the program code written in its class. But if an operation is requested for which there is no method in that class, then in effect the compiler *walks up the tree of superclasses* until it finds a class that *does* have a method by that name. This is the method (subroutine) that gets executed.

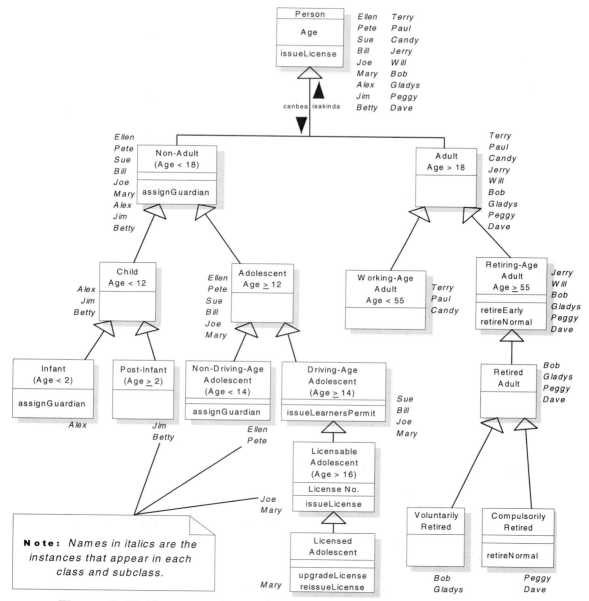

Figure 8-13 More examples of resolving polymorphism: the *issueLicence*, *assignGuardian*, and *retireNormal* methods

This is shown in Figures 8-12 and 8-13. Figure 8-12(a) shows that a request to change the address of a Customer has no trouble finding some code to execute – there's a Change-Address routine right there in the Customer class. A request to change the address for an Other *kind of* Person also finds a piece of program code, but a different piece this time, right there in the Persons class.

Figure 8-12(c) shows what happens when we change the address of an Employee. Since the compiler finds no method called Change-Address in the Employee subclass, it steps up to the superclass Persons and finds one there. This is the code that actually gets executed for Employees. Figure 8-13 shows some more examples.

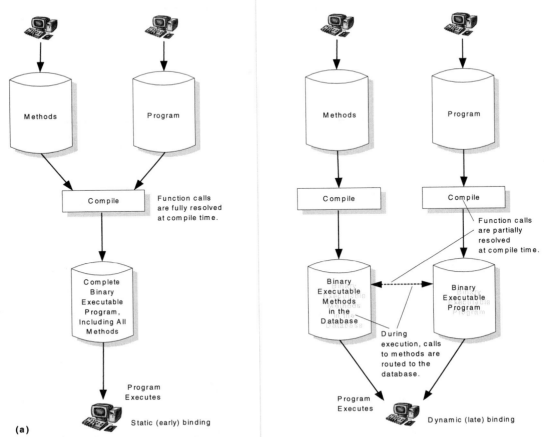

Figure 8-14(a)   Static (early) and late (dynamic) binding

Some OOPLs and ODBMSs actually do it exactly the way I described. Others have their own variations on the theme, but they all achieve the same effect, one way or another. There are a number of differences in the way these things are done by the various compilers, and probably the most significant is the difference between early (static) and late (dynamic) binding.

Static and Dynamic Binding

Some object-oriented products **store the methods as partially compiled object code, which is then linked into the program at compile time.** This is referred to as ***early binding*** or ***static binding.*** Thenthere are others that **store the methods as binary executable code in the database, which at run time is executed directly from the database** which is called ***late binding*** or ***dynamic binding.***

It is important for you to distinguish between these two, because this is sometimes critical when comparing the various OOPLs and ODBMSs. Figure 8-14(a) illustrates the difference.

Static binding may have a very slight advantage in speed, but it has several disadvantages. Compared with *late binding*, it means a larger program size. It also means that if you do change any of the program code for any of the methods within the object, you must recompile every program that uses those methods.

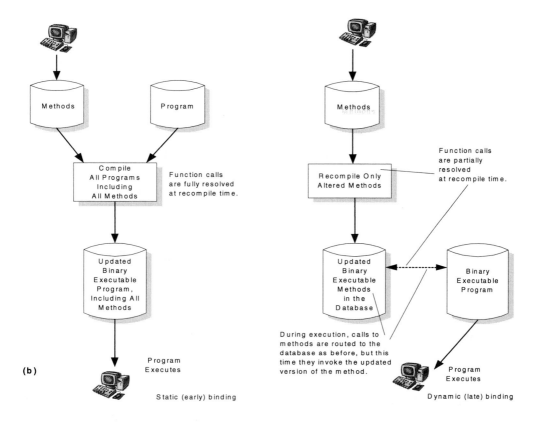

Figure 8-14(b) Updating methods with static (early) and late (dynamic) binding

Dynamic binding is called *late binding* because the methods are compiled and converted to binary executable code, which is then stored *in the database* along with the data for the instances of the class. Later, when the *program* is compiled, the compiler resolves calls to the methods by generating calls to the executables where they're stored in the database.

Later still, at run time, execution simply branches to these pieces of executable code wherever they may be in the database and then returns; see Figure 8-14(b).This way, the program size is reduced because the methods are not included in the executable for the program.

And, a big plus, if you change any of the methods, you simply recompile them and store the new executables in the database. If you need to add a new version of a method in a lower-level subclass, you code it, compile it, and add it to the chosen subclass. *The programs that call the method don't need to be recompiled or altered in any way at all.*

When a method is called (i.e., branched to, or *invoked*), the search will begin up the hierarchy, and the new method will be found and executed. The penalty for late binding is in the time it takes for this search. With *static (early) binding*, the chosen code is compiled right there in the program, and less searching is necessary. The tradeoff is that with *static binding*, changes are more difficult to effect.

It's not only operations that can be changed in the lower levels of a hierarchy. As you'll see in the next section, attributes can also have their properties varied.

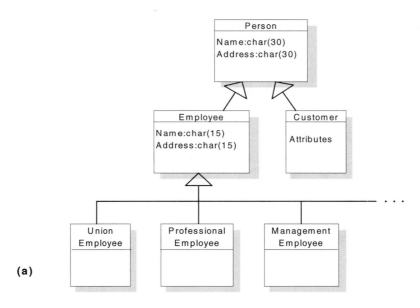

(a)

Figure 8-15 Overriding in a chain of subclasses *(continued)*

Overriding

In the example with The Outhouse, let's examine the Address attribute. For Customers and Other persons we need the full address with city, province or state, and even country, since these persons could have out-of-province (-state), or even out-of-country addresses. Employees, on the other hand, need to live a little closer to their work. (At least, for now we'll say they do. Telecommuting and the Internet may soon change all that!)

So, if we consider Address to be a single data element (that is, a field), then we might save some database space and perhaps some output report space by making the Address field shorter for Employees than for the other *kindsa* persons.

What we've done is to modify the definition of an attribute in the subclass. As I pointed out earlier, a subclass may inherit an attribute exactly as it is, or it may modify the attribute in some way. For example, the attribute may have the same name in both classes, but its domain of permissible values may be different or its size (length or width) or data type may be different.

We say that a subclass feature (attribute or operation) **_overrides_ the corresponding superclass feature; that is, the subclass feature actually replaces the superclass feature *for that subclass and its descendants.***

The reason that the descendent classes also get the new version of the feature is that whenever the feature is referenced in a subclass farther down the tree, the system begins at that class, and walks up the hierarchy until it finds the first class that has a definition for this feature (attribute or operation).

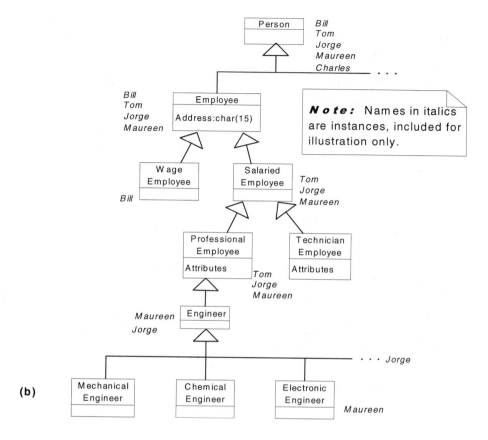

Figure 8-15 (continued)

This means, that it finds the class that has the *new* version of the feature, since we don't get to go all the way up to the class where the old version was written. This is the version that gets used [see Figure 8-15(a)]. Note that a given feature could be overridden several times at different levels in the tree and in different branches. Each time, we simply apply the rule of "walking up the chain of superclasses" until we find some code to execute.

In Figure 8-15(a), the shortened versions of the Name and Address attributes apply to the Employee class and all of its subclasses (unless overridden again in a lower subclass). To print Ted's name and address, we start at the class Union Employee, only to discover there are no such attributes. So we move up the subclass hierarchy to the Employee class, and there we find the short version of the Name and Address attributes.

Now look at Bessie. She's a Customer, but when we need her address we again find there's no such attribute in her class. So we move up the chain, looking for an Address attribute, and in the Person class we find one. It's the original 30-character version of the Address attribute, and so that's the one all Customers and Others end up having available to them.

You'll note that the override doesn't necessarily apply to *all* the descendent classes. In Figure 8-15(b), suppose one subclass of Professional Employees, say, the Engineers, have a need for a 45-character Address attribute. When we list the Professional Employees, we'll call a method called Give-Address, once for each instance of the Employee class.

When we call this method for the instance called Maureen, we'll find she has an instance record in the Electronic Engineer class, but this class has no Address attribute. So we look upward through the subclass hierarchy to the superclass Engineer.

Since Maureen is also an Engineer, she has an instance in the Engineer class, and this one has a 45-character Address attribute. The method searches no further, and returns the value of this attribute as the return value of the function (that is, of the method).

Jorge, on the other hand, is a Traffic Engineer, and the only one on staff. For that reason, we don't have a subclass of Engineers for him. Thus, Jorge has an instance in the Engineer class, but not in any of its subclasses.

We say Jorge is a *direct instance* of the Engineer class (a concept we'll look at in more depth later in Section 8.5). When the Give-Address method is invoked to print Jorge's details, it goes straight to his instance record in the Engineer class and returns the 45-character Address to be printed.

Tom is another matter altogether. Tom is an Accountant. Since the Engineers have the only subclass available under the Professional Employee class [Figure 8-15(b)], Tom and all the other nonengineering professionals go directly in the Professional Employee class.

This, then, is the lowest-level class in the hierarchy where Tom has an instance record. When Give-Address is called for Tom, the system (the compiler) goes to this lowest-level instance record and finds there's no Address attribute. Even though there may be subclasses with Address attributes, Tom is not in any of those subclasses.

So up the chain goes the system, and at the very next level it finds that Tom has an instance record in the Salaried Employee class. This is because Tom is at the same time *both* a Salaried Employee *and* a Professional Employee. Salaried *isakinda* Employee, and Professional *isakinda* Salaried Employee, but neither of these classes has an address attribute.

We go up the tree one more level, to the Employee class. Here we find a 15-character Address, and this value is then returned to the caller as the value of the method.

So you'll see from all this that the attribute that gets used is the one *lowest in the hierarchy*, in the classes where this particular object has instance records. You may also have noticed that Maureen, being an Electronic Engineer and an Employee of this company, has numerous instance records. She has one in Electronic Engineer, one in Engineer, and one in Professional Employee (because she's one of those also). Since Maureen is also a Salaried Employee, and of course an Employee, she has instance records in those classes as well.

In this way, you see that any instance of a subclass is also, at one and the same time, an instance of each and every one of its ancestor classes. There is a chain of superclasses extending upward from the lowest one that our object is an instance of. But we have only the *one object*. There's only one Maureen. ("I'll never find another You!") Our one Maureen object, then, is simultaneously an instance of every class on her superclass chain.

And you see that often somewhere down the chain of subclasses from where we introduced the new version of a feature (attribute or operation), there can be another, newer one. This brings about a further redefinition of the very same feature. So any more subclasses farther down the chain will get to use this redefined version, rather than the one we introduced a little farther up. This is true as far down as the point where yet another subclass may redefine it.

Multiple Inheritance

Multiple inheritance is not available in all OOPLs and ODBMSs, notably missing from current versions of Smalltalk (but perhaps soon likely to be added). And in those that do offer it, there are some problems and anomalies that must be dealt with. Each object-oriented product handles these in its own way.

However, multiple inheritance does exist in the real world, so we must allow for it in our analysis models. At design time, we can make adjustments if necessary to take into account how our OOPL or ODBMS does or doesn't handle it. Some languages allow ***dynamic typing,*** **where an object can switch from one class (or type) to another.**

Smalltalk allows this with what it calls "roles." You'll find a more in-depth discussion of this in Chapter 14. Java avoids the need for multiple inheritance by providing a construct it calls "interfaces."

There are two flavors of multiple inheritance, depending on whether we inherit from two branches that go up to independent classes (multi-origin) or two branches that join higher up into one (single-origin).

MULTI-ORIGIN MULTIPLE INHERITANCE

"Mobile homes" are very common in North America, although readers elsewhere in the world may not have encountered them. They provide semipermanent housing with a considerable amount of space, but with portability too. At any time, the wheels can be put back on, a truck hooked up, and it becomes a 20 x 4 meter (60 x 12 foot) trailer to be towed to a new site, across the city or across the country.

The question is, *Is this a house or is it a vehicle?* The answer is, of course, "All of the above." At one and the same time, it *isakinda* house and, because it travels on the road, it *isakinda* vehicle. It must have a building permit since it's a house, and it needs a license number (or a temporary permit) since it's also an unpowered vehicle, that is, a trailer. Figure 8-16 shows where it might fit in the scheme of things.

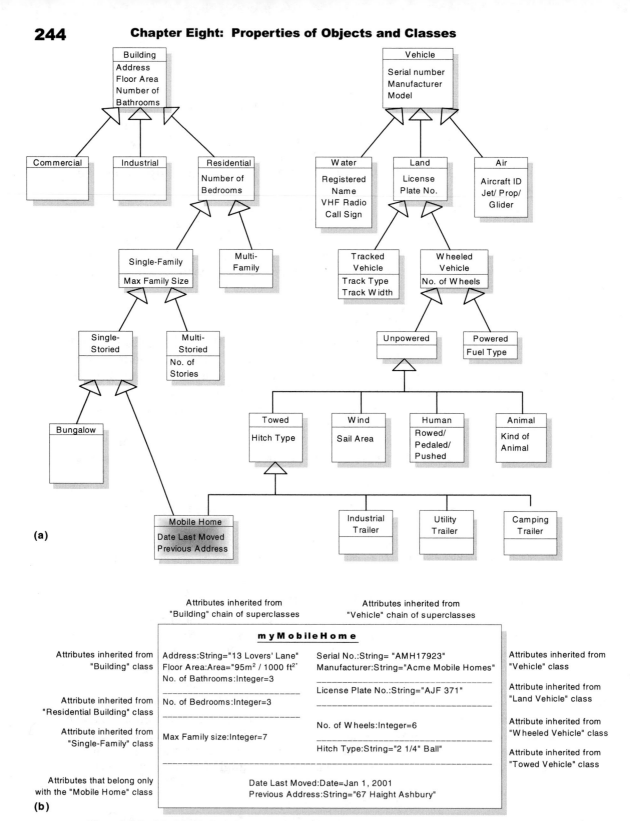

Figure 8-16 Multiple inheritance for a mobile home: (a) Class Diagram and (b) Instance Diagram showing attribute values

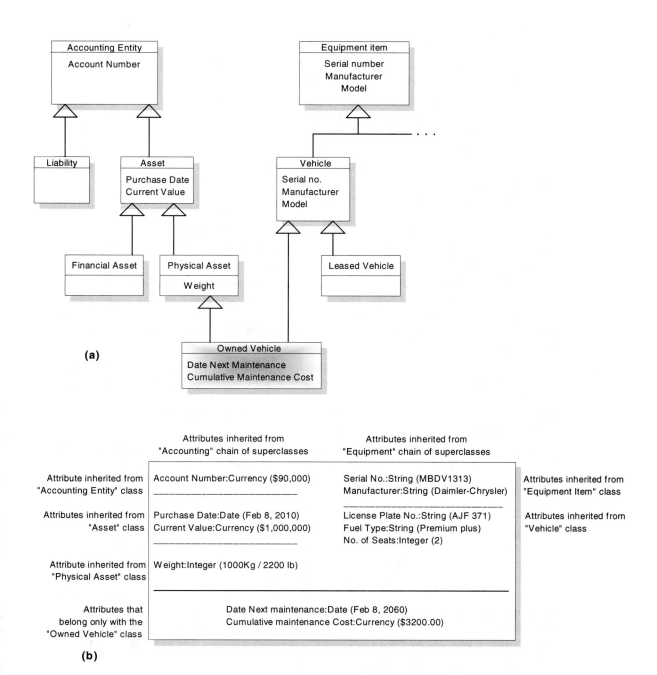

Figure 8-17 Multiple inheritance for a Dodge Viper: (a) class diagram and (b) instance diagram that shows *my* Dodge Viper with atribute values shown in brackets (note the purchase date!)

Now take a look at Figure 8-17. This company has a class of Leased Vehicles and a class of Owned Vehicles. Since an Owned Vehicle *isakinda* vehicle, this is a subclass of the class Vehicle, which in turn *isakinda* Equipment Item. This, then, is the way the fleet manager views an Owned Vehicle.

The accountant, on the other hand, has a rather different view. To him, an Owned Vehicle is simply an Asset, which *isakinda* Accounting Entity. Further, an Owned Vehicle *isakinda* Physical Asset, as opposed to Financial Assets such as stocks, bonds, promissory notes, and mortgages.

In this way, an Owned Vehicle is able to inherit from two chains of superclasses: the Equipment Item chain and the Accounting Entity chain. Figure 8-17(b) shows a Toyota Camry instance.

Because it *isa* Equipment Item, the Camry has Make, Model, Weight, Color, and Serial Number attributes, with (among others) Change-Color and Return-Serial-Number operations. Since it also *isa* Vehicle, it has License Number, Odometer Mileage, and Seating Capacity attributes, along with operations such as Take-A-Trip, Change-Seating-Capacity, and Assign Vehicle To Employee.

From the accounting side, the Camry has an Account Number attribute, a Current Value (balance), and a Description, since every Accounting Entity has these. Like any Accounting Entity, it has operations for Return-Your-Description (to an object who needs it), and Adjust-Current-Value.

And since it is at the same time an Asset, it has a Purchase Date, a Purchase Price, and a Market Value. (For its book value we would use the Current Balance from the superclass.) It will have suitable methods in the Asset class to alter or adjust any of these. Then, as a Physical Asset, our Camry will have a Weight attribute and a Depreciate operation.

Finally, there will be some attributes and methods contributed by the Owned Vehicle class itself. These are not shared with any superclass but are specific to this class only. They're shown in Figure 8-17 (a) as the Cumulative-Maintenance attribute and the Update-Cumulative-Maintenance operation. (In this company, we make sure maintenance is always included when we lease, so these would not be relevant in the Leased Vehicle class.)

You'll note, by the way, that a Leased Vehicle is not considered an asset. If anything it should be considered a liability (or at least its lease agreement should be), and would that ever complicate the diagram!

However, these examples do show that ***multi-origin multiple inheritance*** **is when a class is simultaneously a subclass of two (or more) independent superclasses and inherits from both (and from the chain of superclasses above each), and these two chains of superclasses *do not* link up at the top.**

Single-Origin Multiple Inheritance

Figure 8-18(a) shows land vehicles, watercraft, and aircraft descended from the superclass Vehicle. But farther down the tree, we see that the Hovercraft class shows multiple inheritance from all three of these.

Since it can travel on land, it will require a vehicle license number. As an instance of the Watercraft class it'll need a Marine Radio Call Sign. In some places, it's regarded also as an aircraft, and so will need some Aircraft attributes and methods.

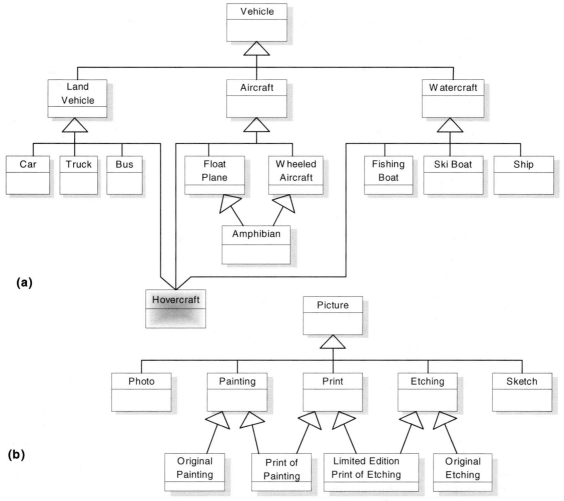

Figure 8-18 Single-origin multiple inheritance: (a) vehicles and (b) works of art

Figure 8-18(b) shows something similar with works of art. This shows the other way that multiple inheritance can happen – ***single-origin multiple inheritance***, **where two or more branches of a class hierarchy *join up* after having sprouted from a single common ancestor class.**

DIFFICULTIES WITH MULTIPLE INHERITANCE

As with most things, there's good news and bad news about multiple inheritance. The good news is the power and flexibility it adds to the object-oriented way of doing things. So much so, in fact, that there is strong pressure from the user community being applied on the manufacturers of Smalltalk, one of the most widely used of the pure object-oriented languages.

Inexplicably to some people, Smalltalk was designed without multiple inheritance. However, many software developers have sorely felt the lack and are beginning to ask for it to be added to the language in a future revision. As a *very rough* generalization, we could say that, at the current state of the art (year 2001), most ODBMSs allow multiple inheritance and most OOPLs do not.

The bad news is that it adds some complications. The biggest one, for which there is as yet no standardized solution, is *what happens when a subclass inherits two attributes of the same name* from two different superclass chains. Of course, this complication also arises when it inherits two *methods* with the same name from two superclasses in different chains. The question is, How do we decide which one to use?

There are a number of ways this impasse can be resolved, but none of them works perfectly. Each of them has its strengths, its devotees, and its problems. Every ODBMS and OOPL uses one or another of these or a variation or combination:

(a) Force the programmer-designer to choose each time.

(b) Require the programmer to code a new method (or attribute) in the subclass to override both inherited ones.

(c) Execute first one and then the other. (But then how do we choose which to do first?)

(d) Name them differently.

Out of all this talk of polymorphism and inheritance comes yet another powerful feature that's not available with conventional ways of writing programs. This is the ability to add to the functionality of a subroutine or function library, *without having access to the source code*.

Object Class Libraries

Most programmers who sell, or otherwise distribute, their work don't want the purchasers dabbling within the source code. Obviously, this is going to cause problems, and in the worst case it could become a fight over who is to blame for some disaster. This is reflected in a couple of ways.

If you were shopping for a C or Pascal function library – say, for accessing Paradox files or MSAccess tables on your PC – most vendors won't allow you to have the source code at all. Others will sell it to you for about three or four times the price of the original library. In the mainframe world, it's sometimes easier to arrange, though no less expensive, but the problems are still the same.

If instead you buy an object class library, a number of things will be different. What you get for your money is not just functions but a set of *class definitions*.

These consist of data definitions, along with the methods to handle them. You can't modify them directly, but if you need to change either the data definitions or the methods, you do it by defining a subclass that inherits from one of the classes in the library. Then you may extend the class library to do exactly what you need by doing one or more of the following:

(a) Code a new method to override the one in the library when applied to the new subclass (and any descendants).

(b) If a new method simply adds steps to the old one, it may include a call to the old method in the library superclass (in most OOPLs and ODBMSs).

(c) Define a new attribute to override one in the library superclass.

(d) Add some totally new attributes and methods.

So we get the best of all possible worlds. With object class libraries, we can buy the functions we need and extend them *without having the source code*. We can sell class libraries and allow the users to extend them, without the risk that they might devastate our handiwork. And if the worst comes to the worst, when there arises a dispute over who caused a disaster, it's easy to tell who wrote which parts of the code.

The object-oriented front-end tools such as PowerBuilder, Visual C++, and ObjectVision work from class libraries. They contain class definitions for such screen objects as windows, buttons, and scroll bars, and you design a user interface for your system by instantiating these classes.

Although somewhat ungainly, *instantiate* has become part of the official object-oriented jargon (OOJ, pronounced "ooh-jay.") To **_instantiate_ a class is simply to create instances of it.** Inprise/Borland C++Builder, for example, comes with a package of *application frameworks*, which in reality are a huge library of object classes. All OOPL and ODBMS products are shipped with extensive class libraries.

In-house class libraries are equally valuable if not more so. As you work on projects in the object paradigm, you'll be creating more and more classes and instances of them. As you move from one project to the next, you'll find that each project needs some of the classes and objects from earlier projects. You'll find that you need to do some or all of the things that I mentioned above, when we were discussing purchased class libraries.

In other words, prior projects can serve to provide an in-house class library. And I have some warnings to pass on about that, too. The move to object-oriented working involves more than just new languages and software tools. It requires a whole new way of thinking, of viewing the business of software development. This is why it's truly a paradigm shift.

On top of that is the learning curve for the new languages and tools. Then there's the need to spend time building the initial in-house class libraries.

The net result is that you can expect your first object-oriented project to take *longer* than it would have with the old methods. The usual experience is that *by about the **third** project* the learning curve and the thinking shift are about done, and the in-house class library has grown to a useful size. So you can expect that the third or fourth project will show significant benefits from this new way of doing things.

After that, the full predicted benefits will start to become apparent, and the in-house class library will continue to grow under the watchful eye of the object-oriented database administrator (OODBA). Since in the object-oriented paradigm the function libraries have now moved in with the databases, their management and administration becomes a database administration (DBA) function. This may well dictate some reorganizing of how your DBA department works.

Here is a summary, then, of how polymorphism works, and how it allows increased reusability of program code:

- Some object-oriented products store the methods as object code, which is then linked into the program at *compile time*. This is referred to as *static (early) binding*.

- Others store the methods as binary executable code in the database, which at *run time* is executed directly from the database. This is called *dynamic (late) binding*.

- A subclass may inherit an attribute exactly as it is, or it may modify the attribute in some way.

- We say that the subclass feature (attribute or operation) *overrides* the corresponding superclass feature. The subclass feature actually replaces the superclass feature *for that subclass and its descendants.*

- When overriding *operations*:
    - **Extension:** Add some new behavior, usually affecting new attributes.
    - **Restriction:** Operation works for a subset of values of argument.
    - **Optimization:** Take advantage of constraints to improve code.

- When overriding *attributes*:
    - **Restriction:** Type of attribute is a subtype of the one in the superclass.
    - **Changing Size:** New attribute has different width or decimal places.
    - **Number/Type:** Preserve the number and type of attributes.

- Multiple inheritance is not available in some OOPLs and ODBMSs, notably Smalltalk. Some object-oriented environments offer both multi-origin multiple inheritance and single-origin multiple inheritance.

- Resolving multiple inheritance can be complicated when the same feature is inherited twice. The different products have various ways that they decide which one to use.

- If you buy an object class library, you can change either the data definitions or the methods by defining a subclass that inherits from one of the classes in the class library. Then you can extend the library by redefining the attributes or methods in your new subclass. *You do not need the library source code.*

- As you do more projects, you'll create classes. As you move from one project to the next, each needs some of the classes from earlier projects. In other words, prior projects can develop an in-house class library.

- Your first object-oriented project will take longer. By the *third* project the in-house class library grows, so the *third or fourth* OO project will show significant benefits.

The greater reusability of program code has the effect of reducing the total amount of coding we do. In addition to the savings in work, time, and expense from class libraries, there's another trick that takes further advantage of inheritance and polymorphism to reduce the coding effort.

8.4 ABSTRACT CLASSES

Something else we discovered during the analysis phase at *The Outhouse* was that both the Person class and the Vendor class needed a Change-Name-and-Address transaction. Vendors were defined as "businesses that supply products to *The Outhouse*," so they're quite different from Persons, be they Customer Persons or Employee Persons.

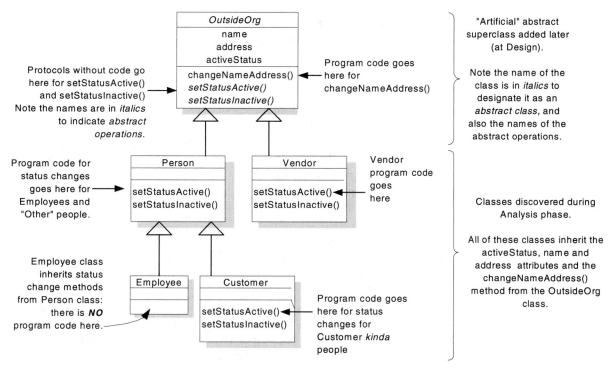

Figure 8-19 Creating an "artificial" superclass

But Persons and Vendors both have a need for this Change-Name-and-Address operation (and one or two others besides, but we'll stay with this one for now). As I mentioned earlier, we'll sometimes find a need to add a class just to take advantage of inheritance and polymorphism, and this is just such a time. We'll create a class called Outside Organization, or OutsideOrg for short (Figure 8-19).

By allowing both the Person class and the Vendor class to inherit from OutsideOrg, we only have to write the Change-Name-and-Address method once. Not only that, but we can also define the Name and Address attributes in the new superclass and take them out of the Person and Vendor classes (which have now become subclasses).

By inventing an "artificial" superclass, we've simplified our model, and reduced the amount of work needed when we build the database and code the methods in the construction phase. We can also expect a reduction in maintenance effort, since there's only one Change-Name-and-Address method to modify and keep track of.

There's something different about this new class, however. While every Person is also an OutsideOrg, and so is every Vendor, these are the **only** OutsideOrgs; that is, *there are no other OutsideOrgs except the ones that come from the Person and Vendor classes.*

We say that the OutsideOrg class has no *direct instances*. A **_direct instance_ of a class is one that's an instance of this class, but not of any of its subclasses.** So the only instances that the OutsideOrg class has are those provided for it by its two subclasses, Person and Vendor.

Whenever a class is "covered" in this way by its subclasses, we say it is an **_abstract class_, a class that has no direct instances.** Alternatively, a **_concrete class_ is one that _does_ have direct instances; it is said to be _directly instantiable_.**

In UML, we show an abstract class by writing its name in italics.

You'll remember that we also mentioned Jorge as being a *direct instance* of the Engineer class in Figure 8-15(b) because there was no subclass for his specialty, Traffic Engineer. Doing this made Engineer a concrete class in that example, because it has one direct instance – Jorge.

Another thing we can do is to move up into the OutsideOrg superclass an attribute called Active-Status, a Boolean or yes/no value that tells whether we're currently allowing any dealings with this Person or Vendor. We may set the Active-Status to Inactive if we're dissatisfied with deliveries from a vendor or with payments from a customer, or for an employee who is temporarily unavailable for work. (Many of our employees are part-time.)

Since the rules and procedures (the algorithm) for changing this status are very different among the three kinds of objects, it was apparent that we would need six different methods to do the changes. We needed three methods to set the Active-Status to Active and three more to set it to Inactive.

So we coded six methods, two in each subclass, which works, since these methods have access to the attributes in the superclass. However, to control future changes and to force maintenance programmers to preserve the format of the messages (the function calls), we defined the *protocols* (interfaces) for the two operations Set-Status-Active and Set-Status-Inactive *in the OutsideOrg superclass.*

But we didn't write any program code in the OutsideOrg class. The **_protocol_ for an operation consists of its name and the names and types of its arguments,** along with its **_semantics_ – the meaning of the operation and what it does.** All this we placed in the OutsideOrg class, so that the methods in the subclasses would inherit it. The program code, the methods themselves, we wrote in the subclasses, that is, Person (to cover the Employees and Others), Vendor, and Customer.

What we've created in the OutsideOrg superclass is called an **_abstract operation_, one that has no program code in the class where it's defined, the methods to implement the operation being provided by the subclasses** [see Figure 8-19(b)]. The subclasses containing the methods may be concrete, or may themselves also be abstract. As with abstract classes, the name of an abstract operation is always shown in italics.

You'll note that an abstract operation is an *operation*, and *not* a method. This is because it has no program code, and a method is defined to be a *piece of code*. In contrast, the same operation in Customer class is considered a **_concrete operation_** there**, because it _does_ have a method (i.e., some code) in that class.**

Similarly, the Change-Name-And-Address operation in the OutsideOrg class, as we discussed in the previous section, is a concrete operation, since it has program code in that class. It's totally okay for an abstract class to have a concrete operation. But what about a concrete class? Can a concrete class have an abstract operation? What do you think?

What if we wish to record some dealings with an OutsideOrg that was neither a Person nor a Vendor? Say we wish to sponsor a sports team or a charity. By creating this entity as an instance of OutsideOrg, but not as an instance of any subclass, we've suddenly converted OutsideOrg from an abstract class to a concrete one.

This highlights the fact that *the abstract or concrete status of a class is always provisional.* At any time, a system maintenance request may necessitate some "other" instances that get created as direct instances, thus turning it into a concrete class. Or, for a concrete class, the system maintenance request may cause us to create an Other subclass, so that the subclasses now completely cover it, making it abstract.

But there's another more critical problem. Now that we have direct instances in OutsideOrg, what happens when we try to change the Active-Status on one of them? This attribute is defined in this class, so finding the attribute is no problem.

But much more serious is the difficulty finding some program code to execute! The system, in its usual way, will see that there is no method for this operation, so it will attempt to climb the hierarchy looking for one, except there's nowhere to climb! The methods are all in the subclasses, *down* the hierarchy, so our concrete class finds it impossible to execute this abstract operation. So it bombs.

The rule, then, is that a concrete class cannot have abstract operations, since there is no program code in that class to perform these operations on its direct instances.

Analysis or Design?

When we create additional "artificial" (and frequently abstract) classes in this way to capitalize on inheritance and polymorphism, should we be doing it at analysis or during design? Strictly speaking, this should be a design issue. In analysis we should be modeling the requirements as the users see them. Then later on in design, we should make use of any tricks or techniques to make the programmers' job more effective and efficient.

However, if during analysis the *users* spy an opportunity to create one, you probably should include it in the models right then. If *you* or the *analysts* see such an opportunity, you'll have a judgment call to make on whether to add, it or make a note and add it later in design. Your judgment will need to be based on whether you feel that doing it now will help the process of understanding and model building, or whether you think it would only cloud the issue.

Many developers will tell you it *must* be done at design time, and they're not wrong. My personal preference, however, is to use judgment on whether it will *help the users understand* better if we do it right now, in analysis. Otherwise, I *make a note* and delay it to design.

Here is a summary list of points about "artificial superclasses" and abstract classes:

• When there are no other instances except those that come from the subclasses, the superclass has no direct instances. A *direct instance* of a class is one that's an instance of that class, but *not* of any of its subclasses.

• When the only instances in the superclass are those provided for it by its subclasses, we say it's *covered* by its subclasses, and we say it's an *abstract class,* that is, a class that has *no* direct instances.

• A concrete class is one that *does* have direct instances; it's said to be *directly instantiable*.

- An abstract operation has no program code in the class where it's defined; its methods are provided by the subclasses. The subclasses containing the methods may be concrete or abstract.

- A concrete operation has a method in its defining class. An abstract class can have a concrete operation.

- The abstract or concrete status of a class is always provisional.

- A concrete class cannot have abstract operations, since there is no program code to perform these operations on its direct instances.

- Add "artificial superclasses" later at design time, or right now in analysis if you judge that they'll contribute to understanding, communication, and development of the project.

The key thing about subclasses and superclasses is that they deal with *kinds of*, where we're talking about a single instance that belongs to *both* the subclass and superclass. There's another important relationship we need to discuss, where we have two *different* kinds of objects. Each belongs to a different class, but here one object is *part of* the other in some way.

8.5 AGGREGATION: COMPONENTS AND WHOLES

There are actually three different relationships to introduce here, all different but related. In the literature, you'll find that some authors distinguish among the three and some lump them together under the label "components and parts." I prefer to use the more generic term *aggregation* to subsume the three more specialized terms, which are:

(a) Whole–part or component–assembly

(b) Container–contents

(c) Collection–member

The importance of these is twofold. First, they are fundamental ways that we humans use to organize our world. Or perhaps I should say, to organize the masses of data we carry in our heads to describe the world around us. Along with all the other concepts we've been studying in this book, from classes and objects to inheritance, these concepts are being used in our heads all te time.

And since systems analysis is an art and is not done by merely applying a recipe, sometimes small and unlikely ideas make a great difference to both the efficiency and effectiveness of our work. Basing our methods on these "natural" factors has dne just that – to a perhaps surprising degree. These factors are really the core reasons why first ERDs, and now object-oriented models, have worked so well.

Second, we sometimes discover associations that just don't "feel right" (after a while you develop quite a "gut feel" for these things). Often it turns out that, for the purposes of the current project, the association is really meant to go to something "within" the object. Then, when we redo the model to add this fact, we find that it gives a more accurate picture of how the users' world really works.

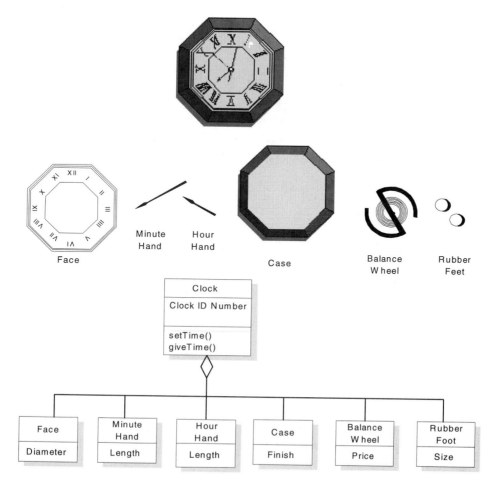

Figure 8-20 Components and models

It may turn out that our users are not really interested in the entire object, only a certain part "within" it. The phrase "within the object," however, could mean any of these three different relationships, as we'll shortly see.

We begin by looking at the whole–part or assembly–component relationship, since it's perhaps the most common, and certainly the least abstract and thus the easiest to grasp.

Whole–Part or Component–Assembly

Who among us doesn't remember, as a child, taking something apart to see what made it tick? And were Mother and Father impressed? We often manifested the curiosity of childhood by taking something apart – and *maybe* getting it back together before we were found out.

This is a very natural way to treat something in order to understand it. As adlts we've learned to avoid trouble by sometimes taking things apart mentally, imagining or visualizing each piece being removed.

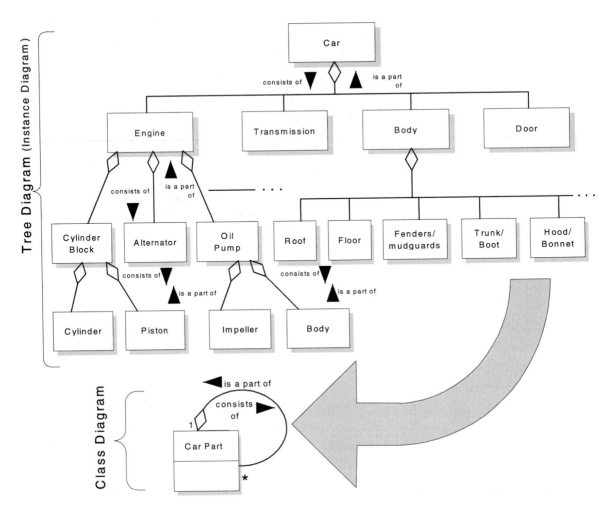

Figure 8-21 How to model a tree structure: (a) a car   *(continued)*

Often we're lucky enough to have a sequence of pictures in a book, or better still, a movie or videotape to watch. The point is that we can learn, understand, and make sense of something by thinking of it as being made up of components. There even are times when the component–whole relationship turns out to be the key to what we'r attempting.

Figure 8-20 shows some examples of whole–part or component–assembly relationships (or call them by any mixture, such as assembly–part or component–whole). A car is made up of wheels, an engine, a body, some brakes, and so on. A book such as the one you're holding in your hand consists of a cover, some pages, and a binding, that is, its physical components.

Viewed another way, a book consists of logical or conceptual components, such as title page, contents, body, and index. The body of the book then consists of a preface and a number of chapters. A house is made up of rooms, walls, doors, windows, and so on.

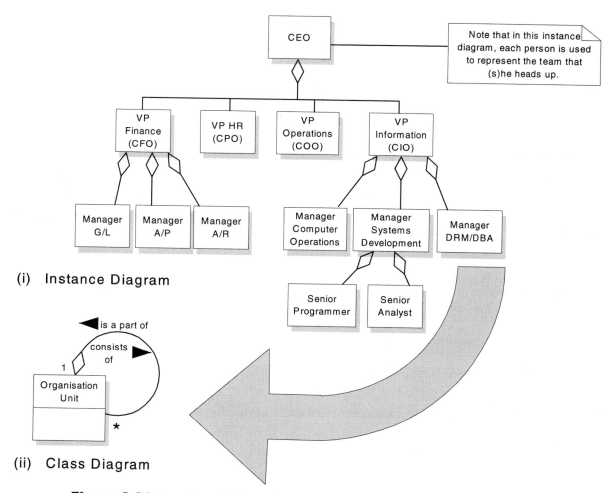

(i) Instance Diagram

(ii) Class Diagram

Figure 8-21 (continued) Tree structures: (b) an organization chart

You'll note that in Figure 8-21 I've used the UML notation with a diamond to show the component relationship. The verb on this relationship is *is a part of* and is very different from the *isakinda* verb we used for subclasses. Other suitable verbs would be *consists of* or *is made up of* if we start at the whole, rather than at the component. (You'll note that I've been careful to place my verbs so that you may read each one as a sentence, as in Figure 8-21.)

One way to tell whether you're dealing with a component relationship is to think about what would happen if you took the "component" away. Would the "whole" still work? Does a clock work if you take out one of its gears? Does a bicycle run without one of its wheels? Questions such as these can't always give a definite answer, but they'll certainly point the way to understanding.

(Overleaf, p258) **Figure 8-22** A Bill-of-Materials structure: (a) An instance Diagram of a car; (b) An extension of the diagram from part (a), showing components of components; (c) A class Diagram. The Engine, Alternator and Cylinder Block [parts (a) and (b)] each have a half by three-quarter inch bolt as a component. Compare this with the Class Diagram in part (c), which is much simpler.

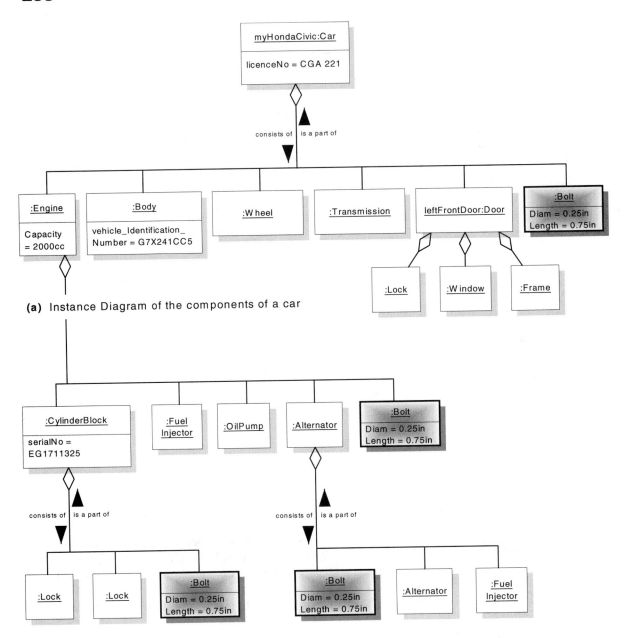

(a) Instance Diagram of the components of a car

(b) Components of components - the engine disassembled

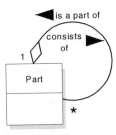

(c) "Many Parts *are part of* one Assembly" or "One Assembly *consists of* many Parts

Some objects can be taken apart into components

There's one special case of assembly–part that's complex and interesting enough for us to treat it separately.

BILL-OF-MATERIALS STRUCTURE

Think for a moment about a product, perhaps a car (if you like that sort of thing) or an item of clothing (if that's more your "style"). The car [Figure 8-21(a)] is made up of many components.[3]

Some of those such as the engine, transmission, alternator, and doors are in turn made up of smaller parts. Traditionally, this was described as a "bill-of-materials structure," because it detailed all the materials (components) needed to build something. Figure 8-22 illustrates how we would show this on an object model.

But take a closer look at Figure 8-22(b). This shows a complication. The "bolt, ¼ x ¾ in." turns out to be a very versatile little piece of equipment. Not only is it used in the engine, but also in other subassemblies such as the cylinder block, transmission, and alternator. And it's used directly in some parts of the car without the help of any major subassemblies. (Note that **a _subassembly_ is a _component_, which in turn breaks down into components.**) In Figure 8-22(c) you'll see how this is modeled.

---

[3] An average car has about 3000 parts. By contrast, some of my students who were technical manual writers on the Hercules aircraft assured me that the Herc has 3 *million* parts! That's why its parts book and manuals are in an Oracle database. What an opportunity for an object-oriented Oracle (O-O-O) project!

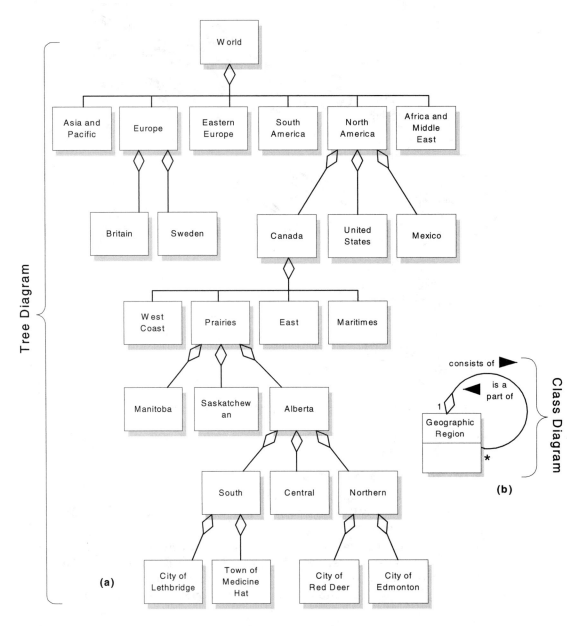

Figure 8-23   More examples of tree structures: (a) an instance diagram of a sales report by region, and (b) The same thing drawn as a class diagram

In Figure 8-22(c), which is a class diagram, you'll see that the relationship is represented by a loop from "Part" to "Part." (We'll assume that it's usually to a *different* instance of the Part class; otherwise, none of this would make sense.) The multiplicity shown in Figure 8-22(c) indicates that we have a one-to-many relationship from one instance of Part (the assembly) to a group of other instances of Part (the components). Figure 8-22(a) shows how this looks in the general case.

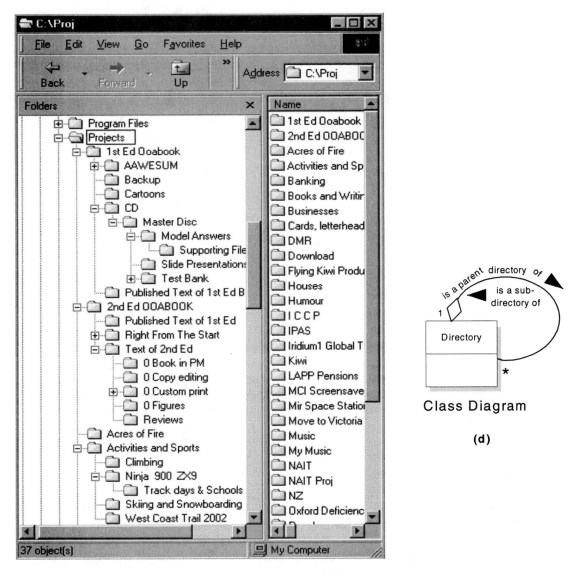

Figure 8-23 (continued) (c) A small sample from the Windows directory structure of my PC, drawn as a tree structure, i.e., as an instance diagram, and (d) the same thing drawn as a class diagram, which covers my *entire* directory structure, current, past and future.

Then in Figure 8-22, we see what happens if one of those subassemblies is in turn also related as an assembly to a bunch of other parts, its components. In short, what we're diagramming here is a tree structure. This is something that occurs in object-oriented analysis whenever we find a class of objects where each is related to some others that are also in the same class. In this case, they're all car parts.

Another example is the organizational units in a company, the divisions, departments, branches and sections. In this case, the tree we're describing is the organization chart. (Figure 8-23 shows more tree structures.)

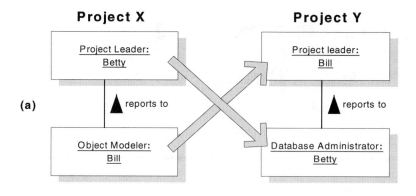

(a)

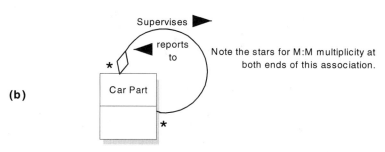

(b)

"One Employee *reports to* many other Employees;
each Employee *supervises* many other Employees."

Figure 8-24   (a) An instance diagram of matrix management; (b) a class diagram of the same thing; (c) an instance diagram of family "trees", showing what a horrible mess such a diagram could become if it is at all complicated; (d) a nice, simple class diagram of part (c), containing all the information we need.

MATRIX STRUCTURE

My wife Nina now works for DMR Group, a consulting firm that has a rather fluid reporting structure. Instead of the usual top-down chain-of-command military structure found in most organizations, they have reporting relationships that change with the project. For instance, Betty may be project leader on a project for Client X, and Bill the object modeler may spend a few weeks working for her, doing the analysis models.

Then Bill goes off to start and lead a project for Client Y. Later, Bill's project has need of someone with experience on a particular database product, and it just so happens that Betty has worked a lot with that product.

So, after finishing her project for Client X, Betty comes to work for Bill for a while and then goes off to head yet another project. The reporting relationships could get somewhat convoluted, to say the least! What we have here is termed *matrix management* and, although unheard of a few years ago, it's becoming more and more common.

How would we diagram this? Figure 8-24(a) and (b) shows an instance diagram and a class diagram. The M:M multiplicity on the class diagram indicates that one Employee *reports to* many Employees, and that one Employee *supervises* many Employees.

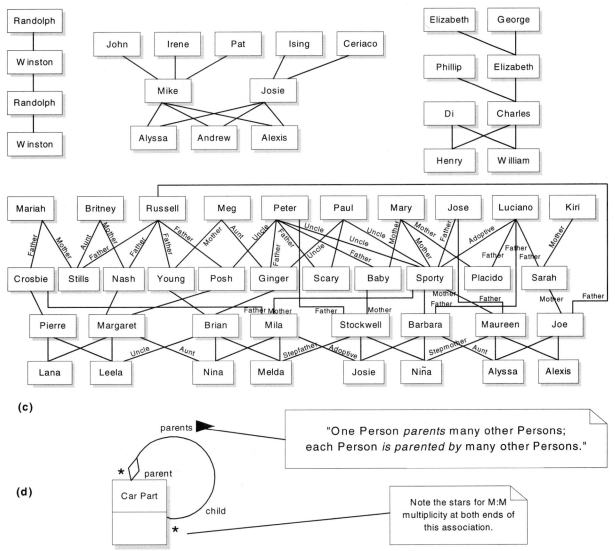

(c)

(d)

"One Person *parents* many other Persons;
each Person *is parented by* many other Persons."

Note the stars for M:M
multiplicity at both ends of
this association.

Figure 8-24 (continued)

A matrix such as this can be viewed as a "two-way tree." In a regular, or "one-way" tree, a "parent" can have many "children," but a child can have only one parent. In a matrix, parents can have many children, and children can have many parents. And that very turn of phrase suggests another example: family "trees" [Figure 8-24(c) and (d)]. I say "tree" in quotes because really it's a matrix rather than a tree, since everybody has at least two parents.

The matrix is relatively rare for component–assembly structures when dealing with individual items, because it's difficult to find a situation where a component is part of two wholes at the same time, but it may easily happen *over time*.

A system to track computers and their components may need to track which computer a given board was installed in before, in addition to its present location. Similarly, a factory equipment application may need to know which machine a particular subassembly is installed in and its installation history.

The same thing can happen with trucks or buses and their engines, or airplanes.

Matrix structures will also occur with contents moving from one container to another, and with members who belong to several collections or organizations either at the same time or else over time. You'll see how this can happen as we explore container–contents and collection–member relationships in the next two sections.

Container–Contents

A container and its contents are a little different from component-assembly. Consider a pot of honey; take away the pot and the honey is still fine, albeit a little messy. Take away the honey, and you still have a perfectly good pot, "Useful for putting things in," as Pooh once said to Eeyore.

A 6-meter-long (20-ft) shipping container is a perfectly good shipping container, empty or full. Its contents are in fine shape, before being loaded into it, while they're inside it, and even after being taken out of it. In other words, the container and its contents exist independently of each other. They do have a relationship, in that the container *contains, holds*, or *houses* the contents, and in that way provides a service for those contents.

But the container doesn't depend on the contents for its existence, nor vice versa. This is unlike components and wholes. Generally, an assembly is incomplete when it loses some of its components, but a container is still complete and fully functional when it loses some or all of its contents. This is one of the clues to look for when modeling, to help decide which form you've encountered.

Collection–Member

Yet another variation on this theme of aggregation is the collection–member. Collections can take many forms. Besides the more obvious stamps, books, art, and other collectibles, there are many organizations that can be viewed this way. Think for a moment about a sports club, a church, or perhaps a military regiment. Each organization has a history, a tradition, even what might be considered a subculture. It has a distinct identity, recognizable to people within it and around it.

Each organization depends on its members, past and present, for the development of this organizational character, but not upon any individual member. Over the years, members come and go, and the group may move to new premises across the city or across the nation. All of the group's possessions, equipment, furniture and the like may be disposed of and replaced (except for a few symbols and icons associated with this "character" the group has).

Practically everything may change, but the group retains its identity. The prestigious Black Watch regiment, for example, has none of its World War II personnel or equipment still on active service, but like such regiments in many countries, has retained its tradition, identity, and character to this day, right on into the new millennium.

Where are you most likely to meet collection–member relationships? It's certainly conceivable that you might develop a system for a library, gallery, museum, or some other actual *collection*.

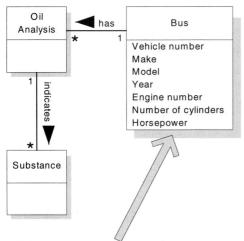

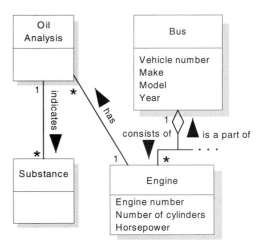

(a) Because this class has a mixture of attributes that belong some to Bus and some to Engine (and presumably does the same with its operations), this diagram is unnormalized by the definition used in this text.

(b) This diagram is more explicit, precise and accurate, all good things for a diagram to be. It is so because the "has" relationship is now a 1:M from the Engine class rather than from Bus. In this sense, the diagram more accurately reflects the real world of our Transit Co. users.

Figure 8-25   Relationships with a Component-Assembly structure: (a) the "wrong" way and (b) a "better" way

On the other hand, the connection may be more subtle. You may encounter a fleet of vehicles, aircraft, or watercraft that behaves as a collection. You may find a furniture or equipment inventory that fits the mold. Or you may sometimes find that a herd, flock, school, mob, gaggle, or skein[4] of animals can best be handled by considering it this way.

Webster (1975) defines **_aggregation_ to be "a group, body or mass composed of many distinct parts."** *Oxford* (1998) says it is **"A whole formed by combining several elements."** These examples show that for our purposes we can say **_aggregation_ is a relationship between two classes where the instances of one class are in some way _components, members_, or _contents_ of the instances of the other.**

Associations with Aggregation

A friend of mine has a business that does a computerized analysis on the used oil from diesel truck and bus engines (including Edmonton Transit). An analysis is done at each oil change, and the various readings are represented as the attributes of an instance of an Oil Analysis class. The object model for this company includes the portion shown in Figure 8-25.

As you can see from Figure 8-25(a), there appears to be a one-to-many association from Bus to Analysis. But what if, as is sometimes the case, an engine is removed from a damaged bus and reinstalled in a bus whose original engine broke? We'll either lose some information or end up with a misleading result. The Oil Analysis history for the second bus will actually cover two engines!

---

[4] In case you're wondering, these refer respectively to cattle, sheep in England, fish, sheep in New Zealand and Australia, geese on the ground, and geese in formation flight.

To avoid this potentially embarrassing situation, we need to model the Engine as a *component* of the Bus, as in Figure 8-25(b). We must then set the one-to-many association to involve the Engine rather than the Bus. This will ensure continuity in the history of an engine.

Wherever you find these subclassing and aggregation structures in your users' world, it's important to identify them, and sometimes one of the most difficult things is distinguishing the aggregation structures from the subclass hierarchies. In the next section, we point out some of the differences between the two kinds of structure and discuss how they behave.

Figure 8-26 A Person (and a Bear) consists of Hands, Feet, and other Parts

8.6 THE DIFFERENCE BETWEEN SUBCLASSING AND AGGREGATION

These are two very different structures, but they look enough alike that people often have a hard job telling them apart. The difference shows in the choice of verb. For a subclass hierarchy, there's only one possible verb in each direction.

To say "a Person *canbea* Employee" is to say that this object *isa* person and possibly also *isa* Employee, *both at the same time*. From the other direction, we know when we first meet an Employee that she's also a person, since an Employee *isakinda* Person. In both directions, the most important part of the verb is the "*is*."

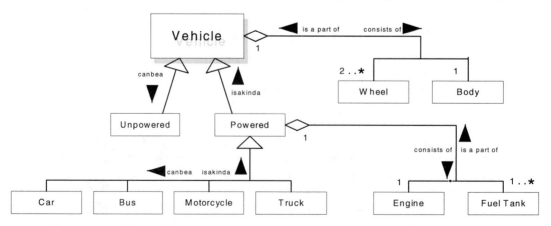

Figure 8-27 Components and subclasses both shown on the same class diagram.

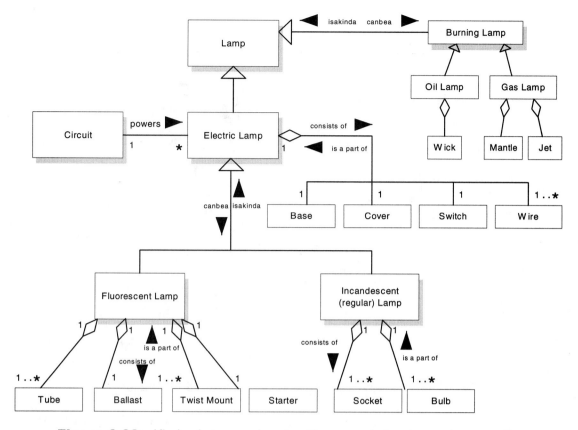

Figure 8-28 Kindsa lamps and parts of lamps: subclassing and aggregation together on one class diagram

On the other hand, any person (including Employees) can be taken apart into hands, feet, tongue, and other interesting pieces. These are *components*. A Person *is not* a Hand, but a Person does *have* a Hand or two. Or a Person may be said to *consist of* Hands, Feet, and so on. (Of course, the actual choice of verb in these cases has to be the one your users feel most comfortable with. The verb they choose may well give you a clue to which of the three types of aggregation relationship you've discovered.) Figure 8-26 shows how this one works.

In the same way, an Engine *is not* a Car, but it's *part of* a car and thus has a component relationship with a Car. However, a Car *isakinda* Vehicle. It's not *part of a* vehicle, it *is* one. This makes the class of cars a subclass of the class of vehicles, and most vehicles, including cars, have a component called an engine. Figure 8-27 suggests how this might work.

When you develop a system with an object-oriented graphical user interface (OOGUI), you have a class of objects called *Windows*. There are various *kindsa* Windows for you to use. A Dialog Box *isakinda* Window, and a User Data-Entry Screen *isakinda* Window, as is a Drop-Down Menu. Any Window can have a Check Box or a set of Radio Buttons as *components*. Check Boxes and Radio Buttons are themselves also Windows, but they can only exist as *components of* another Window.

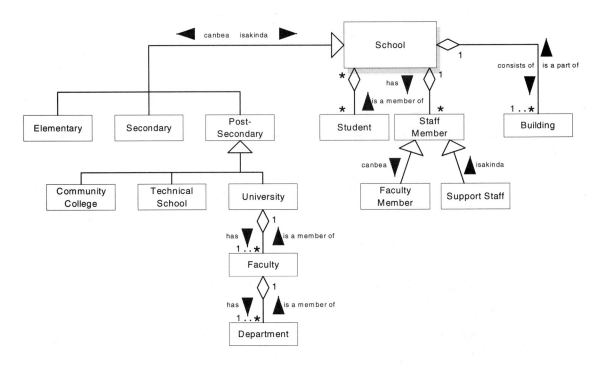

Figure 8-29 Subclassing and aggregation: school administration

Figure 8-28 shows a Lamp class. The figure shows that every lamp is made up of a base, a cover, a switch, and some wiring; these components are common to all *kindsa* lamps. There are two *kindsa* lamps: incandescent (ordinary bulb lamps), and fluorescent. A fluorescent lamp – in addition to the base, cover, switch, and wiring – is also made up of a ballast coil, a twist mount, and a starter, and these are things an incandescent lamp doesn't have. The extra parts for an incandescent lamp are a socket and a bulb, neither of which is found in a fluorescent lamp.

Exercise 8.2 is the object-oriented treasure hunt (OOTHunt), designed to demonstrate and highlight the differences between subclassing and whole–part relationships. It also works on several *learning modes* at the same time (see Chapter 16), and can even be fun.

Figures 8-29 and 8-30 show a school administration and a shipping business, respectively. Both diagrams show subclass relationships (*isakinda*), as well as several forms of aggregation. Figure 8-29 shows three subclasses of School, and Postsecondary school in turn has three subclasses (*kindsa*).

A School also *has* many Students and Staff, who are *members of* their respective Schools (collection–member). There are two *kindsa* staff, too. You'll also note that a University *is made up of* many Faculties, each of which *is made up of* a number of Departments (assembly–component or whole–part). You should now go through this same analysis on Figure 8-30, before you move on to "Deliverables."

DELIVERABLES

There are no new documents introduced in this chapter, but we've added information to the diagrams that we've already been producing. The knowledge you've gained from this chapter will allow you to capture much more information on the models, by identifying and drawing the hierarchies and aggregations. Each class and subclass in these structures must be fully documented, just like any other class.

You'll need to document the name of the class, the unique identifier, the definition, the lists of attributes and operations, definitions for attributes where needed, and specifications for all the operations. All the associations that used to go to the superclasses or to the "whole" class need to be reconsidered, and some of them may be directed to the subclasses or component classes, respectively.

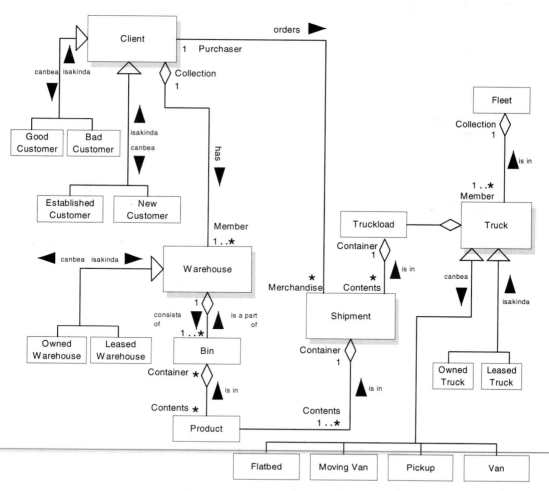

Figure 8-30 Subclasses and aggregation: a shipping application, showing all three types of aggregation, Component–Whole, Container–Contents, and Collection–Member

Further Reading

One of the best – although brief – explanations of objects, classes, subclasses, and inheritance is in the first few pages of the first chapter of Timothy Budd's (1991) book, *An Introduction to Object-Oriented Programming*, the one with the platypus on the cover. Budd says of the platypus, "This egg-laying mammal represents an excellent example of inheritance with overriding . . . ." although sometimes I think the platypus is more like multiple inheritance gone mad!

Coad and Yourdon (1991) also do quite well in their book, *Object-Oriented Analysis*. In Chapter 2, they introduce many object-oriented concepts by discussing Smalltalk, and then in Chapter 4 they introduce more ideas about structures (hierarchies and aggregation) and how to identify them.

All object-oriented authors spend some time and effort explaining this part. Any of the more readable among them are worth reading, in particular, of course, David Taylor (1990, 1992).

Chapter Summary

- A subclass instance *inherits* all the attributes of its superclass.

- The verb for the subclass relationship is *canbea* (a superclass instance *canbea* subclass instance). A subclass instance *isakinda* superclass instance.

- A subclass instance inherits both the attributes and the behaviors of the superclass.

- An object that is an instance of two subclasses has all the attributes and all the behaviors from all three classes.

- An instance that belongs to a subclass also belongs to the superclass automatically and simultaneously. It is at one and the same time a member (instance) of *both* classes.

- An object is an instance of *every one* of its ancestor classes. Its state includes a value for every attribute of every one of its chain of superclasses.

- The *isakinda* verb expresses an identity relationship, which is like equality only stronger. A subclass instance *isakinda* superclass instance (and thus also *isa* superclass instance).

- By definition, an OOPL or an ODBMS *supports* classes, subclasses, inheritance, and polymorphism. A language *supports* a feature if it is *easy and convenient* for programmers to use the feature. To be considered truly object-oriented, it should not only *allow* subclassing and inheritance but should actively *support* them both.

- When an association involves only instances of the subclass, the line to represent it is drawn *to the subclass*. An association that involves instances of the superclass (including instances of the subclass) should be drawn *to the superclass*.

- We can begin from the superclass, and treat the subclasses as special cases. Or we can begin at the subclasses and find common attributes and behavior to make a superclass. Both approaches will be used at different places in the modeling process.

- Subclasses *specialize* the parent class. A superclass *generalizes* its subclasses.
- Polymorphism means behaviors that have the same name and meaning but are actually different, depending on which class they are in.
- Polymorphism means a behavior may be inherited unchanged, or it may be different between the parent and child classes, and this allows us to *specialize* a behavior for particular subclasses.
- Polymorphism is possible only in object-oriented environments and is part of the definition of that term.
- Abstract classes have no direct instances, and are often introduced to exploit inheritance and polymorphism.
- Some object-oriented products store the methods as object code, linked at *compile time*. This is referred to as *early*, or *static, binding*.
- Others store the methods as binary executable code in the database, executed at *run time* directly from the database. This is called *late*, or *dynamic, binding*.
- A subclass may inherit an attribute exactly as it is, or it may modify the attribute in some way.
- We say that the subclass feature (attribute or operation) *overrides* the corresponding superclass feature. The subclass feature actually replaces the superclass feature *for that subclass and its descendants*.
- When overriding *operations*:
    ° **Extension:** Add some new behavior, usually affecting new attributes.
    ° **Restriction:** Operation works for a subset of values of argument.
    ° **Optimization:** Take advantage of constraints to improve code.
- When overriding *attributes*:
    ° **Restriction:** Type of attribute is a subtype of the one in the superclass.
    ° **Changing Size:** New attribute has different width or decimal places.
    ° **Number/Type:** Preserve number and type of attributes.
- Multiple inheritance is not available in some OOPLs and ODBMSs such as Smalltalk and Java. Some object-oriented environments offer both multi-origin multiple inheritance and single-origin multiple inheritance.
- Resolving multiple inheritance can be complicated when the same feature is inherited twice. Different products have various ways to decide.
- With an object class library, you can change either the data definitions or the methods by defining a subclass that inherits from a class in the library. You may extend the library by redefining the attributes or methods in new subclasses or by adding new ones. You don't need the library source code.
- Each new project needs some classes from earlier projects. Prior projects provide an in-house class library.

- Your first object-oriented project will take longer. By the *third* project the in-house class library grows, so the *third or fourth* project will show significant benefits.

- When there are no instances except those from the subclasses, a superclass has no direct instances. A *direct instance* of a class is one that is an instance of that class, but *not* of any subclasses.

- The only instances of an *abstract class* are those provided for it by its subclasses. It's *covered* by its subclasses and has *no direct instances*.

- A *concrete class* is one that *does* have direct instances; it is said to be *directly instantiable*.

- An *abstract operation* has no program code in the class where it's defined; its methods are provided by the subclasses. The subclasses containing the methods may be either concrete or abstract classes.

- A *concrete operation* has a method in its defining class. An abstract class can have a concrete operation.

- The abstract or concrete status of a class is always provisional.

- A concrete class cannot have abstract operations, since there is no program code to perform these operations on its direct instances.

- Add "artificial superclasses" later at design time, unless you judge that if created during analysis they'll contribute to communication and development of the project.

- *Aggregation* is used to subsume these three terms: whole–part or component–assembly, container-contents, and collection–member. These are fundamental ways in which we humans organize our world.

- When for the current project the association really goes to something "within" the object, adding this fact gives a more accurate picture of the users' world. They're not interested in the entire object, only this part "within" it. The verb is *isapartof* (or *consists of* or *is made up of*).

- The Bill-of-Materials structure is a special case of assembly–part. A M:M multiplicity in the class diagram shows a many-to-many relationship from the Assembly to the Components, all in the same class. It shows that an Assembly *consists of* many Components and a Component *can be used in* many Assemblies.

- A tree structure occurs with a class of objects where each is related 1:M to others *in the same class*.

- A matrix is a "two-way tree". In a regular one-way tree, a child can have only one parent. In a matrix, a child can have many parents.

- Matrix structures can occur with Contents moving from one Container to another, or Members belonging to several Collections.

- A Container and its Contents exist independently. The container contains, holds, or houses the contents.

- For a Collection, the Members may change, but the group retains its identity.

- Associations can involve the component/content/member rather than the whole.

Chapter Glossary

abstract class A class that has no direct instances.

abstract operation One that has no program code in the class where it's defined, the methods to implement the operation being *provided by the subclasses.*

aggregation (1) A relationship between two classes where the instances of one class are in some way components, members, or contents of the instances of the other. (2) "A group, body or mass composed of many distinct parts" *Webster* (1975). (3) "A whole formed by combining several elements" *Oxford* (1998).

concrete class One that *does* have direct instances; it is said to be *directly instantiable.*

concrete operation An operation on a class that has a method *in that class.*

direct instance An instance of a class, but *not* of any of its subclasses.

dynamic typing Where an object can switch from one class (or type) to another.

early binding or **static binding** Storing the methods as partially compiled object code, which is then linked into the program at compile time.

inheritance When a subclass instance, in addition to the attributes and behavior it has *by virtue of belonging to the subclass,* also has all the attributes and behavior that instances of the superclass have.

instantiate To create instances (of a class.)

generalization A superclass *generalizes* its subclasses by including all those features that are "general" to all the subclasses.

late binding or **dynamic binding** Storing the methods as binary executable code in the database, which at run time is executed directly from the database.

multi-origin multiple inheritance When a class is simultaneously a subclass of two (or more) independent superclasses and inherits from both (and, of course, from the chain of superclasses above each), and these two chains of superclasses *do not* link up at the top.

override To use the version of some attribute or operation from the *subclass,* in preference to the *superclass* version, *for that subclass and its descendants.*

polymorphism (1) The ability to write *several versions* of a method (function, subroutine) in different classes in a subclass hierarchy, give them all exactly the *same name,* and rely on the object-oriented environment to establish which version should be executed depending on the class of the target object. (2) "Occurring in various forms" (*Webster,* 1975). (3) "Having, assuming or passing through many forms." (*Random House Webster,* 1998)

protocol Consists of the name of an operation and the names and types of its arguments, along with its *semantics.*

semantics The meaning of an operation and what it does.

set intersection The *intersection* of two sets A and B is a set consisting of every element that is a member of *both* set A *and* set B.

single-origin multiple inheritance Where two or more branches of a class hierarchy join up after having sprouted from a common ancestor class.

specialization A subclass is said to *specialize* its superclass(es) by including only certain of the superclass instances.

subassembly A component, which in turn breaks down into components.

subclass A class made up of selected instances from another class, referred to as the *parent class* or *superclass*.

superclass A class that includes all the instances of the subclass, plus possibly some more (see Chapter 5).

support To contain constructs and mechanisms that make it *easy and convenient* for programmers to take advantage of a feature.

WHAT COMES NEXT

Now that we've explored some of the most complex and powerful features of object orientation, we come to the exciting part: how to go out into the real world, find all these marvelous classes and structures, and build them into actual models. Chapter 9 has the step by steps, and also explores many user-related issues that can make or break your model, make it a poor one or a great one. Remember, the *adequacy of your models* will directly influence the success of your systems development project!

CLASS/GROUP EXERCISES AND PROBLEMS

Ex 8.1 In The Outhouse example in Section 8.1, and Table 8-1, can you think up six more data items (attributes) that we might need to know about each of the following groups? Keep your answers for Exercise 10.4.

(a) Data items that we would need to know only about the Customers and not about other *kindsa* Persons.

(b) Data items that we would need to know only about the Employees.

(c) Data items that we would need to know about all *kindsa* persons, be they Customers, Employees, or perhaps even *Others* who are neither Customers nor Employees.

Ex 8.2 **"The Object-Oriented Treasure Hunt (OOTHunt)"**

Objective: The objective of this exercise is first to demonstrate the principles of subclassing and aggregation. But it also has a secondary objective of doing so in a way that's easier for people to grasp who have different "learning modalities." Many highly intelligent and capable people do their best learning in some mode other than reading and lecture, both of which are verbal modes, combining elements of both visual and aural learning.

All of you who have progressed through the system to a level where you need to read this book, are obviously capable of learning verbally. But even among my readers, there are some of you who learn better in other modalities.

Some of you, like me, are primarily visual learners, and there is a considerable amount of graphical and video material around to assist you. Others among you are primarily kinesthetic, learning best from touching, handling, and physically manipulating things. My experience with this exercise has been that it helped many students get a better grasp of these ideas. Everybody, I'm sure, will gain some level of insight from an alternative presentation of the concepts.

Setting: This exercise is best done in groups of three to six participants. Each group should be gathered around a table, with room to move about freely.

Materials: Each group will need a large sheet of paper or cardboard (flip-chart paper or its cardboard backing are ideal), some Scotch and/or masking and/or duct tape, and felt pen(s).

Step 1. Assemble a pile of objects. Each group member contributes some objects to the pile in the center of the table. Dig into your pockets, purses, and briefcases or just use anything you can lay your hands on (preferably not the other group members). Be imaginative, resourceful, and courageous, but stay with things you can attach to the paper or cardboard (it has to go up on the wall later). Appropriate items of clothing can be included (with the permission of the wearer), but don't use any valuables. Use things that can stay up on the wall until the end of the course (or at least until tomorrow, or maybe next week.)

Step 2. Organize the pile of objects into classes. Any classes that make sense to you are okay.

Step 3. Look for subclasses among your classes. Divide your objects into piles that represent subclasses several levels deep. Can you find any multiple inheritance?

Step 4. Draw your subclass hierarchy tree on the paper and tape the objects (instances) to their boxes (classes) on the diagram.

Step 5. Dismantle at least one object (instance) into its components, add this component–assembly relationship to the diagram, and tape the component instances to their class boxes. Can you also find examples of container–contents and/or collection–member?

Step 6. Add to your diagram any other relationships and associations you may become aware of, in addition to subclass and whole–part.

Step 7. Tape the finished product to the wall and have one of your group present it to the class. They should explain how you decided on all the significant classes and associations, and how you explored subclasses and aggregation relationships, along with any significant discoveries or insights you may have had along the way. Make a copy of your model on paper to file in your class notes for Exercise 10.2.

INDIVIDUAL EXERCISES AND PROBLEMS

Ex 8.3 Prepare a class diagram for a membership system for a group of sports/ hobby/ interest clubs. If you have some real users available, use them. Otherwise, be your own user when it comes to making decisions about the business of the club. Allow for several clubs in a group, such as a sports league. Allow for several *kindsa* members in each club. Allow for a club to have members go on trips and for each trip to be in several vehicles. Keep track of who is to ride in which vehicle.

Look in particular for subclasses, collection–member structures, and container–contents structures. Keep your answers for Exercise 10.5.

PROJECTS AND CASES

P 8.1 In your small-business project from Project 7.2, examine what you've produced so far and check for the three kinds of aggregation and for subclasses. If none are apparent, look for places where they might conceivably occur. Be imaginative. Write up your potential structures and present them to the class. Keep this write-up separate from the rest, since it doesn't as yet form part of the permanent documentation for the project. Use it for inspiration later as you work toward completion of the project.

SELF-TEST QUESTIONS

Note: The Appendix has answers to the Self-Test Questions.

Q 8.1 Define polymorphism and give at least three examples of polymorphic operations in the real world.

Q 8.2 Check one box on each line to show what this is an example of.

Q 8.3 Define static (early) and dynamic (late) binding.

Q 8.4 Describe how overriding takes place and the way object-oriented compilers typically resolve polymorphic methods.

Q 8.5 Concrete classes:
- (a) Don't need methods for all their operations
- (b) Must have methods for all their operations
- (c) Must not have methods for all their operations
- (d) Must have abstract operations
- (e) Need program code
- (f) Are better than brick

Q 8.6 Abstract operations have
- (a) No program code in the subclasses
- (b) Program code in the defining class
- (c) Program code in the subclasses
- (d) No program code in the defining class
- (e) All of the above
- (f) Some of the above
- (g) None of the above

Q 8.7 Why is it that a concrete class cannot have abstract operations?

Q 8.8   A concrete class must have

   (a)   Program code for many of its methods

   (b)   No program code for any of its methods

   (c)   Program code for some of its methods

   (d)   Program code for all of its methods

   (e)   No program code for some of its methods

Q 8.9   _____ means a behavior may be _____ unchanged, or it may be _____ between the parent and child classes, and this allows us to _____ a behavior for particular subclasses.

Q 8.10 A _____ class cannot have _____ operations, since there is no _____ _____ to perform these operations on its _____ _____ .

Q 8.11 With an object class library, you can change either the _____ _____ or the _____ by defining a subclass that _____ from a class in the library. You may extend the library by redefining the _____ or _____ in new subclasses or by adding new ones. You don't need the _____ _____ _____ .

Q 8.12   _____ classes have no _____ _____, and are often introduced to exploit _____ and _____ .

Q 8.13 Some object-oriented products store the methods as object code, linked at _____ _time_. This is referred to as _____, or _____, binding.

Q 8.14 We say a language _____ a feature if it is _____ and _____ for programmers to _____ the feature.

Chapter Nine

Finding Objects and Classes in the Real World

WHAT YOU WILL LEARN IN THIS CHAPTER

In this chapter, you'll learn how to build a Class Diagram to serve as the foundation of your object models, using the KRB Seven-Step method. You can be satisfied that you understand this method when you can:

1. List and explain the KRB Seven Steps.
2. Describe the deliverable(s) from each step.
3. As a member of a team, given a business scenario, use the Seven Steps to produce a class diagram for a small project.
4. Document this class diagram as described in the chapter.

WHAT YOU SHOULD KNOW TO START THIS CHAPTER

This chapter doesn't discuss what a class diagram is, but assumes you know that and want to find out how to build one. You can expect, however, that if your understanding is less than perfect, then this chapter will help to clarify many things for you. Most of this chapter applies to entities as well as objects (except the terminology, of course), so you can get started here if you know how to read ERDs and you know what *classes, associations*, and *multiplicity* are.

CHAPTER OVERVIEW

We'll go through the first six steps of the KRB Seven-Step method in detail, showing you how to actually *do* each one. This will provide you with guidelines, hints, precautions, and warnings – all the DOs and DON'Ts for finding the classes and building the class diagram. This then serves as the foundation of all that you'll do later.

After the how-tos, the chapter will discuss the sometimes difficult and subtle question often faced in deciding whether something should be modeled as a *class* or as an *attribute*. Then we'll look at finding subclass hierarchies and aggregation relationships, and finish with a discussion of how to adapt this method to the varying and imperfect circumstances of the real world of systems analysis.

KEY CONCEPTS

- Candidate classes
- Brainstorming
- Delphi method
- Real-world identifier
- Class definition
- Sample attributes and behaviors
- Verbs and nouns
- Capturing all possible associations
- Individual objects or object types
- Refer to your definition
- Expanding many-to-many associations
- Placing event data attributes
- Intersection classes
- Collapsing events
- Normalization
- Unanticipated queries vs. denormalizing for efficiency
- *Sufficient* time commitment from *suitable* users.

"THE OUTHOUSE BATHROOM BOUTIQUE" SALES REPORTING SYSTEM – EPISODE 9

"So is there an association between Sales and Products?" asked Nancy. "What does a Sale *do* to a Product?" Everybody stared blankly for a moment. Nancy went on, "Would it be true to say that a Sale *is of* a Product? And what would a Product *do* to a Sale?"

"It *has* Sales?" ventured Bill a little uncertainly.

"Good," said Nancy, "That'll do just fine. And then the next question is, *How many*? Let's start by asking 'How many Sales does a Product participate in?'"

Hartmut grinned. "Plenty!" he said. "Or at least, we sure hope so. We've got a business to run."

Bill looked puzzled. "Well, I suppose that's OK for towels and soap and stuff," he said slowly, "But what about water heaters? For those, we only sell the product once. It doesn't make sense to talk about a Product having several Sales when we're talking about big-ticket items like water heaters, and toilets, and stuff like that."

"This is where we need to refer back to our definition," said Nancy, and Deanna obligingly held out to her a page from the minutes. Nancy scanned the page, and began reading aloud. "Product: An item stocked for resale by The Outhouse," she quoted.

"Well, that doesn't tell us a whole lot, does it?" observed Bill, perhaps a trifle peevishly.

"Sure it does," rejoined Nancy. "It tells us that while our definition is perfectly true, it's also a little less than adequate."

Bill grinned. "I guess I'll have to go along with that. So what do we do with it?"

"We extend it," asserted Nancy. "We need to change the definition so that it can accommodate both kinds of product. I think we're going to need two classes here, one called Product and another called Product Type. Only certain types of product will need to have an instance in the Product class, and there the identifier will include the serial number. Other types, like soap, will just have an instance in the Product Type class, with a Quantity-on-Hand attribute."

Nancy began drawing boxes and lines on the board. By the end of the three-hour meeting, she had done a lot of drawing and erasing, and felt good about what had finally been produced.

THOUGHT QUESTIONS

1. In your group, discuss and document an incident from the past of one of the group members, in any walk of life, not just systems development You want a time when it was necessary to go right back to the definition of the terms, in order to solve or prevent a problem. Discuss how this illustrates and relates to the incident above, where Nancy took the group back to their definition of *Product*. Each group present the discussion results to the class.

2. Think about how you might introduce subclasses into the model discussed in The Outhouse episode. Draw the class diagram so far showing the Sale, Product, and Product Type classes and any subclasses that you think might be helpful. Refer to this drawing as you read the chapter.

9.1   THE IMPORTANCE OF THIS STEP

By now, you've probably gathered that the *class* is one of the core concepts of object-oriented analysis. And indeed, one of our major tasks will be discovering those classes in the users' world, that are significant for our system.

How do we tell which ones are important and which are not? The short answer, as usual, is "it depends." In this case, it depends on the users and their view of their world. The next step is for you and your users together to identify the interface, entity, and control classes, and the associations among them. These will form the Class Diagram.

The Basis of All That Follows

The class diagram really is the foundation on which your whole system will rest. If that's done well, then your project has an excellent chance of success. If the Class Diagram is all wrong, nothing else will work right either, and you'll end up at the later stages patching your system and then patching on patches. This is where we come face-to-face with the unfortunate truth of the saying "There's never time to do it right, but always time to do it over!"

Time, effort, and care spent on this early stage of your project will pay off later in terms of reduced errors, earlier discovery of errors, and ease of correcting them. This is especially true of time, effort, and care spent on the human side of the process. Some of the people issues were discussed in Chapter 6, and you'll find more at the end of this chapter. Chapter 16 has some specific techniques useful for working with the people during this part of the modeling.

Next I'll describe the actual procedure to follow. You'll need to ensure that all the preparations detailed in the checklist at the beginning of Chapter 6 are in place before you try this.

9.2 THE KRB SEVEN-STEP METHOD

This method is not the only one that works, but it is one that works. I've dubbed it KRB since Anil Kapur, Ravi Ravindra and I (Brown) documented, formalized, and taught it initially as part of an entity–relationship modeling course. The steps were actually put together by a variety of people, mostly at the City of Edmonton Transportation Department, and you'll find the same or similar methods in many articles and books.

The Seven Steps are not a formal methodology or even a defined "method." They're actually just a handy set of steps that can be adapted for use within almost any methodology. They're simply a structure to combine ideas and practices that have accumulated from many sources.

There are parts of this that just sort of evolved in the industry, without being the work of any identifiable person or group. Anil Kapur, Ravi Ravindra, and I don't take any particular credit for this, except to say that we used it and wrote it down.

The "method" may thus be used in its entirety or adapted freely, or individual steps or portions may be borrowed and grafted productively onto whatever other methods you may be using.

Should you be lucky enough *not* to be saddled with a preselected methodology on your first OO project (lucky you!), my recommendation is that you first begin by using the Seven Steps in their entirety, as I describe them here. Once you've tried them, then feel free to customize, or to select and keep only what you need.

These are the Seven Steps:

Step 1: Candidate classes

Step 2: Define classes

Step 3: Establish associations

Step 4: Expand many-to-many associations

Step 5: Attributes

Step 6: Normalization

Step 7: Operations (i.e., *behavior*)

Now let's look at these in detail and see how they're done.

Step 1: Candidate Classes

Our task here is to discover all the interface, entity, and control classes that are significant to the system. I'll discuss methods for working with the users to find these classes, and what we come up with in this step will be a list of *nouns* that *might* name classes we're interested in – hence the term ***candidate classes,*** since they are **possible class names that are being considered as *candidates* for inclusion in the system.**

In Step 2, Define Classes, we'll examine each candidate class and subject it to some tests to see whether it really is a class of interest to our users. For now, I'll present several methods for *finding* candidate classes, so that in a real-world project you'll have a repertoire of techniques that you can use. We'll look at the three kinds of classes and ways to find them:

- Entity classes, relating to the users' real-world entities, and four ways to find them

- Interface classes, to people and to other systems

- Control classes, for behavior that spreads over many classes

Let's begin with entity classes, since these are not only easier to find, but also more meaningful for your users. Your users will be able learn about object modeling and become comfortable with the concepts of *object* and *class*, by working with words and concepts they're already familiar with. This can be of immense benefit, particularly if you have new users with little or no experience of object or entity modeling.

ENTITY CLASSES

Whether we call them entities, objects, or just *things*, the world of our users is populated by *things* that they need to keep data about. Since we're planning to organize the data around *things*, we begin our search with these. A *thing* is represented in English as a noun. I'll present four ways to generate a list of nouns for candidate entity classes:

- Client interviews

- From the requirements model and other documentation

- Brainstorming

- The Delphi method (nothing to do with *Inprise*, née *Borland*)

Each method has its time and place, and each will work. There are many other ways of doing this, and you may well find other members of your team, or other authors besides myself, who prefer to do it otherwise.

Generally, the most effective way is to combine brainstorming with the requirements model and documentation. You may choose the method, or combination of several, that you judge is right for each situation you meet, or you may find that your client or employer insists on a particular method.

First Method: Client Interviews

You may need to do it this way when dealing with busy senior users. You can adapt the group methods from the following sections to an individual or small-group setting, or you may need to interview the users to get the basics and then on your own develop the definitions and the rest of the model.

You'll need to bring this model back to the users regularly for verification. For this stage, ask each user (if necessary in separate interviews) for a list of nouns and then combine them into a larger list to recirculate among the users for further additions. Most of what I describe in the next two methods you'll still need to do as well, except you'll be doing much of it away from the interactive JAD/FTS environment.

Second Method: From Requirements Model and Other Documentation

This idea works just fine by itself or even better combined with the other methods. You need **nouns** relevant to the users' business. So start with the Systems Request Document or Change Request Document from the user, the one that gave rise to the project in the first place. Scan it for nouns and write them down in a list. Then examine the Requirements Model, in particular the Use Cases, picking out the *nouns*.

Then examine other documentation that describes your users' operation, or tells about the business they're in. Pick out the nouns. Check memos, correspondence, and so on that are on the topic of the users' business. Pick out nouns you think might be important for the part of their business that you're modeling.

Third Method: Brainstorming

This is my personal favorite, and the one I recommend for most situations. Many experts argue that the downside of use cases is that they tend to focus too much on the system, on the current project. To provide true resilience to change, however, we need to build our class diagram based not on the data needs of the current project but on the total data requirements of the business area. This brainstorming method does just that.

Brainstorming as a technique has been around for twenty years or more, but in recent years it has fallen into a little disfavor. This is because it does depend very heavily on the skill of the leader. However, far from seeing that as a reason for abandoning the method, I see it as an opportunity for you and me to develop some new and effective people skills, and to hone them in a real-life process.

Brainstorming means more than just a bunch of people getting together to "toss around a few ideas." ***Formal brainstorming* takes place in two or more distinct and separate phases. The first phase is for *generating* ideas, and the second is for *evaluating* them.** In the KRB method, the first phase consists of our Step 1: Candidate Classes. The second phase, that of evaluation, is looked after in KRB Step 2: Defining Classes.

In the first phase, we want to generate a rapid flow of ideas, one after another. It doesn't matter how good the ideas are, and there is no such thing as a bad idea.

No matter how silly or trivial someone may think his idea is, *we want it*, for one or other of two possible reasons. One is that he might be unaware of some of the implications of this idea, and he may be surprised how important it turns out to be.

The other possibility is that even if this particular idea does turn out to be less than earth-shattering, it may *stimulate someone else* to come up with a major contribution. We never know in advance which ones matter, so we need to get *all* ideas up on the whiteboard.

Along with the need to get *all* the ideas out and onto the whiteboard, there are some very necessary rules about how we treat each contribution. As each person calls out a suggestion, *it goes on the board*. Regardless.

And as it does, *no one is allowed to evaluate it* in any way. *No* "Oh, I don't think so"; *no* "Forget it!"; *no* "There goes Joe again"; *no* "Joe, you sure have some funny ideas"; *no* groans, *no* comments, *no* raised eyebrows, *nothing*!

People must feel that their contributions are valued and welcomed. You can help to do this by recognizing *each and every offering* with a small "Yeah," "OK," "Good," "Uh-Huh," "Thanks," or just an encouraging grunt. Some token of recognition is all that's needed to keep the feeling positive and keep the ideas flowing. As you can readily see, this is a *people* process, and this is one place where the skill of the leader is critical.

To illustrate how to do this, let's eavesdrop on Nancy as she leads a facilitated team session (FTS) for *The Outhouse.*

"THE OUTHOUSE BATHROOM BOUTIQUE" SALES REPORTING SYSTEM – EPISODE 9A

"It's time for the brainstorming part. It goes like this. What we need on the board is a list of *things*, so the words will all be *nouns*. These are the things you might need to keep information about in your database. I don't want the data, that's just the stuff you need to know; I want you to give me the things you need to know *about*. Let's start with a couple that I can think of: Product and Customer." She wrote these on the board.

"How about Sale?" ventured Tim.

"Good," responded Nancy, continuing to write.

"Selling Price?" queried Allana.

"Okay," said Nancy.

Hartmut called out "Vendor!"

"Yeah," said Nancy.

"Quantity in Stock," said Steve.

"Right," affirmed Nancy, still writing.

"Isn't that an attribute or something?" queried Tim.

"No evaluating!" admonished Nancy. "We'll look after that in the next step."

"Oh, sorry," said Tim, and Nancy gave him a reassuring smile.

"Who's next?" she asked.

"Uh, Quantity on Order!"

"Yes."

"Back-order Quantity!"

"Okay."

"PO Number."

"Uh-huh."

"PO Request."

"Good."

"What about Vendor?"

"Got that already."

"Oh."

"Salesperson."

"Yes!"

"Inventory."

"Good."

"Catalogue."

"Okay."

"Bin."

"Good."

"Oh, yeah, Warehouse!"

"Okay!"

Nancy wrote furiously, briefly acknowledging each contribution. The words came freely for a while, then began to slow. "Okay," she said, "that looks like a pretty good list."

Scanning the board, Nancy could see that some were obviously not classes, but she refrained from comment. "Now let's move along to step 2."

And we'll pick up with Nancy & Co. later, but for now let's finish talking about the other methods for finding classes.

Fourth Method: The Delphi Method

This is really a kind of "brainstorming by mail," or "brainstorming in slow motion." It can be used when you have difficulty getting the users together for a brainstorming session.

The **_Delphi Method_ is to mimic the brainstorming in slow motion, by first meeting with or writing a memo to each participant and getting them to write a list of candidate classes. Then you combine the lists and circulate the complete list to all participants, for inspired additions.** You may wish to repeat the circulating one or more times. Eventually, you hope to end up with a list much like you would have had from a brainstorming session.

Now that you've seen the four methods that I recommend for finding entity classes, you can combine them up as you need. There's one further suggestion, which I've heard but never tried, and you'll find it works well in some situations. That is, put the list up on a whiteboard or a bulletin board in the hallway, lunchroom, or some other busy common area, for people to update as they think of things.

I've spent quite a bit of space explaining the brainstorming method, since I find it gives the most complete list. However, even if your list is incomplete, this won't ruin your model. Don't get worried or anxious that you might miss some classes, because the method is self-correcting.

When you build a model top-down with the Seven Steps, in a user-driven way, anything you miss in the earlier steps shows up later. It's really quite amazing sometimes, but if you miss something early in the piece, then later on you'll find something else that just won't work. It just doesn't fit or doesn't feel right, and when you do find the solution, it turns out to be something you missed earlier!

INTERFACE CLASSES

User Interfaces

If you've purchased (or written) an OOGUI class library, then all or most of the user interface classes will already be defined in the library.

Data Communication Interfaces

These will normally involve published communications protocols. You'll need some objects to represent the communications link(s), but the details of the protocols can remain in the published form and simply be referred to from your documentation.

Interfaces to Systems Being Monitored or Controlled

If your system must monitor or control a real-world system, then you're likely to have part of the work done for you. The external system might be an industrial process, a patient in an intensive care unit, a traffic light, a student, or the player in a video game. There will usually be a combination of home-grown or customized equipment, along with parts or components where the manufacturer has already published the protocols.

Begin with a class with a single instance, representing the external system, and check for things about it that may be represented as components or subtypes (that is, subclasses). Then follow through the normal process of finding attributes and operations, as with any other class, and as described in the later steps.

CONTROL CLASSES

These will mostly be discovered in the design phase. As usual, however, if you see the need during analysis, I would consider it a judgment call. You need to decide whether to include them in the analysis model or make a note and hold them over until design.

Control classes are created when you come across an operation that calls for data and operations from a large number of other classes. Often it may be that this operation simply doesn't appear to belong to any of the classes you have so far. The control class may end up with only this one operation, and a couple of attributes to support it, and that's okay.

Let's just stop for a moment and review what we've said so far about discovering classes:

- The class diagram really is the foundation upon which your whole system will rest.
- The Seven Steps for the complete Class Diagram are:
  - Step 1: Candidate classes
  - Step 2: Define classes
  - Step 3: Establish associations
  - Step 4: Expand many-to-many associations
  - Step 5: Attributes
  - Step 6: Normalization
  - Step 7: Operations (i.e., behavior)
- **Step 1: Candidate Classes.** Discover all significant candidate classes, for interface, entity, and control classes.
- A *thing* (entity) is represented in English as a *noun*.
- List nouns that might name classes, candidates for inclusion in the system.
- There are a number of ways recommended to generate a list of nouns for candidate classes:
  - **Client Interviews.** For busy senior users. Adapt group methods to an individual or small-group setting. Or interview users to get basics, then on your own develop the model. Bring the model back to the users for verification, *often*.
  - **From the Requirements Model and Other Documentation.** Start with the Systems Request document. Scan for nouns and list them. Examine the requirements model and use cases, picking out nouns. Examine other documents describing users' operation.
  - **Brainstorming.** The downside of use cases is that they focus on the current project. For resilience to change, class diagrams are based not on the data needs of the current project but on data requirements of the users' business or business area. Formal brainstorming has two separate phases, *generating* ideas and *evaluating* them. No evaluation of any kind is allowed during the generating phase, just a nonstop flow of ideas.

- **The Delphi Method.** "Brainstorming by mail" can be used when you can't get the users together for a brainstorming session. First, meet with or memo each participant and get them to write a list of candidate classes. Then combine the lists and circulate the complete list to all users for additions. Repeat until done.

- **Interface Classes.** If you have a OOGUI class library, then most of the user interface classes will be defined in the library. Published protocols can be used freely for data communication links and process control.

- **Control Classes.** Created for operations that need data and operations from many other classes, or don't appear to belong to any of the classes you have. It might have just this operation and a few attributes to support it.

Now we'll continue with the rest of the Seven Steps.

Step 2: Define Classes

Once you have the list of candidate classes, you're ready to examine and evaluate each one to see if it really is important to this project. For many people, this is where it becomes apparent that this modeling business is an art, not a science.

Like every art, however, it has a technology underlying it. But it's rightly viewed as an art because there's no guaranteed way to get the right answer. I can give you guidelines and techniques, and then you must go out there in the users' world and do the best you can. What I *can* guarantee is that you'll get better with practice.

Each candidate class must be subjected to three checks:

- Real-world identifier
- Definition
- Sample attributes and behaviors

These checks don't guarantee to come up with a definite "yea" or "nay" as to whether this is truly a class of interest. Rather, as you ask and answer the three questions, it'll become apparent whether this is a class that matters, or whether it should be an attribute somewhere.

There's a certain amount of judgment operating here, much to the discomfort of those systems analysts who are used to things being more cut-and-dried. This apparent lack of rigor bothers some people who may have an engineering or scientific background, but it's a fact of the real world. In some ways, we can actually capitalize on it, as you'll see shortly.

There's no necessary order for these three tests, but I'm presenting them here in the order that I've found seems to work best. The first two, the *unique identifier* and the *definition*, will form part of your permanent documentation for the model. The third, *sample attributes and behaviors*, if used, should be written as notes to be reused in Step 5. To begin with, we check into the *identity* of the objects.

Real-World Identifier

As we saw in Chapter 5, *objects have identity*. So we could reason that, if the name we have on the board is the name of a class that matters to us, then its instances must have identity. That is,

- They must be *distinct*.

- There is usually *some way of telling them apart*.

Thus, the question we must ask is, How do we tell one from another? This is exactly the way I like to phrase the question for my users in the FTS/JAD session. "How do we tell one Customer from another?" "They all look different!" Sorry, that won't do. "They all have different names." Wrong. Last time I counted, there were seventeen "David Browns" in the Edmonton phone book (two of which were me). And there are dozens of David Browns who have written books – just do a search at amazon.com

And even if names were unique, they're far too sensitive to spelling and punctuation errors to be of any practical use to us. That will have to await artificial intelligence. So, for a class such as Customers, we usually create an artificial identifier – in this case, Customer Number, which we can guarantee to be unique.

But even if the identifier is not unique, as long as one exists it indicates that the instances are distinct and therefore have identity. The U.S. Social Security Number is one such, as I mentioned earlier. I understand the rules have changed now, and they're no longer reissuing numbers ten years or so after the original holder died.

However, this will take an entire generation for the change to become effective! And even then, the past reallocations can't be undone. Yet the *people* these nonunique numbers refer to are most certainly unique themselves. Each is distinct from all the others, and they do have identity.

What matters is simply that an identifier should exist. If you suspect that the real-world identifier might not be unique, then you may still record it, although in the implementation you'll have to rely on OIDs for uniqueness (see Chapter 14).

So if the candidate is in fact a class that's important to us, then that implies that its instances have identity. Unfortunately, it doesn't work the other way around. Even if the instances can be demonstrated to have identity, that doesn't decisively say that this is a class for our project.

Vendors might be a good example. They have names and vendor numbers to tell them apart, and they're not the same, nor are they all the same vendor. So they definitely have identity.

But do they represent a class of importance to our system? Perhaps. (Read: "It depends!") Do we need to keep and process information *about* a vendor? If not, then we can simply keep the name or number of the vendor as an attribute of Product.

So, while *class* implies *identity*, we see that *identity* doesn't always imply a *class*. But we find that if we can establish an identifier, then it's a good first indication that we may have found a significant class. It needs further checking, however, which is where the other two tests come into play.

Definition

The second part that needs to go into the permanent documentation is a *definition* for each class:

- It documents the users' jargon, the words they use every day in their jobs. This allows us as outsiders to begin understanding their world and their operation.

- It provides a "dictionary," which we shall have frequent need of in the remaining steps. Often, when conceptual difficulties or misunderstandings occur during analysis or the later stages of development, they can be resolved simply by referring to these definitions, as Nancy did with *product* at the beginning of this chapter.

- Formally defining their terms is probably something your users have never done. This step is a chance to uncover and resolve some ambiguities, misunderstandings, errors and unexamined assumptions, some of which may have been there for years!

The way I like to ask the question is: "So tell me, then, what *is* a _____?" Then I write down the answer, usually after some discussion. At Edmonton Transit, we asked the following question (among others): "What is a bus?" Answer: A *type of vehicle* used by Edmonton Transit for the transportation of the public of Edmonton, usually for compensation.

You'll note the italicized phrase "*type of vehicle.*" By now, this should immediately suggest to you a chance for some inheritance from a class Vehicle. "*Type of*" is just "*isakinda*" and frequently (but not always) suggests subclasses. This would deserve at least a mental note (and perhaps a paper one).

The word *public* is also worth noting. Initially, the definition had the phrase "Citizens of Edmonton," but very quickly we realized that the service was available to *any* person who happened to be in Edmonton, so the more general phrase was coined and substituted. Again, it's fairly plain to see that the Citizens of Edmonton are a subclass of the Public of Edmonton, so again we write that down in case it turns out to be important later on.

The phrase "usually for compensation" is an interesting one. While it doesn't actually define a bus and though it's not true in every case, the users felt it important to indicate that the passengers mostly are paying for their ride.

Since the users were not completely comfortable without it (and after all, it's their model), it stayed. This kind of thing may not be terribly rigorous, but I feel it's justifiable if it enhances communication and understanding.

There will sometimes be different opinions among the users about the definition, and this is fine. We may have several views on whether the term *Employee* should include former employees, for example. Typically, these differences of meaning or interpretation will be resolved, after some discussion, in one of two ways:

- We'll have several *kindsa* things. We could have Current Employees and Former Employees. We might further divide Former Employees into three groups: Quit, Fired, and Laid Off.

- We may realize that we actually have two (or more) conceptually different classes. Sometimes the similar English names can mislead us into believing they're one class.

Edmonton Transit provided an excellent example of this process when we developed a dispatch system. With four users from different areas of the organization, we had quite a discussion over the word *shift*. As it turned out, one user was thinking in terms of *day-shift* vs. *night-shift* vs. *graveyard shift*, while another was thinking of *split shifts* vs. *full shifts* vs. *partial shifts*.

The third viewed a shift as a record of the hours actually worked by a certain bus driver on a given day. After a couple of hours on this one topic, we thought we had it, with only one definition for *shift*.

But two meetings later, we found something else that didn't fit, and we were forced to revisit our definition of *shift*. After another half-day of arguing (and some help from the dictionary, see below), we wrote up the three conceptually different classes, each with its own distinct definition.

You'll notice that these are not subclasses. They're three completely different *meanings* for the term *shift*. That is, they have different *semantics* and so are not related. (Those of you who are still awake may also have noted, however, that each of the first two potentially has three subclasses.)

One way or another, we must end up with a clear definition for each and every class and ensure that everyone understands it and accepts it. Coming up with definitions is often hard, slogging work. You must go down your list of candidate classes and request an identifier and a definition for each, then argue and discuss as necessary.

If users easily come up with a good definition, then the class is most likely something significant in their world, and thus it's something we need in the system. But if the discussion appears to be going nowhere, there's one more arrow you'll need to have in your quiver.

Your *recording analyst* needs to have both a dictionary and a thesaurus. She should have them both open at the appropriate pages as you begin the discussion of each candidate class. When things start to bog down, you'll simply need to cast a hopeful eye in the direction of your recording analyst, who will have preselected from among the meanings given in the dictionary. She will then read out a definition, and most times the users will just say "Yeah, that's it!" Sometimes they'll want to modify it a bit, but usually not much.

Have you noticed what it is that we're producing here? Our set of definitions constitutes a *dictionary of the corporate jargon*. Chances are good that it will be the first one ever produced for this company's internal language.

There are books on computer jargon, and so on. Legal and medical secretaries take courses on how to type and spell their respective jargon. But apart from systems analysts, nobody bothers to document a specific organization's own specialized variation of the industry jargon.

These are the words that they use day in and day out, every hour of the day. And, in the same way that language gives an anthropologist insights into a culture he's studying, so our little lexicon proves to be of enormous help in learning to understand our users' operation.

But there's still one more test that we may need to apply to our candidate class, the one about sample attributes and behavior.

SAMPLE ATTRIBUTES AND BEHAVIORS

Once you have an identifier and a definition, it's *usually* clear that you're dealing with a class that matters to your project. However, sometimes even those two are not enough to tell clearly, and you'll need to look at some *sample* attributes and behaviors. This means that if it's a class of objects, it must carry some data and/ or be capable of some behavior. So the idea of this test is: "Tell me something you would need to know about a _____."

For the Vendors in the previous example, having chosen Vendor Number as the identifier, we may realize that we need to record the Name, Address, and Phone Number of each Vendor. In other words, you're looking for an attribute, for a data element that this kind of object needs to carry. Right there we have some attributes, so we know that we'll need a class of objects to hang them on.

Alternatively, we could ask, "Tell me some things a Vendor can do that would affect our system" (or "... that would need to be recorded in our database"). The users might suggest "*Ship* an Order" or "*Send* us an Invoice" or "*Receive* our Payment" or "*Back order* a Product."

All of these are events or transactions that our system will need to know about when they happen, and they're things a Vendor will *do*, so they tell us that for sure Vendor will be a class for this project.

It could still be that on another project in another (hypothetical) company, in their Personnel System, it turns out to be different. Over there, for example, they may discover that an Employee needs to be designated as the primary contact person for a Vendor, and nothing more. They determine that they have no data that they need to store about Vendors and no behavior to worry about in relation to Vendors. So for them, a Vendor Number attribute in the Employee class is all that's required. *For that project*, Vendor turns out not to be a class of any importance.

Here's a summary:

Summary of Step 2: Define classes.

- Once you have the list of candidate classes, you're ready to check each to see if it's really a class and whether it's important to this project.

- Each candidate class must be subjected to three checks:
    - Real-world identifier
    - Definition
    - Sample attributes and behaviors

- These checks don't guarantee to come up with a definite answer to whether this is a class of interest. Instead, as you ask and answer the three questions, you'll see whether this is a class that matters or whether it should be an attribute somewhere. Remember, modeling is an *art*.

- Question 1: Real-world identifier
    - Objects have identity. If this candidate is the name of a class that matters, then its instances must have identity. They're *distinct*, and there's *some way of telling them apart*
    - The question to ask the users is, "How do we tell one of these from another?" Even if the identifier is not truly unique, as long as one exists it shows that the instances are distinct and therefore have identity. Even though a few of their Social Security Numbers are not unique, U.S. citizens certainly do have identity!

- Question 2: Definition
    - A *definition* for each class needs to go into the permanent documentation for a number of purposes. It documents the users' jargon, the words they use every day in their jobs, which helps us to understand their operation.
    - The definitions provide a "dictionary." When conceptual difficulties or misunderstandings occur during development, they can mostly be resolved just by referring back to these definitions.
    - Users will sometimes have different opinions about the definition, and this is okay. Typically, these differences are resolved, after some discussion, in one of two ways:
        - We'll have several *kindsa* things that is, *subclasses.*
        - We may have two (or more) conceptually different classes. Sometimes similar English names can mislead us into believing they're one class. (See *shift* above.) We must end up with a clear definition for each and every class, and ensure that everyone understands it and accepts it.

- Question 3: Sample Attributes and Behaviors
    - Sometimes even an identifier and a definition are not enough for a clear indication that this is a class of interest. But if it's a class, it must carry some data and be capable of some behavior. So you're looking for an attribute that this kind of object needs to carry. Or, you may look for events or transactions that our system will need to know about when they happen and that this class will need to respond to.

THE LEFT-LIST

I've found an interesting side issue to these definitions. As we worked down the list of candidate classes, we found some that were not classes. These I usually crossed off or erased, but two things occurred to me:

- These words always seemed to turn up later in the project. In fact, with a little experience, as they go up you'll find that you can recognize most of them as attributes of something. I always went ahead and put them up on the board, since the principle of brainstorming is *"No evaluation until phase 2."*

    And it seemed important that I accept the contributions of the shy, nervous, or scared user, in particular. But what do I do with them when in phase 2 we decide they don't fit?

- I didn't want the technophobe users to see their contributions erased, which some of them would experience as a rejection or perhaps even ridicule. So instead I transferred each of these to a list in the far-left corner of the board, which my students christened the "Left-List."

This seemed to work well and to be far less demoralizing to the occasional fearful user. I believe it encouraged a number of them to contribute a little more freely. Several of my students have reported back that it worked well for them when they went out into the real world, also. Have your recording analyst keep your Left-List for use in Step 5, Attributes.

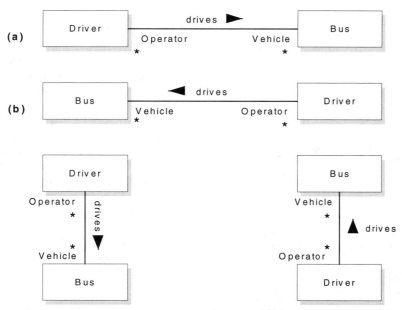

Figure 9-1   How to lay out an association on your diagram. The sentence should read "Driver drives Bus," reading in the direction of the arrow.

Once the hard work of defining and weeding out the classes is over, we can begin looking for the connections among them. These are in the form of ***interactions***; **"actions" in that the objects do things and "inter" meaning they do them *between* objects, that is, to one another.**

Step 3: Establish Associations

Here, we'll be concerned with the question, "What does one of these *do* to one of those?" In finding and handling the answer to this question, we'll need to consider a number of factors:

- Discovering the verb
- Establishing the multiplicity
- Capturing all possible interactions
- Attitude of the users

DISCOVERING THE VERB

When looking at the classes Bus and Bus Driver, the first question I ask of the users is something like "What does a Bus Driver *do* to a Bus?" The answer, surprisingly enough, is that she *drives* it! That then gives us the sentence "Bus Driver *drives* Bus." I then begin the diagram by drawing a box in the center of the board for Bus and another for Bus Driver, joining them with a straight line.

In Figure 9-1(a), you'll see that the verb appears above the line, with nouns below to indicate the *role* that each class of object plays in the life of the other class. We're reading the sentence from left to right as shown by the arrow. In Figure 9-1(b), the diagram happens to be organized differently with the Bus class on the right. The verb is the same, with the arrow and the roles reversed.

(a) "Knight *attacks* Dragon."

(b) "Dragon *burns* Knight."

(c) "Knight *slays* Dragon."

An association is an interaction described by a verb.

To simplify the formal UML definition a bit, **a *relationship* can be viewed as a connection between objects (and sometimes between other things as well.)** So, in UML parlance, an ***association* is a relationship expressing the interactions between instances of two classes, represented by the verb that describes what they do to each other, and/or by the nouns for the roles that each plays in the life of the other.** And we say that an ***association name* is a verb attached to an association describing what one class of objects does to the other.**

The relationships of interest to us, the ones that will go on our model, are all those that contribute in some way to the running of the business we're modeling. We will focus here on the *interactions* among our entity classes. Note they are "actions" in that the objects *do things*, and "inter" meaning they do them *between* objects, that is, *to* one another.

In a retail operation, such as The Outhouse, you might ask, "What does a Customer *do* to a Product?" The answer is likely to be, "He *buys* it." This would look like Figure 9-2(a). Again, you might ask "What does a Salesclerk *do* to a Customer?" and the answer would be, "She *serves* him." (Perhaps we should make this sentence gender-neutral, by saying "a Salesclerk *serves* a Customer.")

We might also ask, "What does a Customer Service Clerk *do* to a Complaint?" The answer would be "*handles* it" or perhaps "*deals with* it." Again, "What does a Vendor *do* to a Product?" A Vendor *supplies* a Product. "What does an Order *do* to a Product?" An Order *includes* a Product. What does a Customer *do* to an Event?" A Customer *registers for* an Event, and a Customer *attends* an Event.

Remember, since this is your users' world we're documenting, you need to be sure that the terms you use are terms the users are used to using. As Booch (1994, 1999) would put it, these terms must "be drawn from the vocabulary of your project." In each case, what we're really asking is, "Does an association exist between this class and that class?"

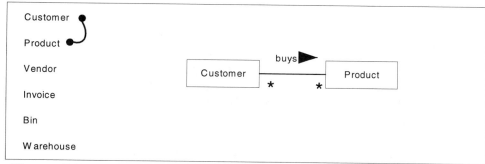

(b)

Figure 9-2 (continued)

The deciding factor in the answer is whether we can come up with a verb that:

- Describes some interaction between instances of the two classes
- Is significant in the operation of the users' business

You may quite often discover two or more verbs that make sense. It's perfectly normal to have several associations joining a pair of classes. Just make sure each has its own verb and that each is telling about a different kind of event or transaction. They must be *independent* in the sense that we don't want two verbs describing the one happening. If two events are actually different but are constrained always to happen together, they should probably be treated as one.

This is all very well; I've shown you what question to ask. But, you may say, how do we organize it? How do we approach the finding of associations in some rational, logical way, so as to ensure that we find them all and don't miss any? And well you may ask, because there's a very good chance of missing a whole bunch unless we ask the questions in a rigorous sequence.

Capturing All Possible Associations

This is one of the few places in this modeling business that I am *religious* about how something must be done. Unless you do it this way, Murphy's Law guarantees that you'll miss some; this method guarantees that you *won't*.

Actually, there are a couple of ways to do this. Perhaps the most logical, at least on the surface, is to use a matrix. You would list all the classes across the top, and again down the side. As you test each combination of two classes for an association (see below), you check off the box to show they're done. You'll only need the top half.

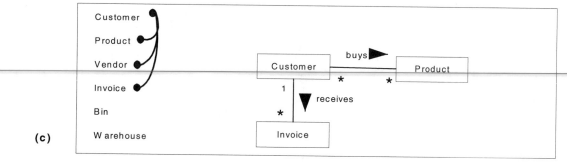

(c)

Figure 9-2 (continued)

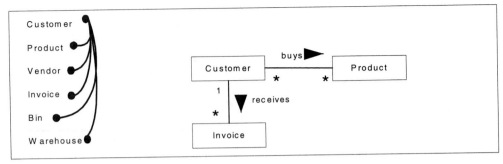

(d)

Figure 9-2 (continued)

I prefer this method below, however, precisely because it is less "mathematical" in nature. Working with non-technical users, it seems to help as the picture grows on the board before their eyes. You'll see what I mean in the next few paragraphs. Either way, what counts is that you do *something* very rigorous about ensuring that you don't miss any associations.

CHECKING FOR ASSOCIATIONS

Begin with a list of all the classes so far discovered, as you see in Figure 9-2(a); now draw a box in the center of the board and label it with name and identifier of *the class at the top of the list* – Customer in Figure 9-2(a). Ask your users, "Is there an association between these two classes?" As you do so, draw a curved line down the side of the list, from the first name (Customer) to the second name (Product), as on the left in Figure 9-2(b).

This line you've drawn signifies that you've *checked for an association* between these two classes, but it doesn't say that an association exists. It just says you *checked* for one. If the users' answer is no, then you go on to the next pair. But if it's yes, then you must ask, "What does a Customer *do* to a Product?" Draw the other box on the diagram, label it Product, and join the two boxes with a line, as Figure 9-2(b) shows.

As part of their answer, the users will no doubt have given you a verb, so you write it abovethe line with an arrow, as in Figure 9-2(b). Now check the first entry on the list, Customer, against the third entry, Vendor.

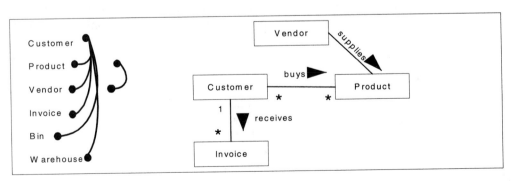

(e)

Figure 9-2 (continued)

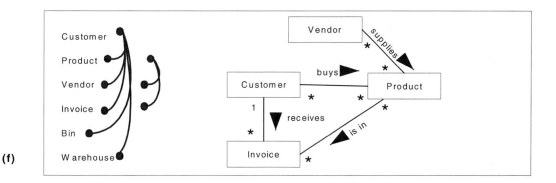

Figure 9-2 (continued)

At the same time, draw a line down the class list from Customer (item 1) to Vendor (item 3), as in Figure 9-2(c). Since the users tell us there is no such association, we simply move on to test Customer (#1) against Invoice (#4). Since we find that the users like the sound of "Customer *receives* Invoice," we add the Invoice box and the association line to the diagram, as in Figure 9-2(c).

We continue this process, until we've matched Customer against all other entries. By this time, the list and the diagram will look like Figure 9-2(d). Notice that the lines on the diagram show we did indeed test for associations from Customer to Bin and from Customer to Warehouse. However, when we checked these, our users said there were no direct associations, so we didn't add anything to the drawing.

With this process, we've checked item 1 on the list, Customer, against every other class possible, to see whether associations exist. By checking item 1 against items 2, 3, 4, and so on, *in order*, we've made absolutely sure we didn't miss any. Then we're ready for the second pass. This time we begin with item 2 on the list, Product, and draw a line to item 3, Vendor.

We then ask the users, "Is there an association between Product and Vendor?" As you may have guessed, there is. (At least, there is in any normal retail business, but you may well find occasional anomalies.) Assuming the users want the verb to be *supplies*, the list and diagram will now look like Figure 9-2(e). Next, we match Product (item 2) against Invoice (item 4) and draw a line down from Product (item 2) to Invoice (item 4), as in Figure 9-2(f).

In this case, though, there's no direct association. The users may think up a verb – in this case, probably *includes*, or some such. As an experienced object modeler, you'll realize that while the two are certainly related, it's only through another class, not on the list, called a Line Item.

You realize, of course, that whenever a Product *is included in* an Invoice, this is done by creating a Line Item on the Invoice for that Product. You may wish to check this with the users, by asking if there's any way that a Product could be "included" in an Invoice without a Line Item, and I'm sure they'll say there is not. For now, however, we'll defer line item to Step 4, *Expanding many-to-many associations*.

So having drawn a line from item 2 (Product) to item 4 (Invoice), we make no additions to the model but simply move on to check Product against item 5, Bin. In this way, we proceed down the list, this time matching Product against every item that follows it in the list. When we reach the bottom, we can expect the list and diagram to look something like Figure 9-2(g).

Now we start again with item 3, Vendor, and match it against items 4, 5, and 6. Each time, we check whether an association exists. (What does a Vendor *do* to a Bin?) The final check we'll make in this example will be item 5 against item 6, "What does a Bin *do* to a Warehouse?" By the time they're completed, the model looks like Figure 9-2(h), and the complete set of lines against the list in Figure 9-2(h) shows that we've checked every possibility.

I've regaled you with the description of this method at some length because I believe it's that important. I do want to encourage you to follow the method of the "lines against the list" with *religious* fervor. It's essential that you do *something* of this nature when finding the associations – either this or a matrix. Otherwise, Murphy will get into your model and spirit away a couple of your precious associations.

And, as we discussed in Chapter 3, when you eventually do discover that you've missed them, the errors will cause much more hassle and be more expensive to fix at that late stage. And now the next step, figuring out "how many."

ESTABLISHING THE MULTIPLICITY

As you discover and draw each association, you'll initially draw it as a simple line joining the two boxes. Once you've placed the verb(s) with their arrows, then it's time to check with the users for the multiplicity. Once you've established that a "Customer *buys* Product," then you'll ask the question, "How many Products does a Customer buy?" The answer (your users sincerely hope) is that a Customer buys *many* Products. So you place an appropriate multiplicity symbol on each end of the line, as shown in Figure 9-3(a), which is really just a piece taken from Figure 9-2(b). Now from the figure you can see that, by following the arrows, you build a sentence that goes:

> A Customer   *buys*   many   Products.

Sentence = Subject   + Verb + Number + Object

(*Object* here is in the grammatical sense, of course, not the object-oriented sense.)

And now we're ready to go the other way. The implied verb in the other direction (which we won't bother writing on the model) will be *is sold to*. Check it out:

A Product　*is sold to*　?????　　Customer(s)?

Sentence　=　Subject　+　Verb　+　Number + Object

The ***multiplicity*** **of an association is the number of instances of each class that can participate in an occurrence of the association.**

You'll notice that I'm a little uncertain of the multiplicity in this *is sold to* association. This is something you'll need to resolve each time with your users. Realistically, can a product be sold to many Customers? As usual, *it depends*. It depends this time on just what you (or at least your users) mean by the term *Product*.

You may recall that back in the section on definitions I suggested that we would have frequent need of a dictionary of the users' definitions of their jargon and technical terms. Well, here is just such a place, because we're about to find out, as Nancy did, that the multiplicity is determined by how we define 'Product.'

Let's say our users felt that a Product is something like a Jar of Pickles, 350 ml, or a Nail, 10 cm. (That last, by the way, is a 4-inch nail, for those of you still using the old-fashioned units.) Do these products have identity? Yes, of course. Any two 10-cm nails are two different nails; they're not the same nail.

But do they have identifiers, for us to tell them apart by? Well, not the individual nails. There are no serial numbers on nails or jars of pickles! They always have a Universal Product Code (UPC), the familiar bar code for the computers, and this is carefully maintained to be unique. The UPC, as you're no doubt aware, identifies not the individual nail, but the *type* of product called "Nail, 10-cm."

For these kinds of Products, we can sell one Product to many Customers. No two Customers will buy the same nail, or the same jar of pickles, but many will buy a kilogram of Nails, 10-cm (that's about 2 pounds of 4" nails).

Many Customers will buy a jar of pickles. They won't all buy the same jar, but our system will treat them all as the same Product, really meaning *product type*. Note that in this case each sale will need to have a Quantity or Amount attribute, to tell how many individual jars of pickles or kilograms of nails each Customer purchased.

In this case, the association between Customer and Product will look like Figure 9-3(b), where the Customer-to-Product association is shown as many-to-many (see the two stars below the line.) Our definition of Product will need to be modified. Here is a repeat of the original one that we had as an example in the section on definitions above:

Product: An item inventoried for sale by The Outhouse

As you've surely observed, this doesn't clearly indicate whether our Products are individual products or product types. The following might be a more suitable definition:

Product: A type of item inventoried by The Outhouse for sale by quantity or by measure.

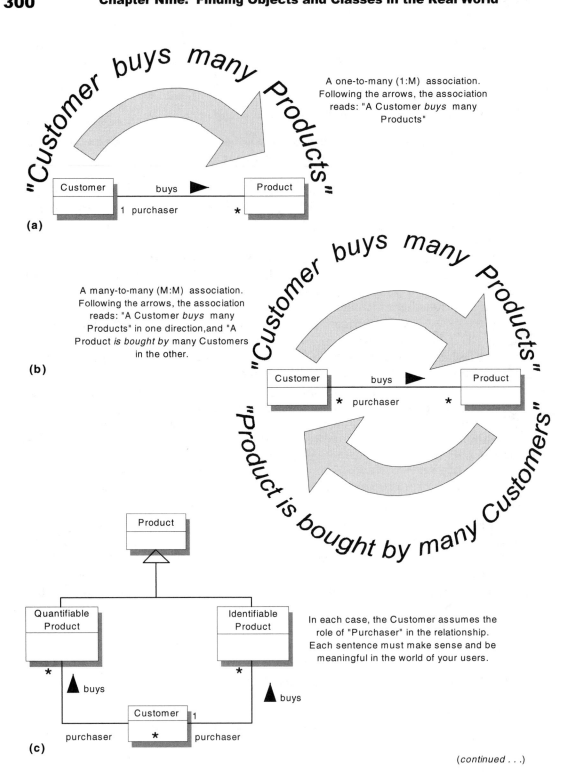

(a) A one-to-many (1:M) association. Following the arrows, the association reads: "A Customer *buys* many Products"

(b) A many-to-many (M:M) association. Following the arrows, the association reads: "A Customer *buys* many Products" in one direction, and "A Product *is bought by* many Customers in the other.

(c) In each case, the Customer assumes the role of "Purchaser" in the relationship. Each sentence must make sense and be meaningful in the world of your users.

(*continued . . .*)

Figure 9-3 Verbs and roles

On the other hand, products such as cars, stereos, bicycles, dishwashers, and other big-ticket items do have serial numbers. These serve to identify the *individual* bicycle, car, stereo, and so on. Dwellings have addresses, tax-roll numbers, and legal descriptions, all of which serve to identify the *individual* house. So when we sell one of these, we're concerned with the sale of a particular *individual* car, house, or stereo, and we write down the identifier as part of the sale.

On these sales, the quantity will always be one, so there will be no need for a Quantity attribute. We'll need an attribute in the Sale class, however, for the serial number (or whatever the identifier is for our Products). And the normal thing is for one of these kinds of Products to be sold to only one Customer! (In order to keep it simple, we'll ignore for the moment the possibility of joint ownership.)

For Products such as these, our association will need to look like Figure 9-3(a), showing the Customer-to-Product association as 1:M. The definition would be along the lines of:

Product: An individually identified item inventoried by The Outhouse for sale.

This fits a lot better for this kind of Product. Did I say *kinda* Product? Could it be that "an Identifiable Product *isakinda* Product?" And that "a Quantifiable Product *isakinda* Product?" Almost. In many real-world inventories, you'll find both kinds of Product, and one possible way to handle this in your model is (you guessed it!) *subclasses*.

Another way is to define a class called Product Type with two subclasses, Identifiable Product Type (these products have serial numbers or some other individual identifier) and Quantifiable Product Type (these products are stored and sold by quantity or measure). The Product Type class would have attributes such as Unit Price, Unit Cost, Quantity on Hand, and Quantity on Backorder, which would be inherited by both subclasses. We would then have a class called Product, which would have a 1:M association from Product Type, as in Figure 9-3(d).

But this still isn't good enough. The Product class has instances only for Identifiable Products, that is, whose type is an Identifiable Product Type. The Product class would have an instance for each individual car, stereo, dishwasher, and so on. First, this means that for clarity we can rename the Product class to be the Identifiable Product class, as in Figure 9-3(e).

Second, as you see in the figure, there's a 1:M relationship to Identifiable Product, not from Product Type the superclass, but from Identifiable Product Type, the subclass. And then we would also need a *buys* association from Customer to Quantifiable Product Type, to handle sales of these products. The processing would have to be somewhat different for these two sale types.

Note this is only one of a number of ways this could be handled. The choice, of course, depends on what is comfortable for your users. The skill you need to develop here is the ability to discern how ***your users*** *actually view all these transactions* and associations, as distinct from your own view, or worse still, *my* view, of how things *should* be.

Note that there's no *Quantifiable Product* class, since we don't record any details of individual products for those ones. In other words, our system doesn't concern itself with any data or behavior for these instances, so they don't form a class of any importance to this system.

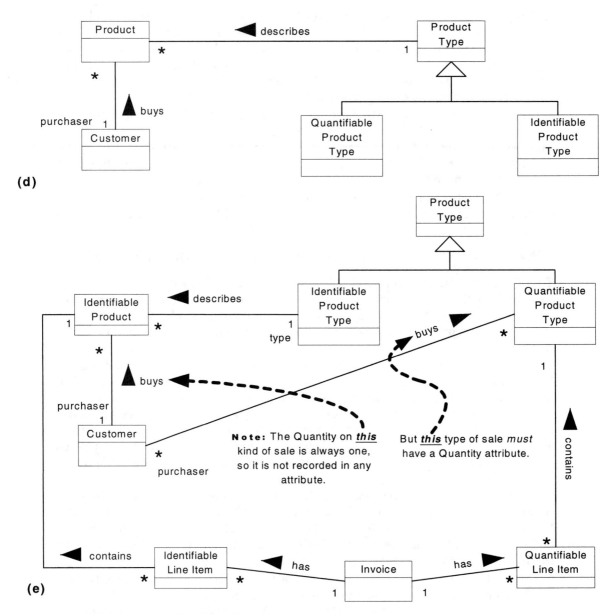

Figure 9-3   (continued)

All this leads to further subclassing in the invoice, as shown in Figure 9-3(e). There would need to be two subclasses of Line Item, one for Identifiable Products and one for Quantifiable Products. You can see that the Identifiable Line Item class has an association to the Identifiable Product class, and that class has one to Identifiable Product Type. The Quantifiable Line Item class has an association directly to Quantifiable Product Type.

Finally, there is a point that I wish to stress about the discussion we just went through. You'll notice it all began with some confusion over the multiplicity of the Customer–Product association. The sequence of discovery that we went through here is very normal. Often you'll find that, having laid down a definition, later (for example, when deciding multiplicity, as in the example above) you'll find something that just won't work. When these anomalies occur, the first thing you do is:

Refer back to your definitions

Usually, as soon as you reread the definition, the confusion comes clear. In The Outhouse example above, it would have been a scene typical of many modeling sessions had we found two users thinking different ways about Products and Sales. One may well have been thinking of identifiable products, while the other may have been viewing the products as quantifiable.

The session leader, sensing the conflict, would call time out to look up the definition of Product. At that point, the reason for the conflict becomes clear, and so the group can embark upon a more rational search for a solution. (You can't solve a problem until you've accurately defined just what that problem really is!)

The solution that suits this particular set of users may be to add subclasses as in the example, and so allow for sales of both types of product. Alternatively, you may find that your users don't really need to track serial numbers and individual products, even though the products may actually be identifiable.

In the latter case, you would drop all reference to identifiers and/or identifiability, and model the inventory with only one class of Product Types, which would in fact be quantifiable in nature. My guess is that your users would probably want to name this class simply "Product."

The important point here is the need to *refer back to the definitions* as soon as your group gets into any kind of wrangling over how associations should work, or anything else. Nine times out of ten, you'll find that the problem is solved as soon as you do this, and the tenth time you're still going to need the definition anyway as a base and a guide for finding a solution.

Difficult and laborious as all this association work may seem, I have an interesting and hopeful comment to make next.

ATTITUDE OF THE USERS

Modeling is hard work. We're expecting our users to spend hours and hours performing strange, unfamiliar rituals with strange words and our cryptic art forms. We expect them to take it on trust that all this will actually bear fruit, with some significant benefit to them in their work. Given their inherent mistrust of technology and of us technoids, and all the other fears that many users experience (as I mentioned in earlier chapters and will again later in this one), it's sometimes surprising to me that they'll follow along this far.

But the nice thing about object-oriented modeling is that at some point the users start to see that what we're doing actually has relevance to them and their jobs. Although it can happen at any stage, this sometimes surprising insight will often happen during the association exercise.

(a) A M:M relationship

(b) A 1:M relationship

(c) Is this a 1:1 relationship?

They see the diagram growing, and begin to recognize in the associations some sentences that describe what happens in their own world. If we're doing it right (or at least close), then we're being user-driven, and they begin to feel that the model is being built from *their* input. They also tend to feel an increased sense of ownership in the project. They begin referring to it as "our system" (meaning them, the users), and not "your system" (meaning us, the techies).

Of course, if your users are experienced at this sort of thing, this all happens right from the word Go. Either way, this little serendipity of increased ownership and cooperation can have some major positive effects on all aspects of the project. So saying, we're ready to move on to the next step, which is to simplify some of the associations we've discovered.

But first, here is a summary to quickly review how we go about Step 3:

• Step 3: Establish Associations. The connections among classes are interactions: actions in that the objects do things, and inter meaning they do them between objects, that is, to one another.

• The question we must ask the users is, "What does one of these *do* to one of those?" In the answer to this question, we'll need to consider:

- Discovering the Verb
- Establishing the Multiplicity
- Capturing All Possible Associations

• **Discovering the verb.** Begin the diagram by drawing a box in the center of the board for Bus, and another for Bus Driver, and then join them with a straight line. The verb is above the line for reading according to the arrow. If the roles are obvious, write either or both below the line as well.

Since this is your users' world, be sure the terms you use are terms your users are comfortable with, and use in their normal conversations. The main thing is whether we can find a verb that (1) describes some interaction between instances of the classes and (2) is significant in the users' business.

You may discover several associations joining a pair of classes. Each must have its verb, and each must be a different kinMd of event, that is they must be *independent*. If two events are different but always happen together, they should be treated as one.

- **Capturing all possible associations.** You must be *religious* about how you make sure you capture all possible associations. Unless you use my method or something like it, Murphy's Law guarantees that you'll miss some. The method of joining the classes in the list with lines guarantees that you won't miss any.

- **Multiplicity/Cardinality.** Ask the question, "How *many* Products does a Customer buy?" That is, "How many instances participate in this association at a time?"

A Customer *buys*   many   Products.

Sentence = Subject + Verb + Number + Object

- Often, having laid down a definition, later you may find something that just won't work. Your modeling group may get into a big argument over something.

Refer back to your definitions

When these anomalies occur, the first thing you do is:

Then, once we have the associations, there's a certain operation we must perform on all of the *many-to-many* associations in our model.

Step 4: Expand Many-to-Many Associations

The many-to-many (M:M) association has some interesting features. Compared with its simpler cousin, the one-to-many (1:M), it's much more complex to actually implement or build in a database.

Employee				has ▶	Absence		
*Employee Number	1			*	*Employee Number + Date		

Employee Number	Name	Hourly Rate	. . .		Employee Number	Date	Reason Code	. . .
7	Jo	1.49			13	Jan 3	12	
5	Mo	2.10			7	Jan 17	42	
13	Bo	1.00			11	Feb 29	17	
11	Slo	0.50			5	Jan 13	21	
					5	Jan 17	21	
					7	Feb 29	17	
					5	Jan 31	42	
					5	Jan 29	17	

Primary Key — In this table, Employee Number is the *entire* Primary Key.   Primary Key — In this table, Employee Number is a Foreign Key; it is only *part* of the Primary Key.

Figure 9-4   Using a foreign key to implement a 1:M association

SIMPLICITY OF THE **1:M** ASSOCIATION

The 1:M association is implemented in a database either as a *pointer* or (in a relational database) as a *foreign key*. For this explanation, I'll stay with the relational model, since more people are familiar with it. Also, it's conceptually simpler, and, for the moment, we're dealing strictly with the data side of things. In Figure 9-4 you see a 1:M association from Employee to Absence, taken from the personnel system model at *The Outhouse*.

If we think of a simplified data-only version of these two classes, we can view each class as if it were a flat file of data, with one record to represent each object instance. We'll have a file of Employees, and a file of Absences. All the absences are mixed in together, however, so the absence record will need a field to tell which Employee it was who was away on this date.

To do that is simple — we just put the Employee Number as a field in the Absence record, so that it becomes a *foreign key*. Now the DBMS software can trace in either direction; given an Employee Number, it can search the Absence file for all records that match. Or, for any Absence record, we can find the matching Employee record. In Figure 9-4 you can readily see that Mo was having some attendance problems in the month of January.

COMPLEXITY OF THE **M:M** ASSOCIATION

For a M:M association, it's more difficult. For the M:M association between Customer and Product, we need to connect each Customer record to many Product records, and each Product to many Customers. If we attempted to build this one in a database with a foreign key as before, we would need not one but many. To connect a Customer to many Products, we would put the Customer Number field in the Product record, as before. So far, so good. But a Product needs to be connected to many Customers, so we would need not just one but *a whole bucnh* of Customer Number fields in the Product record!

Apart from the fact that this would violate the rules of normalization (more about this later), there is a very practical difficulty with that arrangement. How would we know how many Customer Numbers to allow in the Product record? We cannot in practice allow for an unlimited number, and Murphy's Law says that however much room we leave, Murphy himself will sell the one Product to such a large number of Customers that he'll crash the database!

Now let's look at a manual, noncomputer system for Customers and Products, because the problems and their solutions turn out to be the same. Imagine we're tracking our Customers and Products on 8 x 10 cm index cards (3 x 6 inch for you old-fashioned folk). We have a tub of cards for each, arranged in Customer Number and Product Number order, respectively, as in Figure 9-5(a). In this marvelous semiautomated system of ours, we've decided to represent associations, or rather the links that are instances of associations, with strings, each connected from a Customer card to a Product card.

As you can see in the figure, Jo has been busy shopping, because (s)he has purchased some coffee, donuts, a dictionary, and a thesaurus. (Must be planning some object-oriented modeling sessions!) Other customers also have strings leading to the products they have purchased, including two other people who bought donuts. As you can readily see, our card-and-string database really does handle a M:M association.

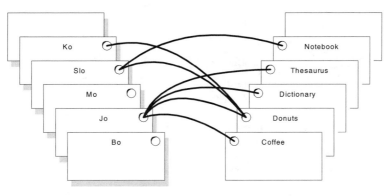

(a) Sales database with card-and-string DBMS, showing strings used to implement the M:M association

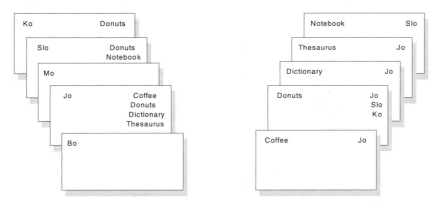

(b) The same sales database with cards but no strings, with the M:M association implemented using repeating fields   (*continued*)

Figure 9-5   A sales database built in a variety of ways, using different DBMS "technologies"

But what can we actually *do* with this rather stringy-looking database? Well, given a customer, we can identify all of her purchases simply by pulling the Customer card. Because of the strings, all the connected Product cards will be dragged along, too. Then we have all the information we need to produce a sales report by Customer. Similarly, if we pull Product cards, the strings will present us with the sales data by product, and identify the customers who bought each product.

And what if we decided the strings were too tangly and we wanted to replace them with foreign keys? Not too difficult. As we cut each string away, we simply write the customer number from one end of the string onto the Product card at the other end of the same string. Then we write the Product Number from that end onto the Customer card at the other end, as in Figure 9-5(b). (Actually, we don't need to do both – one of these is redundant. We only need to write the foreign keys into one of the two files for it to work. But for completeness and symmetry, here we'll write both.)

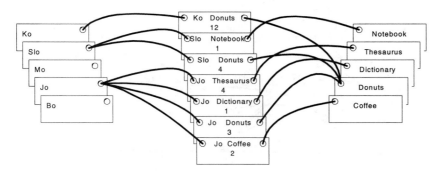

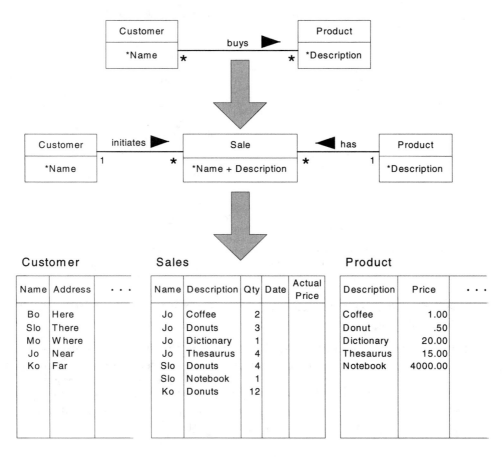

(c) Sales database with the M:M association expanded and the strings in place, showing the foreign keys. The quantities and other Sale attribute values may now be written on the new (center) cards.

Customer

*Name

buys ▶

Product

*Description

Customer

*Name

initiates ▶

Sale

*Name + Description

◀ has

Product

*Description

Customer

Name	Address	. . .
Bo	Here	
Slo	There	
Mo	Where	
Jo	Near	
Ko	Far	

Sales

Name	Description	Qty	Date	Actual Price
Jo	Coffee	2		
Jo	Donuts	3		
Jo	Dictionary	1		
Jo	Thesaurus	4		
Slo	Donuts	4		
Slo	Notebook	1		
Ko	Donuts	12		

Product

Description	Price	. . .
Coffee	1.00	
Donut	.50	
Dictionary	20.00	
Thesaurus	15.00	
Notebook	4000.00	

(d) The same sales database, shown this time beginning as a Class Diagram, and implemented as (extended) relational tables. In this case, the foreign keys perform the same function as the strings did in part (c).

Figure 9-5   (continued)

But what if everybody buys donuts, and we run out of room trying to write all the customer numbers on the 8 x 10 cm card? This is the same problem we mentioned earlier in the flat-file database, so how would we solve it? We need the strings. We need something to connect a Customer card with a Product card.

In our string-and-shoebox card system we create another tub of cards, each card with *one* customer number and *one* product number and nothing else, as in Figure 9-5(c). In the database, this would be done by creating an extra file (i.e., *table* or *relation*) as a cross-reference, as in Figure 9-5(d). The only fields it needs are the customer number and product number.

In other words, each record in this file (each row in this table) represents a string *by recording its two end points*. Now, every time a Customer buys a Product, *we create a row in this new table* as a record of that event. Figure 9-5(d) shows the progression from two classes with a M:M, to three classes with a pair of 1:M, to three tables with a pair of foreign keys.

PLACING EVENT DATA ATTRIBUTES

This new table in the middle can perform another function for us too. There's a certain kind of data in this transaction that we haven't yet considered. For instance, where would we record items such as the Date the Customer bought the Product, or the Actual Price charged? Should we put the Date as an attribute of Customer? If we did, we would be back to the repeating-field problem, with no idea of how many spaces to allow in the record for the dates of all the purchases this customer might make. And remember, however many spaces you might leave, Murphy is still one of your Customers. . . .

The Actual Price is an interesting attribute. Why would we even need it, when we're bound to have a Unit Price attribute in the Product class?

Well, if we *did* rely on the Unit Price field in the Product, then say we sold a Widget to Jo on January 29 for $1.49.

Then let's say we had a price change on February 1, so widgets now cost $2.00. If we did an enquiry on February 3, at what price would the sale to Jo be reported? Well, the only price anywhere in the database is the $2.00 current price, so all our historical sales will be inflated in value in our reporting!

The simplest solution is to record the Actual Price that the Product was sold for. But where? We can't put it in the Customer record, since a large Customer may buy thousands of things from us, and not all of them Widgets. This would mean thousands of repeats of the Actual Price field in the Customer record.

And we may sell Widgets to thousands of Customers, which would mean many repeats of the Customer Number, Date, and Actual Price fields in the Product record. Either way, it just doesn't work, and watch out for Murphy's Law if you try it.

The way to find the official answer to this little conundrum is actually part of the discussion of normalization, later in this chapter. Think about this Date and this Actual Price for a moment. What do they *actually describe*?

Is it the Customer? No, this Date is not something unique about a Customer because he could have thousands of Dates. Nor does it describe a Product since a Product could be sold on many different dates. In fact, what the Date and Actual Price really describe is another type of *thing* (i.e., object) altogether. Can you think of some*thing* that comes into existence the moment a Customer buys a Product? Of course you can, it's a *Sale*! Or your users might prefer to call it a *Purchase*.

With our string-and-shoebox database, we already have a string in place to represent each sale. We could attach a tag to each string, and on it we could write the Date and the Actual price. This would work, and what is more, it would be properly normalized to Third Normal Form (explained shortly), although perhaps a little clumsy. But what it demonstrates is that we do need *something* in the middle to record the data attributes that describe an event, in this case the Sale event.

THE INTERSECTION CLASS

So we've discovered yet another entity class, called Sale. Now we must iterate this new class through Steps 2 and 3 of the Seven Steps and then include it as we continue forward. But in Step 2, the first test we apply is to find an identifier. So how do we tell one Sale from another?

If you were the local super-salesperson and I came running into your office one day and said "Remember that sale you made last week?" what would be your most likely response? "Oh, come on, Dave! I'm the top salesperson round here, and I made dozens of sales last week! Which one are you talking about?"

What information would I need to give you, in order for you to figure out just which Sale I mean? Based on the attributes we have in our example string database, as a minimum it would have to be customer number and product number. But we already have these two attributes together in the little table we invented way back in this discussion, to replace the strings.

So, putting all of this explanation together now, we see that we can record the Date and the Actual Price as *columns* in the cross-reference table. Since in the object paradigm, data can only reside in objects, this is equivalent to putting the "Date" and "Actual Price" *attributes* in the *Sale class*.

In the tub-of-cards example, this would be the equivalent of writing the Date and Actual Price data on the string itself. There are many object notations (and ERD notations) around that do exactly that – they allow *an association* to have *attributes*. But, by and large, they eventually resolve that association into an additional class at some stage, so I prefer to do that right up front.

Having these attributes in a Sale class (that is, having these *columns* in the Sale *table* in the example) means that we now have the ability to record a Sale event that occurs in the real world of the users. To do this, we create an *instance* in the Sale *class* (compare this with the idea of creating a *row* in the Sale *table*, or a *card* in the Sale *shoebox*). Since we can have a virtually unlimited number of such instances (or rows or cards), we've now overcome all the difficulties we found earlier.

Now we should look at the structure of what we've created. Figure 9-6 shows the Class Diagram before and after this process. The ***Intersection Class* or *Associative Class* is the new class we create in the middle of a many-to-many association in order to break it up into a pair of one-to-many associations.** The pattern we can observe here is an important one.

It goes like this:

> # *Every M:M association*
>
> ## breaks out into a pair of 1:M associations,
>
> ## with the many ends pointing at this new
>
> ## *Intersection (Associative) Class.*

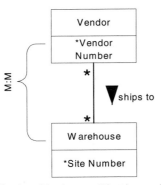

"A Vendor *ships to* many Warehouses"
"A Warehouse *receives from* many Vendors."

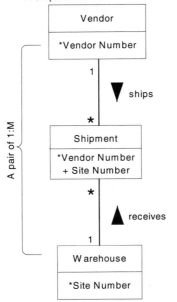

"A Vendor *ships* many Shipments,
A Shipment *is from* one Vendor"

"A Warehouse *receives* many Shipments,
A Shipment *is to* one Warehouse"

Figure 9-6 Breaking out M:M associations:

"Vendor *ships to* Warehouse."

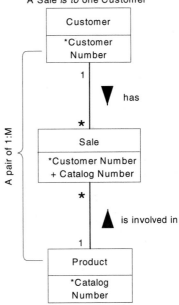

"A Customer *buys* many Products"
"A Product *is bought by* many Customers."

"A Customer *has* many Sales,
A Sale *is to* one Customer"

"A Product *is involved in* many Sales,
A Sale *is of* one Product."

Figure 9-7 Breaking out M:M associations:

"Customer *buys* Product."

Next, we need to go through the entire class diagram and repeat this process with each M:M association. We'll redraw the diagram, converting each M:M to a pair of 1:M, with the two *many* ends pointing to the new *intersection class* in the center. Figures 9-6 to 9-10 show this for The Outhouse project.

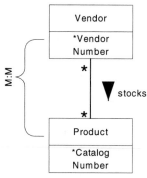

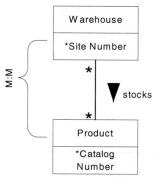

"A Vendor *stocks* many Products"
"A Product *is stocked by* many Vendors."

"A Warehouse *stocks* many Products"
"A Product *is in* many Warehouses."

"A Vendor *has* many Product-Vendor records,
A Product-Vendor record *refers to* one Vendor"

"A Warehouse *has* many Product-Warehouse records,
A Product-Warehouse record *refers to* one Warehouse"

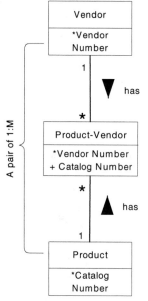

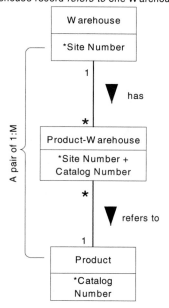

"A Product *is involved in* many Product-Vendor records,
A Product-Vendor record *refers to* one Product."

"A Product *has* many Product-Warehouse records,
A Product-Warehouse record *refers to* one Product"

Figure 9-8 Breaking out M:M
associations:

"Vendor stocks Product."

Figure 9-9 Breaking out M:M
associations:

"Warehouse stocks Product."

To do this with your users, you'll ask them a question for each M:M association. The answer must be a simple sentence that not only makes sense, but *actually describes something that happens in the users' world:*

What does a Customer *do* to a Product (Figure 9-6)?

A Customer *buys* a Product

What does a Customer create for us by *buying* a Product?

She creates a *Sale*.

or

What does a Vendor *do* to a Warehouse?
(Figure 9-7)

A Vendor *ships to* a Warehouse.

What do we create by *shipping to* a Warehouse?

We create a *Shipment*.

In other words, we want to discover what comes into existence, *that did not exist before*, when we perform the sentence that expresses the association. Typically, this newly created object will be a conceptual or event kind of object. Very often it will have a name in the users' world, as *Sale* and *Shipment* do. But sometimes your users will just not be able to come up with a name for this thing, no matter how hard they try.

This doesn't invalidate the class; what we do is name it after the two classes that gave rise to it:

What does a Vendor *do* to a Product?

A Vendor *stocks* a Product.

What do we create when we *stock* a Product?
(Should we call it perhaps a "*Stocking*?" I really *don't* think that will work!)
It has no natural name, so we'll call it the ***Product-Vendor*** class.

"A Vendor *stocks* many Products."
"A Product *is stocked by* many Vendors."
"A Vendor *has shipped* many Products."
"A Product *has been shipped by* many Vendors."

Figure 9-10   Multiple associations

The convention is that you *hyphenate* the names of the two classes. Don't leave out the hyphen! It's imperative that everybody who reads this name should think about it the same way as the person who wrote it. Putting in the hyphen makes sure of that.

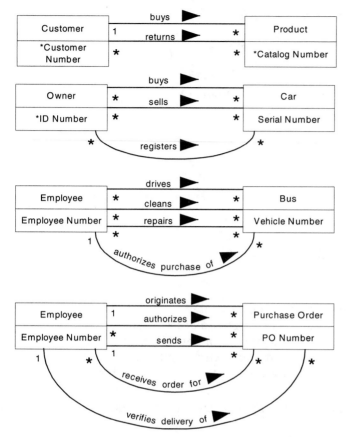

Figure 9-11   More multiple associations

The order of the two names is not significant, but there are some things to watch out for. You'll notice I didn't call this one Vendor-Product. This is because I was afraid the phrase "Vendor Product" might have some meaning for someone, which could be misleading when they read it in the model.

In the same way, "Warehouse stocks Product" might also have given us a class called *Stocking*. But not only is it not suitable, if we had used it we could have had two classes with the same name! So here we'll use Product-Warehouse. We avoid Warehouse-Product because, again, that sounds misleadingly like it might be some kind of product.

MULTIPLE ASSOCIATIONS

Take a look at Figure 9-10, which shows two associations between Vendor and Product. The fact that a Vendor may stock a certain Product is quite independent of whether that Vendor actually ships that Product to us. She may have stocked it for years, but we may never have ordered this particular Product from this Vendor. We normally may buy it at a better price from another Vendor, but we need to know that this one stocks it in case of shortages.

You'll often find two or more parallel associations like these, and the only thing you need to watch is to establish with your users that these are *independent* associations. You need to be sure that they are in fact two different associations, and not just the same one cropping up twice as you build the model. Figure 9-11 shows four more examples of multiple associations.

COLLAPSING EVENTS

You may think "collapsing events" is kind of a funny title for this section, but I really couldn't think of anything else to call it. In Figure 9-12(a), we have three M:M associations. In Figure 9-12(b), we've broken out the Vendor *ships to* Warehouse association.

What comes into existence when a Vendor ships to a Warehouse? Why, a *Shipment*, of course. Then in Figure 9-12(c), we break out the M:M association between Product and Warehouse. And what is it that we create when we ship a Product to a Warehouse? Again, a *Shipment*.

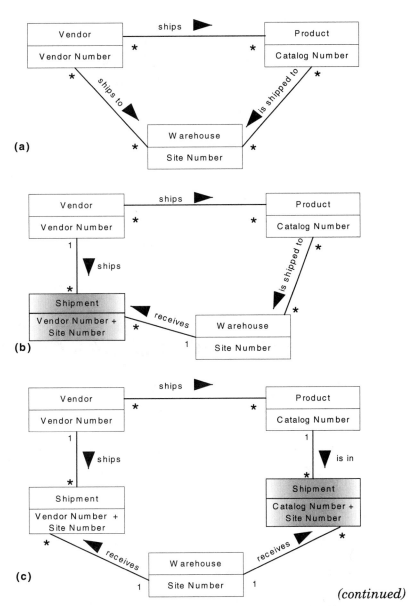

Figure 9-12   Breaking out M:M associations: "Vendor *ships* Product"

Then let's break out the final M:M association in the example: Vendor *ships* Product. Strangely enough, the intersection class looks like it's going to be a *Shipment* also. But how can this be? We already have a Shipment class between Vendor and Warehouse, and another between Product and Warehouse. Do we have three classes of the same name? That's what Figure 9-12(d) would appear to indicate.

But think for a moment. When a Vendor *ships* a Product, where does he ship it to? Why, to a Warehouse! Can a Vendor ship a Product without involving a Warehouse? Normally, *no*. Can a Vendor ship to a Warehouse without involving a Product? Also *no*. In other words, this is the same *Shipment* class turning up in three associations! Figure 9-12(d) would then collapse into Figure 9-12(e), where the Shipment class is shown with three 1:M associations to Vendor, Product, and Warehouse.

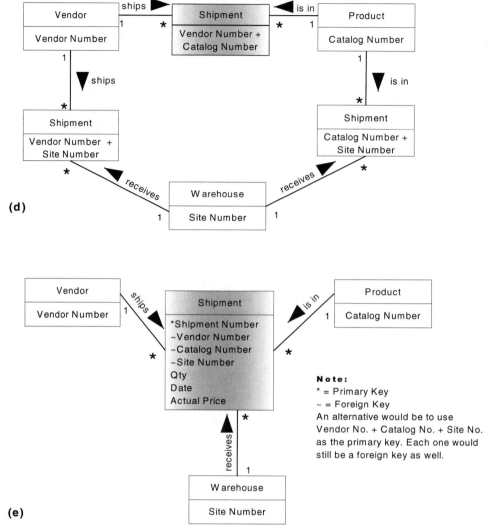

Figure 9-12   (continued)

This is a fairly common thing. Often you'll find two (or more) associations from one class to others, where they turn out to be representing the same event. There can be a triangle of M:M associations that collapse into a single event class. Or there may be two associations showing in your model, which collapse into a single intersection class.

You'll notice that the attributes listed against the Shipment class in Figure 9-12(e) include a Shipment Number We could have used Vendor Number plus Catalog No. plus Site No. as the unique identifier (key), but to make it truly unique we would need to add the Date and Time of Day. Since this would be far too cumbersome, we would normally invent an "artificial" key – in this case, Shipment Number We must still have the Vendor, Catalog, and Site numbers in the Shipment class as nonkey attributes, however, to serve as foreign keys for the three associations.

Remember, for this explanation, we're thinking extended relational. In many ODBMSs, we would not have the foreign keys since they use pointers to establish associations. In that case, these three attributes would not need to appear in the Shipment class. In addition to those, we shall need a few "useful" attributes, such as Quantity and Date, since these ones are why we even bother to have a Shipment class.

Whenever you see a triangle of associations, such as in Figure 9-12(a), this should trigger a warning bell in your head. You'll need to check them carefully to see whether they're truly independent. If they really do represent different actions, or different events, then they stay. But if, as in this case, they're all the same event, then they must all collapse into a single intersection class.

A rule of thumb comes out of this: Whenever you notice that you have a class with three or more 1:M associations, with all or most of the many ends on this class in the center, chances are that what you've discovered is an event class.

Lastly, there are two more kinds of relationship that I haven't mentioned in this discussion. These are subclassing and aggregation, *isakinda* and *isapartof*. We'll discuss how to find these, later in this chapter.

However, if you notice any of these during the association analysis, or something you think might be one of these, *write it down* as a note attached to your documentation. Then you may consider it in depth later. Or, you may feel that you need it to be in the model, so go ahead and add it to the model now if you feel more comfortable doing that.

When you've been through and around the association process enough times, you'll end up with a complete class diagram. You'll probably discover a few more classes as you work through the attribute and normalization steps, and maybe one or two more as you continue through the rest of the analysis phase. Each extra class that you discover must then be run through Steps 2 to 7, defining it and checking for associations and operations.

So now let's look at the next step, searching for attributes.

Step 5: Attributes

After the complexities of the hunt for associations, you may well find this step a welcome break. There may be lots of work to do, but it's relatively simple in concept. You and your users simply go through the model, box by box, and list for each one all the attributes that you and they can think of. You'll find that between you there will be no problem coming up with a solid list for practically every class. If you miss any, they'll turn up in your later work, so you just add them to the documentation when that happens.

For a small model, you may wish to document the attributes either within the boxes or as a list beside each box. Be sure to indicate which one(s) form the primary key (unique identifier), usually done with an asterisk (*). On a larger model with more boxes to draw, you'll need to write the lists in the textual parts of the documentation, and show just the key attribute(s) in the box.

As you list the attributes on the board, you may also need to define them. For all except the ones you're quite familiar with, have the users tell you what each attribute is and use your judgment as to whether it's something that should have its meaning documented. Make free use of the dictionary, as before.

Now that we've discovered all the classes and the attributes, we need to talk about getting the attributes attached to the correct classes.

Step 6: Normalization

This is a topic that usually scares everybody away. Most books and courses treat it at a very theoretical level, but I think it's possible to do it justice without getting too esoteric. Let me begin by defining it in terms of the attributes and classes we've already discussed: ***Normalization* is the process of ensuring that every attribute is attached to the class of objects that it truly describes.**

Normalization is primarily a database design technique, but it has been found to have value at all stages in systems development. I do not advocate a formal normalization procedure in object-oriented analysis, although you (or your employer or client) may wish to do that as a final step in building the object model. My preference is that you finish this book *understanding* normalization and that you bear its *principles* in mind throughout each project.

Normalization is a practice that has had a rough transition to the object world. In the relational paradigm, normalization became a big deal, although it's really just a form of applied common sense. Most of us old-timers had been at least part-way normalizing our files and databases long before we saw the term formally defined. In the object-oriented paradigm, normalization sometimes becomes impossible because of complex and multivalued attribute types.

At the same time as object methods have been emerging, computing power has become cheap enough that everybody is starting to process graphics, audio, video and such in their databases. Objects have turned out to be an excellent way of handling these and other complex attributes, such as graphics and sound and video clips. Objects also lend themselves to attributes that are *lists of values* (linked or not), or queues, and all kinds of things.

Some languages (notably Smalltalk) even allow attributes that are classes of other objects. As you'll see in a moment when we define it, any multivalued attribute automatically violates the First Normal Form of normalization. For this reason, formal normalization has fallen out of favor with object-oriented theorists and practitioners.

However, the principles behind normalization and why we do it are still valid. The problem is that the normal forms are cumulative in nature. A database that has been designed to be in Second Normal Form (2NF) is also in First Normal Form (1NF). A database in 3NF is also automatically in 2NF (and therefore also in 1NF). Thus, if a complex attribute type causes us to violate 1NF, then we've automatically violated all the others as well.

So it has become necessary to redefine what we mean by *normalization*. The old way of explaining it, deriving the technical definitions of the *normal forms*, used to scare everybody off, anyway. What is needed is a statement describing the very essence of normalization, the part of it that's still true and necessary even when we have complex data types that screw up the technical definitions.

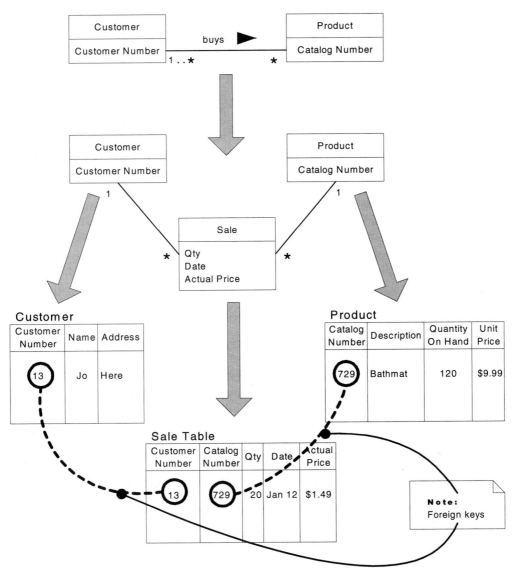

Figure 9-13 Sales with the M:M association correctly broken out into a pair of 1:M

So, for the moment, we'll ignore complex data types and discuss normalization as if we were still in the relational paradigm. As we go through it, you'll be able to see why the complex types are awkward and, I hope, why the *principles* are still important. And once we define 1NF, you'll see why a list-valued attribute would violate it.

There are many levels of normalization. We'll focus on the first three, which are known as First, Second, and Third Normal Form or 1NF, 2NF, and 3NF, respectively. Their purpose is to develop an object-oriented database that stores data in an *accessible manner* and is *resilient to change*. (We saw some of the problems from nonnormalized data in *The Outhouse Saga*, Episodes 3 and 4.) We want the database to be flexible enough not only to produce the set of outputs that we're now aware of, but also all the *unanticipated queries* that we *know* are going to come along over the years.

Record Number	Cust-omer No.	Cat. No.	Date	Qty	Actual Price	Customer Name	Customer Address	Sales-person No.	Sales-person Name	Tenure	Comm %
#1	13	729	Jan 12	20	$1.49	Murphy	Here	1152	Bill	12	5
								1140	Naz	2	5
								1010	Eli	7	15
								1201	Fred	5	10
								1149	Kathy	3	10
								1210	Eric	3	10
								1204	June	5	10
								1133	Julie	7	15
								1175	Oz	11	10
								1169	Kelly	5	5
								1132	Tania	5	5
#2	13	845	Jan 12	30	$2.00	Murphy	Here	1132	Tania	5	100
#3	17	961	Jan 20	1	$100.00	Cissone	There	1132	Tania	5	100

Key: Customer No. + Catalog No. + Date

(a) Sales with additional attributes unnormalized (Note that this table has only 3 rows, that is, 3 records.)

Record Number	Cust-omer No.	Cat. No.	Date	Qty	Actual Price	Customer Name	Customer Address	Sales-person No.	Sales-person Name	Tenure	Comm %
1	13	729	Jan 12	20	$1.49	Murphy	Here	1152	Bill	12	5
2	13	729	Jan 12	20	$1.49	Murphy	Here	1140	Naz	2	5
3	13	729	Jan 12	20	$1.49	Murphy	Here	1010	Eli	7	15
4	13	729	Jan 12	20	$1.49	Murphy	Here	1201	Fred	5	10
5	13	729	Jan 12	20	$1.49	Murphy	Here	1149	Kathy	3	10
6	13	729	Jan 12	20	$1.49	Murphy	Here	1210	Eric	3	10
7	13	729	Jan 12	20	$1.49	Murphy	Here	1204	June	5	10
8	13	729	Jan 12	20	$1.49	Murphy	Here	1133	Julie	7	15
9	13	729	Jan 12	20	$1.49	Murphy	Here	1175	Oz	11	10
10	13	729	Jan 12	20	$1.49	Murphy	Here	1169	Kelly	5	5
11	13	729	Jan 12	20	$1.49	Murphy	Here	1132	Tania	5	5
12	13	845	Jan 12	30	$2.00	Murphy	Here	1132	Tania	5	100
13	17	961	Jan 20	1	$100.00	Cissone	There	1132	Tania	5	100

Key: Customer No. + Catalog No. + Date

(b) Sales with additional attributes in First normal Form (Note that this table has 13 rows.)

Figure 9-14

The highest I've heard of is Eighteenth Normal Form (18NF), but we won't go near that! The theorists tell us that in the relational paradigm we rarely need to go beyond 3NF – less than 5% of the time – and I have only once in a great while seen a contract that requests 4NF or 5NF.

The normal forms were developed initially by Codd (1970) with more work later by C. J. Date and W. Kent. The whole purpose of normalization is to make sure that *every data element (attribute) is attached to the class of objects that it truly describes.* Unnormalized Data

In the discussion on breaking out many-to-many associations, we observed that it doesn't work to have an attribute repeated within an object instance (which in conventional programming terms would correspond to a field being repeated within a record). Figure 9-13 shows how we might build a set of three tables to describe a sale at The Outhouse.

We take a M:M association, split it apart, and then develop a table from each of the resulting classes. Figure 9-14(a) shows how it might look if we were instead to put all the data in a single table, and Figure 9-14(b) if we decided to record the salesperson's number and name as attributes in the Sale class for calculating her commission.

But what if we sometimes needed to share the commission between two salespersons? Perhaps it frequently happens that the salesperson originating the sale needs the knowledge and experience of one of the longer-standing employees. In the interests of customer service, the company wants to encourage these people to seek help when this happens.

For us as analysts, this means adding not one but two sets of salesperson data to the Sale class. As we've observed, this is not good design, but Figure 9-14(b) could handle it.

But what if we built the system, only to have the ubiquitous Murphy wander into the store, determined to outfit his new hotel with bathroom accessories from The Outhouse. This project would require the combined efforts of all eleven employees in the store, and would generate a vast commission that must be split eleven ways! Where do we put the eleven names?

First Normal Form

We could simply put in eleven attributes for Salesperson Name (SName1, SName2, and so on), and eleven more for their numbers. What we have then would be considered more or less totally nonnormalized. We *could* fix things by having 11 Sale records, each with one Salesperson Name.

There are a number of obvious disadvantages, but it does solve the repeating-attribute problem, which puts this version in 1NF [see Figure 9-14(b)]: ***First Normal Form* is when there are *no repeating fields* – that is, at each intersection of a row and a column within the table, there is only one value.**

In the following sections, I'll explain the problems that still remain, but note that we now have the Sale data duplicated eleven times over, which can't possibly be healthy. To my mind, this set of records looks ripe for misunderstandings and errors. To a new person on the project, this would look for all the world like a set of eleven different sales, but you and I know it's eleven records describing one sale, with a lot of duplicated data.

It gets even worse if we decide to include the years of employment (tenure) and other details of the salesperson, and a percentage of the commission for each salesperson, rather than splitting it evenly. Let's say also that the percentages used depend on the tenure of the salesperson. Figure 9-14(b) illustrates this, showing the data parts of the classes only (ignoring behavior, since normalization is a data issue). You may need to check this figure and this paragraph carefully before you proceed.

As you can see, Figure 9-14(b) has a great deal of redundant data. One of the goals of normalization is to minimize (but not eliminate) data redundancy, so we can expect to see this diminish as we develop these tables to Third Normal Form (3NF) over the next few pages. Remember, the 11 records in this table all refer to a single sale, involving 11 salespersons. The final column shows how the commission earned is then distributed among these salespersons, so this column totals to 100% for each sale.

You will also have noticed that Customer Name and Address have been added to the table. This is another questionable practice that many inexperienced database designers fall into. What we've done is to put Customer data in a Sale record, so now we have a very poorly designed, highly redundant database. When we consider Second Normal Form (2NF), you'll see some of the theory behind why this is not considered a good idea.

Even though it's way better than being unnormalized, there are several issues that arise with 1NF. These can be seen in Figure 9-14(b).

- We're wasting a lot of disk space, and therefore processing time also. While this is really a design issue rather than an analysis issue, it's worth mentioning here.

- If we need to change any of the Sale data that has been duplicated – for example, Jo gets married and changes her name – we're faced with the problem of finding all the records that need changing. Murphy says that we're bound to miss some from time to time.

- With the Customer data held in the Sale table instead of in a separate Customer table, we have nowhere to keep information about Customers who have not yet bought from us, or Customers whose sales have all been archived and deleted from the Sale table. Customers and Sales are independent objects (though related) and should not have their data mixed in this way.

Second Normal Form

In Figure 9-14(b), if we know only one of the two values that go to make up the key – say, Customer Number – the table would return us 12 records. These would yield some conflicting data values. We would get two values each for Quantity, Date, and Actual Price. It would return us no fewer than eleven different values each for Salesperson Number, Name, and Tenure and four different values for Percent of Commission.

Only the Customer Name and Address would be uniquely determined, which should not really be surprising if all we know to start with is the Customer No. So the Name and Address are not really dependent on all of the key, but only on part of it. That is, they depend on only one of the two columns that go to make up the key.

Customer Table

Customer Number	Customer Name	Customer Address	Phone Number
13	Murphy	Here	555-1313
19	Stallone	There	555-4242
17	Cissone	Where	281-7416
16	Murphy	Nowhere	555-6529

Key: Customer Number

Product Table

Catalog Number	Product Description	Qty On Hand	Unit Price
729	Bathmat	120	$1.49
845	Soap	97	$2.00
961	Toilet	11	$100.00

Key: Catalog Number

Sale Table

Customer Number	Cat. Number	Date	Quantity	Actual Price	Sales-person No.	Sales-person Name	Tenure	Comm %
13	729	Jan 12	20	$1.49	1152	Bill	12	5
13	729	Jan 12	20	$1.49	1140	Naz	2	5
13	729	Jan 12	20	$1.49	1010	Eli	7	15
13	729	Jan 12	20	$1.49	1201	Fred	5	10
13	729	Jan 12	20	$1.49	1149	Kathy	3	10
13	729	Jan 12	20	$1.49	1210	Eric	3	10
13	729	Jan 12	20	$1.49	1204	June	5	10
13	729	Jan 12	20	$1.49	1133	Julie	7	15
13	729	Jan 12	20	$1.49	1175	Oz	11	10
13	729	Jan 12	20	$1.49	1169	Kelly	5	5
13	729	Jan 12	20	$1.49	1132	Tania	5	5
13	845	Jan 12	30	$2.00	1132	Tania	5	100
17	961	Jan 20	1	$100.00	1132	Tania	5	100

Key: Customer Number + Catalog Number + Date

Figure 9-15   Sales in Second normal Form

On the other hand, we can easily see that the Quantity, Date, Actual Price, and so on all depend on the entire key, and not just on part of it, since they're attributes that truly describe a *Sale*. The table in Figure 9-14(b) is not in 2NF, since some of its columns (Customer Name and Address) don't depend on the entire key. It's in 1NF, however, because it has no repeating fields, but even in 1NF there are some anomalies to deal with.

By adding the Customer table to the database (and thus a Customer class to the Class Diagram), we can isolate the Customer data from the rest. So the usual way of resolving anomalies in a 1NF table is to create another class and move some of the attributes into it, as we do with the Customer class in Figure 9-15.

In our new Customer table, you'll see that we have Customer Number as the key, by itself this time. Then we have the Name, Address, Phone, and so on. These are all dependent on the Customer No., in the sense that if you know the Customer No., then the table will allow you to look up the Name, and it guarantees to give you the correct name.

That is, the Name is *uniquely determined* by the Customer Number, without chance of ambiguity or error. It's important to note also that each Customer Number uniquely determines only one name, although there may be several

Customer Numbers with that same name. In Figure 9-16, you can see that Customer Numbers 13 and 16 will both return a name value of "Murphy."

This tells us that we have a mapping from Customer Number to Name, which is unique in one direction only, as is shown in Figure 9-16. Mathematicians this a **_functional dependency,_ a mapping between a set A and a set B, such that for every A there is exactly one B, and for each B there are any number of A, that is, zero, or one, or many.**

This is demonstrated in Figure 9-16. This definition is consistent with the term *function* as used by both mathematicians and programmers. The important thing about our new Customer table, however, is that **all of the nonkey fields are now functionally dependent on the *entire key*, and not just on a part of it. That is to say, they are _fully functionally dependent_ on the key.** This is not all that difficult to achieve in this table, since the key is not divisible—it consists solely of the Customer Number column.

In our Sale table, it's now also true that every nonkey attribute depends on the *entire key* and is therefore *fully functionally dependent* on the key. The key in this table is Customer Number + Catalog Number + Date. If we know all three of these, the table in Figure 9-15 will return us a unique value for each nonkey attribute. On the other hand, if we know only one of those – say, the Customer Number is 13 – then the table would return us 12 records. This would give us multiple values – that is, nonunique values – for several of the columns.

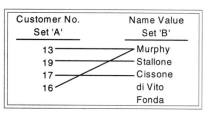

Figure 9-16   Functional dependency

Remember that we're looking only at the data parts of the classes. Now we've arranged things so that each attribute depends on (or is determined by) the *entire* primary key of the class it's in. When this is so, we say that they're *fully functionally dependent* on the key. Each attribute depends on the whole key, and not on just a part of it.

In Figure 9-15 you'll notice that the Customer Name (now in the Customer table) depends on the Customer Number , but that's only one field out of the three that make up the key for the Sale table. **_Second Normal Form_ is when _all_ the nonkey attributes are _fully_ functionally dependent on the key – that is, they depend on the whole key.** Check Figure 9-15 and you'll see that this is so. Don't worry about the significance of 2NF, however, since we never work there. We always work to 3NF, so let's see how that works.

THIRD NORMAL FORM

There's still an anomaly in Figure 9-15, however. If you think about it for a moment, you'll realize that it's not really logical to say that the Salesperson details depend on the Customer Number plus Catalog Number plus Date. The Name, Tenure, and Percentage have no real-world connection to the three attributes that make up the key. These things are nothing to do with who the Customer is or what Product he bought.

And if you look at the last three rows of the Sale table in Figure 9-15, you'll see that we still have some duplicated data, specifically Tania's details. The problem here is that the Salesperson's Name actually depends on the Salesperson's Number, and not on the Customer Number and/or the Catalog Number .

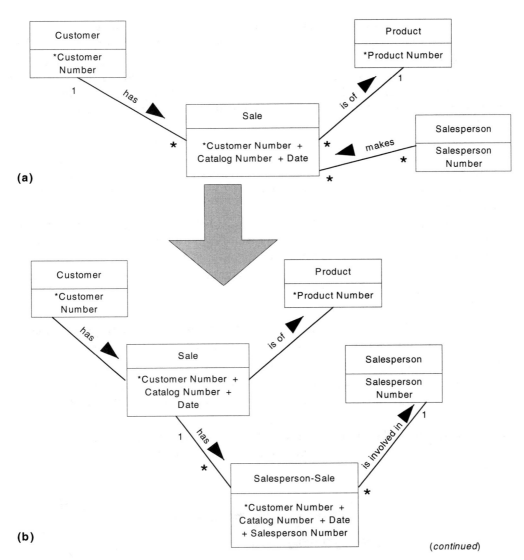

Figure 9-17 Sales in Third Normal Form (showing only the key attributes)

We have some *nonkey* attributes here that are dependent on *another nonkey attribute*, instead of on the key. There's a name for this: **A _transitive functional dependency_ is when one nonkey attribute is functionally dependent on another nonkey attribute.**

We can eliminate this situation by adding another couple of classes. In Figure 9-17(a), we've separated out the columns that describe a Salesperson, the Salesperson No., Name, and Tenure, into a class (and table) just for Salespersons. But you'll notice that the association between Salesperson and Sale is M:M. This is as it should be: "Salesperson *makes* many Sales"; "Sale *is contributed to by* many Salespersons."

Apart from the rather clumsy grammar in that last one, it works. So in Figure 9-17(b), we break out this M:M association into a pair of 1:M. By an incredible stroke of good fortune, the new intersection class turns out to be just the vehicle we need to carry the Percentage attribute. This you can see in the tables in Figure 9-17(c).

It works because the percentage actually depends on which Salesperson was involved and on which Sale it was, out of that person's many Sales. Tania is a case in point, earning only 5% of the total commission awarded on the bathmat sale, but keeping the entire commission for herself on the soap and toilet sales.

This new class I've given the name *Salesperson-Sale*, and the key is a fairly cumbersome one made by concatenating the keys from the Salesperson and Sale classes. I might well have asked the question, "What comes into existence that wasn't there before, when a Salesperson *is involved in* a Sale?" The answer would have been "an Involvement," but I have difficulty seeing that as an appropriate class name in most retail organizations.

Careful inspection of the tables in Figure 9-17(c) will reveal that each column depends only on the key, and not on any nonkey columns. In other words, every nonkey attribute is now fully functionally dependent on the key and only on the key.

So now you can see from the figure that where we began with the single class Sale, we now have the following classes:

- Customer, with Customer Number as the key
- Sale, with Customer Number + Product Number + Date as the key, being the intersection class between Customer and Product
- Salesperson, with Salesperson ID as the key
- Salesperson-Sale, with Customer Number + Catalog Number + Date + Salesperson Number as the key, being the intersection between Sale and Salesperson

Which leads me to the following cutesy (but technically correct) statement, which delightfully and very succinctly summarizes all we have said above about 1NF, 2NF, and 3NF:

Third Normal Form is when

"Everything depends upon

the key, the whole key, and nothing but the key,

so help me Codd."

If you want to be more technical, the official definition is that ***Third Normal Form*** **is when there are *no transitive functional dependencies*.** Any relation that is in 3NF is also automatically in 2NF, so all the nonkey attributes are fully functionally dependent on the key (that is, on the whole key). It's also in 1NF, so there are no repeating fields.

The *principle* of normalization, then, is to make sure that every attribute is attached to the class that it truly describes. The purpose is to reduce redundancy[1] and to remove the anomalies described above. The downside is increased complexity. You'll have noticed in the example that, as we progressively normalized the Sales database, we generated more and more classes.

In the extreme (which I'm sure in the future will be well beyond the current 18NF limit), we could end up with a zillion classes, most with only two attributes! The primary classes would each have a key attribute and a single nonkey attribute, and the intersection classes would have several attributes to make up the key, along with one or zero nonkey attributes. The overhead in analysis and design time, programming time, and response time for the users in the final system, makes this clearly an impossible solution.

Normalization is a tool to be used with discretion, rarely beyond 3NF. And at design time, you may often deliberately *denormalize* your design because of the machine time needed to handle a system that's in pure 3NF. What is important is that the designer needs to be aware of how much flexibility she's sacrificing for shorter response times, because this is very likely to cause long-term problems.

For further discussions in this area, I would recommend Whitten et al. (1994, page 510), although you should probably start at the beginning of the chapter at page 504. Also, Modell (1992) has a good section from page 248 on.

So now that you understand the definitions, you'll see how a list-valued attribute, for example, violates 1NF and therefore 2NF and 3NF as well. Yet the *principle* still matters – that every attribute should be attached to the class *that it truly describes*. If we take this as our approach to normalizing, then it's still worth doing. If our classes and attributes follow this principle, then our database is indeed ready for those *unanticipated queries* that we all know lurk in our misty future.

So much for data. The final step is the one that makes object-oriented modeling different.

Step 7: Operations (Behavior)

This is such a huge and important topic, that I've allocated the next two chapters to ways to find and specify the operations. I mention operations here in order to place them in sequence for you. There are many techniques available, and as is my usual style, I'll present a number of them so that you may have a variety of tools in your quiver (pardon the mixed metaphor!). My intent is that you should be able to choose an appropriate technique for each different situation you may encounter.

In Chapter 10, we'll visit object states and the statechart diagram, as one of the available tools for discovering behaviors. Then in Chapter 11, we'll take a look at Rebecca Wirfs-Brock's (1990) methods using responsibilities and collaborations, and also look at sequence diagrams.

---

[1] The theorists insist that about 20% to 30% redundancy is needed for foreign keys and for such things as improved response times, for a smoothly-working database. In other words, we can't totally eliminate redundancy – that would leave your database looking somewhat anorexic!

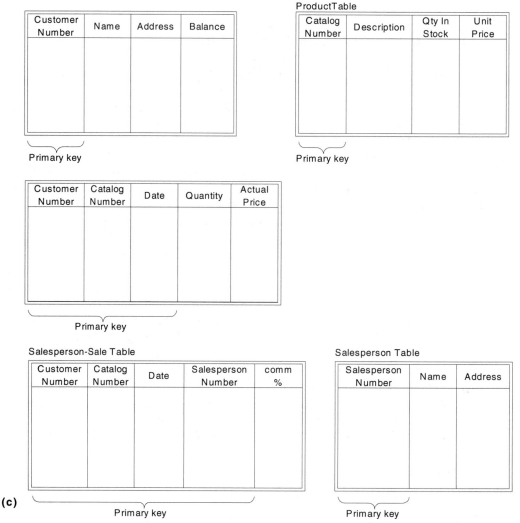

Figure 9-17 (continued) The final set of tables for the sales application in Third Normal Form

Here now is a summary of the last four of the KRB Seven Steps:

• Step 4: Expand Many-to-Many Associations.

- An M:M association has nowhere to place event data attributes, so a new intersection class must be created to carry them.

- Every M:M association must break out into a pair of 1:M associations, with the many ends pointing at this new intersection class.

- Sometimes several adjacent M:M associations will appear to break out into several intersection classes with the same name. If they turn out to actually be the same class, then you must collapse them all into one class, with multiple 1:M associations, all with their "many" ends against the new intersection class.

- Step 5: Attributes.
  - You and your users simply go through the model, box by box, and list for each one all the attributes that you and they can think of.
- Step 6: Normalization.
  - The principle of normalization is to make sure that every data element (attribute) is attached to the class of objects *that it truly describes.*
- Step 7: Operations (behavior).
  - The next two chapters show ways to find and specify operations. I mention them here to place them in context for you.
- At design time, we may choose to reduce complexity and improve response times and maintenance by *denormalizing.* The penalty is that this makes it more difficult to extract the data later.

There are just a couple more topics needed to round out this chapter. We'll now check on some of the ramifications of choosing between modeling something as an attribute or as a class.

9.3　Is It a Class or Is It an Attribute?

Sometimes when modeling with your users, you'll find yourself unsure about this decision. The Commission Percentage class in the normalization example above is a typical case. The thing that usually solves this one is to ask for *sample attributes* (remember those?).

In the example, let's say we initially decided to model the Tenure as a class, with an association to Salesperson, because we had a sample attribute, Percentage. We can view the Percentage as something that describes the Tenure – that is, it's an attribute of Tenure – or we can say that the Percentage is *dependent on* the Tenure. Either way, this indicates that we need Tenure to be a class.

Then at design time, we may wish to reduce complexity and improve response times and maintenance, so maybe we'll decide that in this case we'll denormalize and put both the Tenure and Percentage attributes in the Salesperson class. The penalty is that we make it that much more difficult and less straightforward to extract or update these things later. In particular, we make it more complicated to try to link them with other data in the database. In the extreme, if we do this too often or in an unplanned and uncontrolled way, we end up with the mess Tim described in his old original Outhouse system, in Episodes 3 and 4.

There's no doubt that your system will have more power and flexibility if Commission Percentage is modeled as a class, but this will introduce more complexity. There's more work to be done (read: "more money to be spent") since we must build, debug, and maintain the extra class.

As I suggested earlier, we often must denormalize our designs to allow adequate response times, or for other hardware or platform considerations. Typically, we analyze for a perfect implementation with no trade-offs, and then we make *informed trade-off decisions* during the design phase. As we saw in Chapter 3, it's important to delay these kinds of decisions until as late as possible in the development process, so as not to limit our freedom of choice.

So the rule of thumb is: If in doubt at analysis time, model it as a class. Then at design time, you may elect to change it to an attribute or to denormalize by adding two or three attributes where there should be a foreign key.

Then, when all the work is done finding classes, we need to reevaluate the model to see if there are any further subclass or aggregation structures that we could use to our advantage.

9.4 FINDING AGGREGATION AND SUBCLASS STRUCTURES

You will, of course, be alert for these structures throughout the analysis and design phases. We'll discuss them briefly here, though, as a convenient place to introduce some relevant ideas.

Periodically, you'll need to review the models as they are so far, checking for any subclassing or aggregation opportunities. You may find some structures that will simplify things, or some that will highlight classes you may have missed. Subclass structures will give you opportunities to benefit from inheritance.

As your analysis models are nearing completion, you'll do well to check models from other organizations in the same or a similar business. Different companies do things differently even within the same problem domain. Even so, there will be many classes, associations, attributes, and structures that appear in both your models and theirs.

You can do this no matter whether they're using object-oriented models or entity-relationship diagrams (ERDs). ERDs may or may not show structures explicitly, but even without them, a comparison with your own models may well lead to some inspirations.

Subclass Hierarchies

You'll find some of these as specializations of classes you've discovered, where you realize later that there are several *kindsa*. You'll find others as generalizations, where you see commonalities among some of your classes. As you build your class diagram with your users, watch for subclass structures as you go.

When you think you see one, check it out with the users and include it in the model if they agree. Even if the users don't agree that what they see is a subclass, make note of it in your private notes anyway.

As you progress through analysis to design to construction, review these notes from time to time. You'll occasionally find your early intuition vindicated, when it later becomes more obvious that this indeed is an important subclass relationship. Other times, you'll find the ideas in your notes will inspire you to think of another subclass that you hadn't noticed.

Specializations

- Look for *kindsa* in all the classes you've identified.

- Are there some attributes or operations that are only needed for certain instances?

- Do some associations affect only a subset of instances within the class?

- Could this class be viewed as a subclass of something in your class libraries?

Generalizations

- Does there seem to be a cluster of attributes and/or operations and/or associations that appear in several classes?

- Consider the semantics. Do these words actually mean things that are *kindsa*? Remember the cow and the barn.

- At design time, you'll need to ask, "Are there some significant benefits to putting a subclass relationship here, even though the semantics don't quite fit properly?"

Components and Wholes

You need to check each class in your model and ask yourself if these objects have any kind of internal structure.

- Do you have any attributes on this class that don't really describe an object of this kind, but some object "within" it?

- Do you have any operations that are performed by a "piece" of the object, rather that the object itself? Do you have associations that should involve only a "piece" or "part" of the object?

- Check other models in the same general business area, from other organizations.

This brings us almost to the end of the how-tos, the specific steps for finding classes in object-oriented analysis. The last thing to consider is a few comments on how to begin making this process work in a real-world business environment.

9.5 ADAPTING THE METHOD

I have focused strongly in this chapter on the method as applied in Facilitated Team Sessions (FTS) or Joint Application Design (JAD) sessions. However, there are many situations where such meetings are impossible, or at least only occasionally possible. Busy senior executives will have a strictly limited time budget for your project. You'll need to adapt what I've described and prescribed, to each different company and each different project and each different user.

The Delphi method is a good start. By "brainstorming in slow motion," you can gain many of the advantages of brainstorming within the constraints of users' schedules and commitments. However, while this will allow you to get input from otherwise unavailable senior users, it is *not* a substitute for *full user involvement*.

Whatever form the users' involvement may take, there must be an *adequate* commitment of time from users at various levels. Without user commitment, your project is likely to go the way of so many other wonderful ideas and end up being just another good intention. Or worse, it could be a system designed for *our* view of the users' needs, and believe me, we have a habit of being out to lunch on such things without the users' direct involvement.

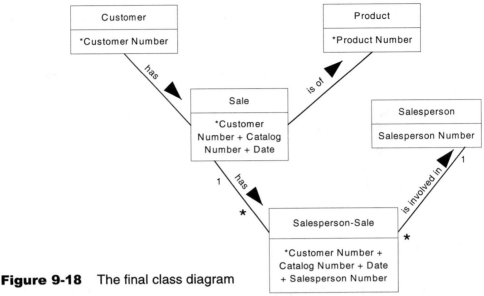

Figure 9-18   The final class diagram

Inaccessible users just don't cut it. Sometimes their resistance takes the form of overflexibility. One of the neatest cop-outs that a few users may try to use is: "You're the expert. You tell me what my requirements are!" This approach is doomed to failure, since you and I as techies just do not know enough about their operation.

But not only that, if we buy into this, we get set up as the scapegoats who are obviously responsible for the entire dismal failure, because we accepted sole responsibility for making it work! Tom DeMarco has been quoted as saying: "Systems analysis is like child-rearing – there are no guaranteed solutions, and thousands of ways to screw it up. If we succeed, the other guy (child or user) gets all the credit, and if we fail, *we* get all the blame."

Inaccessible users can doom a project. While it's understandable that certain users, especially senior management, have only limited time for systems projects, the project simply can't succeed without *sufficient time commitment from suitable users.*

Inaccessible users are a nontechnical problem that requires a nontechnical solution. In the extreme, figuratively speaking, you may have to drag them kicking and screaming to your modeling sessions, and nail them to the chair!

In many organizations, especially government bureaucracies (of which I've worked in a few), often the only feasible solution is to escalate up the chain of command. Get your boss (at a suitable level) to talk to his boss, since the users will only respond to pressure if it comes from directly above them, from the person who signs their paycheck.

The "right" way to do this is to begin the project under the auspices of a "champion" or sponsor in senior management, who has a vested interest in the success of the project, and above all who believes in it. This person needs to be high enough in the hierarchy to wield some clout when these problems occur.

Barbara Bouldin (1989), in her excellent little book *Agents of Change*, goes into great detail with very practical ways to handle difficulties of this sort. Although her book is about the introduction of new methods and software tools into an organization, her ideas apply in any project involving change to the way things are done.

. . . .

DELIVERABLES

The major deliverable from this stage is the class diagram, as shown in Figure 9-18. This needs to be supported with a list of class definitions, attribute lists for each class, and, where necessary, definitions for attributes. As outlined in the chapter, it's my practice to use the system documentation as minutes when modeling in a series of JAD/FTS or interview sessions. By adding the attendees at the front and notes on the end, it works quite well.

To begin with, it's just the attendees and the list of candidate classes, and then the candidate list shrinks and the rest grows, as we proceed. Both the conceptual model and the logical model should be included, for completeness, and as an aid in going back over what we did when confusions and disagreements arise. Most participants will need to keep only the latest version of this document, but the recording analyst should file all the progressive versions for reference.

FURTHER READING

Sally Shlaer and Stephen Mellor, in their earlier book *Object-Oriented Analysis, Modeling the World in Data* (1988), give a good explanation of data modeling, couched in object terms. Their Chapter 8 on techniques, although brief, has some excellent pointers. Chapter 9, not quite so brief, then explains where data modeling fits in the object-oriented development process and how the class diagram will be used in the later stages.

There are also good explanations to be found in John Shepherd's *Database Management: Theory and Application* (1990), in Chapter 2; and in Chapter 8 of Whitten, Bentley, and Barlow (1994) *Systems Analysis and Design Methods*, third edition or 5th ed by Whitten, Bentley and Dittman (2000).

I should point out here that I specifically said "third edition" (or later) since they changed their approach to building the ERD a little. In the earlier edition, their approach was heavily bottom-up, working from detail to diagram. Their later ideas are more top-down, somewhat more in line with my own thinking.

For those who would like a more rigorous, in-depth, approach yet without too much math, Martin Modell (1992) spends the entire second half of his book on ERDs. Half of this is explaining them, and half is about developing them. He has a good discussion of normalization beginning on page 248. This has to be the only book around with "Modell models!" (Sorry for the pun – even Modell himself doesn't sink that low!)

And finally, those who prefer the full mathematical derivation in this kind of stuff would do well to try James Martin (1977) *Computer Data Base Organization*.

CHAPTER SUMMARY

- The class diagram really is the foundation on which your whole system will rest.

- **Step 1: Candidate Classes.** To discover all significant candidate classes for interface, entity, and control classes, list all nouns that *might* name classes, "candidates" for inclusion in the system.

- **Client interviews.** For busy senior users. Adapt group methods to an individual or small-group setting. Or interview users to get the basics, then on your own develop the model. Bring the model back to the users for verification, *often*.

- **From the requirements model and documentation.** Start with the systems request document. Scan for *nouns* and list them. Examine the requirements model and use cases, picking out *nouns*. Examine other documents describing users' operation.

- **Brainstorming.** For resilience to change, the class diagram is based not on the data needs of the current project but on the fundamental data requirements of the users' business. Formal brainstorming has two phases, *generating* ideas and *evaluating* them. *No evaluation of any kind is allowed during the generating phase.*

- **The Delphi method.** First meet with, or send a memo to, each participant and get them to write a list of candidate classes. Then combine the lists and circulate the complete list to all of them for additions. Repeat.

- **Interface classes.** If you have a OOGUI class library, then most of the user interface classes will be defined in the library. Published communications protocols can be freely used for data links and process control.

- **Control classes.** These are created for operations that need data and operations from many other classes or don't appear to belong to any of your existing classes. It may have only this one operation and some attributes to support it.

- **Step 2: Define Classes.** Each candidate class must be subjected to three checks:

  - **Question 1:** Real-world identifier.
  - **Question 2:** Definition.
  - **Question 3:** Sample attributes and behaviors.

- These checks don't guarantee to come up with a definite answer to whether this is a class of interest. Instead, as you ask and answer the three questions, you'll see whether this is a class that matters, or whether it should be an attribute somewhere.

  - *Question 1*: **Real-World Identifier.** Objects have identity. If this candidate is the name of a class that matters then its instances must have identity. They're distinct, and there's some way of telling them apart. The question to ask the users is," How do we tell one of these from another?" Even if the identifier is not truly unique, as long as one exists it shows that the instances are distinct and therefore have identity.

  - *Question 2*: **Definition.** A definition for each class needs to go into the permanent documentation. The definitions provide a dictionary. When conceptual difficulties or misunderstandings occur during development, they can usually be resolved by referring to these definitions.

Users will sometimes have different opinions about the definition. These differences are resolved in one of two ways:
- We'll have several kindsa things, that is, subclasses, or
- We may have two (or more) conceptually different classes. We must end up with a clear definition for each and every class and ensure that everyone understands it and accepts it.

- *Question 3*: **Sample attributes and behaviors.** If it's a class, it must carry data and be capable of behavior. So look for an attribute that this kind of object needs to carry. Or, look for events or transactions that this class will need to respond to.

• **Step 3: Establish Associations.** Ask the users, "What does one of these do to one of those?" Consider the verb, the multiplicity, and capturing all possible associations.

  • **Verbs.** Ensure the verbs you use are ones the users use. The main thing is whether we can find a verb that:
    - Describes some interaction between instances of the classes
    - Is significant in the users' business. You may have several associations joining a pair of classes. Each must have its own verb, and each must be a different kind of event, that is, they must be independent. You must be *religious* about how you make sure you capture *all* possible associations.

  • **Multiplicity.** Ask the question, "How many instances participate in this association at a time?"

A Customer   *buys*   many   Products.

Sentence = Subject   + Verb + Number + Object

• Often, having laid down a definition, later you may find something just won't work. When these anomalies occur, the first thing you do is: Refer back to your definition.

• **Step 4: Expand Many-to-Many Associations.** An M:M association has nowhere to place event data attributes, so a new *intersection* class must be created to carry them.

  • Every M:M association must break out into a pair of 1:M associations, with the many ends pointing at this new intersection class.

  • If several adjacent M:M associations resolve themselves to be actually the same class, you must collapse them all into one class, with multiple 1:M associations, most with the many ends on the new intersection class.

• **Step 5: Attributes.** You and your users simply go through the model, box by box, and list for each class all the attributes that you and they can think of.

• **Step 6: Normalization.** The principle of normalization is to make sure that every data element (attribute) is attached to the class of objects that it truly describes.

- Third Normal Form is when "everything depends on the key, the whole key, and nothing but the key, so help me Codd" (i.e., there are no *transitive functional dependencies)*.

- **Step 7: Operations** (i.e., *Behavior*). The next two chapters cover this in detail.

- In the design phase we may improve complexity, response times, and maintenance by *denormalizing*. We make it more difficult to extract this data later, and more complicated to link it with other data.

- You will be alert for structures throughout the analysis and design phases. You need to watch both for subclass hierarchies and for components and wholes (aggregations).

- Inaccessible users can doom a project. We understand that users have limited time for systems projects, but projects can't succeed without *sufficient* time commitment from *suitable* users.

- Begin the project with a "champion" in senior management, who has a vested interest in the success of the project and who believes in it, high enough in the hierarchy to wield some power when problems occur.

Chapter Glossary

association A relationship expressing the interactions between instances of two classes, represented by the verb that describes what they do to each other, and / or by the nouns for the roles that each plays in the life of the other.

association name A verb attached to an association describing what one class of objects do to the other.

brainstorming A search for ideas, that takes place in two distinct and separate phases. The first phase is for *generating* ideas, and the second is for *evaluating* them.

candidate classes Possible class names being considered as candidates for inclusion in the system.

cardinality (multiplicity) In an association, the number of instances of each class that can participate in an occurrence of the association.

Delphi method To mimic brainstorming in slow motion, by first meeting with or writing a memo to each participant, and getting them to write down a list of ideas (nouns).Then you combine the lists and circulate the complete list to all of them for inspired additions.

Every M:M association breaks out into a pair of 1:M associations, with the many ends pointing at this new intersection class (Associative Class).

First Normal Form When there are no repeating fields – that is, at each intersection of a row and a column within the table, there's only one value.

formal brainstorming (See *brainstorming*)

fully functionally dependent When each attribute depends on (or is determined by) the *entire* primary key of the class it's in.

functional dependency A mapping between a set A and a set B, such that for every A there is exactly one B, and for each B there are any number of A, that is, zero, or one, or many.

__interaction__ An "*action*" in that objects do things and "*inter*" meaning they do things *between objects*, that is, *to* one another.

__intersection class__ or *__associative class__* The new class we create in the middle of a many-to-many association in order to break it up into a pair of one-to-many associations.

__normalization__ The process of ensuring that every attribute is attached to the class of objects that it truly describes.

__relationship__ a connection between objects (and sometimes between other things as well.)

__Second Normal Form__ When all the nonkey attributes are fully functionally dependent on the key, that is, they depend on the whole key.

__Third Normal Form__ When there are no transitive functional dependencies. Third Normal Form is when "everything depends on the key, the whole key, and nothing but the key, so help me Codd."

__transitive functional dependency__ When one nonkey attribute is functionally dependent on another nonkey attribute.

WHAT COMES NEXT

This brings us to the task of finding the behaviors to go with all these classes we now have. The next two chapters are devoted to this, introducing two methods that can be used in addition to or along with the Use Cases, to discover the operations in each class.

First, in Chapter 10, we'll look at statechart diagrams, which we use to document the changes an object goes through during its existence. Then in Chapter 11, we first see a method developed by Rebecca Wirfs-Brock (1990) and her group and going by the name of *Responsibility-Driven Design*.

We'll finish Chapter 11 with a look at *interaction diagrams* as an alternative or complementary way to follow a sequence of message calls and method invocations.

CLASS/GROUP EXERCISES AND PROBLEMS

Ex 9.1 Refer to Exercise 7.4., use the KRB Seven Steps (or at least the first six of them) to produce an object class diagram for each project that doesn't already have one.

Ex 9.2 Develop an Object Class Diagram for Two-Bit Pizza. Keep your answers for Exercise 10.6.

Two-Bit Pizza (formerly, *Binary Pasta*).

Apply the first six of the KRB Seven Steps to the following scenario, which has deliberately been worded the way a user might be expected to say it.

Also, to simplify the example and focus on the modeling process, it has been worded more as a rough description of a system design. The typical poorly structured business problem would be something like:

"We need a computer to keep track of all this! We need a central phone number, and some way to verify delivery and the amount paid by the customer. The way things are, it's just too easy for our delivery drivers to rip us off!" However, for this exercise you'll need the problem to look a little more like this:

The customer calls in to a central number. The orders clerk keys in the phone number to get the customer's first name, their favorite type of pizza, and what the customer ordered last time.
Then the clerk manually assigns the order to one of the stores around the city, from a map of delivery zones. The order appears in a queue on the screen at the store and prints out in three copies for the cook.

The completed order is taken by the delivery driver, who gives the customer one of the three copies as a receipt. Then she gets the customer to initial the third copy, and she brings it back to put on file. We need the system to keep track of the ingredients used and to print out a weekly usage report for the buyers, but the system won't actually do any reordering.

INDIVIDUAL EXERCISES AND PROBLEMS

Ex 9.3   Refer to Exercises 4.3 and 4.4. Which column(s) are unnormalized? What is there in each of the column(s) that violates 3NF? What normal form are they in?

Which data element(s) in which column(s) violate the rule of atomicity for data elements? What entity type should this/these data element(s) be moved to?

Ex 9.4   For the hotshots: If you're finished Exercise 9.2 and you're ahead of the other students, you may fill in the missing parts of the Two-Bit Pizza project in Exercise 9.2. Backtrack to the beginning and produce a complete requirements model for Two-Bit Pizza, based on the scenario in Exercise 9.2.

PROJECTS AND CASES

P 9.1   For your small-business project from Project 7.2 and Project 8.1, use the first six of the Seven Steps to produce an object class diagram for the project. Set up one or more FTS/JAD sessions with your users, taking care to address adequately the eight factors discussed in the beginning of Chapter 7. Document this class diagram as described in the chapter.

SELF-TEST QUESTIONS

Note: The Appendix has answers to the Self-Test Questions.
Q 9.1   List the KRB Seven Steps for building an object class diagram.

Q 9.2   State the deliverable from each step:

Step   Deliverable

1.

2.

3.

4.

5.

6.

7.

Q 9.3   In brainstorming:

(a) Every idea is recorded, regardless of merit.

(b) No evaluation of ideas is allowed until later.

(c) Everyone needs to feel comfortable contributing.

(d) All of the above are true.

(e) Some of the above are true.

(f) None of the above is true.

Q 9.4   Each candidate class must be subjected to three checks, to determine whether it's a class that's important to our project. These checks are:

Question 1: _____

Question 2: _____

Question 3: _____

Q 9.5   Which of the following is not a true statement?

(a) Users will sometimes have different opinions about the definition.

(g) When misunderstandings occur, they can be resolved by referring to the definitions.

(h) We must end up with a clear definition for each class and ensure that everyone understands and accepts it.

(i) Sometimes an identifier and definition are not enough to show that this is a class of interest.

(j) If it's a class, then its instances must carry some data and be capable of some behavior.

(k) The question to ask the users is, "How do we tell one of these from another?"

(l) None of the above.

Q 9.6   An association is:

(a) A straight line on an object class diagram.

(b) Represented by a noun that describes the interaction.

(c) An relationship between instances of two classes.

(d) Often M:M and occasionally 1:M.

(e) Often M:M and never 1:M.

Q 9.7   Multiplicity (cardinality):

(a) Tells how many instances can be involved in an instance of the association.

(b) *Isakinda* sin.

(c) Tells how many associations an instance can be involved in.

(d) Tells how many users can be involved in an association before it becomes too sinful.

(e) Tells how many senior bishops there are in the Roman Catholic Church.

Q 9.8   Name the Roman Catholic Archbishop of the Philippines. (You just won't believe this when you see the answer! But it's true. Really.)

Q 9.9   An association must:

(a) Be described by nouns.

(b) Have attributes.

(c) Be described by a verb or nouns.

(d) Have a 1:M component.

(e) Be described by *isa* or *isakinda*.

(f) Be based on events.

Q 9.10 To discover all significant _____ classes for _____ , _____ , and _____ classes, list all _____ that *might* name classes, " _____ " for inclusion in the system.

Q 9.11 List the four methods we mentioned for interviewing users to discover classes.

Q 9.12 Here are some methods for interviewing users to discover classes:

- _____ _____ to get the basics, then on your own develop the model. Bring the model back to the _____ for _____ , _____ .

- Scan all your _____ , and other _____ describing users' operation, for _____ and list them out.

- _____ in two _____ , _____ a list of _____ and then _____ them.

- _____ _____ , or _____ a _____ to each participant and get them to write a list of _____ _____ . Then combine the lists and circulate the complete list to all of them for _____ _____

Chapter Ten

. . . .

Object States and the Statechart Diagram

WHAT YOU WILL LEARN IN THIS CHAPTER

In this chapter, you'll learn how objects always exist in some *state*, and are able to switch, or transition, from one state to another. You can be confident you understand state machines and statechart diagrams when you can:

1. Define the terms *state, event, transition, activity,* and *action* as they're used in this chapter.
2. Describe how an object typically navigates through its life cycle.
3. Draw a statechart diagram for a class with a simple life cycle and explain the transitions involved.
4. Explain why transitions shown in your statechart diagram are permitted, while other possible transitions are not.

WHAT YOU SHOULD KNOW TO START THIS CHAPTER

A general understanding of objects is all that's needed for this chapter. It's not necessary to know the details of the modeling techniques from Chapter 9 or about the OODLC to make sense of what is in this chapter.

CHAPTER OVERVIEW

We'll start out examining what happens to an object during the time it exists – that is, its "lifetime" – and then look at the various states it can exist in, and the events that can affect it when it's in each state. We'll then consider how certain events can cause the object to transition to another state and the actions and activities it must perform as it arrives at and waits in each new state. The main part of the chapter covers the statechart diagram, which documents all of this, and then we finish with the state transition table (STT), an invaluable aid to building statechart diagrams.

KEY CONCEPTS

- State
- Object life cycle
- Event
- Synchronous and asynchronous messages
- Calls and signals
- Domain
- State transition
- Internal transitions, self transitions

- Atomic actions, non-atomic activities
- Guard condition
- Statechart diagram
- State machine
- Coordinated life cycles
- Conservation of events
- Consistent arguments
- state transition table, STT

"THE OUTHOUSE BATHROOM BOUTIQUE"
SALES REPORTING SYSTEM – EPISODE 10

"You know," said Allana, the senior buyer," I sometimes wonder why it's so complicated to get a purchase order to the vendor."

"What do you mean, Allana?" asked Tim, puzzled.

"Well, when my staff want to buy a new line for the shelves, they fill out a Purchase Recommendation form and sign it, and I sign it, and you sign it, and then from it they fill out a Purchase Order Requisition form, which they sign and then I sign. Then that goes to Mary in Accounting, and from it she fills out the actual purchase order that goes to the vendor.

"Then, when the goods come in, the actual goods received are reconciled against the PO, and we do Back-Order forms for the stuff that didn't arrive, then when everything has been received (or in some cases canceled – yet *another* form), the PO is stamped 'Fulfilled', and then filed. Wouldn't it be a whole lot simpler and easier," she continued thoughtfully, "if we did this all on one piece of paper?"

Tim spoke with a brusque voice and a manner that suggested he didn't want to continue along that particular line. "We can't do away with any of those," he said a little shortly. "There's new information added at each step. No, we'd be wasting our time. It can't be shortened. Every step is needed." He shook his head, as if to stress how totally inevitable his negative answer was.

"I think it can," responded Allana. "I think we could start with one form in several parts and just keep adding information to it. The last part that goes to the vendor only needs to show the information that goes to the vendor, and none of our internal stuff."

Nancy felt it was time to intervene, before Tim could stop this idea in its tracks. "What I hear you saying, Allana, is that all these forms – what were they? The Purchase Recommendation, the PO Requisition, the PO proper, Back Orders, Order Cancellation, and so on – they're really just phases in the life of a PO. They're not fundamentally or conceptually different things, but the same thing at different stages of its development."

"Yeah, that's right," beamed Allana. "Now that you put it that way, I realize I've known that for several years now, but I've never been able to put it into words."

"As a matter of fact," said Nancy, "I thought of it when you and the others were working through the use cases involved in originating a PO, but I thought I'd wait a bit and see who came up with this little bit of inspiration on their own."

"Now, wait a minute," Tim broke in, a slightly uncomfortable expression on his face. "You mean you agree with her? You think it can all be done with one piece of paper?"

"Yes, Tim, I'm afraid I do agree with Allana. But actually I don't propose we do it with paper at all. I think it can be done entirely with screens and electronic transfers, perhaps even going to the vendor electronically. And –" Nancy shuffled through her papers for a second or two and stopped when she had found the page she was seeking. "– my thought is that if we combine use cases 27, 28, and 29, that will give us a good picture of the complete life cycle of a purchase order in The Outhouse."

THOUGHT QUESTIONS

1. Tim appeared to be feeling a little uncomfortable during this little interchange. Discuss some possible reasons why you think this might be so. Discuss the way Nancy handled Tim's feelings of discomfort. Should she have done more? Or less?

2. What effects might Tim's attitude have on subordinates like Allana and the others? What are the likely results of a subordinate standing up to a disgruntled boss in a case like this? What if she didn't stand up to him?

3. Discuss an actual specific instance from the past, where you or one of your group members encountered a case where the boss didn't want to consider an issue, but the subordinates forced him to do so. Comment on what happened, in the light of your answers to Questions 1 and 2.

4. Discuss an actual specific instance from the past, where you or one of your group members came across a series of related transactions (or pieces of paper) that you thought (or now think) might actually be different states or stages in the life of one type of transaction.

10.1 LIFETIMES AND LIFE CYCLES

In Chapter 5, we discussed how an object is born, lives its (hopefully useful) life, and eventually either "dies" or is put out to pasture. After it's "born" (created), an object moves from one state to another, in some cases repeatedly. Finally, either it gets destroyed, or it is archived for some incidental (but nonetheless important) purpose, such as reusing it, or for occasional reference, or as required by law.

For some classes of objects, our system will be concerned primarily with this cradle-to-grave kind of lifetime. For other classes, we'll only be concerned incidentally with this, or sometimes not at all. Often we'll be more concerned with a different kind of cycle. Here are a couple of examples, and after these we'll take a slightly more formal look at how it all works.

You'll need to keep in mind as we do this that changes of state in an object will eventually lead us to discovering more of the *operations* (behavior) that the object needs to be capable of. This will both confirm and extend what we already discovered from the use cases, giving us a more complete and more accurate picture of the *methods* that our object class will require in the final system.

Let's begin with a visit to the library.

A Day in the Life of a Book

In a library system, we would certainly need to provide mechanisms for creating a new book in the database, but once created, each book would then be lent out, perhaps thousands of times. Considering only the cycle of loans and returns, Figure 10-1 shows what happens during the normal working day of a busy library book, diagrammed in three very different styles.

As you can see from Figures 10-1(a) and (b), a Book object rests for an indefinite period in the Shelved state, until a Subscriber object sends it a message saying: "Book, *sign out* yourself to me!" This could physically be done, say, by a scanner at the checkout counter. The Book object then changes its state to Signed-Out. At the same time, it establishes a link (an instance of an association) to the Subscriber and updates a date/time attribute.

When the physical book is returned, the Subscriber sends another message to the Book instance, this time saying: "Book, *check-in* yourself." At this point, the Book instance changes its state to Checked In and updates another date/time attribute.

Then it waits in the Checked In state until a Librarian returns the physical book to the shelf. As she does so, the Librarian scans the physical book for the final time in this cycle. This sends a message to the Book instance saying "Book, *shelve* yourself," whereupon the Book changes its state to Shelved, updates yet another date/time stamp, and waits patiently to be wanted again. (It can be very lonely waiting on the shelf!)

In a real library, this cycle would be more complicated, with options at various points, such as reserving or repairing the book, and so forth. There would also be the birth–life–death pattern (that is, acquisition–utilization–disposition) superimposed upon this one. For now, however, we'll keep it simple. Figure 10-1(c) has been drawn as a flowchart, to illustrate what might be one way of showing the cyclical nature of the flow of events.

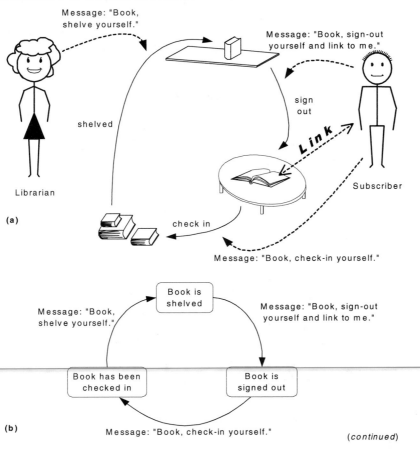

Figure 10-1 The operational life cycle of a library book

(*continued*)

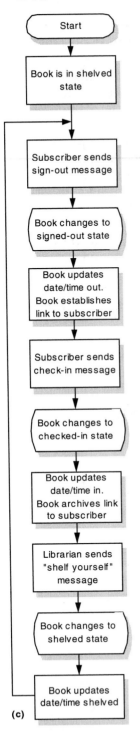

(c)

Figure 10-1
(continued)   A
flowchart for the life
cycle of a library book

We refer to a loop such as this as an *operational life cycle* since it's concerned with the regular operation of the users' business. These life cycles exist for many classes of objects in the real world. We would expect to find similar cycles in vending machines, automated teller machines (ATMs), robots, and many other pieces of equipment.

In these cases, the equipment snoozes in its idle state until called upon to do its thing, and afterward goes back to sleep. Many software systems, especially real-time systems, are concerned only with this operational life cycle. Some systems are concerned only with the birth–life–death kind of lifetime, and many must handle both.

Like the purchase order we saw in Chapter 5, business documents and transactions also follow a pattern of states, a *lifetime* and/or *life cycle*. So also do entity objects such as Employees, Customers and other people objects, Products, assets of all kinds, Accounts, Services, Courses; basically, *everything* does. And then there are associations.

ASSOCIATIONS FOR A LIBRARY BOOK

Did you notice that in describing Figure 10-1, I kind of glossed over how the Book created a link from itself to the Subscriber? This would no doubt be a M:M association, since a Subscriber *borrows* many Books, and a Book *is borrowed by* many Subscribers. So it resolves into an associative class that might be called *Sign-Out.* (What is it that comes into existence when a Book *signs itself out* to a Subscriber? Why, a *Sign-Out* of course! Though it might also perhaps be called a *Loan*, so from here on we'll use that name.)

In creating the link (an instance of the association), the Book would send a message to the Loan class requesting it to create an instance, one that quotes the identifiers for both this Book and this Subscriber. (Incidentally, for proper normalization, the three date/time-Stamp attributes all belong in the Loan class.)

Here is what we have so far discovered about object life cycles, in this chapter and previously:

- At any moment in time, an object exists in a certain manner or condition, which we say is its *state*.

- If anything at all about the object changes, we say it has undergone a *transition* into a new state.

- The various permissible states and the permissible transitions among them form the *life cycle* for that class of object, as it is "born" (created), "lives" (exists), and eventually "dies" (is deleted or otherwise appropriately disposed of).

- For all intents and purposes, the values of its attributes are, or at least represent, the state of the object.

- The statechart diagram is a powerful tool used to model object life cycles.

10.2 EVENTS AND STATES

You may have noticed in Figure 10-1(c) that the actions (shown in ANSI-standard rectangular boxes) come in threes. At all three places in the life cycle where actions occur, first an actor sends a message, and then this causes an object to do something in response. The next thing in the sequence of events – that is, next on the flowchart – is that the object changes from one state to another, which I've shown as an oval. Then each time it does some behavior that goes with that state change – in this case, it updates an attribute each time.

In the terminology we've been using in earlier chapters, this can be described by saying that an actor caused a message to be sent to an object, commanding it to change its state and to do something (e.g., create a link or update an attribute). Something must happen to make it do this – we speak of an **_event_, which we describe as a noteworthy happening** (*Webster*, 1975).

This definition is almost good enough for us, but we need to note one more thing. An event is when something happens, and when things happen, they do so at a certain point in time and at a certain place. So an event always has a *time* and a *location*.

There are several kinds of events, including these:

- *Signals.* These are **_asynchronous_ messages, where the objects that send them do not expect any response from the receiving object, and nor do they wait around for one.** The sending object just sends the signal, and then carries on with whatever it was about to do.

- *Calls.* These are regular function or subroutine calls. They are **_synchronous_ messages, where the calling object stops what it was doing and waits for control to be returned, along with some results, before it carries on.**

- *The Passage of Time.* This is like setting a timer, and when it goes off a transition occurs (provided the *guard condition* evaluates to TRUE. You'll find guard conditions defined a couple of pages further on.)

- *A Change in State.* When one object changes its state, it can execute one or more actions. (You'll find actions discussed a couple of pages over, too.) There can be an exit action for the state it's in, an entry action for the state it moves to, and the transition can have another action attached to it. Any or all of these actions can include steps that send a message to another object. This message would then appear as an event in the state machine of the receiving object (and in the statechart diagram for its class.) (See "Coordinated Life Cycles" later in this chapter.)

An event is *received* by an object (or by the class for some, such as Create Instance). What *receiving an event* really means is that the event is *happening to* this object. Of course, there may be other objects that also experience this event, so it could cause state changes in several objects. Shortly we'll be looking in more detail at the actions and Activities that an instance carries out when one of these events is received.

As we saw in Chapter 5, there are a number of ways we can define the term *state*, and fortunately they're all fairly consistent. To review, from the dictionaries and our earlier discussion:

- **State** "The particular condition that someone or something is in at a specific time" (*The New Oxford*, 1998)

- **State** "Condition, manner or way of existence as determined by circumstances" (*Oxford*, 1979).

- **State** "The condition of a person or thing, as with respect to circumstances or attributes" (*Random House Webster*, 1997).

- **State** "A mode or condition of being" (*Webster*, 1975).

- **State** "A condition or stage in the physical being of something" (*Webster*, 1975).

- The **state** of an object is defined by the set of values currently held by its attributes.

- At any moment in time, an object exists in a certain manner or condition, which we say is its **state.**

A state has the following things:

- **Name**

    A text string unique within this diagram, and *meaningful to your users.* As Booch (1999) would say, it must be "drawn from the vocabulary of your system."

- **Entry and exit actions**

    Things the object must do every time it enters or leaves this state. (See the section on *actions* below.)

- **Deferred Events**

    A list of events that are to be deferred if they occur while the object is in this state. When this happens, each event will be put on hold, until the object reaches a state that *can* accept it.

- **Internal Transitions**

    This is a handy idea that we will discuss later, in the section on *transitions.*

Within our software system, the only things we know about a real-world object are the data values recorded on its matching data-world instance. We use these data values to keep track of the changes of state that the real-world object goes through. The values of the data attributes then reflect the state of the real-world object.

In fact, we could (and some authors do) go so far as to say that the attribute values *are* the state, at least of the data-world object. Or at the very least, we can say that they *represent* its state, or that they represent the state of the real-world object.

The main result from taking this view is that any change in the value of an attribute becomes a change of state for the object. Obviously, however, not all of these states and changes are relevant or significant to our project.

Some classes of objects may even have a status attribute specifically for the purpose of recording the relevant states of the real-world object, as it transitions through its life cycle. The ***domain*, or set of permissible values,** for this attribute can then be found by listing all the significant states for that class of object.

So we can define a ***state transition* as the act or experience of changing from one state to another.** And then a ***statechart diagram* is a map, showing all the permissible states and permissible transitions for a class of objects, along with the events that cause these transitions, and the actions and activities that result from them.**

CLASSES THAT NEED STATECHART DIAGRAMS

As I indicated, the purpose of the statechart diagram is to assist us in finding all the behaviors that our objects must be capable of. Not every class of objects will need one, however. It will sometimes be obvious, and sometimes a bit of a judgement call, deciding when you need one. Here are some clues and ideas to suggest when a statechart diagram is needed:

- If you find a class has an interesting or complex life cycle, it should have a statechart diagram. Often this means classes that create or delete instances, or that create and delete associations.

- If an instance can update its attributes in a variety of ways as it goes through its life cycle.

- If we're talking about a vending machine, library book, or something else with an *operational life cycle.*

- If two classes are depending on each other, in that one of them can start the other on its life cycle, or change the order in which it goes from state to state.

- If you find that the object's current behavior depends on what happened to it before, that is, on its past history.

Generally, you can expect to find more and more suitable classes as you work through all of the various models. Every now and again, you'll uncover another class that has a complex and interesting life cycle, and you'll need to take time out to develop a statechart diagram and a state transition table (STT) for it. Later I'll explain these both in some detail – for now let's look at what happens when a state receives an event.

10.3 TRANSITIONS

At any point in time, an object exists in some *state* in the real world. As time goes by, the object will change. Something about it has changed, with the result that we say it's now in a *new state.*

How do we know something changed? As we noted, within our software system, the only things we know about the real-world object are the data values recorded on the matching data-world instance. We must ensure, then, that we have all the necessary attributes defined on our data objects so that we can record all of the various states of this object, or at least *the ones that are important to our users.*

In addition, we must provide methods that will update the attribute values to record each transition that the object undergoes from one state to another. Thus, we define a *__state transition__* **to be the act or experience of changing from one state to another.**

Or in the words of Booch et al. (1999), **"A** *__transition__* **is . . . between two states (so) that an object in the first state will perform certain actions and enter the second state, when a specified event occurs and specified conditions are satisfied.** When this happens, Booch says the transition *fires*. We'll talk about his "specified conditions" later under "guard conditions."

A transition is made up of:

- *__Source State.__* **The state the object was in before the transition occurred.** Be warned that this state may have an exit action. (See *actions* in the next section.)

- *__Event Trigger.__*   **The event that causes the object to move from one state to another.** But only if the guard condition is met.

- *__Guard Condition__*(optional). **A Boolean expression that will prevent the transition if it evaluates to FALSE.** There may be several transitions tied to one event, providing they all have mutually exclusive guard conditions, so that only one transition can fire each time around. If it happens that they all evaluate to FALSE, then no transition occurs, and that event is just lost.

- *__action__*(optional). **An atomic operation that will be executed during the transition.** That is, it will be done after the *exit action* for the Source State, and before the *entry action* of the target state. (See *actions* in the next section.)

- *__Target (Destination) State.__* **The state the object ends up in after the transition is done.**

As an object "lives" (exists) through time, its state from time to time will change. But that's not all. These are not just passive objects, lying around waiting for someone to change their state. Objects are *active*, they have behavior, and this is shown on the statechart diagram as *actions* and *activities* that can go with each state and each transition.

10.4 ACTIONS AND ACTIVITIES

The way we handle behavior on a statechart diagram is to define *actions* for each state and transition. An action might be as simple as updating a counter or a date/time stamp. Or it might be extremely complicated, with multiple calls to operations (methods) in the same object or other objects. So, an *__action__* **is an atomic behavior that is associated with a state or a transition, and is considered a part of the life cycle.**

__Atomic__ **means that it cannot be split any further without losing or changing the meaning of what it is.**

An *__entry action__* **is an action performed each time the object enters or re-enters a state, regardless of how it got there.** It doesn't matter what state it was in before, or what event triggered the transition. The moment the object lands in this state, it launches the *entry action* for the state.

Later, when the object again changes state, it fires the ***exit action***, **which is an action that the object performs whenever it transitions *out* of the state.**

Actions and Transitions

When a transition occurs, the first thing that happens is the *exit action* for the state the object is leaving. Then, *during the transition*, and before the object gets to its new state, there can be another action that takes place. This one is an action defined to *belong to the transition*. Finally, as the object enters the destination (target) state, it fires the *entry action* for that new state.

Atomic actions

In the original meaning of the word, actions are *atomic*, in that they cannot be divided up or interrupted. (The dictionaries give us *atomic* as being derived from the Greek *atomos*, meaning "indivisible.") For larger tasks, actions can be grouped into chains, or we can use *activities*, and both of these *can* be interrupted when necessary.

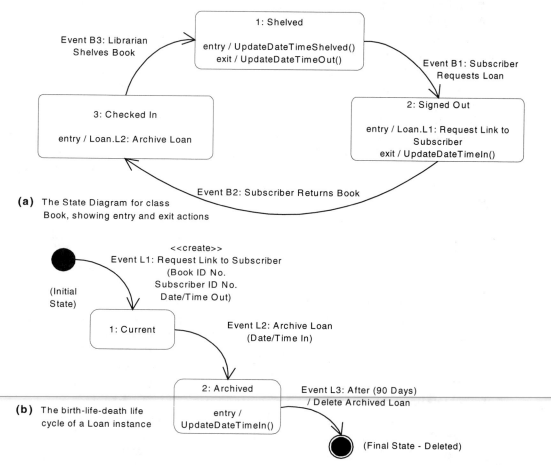

(a) The State Diagram for class Book, showing entry and exit actions

(b) The birth-life-death life cycle of a Loan instance

Figure 10-2　A day in the life of a busy library book

Activities

After an object enters a new state, firing the entry action on the way in, mostly it will simply rest in that state until an event comes along that will kick it out to some other state, thus firing the exit action. But sometimes there will be something you need the object to do while awaiting that next event.

The point is that whatever the object is doing while it's waiting must be something that can be interrupted by the arrival of a suitable event. We have two options here.

One is that we can define a chain of actions. Although each action is itself atomic, an event can break in between them. If the event happened to arrive while one of these actions was underway, it would be made to wait for a gap between actions, and then it can interrupt and cause a transition.

The other way is to define an ***activity,*** **an ongoing process (behavior) that continues as long as the object remains in this state, but can be interrupted by a suitable trigger event.** In this sense, then, an activity is *not* atomic.

The actions and activities may, as usual, be added to the statechart diagram. The names are written inside the state box. You may then spell them out in full detail separately as part of the supporting text.

They may be spelled out in English if fairly simple, or in pseudocode if they start to get complex. Each action or activity will eventually turn into one or more methods, so you'll need to specify them clearly and precisely. For any extra large or complex ones, you should use activity diagrams, which in their simplest form are just flowcharts. Activity diagrams can be found in any advanced UML text, such as Booch et al. (1999), or my new *UML Plain English Users' Guide*, due out in 2002.

Actions and activities can do practically anything. They may update any attributes, which may be in this object, or in other instances of the same class, or in objects from other classes. An entry action might update a status attribute to reflect the transition that just occurred, plus maybe a counter and a date/time stamp.

They update other objects by sending a message to the object, saying: "Please update yourself." (Such a message is, of course, usually an operation or method call, or sometimes a *signal*.) Actions may send messages to other classes or to this same class, requesting that objects be created, deleted, or whatever operations are available in the class.

When an action or activity needs to request some operation from another object, it originates a message. If the receiving object is in a class that has a statechart diagram, and if this message causes the receiving object to change its state, then the message is said to be a *signal*, and appears in that class as an event.

This event will cause the receiving object to fire the exit action for the class it is in. Then there will be a transition as this object switches to another state, followed by the entry action of its new state.

In this way, we can speak of objects communicating by sending signals or calls to one another. More precisely, we speak of the communication, not between the objects themselves, but by sending events between their *state machines*, which will be explained later in the next section.

Let's consider a few examples of things that can happen to our objects, and introduce a most effective way to diagram this whole thing.

10.5 THE STATECHART DIAGRAM

The diagram in Figure 10-1(c) is a flowchart, so it shows the *time sequence of events.* Since the flowchart notation focuses on events and sequences, it has no way of indicating the *state* of an object. To diagram the life cycle of an object, we need a notation whose focus is on the states, showing the allowable transitions from one state to another.

Statechart Diagram Notation

Statechart diagram notation does just that. It shows the states as rectangular boxes with rounded corners, as you can see in Figure 10-2. This shows the library book life cycle in statechart diagram notation. By convention, we give each state a name and a number, *unique within this statechart diagram,* and write them inside the state box. Then we draw arrows to represent all possible transitions.

NAMES FOR STATES AND EVENTS

The UML does not require numbers on the states, just names. But my experience has been that long cumbersome names can get in the way in a discussion, or in a written explanation. I find these things are way easier to discuss, especially with the users, if we give them numbers for short. You'll see when we get to them that I find the same to be true for events, so I like to give them names and numbers also.

The names are made by capitalizing the first letter of each word that makes up the name. You can use several words to make the name, so it looks like an English phrase. You may wish to run the words together, especially if you anticipate the programmers will do so with this name during coding (often referred to as "camel-caps.") Note that, contrary to C++ and Java programming conventions, we *do* capitalize the *first* letter of the name.

In Figure 10-2 you'll see we have State 1: Shelved, State 2: Signed Out, and State 3: Checked In, all of which are valid by these rules. Finally, make sure your state names are mnemonic, that is the name is meaningful and reminds you what the state is all about. The Booch (1999) way of saying this is to insist that we choose our state names "from the vocabulary of the system."

In this particular application (so our users, the library staff, tell us), a book cannot go directly from being on the shelf to being checked in. It doesn't make sense to our users, and it's not something they wish to be able to do. In fact, the only way a book can come off the shelf (so they tell us) is to be *checked out.* So there's only a single arrow out of the Shelved state box, going to the Signed Out state box.

Next to this arrow you'll see Event B1: Subscriber Requests Loan. My preference, which I find works well, is to allocate a one- or two-letter code to each class that we build a statechart diagram for, and then number the events within the statechart diagram. This way the events are identified *uniquely across the whole system,* and across all the statechart diagrams. This is necessary since most events originate in one class and are received by instances of a different class.

Many UML users prefer to use the dot notation, so that my Event B1: would then be written as book.Suscriber Requests Loan, or book.SuscriberRequestsLoan. I think you'll agree that, while they're fine for program code, these names could be a bit of a mouthful to stumble over during a heated discussion!

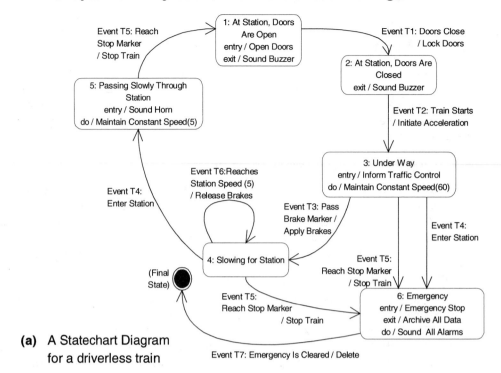

(a) A Statechart Diagram for a driverless train

Figure 10-3 Statechart diagrams (continued)

In Figure 10-2(a), you'll see what happens when Event B1 is initiated by the Subscriber and sent to the Book, where it causes the transition from State 1 to State 2. Event B2 also comes from the Subscriber, and Event B3 from the Librarian. So the events are numbered according to the class of object that *receives* this kind of event, since there could be several sources for the same event type. Remember, these events correspond to the messages (that is, function or method calls) that we talked about in earlier chapters, and they form the vehicle for communication between objects.

In Figure 10-2(a), notice that the entry and exit actions for each state (to be performed as the Book enters and leaves each state) have been written inside the box for the state. In this particular statechart diagram, some of the actions include a date and time update. The entry action for State 2: Signed Out also includes the directive "Send Event L1: Request Link to Subscriber."

This is an event that's received by the Loan class, which responds by creating an instance of Loan, as shown in Figure 10-2(b). You'll see the UML stereotype notation above the event, showing it to be stereotyped as a <<create>> event.

A **_stereotype_ is the notation to use when you create your own local extensions to add to the UML notation. It consists of a name or note enclosed in guillemots,** a.k.a. chevrons, like this: <<create>>. I quote from Rumbaugh, et al.(1999), The *UML Language Reference Manual*: "Note that a guillemet (sic) looks like a double angle-bracket, but it is a single character in most extended fonts. Most computers have a character map utility in which special symbols can be found. Double angle-brackets may be used as a substitute by the typographically challenged."

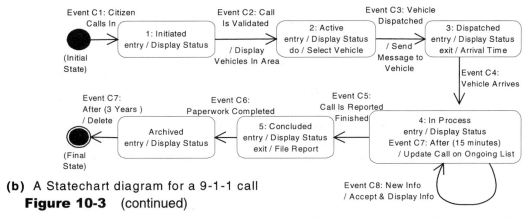

(b) A Statechart diagram for a 9-1-1 call

Figure 10-3 (continued)

The new Loan object carries Book No. and Subscriber No. attributes (possibly as foreign keys, possibly replaced by suitable pointers), so that it records which Book is signed out to which Subscriber.

When the Subscriber returns the Book [Event B2, Figure 10-2(a)], the Book transitions to State 3: Checked In. As it exits from State 2, it performs the specified exit action, that is, it updates the Date/Time In. Then, as it enters Sate 3, it does the entry action and generates Event L2: Archive Loan.

This in turn is received by the Loan instance, which has been waiting patiently in its State 1: Current. (Read this to mean State 1: "I am the Current Loan, and my Subscriber ID attribute will tell you to whom the Book is currently signed out.") Upon receipt of this event, the Loan instance transitions to its State 2: Archived.

Some time later, the Librarian initiates Event B3: Librarian Shelves Book, and this returns the Book to State 1: Shelved. The Book then performs the entry action for State 1, which is to update the Date/Time Shelved attribute. At this point there's no effect on the loan. The loan itself does not need to change state when the book is shelved, so it continues in its Archived state.

Finally, after 90 days, the timer fires, which I've designated as an Event L3: After 90 Days. This event has the action "Delete Archived Loan," which terminates the lifetime of the Loan instance. The termination is shown with a large dot in a circle, a pseudostate representing the destruction of the object instance.

In this case, there is no physical object to be destroyed, since a Loan is an abstract concept, a type of business transaction. For the book, on the other hand, we must be careful to keep the physical book and its database instance in step throughout their lifetime. But whether the real-world object is physical or not, either way this termination means the destruction (erasing) of the instance in the database.

You'll notice that, unlike the Book, the Loan has a *lifetime* rather than a *life cycle*, since its life is not cyclic in nature. Here are a couple more examples, a very cyclic one and a lifetime one.

TRAIN EXAMPLE

Figure 10-3 gives a couple more examples. In Figure 10-3(a), we see a train with five possible states. When we board the train, it's in State 1: At Station, Doors Are Open. A few moments later, Event T1: Doors Close occurs, and the train transitions into State 2: At Station, Doors Closed. The action attached to this event is to Lock the Doors, and one of the more important UML rules is that the action is to be completed before the object can enter the next state.

When all is ready, we have Event T2: Train Starts, which causes the train to enter State 3: Under Way.

The train will then cruise along in this state for a few minutes, with the ongoing activity being "Maintain speed at 60 km/h (40 mph)." Then the next event happens – Event T3: Pass Brake Marker, whereupon the train will apply its brakes (the action defined on the transition), and enter State 4: Slowing for Station.

While in State 4: Slowing for Station, the train should slow down to 5 km/h (3 mph). When it reaches this speed (Event T6) it undergoes a ***self-transition*, which ends up back in the same state.** The action on this self-transition is to release the brakes. *Self-transitions* and the related *internal transitions* are discussed in more detail a few pages ahead.

As the train enters the station (Event T4: Enters Station), it moves to State 5: Passing Slowly Through Station. It executes the entry action for State 5, which is to sound its horn. The ongoing activity for this state is to maintain speed at 5 km/h (3 mph), and of course this activity can be interrupted any time by a suitable event.

Recall that *activities* are interruptible, but *actions* are not. Actions must always run to completion, and no further transitions may take place until that has happened.

So the train continues to pass slowly through the station until there is one such suitable event – it reaches the stop marker (Event T5). This interrupts the ongoing activity and puts it back to State 1: At Station, Doors Open. The action on this transition is to stop the train, and once this has been achieved, the train can enter State 1 and open its doors.

But what if someone were to miss the wide-open door and fall violently onto the tracks? Get out your cell phone and read on.

A 9-1-1 Call

To help in this eventuality, Figure 10-3(b) shows the progress of a 9-1-1 call, which is shown as having a birth–life–archive kind of lifetime.[1] It comes into existence as a result of Event C1: Citizen Calls In. This event creates an instance of the class Call as shown by the «create» stereotype, and places it in State 1: Initiated.

Since this event comes from outside this statechart diagram and starts the whole process, it is shown on the diagram as "coming out of nowhere." The large, solid dot [what Booch et al.(1999) refer to as a "filled circle"] is a pseudostate representing the start of the process.

Event C1: Citizen Calls In causes a transition to State 1: Initiated. The newly initiated Call instance announces its existence on the screen (entry action, State 1), and sits for a while in State 1: Initiated, awaiting further events.

As the events happen one after another [see Figure 10-3(b)], the call progresses through its various states. You'll see actions on several of the transitions in Figure 10-3(b), as well as entry and exit actions on some of the states. In addition, State 2: Active has an ongoing (interactive and interruptible) activity, as shown by the "do / Select Vehicle" entry in the box.

---

[1]Always be sure to say **"nine-one-one"** when discussing 9-1-1 calls. The problem with saying "nine-eleven" is that in a crisis people have been known to panic and freeze, looking for the "eleven" key on the touch-tone telephone pad! The practice recommended by disaster services experts is to make a habit in everyday speech of always spelling out the digits in the emergency number. This gives **"nine-one-one"** for North America, or "nine-nine-nine" or "one-one-one" for some other places. You may have noticed that William Shatner used to call his TV program **"Rescue, Nine-One-One"** for this very reason.

State 4: In Process has two unusual transitions. One is an ***internal transition***, **one that triggers actions or activiies without causing the object to change state. The object ends up in the same state as it started from, without leaving that state, and without firing the exit or entry actions.** You'll see it shown on the third and fourth lines within the State 4 box. This one causes the call to be reported on an "Ongoing Calls List" with an Event C7: After (15 Minutes). The other adds new information to the record as it is received (Event C8).

The difference is that Event C8 is a ***self-transition***, **which *does* fire the exit and then entry transitions of the state (which is acting as both source and target).** This means that after the new information is accepted and displayed (according to the action on Event C8), then the call will re-enter State 4, and in so doing will re-execute the entry action, thus displaying its revised status on the screen.

Finally the call is archived, since in this application the records are likely to be needed for future court cases. Then, after the passage of a preset time (the amount set by law, several years in most countries), the archived call is deleted.

State Machines

It's sometimes useful to be able to talk more specifically about a particular object instance. Most of what I've said so far in this chapter refers to a "typical but unspecified" object. The example statechart diagrams in the previous section talk about the things that are true for *any and every* Book, or Train, or whatever.

All the things I said about to objects applied to any instance you may encounter, but I haven't spelled out or identified any particular one. The statechart diagram describes behavior that's common to all instances, without choosing a specific instance.

However, if we were to take notes on the history of one particular instance as it works its way through the various states of the statechart diagram for its class, the record we would have is a unique set of historical events. It's considered part of the state machine for that object. The rest of the state machine is the *future* set of transitions that the object will make, but has not done so as yet – its "future history."

A ***state machine*** **is the set of events that makes up the execution of a statechart diagram by a *particular specified object*.** This is different from the statechart diagram itself, which is actually an *abstraction* of the state machines of all the objects in this class.

A state machine may include past and/or future events and transitions. We speak in terms of a state machine whenever we are discussing a single object, or a specific instance, and what happens to it. But even so, we mostly refer to things that are common to all objects of that type, in other words all instances of that class. So mostly you'll find you're dealing with a statechart diagram, rather than a single state machine. Be aware, however, that a few authors do confuse the two.

Complex and Multipath Life Cycles

Now let's revisit the library book we last saw in Figure 10-2 and add a slight complication. What if a Subscriber requested a loan when the Book was in the returns bin, rather than on the shelf where it's supposed to be? Do we turn away a customer? Certainly not!

In Figure 10-4(a), you'll see that we've added another transition, this time from State 3: Checked In (in other words, in the returns bin) to State 2: Signed Out. This transition is shown as being initiated by a B1 event, Subscriber Requests Loan. What this is saying is that a B1 event can be accepted by the Book object when it's in either State 1 or State 3. In both cases, it causes a transition to State 2: Signed Out.

The way we word this is to say that the event is *received by the state*, since specifying a state implies a particular object class anyway. So in this statechart diagram, either of States 1 or 3 can accept a B1: Subscriber Requests Loan event.

But what happens if a B1 event occurs while the book is in State 2: Signed Out? I can see two options here that we can present to our users. The first is to say that the system doesn't need to handle this. In other words, a B1 event at this time would simply be ignored by the system. But that won't do, since (so our users tell us) people often come to the desk asking for a book that happens to be out at the time.

The other option is to have the system output a message saying the book is already signed out, and perhaps even to whom. This is shown in Figure 10-4(b), where you'll see a transition from State 2 right back into State 2, driven by a B1 event that occurred while the book was in State 2. This is a perfectly normal "state" of affairs. An object may receive an event, respond to it, and end up in the same state it was in before. This we would call a *self-transition* (see below).

There is a complication, however. Every time the Book leaves State 2, it's obliged to execute the exit action, which means it would update its Date and Time In with an erroneous value. Not only that, but as it re-enters State 2, it must do the entry action, so it would end up creating an unwanted Loan instance. To solve this dilemma, we've introduced an *internal transition*.

Internal Transitions

This is a sort of dummy transition, a response to an event, that leaves the object in the same state it was in before. In fact, the object handles the event without leaving that state. This way, it avoids firing the entry and exit actions for the state. However, you can now take all the things that need to be done, and define them to be part of the action belonging to this transition.

So we can define an ***internal transition*, one that triggers actions or activiies without causing the object to change state. The object ends up in the same state it started from, without leaving that state, and without firing the exit or entry actions.**

In Figure 10-4(c), you see that we have Event B1 shown inside the box for State 2. So when one of these occurs, we will report an exception message, increment an error counter, and remain in State 2: Signed Out. And now, when a B1 event occurs in State 2, we'll do what needs to be done, but we won't corrupt our Date-Signed-In attribute, nor will we create a bunch of spurious Loan instances.

Self Transitions

Let's say we asked the library users what they do about badly damaged books. Their response was a little unexpected. They told us, "We put a new copy on the shelf, give it the same Book Id No as the old one, and update the 'Date Replaced.' We also reset the 'Date Shelved,' because that's the date this copy was put on the shelf."

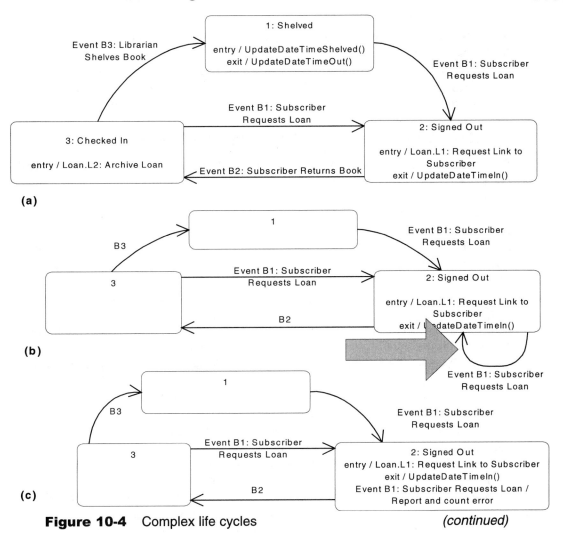

Figure 10-4 Complex life cycles *(continued)*

This tells us several things for our system:

- We need a "Date Replaced" attribute in the Book class.
- We need an action to get it updated.
- This action must execute only when a replacement happens.
- We need to fire the entry action for State 1 to get the 'Date Shelved' attribute updated.

Figure 10-4(d) shows one way we could do this. We define an event B5: Book Is Replaced By New Copy. This causes the book to transition *out* of State 1: Shelved and then right back *into* State 1: Shelved. The action for this transition is to Update the Date Replaced.

But the book actually *did leave State1* and so, as it reenters State 1, it fires the entry action, which updates the Date Shelved attribute. Had there been an exit action defined on State 1, that one would have been the first action to fire. So we can define a ***self-transition*** **to be from one state back into the same state, which** *does* fire the exit and then entry transitions of the state (which is acting as both source and target) as it leaves and then re-enters that state.

And what if our B5: Book is Replaced by New Copy event happens when the book is in some other state? We mustn't lose this event, as it's an important one that must be captured. So if it occurs while the book is in *any* other state, it must be *postponed*.

Postponing and Remembering Events

So a what-if question arises: What if the Book Is Replaced event (B5) happens while our system has not yet reported a Book Is Shelved event (B3)? In other words, while the book is in the Returns bin.

Since an event, by definition, happens *at a point in space and time*, once it has happened it's gone, unless we make some arrangement to store it (that is, to *remember* it.) In this case, the system would not be able to deal with this B5 event and respond to it until finished with whatever it is doing. Once the book returns to State 1: Shelved it can then accept the B5 event.

This timing problem happens often, so as a principle in statechart diagram analysis, we say that *an event can never be lost*. Then, if an object is busy doing something (executing an action or activity), any event that may arrive is considered to be put on hold until it can be accepted and dealt with.

"Dealt with" might mean "ignored," but that's okay. It's a conscious decision to ignore it, as opposed to just letting it fade away unnoticed. For the B5: Book Is Replaced By New Copy event, "deal with" would mean "Postpone until the book is in State 1: Shelved, and then respond to it."

The actual mechanics of how this is done will be up to the OOPL or ODBMS compiler, of course. At the analysis phase, we simply assume that it can and will happen this way. The one thing we must be aware of, however, is how long the event may need to wait. In this example, the book may spend hours or days in the Returns bin, so the programmers must take care that the B5 message is not forgotten.

You'll need to watch for situations where the delay may be long, but the event needs a response sooner. This is especially critical in interactive, process-control, and embedded applications.

10.6 OBJECT LIFE CYCLES
ON THE STATECHART DIAGRAM

Now let's consider what all these examples have told us:

- Most of the objects we'll deal with have a set pattern of stages or states that they go through. This pattern depends on the class of the object; all objects in a class have the same pattern.

- An object moves from one *state* to another in response to an *event*, either from the outside world or from another object within the system.

- Not all of these transitions from state to state are physically or legally possible. The constraints of the users' world will preclude many of them, so only the permissible ones are modeled.

- An *__object life cycle__* consists of the various *states* that an object may transition through, the set of *permissible transitions*, and the *sequencing* of those states and transitions, as it progresses from its initial creation to its eventual disposal.
- The life cycle also includes the actions that are that go with each state and transition, and that are executed each time the object undergoes a transition.
- Not every class has its life cycle modeled, only those with interesting lives.
- Since all the instances in a class have the same behavior, it follows that they must all have the same statechart diagram. But in the execution of the statechart diagram, each separate instance proceeds independently at its own pace in its own state machine, as events arrive to step it through its life cycle.

Coordinated Life Cycles

Let's go back for a moment and retrieve that poor old library book from its comfortable shelf one more time. You'll recall that, in order to record the data that goes with the transition, the Book object will need to arrange for the Loan class to create a Loan instance. This would suggest that an action needs to be able to send events (messages) to other objects so as to get things done when it needs them.

In Figure 10-4(c), look at the action in State 4: *Signing-Out*, where it says: "Generate Event L11: Request Link to Subscriber." What this means physically is "Create (Instance of) Loan." If you check Figure 10-2(b), you'll also notice that the event carries data with it. Because an instance of Loan is to be created, the event must carry the identifiers of both the Book and the Subscriber. These will become foreign keys in the Loan object.

In addition, it also needs to pass the Date/Time-Out data to be recorded in the new Loan instance. Similarly, Event L2: Loan Archived must later carry the Date/Time-In data (when the book was returned) to update this same Loan instance.

Note that Event L2 doesn't show any identifier(s) for the instance to be updated. Most analysts, working at Analysis time, would treat the identifier as implicit, and indeed in some OOPLs it is. In other environments, it needs to be passed explicitly; but if that's the case, it's needed every time, so we can still leave it off the analysis diagrams for clarity. It will need to be added at design time when we spec things out in detail.

In Figure 10-2(b), we have the life cycle for a Loan instance, where the creation is shown as an "arrow from nowhere," triggered by a L1 event. Further inspection of Figure 10-2(b) will show you that as the Book object changes state throughout its life cycle, the corresponding Loan instance must do so as well. We achieve this coordination by having the actions in the statechart diagram for the Book send events to keep the Loan instance in step.

So, as the Book returns to rest in its State 1: Shelved, the Loan instance enters its State 2: Archived. Finally, the Loan instance is deleted sometime later, as you'll see below, and a couple of pages further on under "Terminating a Life Cycle." (Sounds kind of murderous, doesn't it! How did Arnie Schwarznegger. get involved?)

The next time this Book instance is borrowed, a new Loan instance will be created, which will then be archived when the book is returned. Some time later, the Librarian shelves the book. The Book instance will send a message to update the Date/Time-Shelved attribute, which is an attribute in the Loan class, without causing any *relevant* changes to the state in the Loan instance.

(Although technically the Loan instance has changed state since one of its attributes has changed value, this is not a change that matters for this project.)

Some time later yet – say, about three months later for this particular library – the Loan instance will experience an Event L3: Archive Expires. This is a "passage-of-time" event, a timer that fires when the preset time is up. Any Loan instance that has been archived for three months will respond by deleting itself and its state machine.

You'll find many cases where two or more kinds of objects have their life cycles coordinated in this way, where the instances will send events to each other to keep in step. You'll need to do a final careful check your statechart diagrams to ensure that these shared events are handled consistently.

States, Transitions, and Events

Now here are some points about states and events that should be apparent from all these examples.

STATES

While technically every change in the value of an attribute places the object in a new state, you'll find that many, if not most of them, are irrelevant for your project. As part of our abstraction then, our states and their definitions must include only those attributes that are relevant. We don't have to include *all* attribute changes in *all* classes in the statechart diagrams.

A state exists from one event, which caused the transition into this state, until another event brings about a transition out of it. A state has a length – that is, a *duration* – and an event does not. In this sense, a state corresponds to the time interval between two events, and events represent points in time.

So a state separates two events, and in the same way, an event can be thought of as separating two states.

TRANSITIONS

When an event is received by a state, there's normally only one destination state for that event from that state. This means, then, that if state A has possible transitions to states B, C, and D, each would normally be driven by a different event.

There are, however, exceptions. Advanced UML allows concurrent states (Booch et al., 1999; Rumbaugh et al., 1999), where, under certain conditions, an object can legally be in more than one state at a time.

Another exception, that allows several destination states to one event, is when we have *guard conditions*.

GUARD CONDITIONS

In Figure 10-4(e) you'll see that when the book is in State 3:Checked-In, it has two possible responses to the event B3: Book is Shelved. When the librarian takes it out of the returns bin, he checks it for damage. If the book is physically in good enough condition, he puts it in its normal place on the main shelves.

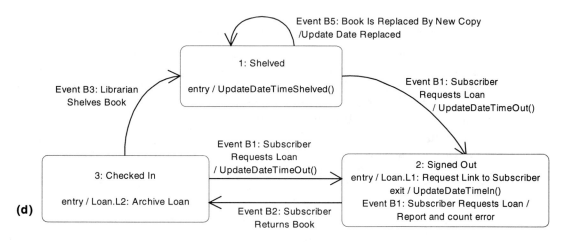

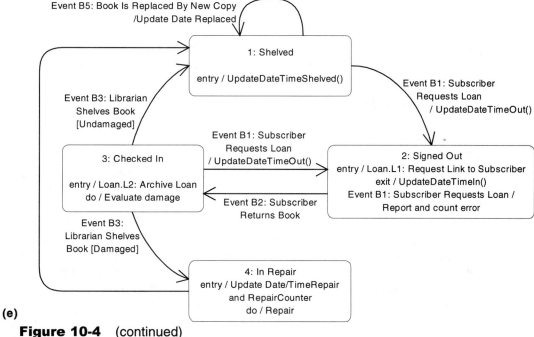

(d)

(e)

Figure 10-4 (continued)

But what if it's damaged? Well, we'll need it to go to the back room for repair. That's shown on the diagram as State 4: In Repair. In this version of the statechart diagram, we get to State 4 if the *guard condition* on the exit from state two is FALSE. The condition reads: *Book Is In Usable Condition*. As you can see, if it's FALSE the book ends up in State 4, and if it's TRUE in State 1.

Note that this only works if these two conditions are mutually exclusive. That way we don't get the book trying to be in two places at once. But they don't have to cover *all* possibilities. If a B3 event happens, but none of the guard conditions are met, then no transition occurs. You'll also note that State 4 includes an internal transition to handle an Event B1: Subscriber Requests Loan, in case it happens while the book is being repaired.

TRIGGERLESS OR "COMPLETION" TRANSITIONS

Then, the way our users asked for it, there is a transition to State 1: Shelved as soon as the repair is completed, firing the entry action and updating the Date Shelved attribute again. This kind of transition can be shown with no trigger event, the implication being that it fires automatically as soon as the source state has finished its activity, in this case the "do / Repair" activity.

But you'll notice that in Figure 10-4(f) we have not one but *two* triggerless completion transitions from State 4 to State 1. What if the book is damaged beyond repair? This is handled by having an exit condition on State 4: In Repair. It just happens to be the same one as on State 3, but this time both transitions have the same target state, and are triggerless.

What's different is that the two transitions have different *actions* attached to them. If the book is in usable condition, meaning the repair was successful, we take the top transition and go to State 1, executing the entry action to update the Date Shelved.

But if the repair was unsuccessful, and the book turns out to be unusable, we *put it on the shelf temporarily*, and this transition [the lower one in Figure 10-4(e)] generates an exception message to the staff, in effect requesting them to initiate a B5: Book is Replaced by New Copy event. Then we enter the new state (State 1) and perform its entry action.

CONSERVATION OF EVENTS

An event is a pretty important thing in a state machine. Events are so important that we can't afford to lose any of them, so we need a couple of rules to guide us. First, as we saw earlier, if an object instance is busy (or, more correctly, if its state machine is busy executing an action), then the event needs to be put on hold. Once the object (or, more correctly, its state machine) has finished what it's doing, then it can accept the new event and respond to it.

What this implies is that, at this level, *an object (i.e., a state machine) can only do one thing at a time.* However, several instances in a class, which all have the same statechart diagram, can each have their separate state machines active all at the same time. There will be no restriction on what they can do – they may all be executing the same or different actions at any given moment.

However, I must then backtrack a little, and mention that in more advanced UML (see Booch et al., 1999; Rumbaugh et al., 1999), you can use *substates* to handle times when you need an object to be doing several things at the same time.

Since an event happens at a point in space and time, the event itself cannot and should not last forever. Each event implicitly knows its own time of occurrence (its time coordinate), so we usually don't give it a Time attribute, unless that time needs to be recorded for reporting or some other future purpose. We've just seen that some events must be put on hold, and that's a somewhat artificial requirement we need to have in order to make the models work.

The point is, that in the normal flow of things, an event should trigger a transition, and then it (the event itself) is not needed any more. For us, an event is simply a message or command to do something, and like a paper message, once it has been read and acted upon, it can be thrown away.

In this sense, Shlaer and Mellor (1992) would say the event has been "used up" and "then vanishes as an event." Once this has happened, the only traces left by the event will be in the changes that may have been made by the action(s) it triggered. The event itself is simply gone.

But events must be consistent. An event B3: Book Is Shelved must always mean that the librarian put the book on a shelf. It must never mean anything else. Especially when it carries a command, an event must always mean the same thing, and always provide the same consistent data to its receiving state machine.

CONSISTENT ARGUMENTS

Events that create instances must always carry the minimum set of data as parameters, that will allow an instance to be created without any inconsistencies. Also, the event will usually need to bring along the identifier for the new instance to be created. This would not be needed if the identifier is to provided some other way. For example, it may be a sequential number automatically generated, or the user could be prompted for it.

Note that, unlike a function call, an event carries data as parameters in one direction only. Data cannot be sent back in the parameters later, because by then the event will have ceased to exist. If one of the steps of the action in the new state is to send some data back as a reply, it must be sent as parameters with a new and different event, generated by completing this action.

This is consistent, however, since when necessary, you can consider a regular message from one object to another (a function call) to be two separate events. First there's a Call event that carries the parameters, and sometime later a separate Return event that sends back the answer(s).

TERMINATING A LIFE CYCLE

There's one transition in Figure 10-2(b) that bears a little more discussion. The library users informed us that detailed loan records are kept for three months, so we needed to arrange for the Loan instance to be deleted after that time. We do this by having a timer that deletes all archived Loans more than three months old.

So Event L3: After (90 days) pops up some time after the Loan enters State 2: Archived. When Event L3 triggers, the Loan is deleted; that is, it simply ceases to exist. This is shown on the diagram as a large dot inside a circle, to highlight the fact that it goes no further; the instance and its state machine disappear totally and permanently.

This is different from the fate of the Book instance. The book, when its useful work was done, was allowed to rest, sitting undisturbed on the shelf until and unless needed again.

Also, in Figure 10-3(b), we saw that the used-up 9-1-1 call finally entered its State 6: Archived, where it remained *quiescent* (in Edmonton for three years). After that it is deleted by an Event C7: After (3 years).

But in Figure 10-4(f) we have added a guard condition to this transition. A hold may have been placed on the record of the call, perhaps because it is needed for a lawsuit or criminal case. If so, the call instance executes an internal transition instead, resets the timer, and waits another 90 days before checking again to see if the hold has been lifted.

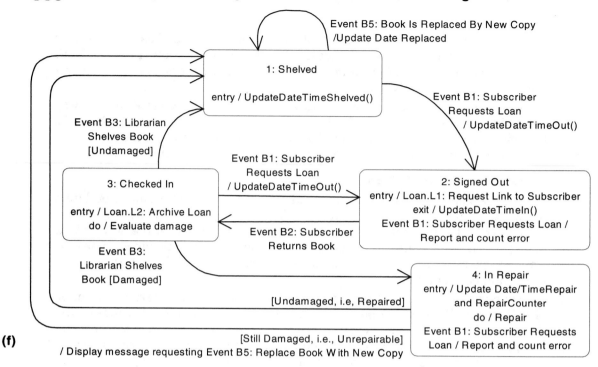

(f)

Figure 10-4   (continued)

Every object life cycle does one of these three things: It cycles forever, or the instance is deleted as soon as it's no longer needed, or it ends with the object entering some kind of archive state or something equivalent.

ACTIONS

As I said earlier, actions can do anything you would expect that a regular program could do. In addition, there are a few things about actions that we should mention specially.

Since an action will eventually translate into program code as a method, it must be specified very precisely. The best way to do this is to begin by using a mixture of English and pseudocode in the analysis phase, probably heavy on the pseudocode. During design the actions may be refined, expanded, and written more clearly in pseudocode.

SUBCLASS HIERARCHIES

There are two things to remember when dealing with statechart diagrams for subclasses:

- A subclass *isa* class, so anything we've said for statechart diagrams for regular classes still applies if your class is a subclass or superclass.

- Actions must take great care when dealing with subclasses. There are a few things they'll need to do in order to leave the hierarchy consistent. For example, when creating an instance, the action must also create all the subclass and superclass instances that go with it. The action will need enough parameter data to know which ones are needed, and then enough to create them.

ERRORS AND EXCEPTIONS

Now is the time to deal with errors and exceptions. After all, they're no different from other types of events. So in your statechart diagram, once you understand the so-called normal course of events, you'll need to check each state and ask, "What could possibly go *wrong* here?"

This could mean unexpected events, events happening at the wrong time, or events happening under the wrong conditions. You must also consider what to do if an expected event doesn't happen, or is late. Should you time it out?

And when an event does occur, does it always mean the same thing (constant semantics)? An event received by your statechart diagram may occasionally be caused by a different happening in the real world, and you'll need to account for these.

If you're thorough, your questioning will give rise to a whole collection of new events, and each must be either added to your statechart diagram (and state transition table – see the next section) or otherwise dealt with. But do be careful not to get too carried away here – beware "analysis paralysis."

It's very important to consider all possible errors and make sure they're handled, so they don't crash the system or give spurious results. On the other hand, it's easy to overdo this, and spend far too much time designing the actions for exception events that most likely will never happen.

Always define an *adequate* response, but don't get too fancy on the ones that will never happen (or almost never). Maintain a balance – don't get bogged down in so much unwanted detail that you lose sight of your goals.

You may find it best to define an event called Other Errors to handle the ones you deem not worthy of their own specialized processing. But do make sure every error or exception produces an adequate error message. By that, I mean it must do three things:

1. Highlight the error.
2. State what the error is.
3. Identify the event or transaction that caused it.

In other words, to the degree possible, give enough information to solve or debug the problem without having to dig further.

By this time, you've drawn a pretty good set of statechart diagrams for your project, and hopefully you have everything on them that should be there. Next we'll look at a way to do a completeness check on your statechart diagrams so you'll be able to tell for sure whether you've checked every possibility.

10.7 STATE TRANSITION TABLES (STTS)

Once you've been through the exercise of drawing a statechart diagram, you need to examine it to see if you've missed any transitions. What we need is a checklist that will force us to examine every conceivable transition and decide whether it's permissible or impossible.

UML does not specifically provide for this, so I will give you a diagram that will do the job for you. I have found it *critical* that I do this with my statechart diagrams, since it is so easy to miss a couple of things – and Murphy's Law ensures that some of them are important things.

State	B1: Subscriber Requests Loan	B2: Subscriber Returns Book	B3: Librarian Shelves Book		B4: Book Replaced	Triggerless Completion Transition	
			[Damaged]	[Undamaged]		[Damaged]	[Undamaged]
1: Shelved	2	Impossible	Impossible	Impossible	1	Impossible	Impossible
2: Signed Out	2	3	Impossible	Impossible	Impossible	Impossible	Impossible
3: Checked In	2	Impossible	4	1	Impossible	Impossible	Impossible
4: In Repair	2	Impossible	Impossible	Impossible	Impossible	1	1

Figure 10-5(a) State transition table (STT) for a library book (compare with Figure 10-2(a))

You will recall that we did something like this back in Chapter 9, in checking for all possible associations on the Class Diagram. There, we could have used a table with check marks, or, as we did, turned the table into a checklist with those curved linking lines down the left. Either way, the principle is to *cover all possible combinations* and make sure we miss none. Any time we need to do this kind of completeness check, a table or matrix is one trick that will always do the job.

The table we use here has all the possible states for the object down the left and all relevant events across the top, as in Figure 10-5(a). Note that when there's a guard condition involved, we need a separate column for each different guard condition (see columns for events B3 and B6.) This time we need more than just check marks because there are four possibilities when an event is received by a state.

One or another of these four must go in each cell of the table:

- **New State.**   The object transitions to another state, in which case the table will show the *target state*. For a small statechart diagram, state numbers are all that's needed. For a more complex one, you may find it helps people to keep track of what is going on if you include state names as well. (Especially for your users. To them, this is just one more piece of technoidia they must wrap their heads around.) Note the one transition in Figure 10-3(a) that leads to the Final State, where the train is deleted.

  But then, of course, the names may run you into the problem of making your table too big to fit on paper. It's a judgment call.

- **Impossible.**   This is an event that simply is not allowed to happen while the object is in this state. To signify this, we write the word *Impossible*, or perhaps *Imp* for short.

State	Event						
	T1: Doors Close	**T2: Train Starts**	**T3: Pass Brake Marker**	**T4: Enter Station**	**T5: Reach Stop Marker**	**T6: Reaches Station Speed**	**T7: Emergency Is Cleared**
1: At Station, Doors Are Open	2	Impossible	Impossible	Impossible	Impossible	Impossible	Impossible
2: At Station, Doors Are Closed	Impossible	3	Impossible	Impossible	Impossible	Impossible	Impossible
3: Under Way	Impossible	Impossible	4	6	6		Impossible
4: Slowing For Station	Impossible	Impossible	Ignore	5	6	4	Impossible
5: Passing Through Station	Impossible	Impossible	Impossible	Impossible	1	Impossible	Impossible
6: Emergency	Impossible	Impossible	Impossible	Impossible	Impossible	Impossible	**Final State**

Figure 10-5(b) State transition diagram for a commuter train (compare with Figure 10-3(a), from which a detail is shown above.)

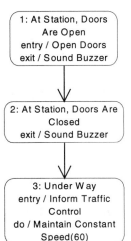

Figure 10-3(a)

(A detail)

There may be a number of reasons why it's not possible:

° In Figure 10-3(a), you'll see that there is no direct transition shown from State 3: Under Way to State 1: At Station, Doors Open. This is because it is physically impossible for the train to be in State 3 one instant and State 1 the next. It must slow down through some intermediate states on the way, so there is no way it can receive a T5: Train Stops event when it's in State 3: Under Way.

° Similarly, when the train is in State 2: At Station Doors Closed, it is physically impossible for the doors to close and give the train a T1: Doors Close event. Often you'll find that a transition is prevented by similar physical or chemical laws, or by other laws of nature.

° In Figure 10-3(b) for the 9-1-1 call, there's no direct transition from State 1: Initiated to State 5: Concluded. This time it's a procedural rule that prevents the transition. The way our users need the system to operate, every 9-1-1 call must go through a certain sequence of states and actions before being concluded and cannot, for example, receive a Call Reported Finished event while in the Initiated state.

° When The Outhouse terminates an employee, the laws of the land (at least here in Canada) require that the records of employment be kept for seven years. Most other countries have a similar rule.

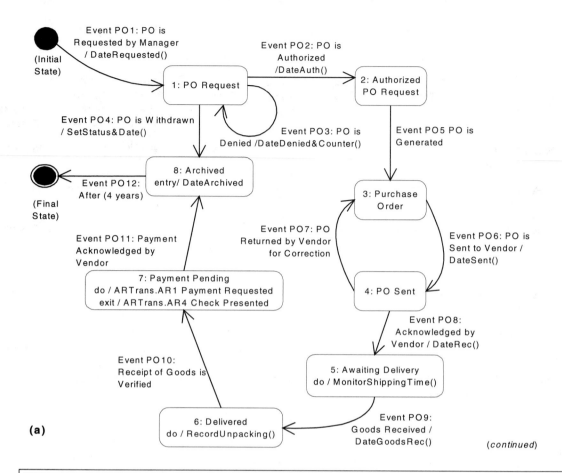

(a)

(continued)

States	PO 1	PO 2	PO 3	PO 4	PO 5	PO 6	PO 7	PO 8	PO 9	PO 10	PO 11	PO1 2
0: Null (Initial State)	1	Imp	Imp	Imp	Imp	Imp	Imp	Imp	Imp	Imp	Imp	Imp
1: PO Request	Imp	2	1	8	Imp	Imp	Imp	Imp	Imp	Imp	Imp	Imp
2: Authorized PO Request	Imp	Imp	Imp	Imp	3	Imp	Imp	Imp	Imp	Imp	Imp	Imp
3: Purchase Order	Imp	Imp	Imp	Imp	Imp	4	Imp	Imp	Imp	Imp	Imp	Imp
4: PO Sent	Imp	Imp	Imp	Imp	Imp	Imp	3	5	Imp	Imp	Imp	Imp
5: Awaiting Delivery	Imp	Imp	Imp	Imp	Imp	Imp	Imp	Imp	6	Imp	Imp	Imp
6: Delivered	Imp	Imp	Imp	Imp	Imp	Imp	Imp	Imp	Imp	7	Imp	Imp
7: Payment Pending	Imp	Imp	Imp	Imp	Imp	Imp	Imp	Imp	Imp	Imp	8	Imp
8: Archived	Ign	Ign	Ign	Ign	Ign	Ign	Ign	Ign	Ign	Ign	Ign	Final State

Events

(Opposite) **Figure 10-6(a)** Statechart diagram and STT for a purchase order (Imp = Impossible, Ign = Ignore)

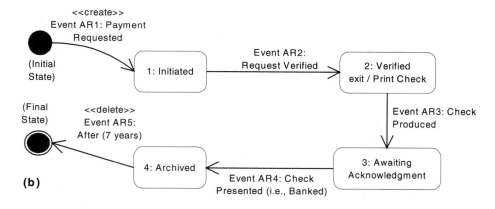

(b)

Figure 10-6 (b) Statechart diagram and STT for an accounts payable transaction

States	Events				
	AR1: Payment Requested	**AR2: Request Verified**	**AR3: Check Produced**	**AR4: Check Presented**	**AR5: After (7 years)**
0: Null	1	Impossible	Impossible	Impossible	Impossible
1: Initiated	Ignore	2	Impossible	Impossible	Impossible
2: Verified	Ignore	Ignore	3	Impossible	Impossible
3: Awaiting Acknowledgment	Ignore	Ignore	Ignore	4	Impossible
4: Archived	Ignore	Ignore	Ignore	Ignore	Final State

So it's just not possible for an Employee instance to move directly from the *Employed* state to the *Deleted* state, without spending a little time in the *Archived* state. That is, an Employee in the *Employed* state cannot receive a 'Deleted' event. This kind of *statutory*, or legal, requirement will eliminate many transitions from your diagrams.

    °   Many professional associations have almost the power of statute in administering their profession and their members. For example, a lawyer cannot go directly from graduate to attorney without a few states in between; in most countries law-school graduates must spend a year working as a legal clerk.

    °   Nor can an instance of Doctor transition directly from state *Intern* to state *Cardiologist* without a term in the *Resident* state. So a Doctor in the *Intern* state cannot accept a Graduate-to-Cardiologist event.

   ° You may on occasion come across an interesting combination of legal
   and physical constraints. Microwave ovens are required by law to
   have interlocks so that the power tube can't be running when the
   door is open. So the oven cannot accept a *Power Tube On* event while
   it's in any state that has the door open.

   ° And in fact, the interlock must be designed in such a way that as you
   press the button, the power goes off the tube before the door latch
   releases. This dictates the sequence of the Power Off and Door Opens
   events.

   ° Also, in most cars these days, it's impossible to have an Engine Starts
   event while in the Transmission-in-Drive state. This restriction is
   also a physical interlock that exists by law (by *statute*) for safety
   reasons.

Any situations you may have in your statechart diagrams that cannot
happen for reasons like these, you mark in your table with the word
Impossible, or the letters *IMP*.

- **Ignored.**   As opposed to impossible events that simply can't happen
  while in that state, there may be many events that *can* happen, but the
  object doesn't react to those events while in this state. In some *other* states,
  it may respond by changing state and executing one or more actions when
  this event occurs, but not in this state.

  These events you'll mark in the table with *Ignored* or the letters *IGN*. Note
  that when an event is ignored, it's still considered to have done what it set
  out to do, which of course was nothing at all. But it has been dealt with
  correctly, and so the event now ceases to exist.

- **Deferred.**   Again, the object doesn't react while in this state, but this
  time the event is put on hold until the object enters a state where it can
  receive this event. The entry in the STT will be marked *Deferred*, or the
  letters *DEF*.

By the time the STT is completed, we should have checked all possible event–state
combinations. At this point, the table becomes part of the permanent
documentation for the project and, of course, is considered to be a deliverable.

DELIVERABLES

For every class where you decide to build a statechart diagram, it's important that
you also build a state transition table (STT) for the completeness check. You'll also
find a List of Events useful, covering all the events in the entire system, as shown
in Figure 10-7 on the next page. You'll need to keep this list in some computerized
form for searching and sorting.

On occasion, you may find a state whose actions turn out to be highly complex.
There are several ways to handle this. One way might be to define subclasses so
that each one gets a piece of the action. Failing that, you'll just have to treat it like
any other sizable program and do an activity diagram, a flowchart, a structure
chart, or whatever other model you may find useful for organizing your coding.

ABC Co. Purchasing System

List of Events

Purchase Order class:

PO1:PO is requested by manager.<<create>>

PO2:PO is authorized.

PO3:PO is denied.

PO4:PO is withdrawn.

PO5:PO is generated.

PO6:PO is sent to Vendor.

PO7:PO returned by Vendor for correction

PO8:Acknowledged by Vendor

PO9:Goods received.

PO10:Receipt of goods is verified.

PO11:Payment acknowledged by Vendor.

PO12:After (4 years).<<delete>>

Accounts Receivable Transaction class:

AR1:Payment requested.<<create>>

AR2:Request verified.

AR3:Check produced.

AR4:Check presented.

AR5:After (7 years).<<delete>>

Figure 10-7 List of Events

Further Reading

Booch et al. (1999), *The UML User Guide*

Rumbaugh et al. (1999), *The UML Reference Manual*

The Three Amigos, led in the first instance by Grady, have produced the definitive user's guide for UML. However, in the classic style of works of genius, it's very complete, but not all that easy to read. You'll find the stuff on events, states, and statechart diagrams spread out over several chapters, notably Chapters 20, 21, and 24.

It's even more spread out, though covered in more depth, in the *The UML Reference Manual* from the same team, this time under the direction of Amigo Jim (Rumbaugh, that is.) Check out Chapter 6, "The State Machine View." (Check this view of your system, and also of UML in general.)

In the alphabetical "Encyclopedia of Terms" that makes up most of the book, check *send, signal, state, state machine, statechart diagram, transition*, etc. For more advanced working, also check *submachines* and *composite states*, and both *concurrent* and *disjoint substates*.

For the earlier notations, probably the best explanation of statechart diagrams (using the earlier name, state transition diagram, or STD) in the object-oriented literature is Shlaer and Mellor's *Object Lifecycles, Modeling the World in States* (1992). They draw on the work of Moore (1956), in particular his notation.

Rumbaugh et al. (1991) give a somewhat more rigorous description in their Chapter 5. They in turn draw on the notation of David Harel (1987), and it is thus no coincidence that UML bases its statechart diagrams on the Harel notation.

Donald Firesmith (1993) has a fairly high-level description of state transition diagrams beginning on page 282. Bruce Douglass (1999a) and (1999b) has some in-depth works on states and statecharts used with UML, with special reference to embedded software.

Chapter Summary

- At any moment, an object exists in a certain state. If anything about the object changes, we say it has undergone a transition into a new state.

- Technically, the values of its attributes are its state.

- The statechart diagram is a powerful tool used to model object life cycles.

- Most objects have a pattern of states they go through. This pattern depends on the class of the object; all objects in a class have the same pattern.

- An object moves from one state to another in response to an event, either from the outside world or from another object within the system.

- Not all transitions are physically or legally possible; only the permissible ones are modeled.

- An *object life* cycle consists of the various states that it may transition through, the permissible transitions, and the sequencing of those as it progresses from creation to disposal. The life cycle includes *actions* that go with each state and transition.

- A statechart diagram is a map of all the *permissible* transitions for a class of objects, along with the events that cause them and the actions that result from them.

- All the instances in a class have the same statechart diagram. But in the execution of the statechart diagram, each instance proceeds independently through the steps of its own *state machine*.

- Often two kinds of objects have their life cycles coordinated where the instances will send events to keep each other in step.

- A state exists from one event, which caused the transition *in*, until another event causes a transition *out* of the state. Thus, a state has a *duration*.

- When an event is received by a state, there's usually only one destination (target) state allowed for that event, from that initial state, unless the transitions have *guard conditions*.

- An event triggers a transition, and then is not needed any more. An event is a message to do something and, like a paper message, can be thrown away. It has been "used up" and "vanishes as an event." The only traces will be the changes that have been made by the action; the event itself is gone.

- When it carries a command, an event must always mean the same and provide the same data to its receiving state machine.

- An event must provide enough data for all the actions that it triggers.

- All the different kinds of events that cause an object to enter a given state must carry the identical data, as a minimum. The same is true for different versions of the same event, for example, from different source states into this one.

- A *state machine* is the set of actual historical events that make up the execution of an statechart diagram by a particular specified instance.

- Every object life cycle does one of these three things: It cycles forever, or it's deleted, or it ends with the object entering an archived state where it remains quiescent.

- Since an action will become program code as a method, it must be specified very precisely. Begin with a mixture of English and pseudocode in the analysis phase. During design, actions are refined and written clearly in pseudocode.

- Actions must take care with subclasses. They must leave the hierarchy consistent; for example, when creating an instance, it must also create the subclass and superclass instances where needed. It will need parameters to know which ones to create.

- You must also model unexpected events, events at the wrong time, or events under wrong conditions. Consider what to do if an event doesn't happen or is late. Time it out?

- Does the event always mean the same? An event received by a state may be sent by a number of different happenings in the real world.

- Each new event must be added to your statechart diagram.

- *State transition tables (STTs)* can have only these entries:

- *New state.* The number of the new (destination) state which the object will enter if it receives this event while it's in this state.

- *Impossible.* There may be a number of reasons why it's not possible: physically impossible, procedural rule (the way our users need the system to operate), statutory (legal) requirement, professional association rules and practices, and combination of legal and physical constraints for example, microwave ovens are required by law to have mechanical interlocks.

- *Ignored.* Events that can happen, but the object doesn't react while in this state. In other states, it may respond, but not in this state. When an event is "ignored," it has been dealt with correctly and now ceases to exist.

- *Deferred.* Again, the object doesn't react while in this state, but this time the event is put on hold until the object enters a state where it *can* receive this event.

CHAPTER GLOSSARY

action An atomic behavior that goes with a state or a transition, and is considered a part of the life cycle. Being atomic in nature, actions cannot be interrupted.

activity An ongoing process (behavior) that continues as long as the object remains in this state, but can be interrupted by a suitable trigger event.

atomic Cannot be split any further without losing or changing the meaning of what it is.

asynchronous Where the objects that send messages do not expect any response from the receiving object, and nor do they wait around for one.

destination (target) state The state the object ends up in after the transition is done.

domain A set of permissible values.

entry action An action performed each time the object enters or re-enters a state, regardless of how it got there.

event (1) "A noteworthy happening" (*Webster*, 1975); (2) An **event** happens at a certain point in space and time.

event trigger An event that causes an object to move from one state to another.

exit action An action that an object performs whenever it transitions out of the state.

guard condition An optional Boolean expression that will prevent the transition if it evaluates to FALSE.

internal transition A transition in which the object ends up in the same state as it started from, without leaving that state, and without firing the exit or entry actions.

object life cycle Consists of the various states that an object may transition through, the set of permissible transitions, and the sequencing of those states and transitions, as it progresses from its initial creation to its eventual disposal.

self-transition A transition from one state back into the same state, which *does* fire the exit and then entry transitions of the state (which is acting as both source and target) as it leaves and then re-enters that state.

source state The state the object was in before the transition occurred.

state (1) "The particular condition that someone or something is in at a specific time." (*New Oxford*, 1998): (2) **state:** "Condition, manner or way of existence as determined by circumstances" (*Oxford*, 1979); (3) **state:** The condition of a person or thing, as with respect to circumstances or attributes. (*Random House Webster*, 1997); (4) **state:** "A mode or condition of being" (*Webster*, 1975); (5) **state:** "A condition or stage in the physical being of something" (Webster, 1975); (6)The **state** of an object is defined by the set of values currently held by its attributes; (7) At any moment in time, an object exists in a certain manner or condition, which we say is its **state**.

state machine The set of actual historical events making up the execution of a statechart diagram by a particular specified instance. This is different from the statechart diagram itself, which is actually an *abstraction* of the state machines of all the instances.

state transition The act or experience of changing from one state to another.

statechart diagram A map of all the permissible states and transitions for a class of objects, along with the events that cause them, and the actions that result from them.

synchronous (messages) Where the calling object stops what it was doing and waits for control to be returned, along with some results, before it carries on.

target (destination) state The state the object ends up in after the transition is done.

transition (1) The act or experience of moving from one state to another. (2) The condition occurring if anything at all about the object changes, putting it into a different state (Booch, 1999). (3) A relationship between two states (such) that an object in the first state will perform certain actions and enter the second state when a specified event occurs and specified (guard) conditions are satisfied. On such a change of state, the transition is said to "fire" (Booch, 1999).

WHAT COMES NEXT

Our next chapter presents an alternative. Instead of drawing statechart diagrams, Rebecca Wirfs-Brock (1990) developed a method that considers the *responsibilities* of each object, that is, what it can do for other objects. This then leads to *collaborations*, where objects cooperate to get things done, and even *contracts* between objects. You'll find all this explained in Chapter 11, as it has been included in the UML.

Then in the second half of Chapter 11 you'll find *sequence diagrams* and *collaboration diagrams*. These are widely used in UML applications, and they're an alternative way to look at how objects can interact in your model. Sequence diagrams are also known as *interaction diagrams* or *event trace diagrams*.

The three methods (statechart diagrams, sequence/collaboration diagrams, and responsibilities/collaborations) are complementary and can be used alone or together.

CLASS/GROUP EXERCISES AND PROBLEMS

Ex 10.1 For all the projects we carried forward from Exercises 5.4 to 6.4 to 7.2 to 9.1, (and will take forward to Exercise 11.1) each group develops a definition for the class and a statechart diagram for each of the following classes. [The (a) to (e) refer to the lists in Exercise 5.4 from which each class is taken]:

(a) Product

(b) Product

(c) Sale

(d) Furniture Item

(e) Listing

Present, compare, and discuss these with the rest of the class. Present all the different groups' versions of the statechart diagram for part (a), then discuss them. Then do part (b), and so on. Each group takes a turn at being the first to present.

Ex 10.2 This exercise refers to Exercise 8.2. Each group selects two important classes from their chart hanging on the wall, develops statechart diagrams for these classes, and presents to the rest of the class.

Ex 10.3 For the imaginary project your group created in Exercise 6.1 and then did further work in Exercises 7.1, 7.3, and 7.4, develop statechart diagrams for your three most significant classes. (You decide which three and justify your choice.) Present and explain these to the class and, where necessary, modify according to the feedback you get from your audience.

Ex 10.4 From The Outhouse example (Sections 8.1 and 8.2, Table 8-1, and Exercise 8.1) develop workable statechart diagrams for these classes:
- Customer
- Employee
- Product
- Sale

INDIVIDUAL EXERCISES AND PROBLEMS

Ex 10.5 This exercise refers to Exercise 8.3. From your club membership model, develop statechart diagrams for these classes:
- Club
- Member
- Trip

Ex 10.6 For the Two-Bit Pizza example in Exercises 9.2, develop statechart diagrams for the following classes:

- Customer
- Employee
- Ingredient
- Pizza Type
- Order

PROJECTS AND CASES

P 10.1   For your small-business project, which you initiated in Project 7.2 and extended in Projects 8.1 and 9.1, develop a statechart diagram for every class in your model. When you've done all of them, examine the statechart diagrams and divide the classes into two groups. One group is the classes that have interesting statechart diagrams, that is, complex and significant ones. The other group has relatively simple (*Borr-ring!*) statechart diagrams. Discard the boring statechart diagrams, and add the others to your permanent documentation.

SELF-TEST QUESTIONS

Note: The Appendix has answers to the Self-Test Questions.

Q 10.1 A State is:

(a) A condition to be satisfied before execution

(b) A condition for an existence criterion

(c) A condition or way of being or existing

(d) A condition to be set before or during a transition

(e) A condition needed for transitioning

(f) A geographical or jurisdictional area

Q 10.2 A transition is:

(a) A passage from one state to another

(b) A change in the way something is

(c) A change in the value of one or more attributes

(d) All of the above

(e) Some of the above

(f) None of the above

Q 10.3 In this chapter, an action is considered to be:

(a) A procedure that is executed each time the object enters or leaves a state

(b) An activity that must be performed during a transition to another state

(c) A process that causes a transition from one state to another

(d) A procedure the user performs whenever the object enters or reenters that state

(e) A process that moves data from one state to another

(f) (a) and (b)

(g) (b) and (c)

(h) (c) and (d)

(i) (d) and (e)

Q 10.4 In this chapter, an Event is:

(a) Something that causes a transition

(b) Caused by an important transition

(c) A noteworthy happening

(d) (a) and (b)

(e) (b) and (c)

(f) (a) and (c)

Q 10.5 An object life cycle consists of:

(g) All possible transitions

(h) All legally possible transitions

(i) All physically possible transitions

(j) All transitions that are physically or legally possible

(k) All transitions that are physically but not legally possible

(l) All transitions that are both physically and legally possible

Q 10.6 A state machine is:

(a) The execution of a particular specified instance

(b) The execution of a particular class of statechart diagram

(c) The execution of a policy by a government behemoth

(d) The execution of a particular specified statechart diagram

(e) The execution of a statechart diagram by a specified instance

(f) A particular specified execution in the class of executions

(g) The execution of a programmer for an object-oriented lifestyle

Q 10.7 Which of the following is a true statement?

(a) A transition in a state machine is an actual physical event.

(b) A state machine may be viewed as an instance of an statechart diagram.

(c) An statechart diagram is viewed as the set of state machines for a class.

(d) All of the above.

(e) Some of the above.

(f) None of the above.

Q 10.8 A state exists:

(a) From one event until another event causes a transition out

(b) For an instant; a state has no duration

(c) With several destination states for a given event when received in this state

(d) Until the next event occurs

(e) (a) and (c)

(f) (b) and (d)

Q 10.9 When an event:

(a) Is received by a state, there is always a transition

(b) Has triggered an action, the event is kept for the next state

(c) Has been handled, it's used up and vanishes

(d) Carries different data, it causes different transitions

(e) Vanishes, all that is left is the results of the action

(f) All of the above

(g) Some of the above

(h) None of the above

Q 10.10 At any _____ , an _____ exists in a certain _____ . If anything about the object _____ , we say it has undergone a _____ into a new state.

Q 10.11 Most objects have a _____ of _____ they go through. This pattern depends on the _____ of the object; all objects in a _____ have the same _____ .

Q 10.12 An object moves from one _____ to another in response to an _____ , either from the outside world or from another object within the system.

Q 10.13 Not all transitions are _____ or _____ possible; only the _____ ones are modeled.

Q 10.14 An object life cycle consists of the various _____ that it may _____ through, the _____ transitions, and the _____ of those as it progresses from _____ to _____ . The life cycle includes _____ that go with each _____ and _____ .

Q 10.15 A state _____ from one _____ , which caused the _____ in, until another _____ causes a transition _____ of the state. Thus, a state has a _____ .

Chapter Eleven
. . . .

Following the Trail: Examining Execution Sequences

WHAT YOU WILL LEARN IN THIS CHAPTER

In this chapter, you'll learn how to examine the responsibilities one class of objects has toward another and how these define collaborations between objects. You can be satisfied that you understand the material in this chapter when you can:

1. Define *responsibility, collaboration,* and *contract* as used by Wirfs-Brock et al. (1990).

2. List the responsibilities, collaborations, and contracts a class has, when it's working in client mode and/or server mode.

3. Prepare an index card (CRC card) for each class in your model.

4. Walk through a use case, using your CRC cards to follow the message calls between classes, either on the desk, or in a role-play.

5. Develop a sequence diagram from your walk-through.

6. Use this information to find further operations for classes in your model.

WHAT YOU SHOULD KNOW TO START THIS CHAPTER

This chapter assumes you understand classes, attributes, and operations. It doesn't require you to know about statechart diagrams, but you'll need to know about operations since this discussion will focus on using responsibilities to find operations. You'll also need to be familiar with use cases as we discussed them in Chapter 7.

CHAPTER OVERVIEW

Responsibility-Driven Design (RDD) is a methodology developed by Rebecca Wirfs-Brock, Brian Wilkerson, and Lauren Wiener and published in their book *Designing Object-Oriented Software* (1990). RDD works well, and has been widely adopted, so I feel this book would be incomplete without some discussion of it. RDD was originally intended to be a standalone methodology, so many analysts use it instead of use cases, statechart diagrams and sequence diagrams.

Some of the concepts from RDD (such as collaborations) have been included in UML, and you should note that Rebecca Wirfs-Brock was on the panel of experts that oversaw the design of UML. Their book presents the RDD method in a complete and practical way, and with my book as an introduction to the object-oriented field in general, I believe you'll find theirs very productive.

We'll begin by defining responsibilities in the OOA context and how collaborations between objects are often needed to fulfill them. We'll look at ways to find responsibilities and collaborations, primarily by working from the use cases we've already identified.

Then in the second half of the chapter, you'll be introduced to some more diagrams that are used to check out the interactions among the objects in your model. These are *sequence diagrams*, a.k.a. *interaction diagrams* or *event trace diagrams*. As before, you'll be shown these so that you can use each one standalone, or together with the others.

KEY CONCEPTS

- Responsibility
- Service
- Operation
- Responsibility-Driven Design
- Client, server, client-server
- Contract
- Collaboration
- CRC cards
- Even distribution of system intelligence

"THE OUTHOUSE BATHROOM BOUTIQUE" SALES REPORTING SYSTEM – EPISODE 11

"There's another method we could use for those difficult classes. It's called Responsibility-Driven Design, or RDD for short," said Nancy at the conclusion of one meeting.

At the next meeting, Nancy turned up with a huge stack of 8-by-12cm (5-by-8 inch) index cards.

"What on Earth have you got there?" asked Steve as she walked in. Nancy grinned. "It's a new game," she explained," one that I think you'll find is not only fun, in a weird kind of way, but we should all learn a whole lot from doing it.

"Okay, clear back the tables and chairs a little, and give us some space at the front here. Good. Now, Steve, as the outsider in the group, I want you to be the Customer object," and she handed him a card labeled 'Customers.' Now, Bill, you know all about being a Salesclerk," and she handed Bill a card that said 'Salesclerk.'

"Okay, Allana, you be the Sale class; Louise, you be the Product class; and Hartmut, you're the Product Type class. Now, everybody got their cards?" She was handing out cards amidst a chorus of "How did I get to be one of these?" and "What do I do with this thing?" and so on.

"Now, Steve and Bill, I want you two to role-play a customer making a purchase. I want you, Bill, to go down the steps of the use case for making a sale, as the role play progresses. If the use case is correct, it should guide you through the steps in the right order. When you need data from the computer at any step of the way, I want you to ask the appropriate class to give you that data from one of its instances. So, when you need a Unit Price, you'll have to ask Louise to give it to you, since she's the Product Type class. Okay? Got all that? Now, action!"

Steve leapt into action. "Good morning, Mr Humphries!" he said brightly. "I'd like to buy some bath towels, please."

"Yes sir, walk this way," said Bill, standing still right where he was.

"I'll take these, then," said Steve, waving an imaginary towel in front of Bill. "And since I'm a friend of Young Mr Grace, I should get a ten percent discount."

"I'll have to check what discount code Captain Peacock has put on this line," Bill responded. "Ms Product class, what discount code do you have for style seven-dash-fifteen towels, please?"

"Code three," announced Louise, stepping to the fore and looking a little bewildered by what was going on.

"Thank you," said Bill, "but I also need the Customer Preference Rating. Sir, what is your Customer Preference Rating?

At this, Nancy quickly checked the list of attributes for the Customer class and found that *Customer Preference Rating* was not there. "Sorry," she called out, "there's no such attribute! I'll add it to the Customer class. Carry on. Steve, you can answer his question now."

"Why, I'm a Class One, of course," said Steve, feigning an offended tone.

"So," Bill said briskly, "since you're a Class One and the product is a Code Three, that tells me you get a ten percent discount. Right on the button, eh?"

"Wait a minute, wait a minute," Nancy broke in. "How did you know that, Bill?"

"Well, everyone knows that," explained Bill in a tone one might use on a four-year-old. "Class One customers get five percent on Codes One and Two and ten percent on Codes Three and Four. Class Two gets five on Codes One, Two, and Three and ten on Code Four. Class Three gets five percent on all four codes, and Class Four gets no discounts."

Nancy held up her hand. "Whoa, that's complicated. Did you get it all, Deanna?" Deanna finished scribbling and nodded. Nancy went on, "Now Bill, does that ever change?"

"No, never," said Bill firmly.

"When did it last change?"

"Oh, about four years ago – Oh! I guess that's hardly 'never' is it?" Bill looked a trifle abashed.

Nancy chuckled. "That's alright Bill, I was trying to trap you. The point is, we need another class here, probably called Discounts. It will have a key of Customer Preference Rating plus Product Discount Code, and a single nonkey attribute, the Discount Percentage."

Nancy and Deanna both quickly scribbled a few notes. Then Nancy took from her notes a page she had been adding to throughout the role-play. "This is the sequence diagram," she said as she handed it to Deanna. "We'll take a look at it a little later."

THOUGHT QUESTIONS

1. In your group, make an estimate of how much more work might have been done before the missing classes and attributes were discovered, had Nancy not introduced the role play. Off the top of your head, what percentage of that work might have needed reworking when the errors were eventually discovered? How many times might this incident be repeated in a six-month project? At the salary you hope to earn upon graduation, estimate a dollar figure for the incident and a total for the six-month project. At each stage, document the process you used to arrive at your estimate.

    Each group present their numbers to the class and construct a table showing the range of the group estimates. Pay particular attention to the strategies the various groups used to come up with their estimates, especially the extreme high and low ones.

11.1 OBJECTS AND RESPONSIBILITIES

An object carries data, and it's capable of doing things. It will always be capable of updating the data it carries, and presenting that data to someone who enquires for it. It may also be capable of a number of other behaviors, such as doing calculations (typically involving some of the data it carries).

Responsibility-Driven Design (RDD) begins by taking a real-world view of the objects and classes. We say that the whole purpose of having an object with data is so that it can *do something for us*. So, in that sense, the object has a *responsibility* to us to be able to do what we need. And any operation that an object is capable of can be viewed as a *service* rather than an operation, a service provided to another object (possibly a user object.) **Wherever a service exists, we can say the object has a _responsibility_ to provide that service to those who need it.**

Now, this definition may sound a little altruistic, but objects are not especially humanitarian. It's just that we build into them only those operations for which there is a definite need. During our analysis, we'll therefore work on the assumption that if a service exists, then there's a corresponding responsibility to provide that service to someone.

(For convenience, we consider that smaller operations, such as those needed to help with larger ones, are just operations and not responsibilities. This works because they don't directly provide a service to another object. If you're ever in doubt about this one, it's your judgement call.)

Putting it the other way around, if we can find all the responsibilities an object has, then we've found all the services it needs to provide. Thus, we've found all the operations it needs to be capable of.

According to Wirfs-Brock et al.(1990),

"Responsibilities include two key items:

1. the knowledge an object maintains, and

2. the actions an object can perform."

In the first of these, the knowledge (data) makes up a group of responsibilities to any actor who needs to use that data. There will be actors who need to make changes to the data values and others who simply wish to request the values. The term *actor* here refers to any user, any other object, or any of the various kinds of actors we discussed in connection with use cases.

Second, "the actions the object can perform" are responsibilities because they're services it provides to actors who need them.

Because services are always provided by one object to another object upon request, we actually have a client–server kind of relationship. The client object requests a service from the server object, which then either performs an action, or returns some requested data, or both. Sometimes an object will be a client, asking for services from other objects, and sometimes it'll be a server, doing things for others.

A Customer object, as client, may request that an Invoice object print itself [Figure 11-1(a)]. The Invoice instance will then oblige by printing the invoice heading, using name and address data provided by the Customer object as parameters with the message. Then it needs some Line Item instances. The Invoice object doesn't know anything about Line Item data, but it knows where to get it. So it then flips into client mode and sends messages to all of its Line Item instances.

Each Line Item instance, in server mode, responds by calculating its own Extended Value (Quantity times Unit Price) and then printing itself. It then returns the Extended Value to the Invoice instance, which adds it to the Invoice Total attribute. The Invoice object then flips back to server mode to do some more on behalf of the Customer. It prints the Invoice Total, calculates and prints the Tax, and adds the Tax to print a Grand Total amount.

Now the Invoice needs to request something from yet another player in this little game. In client mode once again, it sends a message to the appropriate Receivables Account instance, with the Grand Total as a parameter, asking the Account object to update its Balance attribute. Since, in this scenario, the Customer object wasn't expecting any data to be returned, the process ends right here.

You may on occasion have a critical transaction that requires an acknowledgment of successful execution, but often a message, once sent, can be assumed successful. Of course, if it's not, then an error message must occur. This could be sent back to the client object or otherwise displayed directly to the user.

In this story, we can see numerous responsibilities cropping up:

- The Invoice has the responsibility of arranging to print itself.

- The Invoice has the responsibility of updating its Total attribute.

- The Invoice has the responsibility of calculating and printing its Tax and Grand Total.

- The Line Item has the responsibility of calculating and returning its Extended Price.

- The Line Item has the responsibility of printing itself.

- The Invoice has the responsibility of ensuring that the account balance is updated. This responsibility it then delegates to the Account.

- The Account has the responsibility of updating its Balance attribute.

In this little scenario, the Invoice has no responsibility to advise the Customer object that it has successfully printed itself. Instead, it'll have a responsibility to advise the *user* if for any reason it can't complete the task it has been assigned. In a way, there's a kind of agreement between these two objects that the task requested will in fact be done as specified. This gives rise to an interesting way of looking at the association between the two classes.

11.2 CONTRACTS

Each of these responsibilities is a service that the object can provide to some other object. The Invoice object has a responsibility to the Customer object to print itself. Of course, it may also have other responsibilities to other classes of objects that we haven't yet seen.

For the moment, we'll focus on the Invoice and its association to the Customer. If we list all the responsibilities the Invoice has to the Customer, this list may be viewed as a form of agreement between the objects, or more correctly, between the classes. The agreement is that when any Customer instance sends a message, the chosen Invoice instance will provide a service by printing itself. Wirfs-Brock et al. (1990) describe this as a *contract* between the classes, one as client and one as server.

Webster (1975) defines a ***contract*** as a **"binding agreement between two or more persons or parties."** *The New Oxford* (1999) says it is an **". . . agreement . . . that is intended to be enforceable . . ."** Wirfs-Brock et al. (1990) describe a ***contract*** as **"a list of services an instance of one class can request from an instance of another class,"** and further assert that "all the services listed in a particular contract are the responsibilities of the server *for that contract*."

(At first glance, it would appear that we can ignore the other Oxford definition, the one that says a ***contract*** is **"an arrangement for someone to be killed by a hired assassin."** Or can we? It's still an agreement for a server object that *can* provide a service to *do it* whenever requested by a client object.)

This "agreement" between the two classes is "binding" in the sense that what we're listing is all the services that the client instance would expect to be *reliably* performed when requested. Since it's our intention to build a system that does just this, *contract* turns out to be a very appropriate name for such a list of services.

For each of the responsibilities listed above, we need to ask, "Who is this responsibility *to?*" To which other object does *this* object owe this responsibility? Each service or responsibility that an object is capable of means it's a server for that task, so who is the client? Now we're gathering enough information to begin documenting the contracts, and shortly we'll see how that may be done with CRC cards.

However, the Invoice doesn't do all the work itself. It delegates some of the subtasks to objects from other classes.

11.3 COLLABORATIONS

In the preceding story, you will have noticed that the Invoice couldn't do the whole task unaided. Indeed, the Invoice found it necessary to seek help from a number of objects in several different classes. It had to ask the Line Item instances to look after their own calculations and printing, because this is something an Invoice doesn't know about or know how to do. It had to delegate the posting operation to the Account instance, because an Invoice knows nothing about accounting.

As we humans all do in our own world, the Invoice passed on those parts of the task that it couldn't handle personally to "subcontractors," specialists who know how to do those things. Any of you who have ever contracted to have a house built will be familiar with the principle of subcontracting.

Most general contractors don't do heating, electrical, plumbing, or roofing. They pass the specifications (the parameters) over to the specialist subcontractor and wait for the result. More than just housing, this kind of thing happens in practically any large-scale human enterprise. Computer consultants do it all the time.

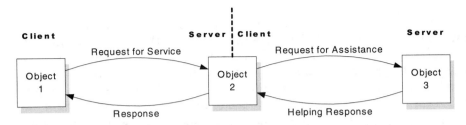

Figure 11-1   A collaboration

Very often a task or service requested by a client object needs more information than the server object has available. Or, sometimes it needs a number of supplementary tasks to be performed before, during, or after the main task. Sometimes the server can fulfill the responsibility by itself, or sometimes it needs help from other objects. These are typically objects from other classes, but they can occasionally be other instances of the same class. We say that the server *collaborates* with these other objects to get its job done.

A *collaboration* takes place when an object has a responsibility it can't handle alone. It then becomes the client for the collaborative task, and sends requests to its helpers (its subcontractors). So a **_collaboration_** **is a request from a client to a server for a service that will help the client fulfill one of its own responsibilities (Figure 11-1).**

Note the last part. The client needs help to satisfy one of its own responsibilities to someone else, so it's asking for help from the server to assist with a client responsibility. Our Invoice found it necessary to collaborate with several Line Item instances and with the Account instance, in order to satisfy the responsibility that it (the Invoice) has to the Customer object.

Here is a summary of what we know so far about responsibilities and collaborations:

- Where there's a service, there is a responsibility to provide that service to someone.

- "Responsibilities include two key items: the knowledge an object maintains, and the actions an object can perform."

- Services are provided by one object to another on request, giving a client–server relationship. The client object requests a service from the server, which performs an action or returns some data. An object may sometimes be a client, and sometimes a server.

- If we list out the responsibilities one class has to another, this list is a form of an agreement between the classes.

- A **_contract_** is "a list of services an instance of one class can request from an instance of another class."

- Sometimes a server needs help from other objects. We say the server *collaborates* with these other objects to do its job. A **_collaboration_** exists when a class has a responsibility that it can't handle alone.

- A **_collaboration_** is a request from a client to a server for a service that helps the client fulfill a responsibility. The client needs help to satisfy one of its own responsibilities, so it seeks help from the server for this "client responsibility."

Now that the example has demonstrated how responsibilities and collaborations work, we need to look at how to find and identify them. But first, let's try a simple and effective way of documenting our discoveries.

11.4 CRC Cards

Rebecca Wirfs-Brock and friends have found a very neat way of recording the responsibilities as we find them. They call them *CRC cards*, for Class-Responsibility-Collaboration cards. These cards are not part of UML, but, like the state transition tables, they're a very valuable tool for checking the completeness of your UML models. They were developed by Beck and Cunningham and presented at the 1989 OOPSLA conference, and have been widely adopted by developers and methodologists.

In Figure 11-2 you'll see the layout of a 10-by-15 cm (4-by-6 inch) or 8-by-12 cm (3-by-5 inch) index card. Many use the "landscape" orientation (short and fat), though I prefer "portrait" (tall and thin), since this gives us more lines to work with. On it we write the name of the class in the top left corner. (As an extension to the method, I also like to add the unique identifier, or key attribute, at the top right.)

If you don't have the right sized cards, any size will do in a pinch, or even sheets of notepaper. Or you can draw up the form in a word processor or spreadsheet, and print them as you need them.

On the back of the card, you can write the class description or definition, although if you've already documented this earlier you may prefer not to duplicate. On the front again, below the name, we have a wide column on the left, where we write each responsibility. On the right we have a narrower one, which is for the name(s) of the class(es) with whom we must collaborate in order to fulfill that particular responsibility.

These cards have become very popular, despite Wirfs-Brock's admonition to the effect that they're just one more way of doing things. She insists that if you and your users are more comfortable using some other medium, such as sheets of writing paper or even a CASE tool, then you should go ahead. Despite these comments, the cards have been found highly useful by many analysts.

It's easy and convenient to spread these cards out on a table or desk, rearrange them, change them, and even throw some out. You can quickly trace a chain of responsibilities from card to card, to see if any links in the chain are missing. The cards are particularly good for checking that each responsibility has been assigned to the correct class.

Wirfs-Brock et al. (1990) also propose a very effective rule of thumb based on the size of the

Class:	Identifier:
Book	Book No.

Responsibilities	Collaborations
Know: Book No.	
Know: Title	
Know Author	
Know Date Published	
Know: Date Purchased	
Know: Purchase Price	
Know:Book (Depreciated) Value	
Know: Date Signed Out	
Know: Date Checked In	
Know: Date Shelved	
Sign Itself Out	Subscriber
	Loan
Check Itself In	Loan
Shelve Itself	

Figure 11-2 (a) CRC card for a Library Book *(continued)*

cards. A 10-by-15cm (4-by-6 inch) card in portrait orientation allows just enough room to write in a "reasonable" number of responsibilities. If you fill it up and need much more, they suggest that the class may be too heavily loaded with responsibilities. You should probably check to see whether some of these responsibilities should be reassigned to other classes.

Should we call these CRC cards an Object-Oriented Cardboard CASE Tool (OOCCT)? What I've found works well is to use CRC cards along with sequence diagrams (see later this chapter), statechart diagrams and class diagrams while looking for all the services/operations/responsibilities. Then you can transfer the "final" list to a CASE tool. (I put "final" in quotes because we're bound to iterate through here again!) So now that we have the documentation tool available, let's see how to go about finding responsibilities and collaborations.

11.5 IDENTIFYING RESPONSIBILITIES

There are a number of places to look when searching for responsibilities. The first place to look is at the data within the object.

Reporting and Updating Attribute Values

Here you need to examine the attributes of each class. You need to see which attributes, and clusters of attributes, will be updated by the various business events that can happen to this class. Also, you must check for attributes and clusters that will have their values requested by other classes.

At the primitive level, each class has at least an Update and a Provide responsibility for each attribute. At a more practical level, these will tend to occur in clusters. Depending on the number of attributes in the class, you may want to write only the larger or more significant responsibilities from here on the front of the card. You can then list on the back of the card all the single-attribute Update or Provide responsibilities.

Remember to check for CRUD – *Create, Read, Update,* and *Delete*. There must be some way for all four of these things to happen to the objects in each class. Then you must also check that your design includes some way to *Read, Update,* and possibly *Clear* each attribute.

Use Cases

Wirfs-Brock et al. (1990) propose a walk-through of the system as a whole, as a means for finding responsibilities. But we're two steps ahead already! We have our use cases, so we can now follow each one through, as the actor involved makes a transaction with the system. At each step, we'll identify which classes of objects are being queried, updated, or otherwise used or affected. Each responsibility you identify is then written on the front of the card for that class.

Input/Output

Every time data is transferred into or out of the system, you know already that it will need Update or Provide responsibilities as a minimum. In addition, input operations will involve Validate responsibilities and the like. The object that receives the input data will have a responsibility to validate the data before accepting it. The object will also have a responsibility to report errors and exceptions back to the actor in a suitable format and to allow corrections where appropriate.

Class:	Identifier:
Invoice	Invoice no.

Responsibilities	Collaborations
Know: Invoice no.	
Know: Customer no.	
Print Invoice Line Item	
Calculate invoice Total	Line Item

(b) Invoice

Class:	Identifier:
Line Item	Invoice no. + Line no.

Responsibilities	Collaborations
Know: Invoice no.	
Know: Line No.	
Know: Product Code	
Know: Quantity Sold	
Know: Unit of Measure	
Know: Actual Unit price	
Calculate Extended Price	
Print line Item	Product
	Tax Rate

(c) Line Item

Figure 11-2   (continued)

(d) Receivables Account

Class:	Identifier:
Receivables Account	~~Account no.~~
Responsibilities	**Collaborations**
Know: Account no.	
Know: Customer No.	
Know: Description	
Know: Balance	
Know: Balance 30 Days	
Know: Balance 60 Days	
Know: Balance 90 Days	
Print Satement	Receivables Transaction
Add Transaction to Balance	Receivables Transaction

Class:	Identifier:
Receivables Transaction	Transaction No.
Responsibilities	**Collaborations**
Know: Account No.	
Know: Transaction No.	
Know: Date	
Know: Cash Amount	
Post to Account	
Print Statement Line	

(e) Receivables Transaction

Figure 11-2   (continued)

For output, various objects will have responsibilities to provide and to format the data, along with responsibilities for calculations, preparing graphics, and so on.

User Interactions

These are largely covered by the use cases referred to above. However, at this stage it's often helpful to bring in some additional users and turn them loose on the existing use cases. Let them walk through parts of the system, and particularly watch for what-ifs that may not have been noticed earlier.

Prompts and Error Messages

If you're aware in advance of some of the prompts and error messages that will be present in the new system, this will help. These may come from an existing system or from some 'what-ifs' and other awarenesses that may occur to you as you work through the earlier stages of the analysis. Each prompt represents input, so some class has the responsibility of receiving, and if necessary validating, that input. So the question is, To which other class does it owe this responsibility?

On the other hand, an error message represents a responsibility to report and therefore to test for some error condition. Also, in considering where the message came from, you may become aware of a process or a responsibility that you might have missed earlier.

Instance Creation and Deletion

Every class has a responsibility to create instances of itself and to delete them (or archive them, or whatever). There may be several different ways that each of these can be performed. Some instances may need to be archived, while others are deleted directly. Yet others may go into some kind of a "suspense" status awaiting deletion or archiving.

By checking when this happens and what external business event(s) give rise to it, you can determine which other classes this responsibility is owed to. That is, which other class will request the *Create, Delete,* or *Archive* service. This way you'll find all the conditions and variations on the creation and deletion responsibilities.

Once you've discovered all (or at least most) of the responsibilities, the next step is to check that they're in the right place.

11.6 ASSIGNING RESPONSIBILITIES

For many responsibilities, it will be obvious which class they belong with. Others will take a little more thought, and a few will end up being judgment calls.

Obviously, the Provide and Update responsibilities belong with the class where the attribute is. So will almost every responsibility that requires any access to or manipulation of the attribute value. Since your object class diagram should be "normalized" already (if you've read Chapter 9, that is), keeping together the data and its manipulation gives a greater level of encapsulation.

All the data that describes one kind of thing goes together in that class, and all the program code to work with it ends up there too. You will recall from Chapter 9 that we called this the *fundamental principle,* or the *essence,* of normalization. Over a large number of classes, the effect is to make the system very much easier to maintain.

Two Principles

There are a couple of principles discussed by Wirfs-Brock et al. (1990) that I find are important whether or not you use Responsibility-Driven Design. The first principle is to be as general as we can in the way we *word* the responsibilities. If we're too specific, too tight, we may sometimes overlook a chance to benefit from inheritance.

The second principle is the even distribution of the power, or "intelligence," of the system. We can consider a class of objects to be "powerful" in terms of how much work it can get done. Roughly speaking, the measure of this power is in the number (and complexity) of the responsibilities this class bears. Very roughly, this gives us a measure of how much this kind of object can do.

You'll find that many classes will have only a few attributes and responsibilities, and so these classes cannot be considered especially powerful or intelligent. On the other hand, you're bound to find a few who are swamped with far too many attributes and responsibilities, and therefore too much power and smarts for their own good. Sharing out this power at an exactly even level is impossible, but here are some reasons why we should at least work in that direction a little:

- If each class had only a little bit of power, then we would need far too many classes to model the whole system. Each extra class means additional overhead in all phases of the project, and in particular adds Create and Delete responsibilities that must be considered, documented, designed, and eventually coded and maintained. Such a fragmented system is very difficult to follow through and understand, let alone trying to find and correct errors.

- Where a few large and powerful classes have unduly large shares of the attributes and intelligence, we reduce the reusability of these classes. The bigger the unit, the more awkward and less portable it becomes. Some applications that will later need to reuse your classes may only be concerned with a few of the attributes and responsibilities, but they'll be forced to take the whole thing. So much of the detail in the documentation will be irrelevant *for that project*, and its presence will be confusing and counterproductive.

In striking a happy medium between these two extremes, the rule of thumb about filling up a class card can be very useful. Once you run out of space on the card for responsibilities, you should consider carefully whether:

- Some of these responsibilities should perhaps be reassigned to other classes.

- Perhaps the class is way too big, and it needs to be split into two or more classes. This might be done either by subclassing, or by extracting out a group of attributes and responsibilities and ending up with a new class, connected by an association. One of the objectives, of course, must be to produce something that we think will have a better chance of being reused in the future.

At the same time that you're discovering and assigning responsibilities, you'll also be watching out for the ones that a class can't fulfill without some help. These will require *collaborations*.

11.7 IDENTIFYING COLLABORATIONS

Although I've placed this section at the end, the process of finding responsibilities and collaborations is actually very highly iterative. You can expect to find, discuss, trace, and document many of the collaborations involved while you're busy in the previous two steps. At the end, however, you'll need to devote some time to searching specifically for collaborations, and you may expect that this will keep plunging you right back into finding, assigning, and reassigning responsibilities.

Finding Collaborations

In this stage, we must go through the entire model, class by class, asking a series of questions. For each responsibility we have, in every class, we must ask:

- Does the class have everything it needs to do this? Does it have all the data attributes? Are there any subtasks and, if so, have they been looked after?

- If not, then what is missing? What data is it missing? What additional tasks are needed before, during, or after the main task?

- What class(es) are there in the model that can supply these? Are there any classes that can do this? If so, we record the collaborations right now. We may find that one subcontractor needs to collaborate with another subcontractor, who needs to contract with some others, and so on.

Any such chain of control that we might find should be followed as far as it goes. If some of the things we need are not available from any class at all, then there are three possibilities:

- ° We can add an attribute and/or a responsibility to one of our existing classes.

- ° We may need to define a new class at this point.

- ° In some cases, we may need to browse the class libraries we have available, be they in-house from previous projects, or purchased.
    Whichever of these three we may choose, and particularly for the second one, we must not forget to iterate as far back as necessary to check for additional associations and responsibilities.

- Once we've answered these questions, we need to take the other point of view and ask about collaborations in the other direction:

  - ° What significant data does this class carry? What are the important functions(operations) that this class is capable of?

  - ° Who needs it? Which other classes have need of these data attributes?

  - ° Which classes have need of the services this class can provide?

The answers to these questions will show you the responsibilities this class bears and to which other classes it bears them.

Record the collaborations on your CRC cards as you become aware of them. Whenever you find a responsibility that needs a collaboration with another class, and then with another, and so on, *follow this trail while it's still warm*. It's important to follow these things to completion when you become aware of them, because if you leave it and come back later you're bound to overlook something.

As you record each collaboration on a client class card, check the server class card as well and make sure the server class knows about this responsibility. You and I are not the only objects around who resent being assigned a responsibility without being told about it!

Then lastly, it's time to go back to the use cases for the final check, but this time I'm advocating a slightly different approach.

Role-Play Use Cases

Again, role-play is something that can be done with or without RDD, but I've found that it does fit very well into this pattern, particularly with the use of CRC cards. Actually, it can fit in with any methodology. If you don't have your model on CRC cards, or perhaps not all of it, you may be able to print your classes on separate sheets from whatever software tool you're using, and these would work just fine for the role-play walk-through.

In your FTS/JAD session, you'll work through each use case in turn this way. Each time, the people hold one or more CRC cards in their hands, or the cards will be lined up on a table in front of them. (Often there are more classes than players, so each person plays several roles.)

One person, who plays the User, starts by reading aloud the steps in the use case. At each step this person asks the appropriate class (i.e., the person who is playing that class and holding that card) for the necessary services and/or data. That person in turn checks their collaborations listed on the card for that responsibility and requests any needed data or services from the next class (i.e., *player*). And so on it goes, with everybody requesting services, passing parameters (in those cases where they have been identified already), and returning results.

The benefit from all this is that, as you follow the chains of interaction among the classes, you'll very often find missing responsibilities, collaborations, and even data attributes. You'll find some responsibilities that just don't fit where you assigned them, and you'll have to move them to a different class. You're also very likely to turn up some missing classes, and have to add them right then to your model.

Document all this on your CRC cards and keep a list of the new responsibilities, collaborations, and classes, since for all the new classes you must iterate back to consider class definitions, associations, attributes, and responsibilities. In fact, for every new class you find, you need to go right back to the Seven Steps in Chapter 9.

11.8 SEQUENCE DIAGRAMS

Once you've understood the pattern of calls among your classes, you'll need a diagram to document them with. So now it's time to look at that extra diagram that Nancy gave to Deanna at the end of the role-play.

Your CRC cards and the role-plays you build around them are an excellent way to discover responsibilities and interactions. The cards are also great for documenting these things, *from the point of view of one class at a time.* This is extremely important for designing and building the classes, where you need complete details of each class, one at a time, as you're coding.

To get a handle on the overall pattern of these interactions, you need a *sequence diagram* showing what messages go where, and which ones cause things to happen, and in what order. This allows you to follow the progress of a business transaction, as it causes a series of things to happen in your software.

So, for discovering what services must exist, and assigning them to the various classes, we need this overview of a group of classes working together to get the task done. This is what Booch and friends variously call "a society of objects," or sometimes, "a collaboration." After doing this many times over for each business event, we end up with a complete picture of all the classes, and of all the services each class must have. At that point, we're ready to switch to a one-class-at-a-time viewpoint, to design and build the classes.

One of the best times to use a sequence diagram is during a role-play, as Nancy did. This is by no means the only time to use them, but it is one of the most productive. As the people discover the messages and responses, you document them on both the CRC cards and the sequence diagram.

As the crew is role-playing the use case, either the leader or the recording analyst should be building this diagram. For this, you should have the CRC cards in the people's hands, or on the desk. The sequence diagram works best on the board, where everyone can see you update it, and they can watch it grow as they progress through the use case.

Sequence Diagram for Outhouse Episode 11

In Figure 11-3(a) you'll see the sequence diagram that describes Steve's attempt to buy some towels from Bill. In Figure 11-3(b) is a piece from The Outhouse class diagram, showing the classes involved and their associations. In both diagrams, the Discounts class is shown on a grey background, to highlight the fact that it was not discovered until we went through this little exercise.

Along the top (X-axis) of Figure 11-3(a) are rectangular boxes labeled for the classes involved. You may have noticed that the box for the Sale class is lower down than the others – I'll explain that in a moment.

Stretching down from each box is a **vertical dashed line that we refer to as the *lifeline* for the class.** Distance down this line (Y-axis) more or less represents time. This is not a linear thing, however. The distance down the line does *not* show how *much* time. What matters here is the *sequence* that things happen, in order, down each lifeline. In mathematical terms, the time axis is said to be ordinal rather than interval.

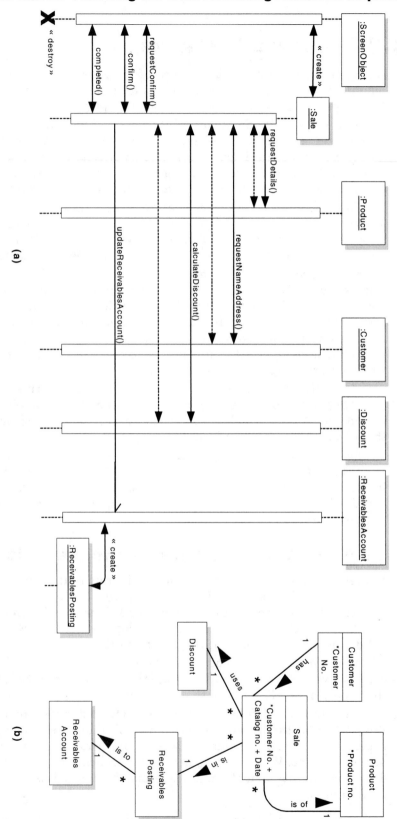

Figure 11-3 (a) Sequence diagram for The Outhouse Episode 11, (b) a section of the corresponding class diagram

On each lifeline you'll see a long skinny box. These are called the *focus of control*, or sometimes *activation lines*, and they show for what part of its lifeline the object is busy doing things. Where you see just the dashed line without the focus of control box, it means that at that point in time the object existed, but it was not involved in doing anything.

The box at the far left is labeled ":ScreenObject," to show that some object on the screen accepts data keyed in by an operator (probably the sales clerk), and then starts the whole process rolling. This object will most likely be a Window or Dialog Box object, or some such, defined in your OOGUI when you design your screens. Or it may be an instance of class SalesClerk.

Either way, this is the object that drives everything else in response to messages from outside the system. For now, we just need to know that there will be some object that does this. We'll refer to it as some kind of screen object, and later we'll figure out exactly what it is, but probably not until the design phase.

It begins by sending a message (an event) to the Sale class to create a new Sale instance, to record the sale. (I use lower case this time for *sale* because this one is the business transaction, outside the software system. The *Sale* instance exists to record the *sale* transaction.) This is why you see the Create line going to the Sale box itself, and not to the lifeline like every other arrow on the page. And this is why the Sale box is lower down the y-axis – the time axis – to show that the Sale object is not created until after we get started.

All the data keyed in by the operator (sales clerk, lower-case because we mean the physical person, not the instance in the database) will be carried as parameters by the create message. This will include the Product Code, so that the Sale is able to send a message (next arrow down) to the correct Product instance, requesting the attribute values for Discount Code and Description. The arrow back from Product to Sale is the response, carrying the requested values, and is lower on the lifeline because, obviously, the response comes *after* the request.

You'll note that the create arrow is shown as a UML stereotype, «create». The stereotypes «create» and «destroy» are more or less standard ones that you should always show this way, next to the message arrows on your sequence diagrams.

Next on the diagram, we see that the Sale uses the Customer Number (also sent as a parameter from the "ScreenObject") to interrogate the Customer instance to get the Name and Address values, the Customer Preference Code, and probably a few other things as well.

The Customer instance responds with this data, and then the Sale is able to use the Customer Preference Code and the Product Discount Code to ask the Discount instance for the appropriate percentage.

Now the Sale is able to do all the calculations, and send the results as a response to the "ScreenObject." This time through, we're considering only the basic use case, so we won't worry about error corrections and such. Instead, we'll assume for now that the sales clerk (lower case) clicks on "OK," and that causes the "ScreenObject" to send a Confirm message.

When the Sale receives this, it *sends* an (asynchronous) *signal* to the ReceivablesAccount instance, telling it to update itself. To do this, it will need to collaborate with the ReceivablesPosting class (i.e., the line items for ReceivablesAccount) and request it to create an instance. (You'll notice that we just followed a chain of collaborations to its end, while it was "still warm" in our minds.)

Since the signal to the Receivables Account is asynchronous (as all *signals* are), it has a "one-sided arrowhead," and there is no response shown. And because for this time through we're assuming that the data (parameters) carried by the signal are all okay, the Receivables Account is expected to take care of business, deal with any errors or exceptions, and not to bother the Sale or "ScreenObject" ever again. *Just Do It*, as they say.

So on our first pass through this process we follow the basic use case, and assume that all is okay, and no errors will occur that the Receivables Account can't handle. Later, when we have a clear picture of the basic process and all that it entails, then we'll go through it all again, this time asking all the awkward and revealing "*What if?*" questions.

So finally, the Sale is able to print a receipt, and then does any other clean-up processing that might be needed. Then it sends a Completed response to the "ScreenObject," which promptly commits suicide. The big X and the «destroy» stereotype at the bottom of the lifeline for the "ScreenObject" shows that its lifeline ends right here.

In other words, the object has been destroyed, or, to put it another way, the instance has been erased. What the operator (sales clerk) will see is that the window closes and disappears.

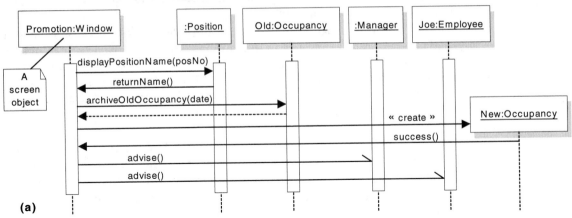

(a)

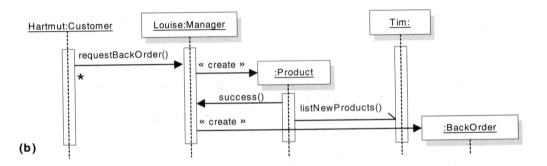

(b)

Figure 11-4 Sequence diagrams for (a) promoting an employee from one position to another within the company, and (b) creating a back order for a product that we do not currently stock.

Rules for Sequence Diagrams

Now let's take a more complete look at how to build these things.

NAMING THE OBJECTS

In Figure 11-4 you'll see that there are several ways to write the object names, here as well as in other UML diagrams. Most times you would use the class name, but sometimes you may find it helps to clarify things if you use the name of an instance.

This is especially useful with the group of users, as you follow a "for instance." What that really means is that you're following a scenario through its use case. Remember that a scenario is really an instance of a use case, where we take real or hypothetical people and things and follow them through the steps of the use case.

By convention, these names are underlined. A colon is used to show the division between the instance name and the class name. This way, the colon appears *after* an instance name used alone, or *before* a class name used alone.

Here are the syntax options for this:

- **Class name only** <u>:ClassName</u>

  You'll see in Figure 11-3(a) that we have <u>:Customer</u>, <u>:Sale</u>, <u>:Product</u>, <u>:Discounts</u>, and <u>:ReceivablesAccount</u>. This style is the best for your permanent documentation.

- **Instance name only** <u>objectName:</u>

  This could be <u>Mary:</u> (who is both an instance of Customer and an instance of Employee) or <u>Joe:</u> (a Customer only; see Figure 7-9.) It could also be <u>MyBathTowel:</u> or <u>YourSink:</u> (instances of Product.)

- **Instance name and class name together** <u>object:Class</u>

  This is the style I prefer when doing instance examples with my users. It has the advantage that it reminds you at each step which instance it is, and which class it belongs to. Try <u>Mary:Customer</u>, <u>MyBathTowel:Product</u>, <u>Joe:Customer</u>, <u>YourSink:Product</u>. Or even something like <u>51796:Sale</u>, which uses an attribute value from the Order Number, which is the identifier attribute (key) for the Sale class.

THE ORIGINATING OBJECT

The object that starts and controls the whole process should be shown at the far left. There are several ways to show it, depending on how you happen to be thinking about this particular one.

- A class or instance, just like all the other boxes along the top of the diagram. In this case, only its position at the far left signifies that it's The One. Do it this way if you're thinking in terms of a screen object (:Window or :SaleDialogBox) or perhaps a database object that drives the process (:Customer or :Sale).

- If you're thinking of something outside the software system that does all this, then show it without the box around the name as in Figure 11-4(b). Otherwise the rules are the same – Hartmut:Manager, Bill:SalesClerk, Allana:Customer, or just :Employee, :Customer, or Louise:

Even if this object or class exists within your system, as long as you think of it as being outside it for this use case, you can show it this way. The key thing is that *the box is missing at the top.*

THE MESSAGES

Each arrow must be labeled with the name of the event, plus the parameters, or at least, whatever we know about its parameters so far. If you already know the details, show the parameters fully in the usual UML notation – eventName(paramType:paramName(defaultValue), . . .) – otherwise, just show it as eventName(params).

Use solid arrowheads for regular (synchronous) calls. This will make them stand out clearly from the asynchronous signals, which have half-arrowheads, like the lowest arrow in Figure 11-4. Rumbaugh (1999) prefers open arrowheads, but this time I side with Booch (1999).

The topmost arrow in Figure 11-4 is shown to be a «create» message, to cause an object to be created. Near the bottom you'll also see a «destroy» message going to the same object. By convention, these are always given UML stereotype names, enclosed in chevrons. You can use double less-than and greater-than symbols, like <<create>> and <<destroy>>, if you happen to be among those whom James Rumbaugh describes as being "typographically challenged." Or you can use true chevrons, which are ASCII codes Alt-174 and Alt-175 respectively.

On a PC, hold down the Alt key with your left hand, and with your right hand use the numeric keypad at the extreme right-hand end of the keyboard. Don't use the typewriter numbers along the top, you must use the numeric keypad at the right. Hold down Alt, and with your right hand type 174, to get a left chevron " « ". Hold down Alt and type 175 for a right chevron " » ". Now you can have «create» and «destroy», which will look somewhat neater on your diagrams and in your documentation.

On the arrow from Hartmut to Louise you will see a star (asterisk, or " * "), which tells us that this event is to be iterated. If you know how many times over it will be iterated, then you should show that on the diagram, along with any other loop-control information that you have available. If you don't know the details yet, just show as much as you can. Use the UML constraint notation fo this, enclosing the iteration conditions in curly braces. That's "{ " for the left, and "} " for the right.

Finally, note that it is possible for a message to go from one lifeline right back into the same lifeline. An instance might send a message to itself, perhaps to invoke one of its own methods. Or it may send the message to another instance of the same class.

This is by no means all there is to sequence diagrams, but it's enough for you to read one that someone else has produced, or to build some yourself as part of your deliverables.

. . . .

Deliverables

The major deliverable for the first part of this chapter is a huge stack of CRC cards. But obviously, while the cards are a great tool for analysis, they're not suitable for the final documentation. You'll need to copy the information from the cards into your documentation, or better still, into your CASE tool.

Either way, however, don't throw the cards away! They are serious source documents, that must be filed for use in resolving conflicts, checking for entry errors and analysis errors, and for use when new responsibilities or classes are discovered later in the development life cycle.

Further Reading

Obviously, Rebecca Wirfs-Brock et al. (1990). As I mentioned at the beginning of the chapter, this book is very practical and gives a complete and usable methodology. The book is useful both as further background in a more general study of object-oriented analysis, or as a guide to development based primarily on RDD. However, it was written before UML came along, so the names and diagrams are not the same as we're now used to.

The Three Amigos don't have very much to say about CRC cards at all, except that Grady (Booch et al., 1999) mentions them a number of times as an alternative or supplement to use cases. However, the Amigos' UML books do have sections on *collaborations*, and what they discuss is really an advanced extension to what I have described of the work of Wirfs-Brock et al.

Chapter Summary

- If a service exists, then that implies a responsibility to provide that service to someone.
- "Responsibilities include two key items: the knowledge an object maintains, and the actions an object can perform."
- Services are provided by one object to another in a *client–server* relationship. Sometimes an object is a client, sometimes a server.
- A *contract* is "a *list of services* that an instance of one class can request from an instance of another class."
- A *collaboration* is a request from a client to a server for a service that helps the *client* fulfill one of its *own* responsibilities.
- CRC cards are a simple and effective way to document OOA models.
- A 10-by-15 cm (4-by-6 inch) card in portrait orientation allows room to write a "reasonable" number of responsibilities. If you fill it up, consider moving some to other classes.
- There are a number of places to look when searching for responsibilities:
  - A class has at least an Update and a Provide responsibility for each attribute or cluster of attributes.
  - Follow each use case through, as the actor transacts with the system. At each step, identify which classes are being queried or updated.

- An object that receives input data has a responsibility to validate the data, to report errors to the actor, and to allow corrections.
- For output, objects have responsibilities to provide and format the data, calculate, prepare graphics, and so on.
- Each prompt represents input, so some class has the responsibility of receiving and validating it.
- An error message is a responsibility to test for and report some error condition.
- Every class has Create and Delete/Archive responsibilities.

- For many responsibilities, it will be obvious which class they belong in.
- Since your object class diagram is normalized already, keeping the data and its manipulation together gives a greater level of encapsulation.
- It's important to distribute the system intelligence more or less evenly.
- Many classes will have few attributes and responsibilities. Some will have too many and thus too much power and intelligence.
- If every class had a little power, we would need too many to model the system. Each class means extra overhead in all phases of the project.
- Where a few powerful classes have large shares of the attributes and intelligence, they're less reusable. Bigger means less portable.
- Some of these responsibilities could be reassigned to other classes.
- Sometimes a class needs to be split into two or more classes. The objective is to produce more reusable classes.
- To find collaborations we must ask the following:
  - Does the class have what it needs to do this? Does it have the attributes? Are there any subtasks and, if so, have they been looked after?
  - If not, then what is missing?
  - What class(es) are there in the model that can supply these?
  - What significant data does this class carry?
  - What are the important functions (operations) that this class is capable of?
  - Who needs it? Which other classes need these attributes? Which have need of the services this class can provide?
- The answers to these questions will show you the responsibilities this class bears, and also to which other classes it bears them. There are three ways to handle these answers:
  - Add an attribute and/or a responsibility to an existing class.
  - Define a new class.
  - Browse class libraries.
- Any "chain of control" should be followed to its end, while it's still warm.
- After creating or modifying classes, iterate as necessary to check for additional associations and responsibilities.
- Role-play the use cases, using your CRC cards.

CHAPTER GLOSSARY

collaboration   A request from a client to a server for a service that will help the client fulfill one of its responsibilities.

contract (1) A "binding agreement between two or more persons or parties" (*Webster*, 1975). (2) ***contract:*** "An agreement . . . that is intended to be enforceable . . ." (*New Oxford*, 1999). (3) ***contract:*** "A list of services an instance of one class can request from an instance of another class," (Wirfs-Brock et al., 1990). (4) ***contract:*** "An arrangement for someone to be killed by a hired assassin" (*New Oxford*, 1999).

lifeline A vertical dashed line on a sequence diagram, extending downward from a class box.

responsibility   Providing a certain service to those who need it.

stereotype The notation to use when you add your own local extensions to the UML notation. It consists of a name or note enclosed in guillemots, a.k.a. chevrons, like this: <<create>>.

WHAT COMES NEXT

These last few chapters have focused on the particular techniques for object-oriented analysis, so now we come to one that looks at problems of managing these methods in the process of building a large model. What I'm talking about is the idea of *subsystems*, ways to break the project into manageable chunks. Chapter 12 will discuss subsystems, in UML called *packages*, which are a "vertical" division of a project, and also *layers*, which are a "horizontal" division. Both are aimed at reducing the complexity of a large system, to make it more manageable.

CLASS/GROUP EXERCISES AND PROBLEMS

Ex 11.1 Refer to Exercise 10.1. For each class where you drew a statechart diagram, have your group list out all the responsibilities they can think of for that class. Prepare a class card (CRC card) for each class on a 10-by-15 cm index card. (4-by-6 inch or thereabouts; use sheets of paper if you have no cards.) Present your results. Here are the classes listed out again [parts (a) to (e) refer back to Exercises 5.4 and 10.1]:

(a) Product

(b) Product

(c) Sale

(d) Furniture Item

(e) Listing

Ex 11.2 Now take your responsibility lists from Exercise 11.1, and for each responsibility list out all the collaborations (if any) that you think it might need with other classes. Add these to the CRC cards.

Choose one of these responsibilities (or some other task that the system must perform) and develop a use case for it. Follow this use case through the CRC cards to find collaborations, and add your new discoveries to the cards. Then draw a sequence diagram for it. Present your results.

Ex 11.3　Repeat the steps from Exercises 11.1 and 11.2 to find responsibilities and collaborations for the imaginary project your group created in Exercise 6.1, and used in Exercise 10.3. Complete by documenting your work on CRC cards, and one or more sequence diagrams.

Ex 11.4　Repeat the steps from Exercises 11.1 and 11.2 to find responsibilities and collaborations for The Outhouse example from Exercises 8.1 and 10.4. Then draw one or more sequence diagrams. Here are the classes listed out again:

- (a)　Customer
- (b)　Employee
- (c)　Product
- (d)　Sale

INDIVIDUAL EXERCISES AND PROBLEMS

Ex 11.5　Repeat the steps from Exercises 11.1 and 11.2 to find responsibilities and collaborations, and produce CRC cards and one or more sequence diagrams, for the two classes you selected from your OOTHunt chart in Exercise 10.2. Compare your results with the other members of your group.

Ex 11.6　Repeat the steps from Exercises 11.1 and 11.2 to find responsibilities and collaborations, and produce CRC cards and one or more sequence diagrams, for your Club Membership model from Exercises 8.3 and 10.5.

Ex 11.7　Repeat the steps from Exercises 11.1 and 11.2 to find responsibilities and collaborations, and produce CRC cards and one or more sequence diagrams, for your Two-Bit Pizza model from Exercises 9.2, 9.3, and 10.6.

PROJECTS AND CASES

P 11.1　For your small-business project from Projects 7.2 and 8.1, develop a responsibility list for one of your main classes and check for collaborations. Prepare CRC cards for all classes, but of course they won't be complete. Choose one of the use cases and follow the processing through, either by role-playing or sitting around a table. Choose a different use case and follow its processing with a sequence diagram. Then, for the first use case, draw an sequence diagram from the CRC cards.

SELF-TEST QUESTIONS

Note:　The Appendix has answers to the Self-Test Questions.

Q 11.1　We say that:

(a) Where there is a service, there's a responsibility to do it.

(b) Responsibilities can include both knowledge and action.

(c) A responsibility always implies a client–server relationship.

(d) Any object can be a client or a server.

(e) A collaboration helps fulfill a responsibility of the client.

(f) All of the above.

(g) None of the above.

Q 11.2 A contract is:

(a) A list of services one class can request from another.

(b) A document detailing the responsibilities of a class.

(c) A list of all the services a class can perform.

(d) A document detailing the responsibilities of the users.

(e) A list of all the responsibilities of a class.

(f) All of the above.

(g) None of the above.

Q 11.3 The most important thing about a class card (CRC card) is that it be:

(a) Measured in centimeters.

(b) Used in portrait orientation to enhance its capacity.

(c) Carefully filed.

(d) An OOCCT.

(e) Used to record responsibilities and collaborations.

(f) 10-by-15 cm (4-by-6 inch).

Q 11.4 Which of the following is not recommended by Wirfs-Brock et al. (1990)?

(a) Being general in the wording of responsibilities

(b) Evenly distributing the intelligence of the system

(c) Having many classes with only a little bit of power

(d) Using a few classes that are very powerful

(e) (a) and (b)

(f) (c) and (d)

Q 11.5 A collaboration is needed when:

(a) A class doesn't have all the data it needs for an operation.

(b) A class needs to pass data back to the calling class.

(c) An operation needs something done that is in another class.

(d) An operation has parameters.

(e) (a) and (c).

(f) (a) and (d)

Q 11.6 The purpose of the role play is:

(a) To have fun.

(b) To discover missing users.

(c) To discover relationships among users.

(d) To discover associations among instances.

(e) To discover missing classes, instances, and associations.

(f) To discover missing classes, associations, attributes, and operations.

Q 11.7 If a _____ exists, then that implies a _____ to provide that _____ to _____ .

Q 11.8 _____ are provided by one _____ to another in a _____– _____ relationship.

Q 11.9 A _____ is "a list of _____ that an _____ of one _____ can _____ from an _____ of another _____ ."

Q 11.10 A _____ is a request from a _____ to a _____ for a _____ that helps the _____ fulfill one of its own _____ .

Q 11.11 Follow each _____ _____ through, as the _____ transacts with the _____ . At each step, identify which _____ are being _____ or _____ .

Q 11.12 An object that receives _____ _____ has a responsibility to _____ the _____ , to report _____ to the _____ , and to allow _____ .

Q 11.13 Each _____ represents input, so some _____ has the responsibility of _____ and _____ it.

Q 11.14 Many classes will have few _____ and _____ . Some will have too many and thus too much _____ and _____ .

Q 11.15 Where a few powerful _____ have large shares of the _____ and _____ , they're less _____ . _____ means less _____ .

Chapter Twelve
. . . .

Subsystems

What You Will Learn in This Chapter

In this chapter, you'll discover how to use subsystems to help manage the complexity of a large project. You can feel confident that you understand subsystems when you can:

1. Define subsystem and list its common synonyms.

2. Draw a UML package diagram, showing a system broken down into subsystems.

3. Describe how subsystems simplify a project and improve understanding.

4. Describe how to go about the subsystem decisions.

5. List the points in the OODLC where one should check to see whether subsystems are needed.

6. Define layer and describe how layers also contribute to simplicity and understanding.

What You Should Know to Start This Chapter

By now you should be familiar with the basics of object-oriented methods for analysis, and this chapter will assume that you are. To handle subsystems you'll need to understand all the various models, so that you can learn how to divide up a project and model each subsystem separately.

Chapter Overview

We begin by defining what subsystems are, why they're necessary, and the different ways that some authors in the field define and treat them. We relate this to the limited capacity a human has for handling complexity. We then look at various techniques and mechanisms for going about the business of dividing up a project, and how to decide where the subsystems should be. This section finishes by describing the UML Package notation.

We discuss several reasons and criteria for these decisions, and the points in the development process where we should be doing the subdividing. We discuss some of the other names that subsystems are sometimes known by, and finish with a look at another, rather different way of dividing a project or business area into more manageable pieces to reduce complexity and improve understanding. This one is *layers*, which are a "horizontal" partitioning of a system, whereas subsystems are a "vertical" division.

Key Concepts

- Subsystems

- Packages, atomic service packages

- "The magical number seven, plus or minus two"

- Dependencies

- Minimal interactions and dependencies

- Look for subsystems early

- Classes that appear in several systems or subsystems

- Subjects, domains, subassemblies

- Layers

- The package diagram

"The Outhouse Bathroom Boutique"
Sales Reporting System – Episode 12

"You know," Tim mused, "there's a bunch of classes over here –" he tapped the paper with his pencil "– that seem to belong together. Look, these classes here. There's Purchase Order and PO Line Item, Back Order and BO Line Item, Vendor, Courier, and Shipment. And then there's this Vendor-Courier thing. Look how many lines are on the diagram between all these boxes. But there's only two lines joining this group to the rest of the diagram, and they both go to the Product. Nancy, didn't you mention this kind of thing the other day?"

"Yes, I did," said Nancy. Picking up a colored marker, she drew a line around the group of boxes Tim had indicated, including a couple more boxes as she did so. This is the thick solid black line shown in Figure 12-1. "Actually, Tim, what these boxes of yours represent is a *subsystem*. If you look carefully, you'll see that this group more or less stands alone. Certainly, it could be delayed until after all the rest of the system is built, without impacting the rest of the system.

"Or it could be developed earlier, as long as we had a *product* file of some kind in place. That's where it joins on to the rest, you see, at the Product class. So that gives us this half of the diagram all about Vendors and how we buy from Vendors, and if you look at what's left, it falls into two more subsystems. There's one group that's mainly concerned with sales, and a smaller group that deals with locations. That one has Shelf, Store, Department, and so on." Nancy drew another line, this time a dashed line, and now her diagram looked exactly like Figure 12-1.

At this point, Nancy noticed that Steve's face was showing a sudden understanding. She looked expectantly at him. "Of course!" he exclaimed. "I'll bet that if we look at the operations in these classes, and which classes call up operations from which other ones, we'll find roughly the same groupings. I mean, I'll bet we would find lots of messages and operation calls within each of thesesubsystems of yours, and not too many crossing the lines you've drawn there. So that would mean that most of the things that happen in the system, and the work that's done, would be contained within each subsystem."

"Right on," said Nancy. "That's just what I was going to suggest next. Let's add the messages to the diagram, the ones that call up operations from other classes. But we'll do it on a transparency sheet over the diagram, so then we can look at things with or without all the messages cluttering up the picture."

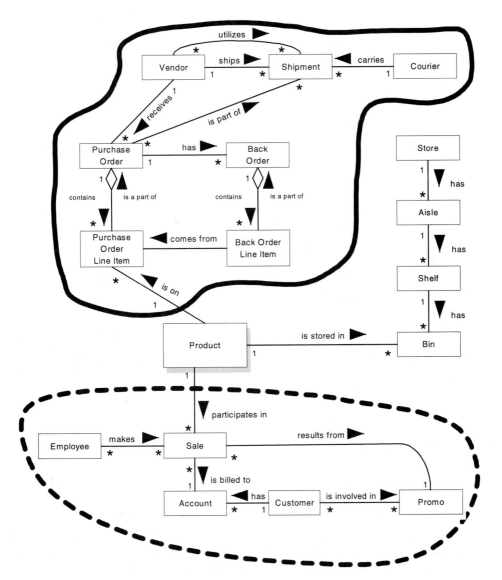

Figure 12-1 Subsystems in The Outhouse class diagram

THOUGHT QUESTIONS

1. Discuss a project that you or one of your group is aware of, where the project needed to be broken into smaller, more manageable chunks. It may have been a systems or programming project, or it may have occurred in any walk of life. How were the decisions made? Did the team do something like we just saw Nancy, Tim, and Steve do? Describe how they went about it.

2. Discuss another project that was not divided into subsystems or subprojects, but you think it should have been or could have benefited. What problems arose that you think might have been avoided in this way?

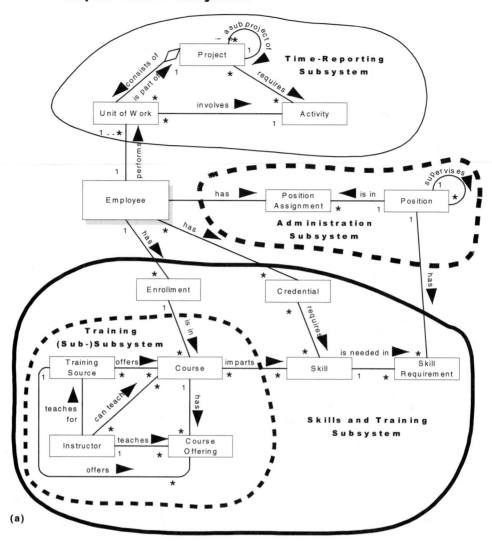

Figure 12-2   Human Resources class diagram from The Outhouse: (a) in full detail, and (b) showing the Skills and Training Subsystem as a single box, but indicating the classes involved in associations that cross its boundary.

12.1 DIVIDING UP A PROJECT

Once you become attuned to the object-oriented way of thinking, you'll find you can apply OOA in projects of all sizes and types. In other words, the method is highly scalable. You'll find it works for projects that take one person a few hours and for projects with teams of hundreds and budgets of millions. The level of rigor that you apply to an OOA project will vary somewhat with the size, but the principles and techniques apply anywhere.

There is a problem managing large projects, simply because of the increased complexity. A medium-sized system might have, say, 30 to 100 classes, which can make a pretty complicated diagram. A large system might have hundreds of boxes on the diagram.

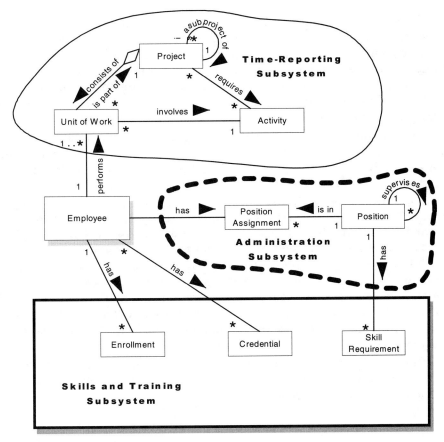

Figure 12-2   (continued)

This could make it physically impossible to draw, let alone comprehend. We need some way to make the model easier to understand, by reducing the complexity. This is usually done with some form of subsystems, which are really another example of *encapsulation.*

Encapsulation, as we defined it in Chapter 5, means hiding the details inside a published, well-defined boundary. The purpose of encapsulation, we saw earlier, is to help us *manage complexity.* To visualize what that means in this context, look at the object class diagram shown in Figure 12-2(a). This shows the classes we might need to handle the administration of Employees and their Position Assignments, Training, and Time Reporting.

The diagram in part (a) has seventeen boxes; as shown in Figure 12-2(b), however, it has only 11 entity-class boxes. This version of the model will allow us to develop the Administration and Time Reporting parts of the system, and encapsulates everything to do with Courses, Skills, Credentials, and Instructors within a box marked "Skills and Training Subsystem." Note the shape of the box — this is the UML Package symbol.

The simplified version of the diagram has all the information we need to develop the Administration and Time-Reporting subsystems, and take them all the way to implementation.

You should also note that the box shown encapsulating the Skills and Training subsystem has boxes within it to indicate which classes the two association lines terminate on. This allows us to show the multiplicity, which in this case is one-to-many (1:M). This being so, we also know that the Employee No. will appear in these two classes as a foreign key (assuming for the moment an extended-relational ODBMS). This also tells us that the Employee class likely won't need any extra attributes to handle the Training subsystem when it's added later.

I think you'll agree that encapsulating a number of subsystems in this way would greatly enhance the readability of a large, complex class diagram. Notice there are only two arrows that cross the boundary between the Training subsystem and the rest of the system; we'll discuss that in detail shortly.

Meantime, here is the formal definition of a subsystem: **A _subsystem_ is a group of classes, relationships, associations, operations, events, and possibly other subsystems, that have a well-defined and (hopefully) small interface to the rest of the system, and are treated as a unit or package.**

Wirfs-Brock et al. (1990) define a **_subsystem_ as a "set of classes (and possibly other subsystems) collaborating to fulfill a set of responsibilities,"** which I think gives us a clearer view of its purpose and structure than the more technical definition. They then go on to point out that the subsystem is strictly an analysis and design construct. Generally speaking, the subsystem boundary disappears during execution of the compiled program code.

But what their definition highlights is that, while a lot of work and interaction happens among the classes _within_ the subsystem, relatively few events cross the boundary to or from the rest of the system.

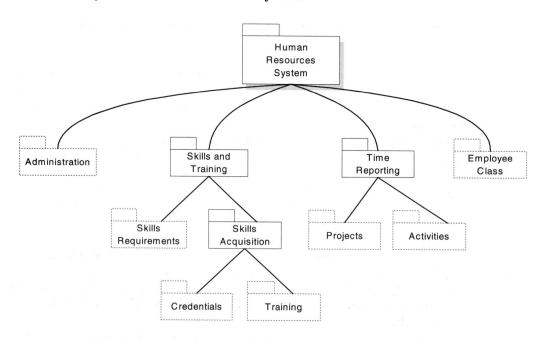

Figure 12-3   Breaking a system into subsystems, or *packages*. The dashed symbols, the "leaves" on the tree, represent Jacobson's indivisible "atomic packages."

Coad and Yourdon (1991) exhort us to "use minimal interactions and dependencies" when identifying what they call "subjects" (see below). What these people are all saying is that a subsystem is a unit or module within the system, with *relatively* few connections of any kind to classes outside the subsystem.

There will of course be plenty of message passing and other interactions going on *within* the subsystem, as the classes and (sub-)subsystems within it collaborate to complete their delegated tasks (that is, to fulfill their responsibilities).

Atomic Packages

No, these are not nuclear-supercharged subsystems! The tree in Figure 12-3 shows a possible decomposition of the Human Resources system from Figure 12-2 into subsystems, or *packages* in UML parlance, at various levels. In this breakdown, it would be pretty well impossible to further subdivide any of the "leaves" of this tree.

The packages at the lowest level shown are the ones we consider cannot be broken into any smaller pieces. These are shown with dashed lines around them in Figure 12-3, which I find to be a useful practice, though it is not part of UML. Note the Administration package, which is atomic as it stands, as is the Employee class, which stands in a package by itself. These, then, are the "leaves" on the tree:

1. Skills Acquisition

2. Skills Requirements

3. Administration

4. Projects

5. Activities

6. Employee Class

Jacobson (1992) takes the view that as we divide a system into subsystems and (sub-)subsystems, we reach a point where no further division can take place. He calls these ***service packages***, **since each must be developed in full or not at all.** In UML, they are usually just called *packages*. In Jacobson's words, "If the customer wants it, he will have the whole of it, otherwise he will get nothing."

These "service packages," then, are to be viewed as ***atomic* in the sense that they cannot be divided any further.** (This is the original meaning of the term, which comes from the Greek *atomos*, meaning "indivisible.") Each service package, then, is an integral whole, a group of classes only (no subsystems this time!) that belong together and need to be built all at the same time.

Now that we've seen what subsystems are, we also need to check why we should bother to use them.

Purpose of Using Subsystems

There's a very good "people reason" for doing all this. Psychologist George Miller (1956) published a landmark paper explaining his observations on how people process multiple pieces of data. Can you memorize a seven-digit phone number? Most of you probably can.

How about an 11-digit number? I find I can never remember "Talking Yellow Pages" numbers because they're seven plus four digits long. My 9-digit Canadian Social Insurance number and my 16-digit VISA number are total mysteries to me until I read them off the card.

In his paper, entitled "The Magical Number Seven, Plus or Minus Two," Miller (1956) proclaimed that the human short-term memory can handle only that many pieces of data, and that we become confused when forced to manipulate more than that. A great deal of later work in cognitive psychology has been based on this idea, and also on Miller's later work (1975) where he modified the formula to "three chunks of three." The point is, there are *limits on our capacity for processing information.*

So in order for you and your users to make full use of your models as tools for communication, we must limit the size and complexity of the chunks, when we break the models down. We must be careful not to over-generalize Miller's work, however. We can certainly have more than 7 boxes on a page, but after about 20 or so it can become a little confusing.

Careful layout and a larger page can help of course, but there's still a definite limit. And remember, often a complex diagram might look just fine to you, but may still be very confusing for others on the project, especially your users.

Once we become aware of the need to break out a subsystem, how do we go about it? The following two sections will show us what to do next.

12.2 HOW TO SUBDIVIDE

Intuitively Obvious

In many cases, the subsystem decision will be intuitive. It will be "obvious" both to you and to your users where the subsystems are. Even so, you would be wise to check the criteria outlined in the rest of this section to see how well your "obvious" subsystems actually fit the bill.

You'll often find you need to make some fine-tuning adjustments, particularly with classes on the edge of the subsystem. These are the classes that could go either side of the boundary, so it's often a judgment or convenience call as to which subsystem they should go in.

Minimal Interactions and Dependencies

This marvelous phrase (courtesy of Coad and Yourdon) is really the core of the matter. As we saw in Figure 12-2, for a subsystem to be an identifiable unit or whole, relatively few connections of any kind should cross its boundary. These connections can be:

- Relationships
- Associations from the class diagram
- Events passed from one state machine to another, in a statechart diagram
- Messages passed to a class from an actor or another class
- Responsibilities that one class bears to another

The last three are really just different ways of describing the same thing, but I think it's helpful to consider them separately.

These then are the various kinds of interaction that can exist among classes. What we need to look for are clusters of classes and subsystems with lots of interactions *within* the cluster and not too many with classes outside it. We can view many of these interactions as *dependencies*, in the sense that wherever there's a responsibility (or a message or event link) between classes, then the one class *depends* on the other to get something done.

Functional Grouping

In Figure 12-2, we saw subsystems for Training, Time Reporting, Personnel Administration, Enrollments, and so on. Each exists to handle some *function* within the users' business. This is a very common basis for subsystems and the one you'll most often resort to. Another project might need an Accounting subsystem, a Scheduling subsystem, and a Statistics subsystem. Another perhaps needs Daily, Weekly, Monthly, and Annual Processing subsystems.

Again, within a system or program, you may sometimes find platform-dependent subsystems such as Printing, Screen Handling, File or Database Access, and so on. The functions we use to divide a system into subsystems can be based either on the users' business functions and processes, or on functions within the computerized system or programs.

Real-Time Considerations

Certain factors are particularly relevant to real-time systems and embedded software, but also sometimes to management information systems (MIS). These factors will occasionally dictate that certain functions must go together in a single subsystem, even when the other criteria we've discussed indicate against it.

One criterion is *physical location*. In systems such as automated cash registers, automated teller machines (ATMs), cellular phone systems, pipeline monitoring, nuclear power stations, petroleum refining, weather stations, and so on, remote processors handle the local details. They're linked to central processors for overall control, monitoring, and recording.

This dictates that certain groups of functions must go in the remote system, whether or not they're related in any other way besides location. In many businesses and in many geographic information systems (GISs), the geographic location dictates this.

Another factor is hardware requirements. Some parts of the system may need to be grouped into a subsystem in order to place them on a particular hardware platform. A similar factor would be the software platform, causing functions to be combined to use a particular OOPL or ODBMS.

Let's summarize what we've seen until now about *subsystems*:

• There is a complexity problem managing large projects. A system might have from 30 to some hundreds of boxes on the diagram, making it impossible to draw or comprehend. To reduce the complexity we use *subsystems*, which are a form of *encapsulation*.

- Encapsulation (Chapter 5) is hiding the details inside a published, well-defined boundary. Its purpose is to help manage complexity.

- A subsystem is a group of classes, subsystems, and the like that have a well-defined, small interface to the rest of the system and are treated as a unit.

- Wirfs-Brock defines a subsystem as a "set of classes (and possibly other subsystems) collaborating to fulfill a set of responsibilities."

- The subsystem boundary disappears at execution time.

- While there's a lot of interaction among the classes within the subsystem, relatively few events cross the boundary to the rest of the system. Thus, Coad and Yourdon say to "use minimal interactions and dependencies."

- Jacobson says that as we divide a system into subsystems there's a point where no further division can take place. He calls these *service packages,* since each must be developed in full or not at all.

- Miller's research says we can only handle "seven, plus or minus two" pieces of data at a time, and we get confused with more than that.

- It will be "obvious" to you and your users where some of the subsystems are. Still, you should check the other criteria.

- The *interactions* referred to include:
  - Relationships
  - Associations from the class diagram.
  - Events passed from one state machine to another, in a Statechart Diagram.
  - Messages passed to a class from an actor or another class.
  - Responsibilities that one class bears to another.

- These are *dependencies*, in the sense that a responsibility implies that one class is *dependent on* the other to get something done.

- Functional grouping, a common basis for subsystems, is the one you'll use most often.

- Find platform-dependent subsystems such as Printing and Screen Handling. The functions used to divide into subsystems can be the users' business functions or inferred computer functions.

- For real-time systems and embedded software, certain functions must go in a subsystem, even when other criteria indicate against it:
  - *Physical location.* In systems such as automated cash registers and ATMs, remote processors handle details, linked to central processors for control. Certain groups of functions must go in the remote system.
  - *Geographic information systems (GISs).* The geographic location dictates some subsystems.
  - *Hardware and software requirements.* Some parts of the system may need to begrouped into a subsystem to put them on a particular hardware platform or a particular OOPL or ODBMS.

12.3 WHEN TO SUBDIVIDE

The major subsystems will be decided early on in the project (see "Architecture" later in this chapter), but many very useful divisions into subsystems may only become apparent during the later phases.

There are a number of points in the analysis process where it may be convenient or even necessary to divide your system into subsystems. However, these are not the only times to do this. I'll describe these important points in detail, but you must remember that these insights may occur to you or your team at any time during development, even beyond the Analysis Phase.

Such awareness has been known to occur anywhere in the object-oriented development life cycle (OODLC), even occasionally during testing or maintenance. As with all changes or errors in the development, it saves a lot of time, hassle, work, and *money* if we can make these decisions as early as possible in the project.

What matters is that any insight suggesting a subsystem should *always* be carefully considered. So sometimes, when at some point in the project someone suggests we need a subsystem, you may choose to pause and decide right there.

You may also deem it necessary to go further and actually design the subsystem (decide and diagram the classes, and so on, that are to be in the subsystem) before going on. Or you may elect to continue on the stream of thought the group was already following, in which case you *must* make a note to come back and look at this potential subsystem as soon as possible.

I've placed some stress on the need to look for subsystems early in the development process, since they have an important side benefit. Besides the benefits I've already mentioned, breaking the project into pieces also helps improve the accuracy of your time and resource estimating for the project. For this reason, some of the break points that I describe next occur very early in the process.

Now for those points where you'll most expect to be looking for subsystems:

- Before you begin
- The systems request document
- Completion of requirements analysis
- As part of the system architecture.
- The class diagram
- During behavior analysis
- Completion of analysis
- The design phase

Before You Begin

Just based on your general knowledge of the users' business or, better still, a prior exposure to it, you'll probably enter the project with some impressions already formed about where to find the subsystems. Be careful, however, not to let these become classical "preconceived ideas." You must keep your mind open enough to be prepared to reconsider and possibly to change these views. As your experience grows, you may expect this process to become progressively more reliable.

The Systems Request Document

Most likely the first thing you see of the project will be a document from the users, in formal or informal format, detailing their view of the problem and requesting a solution. Allied with your experience and the impressions you bring, this may give you further insights.

Completion of Requirements Analysis

While you'll certainly expect some subsystem insights to occur during the requirements analysis, I find it can be productive to pause at its completion and take a careful look for subsystems. Especially, we may see some that are reusable from former projects.

At this stage, depending on the technical sophistication of your users, you may prefer to do this with just the systems people, away from the users. Or you may briefly consider the issue with the users present and again in more depth with just the technical staff.

The System Architecture

On large projects, there is a separate phase at the beginning, where the big decisions are made about platforms, whether to build a distributed or stand-alone system, Internet or leased line for data communications, and so on. Here we are deciding on the **overall shape and structure of the system, which we call its _architecture_.** At this point, it should be fairly easy to see all the major subsystems.

The Class Diagram

Associations give a good indication of the level of interaction, by indicating where many of the collaborations will be. You can expect many of the message interactions will be along the routes marked by the associations.

Since it shows these things graphically, the class diagram is a powerful tool for finding subsystems. We saw this in Figure 12-2. Dividing up the class diagram as we did in Figure 12-2 is one of the easiest, quickest, and most convenient, but by no means the only way to generate subsystems.

Simply draw a freehand line (a "fence") around a group of related class boxes, and you have a subsystem. Of course, you must observe all the guidelines about "minimal interactions and dependencies" and so on.

This works very well at the whiteboard, trying out various divisions and combinations, until you arrive at something satisfactory to both developers and users. By this stage of the development, you can expect that your users will be sufficiently familiar with the process to participate fully in the search for subsystems.

During Behavior Analysis

As you search for the operations for the classes, using your chosen combination of use cases, sequence diagrams, statechart diagrams, responsibilities, role plays, and so on, you'll see groups of functions that belong together, and some of these will then form subsystems.

Completion of Analysis

Finally, when the analysis is deemed to have been completed, you need to pause and check once again, with your users this time, of course. Also, you'll find an important use for subsystems at this point:

SUBSYSTEMS AND DEVELOPMENT SEQUENCE

By inspecting the diagrams of subsystems, especially the class diagrams, you'll find that certain subsystems need to be developed before others. The association connections and message connections will show you that the one subsystem needs data or services from the other, so it must be developed later or at least in parallel.

Also, you'll readily see which subsystems could be dropped from the project altogether without affecting the others, if it should happen that time or resources become severely limited. A map of the subsystems, then, is *the* major discussion tool for deciding on the sequence and options of further development. In UML, this is the package diagram.

The Design Phase

Finally, you'll need to remain alert for subsystems throughout the design phase, since you'll be making the final decisions on many of the factors that I've already identified. You'll be deciding not only on hardware and software platforms, OOPLs, and ODBMSs but also such things as the allocation of functions or data to geographic or physical locations.

Following the design phase, as you proceed through the OODLC, there may be the occasional need for another subsystem, but by this time most of them should have been found. However, before we move on, there are a couple of kinds of classes that need some special mention.

12.4 SOME SPECIAL CLASSES THAT APPEAR IN SEVERAL SYSTEMS OR SUBSYSTEMS

Almost every MIS system you develop will have a need for Employee data, even if it's just to echo back the Name as confirmation of an Employee No. being keyed in. So every project of this type can be expected to include an Employee class. This kind of thing often happens, where data and services from one class are needed by many different systems and projects.

When this happens, if it has not already been done, there must be an "executive decision" to allocate responsibility for that class to some user group. For the Employee class, this would be the Human Resources group. These people and their particular system or subsystem are then considered to be the "owners" of that class, and all other systems and subsystems are granted access or updating rights as needed (when duly authorized).

During the requirements modeling, your users will often come up with a class that already exists somewhere else. A class with a similar name or similar attributes and operations may already have been defined in some other system or subsystem. When that happens, your recording analyst will have the existing definition, attribute list, and operation specs available.

You will of course have done your homework beforehand. You'll have foreseen which existing systems or subsystems your project might need to share classes with. Thus, your recording analyst will have arrived armed with the relevant documentation.

You then run these definitions by your users when the class comes up in the discussion, and ask whether this class will satisfy their needs as it exists already. If not, you'll work out the modifications needed, which usually take the form of additional attributes and operations. Later, you'll need to seek approval for these changes from the owners of the class and, if necessary, do a little negotiating.

Classes on the Boundaries

Other classes that may need some special attention are those whose associations or message connections cross the subsystem boundary. It's very easy to get into a big argument over which side of the boundary the class belongs. It's not worth getting hung up on; make your decision and move on. Here are some guidelines:

- Look for the subsystem to which this class has more association and message links

- Logically and intuitively, which subsystem (or sometimes, which set of users) does this class belong to?

- Which subsystem needs to be constructed first? Can it be built without this class? If the answer is no, but the class strongly belongs in the other subsystem, can we get by for now by constructing a "stub class," having just the attributes and methods it needs to service the first-built subsystem?

- Judgment call, by team consensus ("I can live with it . . . ")

Here, then, is a summary of what we've discussed about finding subsystems:

- The major subsystems and packages will be defined as part of the system architecture.

- There are certain points in the analysis process where you should be dividing your system into subsystems and sub-subsystems, although insights may occur any time, even beyond analysis. It saves a lot of time, hassle, work, and money if we decide as early as possible.

- Subsystems improve the accuracy of project estimates.

- The recommended points are:
  - *Before you begin.* Based on general knowledge of the users' business, you'll enter the project with some ideas already about where the subsystems are.
  - *The systems request document*

- *Completion of requirements analysis*
- *The class diagram.* Associations indicate the level of interaction, where the collaborations will be. Many of the message interactions will be along the associations. Since it shows these graphically, the class diagram is a powerful tool for finding subsystems.
- *During behavior analysis.* As you search for operations with Use Cases, Statechart Diagrams, responsibilities and so on, you'll find groups of functions that go together, and these will form subsystems.
- *Completion of analysis.* You need to pause and check with your users. By inspecting diagrams, you can see that certain subsystems must be developed first. One subsystem needs data or services from another and so must be developed later or in parallel. You also will see which subsystems could be dropped or postponed without affecting others.
- *The design phase.* Watch for subsystems in the design phase, since you make final decisions on platforms, OOPLs and ODBMSs, and allocation to geographic or physical locations.
- *After design.* As you follow the OODLC, there's occasional need for a subsystem, although by now most should have been found.

- Classes that appear in several systems or subsystems:
  - Data and services from one class are needed by many different systems and projects. Allocate that class to an "owner" user group.
  - Users will often discover a class that already exists elsewhere in the company. A similar class may be defined in another system. Take the existing definition, attribute list, and operation specs to the users for feedback. If not satisfactory, work out modifications. Seek approval from the designated "owners" of the class.
- Some associations or message connections do cross the subsystem boundary. Make a decision which side of the boundary the class belongs, and move on. Guidelines are:

  - Find the subsystem to which this class has more association and message links.
  - Logically and intuitively, which subsystem or users does this class belong to?
  - Which subsystem should be built first? Can it be built without this class?
  - Can we use a "stub class," with attributes and methods just for the first-built subsystem?
  - Judgment call.

12.5 COMPARISON OF TERMS

A number of authors have used different names for what we've been calling "subsystems," and some have defined them a little differently. It will be instructive for us to have a look at some of these and what the authors have to say about them.

Subjects (Coad and Yourdon)

Peter Coad and Ed Yourdon (1991, page 106) define a **_subject_ to be "a mechanism for guiding a reader . . . through a large, complex model."** You may notice that while this definition does a fine job of telling us what subjects are *for*, it neglects to tell us what they actually *are*. *Oxford* (1999) does a little better. They tell us it is **"A branch of knowledge,"** to which *Random House Webster* (1998) adds **"That which forms a basic matter of thought, discussion (and) investigation."**

Peter and Ed suggest that the person reading the diagram could be an analyst, a problem domain expert, a manager, or a client, and you'll notice that this list includes both technical and user personnel. This indicates the usefulness of subjects (or subsystems) for communication among all these groups.

They also point out that "subjects are strictly a means to an end – they give an overview of a larger OOA model." This is consistent with Wirfs-Brock's assertion that the subsystem boundaries tend to disappear at execution time. The subjects (or subsystems) are for use during development of the system, as a tool for understanding and communication.

Coad and Yourdon recommend that you use subjects in conjunction with *layers*, which we discuss in Section 12.7.

Domains (Shlaer and Mellor)

These authors refer to *domains*, a term that Firesmith (1993) points out could be confusing since it's used with different meanings in various other contexts. They propose that the domains should be identified before getting started on analysis.

They say that the domain responsibilities should be identified in broad terms, and diagramed with a "domain chart" notation that they have developed. They then take each domain and break it into subsystems. So their "domains" may be viewed as "senior subsystems," or the first level of breakdown from the system level.

Subassemblies (Firesmith)

Donald Firesmith (1993, page 48) has a few things to say about the choice of a name for what we've called *subsystems*. His choice is *subassemblies* since a subsystem typically should also include people, hardware, and the like. He feels the terms *subject*, *domain*, and *cluster* are confusing and that they don't clearly tell that this is a (sub)part of a larger whole. Firesmith is actively campaigning for the adoption of the more correct term *subassemblies* in the object-oriented literature.

He then discusses subassemblies for quite a number of pages. He describes "Master subassemblies," which we would call clients, and "Servant subassemblies," which we would call servers. He talks about "Agent subassemblies," which are those that sometimes assume a server role and then collaborate with other subassemblies by becoming clients to them.

Of all the authors surveyed, Firesmith probably has the most extensive treatment of subsystems (subassemblies). In another section, beginning on page 215 and reaching to the end of the chapter at page 228, he discusses at length a variety of ways to identify subassemblies.

12.6 PACKAGES

According to Rumbaugh (1999), a ***package*** is **"a piece of a model,"** and **"every part of a model must belong to (at least) one package."** This means that your package diagram should begin with one senior or "root" package that represents the system as a whole.

While I have talked throughout this chapter about using the class diagram to break your model out into subsystems, that's not the end of it. Once you have determined the subsystems, it is important that you document all parts of the model for that subsystem within the package that describes it.

This means that, in addition to the classes and their associations, the package must contain all the other diagrams for this subsystem too. There will be state machines (statechart diagrams), use case diagrams, activity and sequence (interaction) diagrams, collaborations, and so on – "anything not contained in some other element." Things like attributes and operations are considered to be contained in the classes, so they don't appear on a package diagram.

Packages may contain other packages, representing "sub-subsystems."

Now, while packages and subsystems are very useful for reducing the complexity of a model, to improve our understanding and communication, they still may not be enough. In addition to this "vertical" sectioning of the system, we may need to improve our model by slicing it "horizontally" into what Coad and Yourdon term *layers*.

12.7 THE MULTILAYER MODEL

The Five Layers

As a further aid to clarity, understanding, and communication with the models, Coad and Yourdon (1991, page 55), propose that we prepare the models in "layers" of increasing detail.

According to *Webster* (1975), a ***layer*** is **"one thickness...lying over or under another."** *Oxford* (1998) gives it as **"A sheet . . . or thickness . . . one of several, covering a surface."** For our purposes, we'll say a ***layer*** is one level of detail, **containing the results of a particular part of the object-oriented analysis process, and it adds information to the other layers.**

Coad and Yourdon suggest five layers, each containing a specific subset of the diagrams:

- Subject/subsystem layer. In UML this is the *package layer*.
- Class diagram layer
- Structure layer (subclasses and aggregations)
- Attribute layer
- Service/operation layer

Think of these as transparencies, arranged so you may lay them on an overhead projector one at a time in the order shown. You may of course use all five at once if you need to. Or you may be discussing with your user the distribution of certain data attributes among the subsystems. For this, you would need only the subject/subsystem layer and the attribute layer.

By using these two together, and only these two, you eliminate the clutter of information about classes, structures, and operations. This will greatly improve your discussion, and may allow you to see patterns or details that would have been hidden in a fully detailed diagram. This, by the way, shows us that subject layers, like subsystems, are another form of *abstraction* as well as being a form of *encapsulation*.

In other discussions, you may wish to begin with the subject/subsystems layer and progressively add more layers to get more detail, in the order that best fits your discussion. In yet another context, you may need to start with full detail and remove layers to show how things fit into patterns. The concept of layers is very flexible, and even more so when combined with subsystems and packages.

Layers Versus Subsystems

Subsystems may be viewed as a "vertical" division of a system, in the sense that we take a small portion of the system and "drill it down" from layer to layer and from phase to phase of the OODLC. With layers, on the other hand, we take an entire system or subsystem and view it only to the limited "depth" of a certain number of layers. So in this sense, layers are a horizontal slicing of the project (or of part of it).

Like subsystems, layers are strictly an understanding and communication device. Like subsystems, they exist only as a help to the development process, and cease to exist at execution time. This last point is even more true of layers, however, since they're merely a documentation device.

We can actually do development work on one subsystem at a time. We might take one subsystem at a time, or a cluster of related subsystems, right through the OODLC to final implementation. We may develop the entire system, then implement one subsystem at a time with the users. So subsystems and packages do, or can, have a physical existence.

Layers, on the other hand, are just a way of viewing the models, and it's simply not possible to "develop a layer" or to "implement a layer." These ideas don't make sense because the layer doesn't exist in the design itself, only in the documentation.

CASE REQUIREMENTS FOR LAYERS

Just how much use you can make of layers will depend to some extent on your choice of CASE tool. While all support subsystems, not all will allow layering. You'll recall that our earlier definition of support for a feature was that it's "easy and convenient" to use. Some CASE tools will allow layering, but others actively support it, in particular, Coad and Yourdon's own CASE tool.

LAYERS AND COMPLETENESS CHECKS

Another helpful result of using layers is in checking at any stage to see if you've missed anything. This is particularly important at the end of each phase of the OODLC, before you present the deliverables to the users or to your own management. It's best to do this in two ways:

1. You'll need to take each package (subsystem), and follow it down through the layers. As a final check, you do the system as a whole. At each level, you must check that all the pieces are present and that they fit with the layers above and below.

2. You'll need to take each layer and check "horizontally" to make sure all the association links and message links are present. Not only that, but you must check that each link shown leaving one package has a matching one across the boundary in another package. And while your at it, make sure it's the right package for that particular link!

DELIVERABLES

The only relevant comment to be made here about deliverables is that they should be the same as before, except now they should be done one subsystem at a time and one layer at a time. You may wish at this stage to add an Enterprise Model to your repertoire. Logically, this should be done as part of the architecture for your system, before all the other models, but for simplicity in this book I've left it out. In simplified form, it could consist of an expansion from the package diagram, showing boxes that represent clusters of classes within the packages, and all associations shown as many-to-many (M:M).

FURTHER READING

You'll find very in-depth discussions of the UML package concept, but not necessarily the easiest ones to follow, in Booch (1999) and Rumbaugh (1999), albeit with not a lot of the how and why of subsystems and packages.

Harmon and Watson (1998) have only a page or so on packages, but it's certainly worth reading if you happen to have the book already. In UML there are three kinds of "implementation diagrams:" *package, component* and *deployment* diagrams. Harmon and Watson also devote a page or so each to the other two, but they're not all that important in your early forays into objects and UML.

Jacobson's (1992) section on subsystems on page 190 is good, if somewhat short. So is Coad and Yourdon's (1991) treatment of *subjects* on page 106.

Firesmith (1993) has an extensive and more technical section on what he prefers to call *subassemblies* beginning on page 45. On page 48, he comments on the terms used by other authors, including *subsystems* (but of course he doesn't mention me because he didn't know that I was coming along). On page 215, he has a comprehensive section on how to find and identify subassemblies (that is, subsystems, or packages.)

Shlaer and Mellor (1992), in their second book *Object Lifecycles, Modeling the World in States*, introduce *domains* on pages 2 and 9, then on page 145 they devote their entire Chapter 8 to subsystem–domain issues.

CHAPTER SUMMARY

- To reduce the complexity problem in managing large projects, we use *subsystems*, or *packages*, which are a form of *encapsulation*.

- *Encapsulation* (Chapter 5) is hiding the details inside a published, well-defined boundary.

- A *subsystem* (or *package*) is a group of classes, subsystems, and so on, that have a well-defined, small interface to the rest of the system and are treated as a unit.

- Wirfs-Brock defines a subsystem as a "set of classes (and possibly other subsystems) collaborating to fulfill a set of responsibilities."

- The subsystem boundary disappears at execution time.

- While there is much interaction among the classes *within* a subsystem, there are minimal interactions and dependencies across its boundary.

- Jacobson says there's a point where no further division can take place. Each *atomic package* must be developed in full or not at all.

- Miller's research says most people can only handle "seven, plus or minus two" pieces of data at a time, and get confused with more than that.

- It will be "obvious" to you and your users where some of the subsystems are. Still, you should check the other criteria, even for these "obvious" ones.

- *Interactions* include:
  - Associations
  - Events from one state machine to another
  - Messages passed to an object, from an actor or from another object
  - Responsibilities

- These are *dependencies*, in the sense that a responsibility implies that one class depends on another to get something done.

- Functional grouping is a very common basis for subsystems.

- We regularly use platform-dependent subsystems such as Printing, and Screen Handling.

- For real-time systems and embedded software, certain functions must go in a subsystem, even when other criteria indicate against it:

- *Physical location* – for example, certain groups of functions must go in the remote system.
  - For geographic information systems (GIS), the *geographic location* often dictates subsystems.
  - *Hardware* and *software* requirements.
- There are certain points in analysis where you should pause to divide your system into subsystems, although insights may occur any time. It saves time and money if we decide early. The recommended points are:
  - Before you begin.
  - System architecture definition
  - The systems request document
  - Completion of requirements analysis
  - The class diagram
  - During behavior analysis
  - Completion of Analysis
  - The design phase
  - After design, as you follow through the rest of the OODLC
- Subsystems also improve the accuracy of your project estimates.
- By inspecting the diagrams, you can often see which subsystems must be developed before another. One subsystem needs data or services from another, so must be developed later. You can also see which subsystems could be dropped altogether if necessary.
- Classes that appear in several systems or subsystems:
  - Data and services from one class are needed by many different systems and projects. Allocate responsibility for that class to an "owner" user group.
  - Users will often come up with a class that already exists elsewhere in the company. Run the existing specs by your users and ask whether this class will satisfy their needs. If not, work out the modifications, but seek approval for changes from owners of the class.
- Classes whose associations or message connections cross the subsystem boundary. *Make your decision* which side of the boundary the class belongs, and move on. Here are some guidelines:
  - Look for the subsystem to which this class has more association and message links.
  - Logically and intuitively, which subsystem or set of users does this class belong to?
  - Which subsystem should be built first? Can it be built without this class? Can we get by building a stub class?
  - Judgment call.

- Authors have used different names for subsystems:
  - *Subjects* (Coad and Yourdon)
  - *Domains* (Shlaer and Mellor)
  - *Subassemblies* (Firesmith)
  - *Packages* (Jacobson, UML)
- A *layer* is one level of detail, containing the results of a particular part of the object-oriented analysis process, and it adds information to the other layers.
- Coad and Yourdon suggest five layers:
  - Subject/subsystem (in UML, the package layer)
  - Class diagram layer
  - Structure layer
  - Attribute layer
  - Service/operation/behavior layer
- Think of these layers as transparencies, added one at a time to make a complete diagram.
- Subsystems are a vertical division of a system, and layers are a horizontal division of the project (or a part of the system).
- How much use you can make of layers depends on your CASE tool. All of them support subsystems or packages, but not all allow layering.
- Completeness-check each subsystem, and finally the whole system, and follow it down through the layers. At each layer, check that all pieces are present and that they fit with the layers above and below.
- Check each layer horizontally to ensure all association and message links are present. Check that each link leaving a subsystem has a matching one in the other subsystem.

CHAPTER GLOSSARY

architecture   The overall shape and structure of the system, including decisions about platforms, distributed processing, and communications.

atomic   Something that cannot be divided any further. (This is the original meaning of the term, which comes from the Greek atomos, meaning "indivisible.")

layer   (1) One level of detail, containing the results of a particular part of the object-oriented analysis process, which adds information to the other layers. (2) "A sheet . . . one of several, covering a surface" (Oxford, 1998). (3) "One thickness . . . lying over or under another" (Webster (1975).

package   "A piece of a model," and "every part of a model must belong to (at least) one package." Represents a subsystem in a UML diagram.

service packages   The smallest possible subsystem, when a point is reached where no further division into subsystems can take place. Each must be developed in full or not at all.

subject "A mechanism for guiding a reader...through a large, complex model" (Coad and Yourdon, 1991).

subsystem (1) A group of classes, relationships, associations, operations, events, and other subsystems that have a *small, well-defined interface* to the rest of the system and are treated as a unit or *package*. (2) "A set of classes (and possibly other subsystems) collaborating to fulfill a set of responsibilities" (Wirfs-Brock et al., 1990).

WHAT COMES NEXT

This chapter has brought us to the end of the analysis process. It's now time to look briefly beyond the Analysis phase, at some of the other phases of the OODLC. We'll begin with the design phase, which is introduced and summarized and a number of issues explored, in Chapter 13.

Following that, in Chapter 14 we'll examine some implementation issues and some of the software tools and environments available for the implementation of an object-oriented design.

CLASS/GROUP EXERCISES AND PROBLEMS

Ex 12.1 Go through all the projects that you've been carrying forward and check each one to see if it has any identifiable subsystems. Be sure you try out all the strategies discussed in Section 12.2, "How to Subdivide." Also check for any of the classes mentioned in Section 12.4, "Some Special Classes." Draw colored lines ("fences") on your class diagrams to show the subsystems and sub-subsystems. Then draw a package diagram for each.

Ex 12.2 Now check through all the projects in Exercise 12.1 and make sure you've subdivided right down to the atomic package level, *but not beyond.*

Ex 12.3 For each project in Exercises 12.1 and 12.2, assume that development resources (mainly people) are in drastically short supply so that only one subsystem can be under development at any time. (We might call this "single-threaded development.")

Develop a schedule for each project showing the sequence in which you recommend the subsystems be developed. Try to sequence them so that, as each new subsystem is developed, it will draw data from classes that have already been built in prior subsystems. Wherever a method of one class draws data from another class that's not scheduled to be built until later, make a recommendation on how to handle this problem. Note that making a recommendation always entails three steps:

- Present a few options. Between two and six is usually enough.
- Recommend one of these options.
- Briefly justify your choice. One or two sentences is the guideline.

Present your results to the class. As before, present the subsystems and schedules for Project 1 from all the groups and compare and discuss the approaches taken. Then present all the versions of Project 2, and so on. Each group takes a turn at being the first to present.

PROJECTS AND CASES

P 12.1 Repeat the process of Exercises 12.1 – 12.3 with your small-business project, the one you began in Project 8.1 and continued in Projects 9.1, 10.1, and 11.1. Justify your scheduling decisions. Use the three-step recommendation process from Exercise 12.3 wherever appropriate. First present your work to the class and seek input and suggestions for improvement. Then present to the client.

SELF-TEST QUESTIONS

Note: The Appendix has answers to the Self-Test Questions.

Q 12.1 A subsystem:

(a) *Isakinda* system

(b) Has a well-defined and small interface to the rest of the system

(c) Is treated as a unit or package

(d) Is a group of classes, relationships, associations, operations, events, and other subsystems

(e) All of the above

(f) Some of the above

(g) None of the above

Q 12.2 Which of the following are words that mean the same as subsystem?
(a) Domain, subassembly, and phase

(b) Domain, layer, and subassembly

(c) Package, layer, and subluxation

(d) Package, domain, and subassembly

(e) Phase, layer, and domain

(f) Subject, layer, subassembly, and domain

Q 12.3 These are the points in the OODLC where one should check to see whether subsystems are needed:
(a) Before you begin and completion of requirements analysis

(b) The class diagram and the design phase

(c) During behavior analysis and at completion of the analysis phase

(d) All of the above

(e) Some of the above

(f) None of the above

Q 12.4 Which of the following is a true statement?

(a) Service packages are subsystems grouped into clusters.

(b) Atomic comes from the Latin *atomos*, meaning "a group"

(c) A layer is a level of detail that adds credibility to other layers.

(d) All of the above.

(e) Some of the above.

(f) None of the above.

Q 12.5 The five layers proposed by Coad and Yourdon are:

(a) Package, data, attribute, model, domain.

(b) Subject, class diagram, structure, attribute, service.

(c) Data, domain, model, structure, attribute.

(d) Model, structure, real time, attribute, package.

(e) Domain, subject, class diagram, structure, subassembly.

Q 12.6 To reduce the _____ problem in managing _____ _____, we use _____, or _____, which are a form of _____.

Q 12.7 A subsystem (or _____) is a group of _____, _____, and so on, that have a well-defined, small _____ to the rest of the _____ and are treated as a _____.

Q 12.8 Wirfs-Brock defines a subsystem as a "set of _____ (and possibly other subsystems) _____ to fulfill a set of _____."

Q 12.9 The subsystem boundary disappears at _____ time.

Q 12.10 While there is much _____ among the classes _____ a _____, there are _____ _____ and _____ across its boundary.

Q 12.11 Miller's research says most people can only handle "_____, _____ _____ _____ _____" pieces of data at a time.

Q 12.12 Interactions include:

- Associations.

- _____ from one state machine to another.

- Messages passed to an _____, from an _____ or from another _____.

- Responsibilities.

Q 12.13 Interactions are dependencies, in the sense that a _____ implies that one _____ _____ on another to get _____ _____.

Q 12.14 There are certain points in analysis where you should pause to _____ your _____ into _____, although insights may occur any time. It saves time and money if we decide _____. The recommended points are:

- Before you _____
- System _____ definition
- The systems _____ document
- Completion of _____ _____
- The _____ Diagram
- During behavior analysis
- _____ of analysis
- The _____ phase

Q 12.15 Subsystems also improve the _____ of your project _____.

Q 12.16 By inspecting the _____, you can often see which _____ must be developed _____ another. One subsystem needs _____ or _____ from another, so must be developed _____.

Q 12.17 Authors have used different names for _____ :

- _____ (Coad and Yourdon)
- _____ (Shlaer and Mellor)
- _____ (Firesmith)
- _____ (Jacobson, UML)

Q 12.18 Subsystems are a _____ division of a system, and layers are a _____ division of the project (or a part of the system).

Chapter Thirteen

Object-Oriented Design

WHAT YOU WILL LEARN IN THIS CHAPTER

In this chapter, you'll meet a number of issues, ideas, and techniques for the design phase of your project. You can be confident that you've mastered the content of this chapter when you can:

1. Explain some of the important issues this chapter raises around the design phase of the OODLC.

2. Define concurrency, threads of control, and multithreaded execution.

3. List some of the issues around the available approaches to the problems of currency and consistency in distributed objects.

4. Describe the work of the Object Management Group (OMG) and the Object Data Management Group (ODMG) and explain why it is so important.

5. Design and spec a test suite, an object(s) that will completely *exercise* an existing class, under polymorphism, inheritance, multiple inheritance, and so on, and under conditions of reuse in an unfamiliar environment.

WHAT YOU SHOULD KNOW TO START THIS CHAPTER

For this chapter, you need to understand objects, but you don't need to know how to do object-oriented analysis (nor how to write object-oriented programs). In terms of this book, that means you need Chapters 4 – 6, and possibly Chapter 8.

CHAPTER OVERVIEW

To begin this chapter, we look at some of the issues confronting the object-oriented designer, such as concurrent execution and the use of abstract classes. Then, after briefly revisiting the OODLC and its smooth, continuous nature, we consider the choice of implementation environment.

After that, we touch on the design of the data part and process part of the system, and the design of the user interface. Two current ideas that are new for many people are *concurrent processing* and *distributed objects*.

Then we take a peek around the corner at what is coming down the line. The standardization work being done in the object-oriented field holds the promise of some really great things. And it's unlike so many previous ideas that held so much "promise." (Are you old enough to remember how CASE was going to make most of us obsolete? Or how computer-based training was going to replace teachers by the end of the 1970s?)

The object-oriented movement, on the other hand, has enough industry support that it looks like it will actually *deliver* on the promise, giving levels of compatibility that we've only dreamed of until now. I'm hoping you'll be as excited as I am when you see it. Then, still in the future, we'll also check out intelligent agents, a seemingly fanciful idea, but one that may not be that far away.

Finally, we look at how testing is and isn't different in an object-oriented environment. It is critically important for the future reuse of classes in your object-oriented designs, that they be exhaustively tested. Here I'll tell you both why and how. We finish with a short discussion of documentation issues.

KEY CONCEPTS

- Concurrency and threads of control
- Multithreaded execution
- Interobject and intraobject concurrency
- Large objects
- Critical success factor
- Pure, extended, and hybrid languages
- Versioning
- Distributed objects
- OMG, ORB, and CORBA
- Class and object naming
- Event notification
- Persistence
- Transaction
- ODMG, voting members, reviewing members
- OpenDoc
- Components
- Intelligent agents

"THE OUTHOUSE BATHROOM BOUTIQUE" SALES REPORTING SYSTEM – EPISODE 13

"So what is this design phase all about?" asked Tim. "You've mentioned it often enough. And you've deferred so many questions to the design phase that I'm really looking forward to just starting to get those answers at last."

"Right," said Nancy. "Now that we've finished the analysis, I think we have a pretty good picture of what you need. And as you've seen, we needed to have it collected and documented in a way that suits the rest of our task."

"Yeah," said Tim, "the UML notation and the statechart diagrams and all that stuff make a lot of sense, now that we've been through it all with you. I would never have dreamed of documenting the problem that way, nor in so much detail, but I can see that it works. What I am a bit puzzled about, though, is what to do with it next. But now that I see how you guys operate, I feel quite confident that you know where to go from here, and I'm ready to do it with you, whatever it is."

Nancy looked directly at Tim. "Well, the design phase is where we start to do some of these things without you. So far, everything we've written down came from you and your staff, and all Deanna and I supplied was the format. From here on, we get into a lot of more technical stuff, which we'll do behind the scenes. We'll still have a lot of stuff to run by you for input, however, so don't think you're off the hook yet. The parts that we do bring to you, you must be absolutely clear on, so please be ruthless about questioning what we write and satisfying yourself that you understand it, and that it works.

"One place where we'll need a lot of input from all your staff is the user interface design. We'll need to work directly with a few of your people to make sure the screens have everything on them that's needed, and in the right places, and in the right sequence. We'll be prototyping these – that is, we'll be designing screens, trying them out with your people, changing them, trying them again, and so on, round and round. We'll look after most of the technical decisions, like choices of language and database, single processor or network, and so on. We also have to decide how much extra stuff we should build in so that we can take advantage of future software products, and new features that are likely to be added to existing software."

"I see," said Tim. "So, I guess from here on, you'll call us as you need us."

"Right," responded Nancy, "we'll still need lots of discussion, but we won't need these regular meetings, so I'll give you a shout in a week or so when we've got started on it. We should have a bunch of questions for you by then."

THOUGHT QUESTIONS

1. What changes would you foresee in the role of the users as we move from the analysis phase to the design phase? Would you see the users being more involved or less as the project moves to design?

2. In your group, discuss the importance and effectiveness of testing, at the class level, program level, and the system level. Would you expect to find that testing is more important or less important in an object-oriented environment? What differences would you expect objects to make to the testing process? Would you see the users being more involved or less as the project moves to the testing phase? Document your answers and the significant discussion points, and review them with your group after studying the chapter.

13.1 OVERVIEW OF DESIGN CONSIDERATIONS

We defined *design*, you'll remember, as the process of producing a *plan*, to show *how* the proposed system will satisfy the requirements, that are outlined in the requirements analysis. This chapter is not intended to be a complete course in object-oriented systems design, but merely to highlight a number of important issues, techniques, and ideas.

There are many of what I usually refer to as "senior" books in this area, as you'll see under "Further Reading" at the end of the chapter. As indicated in Chapter 1, part of the objective of this book is to prepare you for such senior books, or "guru books." I believe that the concepts you've learned so far will enable you to make good use of those books.

So let's begin by asking, "Just what is a *design*?" and "What issues do I need to resolve, or be aware of, while I'm designing one?"

I think also that it would be appropriate here to review what it is we do in the design phase. In Chapter 6, we saw that the design phase is where we modify the analysis models to reflect decisions about the environment that the system will function in. This includes hardware and software decisions, optimization issues such as response times, and so on.

There are two major factors in this process. First, the design models start at the *logical* level and will evolve progressively toward the *physical* level. Second, they'll include a number of new objects and classes that don't directly model objects from the real world. *Abstract classes* are added for machine efficiency or for programming simplicity and code reuse.

Design: The Process and the Issues

Tom Love (1993) points out that there's a lot more to the design phase than just producing a design. In addition to compiling a plan of how we'll build a system to satisfy the requirements, you must also *show it to the users*. More than that, you must make sure they *understand* it. They must work through it in as much detail as you did when you produced it.

This would imply, then, that you and I as developers need to produce designs that are *truly simple and clear*. We must write in *plain English* and draw clear, unambiguous diagrams, and lots of them.

Of course, there will be many technical parts of the design that the users don't need to understand. This is unlike the analysis models, where the users should be able to read and critique the entire documentation. Our analysis is, after all, simply a documentation of *their* business operation, done from our point of view.

Another important thing is the way you go about showing it to them. It's very easy to overwhelm a group of users with page upon page of technical "English" and "PhDese"[1] and acres of obscure diagrams. They can easily be "blinded by science," and some might be scared off computerized systems permanently. If you give them too much at one time, they'll never master it.

But how do you eat an elephant? *One bite at a time!* As we saw in Chapter 12, the system must be broken into manageable chunks. To show the system to the users, we need chunks way smaller than subsystems.

You need to disclose the solution to the users progressively, piece by piece, incrementally. This way they can understand it and check it out for accuracy, practicality, usability, user-friendliness, and all those kind of things and then *feed their criticisms back to us* for *modifications* to our work.

Note that I say *for modifications*. So often, systems designers and course designers (and textbook authors) have a habit of regarding their design as totally adequate. This would seem to imply, then, that the poor user, student, or reader who can't understand it is therefore inadequate.

Not so! To make any progress at all, we must regard the user/student/reader as the standard, and make sure all our work can be read and understood by regular,

---

[1]This is a language that somewhat resembles English, often spoken by PhDs when they get together in groups, or when addressing groups of us mere mortals.

standard users. In practice, this means that anytime a user can't follow your "perfectly clear" directions, or my "perfectly clear" textbook, it's the *directions* and *explanations* that must be adjusted, not the user!

Love also states that a good designer needs to be able to predict the effect that each design decision will have on the overall cost of the project and its timing. According to Love, "The goal is to understand the customer's problem, propose a workable solution that includes costs and schedule, receive approval with modifications – *there's that word again!* – then communicate the final, detailed design to both the customer and construction crew."

Any design that contains unique or unusual features or components complicates the task of the developers. As much as possible, we need to reuse design classes and program code from earlier work. Such modules must be proven by prior usage in other projects, but they must still be tested exhaustively in this new environment (see Section 13.10).

One set of factors that often complicate testing are issues around concurrency and parallel processing.

13.2 CONCURRENCY AND THREADS OF CONTROL

It's at the design phase that we must think about the issue of concurrent processing. In a simple program, there is only one *thread of control*. Think of this as a needle drawing a thread through a "haystack" of program code. At any instant, the needle is pointing to the instruction that's currently executing. The "thread" laid out behind it gives a history of execution, although that's something we would only ever make use of if we were writing a debugger or a compiler, or some such.

So a ***thread of control*** is a path of execution that is currently being followed **through the program code.** The point is that in a simple machine with a simple operating system, there is only *one* such needle and only *one* such thread at any time. Only one instruction can be currently executing. So at any point in time there's only one sequence of steps being followed.

Multithreaded Execution

At the other extreme, a *concurrent computer*, also called a *multiprocessing computer* or *parallel computer,* has several CPUs, all capable of being busy doing something *at the same time*. LANs and all kinds of networks also fit this model. So in this case, each processor has its own independent thread of control.

This is something that standard sequential languages were never designed to handle. Concurrent operating systems for networks and for concurrent machines have had to include all kinds of devices to allow threads of control on the different processors to coordinate.

And in the middle, so to speak, multiprogramming and multitasking operating systems on sequential single-processor machines allow concurrent, multithreaded execution. In effect, they do this by simulating a multiprocessor machine. But we still need the complex communication and coordination features.

No doubt you've already guessed that I'm about to tell you how objects are a natural solution for this problem, too! Since an object is encapsulated, it works away at a task independently, until it's ready to send the answer back to its client object.

Since it's encapsulated, its client need know nothing about how and where it's doing the work. The object could be running as a separate independent task on the local processor, or it could have been sent off to a nearby processor or across the network or the continent to a processor with some free time.

And this can multiply. As our object continues with the task its client requested, it can in turn request data or tasks from other objects. Each of these is in turn encapsulated and thus could run on *any processor anywhere*, as long as it returns its answer to the right instance on the right processor. I can visualize this as producing a cascade of method calls across the nation! And with ORBs and CORBA (see later in this chapter), there are levels of compatibility here now that make this possible.

So the result is that many different things are happening at any point in time. Many objects are active at any moment, in each processor across the machine, the network, and the nation. And for that very necessary communication and coordination, objects make it much simpler. It works like this.

When one object (the client) sends a message to another requesting a service, the receiver (the Server) has several options:

- Act right now. This makes the message equivalent to a simple, synchronous function call. If the client must then pause and await the answer, this could have been equally well handled in a regular sequential language such as FORTRAN, Pascal, or COBOL. In object environments, it's often possible to have the client continue working for a while doing some things that don't depend on the answer, and then make it pause when it runs out of things to do while waiting.

- Wait a certain period or until a certain time, then do something.

- Wait for (an)other event(s) to occur, then act. The other events would appear as further messages.

- The Server object may send additional messages to other objects, for example, to request data or calculations. In this case, the original client object must pause until it receives an answer. It may pause immediately after sending the message, or it may be able to continue for a while doing other things first.

- The Server may send additional messages to other objects to begin completely new independent threads of execution. In this case, the original client object just keeps right on going with its work, while the Server object starts up the new task(s) independently.

  Further along, either or both may finish their task(s) and terminate, or they may "join up" again. This would happen if, say, one of them calculated or retrieved some data that it then provided to the other. That object may have been paused awaiting the data, or it may still be busy with its preparatory work, in which case the data may need to sit in limbo for a while until it can be used.

As Taylor (1995) points out, support for such concurrency was removed from most of the object-oriented languages, such as C++. At the time of writing, Java is the only OO language with threads built into the core of the language. This lonely status may soon change as other languages catch up. There are now concurrent versions of Smalltalk, C++, and other languages, especially among the versions for parallel computers. Parallel computers are an ideal way to exploit the concurrency power of objects, and objects are an ideal way to provide the concurrency needed by parallel computers!

Sometimes, there may be several clients who at the same time request things from a single Server instance. Taylor calls attention to the fact that a single object instance may at these times need to be involved in more than one operation. At the time of writing, this level of concurrency *within* an object is not yet supported by most of the OOPLs or ODBMSs, but the idea can be usefully applied during analysis.

Let me demonstrate the need for both interobject and intraobject concurrency in our analysis objects. Think of all the Person and Department instances in the place where you work or shop. What would be the effect if each one froze and did nothing, after requesting something from another object? We would at any given moment have most of the office standing around waiting for answers!

It just doesn't happen that way in the real world. If you leave a voice-mail message asking someone to send you a piece of information, you don't sit and gaze into space, or go for coffee, until you get it. You carry on with some other task, and most of us have any number of those waiting for our attention. Meanwhile, your friend looks up the item you want, and calls you back. Then you can go on with your original task. In this sense, e-mail and voice mail are asynchronous, and a regular ordinary phone call (POTS[2]) is synchronous.

If we're thinking of Person objects in that example, this is ***interobject concurrency*, where different objects are all working at the same time.**

On the other hand, all of us have been in situations where several bosses, clients, and subordinates have asked us for things, and we end up trying to do six things at once. This is ***intraobject concurrency*, many things happening at once within one single object instance.** Since real-world objects are capable of these kinds of interobject and intraobject concurrency, Taylor argues that it's also needed in the data objects that represent them (us).

I quite agree, and I hope the intraobject variety has been built into all the common development environments by the time you're out there doing object-oriented systems in the real world. I also trust that it will be hidden and automated to the extent that developers will not have to spend time worrying about it. Concurrency is something that should be largely transparent to developers, allowing them to focus on the application, and not the technology.

And one other thing you'll be doing in the design phase is to maximize reuse of classes and code by creating additional subclass hierarchies in appropriate places.

13.3 Adding Class Hierarchies with Abstract Classes

When we talked about subclasses and hierarchies back in Chapter 8 and elsewhere, I mentioned that it's sometimes necessary to add hierarchies during Design. While these may at times appear somewhat artificial, they're by and large justifiable if they lead to increased reuse or a simplified design:

---

[2]POTS: What the telephone people refer to as "Plain Old Telephone Service."

- *Generalize by adding a superclass to link two or more existing classes into a tree.* This allows new methods and data to be defined in one place only, the superclass. Very often this new superclass will be abstract – that is, it will have no direct instances.

  If it was a class with direct instances, it probably should have been discovered during Analysis. But, as you'll no doubt remember, it's okay for an abstract class to have *concrete operations*, with the method coded right there in the abstract superclass. It will then be inherited by the existing classes that have now become the subclasses.

- *Take a class from our analysis model and make it a subclass of an existing class.* This allows access to everything in the old class, with additions and changes in the new subclass. This gives increased reuse of existing methods and data definitions. The superclass may be from elsewhere in the analysis model or from an existing class library. This is how you make use of existing purchased or in-house class libraries, when you need to add or customize.

- Link two existing classes directly so one becomes a subclass of the other. This you do when you suddenly realize a little later that one *isakinda* the other.

There is a caveat, however. Wang and Wang (1994) have pointed out that if classes are being designed for reuse, then the class hierarchies must not be too deep. A potential reuser has a lot to work through to understand your classes, first to make a decision about reuse, and then to actually reuse them in his own project.

If your hierarchies are kept shallow, they're far easier to learn and understand. In addition, this also leaves more room for expansion by subclassing, without getting into overly deep trees. In turn, this makes maintenance simpler as well. As time goes by, many of the patches, fixes, and enhancements that get added to the system in the course of its life will come in the form of new subclasses. Starting with a shallow tree helps keep it all from getting out of control.

Love (1993) has quite a bit to say about developing classes for reuse. He describes the Visual Engineering Environment (VEE) developed by Hewlett-Packard (HP). (Love is convinced that, with the development of a suitable class library, this product would be an excellent system development tool.)

The important point about it for us is that the HP designers built upon the lessons they learned from an earlier project and in this one designed large objects. By that, I mean they tried to use classes with 1,000 lines of source code and 50 to 100 methods in each, although the final average was somewhat lower than this target.

I've also mentioned earlier about need to manage class libraries and how this will be the new job assigned to the DBA. In the Chapter 14, I'll go into this in detail, following a related discussion of software quality. For now, let's revisit another important aspect of objects, the removal of the discontinuities between phases in the OODLC.

13.4 COMMON REPRESENTATION THROUGHOUT THE OODLC

I have already discussed the effects of the discontinuities between phases of the older SDLC. These were changes in notation that we used to encounter as we moved from ERDs to DFDs to structure charts or flowcharts. They had the effect of lowering our productivity and accuracy and generally impairing our overall effectiveness.

The problem is that each different style of model needs a different style of *thinking* for someone to create one, or to work with it. In the old way, we had to keep making a complete turnabout in our way of thinking as we moved among these various models.

With the OODLC, we use the same representation, notation, and most importantly, the same style of thinking, from analysis all the way through to final testing. Iterations around and among the various phases become smoother and simpler. As evidenced by the emergence of the technique of prototyping, iterations are absolutely necessary. Yet when they're too uncomfortable or awkward, they'll often be overlooked or neglected. In the object paradigm, we can avoid this discomfort, so the iterating is done, is done more often, and is done better.

There's only one notation, one style of thinking, to learn. This not only makes it easier and cheaper to train the developers, but also allows us to better educate the users.

For the developers, learning four or five different techniques basically means taking four or five different courses. They then must divide whatever practice and experience time may be available over these various skills. For the users, on the other hand, their time is severely limited. (Not that it's unlimited for developers!)

In addition, many users who may have important information to contribute to the design, and thus need to be on the project, may not have the conceptual learning abilities that developers usually have. Our field, after all, is a highly abstract one.

By reducing the complexity of the whole thing, by reducing the number of difficult concepts, we bring this knowledge within the reach of a larger percentage of people. When more users understand what is going on, we get more and better information and ideas from them. We get more cooperation, enthusiasm, and user ownership of the project.

These last three intangibles, though practically unmeasurable, nonetheless are all critical success factors for any project. A ***critical success factor (CSF)* is any factor, condition, event, or the like, such that no matter what else is done and how much effort is put out, without this factor, success is not possible.** A CSF doesn't *guarantee* success; it's just that, no matter how hard you try, chances are you can't possibly succeed unless this one is also looked after.

So how do we move from one phase to the next through the OODLC? By simply *adding information* to the analysis model, using the same notation in all phases.

Design by Adding to the Analysis Model

In the design phase, then, we proceed by adding things to our existing analysis model:

- **Add classes.** As we saw above, new superclasses and subclasses may be added. Some of these are just to enhance reuse, but others are to handle such things as interfaces to users, other systems, networks, and communication lines. For this last, the communication protocol should be encapsulated within a class, so that a change of datacomm technology would cause changes only within this class.

- **Add methods.**

- **Add specs for methods.** In design, we'll do two things with methods. First, we'll discover a number of new ones; second, we need to spec out all methods so far discovered. Often you'll find that as you spec out a method for some class, it needs a function or a data item from another class. When you check, you find the other class doesn't yet have it, so it needs to be added to the list.

- **Add data attributes.**

- **Add specs for data attributes.** As with the methods, you'll often find that as you spec out a method for a class, you need to add a data item to this class, or perhaps to another class, and some basic methods to handle it. Following this, you must then go through all the attributes in all the classes and decide on data types and sizes, and so on.

  This also implies that you'll make all the appropriate decisions concerning type, format, and capacity of multivalued attributes such as lists; BLOBs (Binary Large OBjects, defined in Section 14.5); and graphics, sound, video, and other complex attributes.

And so the progressive addition of detail to the models takes us toward a fully specified design, *seeking the users' input the whole way.* Then the next phase is construction, where we use products such as OOPLs, ODBMSs, and OODENVs to build the system according to the plan from the final design.

This won't happen in one step or even a linear series of steps, of course. Prototyping is a very appropriate tool to use here, and this can be expected to cause more iterations within the design phase and also back to the analysis phase. By prototyping at this stage, we're actually blurring the boundary to the construction phase, since prototyping is really a matter of a little construction and user evaluation, followed by adjustments to the design; iterate as necessary.

Such prototyping usually begins with user interface prototyping.

13.5 USER INTERFACE DESIGN

This is probably the best-supported activity of all, in terms of the variety and quality of the software tools out there. The screen painters from the fourth generation languages (4GLs) have evolved into wonderful screen-design tools with window and button classes that inherit from all kinds of other classes.

And this should not be surprising, given the importance of an effective, highly usable user interface. We must always remember that, to the user, *the interface* **is** *the system*. Time and effort must be spent on ensuring that users get an interface that does what they *actually need*, as opposed to what we may think is kinda cool. This effort will reap a huge payoff in the level of success of the project as a whole.

These allow you to begin with a prebuilt set of screen object classes, that implement a standard such as Windows or X Windows or whatever. You assemble the pieces on the screen where and how you want them by instantiating those classes, that is, creating instances of them. (I really abhor that word *instantiating*; I use it only because it's so delightfully ugly!)

Customizing is done by defining new classes, as subclasses of the ones provided in the class library that comes with the GUI design product. Of course, any customizing you may do is reusable within that screen, or anywhere else in the system. Put these things in your in-house class library, and they can become standards for the project, or for the whole company.

The list begins with products such as Delphi, PowerBuilder, Visual Basic, and Visual C++ and continues on, growing *monthly*. A scan through the pages of *Component Strategies* magazine, or TAPOS or one of those (see Appendix A1) will give you a good idea of what's out there.

One further thought on user interfaces: Video and audio are now feasible. Since objects can have complex attribute data types, including audio and video clips, these become possible additions to user screens.

Video games and their close relatives, training simulations, have plenty of need and opportunity for video and audio clips in the user interface. But even the formerly staid world of data entry can benefit; point-of-sale data capture, and so on can can all be improved with audio or video. For example, errors could be flagged with sound effects, and correction instructions delivered on the spot by voice or video.

Video will be widely used, especially for computer-assisted instruction, interactive tutorials, and other forms of on-line training and education. Video, graphic, and audio clips sitting in attributes will be available for all the creative uses you can think up for them. For instance, I've seen a remedial reading tutorial where a request for "pronunciation" brought down a video of a mouth and chin covering a quarter of the screen, and the student would both watch and hear the correct pronunciation.

Here is a summary of what we've said so far about design:

- Your design must be in a form such that the users can understand and critique all the nontechnical parts. You "progressively disclose" the design to them in manageable increments (manageable to *them*, that is, not just what *we* would consider manageable), so as not to overwhelm them.

- There is a need for both *interobject concurrency*, where different objects are all working at the same time, and *intraobject concurrency*, with many things happening at once *within* an object. Since real-world objects are capable of both kinds of concurrency, both are also needed in data objects.

- Love suggests you should design *large objects* – try for classes with 1000 lines of source code and 50 to 100 methods in each, although the final average will be less. On the other hand, you must also make sure that potential reusers of your work can quickly and easily understand your classes and hierarchies.

- The same representation, notation, and style of thinking, from analysis on through construction, make for smoother iterations among the phases. When they're too uncomfortable or awkward, they're overlooked or neglected. In the object paradigm, we avoid this discomfort, so iterating happens more freely.

- By reducing complexity, more users understand, and we get better information and cooperation from them, and also more user ownership in the project – these intangibles are *critical success factors* for any project.

- In the design phase, we add things to our existing analysis model:
  - Classes
  - Methods
  - Specs for methods
  - Data attributes
  - Specs for data attributes

- Design a GUI with window and button classes that inherit from other (supplied) classes. Begin with prebuilt screen object classes that implement a standard, and assemble on the screen. Define subclasses of library classes. Customizing is reusable within that screen or anywhere else, and can form standards for your project and company.

Which then brings me to the matter of choosing an implementation language and environment.

13.6 CHOICE OF IMPLEMENTATION LANGUAGE AND ENVIRONMENT

It's a very common fact of life that for most projects the development environment is usually in place before the project even begins. This is often the case when you're employed in an existing IT department, or going into one as a consultant. However, many times you have the opportunity to choose, or at least influence the choice.

This is especially so on small projects for small-business clients, PC-based jobs, and the like. Assuming that you do happen to have some influence, in this section I present some questions and issues for you to think about as your design progresses. You need to make the purchase decisions early in the design phase, since many of your design decisions depend on the development environment chosen. If languages and environments are to be evaluated, this needs to happen even earlier, alongside or before the analysis phase.

Also, you must allow sufficient time for purchase, delivery, installation, and testing of and training on the products you've selected. All these activities need to be included in your project plan, with ample time allowed for problems and delays. They need to be completed comfortably before any construction or prototyping can take place.

Love (1993) has an excellent chapter on these issues, and some of what follows is adapted from his work. I've also drawn on an article by Richard Daley (1994) in a collection edited by Andy Carmichael (1994) titled *Object Development Methods*.

Languages

There are three basic choices: pure, extended, and hybrid languages.

PURE OBJECT LANGUAGES

Smalltalk is probably the purest of the pure. In Smalltalk, *everything* is an object, even files on disks. This is the purest way to go object-oriented. By being forced into a pure object-oriented mode, you'll be sure to gain the maximum possible benefit from using objects.

Eiffel is another one.

While Java is arguably a little "less pure" than those two, I would nonetheless term it "fully pure" in the sense that there is no other way to write Java code except object-oriented. It is also more widely known than Eiffel or Smalltalk. Though some purists may argue that Java is "impure" because it doesn't have *everything* as a class, in practice I believe it belongs in this group.

The major downside of the "pure" languages is the need for training and experience. While virtually all new graduates entering the field these days have had some Java courses, your existing staff will mostly need to be trained from the ground up. Eiffel and Smalltalk experience are not yet common among consultants, but Java is.

EXTENDED LANGUAGES

These are languages where the object-oriented features have been added on while attempting to preserve the structure and rules of the original language. Object Pascal and C++ fall into this group. One of the major advantages is the existing base of programmers in the original language, who need simply to learn the object extensions. But, as we shall see, even that "advantage" may be misleading.

The downside is the *ability to violate encapsulation*, and the temptation to write old-style code in the new language. Mind you, being able to violate encapsulation can be helpful for optimizing, but that tends to make the programs untidy and just as difficult to maintain as the old style.

HYBRID LANGUAGES

These add an object layer to the basic language. A hybrid environment still gives access to the original base language and its operating environment. Objective-C does this by adding Smalltalk-like syntax to C, without altering the C syntax. A hybrid has roughly the same advantages and disadvantages as an extended language.

Note that extended and hybrid languages are often confused, both in the literature and in conversation. Often you'll find either term used to cover both *kindsa* languages, in other words, all "impure" object-oriented languages. Love compares five languages on a number of factors such as strength of object typing, execution speed, memory management, and even number of copies sold, as of his publication date (1993). Java has since changed things somewhat. While such a comparison is, as he says, out of date before it's published, it's still illustrative of the capabilities of those languages.

Related to the issue of language, you'll need to decide on a database and a user interface product, *and make sure they're compatible.*

Databases

At this point in object-oriented history, a lot of systems are being developed using object methods, but are being built around a relational database. It works, obviously. Most of the major relational databases by now have object-oriented front ends and screen builders available. Conversely, all object-oriented user interface products such as Delphi, PowerBuilder, and Visual BASIC and Visual C++ ("The Visuals," as I call them) have interfaces to the popular relational databases, typically through ODBC or SQL.

My personal preference, however, is to do it this way only if forced to because the client has already spent the money on Oracle 7, or has staff with 100 person-years of Sybase relational experience. The object-oriented databases are now mature enough to do the job reliably. Oracle and the other major relational vendors are moving rapidly into objects.

The serious ODBMSs all now have the heavy-duty "industrial-strength" features to handle concurrency, transactions, rollbacks, distributed objects, and security. They now have the things we need to handle serious, mission-critical applications, just as effectively as the relational guys.

My choice is to go objects all the way. Mind you, since all major relational databases are now going object-oriented, this will place Oracle, Sybase, and the rest in contention right alongside Versant, O2, and the others.

Then there are a bunch of administrative issues as well.

Administrative Issues

PROCEDURES

Far be it from me to saddle every developer with the task of memorizing the organization's procedure manual. But everyone needs to know or be briefed on common basic procedures – such as how to book a conference room, a vehicle, or audio-visual equipment; any taboos there may be in the client organization; how to submit purchase orders, mileage claims, meal claims, and the like, or who to get to do it for them. Then there are issues that touch both technical and administrative areas.

VERSIONING

The more sophisticated development environments have comprehensive facilities for handling groups of people all working on the same project. Also, there are a number of specialized version control products on the market. They allow a developer to "check out" a class and then check it back in when finished modifying it. The system must then make sure that all the other team members get to work on the *updated* one.

It gets more complex when two or more of you are working on the same class together. The larger the team, the more critical it is to be able to manage versions of everything, from individual classes and methods to versions (releases) of the final product.

SECURITY AND PERMISSIONS

Along with versions go a couple of other things. Security provisions such as passwords and user IDs are a must. Each developer should be restricted to changing only the parts of the system she's authorized to. It's also important to have traceability on changes and updates. Changes should be automatically date/time stamped and the user ID recorded, in some tamper-proof fashion. Project managers are going to need query facilities, to enquire on change histories and to generate a list of change permissions both by developer and by class.

STAFF RESPONSIBILITIES

Questions such as these should be asked: Who is in charge of support for the development environment? Who do I report bugs in library classes to? Or compiler, database or GUI bugs? How do I get tech support? And who do I go to for office support? And even: Who is my mentor? (Make sure everybody knows who to go to for help.)

CLASS LIBRARIES

You need to evaluate and select class libraries to purchase (and also some that may have been purchased already). You also need to carefully check the classes you expect to reuse from your in-house libraries. Can you use them substantially as is? What classes need to be fine-tuned, optimized, or modified? Which ones need to be subclassed?

TESTING

You need documented testing standards and procedures. Does your environment support the level of comprehensive testing described later in this chapter, in the section on testing?

DOCUMENTATION

Does your environment encourage complete documentation? Does it support everything recommended below under testing?

OTHER ISSUES

In the next few sections, we look at a number of other things that involve you in decisions, such as distributed objects, ORBs and CORBA compliance.

13.7 DISTRIBUTED OBJECTS

Throughout this entire book so far, we've discussed objects under the unexamined assumption that all this data and code is sitting right here, available the moment you need it. It could be on the local hard disk perhaps, or somewhere equally convenient. However, in the words of the incorrigible Sportin' Life, "It Ain't Necessarily So!"[3] It may be that the data and code that make up the object we're dealing with are spread across the company, the city, or the nation.

This can happen several ways. Within a class, some instances may be on the local disk and others across the network. Within a single instance, some instance variables (attributes) may be on one network node and some on another; or on a single machine, some in one file and some in another. The methods might be similarly distributed. And again, we might have multiple copies of an instance or of certain attributes or methods, on different machines in different cities.

---

[3]Title of a song from *Porgy and Bess* by George Gershwin.

There are a number of reasons why this might happen, one of which we'll discuss in detail in Chapter 15, and that's *legacy systems*. In that chapter, we'll see how we can simulate an object-oriented interface to existing older systems by surrounding legacy data with an object-oriented "wrapper." Sometimes, when we attempt to do this, we find that the old designers have splattered the data we need, and the program code that uses it, across the company, nation, or continent.

To assemble all relevant attributes and program code into a usable object-oriented form, we end up encapsulating this inside a *distributed object*. The old data and code could be anywhere, since it was designed without regard to what rightfully belongs in any given object.

When we encapsulate this within an object wrapper, we have to take it from wherever we can get it. But fortunately, we can hide the details of its physical location and format within what is really a pseudo-object. client objects simply send the usual messages, and the methods within the wrapper object are left to sort out the request, locate the data, and prepare an appropriate response.

Another reason could be for optimizing. When the data is needed at several locations around the company, city, nation, or world, response times could be horrific and unstable if we're retrieving across communications links or the Internet. Hence the need for a database to have multiple distributed copies of a single instance.

This then implies a need for such things as two-phase commits, where the various copies of the database communicate back and forth to make sure they're all in step. Either that, or we need some other way of coordinating and updating the data, and then there is a whole slew of problems that go with distributed databases.

All the complexity found with distributed relational databases is still there for distributed objects. The two-phase commit is expensive, and subject to repeated failures and re-attempts, especially when we have hundreds of copies over large distances. Because of this, it's usually reserved for critical data – that is, where human lives may depend on it. Less critical applications can get away with periodic updates (overnight, for example) or other devices to ensure adequate currency for the data.

All of this is then encapsulated within the distributed objects, and the client objects know nothing of it at all. What is more, a switch from periodic updates to two-phase commits, say, would also be invisible to the clients, none of whom would need to be modified to accommodate such a change. They would just one day find themselves working with data that is more current than they're used to getting.

So the actual data and program code can be physically spread among several geographic locations, several hardware platforms, several software products, or any combination of these. This physical complexity is encapsulated within the object, so its clients (be they users, programs, or methods of another object) are not aware of what is going on.

To the client, it appears as just another object, with some data available via some methods. The problems of finding the data across networks, and of coordinating multiple copies of the data, are all hidden from view, that is, they're encapsulated within the distributed object.

Now, all this communication and interchanging of data is going to require a high level of compatibility among the many products involved. This is the province of the newly emerging *object request broker* (ORB) technology.

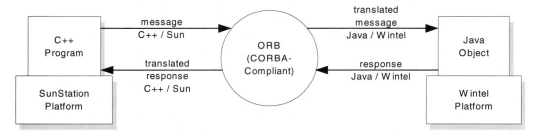

Figure 13-1   The ORB

13.8 OMG, ORBs, AND CORBA

There has been an exciting development in the object-oriented field, promising levels of compatibility that we programmers could only dream of in earlier times. What makes it so exciting is the fact that an industry organization has been formed to set the necessary standards, and with so many members, it represents almost the entire industry.

The Object Management Group (OMG) has been formed with almost 1000 member organizations (at the time of writing) and is still growing. In other words, virtually the entire industry! Its mandate is to develop the standards for a new kind of product called an *object request broker* (ORB). This is how it works.

You may be writing an object-oriented program in C++ on your SunStation, and you need to call a method and/or retrieve some data from a class that you know exists already, elsewhere in the company. So you send off the appropriate message, saying, in effect, "Object, do your thing for me!" Now, the awkward part is that the object you're addressing happens to have been written in Smalltalk on a Mac.

Enter the ORB. In the new scheme of things, your message goes not to the object but to the ORB, as you see in Figure 13-1. The ORB then translates your request into Smalltalk format on the different operating system, and passes it over to the other platform, where it finds the target object residing.

The target, of course, understands the translated message and responds to it in Smalltalk format. This response goes back to the ORB, where it's translated for C++ on a Sun, and is passed on. Your C++ program code understands the translated answer and accepts it joyfully.

In this way, what the ORB does is to *broker* the requests going from object to object, hence the name *object request broker*. And that's not all. Eventually, you won't need to know anything about the target object or even its location. You'll simply request the data you need, and the ORB will worry about where it is and in what format. Thus, we have yet another level of encapsulation!

So, an ***object request broker (ORB)*** **is a software product that intercepts messages from an object, translates them for language, operating system, or other differences in environment, and routes them to the correct object, wherever it may be, geographically or "platformally."**

The OMG standard describes the structure and appearance of an ORB, so it's referred to as an "architecture" for the ORB. Since it's to be common to ORBs from different manufacturers, it has thus been named the *common object request broker architecture* or *CORBA* (be careful to pronounce it correctly, with the *R* sounded *before* the *B*.)

The OMG is not developing any products. Rather, it is producing a *standard*. The OMG will also certify compliance to that standard – that is, the OMG will evaluate a product and issue a certification saying whether it complies. Such products may then bill themselves as CORBA-*certified*.

At a less rigorous level, any product that has been designed within the standard may call itself CORBA-*compliant*, without need for testing and certification.

At the time of writing, the OMG has published the CORBA 3.0 spec. This specifies all rules and standards needed for objects and classes from various authors, and in various languages, to interact successfully via ORBs from various vendors.

The OMG has defined the Interface Definition Language (IDL), which allows us to document the details of a class. We use the IDL to record the attributes, methods and their parameters, classes it inherits from, and so on. Once this has been done, the ORB software will generate globally unique identifiers, so these objects can then be used from anywhere in our system.

The OMG has defined a number of object services that an ORB must provide. These include the following list, and we can expect more to be added as time goes by. You'll note that I haven't defined them in detail, since this is all still in the process of evolution.

Much will change over the next few years, and I include this list just to give you an idea of what can be done. Check current issues of magazines and periodicals in the object-oriented field (see www.wiley.com) to find out what is happening at the state of the art.

At www.omg.org you'll find membership lists for the eight different classes of OMG members. (Should that be "eight subclasses of Member?") The site also provides articles explaining CORBA and the other work of the OMG. There is even a section called "Free Stuff" where you can download ORBs and other software.

Here, then, is a list of object services that an ORB must provide in order to call itself CORBA-compliant:

- Class and object naming (allowing you to assign the class a name and "register" that name, much as a data dictionary registers a data name)

- Event notification

- Persistence (allowing objects to survive from one execution session into the future; this is the primary feature that an object database must provide)

- Object life-cycle management

- Transactions (with commit, rollback, and associated operations)

- Concurrency control (i.e, concurrent access to the database by different users, locking, deadlock avoidance, etc.)

- Relationships and associations

- Externalization
- Queries
- Licensing
- Properties
- Security
- Time

By the time you read this, all of it will have been extended and improved. It is my sincere hope that you'll all be in a position to benefit from CORBA-compliant ORBs, in whatever form the standard has evolved to by then.

ODMG

There's an interesting subgroup that has formed from within the OMG. This not a splinter group, because that would be in opposition. These companies are all OMG members; they're the object database manufacturers.

The Object Data Management Group (ODMG) is committed to developing database interoperability among their ODBMS products, all within the CORBA specification. All of its members are also in the OMG Special Interest Group on Object Databases (SIGDB).

They have a rather unique and effective way of achieving their objectives. It is built around these two commitments:

- It is the intention of the ODMG that, wherever possible, any feature they mandate members to add to their products will be based on a feature that one or more members already have. This way (1) they know it's a workable and useable feature, and (2) they know it *can* be built, and what it should look like.

- Voting members must commit, as a condition of voting membership, that any feature decided upon by the ODMG will be in their products within 18 months of its publication. This ensures that all will do it together, and make it work, over a suitably short time frame.

These commitments, by the way, are in addition to paying the rather stiff membership fee, designed to retain only the very serious and weed out the merely curious.

Atwood (1994) discusses the ODMG and its work. The two current standards, CORBA 3.0 and ODMG 3.0, are discussed in Chapter 14 of this book. The ODMG membership list may be viewed at www.odmg.org and from the website you can buy or download books, articles and "white papers" that explain the work of the group.

The process is gathering tremendous momentum and promises great things for the near future. At the time of formation of ODMG, the five original voting members represented almost 90% of the ODBMS market worldwide. Because of this, whatever they do as a group is a de facto standard anyway.

So now that we're assured of sufficiently high levels of compatibility in the near future, let's talk about building objects for reuse.

13.9 COMPONENTS

Much of the recent literature refers to objects as "parts" or "components." What such terms are trying to suggest is that software should be built from prefabricated "parts" much the same way as an engineer designs and assembles physical machinery.

When an engineer designs a new product, he doesn't do everything from scratch. For a new model of lawnmower, say, our designer would not attempt to reinvent the motor, nor, for that matter, the wheel!

Instead, she would build into the product a motor and wheels that have already been designed (probably by someone else), built, tested, and already proven in production and use. In other words, she would use as many off-the-shelf parts as possible. This has a number of benefits:

- *Reduction in time, effort, and cost.* Reinventing the wheel is costly and error-prone. In engineering we can make far more productive use of our designers' creativity by keeping them working on new stuff. This tends to challenge and inspire them more too, which compounds the benefits. In the software business we gain precisely the same things by reuse of software components, by which I mean reusing classes that already exist.

  For us, this reduction in cost would seem to be by far the major benefit. But there are a number of intangibles involved here, such as fatigue and boredom, inspiration and motivation, the effects of working under deadline pressure, and so on. When summed, these various intangibles could make this one of the most important benefits of component reuse.

- *Economies of scale.* When we produce larger quantities of a single hardware product, this is better than spreading the required total quantity over several different kinds of products. We find that the unit cost is reduced because, among other things, we have longer production runs and thus fewer production setups.

  The parallel benefit with software is that we save a little on distribution costs for copies of the classes. Also, we're doing maintenance on a smaller number of classes. And there's a finite saving on making the copies, but this is negligible since the costs of copying software are so minuscule.

- *Inventory reduction.* When we sell or use twice as many of one hardware item, rather than half as many of two items, we don't need to keep double the stock on the shelf. This way, we find that fluctuations in demand are smoothed somewhat, and "safety stock" can be greatly reduced. In a physical inventory, this represents a reduction in the amount of capital tied up in shelf stock.

  For software components (classes), the parallel benefit is that we reduce the size and complexity of our class libraries. This makes browsing them simpler and more effective. When searching for a suitable class to reuse, we're less likely to overlook a good one.

Systems designers have always been aware of the need to reuse software components, but it's only with the advent of the object paradigm that this has become a truly attainable goal. Objects are encapsulated the same way motors and wheels are, giving the possibility of what we might call "off-the-shelf" classes. In the words of Orfali et al. (1994), we'll end up with "live blobs of intelligence and data in an infinite number of Lego-like arrangements."

And now a summary about language issues, compatibility, and components:

- If languages and environments are to be purchased and evaluated, this will need to happen with or before the analysis phase. Allow time for purchase, delivery, installation, testing, and training on the products. Include these activities in your project plan; allow for problems and delays. They'll need to be completed before construction or prototyping.

- There are three kinds of OO languages: pure, extended, and hybrid.

  - *Pure object languages.* In Smalltalk, *everything* is an object. In Java, there is no other option except to code in objects. Eiffel is another one. The downside is the need for training and experience.

  - *Extended languages.* These have added object-oriented features while preserving the structure of the original language, for example, Object Pascal and C++. The advantage is the existing base of programmers. The downside is the ability to violate encapsulation and write old-style code in the new language. Violating encapsulation is sometimes OK for optimizing (with the help of a true expert), but makes programs difficult to maintain.

  - *Hybrid languages.* Add objects to the base language. A hybrid gives full access to the base language. Objective-C does it by adding Smalltalk-like syntax to the C syntax. A hybrid has roughly the same advantages and disadvantages as an extended language.

- Hybrid and extended languages are usually lumped together under either name.

- Compare languages on factors such as strength of typing, execution speed, memory management,

- Serious ODBMSs now have heavy-duty "industrial-strength" features for concurrency, transactions, rollbacks, distributed databases, and security for mission-critical applications, as do current RDBMSs.

- My advice is go *objects all the way.* Relational databases will soon all be object-oriented, so Oracle, Sybase, and the rest will compete with Versant, Objectivity, and the others.

- In design we must deal with issues around procedures, versioning, security, permissions, responsibilities, class libraries, testing, and documentation.

- The Object Management Group (OMG), with almost 1,000 member organizations, develops standards for object request brokers (ORBs). An ORB intercepts messages from objects, translates them, and routes them to the correct object, wherever it may be, geographically or "platformally."

- The OMG is producing a standard, rather than products. The OMG certifies compliance to that standard, which describes the architecture for the ORB – that is, the Common Object Request Broker Architecture (CORBA).

- The OMG has defined object services that ORBs must provide; more will be added over time.

- The Object Data Management Group (ODMG) is developing database interoperability among their ODBMS products, all within the CORBA specification.

- Any feature the ODMG mandates members to add to their products will be based on a feature that one or more members already have. This way, they know it's a workable feature, and they know it can be built.

- Voting members must commit, as a condition of voting membership, that any feature decided upon by the ODMG will be in their products within 18 months.

- With software components, a designer would use as many off-the-shelf "parts" as possible.

- By reusing classes that already exist, we reduce time, effort, and cost, and challenge and inspire designers by keeping them working on new stuff.

- Reuse gives a reduction of inventory. Fluctuations in demand are smoothed, and safety stock is reduced. Reuse reduces the size and complexity of class libraries and makes browsing simpler and more effective; reuse makes us less likely to overlook a good class.

- There are a number of intangible benefits from reuse, such as reducing fatigue and boredom, effects of working under deadline pressure, and enhanced inspiration and motivation. The intangibles could be the most important benefit of component reuse.

- Systems designers have always been aware of the need to reuse software components; only with objects has this has become attainable. Objects are encapsulated the same way motors and wheels are, giving the possibility of "off-the-shelf" classes.

There's another kind of object looming on the horizon. The *intelligent agent* is a concept that has been dreamed up but awaits advances in both artificial intelligence and object technology (including CORBA) before it can really become practical.

Intelligent Agents

There has been much focus in the popular literature on the development of robots in industry over the last few decades. Movies such as the *Star Wars* series (still growing!) have depicted anthropomorphic robots like R2D2 and C3P0.

Most of us think of robots as physical entities, pieces of electromechanical machinery that can think and act independently. This has tended to obscure the fact that, like any artificial intelligence (AI), *the intelligence of a robot lies in its software*. AI research doesn't require special hardware; it uses AI *software* running on PCs, Macs, VAXen, and UNIX boxes.

This in turn would suggest the possibility of *software robots*, which we can call *agents*. Think for a moment what a software robot might look like. It would need some program code to make things happen and some data to work with. If you think this sounds suspiciously like an object, you're right.

The difference is that an agent carries on with its assigned task without further direction from the user or other object that invoked it. In fact, an agent is an object that, once created, carries on an independent existence, determined to complete the task it was designed for. Because it carries on independently, an agent requires an environment that supports multithreaded execution and concurrent processing.

There are agents already in use, with varying amounts of "intelligence." Web-crawlers and such fit the definition of an agent. But AI will be the key that brings out the full potential – as it will for most things in society, not just for software agents.

Let's illustrate how an intelligent agent might function by looking at a hypothetical "GPA Agent," designed to assemble a transcript of a student's college career and calculate the grade-point average (GPA). What follows is perhaps somewhat fanciful, but real agents can do these things, or soon will be able to.

I've described how I think this might happen a few years from now, assuming that the levels of compatibility promised by CORBA and OMG do come about. We'll follow this agent through its life cycle, from when it's created through the completion of its assigned task and its eventual destruction.

The process begins when a student or clerk keys in a request for a transcript, and the GPA-Agent class creates an instance of itself. This GPA-Agent instance then initiates a search of the student records by invoking methods in the Student class.

An instance is created in the Transcript class, and then messages fly back and forth among a variety of classes, as Grade attribute values from the enrollment instances are sought and found and fed into the GPA calculation. As each line for the transcript is assembled, it is stored in its own instance of the Line-Item class. All of this is facilitated by an ORB, of course.

Then, let's say, a different kind of record is discovered. It seems that some of the courses this student has credit for were taken at another college. Our GPA-Agent instance knows what to do about this. Invoking a method in the Internet-Interface class, the GPA-Agent instance sends an e-mail to the other college. This e-mail just happens to be a complete copy of *itself*. Then it deletes the original local copy of itself (i.e., the original copy "commits suicide.")

In this way, it has "traveled" across a data link. When it arrives in the computers at the other college, it simply begins anew its functions of finding the Student instance in the Student class (in the new computer) and scanning the Enrollment class for grades to use in the GPA calculation.

Eventually, when it has assembled the Line-Item instances it needs, it e-mails first itself, then those details, back to the home college. Then it deletes both itself and those Line-Items from the new college's computer (this time the *second* copy of the GPA-Agent instance commits suicide).

When the returning copy (which is now copy 3) of our GPA-Agent instance arrives back in the home college computer, it adds the Line-Items that it brought back with it to the ones already waiting. When all Line-Items it needs are built, it sends them to the printer, deletes them from the Line-Item class, and then finally deletes itself (suicides for real).

How was it able to check out the student's records in a foreign computer and come back with a grade and course details to appear on the transcript? Because both colleges built their information systems with CORBA-compliant tools, and used "tertiary education industry-standard" naming conventions. (This standard is something I made up for this story, but I'm certain something like it will come into being in the not-too-distant future.)

Thus, our "GPA-Agent instance copy" is able to function when it arrives at the other college, just as if it had been born there. So, ever mindful of its purpose, it simply got busy issuing the same messages it had been issuing at home. Because of the standardized object interfaces, and because of encapsulation, the objects in the new college's system responded with *methods appropriate to their system*. These methods worked differently inside than the ones at home, but they produced compatible results.

So an **_gent_ is an object that, once created, becomes independent. Without further direction, it performs the various functions needed to achieve the task it was designed for.** Agents will be able to "mail" themselves like the one above did or copy themselves as needed, to perform their designated task.

You'll note that in the example I had the original copy commit suicide after sending off the copy to the other college. Of course, it's not really necessary for it to do that.

Earlier we discussed the need and potential for concurrent processing among objects, and here is a place where we can exploit it. The original GPA-agent could have just kept on processing, continuing to build up a stack of Line-Item instances, while its twin did the same across the continent. And if the student's career spanned three or a dozen colleges, our GPA-Agent instance could have mailed copies of itself wherever necessary, and all could be busily processing in parallel.

For some applications, however, a serial agent might work better than a parallel one. Imagine an agent that will check all the hotels in Banff or Aspen, until it finds a room that suits your needs! It could mail itself from one hotel to the next, then as soon as it found a room, mail itself home to your place with the good (or bad) news.

Agents will know how to defragment (*defrag*) your disks, order flowers, buy a ticket for a concert, find you a house or car to buy, schedule a meeting, book a conference room, enroll you in a course, sort and filter data, present and analyze information, and so ad infinitum. Another way to state the definition might be to say that **an _agent_ is an intelligent packet of data and program code – that is, an _intelligent object_ – capable of independent existence, designed to perform a certain set of functions, and carrying the necessary data attributes within itself.**

So far, agents are at a very early stage of development, and intelligent agents are mostly confined to research projects in AI. Because they carry both program code and data, their development is being spurred on by the advent of object technology.

You'll notice that I've included the word *intelligent* in the definition. While simple ones have been built already, agents can't really come into their own until the advent of serious AI. I'm sure you've already imagined a few of the myriad problems and exceptions that could stop the GPA-Agent in the story dead in its tracks. Because an agent receives little or no direction once it's working, it needs to be smart enough – that is, *truly* intelligent – to solve many different kinds of problems.

But here's another thought. What if some of our agents (think of them as "software robots") were as smart as us? (And there's no reason to believe that AI research can't achieve this in a few more years.) What we would then have is the situation depicted in movies such as *Tron, Johnny Mnemonic,* and the last part of *Lawnmower Man I*. That is, we have *sentient* (intelligent, self-aware) creatures inhabiting the computer!

I once used to think that such movies were pure fantasy, but I'm no longer so sure. And I think Isaac Asimov (1950) was right to be concerned about the ethics of robots in their attitude to their makers, and to have his characters develop "The Three Laws of Robotics." But even so, I suspect he may not have been aware of just how important it is that software programmers also maintain those very same ethics, or some improved version.

Asimov's stories bring to light a number of potential problems, particularly with the failure of the Three Laws in their attempt to protect humans. (So your homework this weekend is to rent and watch those three movies, and read *I Robot*.)

Rasmus (1995) has a view of agents that differs in a few points from what I've presented above. He suggests that agents will be "small, relatively fragile, knowledge-based objects" and that they'll "consume and redistribute information (and) exist in communities."

He predicts they'll "behave like tiny digital critters" and that, like bacteria, it'll take swarms of them to do something, each one contributing just a little to the overall task. I think there will be needs and opportunities for both kinds of agents, and for many others in between as well.

Not only that, but Rasmus hints that for agents that can reproduce themselves, we might accidentally or purposely give them some way to mutate. Once that's possible, so is evolution, through some form of natural selection. And since the generations will go by at processor speeds, this evolution and selection could be quite rapid. Fanciful? What kind of Dr Frankenstein have we become? It's just as well that evolving software agents don't leave fossils to clutter up hard disks!

Of course, mutated agents with bugs won't survive many generations. In fact, all forms of reuse depend on libraries of *robust* and *reliable* object classes that have been thoroughly *tested* under all conditions.

13.10 TESTING

Why would we discuss testing in the design chapter? Surely it belongs further along the OODLC, after the construction phase? Well, I'm glad you asked, because thorough and effective testing requires thought, planning, and preparation. Since we defined Design to be the process of producing a plan for the system, it's also the appropriate stage to produce detailed plans for testing the system.

In earlier chapters, we saw that you need to document and save your use cases so they become test cases. These provide a high-level test, covering complete user sessions, but by itself this is nowhere near enough. Before we start testing the users' views of the system, we must begin by testing separately each module, unit, and component the system is made up of. In the object-oriented paradigm, that of course means testing every class.

When testing is unstructured, it usually consists of trying a few (somewhat incomplete) use cases, and fixing any crashes or inaccurate results. Only a small percentage of developers take a systematic approach and test all or most combinations and permutations of the various inputs and situations.

As a result, we normally expect to see a large number of crashes and bugs in the early production runs. Other faults may lurk hidden for months or even years, until one day they manifest themselves. Many developers will attempt to remedy this by asking some of their peers to try and make the system fail, usually referred to as "breaking the system." Then they may ask some users to do the same.

While each of these approaches can certainly be expected to turn up more bugs and crashes, neither is systematic enough to do a thorough job. Many parts of the system will never be "exercised" this way. Many of the less frequent or less obvious user processes may be overlooked. Some of the unusual options, combinations, and circumstances are likely to be neglected. Under these conditions, you'll never know just how much of your system has and has not been tested.

If you were being conscientious, then throughout your analysis you've been thinking up what-ifs (*and documenting*, in case you get moved to another project.) For each class, each attribute, and each method, you must dream up all the what-if's and exceptions that will need testing.

As we've already seen, in the design phase you'll be adding a number of classes, attributes, and methods to your model, for various reasons. As you do this, you must be thinking of test cases at each step. As you design each class, attribute, or method (old ones or added ones), you must also design the test cases it'll need to exercise all its parts. Designing a test case means:

- Identifying just what error or exception it is that we're testing for. The we need to know which use ase it's in.

- Planning the sequence of events that will make up the test, often to the extent of pseudocode.

- Creating the appropriate test-data values.

- Calculating the predicted output, for every combination of inputs and circumstances. Each input must be tried many times, while the object is in each of its allowable states.

Later, in the coding phase, you'll code a stub program or program segment as part of a "test suite" that will invoke the unit to be tested and run all these tests. For right now, you'll produce a *design* for the test suite as part of the design for the class.

Testing and Reusability

Designing for reuse adds its own set of testing requirements. Classes that are reused in another project must be both ***reliable*, meaning they will still give the right answers in a new environment, and *robust*, meaning they will not crash in new environments.** We must also be careful that they have no side effects. **A *trustworthy* class, then, is reliable, robust, and has no significant side effects.**

Many object-oriented developers take the stand that reuse in itself provides enough testing. They argue that by the time a class has been reused a few times, all the errors must have been found. What they're forgetting, of course, are the points I made in the previous section, about unstructured testing. Frequent reuse still can't guarantee that the entire class has been exercised, or even come close.

To ensure trustworthiness in our classes, we must not do it this way. Instead, each time a class is reused, especially if it had a few little changes or additions, we must retest it *completely*.

Often we'll find unexpected incompatibilities, or missing or inadequate behavior when we try the class in its new environment. We can't assume that because a method works properly when invoked by one client object, it always will for other clients.

This level of comprehensive testing can be time-consuming, so it *must be automated*. We must set it up once at the start and then automate it. The way to do this is to have **a program or program segment in place that will run all the tests more or less automatically, or at least interactively. This is your *test suite*, stored as part of the class library, so that developers and reusers can retest the class completely each time they use it in another project.**

This test-case program needs to include your predicted test results, and the automation is a lot more effective if you also automate the comparisons of actual against predicted results. The test program must be updated every time the class is modified or reused, and these changes need to be documented and controlled by the DBAs, along with any changes to the class itself.

All of this must be planned and designed in the design phase, and coded along with the programs and methods in the construction phase. If not, there is a danger it may be skipped or neglected under the pressure of meeting deadlines in the later phases.

Testing Must Happen, Even Under Deadline Pressure

As we saw in Chapter 3, the cost of fixing an error increases as the project proceeds beyond where the error was made. For this reason, we must test each piece of code *as soon as possible* after it's written. Testing is so often skipped, or shortened, or done in a grudging and perfunctory manner.

Yet thorough testing is way cheaper than repairs after the fact, especially when irate users are standing around waiting! Users can become very scared and angry during implementation of a new system, when they're under pressure, and they perceive us as holding them up and making them look bad.

As the project deadline looms and everybody is hustling, testing is very often the first thing to suffer. Under this kind of pressure to "just get it done," developers and users alike will rush or skip the testing. The results are likely to be similar to the *Vasa* project in 1625. Tom Love (1993) has a delightful chapter in which he draws many unfortunate parallels between the Vasa project and much of modern systems development.

In that project, the seaworthiness of the Swedish flagship *Vasa* was tested by having thirty sailors run from side to side of the deck. When this almost capsized her, the problem wasn't remedied, since no one had any idea how to go about fixing it. Not only that, but the user (the king) insisted the project be ready on time. The result, as Love describes it: "About one mile from the harbor, a modest gust of wind caught the mainsail, and the ship 'turned turtle,' sinking immediately, with the loss of some 800 lives."[4]

Binder (1995) declares that the answer to this schedule compression that reduces and interferes with proper testing is to *start early in the project*. Planning and designing the tests, test data, test cases, and test programs as you go, throughout the analysis and design phases, means that when the crunch comes, your preparations are in place.

With relatively little further effort, you can be ready to run through your prepared, automatic, thorough, and above all quick test suite. This way, you and the rest of your team are far less likely to short-circuit the testing procedure.

Binder also mentions repeated studies that have come up with a rather surprising statistic: Teams who thought they were being "excruciatingly thorough" typically end up exercising only one-third to one-half of the *statements* in a program. And that's not considering all the possible combinations that will need testing.

There Is a further warning about testing, and that concerns testing under inheritance.

Testing Under Inheritance and Polymorphism

When we reuse a trusted class and inherit from it, there can be a very strong temptation to assume that it needs no further testing. Since everything in the superclass worked before, it should still be fine, right? WRONG!! This can be a dangerous assumption. In the new (reuse) environment, there can be subtle differences that didn't show up in the original testing. New side effects may well turn up too.

Let's say we define a Preferred Customer class, inheriting from Customer, then we must rerun the entire *existing* Customer test suite against a *Preferred* Customer instance. This will verify that all the methods in the Customer class still work (or it'll show they don't work) in this new environment. Then, and only then, should we run the *new* Preferred Customer test suite against the same instance.

These tests have another step to test because of this added inheritance. Methods defined in the Preferred Customer class must not only be tested alone but also, wherever possible, in combination with methods from the Customer class. What is new is the possibility of interactions and side effects from the combined use of methods from the two classes. So if anything, the test suite needs to be *more* comprehensive, rather than less, when reusing classes with inheritance.

Also, the procedure must start at the top of the hierarchy (as much as the "top" can be defined in some languages). Then the testing must extend down the tree, level by level, to test and retest every method in each subclass and all its descendants.

After the testing is complete, it's time to finalize the documentation.

---

[4]In a footnote, Love mentions that "due in part to the stress, (the shipbuilder) became seriously ill and died a year before the Vasa was completed." Draw your own inferences. Sad to say, this was probably the most fortunate thing that could have happened to him, since had he survived, his embarrassment would have been extreme. Not only that, but in 1625, making a laughingstock of the king could easily have proved fatal anyway!

13.11 DOCUMENTATION

Grady Booch (1995) insists that you write your reference manual and user guide *early in the project*. This forces users to get involved. As they review the user manuals, it's like another level of prototyping. You can expect questions and comments such as, "Why is this in the system?" or "That's not how I wanted it to work!" or simply "I don't understand these directions." Some of these will be problems with the manuals, but many will be things that need to be changed in your system design.

This is the time to find these problems. The earlier they're found, the easier and cheaper it is to fix them. This additional feedback can be very valuable. Don't think that by avoiding it you'll make the problems go away! They'll surface eventually and cause more grief for doing so later rather than sooner.

This causes us to build systems that are more user-friendly. You may also need to consider that if we put something in the system that the user can't understand without six or seven pages of help, perhaps it's the wrong thing to have in the system!

Booch defines two extremes of documentation, which he calls "high-ceremony" and "low-ceremony."

He describes high-ceremony projects or companies as those that insist on having a file with all possible details. Meeting minutes, trip reports, and so on must be kept. They require that a programmer keep a folder with details of everything that occurred for him on the project. This would include speed memos, notes of all phone calls, ideas, comments, and so on.

Detailed documentation of the design work must be done as the design is developed, not after the fact, and must be reviewed regularly. No one is allowed to write any program code until all documentation has been prepared and approved for that part of the job.

This, to both Grady and me, would seem to be a little like overkill. Booch comments that he feels this is suitable only when human lives depend on the software. Control systems for airplanes, ICBMs, and self-guided vehicles would fall into this class.

So would the software on Scottie's "Beam-Me-Up" system (one day when we build it), or monitoring software for chemical and nuclear plants, or for patients in an ICU[5] (see *Systemantics* by John Gall, 1988).

Low-ceremony projects or companies produce zero documentation other than the program code of the final system. Booch considers, and I agree, that this is only appropriate where the software must work once or twice, and then will be thrown away. In these cases, we need to keep an eye on the documentation costs, so they won't be more than the software.

So the recommended compromise is, according to Booch, to spend between 5% and 10% of the total development effort on all forms of documentation. This would include both the external (such as user manuals) and the internal documentation (technical stuff to be used during maintenance and enhancement).

• •

DELIVERABLES

The actual format of the deliverables from the design phase depends quite a bit on the software products used to produce it. By this I mean:

- *Documentation tools*. Most such products are very flexible, but when it comes to style, each one has some styles it supports a little better than others. Not a big deal.

- *CASE product(s)*. These will have a definite influence on the "look and feel" of your documents and diagrams. Any given CASE product supports some styles better than others, and supports some diagrams better than others. And you're bound to find some diagrams it won't even draw.

- *Development products*. Each language, database, GUI product, and the like comes with its own set of documentation capabilities, limitations, and styles.

- *Diagramming techniques*. Again, for the different development products, different diagraming techniques may be appropriate depending on the kind of product – for example, whether your database is relational (nonobject), an extended relational ODBMS, or a pointer-based ODBMS.

- *UML* A great deal of very necessary standardization is coming about as a result of the worldwide adoption of UML notation. Both people and skill sets will be transferable from project to project, and from company to company. You will have less to learn when you join a project, so everyone's productivity will improve.

- *Methodology*. Each of the various published methodologies has its own set of biases to the diagrams, models, and so on. Many will make use of the stereotype provision in UML that allows for a limited amount of customizing the notation.

So there can be a lot of variation as to just what deliverables are produced during design. The one thing I must emphasize, however, is that you must decide what deliverables you'll produce, and settle on suitable formats, *long before you begin the design phase*. Like everything else, you can expect to fine-tune these decisions later, but the groundwork and the major decisions must be taken care of beforehand.

If you're using a published or purchased methodology, either this will be set for you, or you may be given an array of deliverables from which to choose the ones you expect you'll need. These decisions should be in the form of a standard that you intend to apply to all projects in your organization from now on. Keep in mind, though, that you may need to define two or three project size ranges and specify a different set of deliverables for each.

FURTHER READING

Tom Love (1993) in his book *Object Lessons* delivers a lot of good stuff you should read. He has many eminently practical suggestions. His last few chapters are particularly appropriate to the design phase, and his Chapter 12 relates to my Chapter 15, about the move to using objects.

You'll note that in many places, and particularly in this chapter, I've quoted articles from *Object Magazine*, now renamed "*Component Strategies*. While there are a number of magazines in the field (see www.wiley.com), I find this to be one of the best for analysts and designers.

Also appropriate are *TAPOS* magazine and *Object Systems*. Also, ROAD (*Report on Object Analysis and Design*) is another good one for systems analysts. Others mostly focus on OOP or one particular OOPL. Then there's JOOP (*Journal of Object-Oriented Programming*.) As the term *journal* in its name implies, this one has more leading-edge OOP topics, research-oriented articles, and other such things for computing scientists, rather than for systems analysts.

Andy Carmichael's collection of articles under the title *Object Development Methods* (1994) gives a variety of viewpoints on many important topics. It includes Richard Daley's article, "Object-Development Environments," with a lot to say about setting up environments. Daley discusses language and CASE choice, class libraries, and testing and test management. Carmichael's book is divided into sections with the following rather intriguing titles:

- Understanding and Adopting Object Technology
- Methods Comparison
- Perspectives on Specific Object-Oriented Methods
- The Evolving Development Environment

Atwood (1994) in his paper at the Object Expo conference describes the ODMG-93 standard, which at the time was the state of the art. The current standard is known as ODMG 3.0, and is discussed in the next chapter. More importantly, his paper discusses the formation, goals, structure, and activities of the ODMG, and this is what makes it worthwhile reading.

Of course, a lot of interesting and useful work has appeared in the proceedings of later conferences, but much important groundwork was done in those earlier years of the object-oriented era. At www.odmg.org you can get the latest information, and papers describing the current ODMG 3.0 standard.

Object Expo conferences are held annually in several places around the world. There are a lot of good papers from some of the big names in the field, and good ones from the little guys too. The conference proceedings should be available from SIGS in New York. You can also check www.sigs.com.

Finally, for object-oriented design focused on the Eiffel language, Bertrand Meyer, *Object-Oriented Software Construction* (1988) is the standard text , and you can visit www.eiffel-forum.org.

CHAPTER SUMMARY

- Your design must be in a form such that the users can understand and critique all the nontechnical parts. You progressively disclose the design to them in increments so as not to overwhelm them.

- Both *interobject* concurrency, where different objects are all working at the same time, and *intraobject* concurrency, with many things happening at once *within* an object are significant, since real-world objects are capable of both kinds.

- Design for large objects, with 1000 lines of code and 50 to 100 methods in each, but expect that the final average will be less.

- Reduce complexity and more users understand; we get better information, cooperation, and user ownership, critical success factors for any project.

- In the design phase, we add to our existing analysis model more classes, methods, specs for methods, data attributes, specs for data attributes.

- Design the GUI with window and button classes that inherit from screen object classes that implement a standard such as Windows. Define new classes as subclasses of library classes. Customizing can create standards for your company.

- GUI products include Delphi, PowerBuilder, Visual Basic, Visual C++, and others.

- Plan for language and environment purchase, delivery, installation, testing, and training with or before analysis. Allow for problems and delays.

- There are three basic choices: pure, extended, and hybrid languages.

  - *Pure object languages.* In Smalltalk, everything is an object. Java is totally object-oriented. Eiffel is another one. The downside is the need for training and experience.

  - *Extended languages.* Object-Oriented features are added; examples are Object Pascal and C++. The advantage is an existing base of programmers. The downside is the ability to violate encapsulation and to write old-style code in the new language.

  - *Hybrid languages.* Add an object level to the base language. A hybrid language provides access to the base language. Objective-C does by adding Smalltalk-like syntax to C, without altering the C syntax. A hybrid has about the same advantages and disadvantages as an extended language.

- Compare languages on factors such as strength of typing, execution speed, and memory management. Java is fast, strongly typed, and does its own automatic garbage collection.

- Serious ODBMSs now have the heavy-duty "industrial-strength" features to handle concurrency, transactions, rollbacks, distributed objects, and security for mission-critical applications, as do current RDBMSs. My advice is to *go objects all the way*, though currently many projects use OO front ends to RDBMS back ends. Relational databases will soon go object-oriented, so Oracle, Sybase, and the rest will compete with Versant, O2, and the others.

- In the design phase we must deal with issues around procedures, versioning, security, permissions, responsibilities, class libraries, testing, and documentation.

- The Object Management Group (OMG) has been formed to develop standards for object request brokers (ORBs). An ORB intercepts messages from an object, translates them, and routes them to the correct object, wherever it may be, geographically or "platformally."

- The OMG is producing a *standard*, rather than products. OMG certifies compliance to that standard, which describes the architecture for the ORB, that is, the common object request broker architecture (CORBA).

- The OMG has defined *object services* that an ORB must provide and more will be added.

- The Object Data Management Group (ODMG) is developing database interoperability among their ODBMS products, all within the CORBA specification.

- Any feature the ODMG mandates members to add to their products will be based on a feature that one or more members already have. Voting members must commit that any feature decided upon by the ODMG will be in their products within 18 months.

- With "software components," a designer will use as many off-the-shelf "parts" as possible.

- Reusing *classes* that have already been defined brings about reduction in time, effort, and thus cost, for the designers, and challenges and inspires them by keeping them working on *new* stuff.

- Repeated reuse reduces the size and complexity of class libraries, makes browsing simpler and more effective, and makes us less likely to overlook a good class.

- *Intangible benefits*: reduced fatigue and boredom, effects of working under deadline pressure, enhanced inspiration and motivation. Intangibles like these could be the most important benefits of component reuse.

- Systems designers have always been aware of the need to reuse software components; only in the object paradigm has this become truly attainable. Objects are encapsulated the same way motors and wheels are, giving the possibility of off-the-shelf classes.

- Intelligent Agent ("software robot"): an intelligent object, capable of independent existence, designed to perform a certain set of functions, and carrying the necessary data within itself.

- An agent could check hotels to find a room, mail itself from one place to another. Agents will defragment disks, order flowers, buy a ticket, book a conference room, enroll you in a course, present and analyze information, and so on.

- Agents as smart as us could become sentient creatures inhabiting the computer! I once thought that was fantasy, but I'm no longer sure.

- Since Design is producing a *plan for the system*, it's also the right time to produce *detailed plans for testing the system*. Document and save your use cases to be test cases. These give a high-level test, covering complete user sessions.

- Unstructured testing means trying a few use cases and fixing crashes or inaccuracies. A small percentage of developers take a systematic approach and test all possibilities. Many of the less-frequent or less-obvious user processes may easily be overlooked.

- Identify the use case, error, or exception to test for and plan the sequence of events for the test, often in pseudocode. Create appropriate test-data values and calculate predicted output. Each input must be tried many times, while the object is in each of its allowable states.

- Later, in the coding phase, you'll code a stub program or segment, a *test suite*, to invoke the unit and run all these tests.

- A trustworthy class is one that's reliable, robust, and has no significant side effects.

- Frequent reuse *cannot guarantee* the entire class has been exercised. When a class is reused, you must retest it *completely*. Often we find incompatibilities, or missing or inadequate behavior, in the new environment. We can't assume that because a method works when invoked by one client object, it will for others.

- *Testing must be automated.* Have a test suite in place to run all the tests automatically, stored in the class library, so that reusers can retest the class completely. Include predicted test results and automate comparisons of actual against predicted results. The test program must be updated every time the class is modified; this is documented and controlled by the DBAs.

- If not planned in the design phase, this may end up being skipped or neglected under pressure of meeting deadlines in later phases. ***Testing must happen, even under deadline pressure.***

- Teams who thought they were "excruciatingly thorough" exercise only one-third to one-half of the *statements* in a program.

- Methods defined in superclasses must be tested alone and with methods from subclasses, for interactions and side effects from combined use. The test suite must be *more* comprehensive when reusing classes with inheritance.

- Start at the "top" of the hierarchy and test down the tree level by level, to test and retest every method in each subclass and all its descendants.

- High-ceremony: insisting on filing all details, speed memos, notes of all phone calls, ideas, comments, detailed documentation, and so on, reviewed regularly. No program code until documentation approved. This is overkill for most applications. It is suitable when human lives depend on the software, such as monitoring software for chemical and nuclear plants, or aircraft or missile software.

- Low-ceremony: no documentation other than program code. Appropriate where software must work only once or twice. Watch that documentation doesn't cost more than software.

- Recommendation: Spend between 5% and 10% of the total development cost on all forms of documentation, both the "external" and "internal."

CHAPTER GLOSSARY

agent An intelligent packet of data and program code – that is, an intelligent object capable of independent existence, designed to perform a certain set of functions and carrying the necessary data within itself.

agent An object that, once created, becomes independent.

Common Object Request Broker Architecture The OMG standard that describes the structure and appearance of an ORB, referred to as an "architecture" for the ORB. Since it is common to ORBs from different manufacturers, it has thus been named the *Common Object Request Broker Architecture* or *CORBA*. (Be careful to pronounce it correctly, with the R sounded *before* the B.)

CORBA Common Object Request Broker Architecture (Be careful to pronounce it correctly, with the R sounded *before* the B.)

critical success factor (CSF) Any factor, condition, event, or the like, such that no matter what else is done and how much effort is put out, without this factor success is not possible.

interobject concurrency Where different objects are all working at the same time.

intraobject concurrency Where many things are happening at once within an object.

object request broker (ORB) A software product that intercepts messages from an object; translates them for language, operating system, or other differences in environment; and routes them to the correct object, wherever it may be, geographically or "platformally."

reliable Indicates that a method or class will still give the right answers in a new environment.

robust Indicates that a method or class will not crash in new environments.

test suite A program or program segment that will run all your tests more or less automatically, or at least interactively. It is stored as part of the class library, so that developers and reusers can retest the class completely each time they use it in the same or another project.

thread of control A path of execution that is currently being followed through the program code.

trustworthy class A class that is reliable, robust, and has no significant side effects.

WHAT COMES NEXT

After the design phase comes *construction*, or *coding*, call it what you will. In the next chapter, we look at this phase of the OODLC, where it's time to take all this analysis and planning and put it to the test. It's time to actually build something. Finally, we'll have something to show for all the work we put into the earlier phases.

I won't take you through the step-by-step of coding the methods and building the classes. That's highly language-dependent and beyond the scope of this book. It would also be out of date by the time you read this. Instead, I'll limit myself to commenting in the next chapter on some of the various languages and databases available and a number of issues around them.

CLASS/GROUP EXERCISES AND PROBLEMS

For these exercises, you'll need your class diagrams from the exercises in previous chapters. Your group should do each exercise against several diagrams from the different projects until you feel you have the hang of it.

Ex 13.1 Find as many places as you can to add abstract superclasses. You may stretch things a bit if you need to, since this is, after all, an exercise. But you must justify each one. You can expect that most of your justifications will be in terms of common or simplified *features* (attributes and methods).

Ex 13.2 Draw out the tree of subclasses descending from each of the new abstract superclasses. Show the operations inside each box. Show which are abstract operations, by writing the name in italics. Show where the classes inherit methods and attributes and show where some methods are overridden. In at least one abstract superclass, show both some abstract and some concrete methods.

Ex 13.3 Find as many places as you can to link two existing classes into a subclass superclass relationship. Justify each one (or at least explain why it might be reasonable.)

Ex 13.4 Obtain a copy of the full documentation and specs for a class library, either a purchased one or somebody's in-house class library. If it can be done, get access to the library itself as well.

(a) Scan the documentation manually. Use whatever browsers that come with the class library or that came with your language or database, to scan the class library itself. Evaluate classes and select a few that could be reused in some of your projects.

(b) Document your reasons for choosing these particular classes, especially where there were other classes that almost or also could have been chosen.

(c) For at least one other class that narrowly missed being selected, document your reasons for rejecting it and choosing something else.

(d) Present your results and reasoning to the class. Ask the class for comments, corrections, and things you may have missed.

Ex 13.5 Test Suites.

(a) Select a few of your classes from your projects and design a test suite for each. Write pseudocode procedures and create test-data values as well to test each method thoroughly.

(b) Exchange with another group. Evaluate their test suites and document everything they have forgotten or missed.

(c) Now you present their test suite and your "improvements" to it, to the class. (Be gentle, now. You're next!)

This is a golden opportunity to practice those people skills, in preparation for Chapter 16. You'll need to present this in such a way that they won't feel that you're picking holes in their work. They must feel that they did a good job and that you're just helping them make it a bit better. Remember, it's how they actually feel about the critique that tells how successful you were with the people skills, not how you think they should feel nor how you intended them to feel.)

INDIVIDUAL EXERCISES AND PROBLEMS

Ex 13.6 For the GPA-Agent example in the chapter, draw a class diagram showing the GPA-Agent as a class and showing all the other classes it would need to interact with.

Ex 13.7 Draw a statechart diagram showing the life cycle of a GPA-Agent instance. Don't forget to include its travels.

Ex 13.8 List out the names and one-sentence descriptions for all the methods you can think of that your GPA-Agent class would need to have.

PROJECTS AND CASES

P 13.1 Go back to the small-business project that you began for a real business in project Project 7.2 and that you've done further work on in projects Projects 8.1 and 12.1.

(a) Make and document all the design decisions regarding choice of hardware and software platforms, choice of GUI, and so on. Then go through the chapter and do everything we discussed toward producing a design for the project.

(b) Design the screens and reports and other I/O, with feedback from the users.

(c) In particular, develop the testing plan and the test modules for all the classes, to the level of pseudocode.

(d) Develop the draft technical documentation and user manuals, both for the system itself and for the testing procedures.

(e) Complete the design as far as you can, short of actually beginning the coding. Have everything ready so that you could begin creating classes and writing code after reading the next chapter.

SELF-TEST QUESTIONS

Note: The Appendix has answers to the Self-Test Questions.

Q 13.1 The experience they had with earlier projects convinced the HP designers they should try to design:

(a) Large classes with about 1,000 lines of code

(b) Small classes with about 50 lines of code

(c) Small classes with about 50 to 100 lines of code

(d) Small classes with about 1000 lines of code

(e) Large classes with about 500 lines of code

(f) None of the above

Q 13.2 The experience they had with earlier projects also convinced the HP designers they should try to design

(a) Small classes with about 50 methods

(b) Large classes with about 100 methods

(c) Large classes with about 50 to 100 methods

(d) Small classes with about 50 to 100 methods

(e) Small classes with about 100 methods

(f) Large classes with about 50 methods

(g) None of the above

Q 13.3 Concurrency is:

(a) When two objects are working at the same time

(b) When two processors are operating on different programs or methods at the same time

(c) Simulated by time-slice sharing on a single-processor machine

(d) Able to exploit the encapsulation available with objects

(e) Made easier by objects

(f) All of the above

(g) None of the above

Q 13.4 ORB stands for:

(a) Object reuse broker

(b) Object reuse banker

(c) Object reuse booker

(d) Object request booker

(e) Object request banker

(f) All of the above

(g) None of the above

Q 13.5 A critical success factor (CSF) is:

(a) A success rating given to a movie by the newspapers

(b) Everything you need to guarantee a project's success

(c) When a project is successful by responding to comments and advice

(d) A necessary but not sufficient condition for success

(e) An ideal but not practical way to ensure success

(f) All of the above

(g) None of the above

Q 13.6 Match these language categories with the correct descriptions:

Category	Description
(a) Pure	(1) Modified syntax of the original language.
(b) Extended	(2) Object-oriented features added with no change to the original language.
(c) Hybrid	(3) Everything is an object. Object orientation is the only way to do anything.

Q 13.7 Intraobject concurrency is when

(a) Each object has only one method executing at a time

(b) One object has two methods executing at the same time

(c) Two objects have one method each executing at the same time

(d) One object must wait for the other to finish executing before it can begin

(e) Each object must finish executing one method before it can begin another one

(f) None of the above

Q 13.8 A thread of control is

(a) A path of execution recorded for later tracing during debugging.

(b) A series of commands issued by the user at the user interface.

(c) A series of messages to an object requesting execution of various methods.

(d) A line or cord fed through the handles of a series of switches to execute them in the desired sequence.

(e) A path of execution being followed through the program code.

(f) All of the above

(g) None of the above

Q 13.9 *CORBA* stands for:

(a) Common object reuse broker argument

(b) Common object reuse banker architecture

(c) Common object request broker architecture

(d) Complete object reuse banker architecture

(e) Common object reuse banker argument

(f) Complete Object Request broker Architecture.

(g) A sports car designed by Carroll Shelby.

Q 13.10 Software components are

(a) ICs with standard routines embedded in them

(b) .Subroutines to be reused in your software

(c) Precoded data definitions to be copied into your system

(d) Methods to be copied from one object to another for reuse

(e) Object instances that can be copied into your classes

(f) All of the above

(g) None of the above

Q 13.11 Software for driverless trains and nuclear plants requires which approach to documentation?

(a) High ceremony

(b) Medium ceremony

(c) Low ceremony

(d) No ceremony

(e) Wedding ceremony

(f) None of the above

Q 13.12 Robust and reliable classes mean

(a) Robust always gives correct results, reliable never crashes

(b) Robust always gives correct results, reliable usually crashes

(c) Reliable always gives correct results, robust usually crashes

(d) Reliable always gives correct results, robust never crashes

(e) Reliable always gives correct results, robust always crashes

Q 13.13 Software components

(a) Rarely need further testing when reused

(b) Must be rewritten or modified if they don't do exactly what you need

(c) Are useless without their source code

(d) Can be reused only if they do exactly what you need

(e) Are nothing more than precoded and pretested class definitions

(f) None of the above

Q 13.14 What proportion of the total project cost should be spent on all forms of documentation?

(a) 55% – 80%

(b) 45% – 60%

(c) 25% – 40%

(d) 15% – 30%

(e) 10% – 20%

(f) 5% – 10%

(g) 0 – 5%

(h) None of the above

Q 13.15 "Excruciatingly thorough" development teams have been found to test approximately what proportion of the statements in their programs?

(a) 100%

(b) 80% – 100%

(c) 66% – 75%

(d) 50% – 66%

(e) 33% – 50%

(f) 20% – 50%

(g) 20% – 33%

(h) 0 – 20%

(i) None of the above

Q 13.16 Intelligent agents

(a) May be regarded as "software robots"

(b) May be able to mail or copy themselves over data links

(c) Operate independently once created

(d) Require concurrent processing and multiple threads of control

(e) Require levels of compatibility and interoperability that don't exist as yet but are just around the corner

(f) All of the above

(g) None of the above

Q 13.17 Your design must be in a _____ such that the _____ can _____ and _____ all the _____ parts.

Q 13.18 Both _____ _____ , where different objects are all _____ at the _____ _____ , and _____ concurrency, with many things happening at once _____ an object are significant.

Q 13.19 By reducing _____ , more users _____ ; we get better information, cooperation, and user ownership, _____ _____ _____ for any project.

Q 13.20 Plan for _____ and environment purchase, delivery, installation, _____ , and _____ with or before analysis. Allow for _____ and _____ .

Q 13.21 _____ object languages. In Smalltalk, _____ is an object. _____ is totally object-oriented. Eiffel is another one. The downside is the need for _____ and _____ .

Q 13.22 _____ languages. Object oriented features are _____ ; examples are Object Pascal and C++. The advantage is an existing _____ of _____ . The downside is the ability to _____ _____ and to write _____ - _____ code in the new language.

Q 13.23 Compare languages on factors such as strength of _____ , _____ _____ , and _____ _____ . Java is fast, _____ typed, and does its own automatic _____ _____ .

Q 13.24 Serious _____ now have the heavy-duty " _____ - _____ " features to handle _____ , _____ , rollbacks, _____ _____ , and security for mission-critical applications, as do current _____ .

Q 13.25 The Object _____ Group (OMG) has been formed to develop _____ for _____ request _____ (ORBs). An ORB intercepts messages from an object, _____ them, and _____ them to the correct _____ , wherever it may be.

Q 13.26 The OMG is producing a _____ , rather than _____ . OMG certifies compliance to that _____ , which describes the _____ for the ORB, that is, the _____ _____ _____ _____ _____ (CORBA).

Q 13.27 With "software _____ ," a designer will use as many _____ - _____ - _____ "parts" as possible.

Q 13.28 Repeated reuse reduces the _____ and _____ of class libraries, makes _____ simpler and more _____ .

Q 13.29 Intelligent _____ ("software robot"): an intelligent _____ , capable of _____ _____ , designed to perform a certain set of _____ , and carrying the necessary _____ within itself.

Q 13.30 Since design is producing a _____ for the system, it's also the right time to produce _____ _____ for testing the system. Document and save your _____ _____ to be _____ _____ .

Q 13.31 _____ testing means trying a few _____ _____ and _____ _____ or inaccuracies. Only a _____ percentage of developers take a _____ _____ and _____ _____ _____ .

Q 13.32 Later, in the _____ _____ , you'll _____ a _____ _____ , to invoke the unit and run _____ the tests.

Q 13.33 Frequent reuse cannot _____ the _____ class has been exercised. When a class is _____ , you must retest it _____ . Often we find _____ , or missing or _____ behavior, in the new environment.

Q 13.34 Testing must be _____ . Have a _____ _____ in place to run all the tests _____ , so that reusers can _____ the class _____ . Include _____ test results and automate _____ of _____ against _____ results. The test program must be _____ every time the class is _____ .

Q 13.35 If not _____ in design, this may be skipped or neglected under pressure of _____ _____ in later phases. Testing must _____ , even under _____ _____ .

Q 13.36 Teams who thought they were "_____ _____ " exercise only _____ to _____ of the statements in a program.

Q 13.37 Recommendation: Spend between _____ and _____ of the total development cost on all forms of documentation, both the " _____ " and " _____ ."

Chapter Fourteen

Implementation: OOPLs and ODBMSs

WHAT YOU WILL LEARN IN THIS CHAPTER

In this chapter, you'll discover some requirements and issues around object-oriented languages, databases, and development environments. You can be confident that you've mastered the content of this chapter when you can:

1. Discuss some important issues around OOPLs and ODBMSs.

2. Describe some of the different approaches that the various language and database products have taken to such things as persistence of objects, multiple inheritance, dynamic typing of objects, and extended, hybrid, and pure object-oriented languages.

3. Discuss some of the issues and describe the state of the art in the benchmarking of ODBMSs.

WHAT YOU SHOULD KNOW TO START THIS CHAPTER

For this chapter, you need to understand objects, but you don't need to know how to do object-oriented analysis (nor how to write object-oriented programs). In terms of this book, that means Chapters 4 – 6, and possibly Chapter 8.

CHAPTER OVERVIEW

After a few introductory comments about features that an OOPL or ODBMS needs to have, I discuss some of the directions you'll see the industry moving in over the next few years, in particular the work of the OMG and ODMG. Then we examine some technical issues relating to OOPLs and ODBMSs, followed by some comments on the products available at the time of writing.

For databases, you'll find a discussion of how object databases differ from relational and some of the approaches that have been taken to building ODBMS products. We look at a couple of benchmarks that have been published for comparing object databases, and then at a few of the products that are out there already. Finally, there are a few brief comments on object-oriented development environments.

KEY CONCEPTS

- "Complete" database language
- Data/Object Definition Language (DDL/ODL)
- Data/Oject Management Language (DML/OML)
- Data/Object Control Language (DCL/OCL)
- SQL, OSQL and OQL
- OMG, ODMG; OMG object model
- ODMG 3.0
- Language binding
- Garbage collection, memory leaks
- Dynamic Typing
- Pure language, hybrid language, extended language
- ISO/ANSI Ada 95
- BLOB
- Clustering, benchmarking
- Complex objects, complex attributes
- Engineering Database Benchmark
- HyperModel Benchmark

"THE OUTHOUSE BATHROOM BOUTIQUE" SALES REPORTING SYSTEM – EPISODE 14

Meetings during the design phase were less frequent than they had been during analysis, and mostly were attended by only a few of The Outhouse staff, the ones who were directly involved in the topic of the day. The development team had been expanded to include two programmers, Joan and Sam, in addition to Nancy as project manager and Deanna as project administrator. These four developers are meeting with Tim, Hartmut, and Allana. Nancy is reporting on the choice of personnel and the choice of development software.

"Joan has a strong background in all the development tools we've selected," she began. "She's done several Java projects, a couple with the Versant database, and one with Versant's Argos development environment. She also did a big web-based system in Java with Oracle 8, the object-oriented version of the Oracle database. While Sam has not used Versant before, he's thoroughly grounded in the language we've chosen, Java.

"So, we're borrowing two class libraries that were developed on projects with other clients, and Joan and Sam were both involved in developing them. Oh, and don't get all worried about the 'borrowing.' It was part of their contracts that we would be able to reuse classes from their projects. We've also purchased another general-purpose class library, one that Sam knows really well."

THOUGHT QUESTIONS

1. In your group, discuss some projects the members have worked on where several programming languages and/or databases were involved. How compatible were they? What problems were encountered linking between the different languages? How did it affect function and subroutine calls? Data and parameter passing?

2. If you had been given an opportunity to design a product that would assist with those compatibility issues, what would such a product have looked like? What would you call it, both a generic name and a trade name? Develop a rough specification for such a product. Spell out what features it should have, and all the things it should be able to do, and design calling protocols to invoke these various functions and features.

14.1 LANGUAGES AND DATABASES

Much has been learned from the problems and mistakes encountered in the earlier paradigms, and is being done the right way this time around with objects. Manufacturers and users alike are actively seeking standardization in many, many forms.

After all these years of practice, both the American National Standards Institute (ANSI) and International Standards Organization (ISO) have in place their well-oiled mechanisms to form committees and develop standards as the need arises. ANSI has a number of committees that are working on object-oriented standards. Add to this the efforts of the OMG and ODMG, and we can expect an unprecedented level of standards and compatibility in our little corner of the world. And much of it is happening already.

Let's begin our talk of development tools with a discussion of some of the requirements for a successful programming language or database.

Database DDL, DML, and Query Language

Most of you will have encountered SQL, Structured Query Language, which was developed as the world standard language for relational databases. SQL is considered to be a *"complete"* **database language, meaning it has these three parts: a data definition language (DDL), a data management language (DML – including a query language), and a data control language (DCL).**

All three functions are needed for any database to operate, so any *complete* database language needs to have all three. This applies no matter whether it's a conventional procedural language or object-oriented. The corresponding object-oriented variety have been labeled ODL, OML, and OCL. These are discussed further in this chapter, in the section on the OMG object model.

DDL/ODL

The primary function of the *data definition language (DDL)* is to design and build the database. It must have syntax to create a schema, or plan, for the database, and to spell out such things as integrity conditions. In a relational database, this means syntax to create and remove tables, assign columns (attributes) to a table, define the domain of a column, define any constraints or restrictions, and so on.

In an ODBMS, the corresponding functions are to create classes, assign attributes to classes, and define attribute domains and constraints. But more is needed with objects. The ODL must also handle things like methods, set-valued attributes, complex attribute types such as BLOBs (defined later), lists, sound, video, and the like. And it must also deal with subclass relationships, along with inheritance and polymorphism.

DML/OML

The *data management language (DML)* looks after the day-to-day work of adding, deleting, and changing the data values in the database and then retrieving them when needed. In a relational database, this would mean inserting rows, deleting rows, and updating column values.

The retrieval side is the province of the query language. Although it's actually part of the DML, it's often considered separately. It is a *nonprocedural* way of retrieving certain data. It allows users to specify search criteria, so only the rows (instances) that satisfy will be chosen, and only the requested columns will be retrieved.

The result is a subset of the original table and is then passed on to the screen, or to a report, or wherever. In a relational environment, the query language is the most difficult to do, since searches, scans, and relational joins can all be slow and long. Queries are often a bottleneck.

In an ODBMS, the DML and query language must be more even powerful than SQL, to handle the various additional data types that ODBMSs allow. An object query language is sometimes referred to as an OQL.

DCL/OCL

The *data control language (DCL)* is concerned with such things as security, integrity, and optimization. Typically, it handles functions such as the following:

1. Transactions (COMMIT, ROLLBACK, etc.)
2. Access control (GRANT, REVOKE, etc.)
3. Index creation and management
4. Enforcing integrity rules as spelled out by the DDL (or ODL)

The object-oriented version is often called an OCL.

SQL, OSQL, and OQL

Many writers, such as Won Kim, believe that OQL should be a superset of SQL. The ANSI Object SQL committee has done just that. They're developing "an object SQL which extends SQL2 with facilities for defining, manipulating and querying an object database as a superset of a relational database" (Kim, 1994). This one is called OSQL, or Object SQL.

14.2 Directions

In Chapter 13, we met the Object Management Group (OMG) and the Object Data Management Group (ODMG).

OMG and ODMG

The core of the OMG standard is the OMG Object Model. This model has been developed in the form of a set of *components*. These are designed to be assembled in groups into "profiles" that will adequately specify the requirements for a particular product. There will be a profile for ORBs, and one for ODBMSs, and so on. There's one component, referred to as the *core component*, which must be present in every profile. This is the one that defines objects and operations on objects.

The ODBMS profile adds some new parts to the specification. These include persistence, associations, attributes, queries, and transactions. The ODMG has developed their own object model, which can be thought of as a formalized specification of the OMG Object Model.

The ODMG 3.0 Specification

The ODMG 3.0 spec is a statement of requirements for compatibility among ODBMSs. The objective is that you should be able to code a program with calls to a database interface, without knowing which database you'll eventually be using. With a common database interface syntax, and compatible features in the ODBMSs, porting software from one database platform to another will be simplified.

ODMG 3.0 consists of four parts:

1. An object model
2. An object definition language (ODL)
3. An object query language (OQL)
4. "Bindings" to the various OO languages

ODMG 3.0 Object Model

The data model and notation for ODMG 3.0 is based on the OMG Object Model. The OMG Core Model was intended to be a common basis for object request brokers (ORBs), databases, OOPLs, and so on. ODMG 3.0 has added such things as associations to the OMG object model, to make it suitable as the basis for an ODBMS.

Object Definition Language (ODL)

The syntax for this is taken directly from what the OMG has called its *interface definition language* (IDL). It has been labeled IDL to distinguish it from traditional data definition languages, or DDLs.

Object Query Language (OQL)

This is a declarative language, like SQL. That is, it's not procedural, or step-by-step, the way most programming languages are. This allows us to describe what we want done that is, what the output should look like without getting involved in specifying how it should happen.

Bindings

A *language binding* in this context is a syntax, and a supporting set of software (in this case, it takes the form of classes and methods) to allow a programmer in the target language to access features of the database language (such as the ODL, OML, OQL, and OCL). ODMG 3.0 specifies bindings to the several of the most popular languages, including Java, Smalltalk and C++. Others are being added from time to time, and then it remains for each OOPL and ODBMS vendor to implement them in their products.

For those who would like to find out more, or to order copies of the work of the OMG and ODMG, the addresses are in Appendix A4. You can also read Cattell (2000) and Barry (1998), both available at www.odmg.org.

14.3 ISSUES FOR OBJECT-ORIENTED LANGUAGES AND DATABASES

Sutherland (1995) identifies a number of issues in his comparison of Smalltalk, C++, and OO COBOL, which he refers to as "The Good, the Bad and the Ugly" (respectively) after the Clint Eastwood movie. Note that Sutherland's paper was produced before Java was released, so Java would add a whole new category – perhaps to be called "beautiful." He compares these three languages on fourteen factors.

The actual comparison will be, as he puts it, "out of date before you read this" (there's that phrase again!). However, here are some factors that you'll need to consider carefully when evaluating object-oriented languages. Below I've summarized a few of what I feel are Sutherland's more important points.

Garbage Collection

As instances are created during execution of an object-oriented program, they take up space in RAM. Conversely, when one is deleted or destroyed, or made permanent by being copied to disk, it frees up some RAM. But does it? Can that RAM actually be reclaimed and later reused for some other instance creation? In some languages, this is done automatically, and in others manually.

The process of recognizing and reclaiming freed-up memory is referred to as "garbage collection." When it's not available, the programmer has to make sure that unwanted instances are physically deleted from memory, otherwise the system may run out of RAM and crash. Conventional programmers are not trained to watch for this. In Sutherland's words, "This is like handing a COBOL programmer a loaded gun with the safety off!"

Most of the higher-level OO languages such as Smalltalk and Eiffel have automatic garbage collection in one form or another. C++ is the notably typical low-level language without it, and this is one of the limiting factors for C++ in commercial MIS development.

Memory Leaks

This is related to the garbage collection issue. It happens when we're no longer using some parts of memory, but the program is not aware that it can reclaim them or doesn't know how to. Sutherland again: "This is like giving a COBOL programmer a water bucket with holes in it."

Dynamic Versus Static Binding

Dynamic binding (late binding) leads to smaller executables, but marginally slower execution, since the system has to go find and load the code at execution time. With *Static (early) binding*, the methods are compiled right into the program's executable.

The advantages of dynamic binding, on the other hand, are in flexibility and ease of change. With widespread component reuse and the use of ORBs, the multiple recompiles needed with static (early) binding may cause too many complications. With extensive reuse all over the place, how would we ever keep track of which programs had used the method we've just modified (and recompiled)?

Execution Speed

The average Smalltalk programmer has been found to write code that runs just about as fast as code that an average C++ programmer can write. While C++ promises assembler-like execution speeds, *it takes a skilled and experienced expert C++ tweaker to optimize C++ code to that level.*

Java offers an excellent compromise; it has most of the power of C++, without the disadvantages. While it's slower to code than Smalltalk, it's way faster to code and debug than C++. Java is also easier to use for Web-based applications than C++.

Upward Compatibility

Hybrid and extended languages such as C++, OO Pascal, and OO COBOL, according to Sutherland, "make acceptance of the *language* easier at the expense of losing 80% of the *benefits* of object technology." This kind of compatibility is at best a mixed blessing, and at worst can lead to a failed attempt to convert to object-oriented working.

Multiple Inheritance

Sutherland views this as a bit of a "red herring." While C++ and some others do allow multiple inheritance, many programmers decry Smalltalk because it does not. However, Smalltalk has "roles," which in effect allow an object to have several types. That is, it can be an instance of several different classes at once.

Now we saw something like this in subclass hierarchies, but there the object was simultaneously in several classes in a line, up through the hierarchy. Here, the classes involved may have very different attributes and behavior, but once they're specified as roles for an object, it becomes simultaneously an instance of every role class. In effect, we can view it as if there's a copy of the instance in each of its role classes. This is Smalltalk's way of implementing dynamic typing.

Dynamic Typing of Objects

The net effect of this is to allow the object to be treated as a different type, or class, at different moments, and some of these types may inherit down different trees. This then simulates multiple inheritance. However, Sutherland feels that this is still not enough. He suggests that all languages need to support dynamic typing, where the instance can simply be moved from one class to another, without having to make a copy of itself.

While not supported in the first implementation of OO COBOL, from Micro Focus, this is in the proposed ANSI standard. Java achieves something similar with *interfaces* (also available in UML), rather than allowing true multiple inheritance.

Standardized Class Libraries

Porting an application from one compiler to another can be very difficult if they don't have closely matching class libraries. The C++ ANSI standard now specifies certain class libraries as part of the language, but ANSI OO COBOL does not. This has removed a lot of unnecessary work when porting from, say, Microsoft C++ to Borland.

ANSI Smalltalk also includes a standard set of class libraries. Java is built *entirely* around an extensive library of packages and classes.

If things work out the way we all hope they will, ORBs and CORBA may solve this problem by making it possible to port an application from one dialect of a language to another, or from one language to another, and still access the old libraries.

Here, in the proverbial nutshell, is what we've said so far about languages and databases:

- A "complete" database language has three parts:
    - A data definition language (DDL)
    - A data management language (DML)
    - A data control language (DCL)
- Any complete database language needs to have all three functions, whether it's a conventional procedural language or object-oriented. The object-oriented ones are ODL, OML, and OCL.
- A data definition language (DDL) is to design and build the database, with syntax to create a schema, and to define, for example, integrity conditions. An ODL must also handle methods, set-valued attributes, and complex attribute types such as BLOBs, lists, sound, video, and the like. It must also handle subclass relationships, along with inheritance and polymorphism.

- A data management language (DML) is for adding, deleting, changing, and then retrieving the data values in the database. In an ODBMS, the DML and query language (OQL) are more complex to handle all the data types that ODBMSs allow.

- A data control language (DCL/OCL) is for security, integrity, optimization, and so on:
  - Transactions (COMMIT, ROLLBACK, etc.)
  - Access control (GRANT, REVOKE, etc.)
  - Index creation and management
  - Enforcing integrity rules as specified by the ODL

- The OQL should be a superset of SQL. ANSI has an object SQL for defining, manipulating, and querying an object database as a superset of a relational database, calling it OSQL, or Object SQL.

- The OMG Object Model exists as a set of *components*, designed to be assembled into "profiles" to specify a particular product. There will be a profile for ORBs, and one for ODBMSs, and so on. The *core component* must be in every profile.

- ODMG 3.0 consists of four parts:
  - An object model
  - An object definition language (ODL)
  - An object query language (OQL)
  - Bindings to various OO languages

- A *language binding* allows a programmer in the target language to access features of the database language (such as the ODL, OML, OQL, and OCL). ODMG 3.0 specifies bindings to Java, Smalltalk, C++ and others.

- *Garbage collection.* As instances are created, they take up RAM. Deleting unwanted instances frees up RAM to be reclaimed. When not available, the programmer has to physically delete unwanted instances or the system may crash. COBOL and other procedural programmers are not trained for this.

- Most high-level object-oriented languages, such as Java, Smalltalk and Eiffel, have automatic garbage collection in one form or another. C++ does not.

- Memory leaks are related to garbage collection, and happen when we're no longer using parts of memory, but the program can't reclaim them or doesn't know how to.

- Dynamic (late) binding means smaller but slightly slower executables. The average Smalltalk programmer writes code that's about as fast as code an average C++ programmer writes. C++ promises speed, but it takes an expert tweaker to optimize C++ code to that level.

- Multiple inheritance is a red herring. Smalltalk doesn't allow multiple inheritance but has roles, that allow dynamic typing of objects. Java uses interfaces.

- Standardized class libraries come with only some of the languages.

Now that we've seen some of the issues around object-oriented languages, let's briefly examine a few.

14.4 OBJECT-ORIENTED PROGRAMMING LANGUAGES (OOPLs)

I have just a few comments about some of the more popular languages. This is in no way exhaustive but is intended merely to further your introduction to the languages and highlight a few points about each. There's no way I can teach object-oriented programming in one small chapter, so I haven't attempted to do that.

There are many books on object-oriented programming – some general in nature and spanning several languages, others dedicated to one specific language. You'll find a few selections at the end of this chapter under "Further Reading."

Java

Java can be viewed as very loosely based on C/C++, but with a large number of improvements. Java has now become the preferred language for object-oriented programming, despite what Mr Gates and Co. would like us to believe.

Compared with C/C++, most of the opportunities for screwing up have been removed, such as pointers. Because it is fully object-oriented, Java does away with the problems inherent in hybrid and extended languages.

Standardization of the language is one of the beauties of Java. There are numerous Java compilers and development environments available, but because it is controlled by a single company (Sun Microsystems), Java is very consistent across platforms. At my last reading, Sun had licenced Java to 117 vendors, only one of whom had attempted to stray from the defined standard. Very appropriately, they ended up in court over this breach of their contract with Sun.

Part of Java's appeal is that it was set up for use on the web right from the start. Its *applet* concept was way ahead of anything else at the time. Java has now evolved into a highly versatile language, used for everything from the web, to process control and embedded software, to regular MIS applications.

You can download the complete Java Development Kit (JDK) free, along with a host of other exciting stuff, from the Sun server at http://java.sun.com. It includes a Hotjava browser, a Java compiler, libraries, and some documentation. Sun provides a number of lists to which you may subscribe with an e-mail with SUBSCRIBE as the text. Two that I think may be of interest are at java-announce-request@java.sun.com and java-interest-request@java.sun.com.

Smalltalk

Smalltalk is arguably the most "pure" way to go object-oriented, since *everything* is an object, including attribute values and everything else. Smalltalk provides a complete development environment and comes with an ANSI standard basic class library. Until 1998, there were two manufacturers to choose from. This remains true, but with a difference.

The original Smalltalk was developed by Xerox Palo Alto Research Center (PARC) and was marketed as Smalltalk-80 by ParcPlace Systems. The other dialect was Smalltalk V from Digitalk. In 1998 IBM put the stamp of approval on

Smalltalk by bringing out their own version. For a while there, we had three to choose from. But then, in order to combat the might of Big Blue, the other two went and merged!

Smalltalk and C++ used to battle for the lead among OOPLs. Initially, C++ was ahead, boosted by the pool of existing C programmers and its promises of speed and portability. Later, however, difficulties have shown up with these areas in C++, while Smalltalk began to show promise in both areas. But then along came Java and put both to shame!

C++

C++ is complex and detailed. Largely because of this, it's not as programmer-productive as higher-level languages such as Java, Smalltalk and Eiffel. It is, however, good for writing systems code.

With proper optimization, it shines in the areas of execution speed and executable size and other things needed for operating systems, drivers of all kinds, embedded software, and so on. The key here is **proper optimization**. For C++, effective optimization requires real skill and experience in a highly complex business. This is not that easy to come by.

C++ has a much longer learning curve, except where there exists a pool of C skills already. But then, as with any hybrid language, we face the risk of writing old-style procedural code using an object-oriented language. The fact that there is no garbage collection means that the programmer must also guard against memory leaks.

The Visuals

While Visual C++ was of course always object-oriented, at the time of writing (Fall, 2000), Visual Basic has only just become so. Like most Microsoft products, these also show signs of non-standard features which may tend to inveigle you into using only the MS products. Beware.

Eiffel

Eiffel initially showed promise of competing well with Smalltalk and C++, but more recently all three have been overshadowed by Java.

Eiffel was developed by Bertrand Meyer (1992), of Santa Barbara, California. As he says in his preface to *Eiffel, The Language*, it was designed from the ground up to "increase the amount of reuse going on." Meyer was looking to create "a new culture of software development, focusing on the reuse of industrial-grade components, on the development of complete systems rather than just programs, and on the long-term investment in class libraries." He declares himself ready for "meeting the challenge of software quality."

Given these perhaps somewhat lofty aims, Meyer has produced an elegant language, which most users seem to consider every bit as good as Smalltalk, and which addresses some of Smalltalk's deficiencies. Eiffel is arguably a bit less "pure" than Smalltalk, but only religious fanatics would care. (I try to avoid information systems religious arguments.)

Also, Meyer assures us that concurrency has been designed into the language, but is not in any of his books since it has not yet been implemented in the compilers. I guess that gives us something to look forward to in the (hopefully near) future.

One important new development is that Meyer has now passed the responsibility for the specification of the language over to a vendor-independent committee, the Nonprofit International Consortium for Eiffel (that's *NICE*). It seems the best languages have all originated with one person (e.g., Pascal by Niklaus Wirth). However, Meyer maintains there comes a point where this kind of committee is required for the language to grow in the directions needed by its user community. And since there are now alternative compilers on the market, I would agree that such a body has become essential.

Meyer learned well from history. This is what did *not* happen effectively with dBASE, for example, allowing the various dialects to evolve into largely incompatible language products. This fragmented the "xBASE" user community to the extent that most of these languages are no longer around.

 Foxbase/Foxpro and Clipper have survived, the only two out of perhaps a dozen. While both clearly betray their dBASE origins, neither could now be considered in any way *compatible* with dBASE. All three are now niche products, with dBASE itself having the smallest market share.

Meyer has a page at the front of his book headed "About the Status of Eiffel," where he describes how anyone can join NICE and its technical committees. I've included the addresses of NICE and Meyer's own company, ISE, in Appendix A4.

Objective-C

There are a few other languages around such as Objective-C, CLOS, and so on. Each has been developed in an attempt to solve some perceived problems with existing languages and some have succeeded. But, as it has always been and always shall be, no one language will ever turn out to be perfect for all applications.

Objective-C is a hybrid, which as we defined it, means it adds object-oriented functionality to the base C language without altering the C syntax. While perhaps a little more elegant than C++, and arguably less easy to screw up, it has almost completely disappeared from the IT scene.

OO COBOL

At the time of writing (Fall, 2000), still the only implementation of this language is from Micro Focus. However, with the ANSI standard in place, more can be expected. Sutherland (1995) has his reservations (remember, "The Good, The Bad, and The Ugly") and, I must confess, so have I. Fortunately, Java seems to have eclipsed OO COBOL.

COBOL has had its place in the history of MIS, and Grace Hopper is one of my heroes, and now it's time to move on. I had envisaged the move to object-oriented programming as a chance for the world to throw off the tyrannic yoke of COBOL, but perhaps 'tis not to be so. (Oops! My prejudices are showing.) Since OO COBOL is yet another extended language, we must remember that it has all the dangers that old-fashioned COBOL programmers may use the wonderful newfangled compiler to write old-fashioned COBOL code.

But there's one major development that I think is significant enough to mention, and that's Object-Oriented Ada, in the Ada 95 standard.

ISO[1]/ANSI Ada 95

Although the earlier ANSI military standard, Ada 83, did have objects (which it called "packages"), it was considered object-based, since it lacked polymorphism, inheritance, and dynamic binding. Ada 95, however, supports all these, plus dynamic typing and abstract classes.

Not only that, but the language is organized into a core language with standardized class libraries that it calls *annexes*. It also includes explicit support for subsystems, which makes it more suitable for very large systems. It handles several different models of multiple inheritance, and by the use of "dispatch tables" it's able to keep to a minimum the execution time of dynamically bound operations.

To explain the strengths of Ada against other OO languages, I quote Markus Kuhn [see (4) below]:

> "C++ inherits from C the pointer arithmetic and problems associated with it, especially the fact that any code can easily overwrite any part of the data segment of a process, which means that private components of objects are not protected against accidental access in any way. This is a very significant problem for formal correctness evaluation of C++ problems, which is why *standards for safety-critical software do not allow C or C++ to be used in really critical applications.* (My italics.)
>
> "Both Ada and Java provide real object protection and do not use the dangerous pointer arithmetic (although Ada allows unchecked memory access for device-driver development). In addition, both Java and Ada have learned from C++ to avoid the complicated semantics of multiple inheritance and provide alternative simpler structures.

Riehle (1995) gives a number of examples of what can be done with the new Ada and includes some interesting information sources. Following are some that I found particularly interesting:

1. You can request a free compiler for Ada 95 from ftp://cs.nyu.edu/pub/gnat/ along with source code that will allow you to port Ada to your choice of a variety of platforms.

2. There is information available from the (now-defunct) Ada Joint Project office at http://sw-eng.falls-church.va.us and http://sw-eng.falls-church.va.us/ajpofaq.html.

3. Usenet group comp.lang.ada

4. There is a wealth of information available at Markus Kuhn's private web site at http://www.cl.cam.ac.uk/~mgk25/ada.html.

Now, to summarize OOPLs:

- Java has taken over for most OOP work. It is fully OO, and suited to Web, embedded, and MIS applications. It is better standardized across platforms than any other language.

- Smalltalk is the most pure object-oriented language, since everything is an object, even attribute values. It has a development environment and an ANSI standard basic class library. Recently, Smalltalk has begun to catch up on C++.

- C++ is complex and detailed, so it's not as productive as Smalltalk, Java and Eiffel. It's good for systems code. With proper optimization, it gives better execution speed and executable size. Effective optimization of C++ requires real skill and experience.

- C++ has a longer learning curve, except where there exists a pool of skills. But there's risk of writing old-style procedural code in the object-oriented language. No garbage collection means programmers must beware memory leaks.

- Eiffel was designed to increase reuse. Eiffel is arguably less pure than Smalltalk, but concurrency will be added soon. A vendor-independent NICE committee, the Nonprofit International Consortium for Eiffel, has become guardian of the language

- Other languages such as Objective-C and CLOS solve some perceived problems with existing languages, but no one language will do for all applications. Objective-C is a hybrid; it adds object-oriented functionality to the base-C language without altering the C syntax.

- OO COBOL is an extended language and so there is danger of old-fashioned COBOL programmers writing old-fashioned COBOL code.

- ISO/ANSI Ada 95 is truly object-oriented, with dynamic typing and abstract classes. It has a core language, with standardized class libraries (annexes). It has subsystems, which makes it good for very large systems. It handles several different models of multiple inheritance.

- You can request free compilers for Ada 95 and Java.

So this completes our brief survey of languages. Now it's time to look at the issue of persistence and the object-oriented databases.

14.5 OBJECT-ORIENTED DATABASES (OODBMSS OR ODBMSS)

The Current State of the Art

The current state of the art in object-oriented databases can be summarized in one word: change. Expect a lot of it in the next few years. Current ODBMSs are well beyond the experimental stage and have reached a point where they can handle the tough jobs.

That said, we must remember that they're still at a stage of intense development and evolution. Larger companies keep buying smaller ones in this business, sometimes just to acquire their technology. In parallel, OMG and ODMG have developed standards that are still rather young, and the maturation of these standards over the next few years will drive the development of the database and development products.

There will also be competition from Microsoft with DCOM, over which it is maintaining tight control. While it has been talking about links or gateways or interfaces, Microsoft has stopped short of actually embracing the CORBA standard.

As it attempted in the Java arena, Microsoft is choosing to develop to its own proprietary standards. To all appearances, this would seem to be a ploy to encourage its customers into going Microsoft all the way – a trick that Brother Bill no doubt learned from his erstwhile TLM.[1] Perhaps it is significant that said TLM is *no longer* the largest corporation in the world. Careful there, Bill.

I've seen some writers speculate over Microsoft's reasons for holding out on the issue of standards, so I expect there will be some interesting developments as the standards all settle out over these next few years.

This little war over standards has echoes of the VHS/Beta battle in videotapes. Beta gave a better picture and was promoted by Sony, the largest manufacturer in the marketplace. Even so, it eventually lost out to the VHS standard adopted by the entire rest of the industry. The IBM PS/2 suffered a similar fate, and brought Bill's once-powerful mentor that year to its first-ever recorded loss. Could there be a lesson here for Mr Gates & Co?

What this industry needs in order to move ahead is ***standards.***

Differences from RDBMSs

Bertino and Martino (1993) point out that most database applications in the past were for MIS. For these jobs, the demands made on a database are relatively straightforward. Attribute values are limited to primitives such as integers, reals, character strings, and the like, and this was fine for MIS, until now.

In the modern world, we're seeing applications like CAD/CAM; multimedia; geographic information systems (GIS); document, image, and drawing management systems, and so on.

These all have a need for more complex data types, such as graphics, sound, video clips, and such. There are also needs for attributes whose values are lists, sets, or other objects. Sadly, the trusty RDBMS is simply not up to this. There have been attempts to extend the relational model in various ways to handle some of these, but the major progress has been made by moving to ODBMSs.

Some people feel that the major obstacle holding back the development of ODBMSs has been the lack of a solid theoretical base. There's no equivalent in the object paradigm to Codd's thorough and rigorous work in deriving the relational model from set theory. Bertino and Martino are of the opinion, however, that it really doesn't matter very much.

Handling the actual tables, relational joins, and so on is a surprisingly small part of the total product, though these functions can use a big chunk of the running time. Much of the development effort goes into things such as transactions, security

---

[1]TLM: Three-letter mentor – in other words, IBM.

and crash recovery, access control, and concurrent access. They consider that ODBMSs are still in the process of perfecting this part of the technology, and are only now coming into their own.

Approaches to ODBMSs

There have been two basic approaches taken to the challenge of the ODBMS. One has been to extend the RDBMS. The approach has often been something akin to the way dBASE handles its MEMO fields. In that case, a pointer stored in the table points to the variable-length textual data, which is in another physical file.

This has led to the concept of BLOBs. According to Rotzell and Loomis (1994), this is "database speak for *__Binary Large OBjects__*, **large strings of bits which are stored in databases and managed as uninterpreted . . . , well, _BLOBs_.**" The ODBMS doesn't attempt to make any sense of the contents of a BLOB, but simply handles it as a string of thousands or millions of bits. While the application program must be aware of its internal structure and organization, the database is not and doesn't need to be.

To the application program, the BLOB may be graphics, sound, video, or whatever. The ODBMS will simply store it and later make it available when requested, without ever knowing what it was for.

Other types of complex data values, such as lists, sets, object instances, and classes, have been more difficult to add to the relational databases. These have turned out to be a little easier in the alternative approach to ODBMSs, which is to use *pointers*.

Some complain that the use of pointers takes us back to the days of hierarchical and network databases and the CODASYL[2] standard, but not so. What has happened is that with complex objects (objects with complex attributes), rapid retrieval becomes a problem. Just think, in a relational table with attributes (columns) that are *also tables*, the number of joins needed to find anything would be killing, even with modern hardware speeds.

Some of the techniques used by the architects of the old databases have been dusted off and given a new lease of life, however. One of these, for instance, is *__clustering__*, **the technique of physically locating records close to one another when they're logically related and likely to be retrieved together.**

Clustering was a big deal for CODASYL database designers, and now it is again for *some* object database designers. One of the big problems that can do with streamlining, however, since it was rather cumbersome in the old days, is how to change the clustering when the users' data access patterns change.

But the proof of the pudding, as they say, is in the eating. Really, the only way to know whether your database will perform to your needs is to try it. Benchmarks exist for just that purpose, with varying levels of success and appropriateness.

Benchmarking ODBMSs

__Benchmarking__, **the process of comparing one or more products by running them against a standardized task,** is never a simple matter. It's always somewhat

---

[2] **CODASYL:** *C*ommittee *O*n *DA*ta *SY*stems *L*anguages

artificial, in the sense that the standardized task never exactly matches the real-world environment that you or I plan eventually to work in. Even so, by making some intelligent allowances for such factors, we can gain a lot of information from well-designed and properly standardized benchmarks.

Rotzell and Loomis (1994) discuss a number of significant issues around benchmarking ODBMSs and describe the two that at the time of writing (Fall, 2000) show some promise for worthwhile comparisons. They are the Engineering Database Benchmark and the HyperModel Benchmark.

Below I'll repeat some of their comments, after first discussing a few of the issues that they raise. These two benchmarks are by no means the only ones around, and you may expect that others will also come to the fore over the next few years.

I'll begin with a couple of performance issues. Many of the benchmarks that have been developed for relational databases have turned out to be totally inadequate for comparing object-oriented databases. Because the data is often organized in a vastly different way in an ODBMS, we often require very different kinds of access to it.

Relational joins and such have always been a source of bottlenecks in RDBMSs and will continue to be in some ODBMSs, notably the "extended relational" ones (see below). Those that use pointers will have no need of costly, time-consuming joins, but Murphy says you can bet they'll have other deficiencies. (After all, nobody's *prefect*!)

Many object-oriented applications will have need to handle just a few transactions, but large ones, rather than the host of little ones that we typically expect in MIS. By "large" I mean in some cases transactions lasting hours or days. These are likely, for example, in computer-aided design/computer-aided manufacturing (CAD/CAM) applications and in computer-assisted software engineering (CASE).

In both these areas, a designer will frequently have need to "check out" a design or drawing or part thereof and work on it for a period of hours, days, or perhaps even longer. Meantime, clients, managers, or other team members may need to consult that design. Should they be locked out until our friend returns the updated design and "checks it in" again? Their needs may well be too urgent for that.

What we're faced with here is no more than the familiar problem of a multiaccess database, working now to a very different time scale. Because the time scale may span hours, days, or weeks, the needs of other classes of users begin to impact how we handle the concurrent access. The various ODBMS and OOCASE products have taken a variety of approaches to these problems, as you'll find when you begin to learn the products. (Note also that an OOCASE "repository" is simply an ODBMS of ***metadata*, or data about data.**)

Another issue to be considered is that of complexity of operations and queries. In the kind of systems we've been building around RDBMSs, the *updates* are generally relatively simple, but typically the system must handle a lot of highly complex *queries*. In object-oriented systems, we still need to handle the complex queries, but in addition we're likely to be faced with a great deal more complexity in the updates and other processing.

As a result of these and similar issues, we find that the most commonly used relational benchmarks don't measure adequately the features that are now provided by ODBMSs. The things they do measure are often things that don't matter too much to ODBMS users. So the existing benchmarks haven't generally been much help.

Benchmarks are always only a limited help for evaluating a product anyway. Raw performance is only one aspect. "Typical" operations on "representative" data may or may not approximate *your* actual conditions of use. Amount of data, size of objects, and number of objects created – these things all affect performance.

The benchmark tasks are often single user, single application, and single database, where the current state of the art is multiusers, multiple tasks, and distributed objects. Performance may well be impacted by several applications running at the same time, especially if they're all of different kinds, competing with the benchmark program for resources.

Levels of locking can also have an effect. Locking at a *fine granularity*, either record locking or field-level locking, can slow down a single-user application. On the other hand, with multiple users accessing the same database, such fine granularity can help. It can make a larger portion of the database accessible to other users when one program has something locked.

Most benchmarks test only with a single database, where many business applications need to use several. Some ODBMSs don't allow a single transaction to access multiple databases. There's a lot of variation in how object-oriented databases centralize or distribute both the data and the program code that locates objects. The speed and loading of your network can have an effect. Building systems with a client–server approach can make a big difference.

And finally, apart from performance, you need to evaluate such things as ease of interfacing to your chosen OOPL. Such things as programmer convenience and product flexibility can affect productivity and thus system-development time, as well as error rates and the overall quality of the delivered system.

Now let's take a look at a couple of object-oriented benchmarks, as described by Rotzell and Loomis.

Engineering Database Benchmark

Developed at Sun Microsystems by Cattell et al. (1990), this one was designed to check performance problems that relational databases sometimes have when processing engineering-type data. What they wanted to see was whether an ODBMS could do it faster.

The benchmark task is to create a database of 20,000 parts and 60,000 interconnections. A range of different retrieval and navigation operations are then performed on it, both from warm-start and cold-start conditions:

1. Warm-start: Ten repeats of each operation are done before the timed test begins. This ensures there are lots of objects already cached in RAM.

2. Cold-start: Starts with all the data still on the disk and nothing yet transferred to RAM.

The results, as published by Sun at OOPSLA, showed a speed advantage of 30 times for ODBMSs over RDBMSs.

HyperModel Benchmark

Developed at Tektronix by Anderson et al. (1989), this benchmark is based on a hypertext task and covers a wider set of operations than the Engineering Database Benchmark. This one includes component relationships (whole-part) and BLOBs.

The larger set of operations, with more interrelationships among the objects, is intended to give a better comparison than the Engineering Database Benchmark. The HyperModel also does cold- and warm-start tests, and its results were similar, though perhaps a little less dramatic.

ODBMS Products

Given the volatility of the ODBMS marketplace, I won't attempt a survey of products. With new products every few months and frequent new features in existing products, about all I can do that would be of any use at all is simply to list the currently available products. You'll find a very incomplete list of addresses in Appendix A4, and if you browse a current issue of TAPOS or Component Strategies magazine or some such you'll find more. Here they are, approximately in alphabetical order, and by no means a complete list:

- COGNOS Axiant
- Object-Oriented dBASE
- Gemstone (from Servio)
- HP Odapter (formerly OpenODB)
- O2
- Objectivity
- ObjectStore
- ORACLE 8i and 9i
- Paradox for Windows/Object PAL
- Poet
- UniSQL
- VERSANT

14.6 OBJECT-ORIENTED DEVELOPMENT ENVIRONMENTS

We have a similar volatility problem with OODENVs, so again, I list just a few of the better-known ones. I do have one or two brief comments to add in a couple of places, however.

Most of the major C++ manufacturers offer more or less complete program development environments. Inprise/Borland, Microsoft, and Zortech, along with numerous others, all do it this, way, although there are compilers out there that are just that and nothing more, in case you might want that.

Delphi is an excellent offering from Inprise/Borland and shows much promise. Perhaps my next book should be *Delphi for Dummies*. (Has it been done yet?)

Object One and PowerBuilder, like Delphi, are popular as complete development environments, but must compete with the ones that come with C++ and Java.

Smalltalk: As with C++, all current Smalltalk manufacturers provide a full development environment, rather than just a compiler, as do all of the Java vendors.

VERSANT Argos (code generation in Smalltalk), Visual BASIC, and Visual C++ ("The Visuals") are (currently) somewhat impoverished compared with the others in this list. They're easy to learn and very user-friendly, but some of the others are to be preferred for large industrial-strength projects. My earlier comments about Microsoft and their policies should be borne in mind if you are considering any of these products.

DELIVERABLES

Your major deliverable from this phase is a working system! Your secondary deliverable, then, will be a *well-documented* working system.

FURTHER READING

For object-oriented programming, here are a few selections out of the dozens that are on the market. (See the Bibliography for complete publishing data.)

General

- Budd (1991): Timothy Budd, *An Introduction to Object-Oriented Programming* (with the platypus on the cover).

- Voss (1991), *Object-Oriented Programming, an Introduction*.

Java

- Bishop (2001): *Java Gently*, by Judy Bishop. For those interested in Java, who are new to programming, I strongly recommend this one. There are a thousand Java books out there, most of them decidedly *bad*. In my humble opinion, only a tiny few are worth reading, and this is one of them.

- Eckel(2000): Bruce Eckel. *Thinking in Java*. This one is excellent for experienced programmers who wish to learn Java.

Smalltalk

- LaLonde and Pugh (1990), *Inside Smalltalk*.

- LaLonde (1994), *Discovering Smalltalk*.

Eiffel

- Meyer (1992), *Eiffel, The Language*.

- Wiener (1995), *Software Development Using Eiffel*. This one bears the rather tongue-in-cheek subtitle, *There Can Be Life Other Than C++*. Richard Wiener is editor of JOOP magazine (Journal of Object-Oriented Programming).

C++
- Pohl (1993), *Object-Oriented Programming Using C++.*
- Schildt (1994), *C++ from the Ground Up.*
- Swan (1998), *Tom Swan's Mastering Borland C++ 5.* This 8-cm (3-inches) thick weighty tome is a wonderful primer-to-expert learning tool for C++. It starts assuming no prior knowledge of C, unlike most "learn-to-C++" books. Swan includes an excellent section on object-oriented programming and a CD with *all* the sample programs from the pages of the book. (The Borland/Inprise C++ software is available at educational discounts at most college bookstores.)

CHAPTER SUMMARY

- A data definition language (DDL) is used to design and build the database, with syntax to create a schema, and to define integrity conditions and so on. An ODL must also handle methods, complex attributes, and subclass relationships, along with inheritance and polymorphism.

- A data management language (DML) is for day-to-day adding, deleting, changing, and then retrieving the data values in the database. In an ODBMS, the DML and query language (OQL) must handle the complex data types that ODBMSs allow.

- A data control language (DCL/OCL) is for security, integrity, optimization, and so on:
  - Transactions (COMMIT, ROLLBACK, etc.)
  - Access control (GRANT, REVOKE, etc.)
  - Index creation and management
  - Enforcing integrity rules as per DDL/ODL

- A *complete* database language must have DDL, DML, and DCL, whether it's conventional or object-oriented. The object-oriented ones are ODL, OML, and OCL.

- OQL is a superset of SQL. The ANSI SQL3 committee is developing object SQL for defining, manipulating, and querying object databases as a superset of a relational database, calling it OSQL, or Object SQL.

- The OMG Object Model exists as a set of components, to be assembled into "profiles," one for ORBs, and one for ODBMSs, and so on. The *core component* must be in every profile.

- ODMG 3.0 consists of four parts: an object model, an object definition language (ODL), an object query language (OQL), and bindings to the various languages.

- A *language binding* allows a programmer in the target language to access features of the database language.

- Garbage collection involves deleting unwanted instances and frees up RAM to be reclaimed and reused. When it's not available, the programmer must physically delete instances or the system may crash. COBOL programmers are not trained for this.

- Most high-level object-oriented languages such as Java, Smalltalk and Eiffel have automatic garbage collection in one form or another. C++ does not.

- Memory leaks are when we're no longer using part of memory, but the program can't reclaim them or doesn't know how to.

- Dynamic (late) binding means smaller but perhaps slower executables. Smalltalk code is as fast as C++, unless you hire an expert C++ optimizer.

- Smalltalk doesn't allow multiple inheritance; it has roles that allow Dynamic Typing.

- Standardized class libraries come with only a few of the languages.

- In Smalltalk, *everything* is an object. It has a development environment and an ANSI standard basic class library. Recently, Smalltalk has begun to catch up on C++ in usage, speed, and portability.

- C++ is complex and detailed, so not as programmer-productive as, for example, Smalltalk and Eiffel. It's good for systems code. *With proper optimization*, it gives better execution speed and executable size. Effective optimization of C++ requires real skill and experience.

- C++ has a longer learning curve, except where there's a pool of C/C++ skills. But then there is risk of writing old-style procedural code in the object-oriented language. No garbage collection means programmers must beware of memory leaks.

- Eiffel was designed to increase reuse. Concurrency will be added soon. The Nonprofit International Consortium for Eiffel (NICE) has become guardian of the language.

- Objective-C is hybrid and adds object-oriented functions to the C language without altering the C syntax.

- OO COBOL is an extended language, where object-oriented extensions are added to the COBOL syntax. Beware old-fashioned code and coders!

- ISO/ANSI Ada 95 is truly object-oriented, with dynamic typing and abstract classes, a core language, with standardized class libraries (*annexes*), subsystems, and several different models of multiple inheritance.

- The maturation of standards over the next few years will drive the development of the database products. There will also be competition from Microsoft with DCOM, which they're promoting against CORBA.

- CAD/CAM, multimedia, GIS, document, image and drawing management systems, and the like all need complex data types – such as graphics, sound, and video clips and attributes that are lists, sets, or other objects. RDBMS have been extended to handle some of these, but major progress has been made by moving to ODBMSs.

- The approach has often been a pointer stored in the table, pointing to the variable-length data, which is in another physical file. This has led to the concept of *BLOBs*.

- Other complex data types, such as lists, sets, and classes, have been more difficult to add to the relational databases. These work better in the alternative approach, that is, *pointers*. Some say pointers take us back to the network databases and CODASYL. With complex objects, rapid retrieval is a problem. Techniques such as *clustering* are regaining their importance for DBAs.

- Benchmarks designed for RDBMSs are inadequate for object-oriented databases. Data is organized differently and requires different access. Joins are a bottleneck in RDBMSs and will be in "extended relational" ODBMSs. Those using pointers won't need costly, time-consuming joins.

- Many object-oriented applications will need to handle a few large transactions, rather than many little ones, especially in CAD/CAM and CASE. A designer "checks out" a drawing and works on it for hours or days. Other team members may need it and can't wait until she returns the updated design and "checks it in" again. Versioning is important.

- Most common relational benchmarks don't measure the features now provided by ODBMSs. Things they do measure often don't matter to ODBMS users.

- Benchmarks are only limited help for evaluation. Performance is only one aspect. "Typical" operations on "representative" data may not approximate your actual conditions. Amount of data, size of objects, number of objects created – all affect performance. Tasks are often single user, single application, and single database. We need multiusers, multiple tasks, and distributed objects. Several jobs may be running at the same time.

- Locking at fine granularity, record or field-level, can slow a single-user application. With multiple users, fine granularity helps, meaning a larger portion of the database is still accessible to other users when one program has something locked.

- Most benchmarks test with a single database; many business tasks need several. Some ODBMSs don't allow a transaction to access multiple databases. There's some variation in how object-oriented databases centralize or distribute data and program code. Speed and loading of the network can have some effect.

- Also evaluate the interfacing to your chosen OOPL, for productivity and system development time, as well as error rates and the overall quality of the delivered system.

- The Engineering Database Benchmark from Sun checks performance with engineering-type data. It creates a database of 20,000 parts and 60,000 links and does retrieval and navigation tasks, both from "warm-start" and "cold-start" conditions. Shows a speed advantage of 30 times for ODBMSs over RDBMSs.

  - Warm-Start: Ten repeats of each operation before test, so lots of objects cached in RAM.

  - Cold-Start: Starts with all the data still on the disk and nothing yet in RAM.

- The HyperModel Benchmark from Tektronix is a hypertext task and covers a wider set of operations than the Engineering Database Benchmark. This one includes component relationships (whole-part) and BLOBs and also does cold- and warm-start tests.

CHAPTER GLOSSARY

benchmarking The process of comparing two or more products by running them against a standardized task.

Binary Large Objects (BLOBs) Attributes stored in databases and managed as uninterpreted strings. The ODBMS doesn't attempt to make any sense of the contents of a BLOB but simply handles it as a string of thousands or millions of bits. (While the application program must be aware of its internal structure and organization, the database is not and doesn't need to be.)

clustering The technique of physically locating records close to one another when they're logically related and likely to be retrieved together.

complete database language Consists of three parts: a data definition language (DDL), a data management language (DML), and a data control language (DCL).

data control language (DCL) Concerned with such things as security, integrity, and optimization.

data definition language (DDL) Designs and builds the database.

data management language (DML) Looks after the day-to-day work of adding, deleting, and changing the data values in the database and then retrieving them when needed.

language binding In this context is a syntax and a supporting set of software (in this case, it takes the form of classes, methods, and so on) to allow a programmer in the target language to access features of the database language (that is, the ODL, OML, OQL, and OCL).

metadata Data about data.

WHAT COMES NEXT

Now that you've learned a great deal about object-oriented techniques, it's time to see how to make the change in your organization. Chapter 15 is devoted to ideas, methods, and pitfalls involved in introducing these new – and for many people, very scary – ideas into a systems organization, against politics and resistance. Chapter 16 deals with people, and Chapter 17 is a case study, very important to help you put it all together.

CLASS/GROUP EXERCISES AND PROBLEMS

Ex 14.1 Check out all the comments and assertions in the chapter regarding features and problems present or missing in the various object-oriented products that we discussed. While correct at the time of writing (Fall, 2000), much of the information may well be out of date by the time you're reading this. Each person or group take one or more products and research the manuals, magazines, and books, then report back to the class on products that have changed since the book was written.

Ex 14.2 Do this one on all your exercises that you've been carrying forward through the earlier chapters, both group and individual: In light of the information presented in this chapter, go back and review your choices of software/ODBMS/language. Document your justification for any changes, and even if you decide not to change it from your original choice. In that case, document why you decided to stay with that choice.

INDIVIDUAL EXERCISES AND PROBLEMS

Ex 14.3 Now that you're aware of the OOPLs available and the standardization work being done, it's time for you to try one of those agents we met in Chapter 13. In this exercise, I've attempted to get you to create a simplified, simulated, approximated "intelligent agent." It's not really true to life at all, but it's intended simply to illustrate how the principle might work. Do it in pseudocode, but if you know or are learning an OOPL, bias it toward your chosen language. Feel free to code and run it if you wish!

Design an agent class as follows:

(a) The class creates an instance of itself every time the right mouse button is depressed for any reason, within any job. (You may want to look up the relevant interrupt codes.)

(b) Each instance records its own creation date and time in an attribute(s) and then sits waiting for interrupts to occur. It increments counter attributes for each mouse button (left, right, and center) and a counter that tracks the total number of keyboard depressions.

(c) Every time the printer becomes idle, the oldest of the surviving agent instances increments a counter. When the counter reaches 10, the instance prints its counts, creation date/time, and current date/time. Then it calculates and prints each category of mouse clicks as a percentage of the keyboard depressions.

(d) After that it commits "suicide" and leaves the task to someone else. You'll note that there could be several agent instances alive at one time and they'll need to communicate to see who is the oldest. Also, once created, they carry out their task with no further intervention from the "creator."

PROJECTS AND CASES

P 14.1 For your small-business project

(a) Review your platform choices in light of the information in this chapter.

(b) Take a course in your chosen OOPL and/or ODBMS.

(c) Now you're ready to begin coding. Good luck and good testing, too!

SELF-TEST QUESTIONS

Note: The Appendix has answers to the Self-Test Questions.

Q 14.1 Expand the following acronyms. Every one of them, except for one, appears somewhere in this chapter. (Isn't that a scary thought!) Mark the one that *doesn't* appear in this chapter.

ANSI	OCL
BLOB	ODBMS
CAD	ODL
CAM	ODMG
CLOS	DCOM
CODASYL	OML
CORBA	ODBMS
DCL	OOPL
DDL	OQL
DML	ORB
GIS	OSQL
IDL	RAM
ISO	RDBMS
MIS	SQL
NICE	TLA

Q 14.2 A "complete" database language has to have

(d) DDL, DCL, DML

(e) DML, ODL, DCL

(f) DML, ODL, OQL

(g) DCL, DDL, DQL

(h) All of the above

(i) None of the above

Q 14.3 Match each language with the set of functions it performs:

(a) DML	(1)	Design and build database; create and modify schema; assign columns to tables
(b) OML	(2)	Queries on an ODBMS
(c) DDL	(3)	Creating instances; changing attribute values
(d) ODL	(4)	Relational joins

(e) DCL   (5) Assign attributes to classes; create classes; set subclass
                                             hierarchies

(f) OCL   (6) Add and delete rows; change column values

(g) SQL   (7) Transactions; indexes; integrity; access control

(h) OQL

Q 14.4 What three languages did Sutherland list as the name of a Clint Eastwood western?

(a) _____ is the ____   ____   ____   ____

(b) _____ is the ____   ____   ____   ____

(c) _____ is the ____   ____   ____   ____

Q 14.5 Garbage collection is when

(a) You reclaim memory space when a program is deleted.

(b) You reclaim memory space when an instance is deleted.

(c) You reclaim disc space when a file is deleted.

(d) You reclaim disc space when a persistent instance is deleted.

(e) You reclaim office space when an employee is deleted.

(f) They empty your office waste basket.

(g) None of the above.

Q 14.6 Which of the following is true?

(a) Hybrid and extended languages allow easier conversion but may cause us to miss some object-oriented benefits.

(b) Dynamic typing of objects renders multiple inheritance unnecessary.

(c) Dynamic binding gives smaller but slower executables.

(d) Porting among languages, dialects, and platforms will be simplified by CORBA.

(e) Most ANSI OOPL standards don't specify a standard class library.

(f) The average C++ programmer is not good enough to realize the potential execution speed of the language.

(g) All of the above.

(h) Some of the above.

(i) None of the above.

Q 14.7 BLOBs are

(a) Something like the Inkspots, only bigger

(b) A symbol a little like a cloud, used in class diagrams in some OO methodologies

(c) A device to soften the rigid boundaries of a cell

(d) Bit-length ordered bytes

(e) Bit strings stored by a database that is ignorant of any internal structure it has

(f) None of the above

Q 14.8 Which of the following approaches have been used in the development of ODBMS products?

(a) Use pointers, a device borrowed from older DBMS designs.

(b) Extend the CODASYL model to handle methods and complex data types.

(c) Insert methods into tables so as to preserve First Normal Form.

(d) Extend the relational model to handle methods and complex data types.

(e) Borrow pointers from the CODASYL model and add them to the relational model.

(f) Extend the hierarchical model to handle methods and complex data types.

(g) All of the above.

(h) (a) and (e)

(i) (a) and (d)

(j) (b) and (e)

(k) (b) and (d)

(l) (a) and (c)

(m) (b) and (c)

(n) None of the above

Q 14.9 A memory leak is when

(a) A "mole" in your group memorizes your system design and sells it to your competitor.

(b) Your company experiences a brain drain.

(c) A program doesn't know how to reclaim freed-up RAM.

(d) A program reclaims memory space when an instance is deleted.

(e) A program cannot release RAM from objects that have been deleted.

(f) None of the above.

Q 14.10 Which of the following is true?

(a) Most benchmarks test a single database and a single thread of control.

(b) Levels of locking can affect processing differently, depending on whether one or many jobs are running.

(c) Object-oriented applications sometimes need to handle transactions lasting hours, days, or weeks.

(d) Existing benchmarks for RDBMSs have mostly been found adequate for ODBMSs.

(e) All of the above.

(f) Some of the above.

(g) None of the above.

Q 14.11 A data _____ language (DDL) is used to _____ and build the database, with syntax to create a _____ , and to define _____ conditions and so on. An ODL must also handle _____ , complex _____ , and subclass relationships, along with _____ and _____ .

Q 14.12 A data management language (DML) is for day-to-day _____ , _____ , changing, and then _____ the data values in the database.

Q 14.13 A complete _____ _____ must have _____ , _____ and _____ , whether it's conventional or object-oriented. The object-oriented ones are _____ , _____ , and _____ .

Q 14.14 _____ _____ involves deleting unwanted _____ and frees up _____ to be _____ and _____ .

Q 14.15 _____ (_____) binding means _____ but perhaps _____ executables.

Q 14.16 ISO/ANSI _____ 95 is truly object-oriented, with _____ _____ and _____ classes, a core language, with standardized _____ _____ (annexes), subsystems, and several different models of multiple _____ .

Q 14.17 Benchmarks designed for _____ are _____ for object-oriented databases. Data is _____ _____ and requires different access. _____ are a bottleneck in RDBMSs and will be in " _____ _____ " ODBMSs.

Chapter Fifteen

· ·

Moving to Object-Oriented Techniques

WHAT YOU WILL LEARN IN THIS CHAPTER

In this chapter, you'll be given some warnings and introduced to some issues, that an organization faces in the change to object-oriented methods. You can be confident that you understand these when you can:

1. Select a pilot-project team with an appropriate mix of skills and experience.

2. Select a pilot project with regard to the issues discussed in the chapter.

3. Discuss problems that are likely to occur during the transition to object-oriented working.

4. Describe how object-oriented wrappers facilitate the integration of legacy systems.

5. Define quality and describe how objects can improve software quality.

WHAT YOU SHOULD KNOW TO START THIS CHAPTER

This is another chapter where you don't need to be a skilled developer to follow the material. You do, of course, need to understand objects (Chapters 4–6 and Chapter 8).

CHAPTER OVERVIEW

We begin with a few questions about whether you should go object-oriented and whether your company is ready for this. Then we look at the staffing issues – what kind of people should be on the pilot project(s), what skills they'll need, and training, training, training! Then we discuss the choice of the pilot project itself and some very important issues around that choice. We discuss a few migration problems, in particular what to do about your existing, or legacy, systems. Finally, we attempt to define software quality and consider how objects can help us to achieve it.

KEY CONCEPTS

- Planning and time
- People-centered approach
- Team size for a pilot project is around seven
- New hirees versus experienced staff
- Recent graduates versus OOT-experienced consultants
- Complementary skills; live and breathe objects
- Mentors; pilot team become mentors
- Three pilot projects, independent projects
- Some pilots will fail, keep a low profile
- Learn lots, lick wounds, and try again
- Project plan, conversion plan, business area
- Knowledge-rich environment
- Parallel migrations: to client-server, e-commerce, and networks
- Legacy systems, object-oriented "wrapper"
- Objective and subjective errors
- Quality Assurance (QA), quality is customer satisfaction
- Black-box or input-output verification vs. white-box verification
- Goal of testing is to *find* errors

"THE OUTHOUSE BATHROOM BOUTIQUE" SALES REPORTING SYSTEM – EPISODE 15

"You know, there's one thing you're really rather lucky in," said Nancy to Tim one day at lunch in the coffee shop next door.

"Oh?"

"Yeah. You're going into this object-oriented thing more or less right from Day One. You have only one system that has to be redeveloped, and none of the pieces of the old system are going to be kept around to get in the way. Everything else that you do on computers – accounting, payroll, personnel, and so on – is being done with shrink-wrapped software.

"Larger companies have a lot of problems with a change like this. They have so many systems, each with so many programs and subsystems, that the switchover has to be done piecemeal. Some of their older 'legacy systems' they can't afford to rewrite until several years later!"

"And I'll bet they have a lot of trouble with people not wanting to change things," put in Tim. "You know, people just don't like anything to change around them. But I thought that of all people, computer specialists would be the ones who would get excited about new stuff, and even welcome change."

"Don't you believe it!" responded Nancy, shaking her head. "We're often the very worst. That comes as a surprise to many people, of course, because our job involves making changes to the way you guys do *your* job. But don't you dare try and change ours!

"Some people figure it's because we invest so much time in training, and in learning all our software, but I think that's really just an excuse. And like all good excuses, it has just enough truth in it to make it sound plausible. Actually, I think we're just like everyone else, scared of change.

"There are ways to make a properly executed changeover to object methods go smoothly. It's mostly a matter of planning, and of choosing the right people for the pilot projects. In fact, just *having* a pilot project is a big step in the right direction. Selecting the *right* pilot project helps a lot too, and so does knowing how to handle the organizational politics."

THOUGHT QUESTIONS

1. Consider an organization that you've worked for or one of your group members has. Would you consider them ready for a change to object working? Why, or why not? Justify your answers and write them down. Review these answers after studying the chapter and see whether your views have changed any.

15.1 Is OOT the Final Answer?

As Tom Love (1993) puts it, one of those unfortunate facts of a systems developer's life is that users come to us with "vivid dreams of the future, but without

- A clear idea of what they want built
- An understanding of the available technology
- Sufficient time to arrive at the desired product
- Adequate resources to construct their vision."

Koontz (1994) asks, "Is this a revolutionary technology that will solve all our problems?" Emphatically, the answer must be *no*. It's not simply one technology, and it may well *cause* more problems than it solves. It's a matter of staying up to date with the industry or falling way behind. Objects are a new way of thinking and doing, a totally new way of viewing our world.

According to Love, "The technology is not perfect; some projects do have difficulties, *but the developers continue to use objects on subsequent projects*" (italics mine). The implication clearly is that once a developer becomes accustomed to objects, he invariably finds enough benefits to stay with them.

15.2 Is Your Organization Ready for OO?

One of the first things you'll need to do in preparing for a transition to objects is a careful and thoughtful analysis of where your company is currently at. Once you know that, you can gauge how far you have to go. Add to this some estimation of the amount of resistance to change you're likely to encounter and the availability of cash and other resources, and you then are in a position to get some idea how difficult the change will be.

The first step will be to look at how the company currently does the job. A number of groups have developed scales to estimate how sophisticated and up-to-date a company is in its approach to systems development, for example in Humphrey (1989).

15.3 EVOLUTION OR REVOLUTION?

Throughout this book, I've tried to present object methods as an *evolutionary* growth from earlier methods, as you can see from the history in Chapters 3 and 4. Yet, in another sense, objects make such a difference in the way we think about data, information, and systems that perhaps we should be calling this a *revolution*. So we'll say that while its effects are certainly revolutionary, the method itself is evolutionary.

This distinction is not so much a problem, as it is by way of being a warning. Be warned that many of the developers in your organization will view the switch to objects as a revolution and therefore something to be feared and resisted.

Since it's *so* different, these people will see it as something to be feared, as is anything that's new and different, at least to them. This is where you'll need your people skills, the mentors, the training, and the progressive apprenticeships, all of which you'll read about later in this chapter.

These people should not be on the pilot or early production projects. They should move to the object-oriented projects later in the conversion calendar, when there are plenty of experienced peers and mentors for them to lean on for help, support, and the living proof that these weird things can in fact be done. These are not the ones that should be struggling with how to make the new techniques work. Give that part to the *high-achieving* experimenters and challenge seekers in the group.

Note that this doesn't mean *all* the "experimenters." In these early projects, we want only the *high achievers* among them. These are the ones who not only love to try out something new, but are in the habit of *making it work*, successfully and on time. These are the ones who habitually use new technology to do the job better and to gain some benefit from it for the project.

15.4 GETTING STARTED

Do your investigations and decision making early. There's no better way to make sure a conversion fails than to start late. People never *plan to fail*, they just *fail to plan!* Any project needs adequate planning and sufficient time allocation.

In this conversion project, everyone is on a learning curve, there are far more things that can go wrong, and it's all so new that when they do go wrong, no one will know how to fix them! So adequate planning and sufficient time, while always important, here are twice as critical.

Take the time to choose a language and an ODBMS carefully. Make sure the architecture and features really do fit your needs. Many companies have reported that they wish they had taken more care to see that the OOPL and ODBMS that they chose actually had all the features they were going to need.

Get the training and get it early (see the next section).

Get the consultants in early. Don't wait until you're already in trouble before you bring them in. Remember the old saying, "Around here, there's never enough time to do it right, but there's always enough time to do it over!" Give everybody enough time to do it right the first time through. It'll save time and money in the long run, and bring reduced stress and better productivity for everyone.

You'll end up with a better quality product, on time, and you're more likely to have a satisfied user. You will recall the discussion in Chapter 3 on how critical it is to catch errors as soon as possible after they've occurred, and therefore how the early stages (analysis and requirements definition) are where it's doubly critical to avoid errors. Bring consultants in early enough that they can do the analysis *right*.

Koontz (1994) reviews a conference on object-oriented software development at St Thomas University, St Paul, Minnesota. From the variety of companies reporting on their varying levels of success of their object-oriented conversions, he distills a number of observations, among them these two:

1. The first and second projects you can expect will be about 30% more expensive using object-oriented techniques.

2. The third project and onward will be money savers.

You'll note that these statistics are consistent with those reported by other writers, some of whom I've cited elsewhere in this book.

Here's what we've said so far:

- Object-oriented technology is not the silver bullet, the final answer. It's one more step ahead and better than what went before.

- Do your investigations and decision making early.

- Get the training and get it early.

- Get the consultants in early.

- Choose your OOPL and ODBMS carefully. Make sure their architecture and features really do fit your needs.

- The first and second projects will cost about 30% more, and the third and on will save money.

Now let's look at what to do about that most difficult of all the resources we have to have: *people*.

15.5 STAFFING AND TRAINING

At this point in the industry-wide transition to object-oriented technology (OOT), there aren't a lot of experienced OO analysts and designers out there. For this reason, a company should expect mostly to train rather than hire for the new skills.

Having said that, I must also say that it's imperative to have one or a core of experienced outside consultants or new hires. These must be truly experienced in OOT, and will serve not only to guide and manage the project, but also to nurture and mentor your existing staff through the changes.

You must not neglect training your staff in the people skills that are described in Chapter 16. While it would be nice to think that all your current staff and new hires are equipped with adequate interpersonal skills, in reality this could be a bad assumption.

The changes won't be easy for all of your people. There will be the hotshots, who read everything and take a course and are itching to try their new knowledge. Then there are the ACP[1] cadre over in the corner, who will fear and resist change (and hope to retire before it happens).

Perhaps all you can do for those people is buy them a copy of this book! It's essential that the company take a sensible, practical, reasonable, and above all *people-centered* approach to the training plan, and indeed to the whole object-oriented transition. In Chapter 16, you'll find some discussion of training and a number of related issues.

Selecting the Team

MIX OF SKILLS

The ideal team size for a pilot or initial project is around seven. Of these, at least one person must be familiar with the OOPL chosen, and at least one familiar with the ODBMS (not necessarily a different person). The remainder must cover a variety of complementary skills as on any project.

You'll need someone who is a natural administrator, and you'll need a leader, an innovator, and some solid workers. You'll need an operating system expert, or access to one, and if possible someone already familiar with the application area. This last person can be a technically savvy user, perhaps one who has already worked on systems projects in the past.

PROJECT MANAGER

Every project, especially a pilot or early production project in something this new, must have a designated leader. Call her or him *project leader*, *project manager*, or whatever, this person is the central point of reference for everybody connected with the project.

The project manager acts as "traffic cop," accepting and redirecting messages, complaints, and queries (kind of like a human ORB, in a way.) Such messages will come from team members, users, management, and hardware and software vendors, as well as all kinds of unanticipated sources.

This person has the responsibility and must also have the authority to make the day-to-day decisions, or delegate them, or take issues to the users for a decision. You might be amazed how often in real life managers are given responsibility without matching authority! It's a matter of senior managers being able to delegate effectively, to have the courage to share their power, trust their people, and live with the results.

Be careful when you're given responsibilities and make sure you have the appropriate power to make decisions and take action on the issues you've been given responsibility for. But that is, as they say, "a whole 'nother story," for a course in management and delegation. In Chapter 16, you'll find some comments on teams and their formation, and on styles of management.

The project manager is there to make sure no people, issues deadlines, deliverables, or problems fall through the cracks. As a coordinator supreme, he guides and choreographs the project. Above all, this person is the one who must motivate the team and recognize their achievements, large and small.

---

[1]ACP: Ancient COBOL Programmers. ACP itself is simply another TLA.

Recent Graduates

At least one of the team should be a recent graduate, if available. This is for two reasons. One reason is that they (hopefully) are up-to-date and have already had some object-oriented programming and analysis courses (and of course have read this book! I would also hope that they have read one or two others, those that I term the "senior books" or "guru books" in the object-oriented field.)

Another reason is that recent graduates can be expected to bring to the project a fresh outlook and a willingness to try new things. After all, is that not what a pilot project is all about?

Experienced Staffers

Older and more experienced team members can be relied on to provide some important stability and common sense, but they'll be battling the C word, and that is *change*. Undeniably, they'll be a bit more set in their ways and can be expected to feel less comfortable with all the newness.

It's important to choose these experienced team members from among those who *can* handle change well, and who are interested and even excited about the move to OOT. Companies who have made the transition successfully chose pilot-team members who were flexible in their thinking and able to adapt readily. They also provided a high level of support (*including adequate training*) to these people as they learned the new ideas and techniques.

Not for Everybody

It seems not everyone is suited to being in the vanguard of the move to OOT. Some companies have reported that they lost the occasional person who quit because they couldn't handle it. Careful choice of team members will minimize this loss of expensive, highly trained developers.

Those who are not put on the pilot project should continue with maintenance on the legacy systems for a while, until the transition to OOT is well under way. Then there will be plenty of experienced mentors and peers to help them deal with the change.

Training

It is essential that the team receive extensive training and that they get it early in the piece. They'll need vendor training for the methodology, OOPL, ODBMS, and other products used. Many companies also send the team for object-oriented analysis and design courses. Everybody should have a copy of *this* book, and there should be copies available of some of the "guru books," including those of The Three Amigos (Booch, 1999; Rumbaugh, 1999)

Time and time again, reports of post-mortem studies on both successful projects and failed ones have mentioned a need for *more training*. Often, it seems, the need for training is initially underestimated, leading to difficulties that could easily have been avoided.

Mentors

Also, in such a major change, the support of *mentors* has been found crucial. A **_mentor_ is a wise and trusted adviser** (*Gage*, 1983). *Oxford* (1998) replaces "wise" with "experienced," and also gives us **an experienced person in a company,** college, or school who trains and counsels new employees or students. In our context, then, a **_mentor_ is a person with knowledge and experience, who is both willing and able to assist, advise, and nurture those who are beginning their work in this area.**

Mentors provide assistance and support as the team members begin to use their new skills. Initially, they'll mostly be external consultants. The pilot team will need one or more of these.

After the pilot project, the pilot team then become the internal training group, along with any remaining consultants. These people then nurture and mentor the rest of the developers on the early production projects.

Beyond the pilot project, we can learn from the Hewlett-Packard VEE project (Love, 1993). These guys took an approach to object-oriented training for developers that I consider to be an example of common sense and realism in action. (Common sense, unfortunately, is all too uncommon. HP does seem to have quite a bunch of it!)

At HP, new members of the team, after some formal training, for a while were restricted to maintaining existing object-oriented programs. Then they were "apprenticed" to an experienced object-oriented developer, that is, a mentor. These two phases in their training typically lasted *more than a year* before they began working on their own.

15.6 THE PILOT PROJECT

The actual choice of the pilot project is yet another critical item. Be prepared to spend a great deal of time and thought on this. Below I've summarized some points to watch out for.

Choose Three Pilots

Consistent with Koontz's comments above, Taylor (1992, page 286) suggests you'll really need to have not one but *three* projects chosen and planned for when you begin. The first two, which can be expected to take longer with object-oriented methods, can both be considered pilots.

The third, since we can expect it to begin showing some benefit from the use of objects, may be considered either a pilot or the first early production project. Taylor discusses numerous important points in his chapter on adopting object technology.

Taylor has a slightly different perspective on choosing a pilot project. Most of us prefer to be a little more reticent and conservative, as you'll see in the next section. But Taylor recommends for a pilot "a simulation . . . involving complex entities with complex interactions . . . This is where Object Technology really shines . . . and traditional methods have trouble." I would suggest you consider a project like this perhaps for your second or third pilot.

If you have a need for something to impress management or clients and to sell the idea of objects, then provided it's feasible, Taylor suggests a full-blown "controlled comparison test, where two teams develop the same project." Or you could redo an existing project that was well-metricked in its original form.

This kind of comparison is great where appropriate, but it can mean sticking your neck out a bit. These comparison ideas do have a certain merit and may be appropriate in some cases. They may perhaps be best suited for your second pilot than for your first. One problem with both of these comparison ideas, however, is that you may have difficulty maintaining a low profile, as suggested in the next section.

Keep a Low Profile

Your pilot project(s) must be carefully chosen to satisfy a number of requirements.

- Ideally, choose one that you can make highly visible if successful, but play down if not. If it should fail, then *keep a low profile,* learn lots, lick wounds, and try another one.

  A pilot, by definition, is experimental in nature. It is intended for trying new things and struggling to make them work. It's for making mistakes and learning from them. Under these conditions, it can be expected that *some pilots will fail*. But only the pilot project should fail, not the entire *conversion* project with it!

- Be prepared to deal with the possible failure. Have your contingency plans in place, particularly the political ones for making sure this failure doesn't halt the entire conversion project.

  Also, you'll need those people skills again to ensure that your team is not feeling devastated by a failure, can learn effectively from it, and is in good spirits and motivated to try some more. This kind of attitude to failure is characteristic of winners and achievers, so cultivate it freely in yourself and your team, and choose team members who have already demonstrated this ability.

- It should have a graphical user interface (GUI). This is one of the most widespread and spectacular applications of OOT. There's also a large and varied set of software products available, and GUIs receive a significant proportion of the media attention that goes to objects.

- It must be an independent project. That is, it must be separate from any mission-critical processing, so that it can't bring down any part of the company or the existing systems if it fails. It's a proof of concept and a first attempt, so it could fail. Keep it clear of corporate politics.

Other Points

Here is a smattering of things that Taylor feels will help make your transition smoother:

- Select some of your best people. They must be volunteers who have a positive view of the change. They must feel comfortable with the new way of doing things, which means they must be properly trained. ***Don't skimp on training!*** These must be people that the management has confidence in already.

- They should, if possible, be full-time on this project. They must live and breathe objects for the duration of this project and must intend doing so for the rest of their careers (or until the next paradigm comes along).

- Planning is critical. Besides a proper project plan, you need a well-developed conversion plan, with criteria prepared in advance for evaluation at each stage of the project and of the conversion.

- A pilot should be of manageable size. A team of five to seven people is large enough to allow for a lot of interaction and learning, but small enough to keep everyone on the same track.

- While the statistics can be used only as a very rough guideline, something like 50 or more classes, with 200 or 300 methods, is probably an appropriate size for a pilot project.

Once the pilots are done, then we do it for real. Early production projects must also be carefully chosen. They too will be under corporate scrutiny, just as the pilots were.

Steps in the Conversion Process

1. **Model a business area.** A business area is a cluster of functions, activities, jobs, and operations that belong together. Even though they may have been formally placed in different branches of the organization chart – that is, in different organizational units – they actually are related, and generally you'll find that they have similar needs for information.

   Consultants are a good idea for this. They should do most of the work, with your own staff learning from them, for this very first object-oriented requirements analysis. The recent graduates among your staff will have a great deal of useful knowledge, but must learn from the experience and past mistakes of the consultants. Have the models finished for a complete business area before moving on to choose an application.

2. **Prototype and develop an application in that business area.** The consultants and staff should do this together. Koontz suggests a one-to-one ratio of staff to mentors on the first project, that is, *one expert for every novice* (his italics).

   Full immersion is the most successful route, and the least expensive in the long run. It requires a "very knowledge-rich environment." Your own staff should probably do the user interface, since they're familiar with the users and their needs. Your staff should also do the implementation and user training, for the same reason.

3. **Repeat Step 2 with each additional application in that business area.** You may go a two-to-one ratio of staff to mentors on the second project, because by then the managers and users and team leaders will all know what is expected. As you repeat this a for few more projects, your own staff can take over a larger share each time.

4. **Move to a new business area** and repeat from step 1, with all or mostly in-house staff.

This gets you off the ground. As you do more, your new development and redevelopment projects will drive OOT progressively through your organization.

Don't Do It This Way!

If you want an opportunity to be immortalized in legend, try a major mission-critical project for your first baby step!

These sage words, whose source I've been unable to track down, pack a lot of meaning. Don't become a legend! *Choose a pilot project that will not be a disaster if it fails!*

According to Koontz, there is one other sure-fire way to guarantee failure. This is to use the traditional waterfall analyze/design/code/test method, with traditional developers and analysts and team leaders from a data/process procedural background. In other words, old guys doing it the old way.

He predicts this will give rise to a "standard, procedural system that happens to be written in an object language, with none of the benefits, but all the pitfalls, of object orientation." *Get the training and bring in the experience,* ***early!***

Now for a summary of how to choose the pilot project and the staff for it:

- Expect to train rather than hire for new skills, but have some outside consultants or new hirees, truly experienced in OOT. These people will not only guide and manage the project but also mentor existing staff.

- Train your staff in people skills.

- The ideal team size for a pilot or initial project is around seven.

- One person should be familiar with the OOPL, and one with the ODBMS. The others must have a variety of skills as on any project. You need an administrator, a leader, an innovator, some solid workers, an operating system expert, and someone familiar with the application area (a problem domain expert.)

- Not everyone is suited to the vanguard of OOT, and some companies have lost people who couldn't handle it. Careful choice of team members will minimize this loss. You need pilot-team members flexible in their thinking and adaptable. They need a high level of support, including adequate training.

- The team must get extensive training, early. They need vendor training for the methodology, OOPL, ODBMS, and object-oriented analysis and design courses. Everybody needs *this* book, and some of the "guru books."

- Mentors give assistance and support. Initially, they're external consultants. After the pilot project, the pilot team then become the internal training group, and mentor other developers on early production projects.

- On the HP VEE, new members were trained, then they maintained existing object-oriented programs, and then were "apprenticed" to an experienced object-oriented developer as mentor. This took a year or so, before working on their own.

- Choose *three pilots*. The first two will take 30% longer with object-oriented techniques.

- Perhaps for your second or third pilot, "a simulation . . . complex entities with complex interactions . . . is where object technology shines . . . and traditional methods have trouble." To impress management or clients, present a full-blown controlled comparison test: Two teams develop the same project, or redo an existing project.

- Keep a low profile. Choose a project to be highly visible if successful, but play down if not. If not, then keep a low profile, learn lots, lick wounds, and try another one. Pilots are experimental and can fail. Be prepared for failure, have contingency plans in place, and ensure that it doesn't halt conversion. Ensure that the team can handle failure, learn from it, and are motivated to try again.

- It should have a GUI.

- Make it an independent project, separate from mission-critical processing, so it can't bring down existing systems if it fails. Keep it clear of corporate politics.

- Use your best people: those who have a positive view of the change, are comfortable with new things, are properly trained, and in whom management has confidence. ***Don't skimp on training!***

- The staff must work full-time on this project, they must live and breathe objects

- Planning is critical: project plan and conversion plan, criteria prepared in advance for evaluation.

- Keep pilot staff to a manageable size; five to seven people are enough for interaction, but few enough to keep everyone on the same track.

- For a pilot project, 50 or so classes, with 200 to 300 methods, are probably appropriate.

- Steps in the conversion process:

  1. Model a business area. Consultants should do most of the work, with your staff learning from them.

  2. Develop an application in that business area, consultants and staff together. Have a one-to-one ratio of staff to mentors.

  3. Repeat Step 2 with each application in that business area. Have a two-to-one ratio of staff to mentors. Repeat from Step 1 in a new business area, with all or mostly in-house staff.

- ***Choose a pilot project that will not be a disaster if it fails!***

- ***Get the training and bring in the experience, early!***

15.7 MIGRATION PROBLEMS

Those of you who are already in the workforce will be aware of some of the problems inherent in a changeover such as this. For those among you who are preparing to enter the world of work, these are some of the problems you may see if you happen to join a company that has not yet switched. You may be lucky enough to join an object-oriented firm (OOF), but right now there's still a good chance you'll work for an old-fashioned employer (OFE, pronounced "Oaf.").

New Technology Problems

CONFIGURATION

In most companies, other migrations are already under way. While these are not necessarily related to objects, they can certainly be expected to affect the migration to objects. One is the move from stand-alone systems to client–server processing. As it happens, client–server working is an ideal showcase for the power of objects, especially distributed objects, so you can expect to be combining these technologies.

E-commerce is another one. Many MIS applications communicate and do business across the Internet already, and the trend would appear to be in the direction of a totally e-commerce economy.

HARDWARE

In parallel with this, there has been a move away from mainframes to workstations and the UNIX and Windows platforms. As mainframes are dropped, legacy systems are being redeveloped on networks and workstations. This of necessity must be total redevelopment because of the new platform, giving an opportunity for a switch to object-oriented methods.

However, you do end up having to learn and implement two or three new technologies at the same time, which just adds to the difficulties and the stress load.

SOFTWARE

The new object-oriented development tools, compilers, databases, and such are all about the same price as the old ones. This means that the major software-related costs are for training, and the hidden costs of the learning curve. The choice of software tools must not be undertaken lightly or cursorily, as we saw earlier.

TRAINING

Many writers these days talk about the need for proper training when changing tools and technologies. Experience in the 1980s with CASE tools highlighted this. Many copies of Excelerator and Information Engineering Workbench (IEW) ended up being used merely as graphics tools, with the enormous power of the tool left untapped.

The literature abounds with examples of failures and near disasters, where the postmortem opinions say "more training was needed!" So the biggest problem with training is not finding it or doing it, but *making sure that it happens.*

TOOL VERSUS METHODOLOGY

It is important when bringing in a new tool or technology to have realistic expectations as to precisely what it's going to do for you. One of the lessons from the first go-around of CASE tools in the 1980s was that the tool won't fix all your problems.

Neither will OOT. You must understand your own way of working and be fully aware of how you're going about things. In other words, you must have a methodology in place that you both *use* and *understand*. Otherwise, all the tools and object-oriented ideas in the world are not going to help. When CASE tools first surfaced in the 1980s, they were bought by the thousands of copies, were tried out, and then many became "shelfware."

> There's a story about a lumberjack, who brought his old-fashioned hand saw in to the store to be sharpened. The storekeeper talked him instead into buying a shiny new chainsaw, promising he would fell three times as many trees in a day. Off went the happy lumberjack, only to return two days later complaining that he was felling, not more, but fewer trees per day. The storekeeper sharpened the chainsaw, tuned it, and sent him off again. Two days later he was back, with the same complaint. So the storekeeper said to come out the back and let him see how he was using it. They got out the back to a tree, and the storekeeper fired up the motor. The lumberjack recoiled in horror! "What's all that noise?" he cried . . .

If you don't change your way of doing things to take advantage of a new tool or technology, you'll end up doing the old things with the new tool, and probably not doing them as well as before. You must introduce the methodology before or at the same time as the new tools, technology, or techniques.

To switch to OOA&D, you may buy a methodology, along with training, consulting, and other support, from an established consulting firm such as DMR, Andersen, Sierra, EDS, PWC, or any of the myriad firms large and small. Or you might adopt and adapt one of the "guru methodologies" found in the books by Jacobson, Shlaer and Mellor, Wirfs-Brock, Coad and Yourdon, or Meyer, to name just a few. All of these are now available as proprietary methodologies, supported by CASE. The important things are that you *have* a methodology, document it, understand it, and above all *use* it.

As Ivar Jacobson is wont to say, "You can use a method without a tool, but not a tool without a method."

15.8 DEALING WITH LEGACY SYSTEMS

At some point, your new object-oriented systems must interface with your older existing systems. One very effective technique for doing this is to encapsulate the legacy system within what probably should be called a "pseudo-object." We can hide the untidy, nonobject details within an object-oriented "wrapper."

From the outside, the wrapper looks for all the world like a regular object. You send it messages, and you get back data and behavior. On the inside, it's still the same old COBOL system, doing the same old things. But this is invisible to all the object-oriented client objects out there!

Let me explain with an example. Let's say your personnel system exists as COBOL code and a DB2 database. Our super new object-oriented system needs an Employee class with data (Name, Address,...) and behavior (Hire yourself, Fire yourself, Promote yourself, . . .)

The old system certainly has that data, and it also has all the program code to account for those behaviors, since the same business events have been occurring since Day One. However, the code is probably scattered among various programs. Not only that, but the data may be spread among various databases, and some hardcoded into tables in some of the programs. Here is what you would do about that:

1. Analyze and design your new system, perhaps it's "Production Control."

2. Create a class called Employee, with no data attributes.

3. During the analysis, you will discover what methods it needs.

4. In the design phase, specify the protocols for the methods the way the new system needs them to be.

5. For each method, write some object-oriented program code (perhaps in C++ and utilizing bits of COBOL code) to invoke the existing COBOL code in the old programs, to manipulate and/or extract the data. You may even need to go to the extent of simulating calls from an IBM 3270 terminal or a DEC VT100 (the dumb terminals that were commonly used with older mainframes) and stuff like that. You may have to trap and redirect output that the old system used to send to the screen or printer.

6. The rest of the legacy system continues to operate as it always has, gathering, storing, processing, and reporting on the data.

7. Add any new data attributes to the Employee class, those that the legacy system didn't have, and code any additional methods that the legacy system was unable to provide.

8. Your new OO production control system goes into production, drawing employee data from the legacy personnel system via the wrapper object(s).

9. At a later date, redevelop the legacy personnel system with object-oriented technology. Now create data attributes in the Employee class to replace the data fields in the old files. Write methods in an object-oriented language to replace the legacy COBOL code (if appropriate, you may wish to do this progressively, one function at a time).

10. All your existing object-oriented programs (in your new production control system and elsewhere) should still work. Because of the level of encapsulation involved, they need not even be aware that there has been a change from the legacy personnel system to the object-oriented human resources system.

Note that the wrapper could be around the entire program. In some cases, the wrapper receives the messages from other objects, and the wrapper routine simulates the appropriate method for the outside caller. It does this by translating the received message into whatever form the legacy program can handle.

If you're lucky, this could mean function calls. Otherwise, you may need to simulate keystrokes to feed to the legacy system, and then intercept its screen output and translate that back to a form suitable to send back to the calling object as a response to its message.

From the point of view of the legacy system, this makes the client object appear like a keyboard user. From the point of view of the client object, it makes the legacy system look like one or more (server) objects.

Or you may prefer to isolate the functions from within a legacy program and place a wrapper around each individual one. This way you're taking the program apart and making the pieces into classes and methods. Now you rebuild the original program by replacing all of its function calls with messages between these new objects.

The functionality of the old program is still being handled by the original code, but it has been split up into these methods. The execution pathways and logic of the old program have now been replaced by the message calls.

There are two major advantages to doing it this way:

- Each individual pseudoclass with pseudomethods may be replaced separately with a true object-oriented class, allowing incremental evolution to a fully object-oriented structure.

- The legacy functions in their new arrangement as pseudoclasses and pseudomethods can now be reused in new development and in maintenance, just like any other classes and methods. When you do eventually rewrite them in true object-oriented form, however, the systems and programs where they were reused need not even know about the change.

Of course, all the extra processing through the wrapper (in whichever form) to get at the legacy code introduces a performance penalty. This is the price we pay, and something we must live with until such time as we rewrite the system in true object-oriented fashion. Hopefully, advances in faster, cheaper hardware will partially compensate for this.

For now, let's take a look at some of the benefits in testing and system quality that will accrue as we switch to OOT.

15.9 TESTING AND QUALITY ASSURANCE

Consider the following observations:

- *All software fails in its first production run.* John Gall's (1988) book *Systemantics* brings this out well. Have you ever written a (nontrivial) program that worked first try?

- *NORAD uses software.* And a lot of it, too.

- *The first production run for NORAD is **World War III*** (whoever that turns out to be against!).

- *Ergo,* **we're in trouble!**

So it might seem at first glance that the software at NORAD is not very high on quality. In fact, it is of unusually high quality; it just happens to be in a mission-critical application. Mission-critical, that is, only if we want to avoid *TEOTWAWKI!* [2]

I would hope for similar quality in the software if I'm ever being monitored by

---

[2]TEOTWAWKI: *The End Of The World As We Know It.* This acronym (which is definitely *not* a TLA) surfaced in connection with some of the more dire (and fortunately inaccurate) forecasts for Y2k.

computers in an ICU[3] . For a demonstration of what could go wrong at NORAD over quality and security issues, your homework this week is to watch the movie *War Games.* Also note that sometime around 1990 two students, one of them the son of the head of NORAD security, brought down the entire NORAD network with a benign but very busy virus! I do hope the U.S. Army had the foresight to hire them both when they got out of jail.

What Is Quality?

BUILDING IT EXACTLY AS SPECIFIED?

Emphatically NO! *Not good enough!* The problem is that the specs are rarely right! All the ideas, techniques, and so on that we discussed in reference to the requirements analysis, are for the purpose of getting the specs as close to *right* as we possibly can.

But we run into problems of documentation and communication, plus the users' vague vision of the final product typically has gaping holes in it. The "freeze-the-specs" method was one early attempt to deal with this. It wasn't successful, primarily because the users' needs would change and put the specs out of date long before the system was completed from them.

Errors in building to spec may be termed ***objective errors*, where the final product doesn't meet the specification.** In other words, the system doesn't do what the customer said she wants. Provided a written spec exists, these errors are (at least in theory) fairly easy to find and demonstrate. In theory, you simply read the spec and try everything out on the system.

The U.S. Department of Defense found one interesting bug of this nature. It seems the spec for a certain type of missile stated that the computer should arm the warhead immediately after it separated from the main rocket.

Unfortunately, the programmer was unaware that the computer was located in the main rocket! The rocket had left when they separated and so the computer was no longer able to tell the warhead to do anything at all. Since it couldn't possibly arm the now-distant warhead, it was unable to perform "up to spec." I understand the problem was noticed and corrected, but otherwise I'm sure it would have been found on the very first test flight. This is what I would describe as a "mission-critical objective error."

QUALITY *Is* CUSTOMER SATISFACTION

Levi Strauss, in the California gold rush of 1848, invented trousers made from tent canvas. They sold like hot cakes because they protected the miners, kept them warm, and, most important, lasted more than just a few days in the harsh conditions.

This was the origin of the now-ubiquitous "jeans" that we all wear. But in this day and age, jeans must be a lot more than just long-wearing and functional. They must be stylish, and they must carry one of a limited number of socially-acceptable designer labels.

---

[3]ICU: Intensive Care Unit at a hospital. This one *is* a TLA.

[4]GTG Count: Your *"Gee, That's Great!"* Count. Another TLA.

These are requirements that must be clearly understood by the "developer." When the customer asks for jeans, the "developer" of the jeans needs to know, from experience, or from market research, *or by asking the client directly*, just what kind of vision the customer has of himself in jeans.

I could walk the two blocks from my house to Mark's Work Wearhouse at West Edmonton Mall (the largest mall in the *world*), and spend $30 on a pair of jeans for one of my teenage nieces. Would I have a satisfied customer? The product meets the spec for "jeans" and would be great for the bush or the construction site. But if I bother to listen to these young ladies, I find that the 14-year-olds are wearing them baggy from Le Chateau, and the 19-year-olds are wearing them tight from The Jean Boutique. Oh, and either way, they cost not $30, but $130. You see, *when you know what the customer actually wants, you're more likely to come up with it.* Tom Love suggests this will boost your "GTG Count."[4]

What this says to us is that, rather than merely conforming to its specifications, the product must actually *satisfy the users' requirements*. Remember that the specs are merely someone's *attempt* to write down the requirements. You must not consider the spec to be the true requirements.

Subjective errors are where the system doesn't do what the customer wants. It may be built perfectly to spec (what the user asked for), but what if the spec was wrong? Or it may meet the spec, but not quite the way the user wants or needs it. So the answer is that we must first test that the product meets the specs, and in addition test that the specs meet the requirements.

Further, it's no good if the system does what the specs say, and even does what the users need, if they get frustrated and angry trying to use it. The *users' perception* is important. This is why there are designer labels on jeans.

Users' opinions are important, and so are their feelings. It has even been suggested that we videotape users' faces as they try the product and watch their expressions as they meet each problem, bug, or feature. Naturally, we would hope to see more expressions of pleasure than otherwise . . . .

Remember it doesn't matter what technical concerns we've had to address during development of the software, and how technically perfect we know it to be. These are the people who must use it daily, and whose feelings of satisfaction or otherwise will determine how we're rated at doing our job.

Need We See Inside?

Quality assurance (QA) is an important part of the testing. This function should, if possible, be carried out by someone other than the actual system developers, perhaps a designated systems person(s), knowledgeable user(s), or consultants from a second firm, retained for this purpose. *Quality assurance* is a final test of the delivered product against the specs and also of the specs against the users' requirements.

QA must work without knowing the insides of the system and its various parts. They must work on an "Input–Output" model, or, if you prefer, a "black-box" model. **_Black-box verification_ or _input–output verification_ is when the workings of the system are encapsulated and the testing consists of checking that each input generates the expected output.**

That is, they must simply verify that every use case actually works the way the user intended. Recall that the use cases are a key tool for building, and later executing, your testing plan. The system designers, on the other hand, do ***white-box verification*, where the inside workings of the system are visible to them.**

Software quality is a management issue. The three levels of management – corporate, MIS and project levels – all have a responsibility to ensure that quality happens. They're the sources of the time, people, resources, and above all the *motivation* to produce a quality product. Love (1993, page 188) gives a list of books on software quality, some of which I've found very useful. You'll find this list discussed in part in "Further Reading" at the end of this chapter. Now let's examine how objects can help us with quality.

Objects and Quality

Here are some ways that objects affect our striving for quality:

- Encapsulation allows us to first test *inside* a class, and then test from outside the interface to see whether the class performs as expected. Then we can test each other class that we know is going to call this one, and finally do *system testing* covering the whole project. Use cases are also test scenarios.

- Encapsulation reduces the number of connections among classes, reducing the number of test cases needed. In the old days, such links were not controlled, and tended to proliferate throughout design, coding, and maintenance. This led to a lot more work and detail in the testing and to a lot more things that should have been tested but were missed.

- Test cases are built at same time the class is built. Each class has a test suite implemented as a "tester" class, whose sole purpose is to "exercise" the subject class (see Chapter 13).

- Once the object paradigm is established within a company, any program we write is composed to a large extent of prewritten and pretested code. High levels of reuse mean that each class will be used, and must be retested, over and over many times. Each time it's reused, its existing test suite must be run against it as an acceptance test, and then it's tested in relation to the new system.

- Each time we reuse a class, we further test all its methods. From time to time, we can expect to uncover an old error in a class we reuse, thus increasing the reliability of all the old programs that have already used that class.

- In this way, it's tested and retested many times in varying environments, leading eventually to a very stable and trustworthy reusable component.

- Because objects give enhanced traceability from analysis to design to coding to implementation, corrections to the requirements or the design point us directly to the code that needs to be changed, and vice versa. We can be confident that:

     °   There are no hidden pieces of code to change – this is all of it.

     °   The encapsulation ensures that the changes have only a limited effect in other places in the code – that is, there's no ripple effect, no cascade of errors and associated changes after a seemingly small and innocuous correction.

Remember that the goal of testing is to *find errors*. Somewhat paradoxically, if you're finding errors, your method of testing is working. If you're not finding errors, you must not assume that all is okay. If you can't find any errors, the first thing you do is assume that your testing method is suspect!

    Testing must be automated as much as possible so that we may indulge in total and exhaustive testing, without spending ridiculous amounts of people time on it.

Quality and Class Libraries

Love (1993) discusses the need for quality if we're to begin marketing prebuilt classes as "software components." The same things apply for classes we develop for in-house reuse. He raises a number of questions:

- *Searching.* How do we find the components (classes) we need for a given project? Once we know what the class must be able to do, are there better ways to find a class that can do it? This highlights the need for class libraries to have efficient and effective browsers, including your in-house libraries.

- *Geographic location.* How can we find classes we need when they're likely to be on any of a number of processors, possibly spread around the company, city, nation, or even the world? Or a single class or instance could be distributed over several processors anywhere.

- *Maintenance.* Even if a class is built carefully for reuse and tested thoroughly in a variety of environments, it could still fail out there in the customer's world. Who is responsible if your "component" fails after your client embedded it in a product and sold it to her client? This could go several generations and be ported among hardware and software platforms, so who is responsible when it fails in such a distant and foreign environment?

- *Naming.* We must be careful of a proliferation of classes with the same name and slightly different characteristics. The DBA, in his expanded new role, must police and enforce naming conventions and registration procedures, and attempt to minimize the spread of such anarchy.

• •

DELIVERABLES

There are no deliverables for this chapter, save for a completed, successful, smooth transition to object-oriented technology. Good Luck!

FURTHER READING

Love (1993) and Taylor (1992) each have excellent chapters on the switch to OOT, and Barbara Bouldin's book *Agents of Change* (1989) has a wealth of practical ideas for introducing new software development techniques into an IT group.

Jacobson (1992) in the first part of his Chapter 15, "Managing Object-Oriented Software Engineering," has quite a bit to say about conversion to object-oriented methods and about project selection.

You should also read Tom Love's entertaining and at the same time rather scary story in his Chapter 1, about the Swedish flagship *Vasa*. As I mentioned in Chapter 13, she was built and sailed her one and only voyage in 1625. I found it chilling to recognize in the story all the things that I've seen happen to systems projects, with results similar to those of the unfortunate *Vasa* and her crew. Love also has an excellent book list in his Chapter 11, "Building in Quality," on page 188.

There is a wealth of discussion on quality issues in general, not specifically IS, in a book with the rather surprising title *Zen and the Art of Motorcycle Maintenance*, by Robert Pirsig (1975). This enjoyable and definitely enlightening book has little to do with actual motorcycles, and much to say about life, including such issues as *quality*.

CHAPTER SUMMARY

- Do your investigations and decision making early. Get the training and consultants early.

- Choose your OOPL and ODBMS carefully. Make sure their architecture and features really do fit your needs.

- The first and second projects will cost about 30% more, the third and on will save money.

- Train for new skills, but have outside consultants who are truly experienced in OOT. These will guide and manage the project, and nurture and mentor staff. Train your staff in people skills.

- The ideal team size for a pilot or initial project is around seven: one familiar with the OOPL, one with the ODBMS, and others with complementary skills as on any project.

- Some companies have lost people who couldn't handle OOT. Careful choice minimizes this loss. You need flexible and adaptable pilot-team members, well supported, including adequate training.

- The team needs extensive training, *early*; vendor training for methodology, OOPL, ODBMS, and so on. Also, OOA&D books and courses should be provided. Everybody needs *this* book.

- Mentors assist and support. Initially, external consultants, then pilot-team members, mentor other developers on early production projects.

- Choose three pilots. The first two will take longer with OOT.

- Keep a low profile. Choose a project highly visible if successful, but play it down if not. If not, then keep a low profile, learn lots, lick wounds, and try again. Pilots can fail. Be prepared to learn from failure.

- The pilot should have a GUI and be an independent project, not mission-critical, so it can't bring down existing systems if it fails. Keep it clear of corporate politics.

- Use your best people who are properly trained, in whom management has confidence, who are full-time on this project, and who live and breathe objects. ***Don't skimp on training!***

- Planning is critical for the project and conversion plan; have evaluation criteria ready in advance.

- A manageable team size is five to seven people. Plan for 50 or so classes, and 200 to 300 methods.

- The steps in the conversion process are:

    1. Model a business area. Hire consultants, with your staff learning from them.

    2. Develop an application in that area, consultants and staff together, using a one-to-one ratio.

    3. Repeat Step 2 with each application in that area. The ratio is now two-to-one, staff to mentors. Repeat from step 1 in a new business area, with all or mostly in-house staff.

- ***Choose a pilot project that will not be a disaster if it fails!***

- ***Get the training and bring in the experience, early!***

- New technology problems:

    - **Configuration:** We're moving from stand-alone to Client-Server, an ideal showcase for the power of objects, and to e-commerce.

    - **Hardware:** From mainframes to workstations and networks.

    - **Tool Versus Methodology:** The tool (OOT or CASE) won't fix all your problems. Remember the lumberjack.

- To interface with existing systems, encapsulate the legacy system in an object-oriented "wrapper."

- A *wrapper* looks like a regular object, gets messages, and returns data and behavior. COBOL code is inside, invisible to the client objects outside.

    1. Create a class with no data. During Analysis, find what methods it needs.

    2. In Design specify protocols the way the new system needs them.

    3. Write object-oriented code and COBOL code, to invoke the existing COBOL code in the old programs to manipulate and/or extract the data. Trap and redirect output that the old system used to send to the screen or printer.

    4. Later, redevelop the legacy system with OOT, with attributes to replace fields. Write methods to replace the legacy COBOL code. You can convert one function at a time.

    5. All existing object-oriented programs still work. Because of encapsulation, they need not be aware that there has been a change from legacy to object-oriented system.

- Note that the wrapper could be around the entire program – translating a received message to a form the legacy program can handle – with function calls, or simulated keystrokes. Intercept screen output and translate to object-oriented form for the calling object as a response to its message.

- Or, isolate functions within a program and place a wrapper around each one. Rebuild the original program by replacing all of its function calls with messages passed among these new objects.
- The functionality of the old program is still being handled by the original code, but it has been split up into these methods. The execution pathways and logic of the old program have now been replaced by the message calls.
- This has two major advantages:
  - Each individual pseudoclass may be replaced separately with a true object-oriented class, allowing incremental evolution to a fully object-oriented structure.
  - Legacy functions in new dress can be reused like other classes. When eventually rewritten in true object-oriented form, the reusing programs need not know about the change.
- ***The specs are rarely right!*** Requirements analysis is for getting them as close as possible. Errors in building to spec are *objective errors:* The final product doesn't meet the spec. The system doesn't do what the customer *said* she wants.
- Quality *is* customer satisfaction.
- Rather than just meeting *specifications*, the product must satisfy the *users" requirements*. The specs are an *attempt* to write down requirements, they are not actually the requirements.
- *Subjective errors*: the system doesn't do what the customer wants. Test that the product meets the specs, and in addition test that the specs meet the requirements.
- Quality assurance (QA) is a final test of the delivered product against the specs and also of the specs against the users' requirements.
- QA must work black-box or input–output, with the workings of the system encapsulated, and test by checking each input for expected output – that is, every Use Case works as intended.
- Designers do white-box testing, where the workings of the system are visible.
- Encapsulation allows testing inside a class, then from outside to see if it performs as expected; then you test clients and the complete system. Use cases are also test scenarios.
- High reuse means each class will be used and requires retesting every time – that is, each time we use it we must further test all its methods. Sometimes we find (and fix) an old error, increasing the reliability of all programs that have already used that class.
- In this way, it's tested and retested leading to a stable and trustworthy reusable class.
- Enhanced traceability from analysis to design to coding to implementation means corrections to requirements or design point directly to the classes and the code to be changed.

- There is no hidden code to change – this is all of it.
- Encapsulation ensures changes have limited effect, that is, there's no ripple effect.
- The goal of testing is to **_find errors._**
- Searching class libraries: How do we find the classes we need for a given project? Once we know what the class must be able to do, are there better ways to find a class that can do it?
- How can we find classes when they could be on any processor, around the company, nation, or world? Or when a single class could be distributed over several processors?
- Who is responsible if a class fails after your client embeds it in a product and sells it to her client?

CHAPTER GLOSSARY

black-box verification, or **_input–output verification_** When the workings of the system are encapsulated and the testing consists of checking that each input generates the expected output.

business area A cluster of user functions and activities, jobs and operations, that belong together. Even though they may have been formally placed in different branches of the organization chart – that is, in different organizational units – they actually are related, and generally you'll find that they have similar needs for information.

maturity in dealing with systems development A level of sophistication in the way a company goes about developing information systems.

mentor (1) A wise and trusted adviser (Gage, 1983). (2) An experienced and trusted adviser (Oxford, 1998). (3) An experienced person in a company, college, or school who trains and counsels new employees or students (Oxford, 1998). (4) A person with knowledge and experience, who is both willing and able to assist, advise, and nurture those who are beginning their work in the area.

objective errors Where the final product doesn't meet the specification. In other words, the system doesn't do what the customer _said_ he wants.

quality assurance (QA) A final test of the delivered product against the specs, and of the specs against the users' requirements.

subjective errors Where the system doesn't do what the customer wants. It may be built perfectly to spec, but what if the spec was wrong? It may meet the spec, but not the way the user wants or needs it.

white-box verification Where the inside workings of the system are visible to the testers.

WHAT COMES NEXT

The next chapter, the last "information chapter" in the book, is devoted to some of the people skills you'll need to make all this object-oriented stuff happen. After that comes a chapter with a case study, very important in helping you put it all together.

CLASS/GROUP EXERCISES AND PROBLEMS

Ex 15.1 In your group, survey the members and have each person report verbally about how systems are/were developed, at one or more organizations or projects they have been associated with. For students, these may be projects, especially team projects, that you did in earlier courses. The group then ranks each organization or project. Summarize your group's reasons for each decision and be sure to mention any dissenting views expressed by members. Present your findings to the class and seek feedback and opinions.

In the class as a whole, based on the presentations, devise a ranking scheme for software development maturity.

Ex 15.2 Propose your own group as the team for a pilot project. Each member takes a role (or two if the group is small), such as project manager/leader, administrator, language expert, problem-domain expert, recent graduate, or mentor. If you can, try to relate the roles chosen to the actual skills and styles of the group members. Identify training requirements for your group.

Each member writes a paragraph, describing prior experience (real if possible, otherwise make it up – your instructor won't notice the difference). Use these to recommend yourself for your chosen role(s) on the pilot-project team. Put it all on overheads or flipcharts to present to the class. Each group member presents herself or himself and justifies their suitability for the role(s).

INDIVIDUAL EXERCISES AND PROBLEMS

Ex 15.3 Have each person find an article in an object-oriented magazine, book, video, web site, or other form of production, that relates in some way to the conversion to object-oriented technology. Review the article, taking what it says and relating it to the content of this chapter. Present your summary of and comments on the article to the class. Have complete sets of copies of all the reviews to hand out at the beginning of the presentations so that the people may follow along, take notes, and review your notes afterward.

Ex 15.4 For *The Outhouse Saga*, select three or four projects within The Outhouse company that you consider would make good pilot projects. Speculate freely, and use your imagination, then justify your choices according to the criteria discussed in the chapter. Now choose three or four projects that would *not* be good pilot projects, and thus should happen later, and give reasons why. Present both lists to your group or class.

Ex 15.5 From The Outhouse staff and consultants whom you've met throughout this book in *The Outhouse Saga*, select a pilot project team of five people. One of these you may hire from outside, that is, make him up in addition to the people you've already met in the story.

Specify whether you think this person should be an employee or a consultant and say why. Justify each person you choose on the basis of knowledge and skills they bring to the project. Present your team to the group or class and ask for feedback of opinions and other options that you may have missed.

Projects and Cases

P 15.1   Have the members of your group choose one of the real small-business projects (that were begun in earlier chapters) from among all the members. Take your proposed team and their résumés from Exercise 15.2. Add your analysis and design models as they exist so far and put together a project plan and a contract proposal to present to your client. (But this time don't make any of it up!)

Self-Test Questions

Note: The Appendix has answers to the Self-Test Questions.

Q 15.1 Which of the following do users typically have?
 (a) A clear idea of what they want built

 (b) Sufficient time to arrive at the desired product

 (c) An understanding of the available technology

 (d) Vivid dreams of the future system

 (e) Adequate resources to construct the vision

 (f)   All of the above

 (g) None of the above

Q 15.2 Optimal size of a pilot project team is:
 (a) 1 – 3.

 (b) 6 – 8

 (c) 9 – 12

 (d) 10 – 15

 (e) 18 – 25

 (f)   None of the above

Q 15.3 A pilot-project team needs which of the following skill sets
 (a) Administrator

 (b) Leader

 (c) OOPL

 (d) Worker

 (e) ODBMS

 (f)   Innovator

 (g) All of the above

 (h) Most of the above

 (i)   Some of the above

 (j)   None of the above

Q 15.4 People who are not sufficiently flexible and challenge-oriented for the pilot and early production projects should be

(a) Fired

(b) Trained intensively until they have corrected this attitude problem and personality deficiency

(c) Put on maintenance of legacy systems initially, then moved to object-oriented projects when enough mentors have been developed

(d) Trained intensively for legacy system maintenance, since they can expect to be there for at least a year

(e) Put on a desk job and kept away from the users

(f) None of the above

(g) Some of the above

(h) All of the above

Q 15.5 A mentor is:

(a) A person who helps new people

(b) A wise and trusted adviser

(c) An excellent way for object-oriented programmers to learn

(d) A person with knowledge and experience

(e) A person willing and able to assist, advise, and nurture

(f) All of the above

(g) Some of the above

(h) None of the above

Q 15.6 In the HP VEE project, trainees typically did object-oriented maintenance and an object-oriented apprenticeship for

(a) Six months

(b) Less than a year

(c) One year

(d) More than a year

(e) Two or three years

(f) None of the above

Q 15.7 How many pilot projects should you expect to need?

(a) None, since object-orientation is such a natural way of working that we've all been using throughout our lives

(b) One, because object-orientation is so natural and easy to learn that we should have it down by the end of the first OO project

(c) Two, because savings are not expected until the third project, which doesn't need to be a pilot, it can be a production project

(d) Three, because object-orientation is a revolutionary method, different from anything before

(e) Four, since object-orientation has such a long learning curve.

(f) None of the above

Q 15.8 For your pilot project(s):

(a) Keep a low profile.

(b) Make it visible if successful.

(c) Be prepared for failure.

(d) Ensure your team can handle a failure and learn from it.

(e) All of the above.

(f) Some of the above.

(g) None of the above.

Q 15.9 Pilot projects

(a) Are small enough they can never fail

(b) Should have a GUI, so there's something left if it fails

(c) Should be a small, important part of a large mission-critical system

(d) Should be one of the CEO's pet projects to ensure visibility

(e) Can sometimes fail

(f) All of the above

(g) Some of the above

(h) None of the above

Q 15.10 Transition staff

(a) Should not be your best people – those should be on important legacy systems until after the transition

(b) Can be time-shared with other projects that still need them

(c) Can develop the transition plan as they go along

(d) Should be no more than five on the pilot team

(e) Should go back to legacy maintenance after the pilot so the next group can learn by doing

(f) All of the above

(g) Some of the above

(h) None of the above

Q 15.11 The conversion process should

(a) Spawn a crop of mentors for later projects

(b) Focus initially on a single business area

(c) Use in-house staff from the beginning, with consultants added later

(d) Use consultants exclusively

(e) All of the above

(f) (a) and (b)

(g) (b) and (c)

(h) (c) and (d)

(i) None of the above

Q 15.12 Which of the following is a good thing to do and will not bring about a disaster?

(a) Choose a pilot project that other systems depend on for data.

(b) Delay the training until the last possible minute.

(c) Save money on training by letting everyone read a book and then learn on the job.

(d) Choose a low-profile project that can't bring down other systems if it fails.

(e) Use whoever is available to staff the pilot project so the skills are spread around.

(f) All of the above.

(g) Some of the above.

(h) None of the above.

Q 15.13 For legacy systems, an object-oriented wrapper

(a) Surrounds each object in the new system to protect it from violation by the code in the old system

(b) Encapsulates the old code

(c) Must encapsulate the total functionality of the old program or system within a single pseudo-object

(d) Converts messages to old-style calls.

(e) Prevents a pseudo-object from responding to actual messages

(f) All of the above

(g) (a) and (c)

(h) (b) and (d)

(i) (c) and (e)

(j) None of the above

Q 15.14 One of the important steps in software quality is

(a) Building precisely to the specs

(b) Correcting the specs to the requirements

(c) Quality is in the jeans

(d) Yellow-box testing

(e) Opaque-box testing

(f) All of the above

(g) Some of the above

(h) None of the above

Q 15.15 The goal of testing is

(a) To find errors

(b) To get a clean run

(c) To prove there are no errors.

(d) To exercise all or most of the program

(e) To exercise every class

(f) .All of the above

(g) Some of the above

(h) None of the above

Q 15.16 Testing by the input-output model is the same as

(a) White-box testing

(b) Testing keyboard throughput

(c) Yellow-box testing

(d) Opaque-box testing

(e) Black-box testing

(f) All of the above

(g) Some of the above

(h) None of the above

Q 15.17 The _____ down this list, the more people _____ their own _____ _____ _____ .

Q 15.18 Do your _____ and _____ making early. Get the _____ and _____ early.

Q 15.19 Choose your _____ and _____ carefully. Make sure their architecture and _____ really do fit your needs.

Q 15.20 The first and second projects will cost about _____ % more, the _____ and on will save money.

Q 15.21 _____ for new skills, but have outside _____ who are truly experienced in OOT. These will guide and _____ the project, and _____ and _____ staff. Train your staff in _____ _____ .

Q 15.22 The ideal team size for a _____ _____ is around _____ .

Q 15.23 Some companies have _____ people who couldn't handle OOT. _____ choice _____ this loss. You need _____ and _____ pilot-team members, well supported, including _____ _____ .

Q 15.24 Team needs extensive _____ , for _____ , OOPL, _____ , and so on. Also, OOA&D _____ and _____ should be provided. _____ needs this book.

Q 15.25 Mentors _____ and support. Initially, _____ _____ , then _____ - _____ members, _____ other developers on early production projects.

Q 15.26 Choose _____ pilots. The first two will _____ _____ with OOT.

Q 15.27 Keep a _____ _____ . Choose a project highly _____ if _____ , but play it down if not. If not, then keep a _____ _____ , learn lots, lick _____ , and _____ _____ . Pilots can _____ . Be prepared to _____ from _____ .

Q 15.28 Pilot should be an _____ project, not _____ - _____ , so it can't bring down existing systems if it fails. Keep it clear of _____ _____ .

Q 15.29 Planning is _____ for the project and _____ plan; have _____ _____ ready in advance.

Q 15.30 To interface with _____ _____ , encapsulate the _____ _____ in an object-oriented " _____ " which looks like a regular _____ , gets _____ , and returns _____ and _____ . _____ code is inside, _____ to the client objects outside.

Q 15.32 Later, redevelop the _____ _____ with OOT, with _____ to replace fields. Write _____ to replace the legacy COBOL code.

Q 15.32 The specs are _____ _____ ! Requirements _____ is for getting them as _____ as _____ .

Q 15.33 Quality is _____ _____ .

Q 15.34 Rather than just _____ _____ , the product must satisfy the _____ _____ . The specs are an _____ to write down requirements, not _____ the requirements.

Q 15.35 QA must work _____ - _____ or _____ – _____ , with the workings of the system _____ , and test by checking each _____ for expected _____ – that is, every _____ _____ works as intended.

Q 15.36 Designers do _____ - _____ testing, where the workings of the system are _____ .

Q 15.37 _____ reuse means each class will be _____ and requires _____ every time – that is, each time we _____ it we must _____ _____ all its _____ .

Q 15.38 Enhanced _____ from Analysis to _____ to Coding to Implementation means that _____ to _____ or _____ point directly to the _____ and the _____ to be _____ .

Q 15.39 The goal of testing is to _____ _____ .

Chapter Sixteen
. . . .

The People Side of Systems Development

WHAT YOU WILL LEARN IN THIS CHAPTER

In this chapter, you'll be introduced to issues, concerns, and practical techniques in dealing with people. While these are presented here specifically for the analysis stage of the modeling activity, they're important for all stages in systems development. What's more, these are skills that you'll find immensely valuable in all phases of your professional and personal life.

You can be confident that you've mastered the content of this chapter when you can:

1. Observe and note the differences in personality, behavior, strengths, and style among team members, including yourself, and adjust your *own* functioning, both to accommodate and to capitalize on these differences.

2. Identify areas where your own interpersonal skills can be improved, and develop a training/reading/practice plan to achieve this.

3. List and describe the stages a team typically goes through as it develops to a functioning, productive unit, and some of the typical feelings and behaviors that can be expected with each stage.

4. Use the paraphrasing/reflective listening method in a discussion to clarify the meaning of a question or problem.

5. Demonstrate the use of guided paraphrasing to arbitrate a conflict.

6. Perform a feelings perception check during a conversation, using a correctly structured question.

7. Conduct a conversation or interview for a few minutes using open-ended questions exclusively.

8. Explain why training is so important in the move to object-oriented methods.

WHAT YOU SHOULD KNOW TO START THIS CHAPTER

This chapter doesn't assume any specific prior knowledge. However, it will help immensely to make the material relevant, meaningful, and above all *helpful* if you've observed and/or participated in some JAD/FTS sessions and other systems meetings beforehand. Being part of a systems development project will help, or even better, being involved in the project management side of it.

CHAPTER OVERVIEW

After some introductory remarks on the importance of people skills to a systems analyst, we have a section on teams. We look at why a team is necessary, and how to deal with, and take advantage of, the differences among the team members. We consider differences in personality, style, strengths, and skills.

After studying several important aspects of teams and team building, we take a detailed look at the four stages of establishing a team, what I call the *Stormin' Normin'* model (with apologies to General Schwarzkopf).

Next you'll learn some practical methods for some of the critical interpersonal functions in systems analysis. These are for effective listening, refereeing a conflict or dispute in a meeting, dealing with someone's feelings during a discussion, and using open-ended questions to keep a meeting or discussion flowing productively. The chapter finishes with some brief comments on the critical importance of training, and methods for overcoming resistance to change.

KEY CONCEPTS

- Technophobia, cyberphobia
- Team, complementary skills
- The 4 temperaments, the 16 types
- Formal and informal communication
- MBWA: Management By Wandering Around
- MBCIF: Management by Control of Information Flow
- MBAW: Management By Avoidance of Waves
- Commitment, specific performance goals, mutually accountable
- Life cycle of a team
- The Stormin' Normin' model of team formation; norm
- Reflective listening/paraphrasing
- Conflict arbitration by guided paraphrasing
- Feelings perception check
- Open-ended questions
- Mentor, change agent, marketing role

"THE OUTHOUSE BATHROOM BOUTIQUE" HUMAN RESOURCES SYSTEM – EPISODE 1

"Now that the project's getting close to finished," said Tim at yet another lunch in the coffee shop, "I must tell you how much I admired the way you worked with the people all through it. I learned a lot myself just by watching you. I noticed especially how you phrased your questions to get a particular effect."

"Oh really?" smiled Nancy, flattered. "And just what did you notice me doing?"

Tim chuckled. "Well, probably the most dramatic was the time when Allana was just about ready to smack Hartmut across the face in that one meeting, and you just took over and told them what to do. And they did it. And it worked!"

"Oh, yes, that." Nancy smiled again. "Actually, what I did there is a recognized technique called 'guided paraphrasing.' And in fact, it was developed from an effective-listening method called simply 'paraphrasing.' They both are wonderfully simple, and they work just great in situations like that. I'll give you some course numbers and names of some courses offered at the technical college Business Department. The courses teach these techniques in a workshop environment, and I can recommend them for you and for your staff, if you're interested in following these ideas a little further."

"I sure am," said Tim. "And I also noticed that you always ask questions that make people think a bit and make them give an answer that's a whole sentence full of stuff, rather than just a one-word response."

"Ah, yes, another deliberate technique, I'm afraid," laughed Nancy. "The courses teach that one, too, and a bunch of others. And the courses do quite a bit on what makes a team a team, and how a group of random people form into a team. We call it the *Stormin' Normin' model of team formation.* And no, it was not named after General Schwarzkopf, but the association with his nickname helps people remember it!"

Thought Questions

Answer these questions in writing and review your answers after studying the chapter, to see what has changed:

1. Describe everything that is less than perfect about the way you listen. (Be honest, now!)

2. What could you do to improve the efficiency and effectiveness of your listening?

3. How would you handle a violent clash between two participants in a meeting or FTS/JAD session?

4. What kind of things could you say that would encourage someone to voice their true feelings in a discussion or argument?

Write these answers and ideas down and then try them in practice, then if possible in real discussions or arguments. Report the results to your group and analyze. *Review these results after reading the chapter.*

16.1 Sensitivity and People Issues

I've already alluded in earlier chapters to the problems of *technophobia* **(fear of technology)** and *cyberphobia* **(fear of computers).** While the names given them are kind of cute, they are nonetheless very serious problems, especially when we meet them in our users. As I've said before, to do our job well, we need the information our users have in their heads, and often don't know that they have it. And we must watch for the shy little guy down the back.

Of course, he's always in the *back* row in a meeting. He may well be a superb expert in the business (the problem domain), yet be very intimidated in front of you and me. These people are not about to speak up in front of us and their peers and their bosses, for fear of looking stupid if they make a mistake or don't know something. They're afraid of looking bad if they're a little slow catching on to all this techie stuff.

How to deal with all this can be a university degree in itself, or at the very least a series of courses in Organizational Behavior. In this chapter, I discuss the needs that exist, and then give you a brief overview of possible solutions with a few practical, effective techniques that you can use immediately. I've also been careful at each stage to point the way to further learning. This way, you have the option of following up with further work on areas that you think will give you the most benefit.

It's up to us as analysts and developers, with responsibility for the success of the project, to *do whatever is needed* to get the communication going and the ideas flowing. We must take the courses, read the books, and attend the seminars (and read this chapter), to ensure that we have the needed people skills. We must take responsibility for having the necessary sensitivity, communication ability, and other skills detailed in this chapter, to make sure the project works.

That applies equally to all of our own people, our team members. We must work together as a team, with all the shared goals, cooperation, and so on that teamwork implies. But this doesn't simply happen, nor does it happen overnight. Forming an effective team, as we'll see in the next section, is a complex and turbulent process.

16.2 TEAM BUILDING

We can define a **_team_** as *a small group* of people with *complementary skills* who have *commitment* to a common purpose, *specific performance goals*, and a common approach to the task, and for all these things they hold themselves *mutually accountable* (adapted from Katzenbach and Smith, 1993). Notice that I've italicized a few important terms and phrases in this definition, and we need to examine these in a little more detail:

- **A small group** This will lead us into a detailed discussion of individual differences and how they affect working relationships within a team.

- **Complementary skills** Here we discuss the need for
    ° Technical skills
    ° Functional (Process Improvement) skills
    ° Interpersonal skills (Communication skills, trust, leadership skills, arbitration skills)
- **Commitment**
- **Specific performance goals**
- **Mutually accountable**

Small Group

"Two heads are better than one, as the saying goes, but you may have noticed that they take longer to come to a decision. The larger the group, the more difficult they'll find it is to get along. They'll have more trouble agreeing on things, and there'll be more chance of disagreements and squabbles.

A larger group is less likely to resolve their differences. They'll have different personality styles (linear thinking versus random, detailed approach versus big picture) and different levels of achievement orientation, organizing ability, and being *personally* organized. They'll have very different ways of operating. Fortunately, some very powerful methods are available to accommodate and even capitalize on these differences.

Myers and Briggs (1962) were a mother-and-daughter team who in the 1960s did some important work on grouping people according to type of personality. It turns out that personality theorists down the ages – from the ancient Greeks to

Freud, Jung, Adler, and modern psychologists – have mostly grouped people into four "temperaments." It also turns out that they have all used basically the same four groupings.

Myers and Briggs defined these, and further refined them into the "Sixteen Types" that now bear their joint names. They documented the differing needs and characteristics, and the different ways each type needs to interact with other people.

Keirsey and Bates (1978) have produced a wonderful little book called *Please Understand Me* that gives a brief yet thorough and readable explanation of the 4 temperaments and the 16 types. At about $15, I strongly recommend that you buy it *and read it*.

You do the questionnaire on page 5, and after that you just read the parts of the book that are about *you*. Then you read about your boss, spouse ("significant other"), kids, and friends. You'll find this knowledge invaluable in figuring out how to deal with the people around you.

The Myers–Briggs classification system rates people on four *dimensions*, and you score a letter on each. The four resulting letters then give the classification:

1st dimension:	Introvert	(I)	vs	Extrovert	(E)
2nd dimension:	Intuitive	(N)	vs	Sensing	(S)
3rd dimension:	Feeling	(F)	vs	Thinking	(T)
4th dimension:	Perceiving	(P)	vs	Judging	(J)

My own rating, for example, is ENFP. My wife Nina is ISTJ. Opposites (or close) attract. They also have *complementary skills*.

To get the Four Temperaments, we first divide on the Intuitive/Sensing scale. Then we take the Sensing (S) people, and divide them on the Judging/Perceiving scale into SJ and SP. The Intuitive (N) people we divide on the Thinking/Feeling scale, to get NF and NT. So our Four Temperaments turn out to be:

SJ   Sensing, Judging   (Administrator)

SP   Sensing, Perceiving (Live-for-the-moment)

NF   Intuitive, Feeling. (Feeling)

NT   Intuitive, Thinking (Scientist)

To oversimplify drastically, SJs (typically, accountants, administrators, and the like) are highly organized and set a lot of stock by the rules. (I quote Staff Sergeant Johnson of the Canadian Corps of Commissionaires, retired from the Canadian Army, commenting when I requested one of my many exceptions to the rules: "If everyone just followed the rules, we'd all get along a whole lot better around here!")

NFs like me (The feeling group. We like to think we're the creative group!) are ready to change the rules whenever they get in the way. (People made them; people can change them!)

NTs (scientists) take a very thoughtful approach, and SPs (live-for-the-moment) want to *do it now*. In any team, these differences will exist. If they're not accepted and accounted for, then they'll cause disagreements and misunderstandings that will impede progress toward the goals of the group.

A smooth, efficient, and above all *effective* group can only arise when the members have recognized and discussed these differences, and resolved them by a consensus of what is acceptable and what is not, and know how to *take advantage* of the differences.

Each team member needs to take a reasonable and thoughtful stand, being assertive about her own strengths and needs, and tolerant towards the others. Very often we each perceive the differences in the others as weaknesses. It takes much strength of character to be able to recognize that these people are merely *different*, not wrong; that they also have strengths and abilities that are important to the functioning of the team.

SJs (administrators) have a particularly tough time accepting their opposites, the feeling NFs (especially since all of us typically *marry* our opposites!) NTs (scientists) have trouble understanding their opposites, live-for-the-moment SPs.

Here is an example of the kind of conflict the Myers–Briggs analysis can help clarify. All three of the "practical" groups SPs, SJs, and NTs have trouble figuring out the "feelers," the NFs. While these three types may not want to *be* in each other's groups, they can understand that someone else might want to run their life that way.

But NFs are a total mystery to all three of those groups. It can take a lot of patience on their part to accept NFs and to believe that they do actually have something of significance to contribute to the team. So the big challenge to all you SJs, SPs, and NTs is to *accept* that the NFs are merely different, not wrong, and allow them to demonstrate their strengths, rather than rejecting them as dreamers. (*Is anybody out there identifying with all this?*)

The larger the team, obviously, the more chance there will be for these differences to cause disagreements and the longer it will take to come to any kind of agreement over anything, including how to handle the differences. Out of the differences in style among the team members, there will arise a variety of strengths and abilities that we'll need to capitalize on, and make them complement one another.

COMPLEMENTARY SKILLS

No one person can have all the skills needed for a large project. This is one of the reasons that it becomes important to know (or at least to "guesstimate") the personality styles of the people you work with and live with. This is where the Myers–Briggs classification comes in so handy. It can be kind of fun to do the Keirsey Temperament Sorter on page 5 of *Please Understand Me*.

You should try it with friends, co-workers, and family. With your team, you may find some members resistant to this idea, so don't push them. You need full compliance to get accurate results in something like this. However, you can still go quietly through the exercise with the people who like the idea.

Any project big enough to warrant a team can be expected to need a wide variety of skills. The team needs to consist of a number of people, then, who among them have the right *mix* of skills and styles. The first challenge is to find the right people with the right skill sets, and then the second is to weld them together into a functioning team.

Shortly we'll discuss the actual team-building process. For the moment, let's look at the different kinds of skills that the members of a team must bring to the project, and then we'll delve into the *interpersonal skills* since they're the ones related to the topic of this chapter. Each team member will bring some subset of these skills to the project, and certain skills must be present in every member. The skills fall into three major groupings:

- Technical skills
- Functional (or process improvement) skills
- Interpersonal skills

Technical Skills

These are abilities directly related to the task at hand, to the purposes and goals of the team. Programming, analysis, systems design, database design, and so on are all skills that the team obviously must have. The team can't possibly function without them.

However, the downfall of many "teams" turns out to be a total focus on these technical skills at the expense of the supplementary skills. These are the skills needed so that the members can operate as a team. Without these nontechnical skills, our team degenerates into an uncoordinated bunch of disconnected experts. These skills fall into two groups, *functional* and *interpersonal* skills.

Functional (Process Improvement) Skills

These can be called *process improvement skills*. They are skills needed to run the project, as opposed to the technical skills needed to do the work the project was set up for. They include project-management skills; planning, problem-solving, and decision-making skills; and many others. These are non-technical skills, ways to make sure the *right* technical things get done the *right* way, at the *right* time (that is, *on time!*)

We should also consider here the very necessary skills that make each individual team member more productive, and thus the team as a whole. Reading skills are critical in a field such as ours (Cutler, 1993; see also the preface and Chapter 1 of this book). Personal organization skills, stress- and time-management skills, team-building skills, leadership and management skills, and study skills are all important.

Technical writing skills are important. You need to be able to write directions for users and developers during a project, and quality user and technical documentation is one the most important but frequently most neglected parts of a project. These skills will serve to enhance your project's chances of success, and also the quality of the delivered system. Take all the courses you can get in these areas.

Interpersonal Skills

In the next section, we'll look at some specific techniques for various interpersonal needs. Here in this section, we first examine some of the needs that team members have for getting along and functioning together, and the reasons behind those needs. Let's start with communication, the flow of information from person to person.

The skill sets needed by every team member on a project look like this:

Purpose	Skills Group	Examples of Skills
To get the work done	Technical skills	Programming, analysis, etc.
To ensure that the right work gets done and that it gets done right	Functional skills (process improvement)	Project management, planning, problem solving, decision making, reading, writing
To ensure that people work together so all of the above gets done and gets done right	Interpersonal skills	Communication skills, trust, leadership skills, arbitration skills

Communication

> ## The biggest problem with communication is the *illusion* that it has occurred!

This is one of the places where teams so often fall down. **_Communication_ is a matter of sending and receiving signals,** and unless we agree beforehand on the meanings of these signals, we can easily end up at cross-purposes.

One of the crucial parts of this process for an object-oriented project is the definitions for the classes, Step 3 of the Seven Steps (see Chapter 9). This ensures that everyone involved attaches the same meaning to each word, and once you've been through one or two FTS/JAD group design sessions on this, you'll understand its importance.

This kind of prior clarification is also critical for mixed teams of people drawn from varying backgrounds. We may have on our team a variety of technical experts and several different kinds of users. Each group is used to their own jargon and their own way of doing things. It is necessary for us to recognize this and take conscious action to smooth the communication among these diverse groups.

Each team member must always be aware of what the others are doing. There must be frequent formal meetings, and many *informal* ways of exchanging information. Regularly scheduled formal meetings are essential, for several reasons.

It's important to check where we're up to and how we're doing. Each team member needs to know what the others are doing and may often be able to contribute with some advice or suggest a resolution to a problem. Then there's a very subtle effect that can cause serious difficulties if regular meetings don't take place, and which I shall illustrate with a story:

At the City of Edmonton, the three project managers John, Anil, and I, had regular weekly meetings with our director, Hartmut. They were just the basic stuff of such meetings, Hartmut conveying to us his plans and needs, and passing along information from his meetings with his boss (the manager) and from his peers (the other directors, i.e., users). We each in turn would discuss progress of our various projects, staff problems, and the like.

On occasion, however, the four of us would all get so busy with our projects that we would allow the meetings to lapse for a few weeks. One time, however, we had found that our usually cooperative and effective systems group seemed to be degenerating into a den of conflict and misery.

Anil put his finger on the problem, by observing that all this had been caused by the *lack of meetings*. In a meeting, he observed, one of us might mention that something was about to happen, and another might say, "Oh, but that will affect my group because . . ." Agreements would then be worked out to solve or work around this concern, long before it actually happened.

In this way, conflicts and bad feelings were kept to a minimum. But without the regular weekly meetings, there was no chance for this to happen, hence the den of misery. **We realized that one important but unheralded function of these meetings had been to air incidents and concerns before they had a chance to grow into problems.**

In their landmark book, *In Search of Excellence* (1982), Peters and Waterman give a number of examples of how this flow of information is maintained in successful companies. The term they made famous is **MBWA: Management By Wandering Around, which is keeping in touch and gathering information informally by "wandering around" and chatting with the team members.** This management style is important for managers and leaders at all levels.

An excellent example of this is given in the early part of the movie *Mr Mom* from the early 1980s. The hero, while still at that stage employed as a senior manager, is shown on the shop floor, chatting with workers and supervisors and explaining things using examples that they might identify with, in this case football. (Your assigned homework for tonight, then, is to find, rent, and watch *Mr Mom*.)

The biggest difficulty with MBWA lies not in the method itself, but in the minds of the managers. For most of them, wandering around and chatting with the staff doesn't *feel* like work, and if they try it their guilt feelings soon send them back to their desks. They fail to realize how critically important these informal sources of information can be.

The opposite to MBWA is something I've christened **MBCIF: Management By Control of Information Flow. This kind of manager keeps close control of information going up to his boss, out to his peers, and down to his staff. He lets them learn only what he wants them to know, and typically he embellishes or withholds things so as to manipulate his staff, peers, and superiors, thus enhancing his *feeling* of being in control.** (Though you and I and his psychiatrist know he's fooling himself!)

(This style sometimes blends with a favored style of bureaucrats, **MBAW: Management By Avoidance of Waves; these people are preoccupied with keeping out of trouble and thus are not very productive.**

MBCIF managers and team members seem to have a real control issue. They seek to control the people around them by controlling what they know, by filtering and coloring what information goes to those people. If you should encounter someone whom you recognize as one of these, my usual advice would be to resist having them added to your team.

As managers and team leaders, their style automatically makes the team less than optimal by interfering with the very necessary *free* flow of *accurate* information to, from, and within the team. As team members, they're both tiresome and troublesome. They keep things to themselves and resist legitimate requests to share information and knowledge. Perhaps unintentionally, this then becomes a rather insidious form of passive sabotage.

If, by the way, it happens that from my brief description you should begin to feel this might fit *you*, then, in the words of the immortal Anne Landers, please "seek professional help." Change is definitely possible. And when a leader or co-worker distorts or withholds information for their own agenda, typically a *hidden* agenda, it becomes extremely difficult to *trust* them ever again.

Trust

For a team to function as a team, members must be able to depend on one another. Your success and reputation will depend on my commitment and performance, and mine on yours. We must build up a level of trust that allows this to take place. Any team member could at any time fail, quit, or screw up, which would then affect us all. It's thus in our own self-interest for us to help and support each other through whatever may come along.

When one member of a team does a few things for his or her own purposes, rather than for the purpose of the team, this takes away from the team's performance. Whatever time and resources this person may have diverted to their own benefit are no longer available to the team. The trust the team placed in this person has now been betrayed.

One of the strange characteristics of trust, in any part of life, is that while it may take months or even years to build up, it can be destroyed in a few seconds. **Then it takes ten times the original amount of effort to reestablish.** Being able to establish an environment where trust is more likely to occur, and the ability to nurture and maintain that trust among the team members, is a mark of a great leader.

Leadership

A leader must set examples in many ways – for example, getting some action started, such as when the team is faced with a new problem. While many would still be gazing in fear and wonder at the new challenge, a leader will be initiating discussions and brainstorms to begin finding a solution.

A leader draws information, opinions, ideas, suggestions, and concerns from the members and shares her own. A leader clarifies and elaborates the ideas given and points out issues, interpretations, and options.

A leader summarizes the situation, states conclusions for the team to adopt or reject, checks for consensus, and then moves them toward action on the chosen solution. Amid all these ideas and decisions, a good leader must also be able to manage the inevitable conflicts that will occur.

Arbitration Skills

With all the differences among people that I mentioned already, it's important that someone on the team be skilled at helping people resolve conflicts and disagreements. One of the most critical skills of a leader is the ability to keep the team working together, often by functioning as a referee. In the next section, where we discuss practical interpersonal techniques, we'll explore one particularly effective method for arbitrating a serious conflict between team members in a meeting, that of *Guided Paraphrasing*.

Commitment

What is it that makes a team a team? Why is a *team* different from a group of individuals working side by side?

What's different is that they're all there to *get something done*. They're all there for the same purpose, they're committed to helping each other, each pulling their weight, and *together* they'll achieve that goal.

This is what a team is all about. This *commitment to a common purpose* is what makes a *team* different from a *group of individuals*. Such individuals, even though they may be companions and may even help each other, are working each toward their own purpose. A team has a major goal or purpose that *all* members are working for. One of the critical things in generating this kind of commitment is that the members must also take part in the planning for that goal.

Specific Performance Goals

The best teams spend a lot of time identifying and clarifying their own purpose. Even though the purpose is typically set by management (that is, from outside the team), the members will need to discuss it at length and then break it into a sequence of steps and goals. These goals must build on one another, to arrive eventually at the overall goal of the team.

It is a characteristic of professional workers, including analysts and programmers, that they have a need to participate in decisions that will affect them. Thus, the fact that the team members have had major input into the planning process further builds the commitment level. Conversely, it's an unfortunate and all too common experience to find that workers of all kinds have *not* had input into the planning and decisions that affect them, and are typically found to lack commitment.

The goals as they are set need to be "specific, measurable performance goals." Each goal must state clearly that something definite will happen, such as: "Complete the Requirements Definition and submit to client by end of week 3." Or perhaps, "Have 90% of the classes from the analysis model coded and ready for testing by July 1."

Each goal must have a date attached. And each goal must be *measurable* in the sense that:

- We know whether or not we achieved it, and

- We know by *how much* we exceeded it or missed it.

Here are some things that this kind of *specific performance goal* does for a team:

- When everyone knows exactly what it is we're trying to achieve, there's less confusion and much better communication. If you've ever been assigned a task with unclear goals, you know just what I mean. Clear goals also make the inevitable conflicts more constructive, so they actually help the process rather than hinder it.

- When the objectives are clear and the commitment of the team is high, titles, rank, and formality tend to be ignored in favor of finding what works best for the team. The team will focus on the strengths and abilities of each person and how these may best be utilized for the common purpose. The team members treat each other as equals and as *people*, often with more true respect than they would in an environment modulated by titles and rank.

- A sequence of small goals leading toward the major goal allows for "small wins." Each small goal achieved is an excuse for a small celebration and some good feelings about the project. Each marks a step along the way, visible evidence of progress toward that important end. This builds those critical levels of commitment, to the group and its purpose, among the members. When the members feel good about each other and their progress, communication improves and conflicts are resolved more quickly and effectively.

- Well-formulated performance goals have an energizing effect. They become symbols of what we can achieve, and they motivate and compel the team members to stretch and exert themselves. This is enhanced by frequent "How are we doing?" meetings, where the team reviews their progress and approach.

- Reviews of the approach to the project encourage fine-tuning and allow major problems to be aired. This way, drastic changes of approach, when needed, are more likely to be discussed before any action takes place. Then they're more likely to happen, and to happen in a planned and considered manner.

To summarize what we've said about skills and personality styles:

- *Process improvement* skills are *nontechnical* skills needed to run the project, as opposed to technical computer skills. They include project management skills, planning, problem-solving, and decision-making skills, and many others. Also included are the skills that make each individual team member more productive, such as reading and writing skills, and time and stress management.

- For the success of the project, we must *do whatever is needed* to get the communication going and the ideas flowing.

- The larger the group, the more difficult it is to get along. There's more trouble agreeing on things, more disagreements and squabbles. A larger group is less likely to resolve their differences. They'll have different personality styles and different ways of operating.

- Myers and Briggs:
  - Introvert (I) vs Extrovert (E)
  - Intuitive (N) vs Sensing (S)
  - Feeling (F) vs Thinking (T)
  - Perceiving (P) vs Judging (J)

- The Four Temperaments are:
  - SJ   Sensing, Judging   (Administrator)
  - SP   Sensing, Perceiving   (Live-for-the-moment)
  - NF   Intuitive, Feeling.   (Feeling)
  - NT   Intuitive, Thinking   (Scientist)

- SJs (administrators) like rules; NFs (feeling) want to change the rules. NTs (scientists) are thoughtful, and SPs (live-for-the-moment) want to *do it now*.

- In a team, differences exist and must be accepted to move toward the goal. In an effective group, members recognize differences and resolve them by a consensus of what is acceptable.

- Communication is where teams often fail. It is sending and receiving signals, and we must agree on the meanings of the signals. One of the crucial parts of this process for an object-oriented project is the definitions for the classes, step 3 of the Seven Steps.

- You must know what the other team members are doing. Have frequent formal and informal meetings. Regularly scheduled formal meetings are essential, to check where we're up to. Issues can be dealt with before they become problems.

- Use MBWA: Management By Wandering Around.

- Trust: To function as a team, members must depend on one another. My success and reputation will depend on your commitment and performance, and yours on mine.

- A *leader* initiates discussions and brainstorms to find solutions; draws information, opinions, ideas, suggestions, and concerns from members; and shares his own. A leader clarifies ideas given; points out issues, interpretations, and options; summarizes and states conclusions for the team to adopt or reject; checks for consensus; and then moves them toward action on the chosen solution.

- *Arbitration Skills:* A good leader must manage the inevitable conflicts that will occur. Someone on the team must be skilled at helping people resolve conflicts and disagreements.

- *Commitment*: Team members are all there for the same purpose. Commitment to a common purpose is what makes them a team.

- The best teams spend a lot of time identifying and clarifying specific performance goals. Though the overall purpose is typically set from outside the team, the members will need to discuss it at length and then break it into a sequence of steps and goals. These goals must build on one another to arrive eventually at the overall goal of the team.

Mutually Accountable

There's a critical yet subtle difference between saying that "The boss (or the company) holds me accountable" for something and a team saying "We hold ourselves accountable." This kind of accountability is built from the sincere promises that we make to the other team members and to ourselves.

Trust, commitment, and accountability cannot be ordered or mandated by a higher or external power. They come into being only as a result of people working together in good faith. Trust, commitment, and accountability grow together as a team comes together, establishes its team structure, begins its task, and progresses toward its final goal.

Life Cycle of a Team: The Stormin' Normin' Model

You may have noticed that when a bunch of people are thrown together and given a task, especially when under some kind of pressure, that they'll usually do a lot of bickering and arguing before they finally get off the ground and get working (if they ever do!)

This is perfectly normal. Teams don't just magically come together and begin achieving. There's more to it than that. When a group of people is faced with a task that will require cooperation, they will always go through a series of experiences that Weber (1982) has labeled as follows:

- Forming
- Storming
- Norming
- Performing

As a mnemonic, I call this the Stormin' Normin' model (with apologies to General Schwarzkopf, who, so I've read, actually prefers his other nickname, "The Bear"). An existing team facing a new task or challenge, where most of the members have already worked together, will merely need to update a little at the first three stages. They'll go quickly to the fourth and most important one, Performing.

If you understand these stages and the reasons for them, I believe you'll be better prepared to help the group work through them constructively and form into a better team.

For practice and awareness, whenever you see a group forming to do a task under some pressure, observe them and watch for their transitions from one stage to the next. Let's take a look at these in detail; what follows is adapted from the work of Scholtes (1988), based on the stages identified by Weber, and used in seminars and training materials by Joiner and Associates, Inc.

FORMING

Generally, the people want to work together, but they have all kinds of doubts and conflicts, about the group and about the task. There's generally a mixture of excitement and fear and a lot of confusion about the best way to get started, and the approach to the problem.

Feelings

- Excitement, anticipation, optimism
- Pride in being chosen
- Tentative attachment to the team
- Suspicion, fear, anxiety

Behaviors

- Attempts to define tasks
- Attempts to decide acceptable group behavior and how to handle problems
- Decisions on what information is needed
- Abstract discussions of concepts and issues
- Discussions of things not relevant to the task
- Complaints about the organization and impediments to the task

STORMING

As the discussion progresses, there will be a lot of argument about the task, the team, and the members. The arguments at this stage can become quite heated, and besides not losing your temper, you must accept that this is normal. You must work your way through this difficult part of the process in the anticipation that things will eventually settle out, and that the team will then be able to get on with the job.

Many teams founder at this point, as the members become angered and feel like quitting. It's important for all to recognize that it's only a stage in the formation of the group, and that it's necessary to go through this turmoil to establish a healthy, productive team.

Feelings

- Resistance to the task and any suggested solutions
- Sharp fluctuations in attitude
- Disunity, jealousy, tension

Behaviors

- Arguing among members even when they really agree
- Defensiveness and competition, choosing sides
- Questioning the sanity of those who assigned the problem and chose the team members
- Establishing unrealistic goals; concern about excessive work
- A "pecking order" begins to develop

NORMING

Once the "storming" declines and the team begins to agree on more and more things, they start to examine the task and the constraints, and themselves as well, and begin the process of agreeing on how things will be done.

They will look at how the team will operate, lines of command, responsibilities, and how they plan to communicate and coordinate. They'll discuss how to go about finding approaches and solutions, and many other *process-oriented* matters. They'll also consider task-oriented issues, such as agreeing on an approach, finding and agreeing on solutions, and so on. As each decision is agreed on, it becomes a **_norm_ for the project, that is, an agreed-on pattern or standard.**

Feelings

- Ability to criticize constructively

- Acceptance of being part of the team

- Belief that it will work

Behaviors

- Avoiding conflict to get things done

- Friendliness, confiding, sharing of personal problems

- Cohesion, team spirit

- Establishing norms

PERFORMING

Once the norming process has set the stage and cleared the way of issues and stumbling blocks, it's time to get on with it. Each member now has a clear idea of both the group goals and their own part in those goals. Methods and approaches have been agreed on, and now everybody can get productively to work.

Feelings

- Understanding personal and group processes

- Aware of people's strengths and weaknesses

- Satisfaction with progress

Behaviors

- Members experience constructive self-change

- Ability to resolve problems conflicts

- Close attachment to other members

As the team works through these stages, there will be a lot of interaction, some of it probably quite emotional and vociferous. Next let's examine some specific methods that you as a team member or leader may need to draw upon in order to smooth the team's progress toward the performing stage and to handle interactions throughout the project.

But first, to summarize:

- Mutual accountability is built from the sincere promises that we make to the other team members and to ourselves. Trust, commitment, and accountability cannot be mandated by a higher or external power.

Forming

- Generally the people want to work together but have doubts and conflicts.

- Abstract discussions; attempts to define tasks.

- Complaints about the task.

Storming

- Argument(s) about task, team, and members. This is normal. You must work through this difficult process, trusting that things will get better and that the team can get on with the job.
- Resistance to task and suggested solutions; fluctuations in attitude.
- Arguing, questioning the sanity of those who chose the problem and the team.

Norming

- Team begins to agree more, starts to examine task and constraints, and begins agreeing how things will be done.
- Acceptance of membership in the team; belief that it will work, avoiding conflict.
- Friendliness, confiding, sharing. Sense of team cohesion; team spirit and goals; establishing norms.

Performing

- Time to get on with it. Each member now has a clear idea of group goals and own part in those goals. Methods and approaches agreed on, now everybody can get to work.
- Satisfaction at the team's progress; close attachment to the team.

Now let's get more specific and look at some useful methods for dealing with people.

16.3 SPECIFIC INTERPERSONAL TECHNIQUES FOR OBJECT-ORIENTED ANALYSTS

I present these techniques here specifically for use with users during your modeling, and for you as the developers working together in a team, but you'll find use for them in all parts of your life. These are practical methods that work, and are at the same time well-grounded in psychological theory. The tricky part is that these techniques will only work if you *use them*. Simply reading about them in these pages won't make you a better leader or communicator. *Practice will*. We'll examine these techniques in detail after a few comments about the need for effective listening.

Listening Skills

We all know how to listen, right? We've all sat through years of school, hours of parental lectures, and day after day of business meetings. But how often were you actually *there*, in the room, fully focused on what was being said?

If you're like most of us, it was less than half the time. The rest of the time we were off out the window someplace. Imagine the learning, grades, and performance we could achieve if we could *be there* 100% of the time.

I've seen studies that found that the average parent spends less than 12 minutes per day actually *listening and attending* to each of their children. (Other studies, incidentally, have found that the most common complaint of teenagers is that "nobody ever listens to me!").

On a recent team-building workshop, I noted that, in the postmortem debriefing after each exercise, the need for *communication*, especially when under pressure, was consistently number one or two on the list of things we had become aware of.

Barbara Bouldin (1989, page 64) has some very relevant comments on the importance and difficulty of effective listening. As she points out, so-called communications courses usually focus on talking, " . . . but no one ever teaches us to listen." Have you ever seen a book on effective listening? You may have noticed that many books on speaking mention how difficult it is to get anyone to listen!

Remember, the biggest problem with communication is the *illusion* that it has occurred. Teachers, speakers, and writers assume that once they have presented their material, it has been heard and understood.

Unfortunately, this is usually far from the truth. In meetings or discussions, most of us assume that when the other guy stops talking, we have understood his message. This is also rarely true. How often have you found that instead of listening to the second half of someone's sentence, you were busy framing your reply to the first half? When you first begin to use the technique of *Reflective Listening*, which you'll find in the next section, you may get some big surprises. I first learned the technique in the early 1970s at a seminar given by Athabasca University.

AU is a correspondence-only university, and in the 1970s I was a telephone tutor for them. The reflective listening method becomes extremely important in a telephone discussion of abstract, computer-related topics, because the additional clues for understanding from body language and facial expressions are not available to the listener. Even the tone-of-voice clues are distorted.

Many of the tutors taking part in the seminar received unpleasant shocks during the exercises. They would respond with supreme confidence to a problem put to them, only to react with total disbelief when the "student" would say "No, that's not what I meant!" and they would have to start over. Some of the looks on their faces were in fact quite comical. But the experience highlighted for them, and for those of us watching, just how difficult is real understanding, and how easy is the *illusion* of communication.

The sad consequence of this difficulty, as you'll observe in people around you, is that so often we end up answering the wrong question, or proposing a solution to the wrong problem. It's all part of the same issue we discussed in Chapter 3, the need for complete and accurate analysis to define the problem clearly, before we begin proposing and designing a solution. Remember, a perfect solution to the wrong problem gets us nowhere in particular.

So, both at the macro level in systems analysis, and at the micro level in personal discussions, there's a critical need to **get the problem correctly stated and understood** before we move on to an answer or solution. This is why the need is to focus on listening. This is why we can no longer *assume* that we're listening effectively and why we must take steps and learn techniques to *ensure* that we are. *Reflective Listening* is one of the most powerful of these.

Reflective Listening/Paraphrasing

Since I learned this technique and began using it, I've it found in a variety of books under various names. I've seen it called *"Reflective Listening,"* or simply *"Paraphrasing,"* and also *"Negotiating for Understanding."* All three names do in fact describe the method correctly, but I prefer *Reflective Listening* as the most informative, in that it tells more about what is going on. Let me describe how it works, and then you'll see why it's so effective. Begin by considering this little interchange:

CHILD: Mommy, where did I come from?

PARENT: [Oh no! The dreaded moment has arrived!] Well, you see, ah . . . , when a man and a woman, um . . . , fall in love and get married and . . ah . . decide they want babies, . . . there are certain, um . . . , things they need to do . . . so that the baby will begin to grow in the mommy's tummy. . . .

CHILD, somewhat exasperated: But Mommy, Peter says he came from Nevada. Where did I come from?

So what happened here? Can you identify with this somewhat embarrassing situation, either as the parent or as the child? What the parent did was to take the child's somewhat ambiguous words and interpret them in the light of her own frame of reference. That is, she heard what was relevant to the things that were on her own mind (including a fear of having to explain the Facts of Life), rather than checking to see where the child was actually coming from with the question.

What could we do differently? Try this version:

CHILD: Mommy, where did I come from?

PARENT: [Oops! Better check this out.] Do you mean, how are babies made?

CHILD, a little puzzled: I didn't say anything about babies! Peter says he came from Nevada. Where did I come from?

PARENT: [Sigh of relief. Narrowly avoided making a fool of myself!] Oh, you're from right here. You were born in this town, and we've lived here all your life.

A little better? This way is not only less embarrassing, but also far more productive, in that the child was easily able to gain the actual information that he wanted. By reflecting the question back to the child *in different words,* the parent was able to clarify her understanding of the meaning of the question and avoid wasting time, effort, and temper going off on the wrong track. This, then, is the essence of *Reflective Listening*.

The method has four steps and a loop. In the description that follows, take particular note of the "loop control," that is, what it is that lets you out of the loop.

Step 1.   The *Client* (user, student, child, spouse, whoever) expresses a problem of some sort to the *Server* (analyst, teacher, parent, whoever – i.e., *you*).

Step 2.   The *Server* repeats the problem or question back to the Client *in his own words* (that is, the *Server's* own words, *different* from the Client's words).

Step 3.   If the *Client* is not satisfied that the *Server* has properly understood the problem, then the Client says something like "No, that's not what I meant. What I meant was . . . " and then branches back to Step 1 to restate and clarify the problem.

Step 4.   We then iterate steps 1 – 3 *under the control of the Client*, until the *Client* is satisfied that the *Server* has understood the question correctly. Then, and only then, is the Server allowed to try and answer.

You will have noted, I'm sure, that the *Client* is in control of the loop! You and I, as Server, don't get released to begin work on a solution until the *Client* is satisfied that we've correctly understood what she was trying to ask us. You may also by now have realized why the seminar participants were getting so many surprises.

Some of them (especially the younger male teachers, and especially when facing a female "student") would swagger up to the stage for their turn, obviously confident that they knew how to listen and answer a question. Then there would be this horrified look of disbelief when the "student" said, "No, that's not what I said! What I want you to tell me is. . . ." In fact, very few of us got it right first time, but all of us improved with practice.

I've tried to present the method in a way that will show you how it can work both in the technical field of object-oriented analysis and design, and in your personal interactions. As I've stressed throughout this book, the very same ideas and skills that help us communicate in our work are also very helpful in talking with the people we care about. With practice, this simple method can make a difference to your life, in many ways. It's simple, but not necessarily easy. It only works if you ***make yourself do it.***

The key, of course, is *practice*. At the end of this chapter, you'll find some practice exercises, and I encourage you to work with a friend or a group on these. Then seek out chances to try it at work, at school, at home, and with your friends.

Even though it feels awkward at first, your Client probably won't even notice. He will just react by clarifying and afterward feel good that not only were you *listening*, but you also gave some very helpful advice or information. Actually, it was exceptionally helpful just because this time (by way of a change) you gave the *right* advice or information, since you were answering the *right* question.

The impression gained by your Client that you were *actually listening* stems from the fact that you paraphrased the original question, *in your own words*. This tells the Client that you cared enough about what she was saying, to spend the time and energy needed to try sincerely to understand.

Be careful not to simply repeat the Client's words back at her, parrot-fashion. Parroting just gets the Client angry and shuts down the communication before it gets going. You absolutely *must translate* the question into different words before you give it back to your Client.

There's a further important application of the method, which we look at next. It serves as the basis for a highly effective method of resolving conflicts and arguments.

Conflict Arbitration

Have you ever encountered in a meeting, group session, or modeling session a conflict where two people or groups took opposing positions? Of course you have. Most are resolved more or less satisfactorily after some discussion or argument.

Occasionally, however, opposing positions will solidify, tempers will flare, and discussion may degenerate into shouting and name calling. Sometimes the meeting, or even the group itself, will terminate because of such arguments. While I can't guarantee to spare you from such disasters, I can show you a method for defusing them before disaster sets in.

Most arguments and conflicts of this nature stem from misunderstandings and communication errors. **People always hear things through a filter consisting of their own feelings, experiences, prejudices and fears, in other words, their own unique _frame of reference._** For all of us, our frame of reference tends to be selective, so we hear mostly the things that confirm or fit with our fears and prejudices.

In this way, and one or two other ways as well, our view of the world around us becomes somewhat distorted, more so for some people than for others. It turns out that even small misinterpretations of a speaker's words, or of where the speaker is coming from, can cause strong feelings to arise.

You would be amazed how often the fight simply evaporates as soon as the communication is cleared up. One of the best ways to make this happen is to get the antagonists simply to _listen_ to each other.

Reflective Listening, as you may have guessed already, is the key. But, you may well protest, these people are so angry right now that there's no way they're going to stop, learn a totally new technique, and then apply it in a calm and effective manner.

This is where you come in, as meeting leader. Even if you're not the official chair for this meeting, you may need to step in and take over until the crisis is past. Then you'll direct each person through the steps of the reflective-listening process. Here's how you do it. Mary and Joe are in the process of tearing each other's throats out:

YOU: Now just a minute here! I can see we're not going to get anywhere until this is resolved. Joe and Mary, please sit down and calm down for a moment. I'm going to make sure you each have a chance to make your point, and you each get a chance to answer what the other one said. Joe, I'm going to let Mary say her piece first, and you'll get to answer. Then it will be your turn to say yours, and her turn to answer. Now here's how we're going to do it.

Mary, you make your point in a sentence or two. Then Joe, I want you to repeat back to Mary _in your own words_, what it was you heard her say. Mary, you'll say yes or no, did he get it right. And Joe, when Mary figures you have it right, then you'll get to answer. After that we'll do it the other way around. Okay, Mary, say what you wanted to say.

Mary makes her point. Joe sits and sulks.
YOU: Joe, what did she say? In your own words, now.

Joe rephrases Mary's statement and, of course, gets it wrong.

> YOU: Mary, is that what you meant?

> MARY: No! No! I never meant to imply that I would take half of Joe's staff into my department! What I meant to say was. . . .

And she proceeds to restate her point, rather more clearly this time.

> YOU: Joe, what did you hear her say this time?

Again Joe paraphrases what Mary said. Everyone in the room can feel the tension beginning to ease, as they all realize he's got it near enough to right this time.

> YOU: Mary, is that it?

> MARY: Yeah, I think that's pretty much it.

> YOU: OK, Joe, now you can go ahead and answer her.

Joe responds to what Mary said, and his speech is somewhat different from the things he was accusing her of in the initial argument. This is because he's now answering her actual statements, rather than his own version of them, as filtered and distorted by his own problems and fears.

> YOU: Now, Mary, it's your turn. What did you hear him say?

And so the discussion continues, under your firm guidance, with each statement and argument being clarified and clearly understood by the listener (the Server) before (s)he responds to it. At each step, the speaker (Client) is in charge of the loop and thus determines when the listener (Server) is allowed to respond.

I can pretty well guarantee that after a very few iterations through this process, the meeting will be back on a reasonably even keel and progressing more or less smoothly. As tensions begin to ease, you may find one or two places to throw in a feelings perception check (see the next section).

Even if you haven't been practicing and using reflective listening (but of course I'm sure you have been), as long as you *understand* it you can still orchestrate a violent discussion into a peaceful one as I've indicated. This is a very powerful technique and represents the big guns of arbitration. There will also be many other times when feelings intrude on a discussion, in a much smaller yet still significant way. Here is another method that's suitable for these occasions.

Feelings Perception Check

Many times in the course of a meeting, modeling session, or private conversation, you'll become aware that the person speaking is feeling some emotion connected with what's being said. They may betray anger, bitterness, frustration, helplessness, sadness, fear, or any of the myriad of human feelings. Often this will interfere with the discussion, in a number of possible ways.

The speaker's feelings may cause him to react or make decisions in erratic or less-than-optimal ways. His emotions may interfere with his ability to present his ideas or carry on a dialogue. He may make unintended emotional statements that anger or upset others. If the other(s) then have an emotional reaction, we could be launched on the path to the kind of crisis we dealt with in the previous section!

There are very many ways that feelings can get in the way of a productive meeting or discussion, *unless properly dealt with*. It certainly doesn't help to ignore the feelings and hope they'll go away, or to pretend they don't exist. Managers are fooling themselves when they instruct their people to "leave the feelings at the door." That's just running away from a problem they don't know how to handle.

Sometimes the speaker is unaware of his own feelings. Sometimes he will feel vulnerable and frightened at allowing his feelings to show, fearing that he will be ridiculed or that his "opponents" will somehow find a way to use his feelings against him. There are other possible reactions too, but the key to handling any of them is to let the person know that you recognize his feelings and that it's okay for him to have these feelings.

There's a very simple way to do this. You just say something like: "You seem to be feeling frustrated about this, are you?"

You can substitute *angry, scared, bitter, helpless, sad,* or any other **feeling word** where I said *frustrated*. Positive feelings can also be recognized the same way. This is usually less critical but still can have a very positive effect on a discussion. You might use *feeling words* such as *happy, pleased, mellow, satisfied, gratified,* and so on. Either way, the effect is that the person feels *validated* by the fact that you *recognized (and named) the feeling they were experiencing*.

In case you're feeling a little leery about trying to put a label on someone's feelings, the best part is that *you don't have to get it right for it to work!* The way the sentence above is structured, it becomes exploratory in nature, and gives the person an opportunity to either accept or correct your diagnosis.

Either way, they will feel *validated* by the fact that you took the trouble to try, by getting a chance to state their feelings, and by the ensuing discussion about their feelings. Sometimes this will lead to an extensive discussion of some important feelings, thus clearing a lot of air and allowing us to get back to work. Other times there will need to be only a comment or two about the feelings to dispel any negative effects they were likely to have on the discussion.

The key is in the structure of that sentence. It has been carefully engineered to have the desired effect. There's some leeway, which I'll discuss in a moment, but you must be careful to phrase the question as shown. The actual sequence of events is like this:

1. When the person speaks, they'll show some external signs of the emotions they're feeling inside. You may observe their face reddening, breath quickening, voice breaking, fists clenching, tears starting, and so on.

2. From these observations, you come to a conclusion about what they're feeling, and this is where we often go wrong.

Very often we err not only in identifying the feelings, but also in ascribing a reason to them. So in this method we venture a tentative diagnosis, by saying "You seem to be feeling . . ." or "I think you're feeling. . . ."

We then insert the word that we think describes what we think they're feeling, and finish the sentence with the query ". . . are you?" This query at the end is what gives them the opportunity to correct any misdiagnosis, and take the conversation in the direction they need it to go. So we end up with a structure like:

"You seem to be feeling _____ about this, are you?"

There can be some variation, but only like this:

- The word *feeling* is optional.

- The words *about this* are optional, or could be *about that*.

- *You seem to be feeling* could be *I think you're feeling* or *I think you feel*.

- The words *are you?* or *do you?* on the end are **mandatory**. They **must** be there.

So the sentence might look like one of these:

"I think you're angry, are you?"

"You seem to be very bitter about that, are you?"

"You seem very sad, are you?"

"I think you feel gratified about all this, do you?"

A sentence like the last one, recognizing a positive feeling, is particularly appropriate when praise or kudos is due to someone. By recognizing that they feel satisfied or happy or fulfilled and bringing it out into the discussion, you're allowing them to bask in the recognition from the people at the meeting. This is a very effective way of leading a group into giving that much-needed recognition when you think it's deserved. It's also a good way to give lots of recognition and avoid sounding insincere.

While the arbitration technique we looked at in the previous section is for crisis situations, this method is one you can and should use all the time. Like reflective listening, it is effective in work situations and in intimate conversations with the people close to you, and with everyone in between.

Practice it until it becomes natural, and expect to screw it up often. You'll get better with practice. Use it many times in one conversation. Any time you're aware that feelings are showing a little, pop in one of these questions. It's not just for difficult times; it will have a smoothing and facilitating effect on any conversation.

There's another good way to get discussions going and make them more productive, and that is to always try to avoid yes/no questions.

Open-Ended Questions

Have you ever listened to a radio disk jockey who has a kid phone in and puts him on the air? Invariably, the kid, unused to public speaking, says nothing unless the DJ asks a direct question. The DJ, on the other hand, is frantically trying to avoid "dead air," the worst thing that can happen to a radio station.

So the DJ will rattle off a fairly long question, such as "Well, now that school's back in and everyone is getting started on a brand new year, have you got any plans for anything exciting this school year?" only to have the kid say "Nope!" There follows a sequence of these lengthy questions and short, short "Yup!" and "Nope!" answers, with occasionally something a little more informative, such as "Aw, it's okay."

What the poor DJ in this example has not caught on to, is that the way to get a conversation going is to ask questions that require more that a yes/no answer. She could try "Well, now that school's back in, what trips and activities have you got planned for the next couple of weeks?" With luck, this will generate a short list, and the DJ can pick one to follow up on. Of course, it still might get a response like "Oh, not much," in which case she'll just have to try a different topic.

We need to ask questions that generate sentences, lists, feelings, or opinions. Questions that make the person think, reason, remember, or invent will generate more information and keep the discussion going forward.

In a modeling session, rather than "Do the customers need a copy of the invoice?" ask "What information do the customers need to see (on an invoice)?" That should give you a list of items and stimulate some discussion around the need for some of them. Someone may well come up with one or two items that are not usually on invoices, but are needed in this particular system, and may well have been overlooked otherwise.

You'll see a few more examples at the top of the next page.

Again, this also is a simple technique, but not always easy at first. It takes practice, and it can be used anywhere and anytime in any conversation. Practice it at parties or with the person beside you on a bus or plane. Use it with someone you feel awkward around, with a new date, or someone you wish to impress.

Because you'll end up doing the listening while they talk, the other person will always enjoy the conversation. People love to talk about themselves, once you get them feeling comfortable. And they'll be highly impressed with you and your conversational ability, especially your reflective listening and feelings perception checks.

One Question at a Time

Have you ever watched a TV interviewer unleash a string of questions at a subject? "Well, Mr Jackson, just what input does your mother-in-law Priscilla have into the financial affairs of you and your wife? And how much do you think she expects to have? How do you feel about that? How much do you tell her about your family? I think you feel a little resentful about her, do you?"

Now, these are all good open-ended questions, and there's even a feelings perception check at the end. What could possibly be wrong with them? There are too many questions!

When you bombard someone like this, he can't keep track of all those questions in his head and then answer them one by one, checking them off a list. People are not stack-based processors! Watch for this on TV, and what you'll observe is that mostly they *answer the last one* and simply ignore the rest.

You must take great pains to avoid this when interviewing users or leading a FTS/JAD session. The best way is to say something like, "Hold on a minute! I've got a whole bunch of questions for you on that." Or perhaps, "Hold on a minute! That's far too many questions all at once!" Then spin around to the whiteboard and list the questions, speaking them *loudly* as you write them out.

Talking loudly and writing, both at the same time, are important. You may wish to ask the group if they have any more to add. They'll often come up with something fairly important that you had overlooked. Then go down the list and have the person answer each question in turn. It takes a while longer this way, but it gathers a whole lot more information and generates much important discussion.

Then there's another thing about questions. How can we structure them to get realistic answers to the "How would you . . ." or "What would you do if . . ." kind of questions?

Specific Instances from the Past

Tell me what you would do if you had a tire blow out at speed on the highway. "Well, I would hold on real tight to the wheel, 'cause it's gonna be trying to pull outta my hands. And I would stay right off the brakes. Brakes are fatal with a flat at high speed! I'd steer it and let it coast like that until it's down under 30 km/h (20 mph), and then I would brake gently and stop it."

Sounds pretty darned good. I guess I might go ahead and hire you as a driver. Or I might build a software system for controlling cars in the expectation that you (and others) would do exactly this in the event of a blowout at speed. But would you? How do we know? How do *you* know you would do it right, or even close? ***Have you ever had it happen? What did you do that time?***

Try this one: "Tell me about a specific time in your driving career that you had a blowout at speed on the highway. Tell me what you did about it, how well that worked, whether you avoided an accident, and how you felt about your performance afterward."

You may need to have the four questions written down in advance on a piece of paper, to show them as they begin considering their answer (see the previous section on *Too Many Questions.*)

Now here's the kicker. "Take your time. Spend a minute or two thinking and remembering if you need to. I would rather wait for the correct story than rush you into a mistaken one." And give them lots of silent time. Remember that one minute of silence always feels like five.

You see, those of you who have had this particular driving experience and handled it even passably well, can be pretty confident that you both know *and are capable of* the correct response to this little disaster. Those of you who haven't, don't know.

It's as simple as that. If it has never happened to you, then you (and I) have no way of telling exactly how you'll react. Many people do react correctly the first time, and many people do not. Some freeze for a moment, some make incorrect decisions under stress, and occasionally someone dies because of it.

On the other hand, those of you who have experienced the problem before and handled it even half-way well and survived have demonstrated that you're capable. There are, of course, no guarantees in this life, but . . .

The best way to predict someone's future behavior in any situation is to look at their past performance in the same or a similar one!

Past performance, while not perfect, is nonetheless the most effective predictor we have. This fact has led to a questioning technique that is taught in courses on interviewing.

The technique is useful to us for a number of purposes. We can use it for hiring, for selecting team members, and for interviewing users during analysis. It can also be used in user interviews and during modeling sessions to enhance the accuracy of the information we gather. The technique revolves around asking the person to describe what he did in a specific incident in the past that relates to what we're asking about.

The standard "How would you . . ." or "What would you do if . . ." kind of question is really nothing less than a license to fantasize. While the person may be perfectly sincere, believing that this really is how she would react, there's no objective reality for her to compare her theory against. So, strictly, it remains a theory, a hypothesis that can only be tested by trying her out. (If we did that, of course, we now would have a specific instance, with real-world, actual behavior, that we could use for our decision-making.)

And because there's nothing to anchor him in reality, our person can stretch the truth a little, without much guilt involved. Far better, then, to ask about something that *actually happened*. Just the existence of this little piece of objective reality is enough to put most people in a place where they can no longer fantasize, or even stretch things much.

As soon as the story deviates from the facts, *they* know it, whether or not you and I can tell. Being aware of a lie is enough to inhibit that lie for most people. Without that objective reality check, they could easily have convinced *themselves* that the "lie" really is how they would do it, or at worst just a little stretch.

Like all the techniques I've brought you in this chapter, it works really well, *with a bit of practice*. The easiest way to begin is with a more structured "interview" situation, with a new employee or team member or a user. Make up and write down the questions in advance, and you may wish to assign them in advance to different questioners. You'll see a world of difference in the quality of information you get from the answers.

And from now on, watch yourself and the people around you and catch yourself and them any time you're about to ask a "How would you . . ." or "What would you do if . . ." kind of question. Reword the question into a "specific instance from the past" format, and then ask it. Here are some examples:

- Tell me about a time when you needed this service from a vendor. How did you go about setting it up?

- Describe a specific instance in one of your earlier jobs, where your supervisor was wrong and you felt you needed to do something about it. Tell us exactly what you did and what effect it had. How did you feel about doing that? (Too many questions; they need to be written down, or asked one at a time.)

- Tell us about an actual incident in a meeting where you were convinced you were right, and the entire meeting disagreed with you. We want to hear about a time when you were convinced the company would suffer if they didn't listen to you. What did you say and do, and how successful were you at changing their minds? How did you feel about changing (or not changing) their view? (Write down the multiquestions again!)

You may have noticed that I used this style of wording on a number of the team and individual exercises at the ends of some of the chapters in this book. This is because I find that students get more value out of relating the concepts and topics of the chapter to something that really happened.

While I can't do this with every exercise, it's valuable enough that I throw it in wherever I can. You'll find, as with all the techniques in this chapter, that it can also be used in conversation, at home, work, or school or perhaps even when meeting someone for the first time.

Introductions

If you're like me, then you probably share this experience. I've always found it hopeless trying to get the names straight when I meet a bunch of people. At a party it's just embarrassing; at work it could be career-limiting! Eventually, after many years of such embarrassment, I read about a method that seemed worth trying. And, by golly, it worked.

Here are the steps:

1. Listen carefully for the pronunciation of the name. Getting someone's name right is the ultimate compliment you can pay them. (Check this out by wandering into a used-car lot and counting the number of times the salesperson uses your name while trying to sell you a car.)

    Conversely, getting their name wrong is an insult, regardless of any protestations that they're used to having people screw it up. In Canada, for example, my niece Niña gets called "Nina" (which is my wife's name), by all the non-Filipinos except me.

2. Generally speaking, the person who introduces you will use the form of the name that you'll be expected to use. If the host or other introducer thinks it appropriate for you to address this person by first name, they'll introduce them by first name. So listen carefully also for titles such as doctor, professor, or perhaps even "Sir George."

    Whatever way you're introduced, address them that way, at least initially. This rule also applies when someone introduces herself; usually she will do so in the way that she wishes to be addressed. Conversely, when you're introducing yourself or others, be sure to give people these clues. Use the form of address that you think is appropriate for them to use to each other.

3. If necessary, ask for the name to be repeated, several times if you need it. This may sometimes feel embarrassing and awkward, but you'll score additional points if you're the only one who takes the trouble to get it right. I'm such a visual learner that I frequently have to say "How do you spell that?" so I can visualize it in print, to "see" how it sounds.

    This is one reason for exchanging business cards when you meet somebody. Always carry a good supply and give them freely, even at nonbusiness functions. Remember the old Hollywood adage, "Any publicity is good publicity!"

4. *Now this is the kicker for your memory.* When you shake the person's hand, look them directly in the eye and **_speak their name._** You may say "Hello, Joe" or "Hi, Joe" or "How ya doin', Joe?" or, more formally, "How do you do, Joe?" Or the other way around: "Joe! How do you do?"

    Of course, you'll use the form of address that was kindly indicated for you in Step 2. Even though handshakes are not always necessary these days, I recommend you always shake hands this way just for the help in remembering the name. If this is not possible (culturally or physically or whatever), you must still *look them in the eye* and *speak their name.*

So now we've looked at team building, listening and communication, and even meeting people. We've examined some of the skills the team members will need. There's one more thing they'll need before they're ready to be superproductive on the project, and that is *training*, in order to gain and practice the skills we've identified.

16.4 TRAINING

I just want to make a final plug about training. I cannot overemphasize the importance of training. As I indicated a number of times in Chapter 15 and earlier, *training is critical.* Team members must have *sufficient* training in *all* the skills needed for the project.

My experience has been that it can take up to a year for someone to become *proficient* in object-oriented techniques, and very few newcomers can do it in less than six months. Surveys indicate that more training will make people productive sooner. You need to hire the new people *in advance* of the project and then invest in training.

But not too far ahead. Lilly (1995) has written about "The Top Ten Ways to Trash Your OT Training Program." One of her points is that management must time the training program so that people will use it not too long after they learn it. Otherwise, two things can happen:

- Under-challenged and under-utilized object experts have a tendency to leave. You can be sure their newly acquired skills will be in high demand elsewhere.

- If they do stay, there's a real danger that the new knowledge may "rust out." Like bureaucratic budgets, it's a "use it or lose it" problem. Make sure they all have a copy of *this* book, the one in your hand right now.

16.5 OVERCOMING RESISTANCE

I also want to make a few last comments on the topic of *resistance to change*. Change is scary for all of us. Some can handle that fear and view it as a challenge. For others, the fear manifests itself in a variety of ways. It can show as anger, lethargy, hyperactivity (the driven workaholic), mistakes, active rebellion, passive sabotage, desertion (quitting), or a number of other negative, nonproductive behaviors. There are two things I have to say about this:

- Especially for the pilot project(s) and early production projects, you must begin the change to object-oriented methods by choosing the *right people*. You want the ones who have *already* demonstrated an ability and a *willingness* to embrace change and newness productively. I emphasize the word *already* for a good reason. Past performance is always the best predictor of future performance.

  For this critical early work, use people with *proven* ability and flexibility. The others can better make the transition later, when there are more experienced people around to mentor them. For the meantime, they're probably best used on the legacy projects. Love (1993) has quite a bit to say about the choice of people for the early work.

- Whenever you meet some of these counterproductive behaviors, recognize that it's always *fear* that drives them. But people will never admit to this, because that would render them too vulnerable. Most often they're not even aware themselves where the anger or resistance is coming from. So you must never overtly mention the fear. Any mention of the fear and they'll become defensive and probably hostile, for they'll feel it as an accusation of inadequacy.

To deal with these problems, you must quietly make decisions and changes that will reduce the fear, *without telling the person what you're up to*. You may be able to change reporting relationships, assign mentors, and so on. Or you may decide to move this person to a different project, of course pretending that he's desperately needed over there.

When you're able to do something that reduces the underlying fear, you'll reduce or eliminate the overt symptomatic behavior. You'll have only limited success if you try to deal with the symptoms, for example with threats, punishments, or even incentives. Dealing quietly and unobtrusively with the underlying feelings is usually far more effective.

And finally, another viewpoint. Bouldin (1989) devotes her entire Chapter 4, to the matter of overcoming resistance to change. One of her major points is that the "change agent" is constantly in a *marketing* role, selling to both management and users the proposed change with all its benefits. From this, Bouldin develops a number of effective and practical techniques and suggestions.

. . . .

DELIVERABLES

Naturally, there are no deliverables that go with the subject matter of this chapter. However, if you follow the advice and develop the skills described in this chapter both in yourself and in your team, you will significantly enhance the *quality* and *timeliness* of the deliverables that we discussed in earlier chapters.

And don't put it off! Whatever stage your career is at right now, student or practitioner, *start now!* Books, seminars, and courses in any of these people skills and functional skills areas will enhance your functioning in all facets of your career, and indeed of your life. So go out there, buy books and enroll in courses. *Just Do It.*

FURTHER READING (AND SEMINARS)

I have several times referred to Tom Love's book *Object Lessons* (1993), in which he documents many interesting and significant things he has learned in the process of "introducing object-oriented technology into organizations throughout the United States, Japan, and western Europe. These organizations include large computer, telecommunications, and electronics firms, (IT) shops, automobile manufacturers, and some small entrepreneurial companies."

Love has a lot to say about finding, training, and developing the people for these projects in his Chapter 9. In his Chapters 10 and 11, he discusses management of the software development process and quality issues. Chapter 12 is about the change to OOT, and Chapter 13 is a summary of the "Lessons Learned."

For learning by visualization, read Millman's *The Warrior Athlete* (1979) and Lazarus's *In the Mind's Eye; The Power of Imagery for Personal Enrichment* (copyrighted and presumably written in 1977, published in 1984). For more on personal growth and effectiveness, you may enjoy Millman's earlier book *The Way of the Peaceful Warrior*.

There are many, many good books out there on project management, management in general, and personal organization topics, such as goal setting, time and stress management, and others. These skills are perhaps best learned in courses and seminars, with plenty of follow-up reading from books recommended by the instructor(s).

For conducting meetings, you'll enjoy a hilarious learning experience from two training movies by the English comedian John Cleese (of "Monty Python" and "Fawlty Towers" fame, and even an appearance on "Cheers"). The titles: *Meetings, Bloody Meetings!* and *More Meetings, Bloody Meetings!*

In all this, do keep in mind the need for regular review of everything you're learning:

- Same day
- Next day
- Weekly for four to six weeks

As you will have gathered, reading ability is one of my major concerns, since good reading skills are the passport to so much important and necessary learning. This is not to mention that it's a passport to much pleasure as well. Conversely, the lack of adequate reading skills is always a severe impediment to learning, career, effective daily living, and, of course, pleasure. There are many good books out there, such as Cutler (1993) *Triple Your Reading Speed,* or Adams (1989) *Developing Reading Versatility.*

There are also many books on improving your writing, also essential for information professionals. Try Brockmann, (1990) *Writing Better Computer User Documentation.* There are many good courses offered by reputable colleges for improving your reading and writing skills. Take anything that has "reading," "technical writing," "computer user documentation," or "business communication" in the title.

But watch out for exaggerated claims or guarantees. Your improvement, particularly your reading improvement, will depend entirely on how rigorously you make yourself *use* what you've learned, once the course is over.

For personal development in other areas, I recommend Harry Lorayne (1984) *The Page-a-Minute Memory Book,* Lorayne and Lucas (1977) *The Memory Book,* and Lorayne (1988) *Memory Makes Money.* Then there's Fenker (1984) *Stop Studying and Start Learning, or How to Jump-Start Your Brain.*

For your own peak performance, read Kriegel and Kriegel (1984) *The C Zone, Peak Performance Under Pressure.* Robert Kriegel and Marilyn Harris Kriegel describe how to stay out of the frenetic, stressed type A behavior while avoiding the lethargy of type B. They demonstrate the existence of a "C zone" in between, where you're stimulated enough to achieve at your best, but relaxed enough to enjoy it and stay healthy.

An excellent and concise source for the formation and management of teams and groups is Carew et al. (1990): "Building High-Performance Teams: *The Group Development and Situational Leadership II Article;* A Model for Managing Groups," a Blanchard Training booklet [phone (619) 489-5005, item no. HT-0002-04]. This is an update of Blanchard's earlier article, "Situational Leadership II," which itself was an update of a book by Blanchard and Hersey, *Management of Organizational Behavior: Utilizing Human Resources* (1982).

Kenneth Blanchard, of course, is famous as the author of *The One-Minute Manager,* a book that has become a classic in the field. It's concise and pithy and takes only two or three hours to read. This one is well worth reading; check out the "One-Minute Reprimand," in there too.

One superb source for personal development seminars is the Excellence Foundation, which provides the *Pursuit of Excellence* seminars (www.excellencefoundation.org).

For some interesting and significant commentary and predictions, try Peters and Waterman (1982) *In Search of Excellence.* Tom Peters also has several later books that are worth reading.

CHAPTER SUMMARY

- *Process improvement skills* or *functional skills* are nontechnical skills needed to run the project. They include project management skills; planning, problem-solving, and decision-making skills; and many others. They also include the skills that make each individual team member more productive, such as reading, time management, and interpersonal skills.

- For the success of the project, we must *do whatever is needed* to get the communication going and the ideas flowing.

- The larger the group, the more difficult it is to get along. There's more trouble agreeing on things, making more disagreements and squabbles. A larger group is less likely to resolve their differences. They'll have different personality styles and different ways of operating.

- Myers and Briggs defined the 4 temperaments and further refined them into the 16 types. They then documented the differing needs and interaction styles.

  - Introvert (I)   vs   Extrovert (E)
  - Intuitive (N)   vs   Sensing (S)
  - Feeling (F)   vs   Thinking (T)
  - Perceiving (P)   vs   Judging (J)

- ENFP attracts ISTJ. Opposites attract and have complementary skills.

- The Four Temperaments are:

  - SJ   Sensing, Judging   (Administrator)
  - SP   Sensing, Perceiving   (Live now!)
  - NF   Intuitive, Feeling   (Creative, feeling)
  - NT   Intuitive, Thinking   (Scientist, logical)

- SJs (typically accountants and administrators, etc.) like rules; NFs (the feeling, creative group) want to change the rules. NTs (scientists) are very thoughtful, and SPs (live-for-the-moment) want to *do it now*.

- In a team, differences will exist and must be accepted to progress toward the goals of the group. An effective group is when members recognize these differences and resolve them by a consensus of what is acceptable.

- Myers–Briggs is explained in *Please Understand Me*, (Keirsey and Bates, 1978).

- Communication is where teams often fail. It's sending and receiving signals, and we must agree on the meanings of the signals. One of the crucial parts of this for an object-oriented project is the definitions for the classes, Step 3 of the Seven Steps outlined in Chapter 9.

- You must know what the other team members are doing. There must be frequent formal and informal meetings. Regularly scheduled formal meetings are essential to check where we're up to. Issues are dealt with before they become problems.

- Use MBWA: Management By Wandering Around.
- Trust: To function as a team, members must depend on one another. *Your* success will depend on *my* commitment and performance, and mine on yours.
- A leader initiates discussions, and brainstorms to find solutions; draws information, opinions, ideas, suggestions, and concerns from members; and shares her own. A leader clarifies ideas and points out issues, interpretations, and options; summarizes and states conclusions for the team to adopt or reject; checks for consensus; and then moves them toward action on the chosen solution.
- **Arbitration skills** A good leader must manage the inevitable conflicts that will occur. With all the differences mentioned, someone on the team must be skilled at helping people resolve conflicts and disagreements.
- **Commitment** Team members are all there for the same purpose, committed to helping each other, and together they'll achieve that goal. *Commitment to a common purpose* is what makes them a team.
- The best teams spend a lot of time identifying and clarifying **specific performance goals.** Though the overall purpose is typically set from outside the team, the members will need to discuss it at length and then break it into a sequence of steps and goals. These goals must build on one another to arrive eventually at the overall goal of the team.
- **Mutual accountability** This is built from the sincere promises that we make to the other team members and to ourselves. Trust, commitment, and accountability cannot be mandated by a higher or external power.
- A team always goes through these difficult stages as it forms to do its work (the *Stormin' Normin'* model):
  - Forming
  - Storming
  - Norming
  - Performing
- Visualization is a powerful learning tool for skills, motivations, problems, and goals. Use it to rehearse as you learn these skills.
- We need to develop our listening skills. (*Note:* These techniques will only work *if you actually use them*).
- Communications courses usually focus on talking, "but no one ever teaches us to *listen!*" So, we often end up answering the wrong question or proposing a solution to the wrong problem.
- Reflecting the question back to the Client *in different words*, we can clarify understanding of the question and avoid wasting time and effort.
  - Step 1.   Client (user, student, child, spouse, etc.) expresses a problem of some sort to Server (analyst, teacher, parent – that is, *you*).
  - Step 2.   Server repeats the problem or question back to Client *in his own words* (Server's own words).

- Step 3.　If Client is not satisfied that Server has properly understood the problem, then Client says something like "No, that's not what I meant. What I meant was . . ." and then branches back to step 1 to restate and clarify the problem.

- Step *4*.　*If Client is satisfied* that *Server* has understood correctly, then, and only then, is Server allowed to try and answer the question.

- Your Client feels that you were *actually listening* because you paraphrased the question, *in your own words*. This tells your Client you cared enough to try to understand. Don't simply repeat your Client's words, parrot-fashion. Parroting gets them angry and shuts down communication. You *must* translate the question into *different* words.

- Reflective listening can be used for conflict arbitration. The discussion continues, under your firm guidance, with each statement and argument being clarified and understood by the listener (Server) before she responds to it. At each step, the speaker (Client) is in charge of the loop and says when the listener (Server) is allowed to respond.

- Feelings perception check: We venture a tentative diagnosis of the speaker's feelings, by saying "You seem to be feeling . . ." or "I think you're feeling . . ." and finish the sentence with " . . . are you?" This query gives them the opportunity to correct any misdiagnosis and redirect the conversation. So we end up with a structure like: "You seem to be feeling _____ about this, are you?"

- Ask open-ended questions that generate sentences, lists, feelings, or opinions. Questions that make the person think, reason, remember, or invent will give you more information and keep the discussion going.

- *Training is critical.* Team members need training in *all* the skills for the project. It normally takes a year to become proficient in object-oriented techniques, and only a very few newcomers can do it in less than six months.

- Especially for the pilot project(s) and early production projects, begin the change to object-oriented methods by *choosing the right people*. You want the ones who have already demonstrated an ability and a willingness to embrace change and newness productively.

- When people display counterproductive behaviors, recognize that deep down it is *fear* that drives them. Most often they're not even aware themselves where the anger (or whatever) is coming from. So you must *never overtly mention* the fear, or they'll become defensive and hostile. They'll feel it as an accusation of inadequacy. Behind the scenes you must quietly do whatever will truly reduce their fear levels.

CHAPTER GLOSSARY

__communication__ (1) The flow of information from person to person. (2) A matter of sending and receiving signals, and unless we agree beforehand on the meanings of these signals, we can end up confused.

__cyberphobia__ Fear of computers.

frame of reference   The way people always hear things through a filter consisting of their own feelings, experiences, prejudices, and fears.

MBAW: Management By Avoidance of Waves   A favorite with bureaucrats; these people are preoccupied with keeping a low profile and are not very productive.

MBCIF: Management By Control of Information Flow   This kind of manager keeps close control of information going up and down. He passes on only what he wants you to know, and typically embellishes or withholds things to manipulate his staff and superiors, and thus enhance his belief that he's in control.

MBWA: Management By Wandering Around   Keeping in touch and gathering information informally by wandering around and chatting with the team members. *Do this!*

norm   An agreed-on pattern or standard.

team   A small group of people with complementary skills who are committed to a common purpose, a common set of performance goals, and a common approach to the task, and for all these things they hold themselves mutually accountable.

technophobia   Fear of technology. A crippling and debilitating disease.

WHAT COMES NEXT

We've now been through all the parts of object-oriented analysis and looked at some of the other parts of object-oriented systems development. What remains now is to review and reinforce your learning of the concepts with a case study. In the next chapter, we'll progress to something that's a little more realistic in size and scope.

CLASS/GROUP EXERCISES AND PROBLEMS

Ex 16.1   Reflective Listening. This exercise can be done with the entire class, but can be time-consuming in a large class. In that case, do it in your groups. Since it works best with about ten to twelve in the group, you may wish to combine up some of your regular groups.

(a)   Each member of the class or group thinks up and writes down six questions or problems to express to someone. Two are to be targeted at the instructor or group leader, two should be suitable for members of your group or class, and two should be general enough to ask anyone in the room.

(b)   First, each student (group member) expresses one question to the instructor, who will then paraphrase it. The student will then approve the instructor's answer (Yes, that's it!) or rephrase the original question so the instructor may try again. When all students have had a turn, start again with each student using their second question for the instructor.

(c)   Now put two students on chairs at the front of the room. On the whiteboard (or wherever) identify the chairs as "Q: Questioner/Client" and "P: Paraphraser/Server." We'll call them student A in the Questioner's seat and B in the Paraphraser's seat. A poses a question to B, who paraphrases it until A is satisfied that B understands.

(d) Then do the musical chairs thing. A steps down, B takes the Questioner's seat, and C replaces B in the Paraphraser's seat. Now B questions C (using the *third* question on her sheet), and C paraphrases until B says it's okay.

(e) Cycle again, until all have had a turn at both asking and paraphrasing. Don't forget to put A in the Paraphraser's seat at the end.

(f) Now do it in a different order, each person using their *fourth* question. You may wish to reverse the previous order, starting with B questioning A, or any order will do.

(g) Finally, go around the room twice, with each person taking each of their general questions and directing it to whomever they choose, including the instructor.

INDIVIDUAL EXERCISES AND PROBLEMS

Ex 16.2 Go home tonight and find at least two chances to use reflective listening, and two chances to do a feelings perception check. Do this with friends or family, or whoever you spend the evening with. Make notes each time. Describe the interaction and how it went. Report your own feelings both during and after the interchange, and your perception of what effect it had on the other person, in particular on their feelings.

At the next class meeting, each person is to report back to the class or their group and describe what happened. The person will then comment on what he did right and what he can do better next time, with further (sensitive) comments from the other group members. (*Be sensitive*, now. Remember, you're next!)

Ex 16.3 Specific instances from the past

(a) Go through the Class/Group and Individual Exercises at the ends of Chapters 12 and 16, looking for tasks worded in the "specific instance from the past" format. Reword each one as a "How would you ..." or "What would you do if ..." kind of question. Discuss with your group or class what is wrong with them in this form.

(b) Now each person make up some "How would you ..." and "What would you do if ..." kind of questions. Exchange with other group members, then reword them as "specific instance from the past" kind of questions.

(c) Now find some "How would you ..." and "What would you do if ..." kind of questions that have been used in interviews or from books or notes or manuals on interviewing, or anywhere. Group members who are in hiring/firing positions will be useful here, or your instructor. Reword as before.

Ex 16.4 For the questions you found in Exercise 16.3(a) from within this book, now consider the ones you've already answered as you worked your way through the book. Now read the re-worded "How would you ..." or "What would you do if ..." form of the question that you created, and answer it (in writing). If you're doing this as a group, each person answers individually. Now compare the new answer(s) against the original answer to the "specific instance" form of the question. Look for a pattern or trend in how the answers differ.

PROJECTS AND CASES

P 16.1 The objective of this project is for you to enhance the ways you deal with the people around you. The first step is to recognize the style of each person. Remember, just doing that is often enough to make a difference for you.

Choose a partner. This can be a group or class member, friend, co-worker, relative, or spouse (that is, significant other). The exercise actually works best if it's someone you know well and/or interact with on a daily basis, but anyone will do in a pinch. Obtain (beg, borrow, or perhaps even buy) a copy (preferably a copy each) of Keirsey and Bates' *Please Understand Me* (1978). Make a number of photocopies of the answer sheet on page 11. Each of you should read as far as the Kiersey Temperament Sorter on page 5, then both do the test, using the *copies* of the answer sheet.

Once you've established your two groups (e.g., INTJ or ESFP), together read the parts of the book that describe the two of you. Discuss what you discover about yourselves and about each other. Comment on how much you do or do not identify with what the book says about your type.

And remember, this is science, not astrology. Regardless of your spiritual views, for now please stick to the topic, and do not introduce astrological issues or types. You may certainly do that later, outside the classroom.

If you have done other personality style assessments (such as the Controller/Supporter/Promoter/Analyzer breakdown used in the *Pursuit of Excellence* seminars, then it's unlikely that you'll find any serious conflict. Again, later it may be very instructive to see how your own evaluation in the two systems stacks up. (See either www.excellencefoundation.org or www.contextassociated.com)

SELF-TEST QUESTIONS

Note: Appendix A3 has answers to the Self-Test Questions.

Q 16.1 The three major groupings of skills that we identified as necessary in a project or team are

(a) Functional, interpersonal, and complementary skills

(b) Interpersonal, complementary, and arbitration skills

(c) Interpersonal, complementary, and technical skills

(d) Technical, functional, and arbitration skills

(e) Functional, interpersonal, and technical skills

(f) None of the above

Q 16.2 *Mutually accountable* means

(a) The boss has made me responsible.

(b) We are responsible to the company.

(c) I hold myself responsible.

(d) We are responsible to each other.

(e) We have no responsibility.

Q 16.3 In the Myers–Briggs analysis, each person is rated on four dimensions, each represented by two letters. What attribute do the following letters stand for?

(a) E/I _____ / _____

(b) N/S _____ / _____

(c) F/T _____ / _____

(d) P/J _____ / _____

Q 16.4 Again referring to the work of Myers and Briggs, give the short description for each of the four temperaments:

(a) SJ

_____

(b) SP

_____

(c) NF

_____

(d) NT

_____

Q 16.5 For each of the skills shown in the list, indicate whether it's classified as a Technical (T), Functional (F), or Interpersonal (I) skill by entering a T, F, or I in the box beside it:

(a) Leadership   (b) Study skills

(c) Organizing   (d) Scheduling

(e) Planning   (f) Mentoring

(g) Arbitration   (h) Programming

(i) Goal setting   (j) Reading

(k) Feelings perception check (l) Communication

(m) Decision making   (n) Object modeling

(o) Database design   (p) Meeting leading

(q) Technical writing   (r) Listening

Q 16.6 In the Stormin' Normin' model, the correct sequence of the four stages of group or team formation is

(a) Forming, storming, norming, and performing

(b) Storming, performing, forming, and norming

(c) Forming, norming, storming, and performing

(d) Forming, performing, norming, and storming

(e) Performing, forming, norming, and storming

(f) None of the above

Q 16.7 In reflective listening

(a) You make an inspired guess at the speaker's meaning, and adjust later.

(b) You reflect the speaker's words back to her.

(c) You may answer when the speaker says you can.

(d) The speaker clearly defines the problem and then you answer with a solution.

(e) You answer when you're totally satisfied that you understand the problem.

(f) All of the above

Q 16.8 In a feelings perception check

(a) You must guess the person's feelings accurately for it to work.

(b) You identify the person's feelings and then ascribe a cause to them.

(c) You may use any structure you wish for the sentence, as long as you guess the feelings right.

(d) You may leave off the words "are you?" at the end without affecting how well it works.

(e) All of the above.

(f) None of the above.

Q 16.9 The correct sequence of steps in reflective listening is

(a) Question, iterate, paraphrase, and answer

(b) Paraphrase, iterate, question, and answer

(c) Question, answer, iterate, and paraphrase

(d) Iterate, question, paraphrase, and answer

(e) Question, paraphrase, iterate, and answer

(f) None of the above

Q 16.10 In a feelings perception check

(a) You're validating the speaker by recognizing his feelings.

(b) You say "are you?" at the end to allow her to correct any wrong guess at her feelings.

(c) You must be careful to structure the sentence properly.

(d) You observe changes in the speaker's body language and facial expressions and infer what feeling might be causing this.

(e) All of the above.

(f) None of the above.

Q 16.11 In the Stormin' Normin' model of group formation, there are certain feelings and behaviors that group members typically show at each stage. Match the feelings and behaviors listed below with the stage they typically occur at – Forming (F), Storming (S), Norming (N), or Performing (P) – by placing a letter F, S, N, or P beside each one.

(a) Resistance to the task and to any externally suggested approaches

(b) Satisfaction at the team's progress

(c) Disunity; increased tension and jealousy

(d) Insights into personal and group processes

(e) Acceptance of membership in the team

(f) Better understanding of each other's strengths and weaknesses

(g) Lofty, abstract discussions of concepts and issues

(h) Sense of team cohesion; common spirit and goals

(i) Anticipation

(j) Close attachment to the team

(k) Complaints about the organization and the task

(l) Questioning the wisdom of those who selected the problem and appointed the other team members

Q 16.12 Is this an open-ended question?

Q 16.13 Tell me what makes this one an open-ended question?

Q 16.14 Should I use open-ended questions in a self-test such as this?

Q 16.15 What are some of the benefits of asking open-ended questions?

Q 16.16 Give at least three reasons why I should not use open-ended questions in a self-test such as this.

Q 16.17 Which of the previous five questions (16.12 – 16.16) are open-ended, and which are not?

Q 16.18 Process improvement skills or _____ skills are _____ skills needed to _____ the project. They include project _____ skills; _____ , _____ - _____ , and _____ -making skills. They also include the skills that make each _____ team _____ more productive, such as _____ , time _____ , and _____ skills.

Q 16.19 The larger the _____ , the more difficult it is to _____ _____ . A larger group is _____ _____ to _____ their differences. They'll have different _____ styles.

Q 16.20   Myers and _____ defined the four _____ and further refined them into the _____ _____ . They then documented the differing _____ and _____ styles.

- _____ (I)   vs   Extrovert   (E)
- Intuitive   (N)   vs   _____   (S)
- _____ (F)   vs   _____   (T)
- Perceiving   (P)   vs   _____   (J)

Q 16.21 ENFP attracts ISTJ. _____ _____ and have _____ skills.

Q 16.22 The four temperaments are:

- SJ   _____ , _____   (_____)
- SP   _____ , _____   (Live _____)
- NF   _____ , _____   (Creative, _____)
- NT   _____ , _____   (_____ , _____)

Q 16.23 SJs (typically _____ and _____ , etc.) like _____ ; NFs (the _____ , creative group) want to _____ the _____ . NTs (_____) are very thoughtful, and SPs (_____ -for-the- _____) want to do it _____ .

Q 16.24 In a team, _____ will exist and must be _____ to _____ toward the _____ of the group.

Q 16.25 Communication is _____ and _____ _____ , and we must agree on the _____ of the _____ . Crucial for an OO project is the _____ for the _____ , Step _____ of the _____ Steps.

Q 16.26 There must be frequent _____ and _____ meetings. Regularly scheduled _____ _____ are essential to check where we're up to. _____ are dealt with before they become _____ .

Q 16.27 A _____ initiates _____ , and _____ to find solutions; draws information, _____ , ideas, suggestions, and _____ from members; and shares her own. A leader _____ ideas and _____ _____ issues, interpretations, and _____ ; summarizes and _____ _____ for the team to _____ or _____ ; checks for _____ ; and then moves them toward _____ on the _____ _____ .

Q 16.28 With all the _____ mentioned, someone on the team must be skilled at _____ , helping people resolve _____ and _____ .

Q 16.29 Team members are all there for the same _____ , committed to _____ each other, and together they'll achieve that _____ . _____ to a _____ _____ is what makes them a _____ .

Q 16.30 The _____ teams spend a lot of time _____ and _____ specific _____ _____ .

Q 16.31 Mutual _____ is _____ built from the _____ _____ that we make to the other _____ _____ and to _____ .

Q 16.32 A team always goes through _____ as it forms (the _____ _____ ' model):

- _____

- _____

- _____

- _____

Q 16.33 We need to _____ our listening _____ . (Note: These techniques will only _____ if you _____ _____ them).

Q 16.34 No one ever _____ us to listen! So, we often end up _____ the _____ .

Q 16.35 _____ a question back to the _____ in _____ _____ , we can _____ understanding of the question and avoid _____ _____ and effort.

Q 16.36 _____ listening can be used for _____ _____ . The discussion continues, under your firm _____ , with each statement being clarified and understood by the _____ (_____) before she responds to it. At each step, the _____ (Client) is in charge of the _____ and says when the listener (Server) is _____ to _____ .

Q 16.37 Training is _____ . Team members need training in all the skills for the project. It normally takes a _____ to become _____ in object-oriented _____ .

Q 16.38 Especially for the _____ project(s) and _____ projects, begin the change to object-oriented methods by _____ the right _____ . You want the ones who have already _____ an ability and a _____ to embrace _____ and newness productively.

Chapter Seventeen

"The Royal Korona Yacht Club" Membership System

What You Will Learn in This Chapter

This is a chapter that should be read several times through. Being in narrative form, it's fairly quick to read, so you should be able to manage a number of trips through it. In addition, you'll need same-day review and next-day review, at least of the summary, which in this chapter would consist of the "Deliverables" section, along with the Chapter Summary and Glossary. Remember, you should be doing these same-day and next-day reviews of at least the summary, every time you read through any chapter.

You can feel confident that you understand the concepts presented in this chapter when you can:

1. Arrange, invite, organize, set up, and run an FTS/JAD session.

2. Lead a group of users and developers in a productive and effective FTS/JAD object-modeling session.

3. Guide the group through the steps, ensure everyone's point of view is both presented and heard, and deal with all the interpersonal issues that may arise.

4. Produce a well-presented set of analysis models, accurately reflecting the world of your users.

What You Should Know to Start This Chapter

You'll need to know the basics of objects and how to build a real-world object model. This translates into Chapters 4 – 10.

Chapter Overview

In this chapter, you'll go through the process of object modeling to produce a set of analysis models. You'll follow a group of users as they go step-by-step, led by our consultant, Nancy. You'll see in detail how such a session might go with real people.

KEY CONCEPTS

- Context diagram
- Use case, actor
- Brainstorming, candidate class
- Class definition, unique identifier, sample attributes, Left-List
- Associations, 1:M, M:M
- Attributes; operations/behavior
- Sequence diagram
- Statechart diagram, state transition table
- Nonlinear, cycle-back "iterative" progression of the work

"THE ROYAL KORONA YACHT CLUB"
MEMBERSHIP SYSTEM – EPISODE 1

"My wife and I belong to a yacht club," Tim mentioned at yet another lunch. "It's very formal and high-class, but their record keeping always seems to be in a mess. With so many wealthy members, they should be able to afford your rates with no problem. Would you be interested in doing a membership system for them? I've already told the committee all about the work you've been doing for me, and they would really like you to take a look at the problem. They'll pay your regular rate. Could you make it to a meeting either Tuesday or Wednesday evening?"

"Tuesday should be okay," Nancy replied. "I'd love to have a go at that, with all those rich folks. Can we set it up as a modeling session, then?"

"Sure," said Tim, feeling pleased. "After what we've done on this project, I figure I can set it all up properly. It'll be good practice. I'll make a list of who should attend, and run it by you. I'll volunteer as recording analyst. And I'll use the checklist you gave us to set up the room."

"Right," said Nancy, "so we'll plan on two or three hours that night for the initial modeling, and then I'll have enough information to be able to give your committee a quote for the completed project."

17.1 THE CASE STUDY PROJECT AND ITS BACKGROUND

Here we have a sports club with a problem common to every sports, hobby, or interest club; every church, professional association, trade union, and so on. That is, the problem of keeping track of the members, what they're doing or are signed up to do, and what they have and haven't paid for.

In this case study, we'll capture some of the basic structure of the classes for such a club and come up with a model, one that you could possibly use directly for a real-world sports club or other organization. For a small group with a simpler structure, you may find that you can simplify your model from the one we have here. Or you may find that there are additional classes and behaviors that you need to add if your club has more complex needs than the RKYC does.

Structure of the Case Study

The project for this case study is intentionally small. It's intended to illustrate for you the process of doing the analysis. So I've kept it real simple, and I've included a lot of narrative, to show you how it's done. At the same time, the necessary pieces are there, and we build a complete analysis model. It just happens to be a very small one, so you can easily see the big picture, the overall view.

The focus on narrative is so that you can see how the models evolve during discussions with the users. This, after all, is how you can expect to learn about your users' business in the real world.

So let's rejoin Tim and Nancy at the RKYC. You'll notice that for the rest of this chapter I haven't identified episodes of the narrative as I did before. Rather, we'll just slip in and out of the narrative and the explanatory text as we find a need to. In this way we'll follow Nancy as she discovers the structure of the yacht club, and of the data that drives its operation.

17.2 THE PROJECT SCOPE/MISSION STATEMENT

As Nancy and Tim entered the yacht club boardroom, Nancy was pleased to see that all appeared to be ready, just as Tim had promised. Tim introduced her around. She gave everyone a card and took advantage of the moment with each one to practice their names, looking them directly in the eye as she did so. Most gave her their cards in return. Tim then announced that they would "get right down to work," and gave the floor to Nancy.

Nancy quickly scanned the first page of the agenda, which looked like Figure 17-1.

"If you'll turn to the second page of the agenda Tim gave you," she began, "you'll see there a list of the diagrams we'll need to produce for this project. The first part, most of which we should be able to get through tonight, is the requirements analysis.

Royal Korona Yacht Club

Membership System Project

Initial Meeting Jan 13, 2002

Invited:

June Song	Commodore
Brent Figol	Membership Secretary
Michael Kwan	Secretary
Peter Diederichs	Events Coordinator
Alnoor Virji	Treasurer
Diane Bessey	Chief Instructor
Geoffrey Walsh	Safety Officer
Tim Buchanan	Member

Figure 17-1 Sample agenda, first page, as typed up by Tim's secretary

Phase	Activity	Models Produced	Components
Analysis	Object-Oriented **Analysis**	Requirements Model	
			Project Scope Context Diagram Use Case Model Interface Descriptions
		Object Model	
			Entity Classes (data model): Step 1: Candidate Classes Step 2: Define Classes Step 3: Establish Associations Step 4: Expand M:M Associations Step 5: Attributes Step 6: Normalization Step 7: Operations (i.e., behavior) Interface Classes. Control Classes.
		Statechart Diagrams Interaction Diagrams	
Design	Object-Oriented **Design**	Object-Oriented Design Models	

Figure 17-2   Activities and phases of the OODLC – page 2 of Tim's agenda

"As you'll see from the definition there, the ***requirements definition* is the document that spells out what the program we build must do, the information it must produce, and when and where.** You'll see also the *KRB Seven Steps of Object Modeling*, and that's where we'll need to spend a bit of time and get in real deep into your operation." These are reproduced for you readers in Figure 17-2, blended from Chapters 6 and 9, the way Tim had prepared them for Nancy.

Nancy then launched into a 15-minute description of the process, finishing with a promise that it would all come clear as they worked their way through it. "Now for the first thing on the list," she continued, "and that's the Project Scope." On the whiteboard, she wrote a large title: PROJECT SCOPE. Turning to face the meeting, she asked, "Can you tell me, in a sentence or two or three, just what this project is all about?"

After a moment of silence, June, the Commodore of the club, spoke up. "Well," she began, "to put it in words of one syllable, what we need is a program to keep track of our members and whether they've paid their dues."

"Perfect!" responded Nancy, and she began writing.

Then Brent, the membership secretary added, "And we need to keep a record of what races and competitions they've entered, too."

RKYC Membership System
PROJECT SCOPE

A system to track members and their dues paid and owing. The system will record which members enter in events or volunteer to work at events, the event fees paid and owing, and membership of committees.

Figure 17-3   The project scope, first pass"

RKYC Membership System
PROJECT SCOPE

A system to track members and their dues paid and owing. The system will record which members enter in events or volunteer to work at events, the event fees paid and owing, and membership of committees.

The system will report only on fees and dues collected and owing, with no other financial reporting. Fees and dues data will be available for transfer to the financial system.

Figure 17-4   The project scope, final version

And all the social events and everything else," added June.

Then Peter, the events coordinator, broke in. "More than that, we need to know not only what events they've entered, but what ones they've volunteered to work at and what job they've volunteered for at each one."

"Right," said Brent, "and whether they've paid their fees for the event."

"And we need to record committee memberships, too, and responsibilities in each committee," said June.

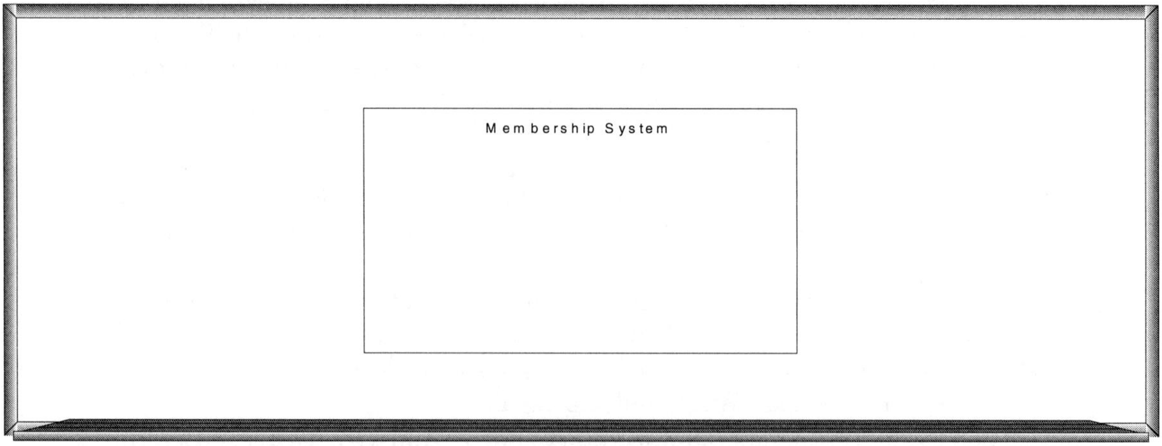

Membership System

Figure 17-5   The context diagram, starting point

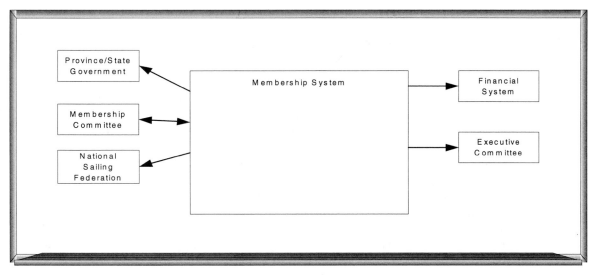

Figure 17-6 The context diagram, final version

Nancy was writing furiously. "Good, good," she said enthusiastically, "that gives me a picture of what's going on. Now try this on for size." Figure 17-3 shows what she had written on the board.

"Okay, how does that look?" she asked. There was a general murmur of assent.

Brent spoke up. "What about financial reporting?" he queried. "We already have all our accounts on a financial package on the computer. We wouldn't want to duplicate that, would we?"

"For sure not," said Nancy. "But the financial system will need to draw data from our membership system, won't it? So let's add a statement of what the system will and will not do for financial data." So saying, she added a couple of sentences to what was already on the board. It now looked like Figure 17-4.

"One thing we must avoid," Nancy continued, "is duplication of data entry. The fees and dues information should be keyed in once, and once only, and then used by as many different programs as might need it. In this case, that's the membership system and the financial system."

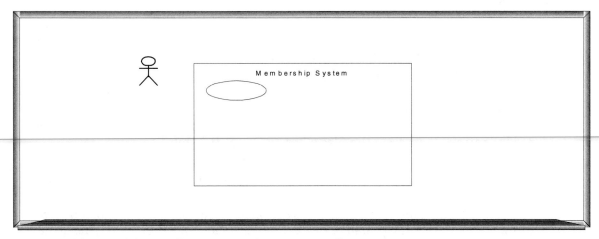

Figure 17-7 First pass at the use case diagram

17.3 THE CONTEXT DIAGRAM

"Okay, are you comfortable with that as the goal for the project?" Another murmur of assent. "And remember that it's not cast in stone. If we feel we need to change it later, we can do so. Let's move on to the context diagram. Mr Recorder, do you have all that?" Tim nodded, so Nancy erased the board and then drew a large rectangle in the center of it. Inside the top of the rectangle she wrote "Membership System," so it looked like Figure 17-5.

She turned to the group and began, "Now, for the context diagram. I need you to tell me all the places, people, systems, and organizations *outside* the membership system that will either feed data into it, or need to get data out of it. We've already mentioned one, and that's the financial system." Nancy drew a smaller square, labeled it, and joined it to the rectangle with a line. "Since the data will flow from the membership system to the financial system, the arrow goes that way," she said, adding an arrowhead. (You can see this in the top right of Figure 17-6.)

"Okay, what others are there?"

"Well," said June, "the Executive Committee will want some reports."

"Good," said Nancy, and she drew another box.

"The provincial government requires an annual report from all nonprofit organizations," contributed Brent. A few more suggestions followed, and before long Nancy's board looked like Figure 17-6.

"Recorder?" asked Nancy, and Tim nodded again. As she cleaned the board she continued, "Okay, next we'll do some use cases." Nancy turned to face the group. "These are really just scripts showing how you would use the system. What I want you to do is imagine yourself sitting down at the computer to add a new member, say. Then describe to me in detail the step-by-steps of how you would use the system to do that. But before we go into all that detail, we need to get an overview by finding and identifying all the jobs or tasks that you're going to want the new system to do for you. Then we give each one a name, and later we describe the detailed steps."

17.4 USE CASES

"What I want you to do," said Nancy," is to think of all the things you might want to do with members. Don't worry about how the system will do it for you, I just need to know all the things you need to be able to do."

"I know what I'd like to do with some of them . . ." chuckled Peter.

"C'mon, now, get serious," said Brent, grinning. "I need to record when someone proposes a new member, and when and if that person becomes a member. Then I need to update addresses, phone numbers, jobs, and all that kind of thing. I also need to remove them from the files when they quit the club."

"What about suspending or expelling someone?" asked Nancy.

"Oh, we've never needed to do that!" Michael broke in quickly, sounding a little offended.

"Not so!" said June. "About six years ago, before your time in the club, Mike, we threw out two families who had been stealing equipment off other boats. And about a year earlier, we suspended a guy for hitting another member over a racing dispute."

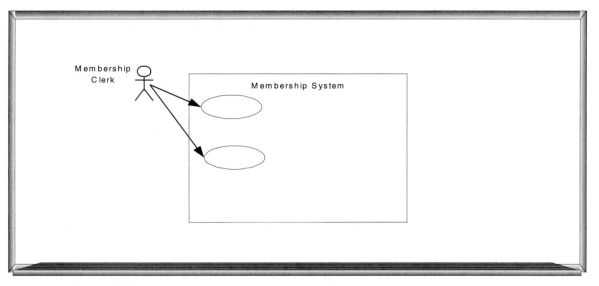

Figure 17-8   Use case diagram, second pass

"Well, I'm sure it's not the kind of thing that happens often," said Nancy diplomatically. "But if it does ever happen, your computer software must be prepared for it, otherwise it'll cause real problems. And remember, Murphy's law says that if we ignore the possibility, then *for sure* it's going to happen.

"We can handle this with just a very little extra work, by providing a *Status* attribute, with values S for Suspended, E for Expelled, and Q for Quit. This same Status attribute can also be used if, down the line a year or two, you come up with some new situations that no one anticipates at this point."

"Wise move," commented Tim, who had been quietly watching all this. "I've seen you do that kind of thing with my project, too. I'll bet it springs from bitter experience!"

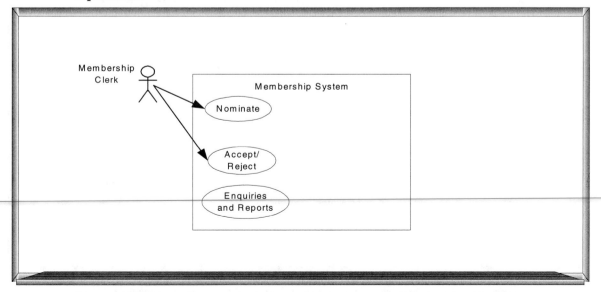

Figure 17-11   Use case diagram, fifth pass, with all tasks identified

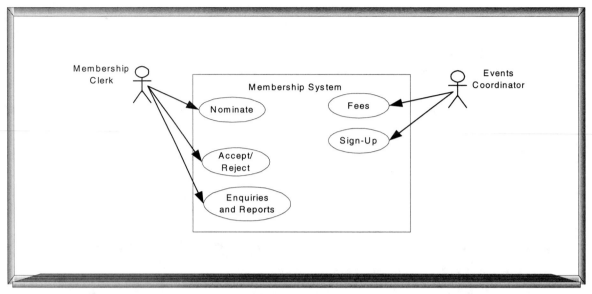

Figure 17-9   Use case diagram, third pass

"Darn right," affirmed Nancy. "Now we'll document all that stuff like this. We'll put a stick figure outside the box that's labeled for the system, and an ellipse inside it. The cute little guy is an actor called Membership Clerk, meaning it could be Brent, or his office staff, or any authorized person. It's really a *role* that could be filled by any one of several different physical people." In her use of the term "role," Nancy was referring here to our definition of an *actor* from Chapter 7, and by now her board looked like Figure 17-7.

Next, Nancy began to label the ellipse with the words Add/Update Members, but Brent stopped her.

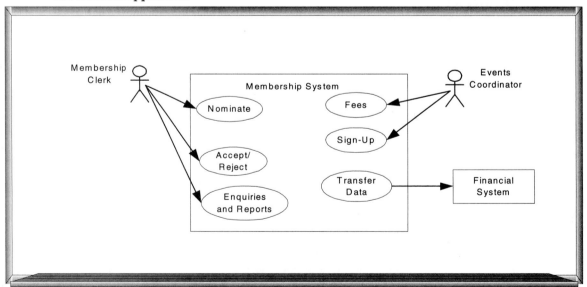

Figure 17-11   Use case diagram, fifth pass, with all tasks identified

"Well, ah, actually," he stammered a little, "it's a bit more complicated than that. New members don't just apply and get entered; they're invited. By two existing members, who propose their name to the Membership Committee."

"Okay, that's what I need to hear," said Nancy. "So I guess step one is to record candidates as they're proposed, and then step two would be to update the ones who are approved as members. And that, by the way, would give us a couple more values for that Status attribute: maybe N for Nominated and M for an approved Member. Oh, and R for Rejected, too."

"Yeah, that would be about it," agreed Brent. "So you found new uses for that Status already!"

The board now looked like Figure 17-8. Nancy explained: "What the ellipses represent is a series of tasks that people (that is, actors) need to use the system for.

And once we've found all of these tasks, or most of them anyway, we'll look at the steps in each one in detail. That process will eventually give us a picture of all the capabilities that we need to design into the system.

"Now," she continued (and readers may wish to glance back at Figure 17-6), "if you look back at the context diagram, you'll see that the Membership Clerk actor can also make enquiries against the membership database, so that gives us another ellipse for another task." So saying, she added another ellipse with an arrow, so it looked like Figure 17-9.

"And there appears to be another actor that we could put over to the right of the context diagram," she went on. "This would be an Events Coordinator actor. In actuality, it could be Peter as the real coordinator, or an event committee member, or any other kind of person you guys may decide should be able to do these things. For now, we'll subsume all these people under the term Events Coordinator."

Nancy drew another stick figure to the right of the board and labeled it *Events Coord.* "Now, what tasks does this little guy need to do?"

"Oh, that's easy," said Peter. "I can see that just by looking at the context diagram. He needs to enter and update members who sign up for an event. He needs to enter and update fees owing and paid, do enquiries, and run the reports, some of them monthly and some ad hoc."

"Good," said Nancy, drawing two more ellipses inside the System box. "We'll put the enquiries and reports in here as a single task, available to both actors." Her diagram now resembled Figure 17-10.

"And then I see a couple more tasks. We'll need someone to run the reports monthly, and also whenever needed by the Executive Committee and the government. That, I would imagine, will be done by the Membership Clerk actor."

"Right," spoke up Alnoor. "And then there's the monthly transfer to the Financial System. I think that should probably happen as a part of running the Financial System, wouldn't you say?"

"Yes," agreed Nancy, "so we'll have another task, here." She drew one more ellipse, as in Figure 17-11. She connected the Enquiries ellipse to the stick figure on the left. "I'll put the reports in with the Enquiries here. And you're right, Alnoor, the actor requesting the transfer to the Financial System is indeed the Financial System itself. So we'll show that as a box, same as before," which she then drew.

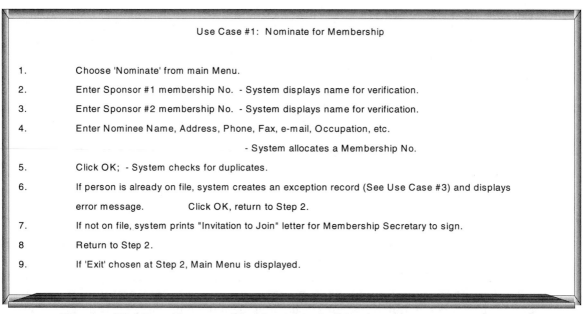

Use Case #1: Nominate for Membership

1.   Choose 'Nominate' from main Menu.

2.   Enter Sponsor #1 membership No. - System displays name for verification.

3.   Enter Sponsor #2 membership No. - System displays name for verification.

4.   Enter Nominee Name, Address, Phone, Fax, e-mail, Occupation, etc.

                                              - System allocates a Membership No.

5.   Click OK; - System checks for duplicates.

6.   If person is already on file, system creates an exception record (See Use Case #3) and displays

        error message.   Click OK, return to Step 2.

7.   If not on file, system prints "Invitation to Join" letter for Membership Secretary to sign.

8   Return to Step 2.

9.   If 'Exit' chosen at Step 2, Main Menu is displayed.

Figure 17-12   Use case #1: Nominate for Membership

"I think we've uncovered all the major tasks," said Nancy. "Let's move on, and if any more turn up we can add them later. For now, it's time to expand each task into a set of detailed step by steps. What I suggest we do is this: I'll guide the group through one of these things, and then I'll split you up into three groups to work on different tasks at the same time. Then afterward, the group can review each one.

"And don't worry if we don't get them quite right. This is only a first pass through all this stuff. Later on, in the design phase, we'll bring in some of the people who will actually do the work at the computer. They'll try each task against a set of dummy screens, and we'll adjust everything until we have it the way they really need it. We call that process Prototyping."

"Ahh, 'Prototyping for Dummies'!" breathed Peter, ever the comic.

Brent managed to ignore him. He looked impressed. "I wish the consultants I hired two years ago at my company were half as thorough," he complained ruefully.

Tim grinned. "You'd better come and sit in on one of her meetings at my shop! See me after, and we'll get together so you can see what we've produced so far. I told you she's good."

"Tim, you're going to embarrass me," complained Nancy. "Let's get started on the *Nominate* use case." She quickly cleaned the board, and then wrote the title from Figure 17-12 at the top.

"Now, the Membership Clerk, and remember that might be you, Brent, with your clerk's hat on. He'll be looking at the Main menu to start with. He'll choose Nominate. Then he'll see a screen for that purpose." Nancy began writing on the board, as in Figure 17-12. "Brent, tell me what you think you would do next."

Brent looked thoughtful. "I'd enter the name, address, phone number, and all that stuff, I guess. And the names of the two sponsors. Could the computer check for me whether this person had been proposed before? Or even might be a member already? Sometimes a member is not very active, and someone goes and nominates them, not knowing they're already in!"

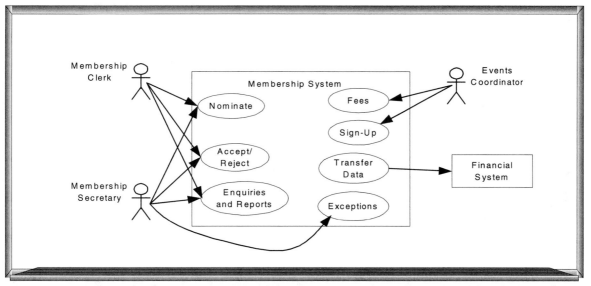

Figure 17-13 Use case diagram, sixth pass, "complete" so far

"Sure," said Nancy, writing some more. She had now completed the board as you see it in Figure 17-12. "How do you want to handle these exceptions? Is this something the membership secretary should do in person, rather than leave to the clerks?"

"Yes, I think so," said Brent, "and, come to think of it, I'm not so sure the clerks should deal with the rejected candidates, either."

"That's fine," Nancy assured him, "We'll just add another actor that represents you, or your replacement when you're not around. So this actor will be called Membership Secretary, and will get the arrow from the *Reject Candidates* task. And in fact, what we can do is rename that task to be *Process Exceptions*, so then it includes those new ones as well. And, of course, anything your clerks can do, so can you. So you get arrows to these other three ellipses as well." As she spoke, Nancy was hurriedly sketching an incomplete version of Figure 17-11 in one corner of the board, showing these new changes as she described them. Figure 17-13 shows it as Tim drew it in his notes.

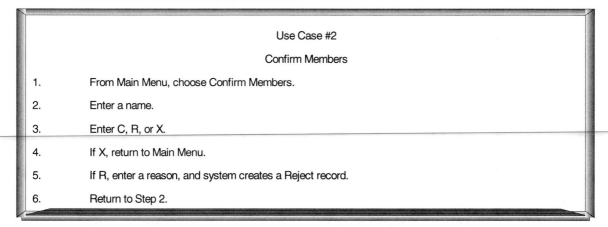

Figure 17-14 Use case #2: Confirm Members, first pass

Use Case #2

Confirm Members

1.   From Main menu, choose Confirm Members.

2.   System displays a scrollable list of all Nominees. Each has buttons marked 'C' and 'R', and a blank 'Status' column. Choose a Nominee name by scrolling to it and clicking.

3.   Click on C or R.

4.   If C, system places 'M' in Status, changes color, prints a letter to be mailed out, and returns to Step 2.

5.   If R, system enters 'R' in Status, displays a dialog box for a reason. Enter a reason, click OK, and system creates a Reject record.

6.   Return to Step 2.

7.   Exit button returns to Main Menu. System gives warning message if some Nominees not yet processed.

Figure 17-15   Use case #2: Confirm Members, second and final pass

"Now let's split up and get three things done at once," said Nancy. "Brent, June, and Mike, would you do the rest of the Membership Clerk and the Membership Secretary. Peter, Geoff, and Diane, would you do the Events Coordinator, and Alnoor and Tim, I'd like you two financial geniuses to take a look at what needs to be transferred financially.

"I'd like you to do each one on a sheet of this flip-chart paper, and then we can put them up for the whole group to look at afterward," she said.

With much scraping of chairs and some good-natured ribbing, the three groups retrieved a few sheets each from the flip chart, and got down to work. Nancy went from one group to another, coaching, coaxing, and advising.

After half an hour or so, they seemed to be ready. Nancy called for attention, and when the chair scraping was done and they were all facing forward once more, she hung up the *Confirm Members* use case, which you can view in Figure 17-14.

Use Case #3: Membership Enquiries

1.   Choose 'Enquiries and Reports' from Main Menu.

2.   Selct 'Membership Enquiries.'

3.   Enter a search condition.

4.   Choose screen or printer.

5.   Click on 'Run' button; system produces list.

6.   Return to Step 2.

(a) Use Case #3: Membership Enquiries.

Figure 17-16   Use cases #3 to #9   (continued)

Use Case #4: Process Nomination Exceptions.

1. Choose 'Exceptions' from Main menu.
2. System displays list of all exception records.
3. Click on a record. System displays full screen of details.
4. Make adjustments to any data if needed.
5. Enter comments.
6. Choose appropriate action from Action List.
7. Return to Step 2.

Figure 17-16(b) Use case #4: Process Nomination Exceptions"

Well, this will do what we need," she said. "Can anyone think of a way to improve on it?"

This time it was Tim who looked thoughtful. "Well, you know, maybe it would go quicker if the clerk could put all the candidates on the screen and just click on the ones that were approved."

Use Case #5: Reports for Executive Committee and for Province.

1. Choose 'External Reports' from Main Menu.
2. System displays a list of report titles.
3. Choose a report. System displays appropriate dialog box for additional details.
4. Enter any additional details needed for this report.
5. Click on 'Run.' Report is printed.
6. Return to Step 2.

Figure 17-16(c) Use case #5: Reports for Executive Committee and government

Use Case #6: Sign Up for Events

Choose 'Sign Up for Events' from Main Menu.
2. System displays scrollable list of events in Date order.
3. Scroll to an event and select it.
4. Choose Add, Update, List or Delete.
5. If 'Add,' system displays a form, key in Membership No. and go to Step 9.
6. If 'Update,' system displays a form, key in details. Go to Step 9.
7. If 'List,' system lists all signed-up Members, each with a check box for print. Select Members and go to Step 9.
8. If 'Delete,' system displays Confirm dialog box; enter confirmation. Go to Step 9.
9. Choose 'Next Person' and return to Step 4, or 'Next Event' and return to Step 2.

Figure 17-16(d) Use case #6: Sign Up for Events

Use Case #7: Receive Fees Paid.

1.   Choose 'Receive Fees and Dues' from Main Menu.

2.   System displays dialog box with prompts for Membership No. and for Event No.

3.   Enter Membership No.; system prompts for Fees or Dues. Enter dues, or enter Fees and Event No.

        Return to Step 2.

4.   Enter Event No.; system lists Members. Select one, enter Fees Paid. Return to Step 2.

Figure 17-16(e) Use case #7: Receive Fees Paid

"Good idea," agreed Nancy. "Will we need to record a reason or a vote against the rejected ones?""Oh, yeah, that would be a great idea," said Brent, excited at the thought. "Then, when I process the exceptions later, I would have all that information right there in front of me. Yes, I like that idea. Let's record both the reason *and* the vote. And can I have the full vote, with how each committee member voted?"

"If it's going to be valuable to you, we can certainly do that," responded Nancy. She then wrote on the board an alternative version, as in Figure 17-15.

By this time they were all getting the hang of it, and the rest proceeded fairly quickly. Figures 17-16(a) – (g) show how they finally looked.

"Now," said Nancy," this next one, although we've done it as a use case, really covers the next step on the list, which is *interfaces*." The list she mentioned is, of course, Figure 17-2. "This one is the interface to the Financial System. The *user* interface screens we'll design later."

Nancy proceeded to tape all the sheets onto the wall. "We'll need to be able to see these as we go through the next part, which is where we have to find all the objects that matter in the system."

Use Case #8: Event Enquiries and Reports

1.   Choose 'Enquiries and Reports' from Main Menu.

2.   Select 'Event Enquiries.'

3.   Enter a search condition.

4.   Choose screen or printer.

5.   Click on 'Run' button; system produces list.

6.   Return to Step 2.

Figure 17-16(f) Use case #8: Event Enquiries and Reports

17.5 THE OBJECT MODEL

"In the modern methods for designing software, we build our databases around the *objects* that we find in your operation. We have certain techniques that we use to discover what those objects are, and that's what we're about to do next. We'll mostly be talking in terms of *classes of objects*, and sometimes in terms of individual objects." Nancy continued in this way for a few more minutes, and then gave an example.

"One of the more obvious objects in your operation is a *Member*. There are a number of points about the object called Member that are important for us." And as she spoke, she counted the following points on her fingers:

- "A *Member* is a kind of *thing* in your world that you need to keep information about. *Object* is just another word for 'thing.'

- "Being a *thing*, it's represented by a *noun*.

- "The stuff we need to know *about* a member will be things like Name, Address, Membership Number, Fees Paid, Fees Overdue, and Status – remember that one? – and so on. These are called *attributes*, which is the word I used for the Status earlier.

- "The term *Member*, then, represents a class of objects that are important to our project. The trick to finding these classes, and this is what we're about to get into, is for you guys, who understand the business of the club, to come up with a definition for each *noun* that we can find. If you can come up with a reasonable definition, then it's probably important enough to be included in our system.

"But that's not the final criterion. There are two more questions that we may need to ask about each class of objects before we're sure it's one we need. The first is, 'How do we tell one Member from another?' The answer this time is fairly obvious: I'm guessing its Membership Number. We call this a *unique identifier*. As long as one of these exists for the class, it tells us these things have *identity*, which says they truly are objects.

"And then, if we're still not totally certain that this is an important class for us, the third check is to ask if there are some things we need to know *about* these objects. That is, find a couple of *sample attributes*. If we have some attributes, then we must have some objects for them to describe, right? So that automatically means we must have a class to hang these attributes on. In this case, the sample attributes might be Name, Address, Status, and Fees Paid."

Use Case #9: Transfer to Financial System
1.   Financial System as Actor sends message requesting transfer.
2.   membership System extracts the necessary data and performs some calculations.
3.   Results passed to Financial System in required format.

Figure 17-16(g) Use case #9: Transfer to Financial System

Candidate Classes

nominee	invitation	financial system	membership	sponsor
dues	menu	race	name	exception
event	date	officer	address	clerk
error message	volunteer			

Figure 17-17   List of candidate classes, first pass

Nancy paused for breath. "Bravo," applauded Brent. "You said a whole lot of stuff there. Do you always talk in bulleted lists like that?"

"Only way I can keep my thinking straight," grinned Nancy. "Now, let's find some nouns. We're going to do several little exercises here, and each one will find a bunch of nouns for us. First we'll develop a list of words by brainstorming, then we'll look in a few other places to add to it. This list we'll call the *candidate classes*. On page two of your agenda" – which readers will recognize as Figure 17-2 – "you'll see this is shown as Step 1 under Entity Classes. Then in the following steps we'll analyze them all and see which ones we want to keep."

17.6 THE KRB SEVEN STEPS

Step 1: Brainstorming

"Now, to the brainstorming." And here Nancy spent a few minutes defining and describing brainstorming, as we saw it in Chapter 9. She concluded with: ". . . And there'll be *no evaluation* until Step 2. Now I want you to just throw some words at me, *nouns* that is, *thing words*; any noun that you can think of that's something the club needs to keep track of, something the club needs to keep information about. I'll start with *Member*. Tim, you've done this before. Get the ball rolling here." And Nancy wrote the word Member at the top of the board.

Tim began, "Ah, how about, uh . . . , yeah, *nominee*. And how about *dues*."

"Event is a noun," said Diane.

"What about name and address. They're nouns," contributed Geoff.

Candidate Classes

nominee	invitation	financial system	party
dues	menu	race	meeting
event	date	officer	event chairman
name	exception	committee	boat
address	clerk	duplicate	fundraiser
membership	sponsor	complaint	bingo
error message	volunteer	reason	

Figure 17-18   List of candidate classes, second pass

"Membership," said June. Nancy wrote all these on the board as the contributions flew.

"Error message," said Tim. And then, "Oh, no, I guess that would be an output!"

"No evaluating, Tim," Nancy reminded him and added the term to the list.

Alnoor then called out "Invitation!" and Nancy dutifully wrote it up, even though she and Tim could both see, as I'm sure you can too, that it was another output, rather than an object class. After a few more minutes, Nancy called a halt. Her board at this point looked like Figure 17-17.

"Well, that was good," said Nancy. "You're to be congratulated for catching on so quickly to this brainstorming idea. And now we've got a couple more places to look for nouns that might turn out to be classes. Some systems analysts like to use these as their primary way to find classes, but I prefer to use them along with the brainstorming."

OTHER PLACES TO FIND CANDIDATE CLASSES

"What we need to do next is look at everything we've written down so far, and anything written or printed that we may have brought along to the meeting. From these we pull out all the nouns that look like something we might need to track in the system. Something we might need to keep information about, in other words. Tim, bring your notes over to the table here, and we'll go through them quickly. Does anyone have any other documentation?"

"I have the club's annual report," offered June.

"I have the Safety and Procedures Rulebook," Geoff called out.

"And I have the Members' Manual, with the club rules and the code of ethics and stuff like that," said Mike.

"Good," said Nancy, taking the various documents and laying them out on a couple of tables. "Now everyone gather around so there's at least two people working with each document, and let's start looking for nouns."

Everyone moved around as she directed, and a hubbub arose as they perused the various documents. After a minute or so Tim cried out excitedly, "In the project scope here," he said. "What about *Committee*? We don't have that in yet."

"Right, Tim," Nancy said, and turned to write it on the board. Over the next ten minutes or so, there were a few more suggestions, and by then her board looked like Figure 17-18.

Step 2: Define Classes

"I think we're ready to move on to the next step," Nancy observed, gazing thoughtfully at the list. She cleared the whiteboard and turned to face the group. "What we need to do now is to take each of the words in the list and check it out to see whether or not it really should be in our system. We do this by asking these three questions that I mentioned earlier.

"First, we ask 'What is it?' We want to come up with a *definition* for this word, the way you guys use it in your operation. Then as a further check, we ask 'How do you tell one of these things from another?' For Members, that might be the Membership Number. And finally, if we need to, we ask 'What might we need to know about one of these?' In other words, what data would we need to keep in the database to describe a Member, say?

Member: A person who belongs to the Royal Korona Yacht Club.

Figure 17-19   The first-pass definition for Member

"Let's get started, and if any of that seems a bit mystifying, I can promise it will come clear as we do some of it. Let's start with Member, which we mentioned first, but," and here she grinned broadly, "we forgot to put it on the list! Well, it's never too late." So saying, Nancy wrote the word Member near the top left of the board.

"Now tell me," she continued, "just what exactly *is* a *Member*?"

Brent spoke up. "Someone who belongs to the club, I guess."

"Well, that sounds reasonable enough," responded Nancy, "but we'll need to address a few details. For instance, what kind of a *someone*? Is it restricted to being a person? Or do you allow some kind of corporate membership or family membership?"

"We don't have corporate memberships yet," said June "but we were thinking of adding them We do allow family discounts, but the family itself doesn't become a member, only the people in the family do. They're all registered as being related, though."

"Good, that tells me *Members* are all *people*, but that may not be so forever. And it also tells me about an association that we'll need to document in a later step." Nancy wrote on the board the definition you can see in Figure 17-19. "Tim, will you make a note that we should check out an association 'Member *is family to* Member.'"

"But there's more. What about the first guy on the list I just cleaned off the board, *Nominee*?" she asked.

"Well, they're not members yet," protested Brent. "We can't go putting them in the Members file!"

Tim broke in. "Ah, but I think I see what you're getting at, though. A *Nominee* is really just a *Member* in an earlier status. Are you suggesting we put them in the member database, with that Status attribute you talked about, to show that they're not full members yet?"

"Something like that," affirmed Nancy, "and the added advantage is that you'll be able to keep historical records of nominations and rejections. And if you want you can include all or some of these people in some of your mail-outs, too."

"Yeah, that could be useful," Brent began with some enthusiasm. Then he looked a little confused. "But wait a minute. Now that doesn't fit the definition any more!"

"Right," said Nancy, "so we'll need to change it to fit." And she erased the last part of the definition and rewrote it, as in Figure 17-20.

Member: A person who belongs to or is being considered for the Royal Korona Yacht Club.

Figure 17-20   The second-pass definition for Member.

Member: A person who belongs to or used to, or is being or has been considered for, the Royal Korona Yacht Club.

Figure 17-21   The final definition for Member.

"But there's some more yet," said June. "If we're going to have potential Members, we should also have former Members. We've already implied that by allowing for Suspended, Expelled, and Quit in the Status attribute. So I think we need to add 'or used to' at the end."

Nancy wrote some more, so her board looked like Figure 17-21. "Like that?" she asked. Heads nodded.

"Well, I think we've got it," said Nancy. "So now let's try the first on the list, and that's *Nominee*. So tell me then, what *is* a Nominee?"

"Oh, I can see where that goes," said Tim, "a Nominee *isakinda* Member! And so is an Officer."

"Yeah," said Brent, "There's a whole bunch of them. Look, there's *Volunteer*, and *Event Chair*, and *Sponsor*. They're all *kindsa* Members, too, aren't they?"

"Right on!" said Nancy, "So would it work for you, to say that a Nominee is a Member whose Status shows that they're being considered for membership?" There was another of those general murmurs of assent, so she wrote it up. After some further discussion, the board looked like Figure 17-22. You'll note they identified that Committee Member *isakinda* Member, and Event Chair *isakinda* Committee Member. By now, Tim's list of candidate classes looked like Figure 17-22(b), after he crossed off the classes they had defined. And if you compare parts (a) and (b) of the diagram, you'll notice that the name of the Event Chair class underwent a little evolution during this process.

"And now," announced Nancy with an exaggerated flair, "for the next item on the list, and that's *Dues*. Can someone tell me please, what is a *Due*?"

Brent answered. "Well, it's an amount of money owed by each member so they can be a member," he said.

"Okay." Nancy paused. "Yes, it's noun alright, and you have come up with a definition for it. But I don't think it's going to work. Let's try the second question against it: How do we tell one Due from another?"

"Well," began Brent, somewhat uncertainly, "One member pays $1,000 a year for a single membership, and another pays $1,500 for a family, is that what you mean?"

"No, not exactly," said Nancy gently. "I meant more like the membership number that we use to tell one member from another."

"But that doesn't make any sense for dues," complained Mike.

"Exactly. So that tells us that Dues is not a class of objects, because dues don't have identity the way members do." Nancy moved to the left, and wrote the word *dues* at the extreme top left of the board. Then she erased the word from where she had it at on the list at the center of the board. "But I don't want to lose the word, though. It's bound to turn up later. In fact, I would predict that this one will turn out to be an attribute of something. Probably of Member, I'd say. So I'll put it up here on the *Left-List* in case we need it for something later.

"Now, what's next? Ah, Event. Okay, what *is* an Event?"

"I guess it's a party or a dinner. Or a fundraiser, like we sponsored an art show last year and a folk concert a couple of months ago," said Geoff.

Peter broke in. "But I look after races and competitions, as well as those things. So they should be Events, too."

Nancy scribbled on the board, as in Figure 17-23.

"Will that do it?" Again assent. "So the next question. How do we tell one Event apart from the next?"

Member: A person who belongs to or used to, or is being considered for, the Royal Korona Yacht Club.

Nominee: A Member whose status indicates that (s)he is being considered for membership.

Sponsor: A Member who has recommended a Nominee for membership.

Volunteer: A Member who has agreed to work on a club project or event.

Officer: A Member who holds an executive position in the club.

Event Chair: A Committee Member who is elected or volunteers to be chairperson of the committee for some event.

Committee Member: A Member who is one of the committee for some club project or event.

(a)

Candidate Classes

~~nominee~~	invitation	financial system	party
dues	menu	race	meeting
event	date	~~officer~~	~~event chairman~~
name	exception	committee	boat
address	clerk	duplicate	fundraiser
membership	~~sponsor~~	complaint	bingo
error message	~~volunteer~~	reason	

(b)   **Figure 17-22**   (a) Definitions for Member and kindsa members. (b) Tim's notes with used-up candidate classes ruled out.

"They all have different dates," offered Diane.

"But I think the problem there," said Peter, "is that we can have several events on the same day. And some events extend for several days. And some events happen several times each year, and some every month, some weekly or daily, and some several times a year or a month, sometimes more or less randomly." He paused as if for breath.

"Yes, of course," Diane pondered, "so I guess we'd need the name of the event, as well as its date."

Nancy judged it was time to resume control of the discussion. "Good, you're on the right track, you guys. Let me take what you just told me, extend it a bit further, and see if it fits for you."

"I'm sure it will," said Tim with a disarming smile, "it always seems to!"

Nancy smiled back at him appreciatively and began. "What I see happening here is that the *Name* of the event tells you what *kind* or *type* of event it is, and then that along with the date pins it down to an actual specific event. But for any given name, or type, of event, there are a whole bunch like it, all on different dates. This suggests to me that we have a new class here, which I think would be called *Event Type*, and its unique identifier attribute would be *Name*. It would have an association to Event, and the verb would be *describes*, or *qualifies*, or something like that."

Nancy began drawing, so the board began to look like Figure 17-24. "And then there are some things you've said that told me a lot about Event Types too. There are Races and other kinds of competitions. So a Race *isakinda* Competition, which *isakinda* Event. And a Fundraiser *isakinda* Event, and so is a Social Event. And a Bingo *isakinda* Fundraiser, and so is a Concert and an Art Show. And then Parties and Dinners are *kindsa* Social Events."

She turned to face them and pointed to the tree diagram she had drawn. "All this stuff about '*kindsa*' gives us subclasses, with a hierarchy like this. We'll talk about all this in detail in a later step. Of course, even then, we may decide that even though these subclasses are perfectly true and very interesting, maybe they'll turn out not to be something we need in the database.

"Tim, you got that?" Tim nodded, so she erased it, and wrote up the next word from the list, *Name*. "Now, can you define a Name for me?"

"Oh, that's easy," said Mike, "it's a string of letters and words that belongs to someone."

"Okay, that's a definition, I suppose," said Nancy, smiling, "but how do you tell one Name from another?"

"Why, by its Name, of course!" grinned Mike.

"How do you mean?" Now Mike looked puzzled.

Event: A party or other social or fundraising activity, or a race or other competition.

Figure 17-23   What is an Event?

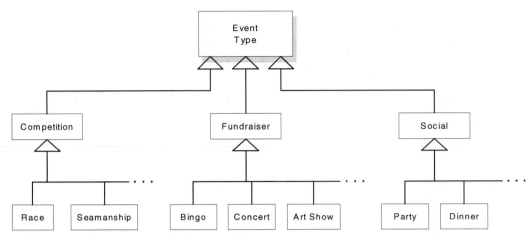

Figure 17-24 Event Type hierarchy

"True," said Nancy, looking a trifle bemused. "So let's try the third question on this one. Can you tell me some item you might need to keep on file about a Name?"

"Well, in the same way that you would keep Age and Sex and Date-Joined information about a Member. Or for a Race you might keep Date and Time, Distance, Number of Boats. What might you need to keep track of about a Name?"

"I think I see what's happening here, now," said Geoff thoughtfully. "What you're getting at is that there isn't anything we would need to keep about a *Name*. Rather, the *Name* is something we need to know about a *Member*! It's an attribute of the Member class, not a class by itself."

"Right on!" Nancy beamed. "The third question is an attempt to find some sample attributes for this thing that we think might be a class. If we do have some attributes, then it must be a class, because we need a class to hang the attributes on. But if we can't think of any attributes, then that suggests this isn't a class at all, but, as Geoff said, it's an attribute of something else. And you're right, Geoff, it's an attribute of the Member class, and possibly of one or two other classes as well."

"I see," said Mike, "the Name is how we tell one Member from another. So it's an identifier. Except some people have duplicate names, so it can't be a *unique* identifier. And the next one on your list, Address, that's also an attribute of Member, isn't it?"

"Right again," said Nancy approvingly, and Tim crossed another one off his list. Nancy wrote Name and Address on the Left-List, and continued. "Now let's try *Membership*. In your club, what is a *Membership*?"

June had been silent for some time, observing and absorbing. Now she spoke up. "Well, you know, we have quite a variety of memberships. There's individual and family memberships, student memberships, sponsorships, and so on, and corporate memberships before too long. There's honorary memberships for celebrities or benefactors, and if someone has been a member for twenty years, they get a lifetime membership."

"Well, that's very good," said Nancy, "so exactly what is a Membership, then?"

"Mm, it's a bit difficult to put in words, exactly."

"Well, give it a shot," encouraged Nancy. "Just spit it out. The first thing that comes to you, and then we can check it out and massage it where needed."

June gathered herself and announced: "A *Membership* is an agreement between a person and the club about how that person is to be treated and what rights and benefits they get."

"Excellent!" breathed Nancy, writing it up on the board. "Now, let's examine it. First, who's that *person*? What kind of *person* is that?"

"Ah – should that be *Member*?" asked Brent.

"I think so," said Nancy, making the two changes. "But is it just one member?"

"Well, yes . . . ," began June, but Mike interrupted her excitedly.

"No," he said, "what about family and corporate memberships? Each *Membership* covers a whole bunch of people."

"Right," said Alnoor, suddenly coming to life. "So it's an agreement between one or more Members, on the one hand, and the club. Like June said, it's about what rights and privileges they have as members." Nancy had already begun writing, so he dictated for her: "It's an agreement between one or more Members as the first party, and the Club as the second party, governing the rights, privileges, and conditions under which they have become Members."

Nancy finished writing it up, and raised an eyebrow at Tim, who nodded that he had it. "So how do I tell them apart?"

A pause. "Membership Number!" said a couple of voices at once.

"Not quite enough," said Nancy. "If it was, then a Member and a Membership would be the same thing."

"Well, aren't they?" queried Mike.

"No, Mike, you just said that a membership can serve several people," explained Diane.

"Oh, yeah, so I did," said Mike, "so how *do* we tell them apart?"

"Try this," Nancy said. "Mike, if you were membership secretary and I said to you, 'Mike, you know that membership you signed up yesterday?' What would be your response?"

"Oh, well, I'd say 'But I signed up dozens!'"

"So what information would I have to give you, so you would know which one I meant?"

"Well, I'd need the Membership Number, for sure. But I see what you mean, it wouldn't be enough 'cause no, wait a minute! This isn't working. If there's more members than memberships, then the Membership Numbers can't match."

"You're right," said Nancy, "that's not going to work at all. In fact, I think Membership Number should identify Memberships, but the Members will need a different identifier."

"You mean, like *People Number*?" suggested Alnoor, with a rather quizzical look.

"How about *Member ID*?" said Geoff.

"Yes, I think that would work." Nancy wrote it on the board. "Do you all feel comfortable with that?" she said to a "chorus" of nodding heads. "Next we have *Error Message*," she went on, turning back to the list. "So what *is* an *Error Message*?"

Figure 17-25   Beginning of KRB Step 3

Geoff replied to that one. "It's an advice to the users of the system that something needs correcting. And I guess to tell them apart we'd need some kind of an Error Code."

"Okay, so you've answered the first two questions at one fell swoop," said Nancy. "But what about the third? What information might you need to keep about an Error Message?"

"Oh, well other than the code and what the message says, I don't think there's anything else, is there?" said Geoff.

"I think you're right," agreed Brent.

"Yes, I think so," said Nancy. "What we have here is an *output* from our system, rather than a class of objects that we need to track within the system. It would have been a class of interest to us, however, if our mandate had included keeping statistics on error messages, or something like that. But for this project, it becomes a Left-List item. Tim?"

"Aye, Skipper, the Left-List it is!" mocked Tim, writing.

Nancy smiled. "Now, what about *Invitation*?"

"That's another output, isn't it?" asked Geoff.

"Yes," said Peter, "there's nothing we need to know about an invitation. We'll just print them from the database once we have some nominees entered."

"Right," said Nancy. "Tim, another Leftie," to which she received another "Aye" from her scribe.

And so they continued down the list, defining and keeping some, and consigning others to the Left-List. By the time they went home that night, the list of definitions looked like Figure 17-47(a), and the Left-List and Tim's Candidate List like Figure 17-47(b) and (c). (Figure 17-47 is in "Deliverables" at the end of this chapter.)

Step 3: Establish Associations

"Which brings us to the associations," said Nancy as the second meeting began a week later. Glancing first at Tim's minutes from the earlier meeting, she drew two boxes to one side of the whiteboard, as in Figure 17-25. Toward the left of the board, she listed the four main classes from Tim's notes.

"Now that we've discovered all the classes of objects," Nancy began, "we need to look at how these things can be connected. The connection can be described with a verb or verb phrase, because it typically involves some kind of *action*. There are other ways to do this besides verbs, but for now we'll keep it nice and simple.

Figure 17-26   More of KRB Step 3

"You see, it's nice to have a whole bunch of Members, and a whole bunch of Committees and Events, but does that give us a club that's worth anything? The club is not functioning at all, until someone *joins* a committee, and a committee *organizes* an event, and so on.

"The question we need to ask is, 'What does one of these things *do* to one of those?' And we have to check all the classes in pairs, and you'll see as we go how I make sure that we don't miss any possible pairs. For each pair, I'll ask you the question, for example, 'What does a Member *do* to a Committee?' You'll then give me a verb if you can; otherwise, we'll say that there's no such association.

"Okay, then, for this one, just what is a Member likely to *do* to a Committee?"

Geoff ventured an opinion. "Well, your suggestion of *joins* is good, but it doesn't quite do it for me."

"I agree," said Diane, "a member does more than just join a committee. That's just the *first* thing they do."

"We need them to work," June added emphatically.

Nancy summarized in her typical group-leader style: "What I hear you saying is that a Member *works on* a Committee. That's a perfectly valid verb phrase for this kind of thing. But is it the right one? Does it say what needs to be said? How well does it describe the interaction between a Member and a Committee?"

"Hey, not fair!" complained Brent. "That's three questions at once."

"Not really," Nancy smiled, "it's the same question phrased three ways."

"OK," Brent grinned, "well, the one answer for all three is Yes. '*Works on*' is the right way to say how a Member interacts with a Committee."

Nancy joined the two boxes with a vertical line, as you'll see in Figure 17-26. To the right of it she wrote *works on* beside a downward arrowhead. "That gives us 'Member *works on* Committee.'

"But there's one more thing. I said I have a way to make sure we check every possible pair of classes. Well, we do that by drawing a line down the side of the list of names." And Nancy added the curved black line you see to the left of the list of names in Figure 17-26.

"And now, we have to check *how many*. We need to ask, '*How many* Members can belong to one Committee?' We call this the *multiplicity* of the association. What I need to know here is this, is it only one, or can a whole bunch of Members belong to one Committee?"

Figure 17-27 KRB Step 3

"Oh, that's easy," said Peter, "the answer is 'a whole bunch.' But I suppose we might sometime need a one-man committee, though."

"That would never work!" exclaimed June, causing surprised looks around the room. But the faces relaxed when she went on, blithely feigning innocence, "But a one-woman committee could sure get things done!"

Nancy was adding the '*' to the diagram, as in Figure 17-27. "One for our side, June," she said. "But all I need to know is whether *more than one* is allowed, and in this case it is, and whether *one* is allowed, and it is. We show the *many* with this asterisk, and the *one* with a digit '1'." She turned to face them. "And what about the other way? How many Committees can a member work on? One or many?"

"Oh, many, we hope. We need everyone to volunteer," said Peter.

Nancy added another asterisk, as in Figure 17-28. "And because a member might not be on any committees at all, we put a zero beside the star on that line, to say we allow zero or more committees for a member," she said.

"So let's read it," she said, pointing to the board that was now Figure 17-28. "We get 'A Member *works on* zero or many Committees,' and 'A Committee *is worked on by* one or many Members'."

"And now, we'll try Member and Membership," Nancy continued, drawing another black line down the left of the list of names (see Figure 17-28 again). "Is there an association here? What does a Member *do* to a Membership?"

"Signs up for it?" suggested Alnoor.

"How about a Member *is part of* a Membership?" ventured Mike.

"I don't know. Neither of those seems to quite fit," said Tim.

Nancy broke in. "How about *has*? That should cover it. And *has* is the old standby if you ever get really stuck."

Figure 17-28 KRB Step 3

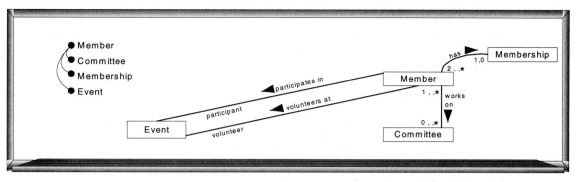

Figure 17-29 KRB Step 3

"Yeah, I think so," said Mike. "A Member *has* a Membership. Yep, that works."

"Okay, so how about the multiplicity?" asked Nancy. "A Member can have *how many* Memberships? One or many?"

"Well, a whole family can join on one membership," said Brent.

"But how about the other way around? Can one member join up several times over, on several different memberships?" Nancy queried.

"Oh no, I guess not. That way around it's only one," Brent nodded, "if any. It could be none."

Nancy placed an asterisk at the Member end of the association line and "0,1" on the other end, as in Figure 17-28. "So we read this one as 'A Member *has* one Membership, or maybe none'," she said."And the other way it reads, 'A Membership *has* many Members.' But can a Membership exist with one Member? Or none at all?"

"Oh, no, never," said Brent firmly. "We only need the Membership record when it's a multiple one. Regular ordinary old single members don't need it. So I suppose the minimum would be two members."

"Okay," said Nancy, "so the asterisk at the right end gets a '2' added to it. Now, what about Member and Event?" And she drew a curved black line down the left of the board from Member to Event, as in Figure 17-29. Then she added a box for Event. "What does a Member *do* to an Event?"

Geoff spoke up. "A member *competes in* an Event," he said.

"*Enters* an Event," said June.

"No, you're both wrong. He *volunteers for* an Event," said Brent.

"But what about 'A Member *organizes* an Event'?" asked Peter.

Nancy held up both hands. "Whoa, just a minute there. I think we're going to need all of those things. Let's take them one at a time. Not all events are competitions, right? So I think *participates in* would cover both *competes* and *enters*. Will that work?"

"Well, I suppose so," said Peter just a little doubtfully. "But what about the volunteers and the committee? They don't enter or compete, but they do participate in a way."

"I'm just coming to those, guys" Nancy assured him. "What we have here is two – no, I beg your pardon, *three* – separate, independent associations between Member and Event. First, a Member can *participate in* an Event, so I put a line from this box to this box, and the verb here, above the line, with the arrow so we read the sentence from right to left as 'Member *participates in* Event.'"

"Or," and here she began writing below the line, "we could phrase it differently by saying that the Member plays the role of *participant* in the Event. So then we would write 'participant' as the role name below the line, at the Member end of the line. And you, dear Reader, can see all this in Figure 17-29.

Nancy continued, "Then we draw another line parallel to that for the association *volunteers at*. Put the verb above the line, and we get 'Member *volunteers at* Event.' And we can put the role name 'volunteer' below the line. The two interactions are quite independent, *volunteer* and *participant*. A member can volunteer at one event and compete in a different one. Or sometimes she may volunteer and compete, both at the same event. The two connections both need to be recorded separately in the database."

"And what about the organizing committee?" asked Peter.

"Ah, that's something I need to check with you. Are volunteers and committee members the same thing? Are they just two different jobs at the event?"

"No, they're not," said Peter. "Committee members attend all kinds of meetings and do all kinds of work, contacting outside people and groups, writing letters and stuff, all that kind of thing. And all this happens way before the actual event. Volunteers just turn up on the day to do whatever job they've signed up for."

"Okay," said Nancy, "that's what I needed to know. But one more thing. Can someone be involved in all that planning and organizing and still be just a volunteer, without being a committee Member?"

"Well, basically no," said Peter. "The odd time the committee needs help from someone, we usually add their name to the committee list. So even if they never come to a committee meeting, we would consider them a de facto committee member."

"Good, and can one person actually do both things? Could they be on a Committee for an Event and also volunteer for some job at that same event?"

"Oh yes, that happens often," Peter nodded.

"So volunteering for an event is one association," Nancy summarized, "and being on a committee is something separate and independent. And this one is not an association from Member to Event directly, because it can only happen through a Committee. So I'll leave that one off the diagram for now, and you'll see it appear when we check Member against Committee, and Committee against Event, in a few minutes time.

"And multiplicity?" Nancy looked around the room. "I think they're both many-to-many, aren't they? And a member isn't *required* to do any of this, right?" Most heads nodded, so she added the asterisks and zeros as you see them in Figure 17-30.

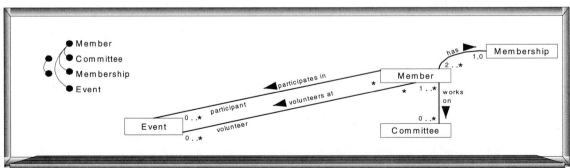

Figure 17-30   KRB Step 3

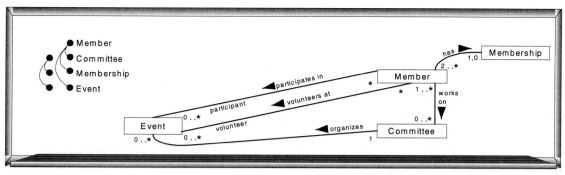

Figure 17-31   KRB Step 3

"So now we've checked Member against Committee, Membership, and Event in other words, Member against everything that's *below* Member in the list. Now here's my secret weapon for making sure we don't miss any associations.

"What we do next is go to the second class in the list, which is *Committee*, and now we check that one against everything below it. And I'll draw one of these little lines each time." So saying, she drew the black line you can see at the far left in Figure 17-30, from the word Committee to the word Membership. "So how about this one? Is there an association here? What does a Committee *do* to a Membership?"

"I'm not sure what you mean," puzzled Mike.

"Apart from the membership committee, nothing," said Brent.

"But even then," said June, "the membership committee deals primarily with members and their applications. That may or may not involve one of these

Membership things we've been talking about, depending on whether they're a single or a family or a corporation or whatever."

"You're both right" said Nancy. "We have to be careful to distinguish between the Membership class of objects in our system, and the general usage of the term *membership* in conversation. It's like, one has a capital *M* and the other a small *m*. When we talk loosely about someone's application for membership, that's a small *m*. When a family signs up, we create for them an instance of the Membership class, with a big *M*.

"And the reason for all this confusion, including yours, Mike, is that I really don't think we have an association here. I don't think a Committee does anything to a Membership at all."

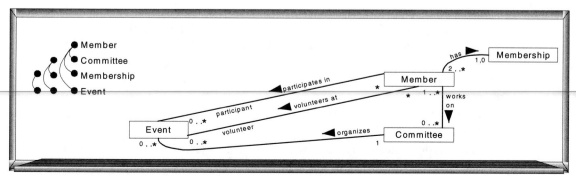

Figure 17-32   Final diagram for KRB Step 3: Conceptual Model

"Oh, I see. No wonder I was confused," said Mike.

"Right, so on we go to the next one," continued Nancy. "What does a Committee *do* to an Event?" . . "Organizes it!" came a chorus from several voices. Nancy drew another curved black line down the left of the list of names on the board, from Committee to Event, and joined the two boxes, as in Figure 17-31. Above the line she wrote the verb *organizes*, with an arrowhead pointing to the left.

"And," said Mike happily, "I can figure this one. A Committee can organize several Events that's zero, or one, or many, but an Event is only ever organized by one Committee!" Nancy added an asterisk and a zero at the left end of the line, and a digit '1' to the right, as you can see at the bottom of Figure 17-31.

"Good. Now there's just one more," she said, drawing a curved line down the left of the board from the word Membership to the word Event. "What does a Membership *do* to an Event?"

"Nothing at all!" cried out a gleeful Mike. "We're done! See, by the list of names, the lines prove that we've covered every possible pair of classes. There are no more associations to find." And he was right, of course, as you can see in the final diagram in Figure 17-32.

"Well, we're done Step 3, Mike," said Nancy, "but we've still got a lot more to do yet. Moving right along, we're into Step 4, where we have to adjust the many-to-many associations. As it stands, we call it a *conceptual model*, roughly because it corresponds to the users' concept of their operation. The next one is a *logical model*, and you'll see the difference in just a moment."

Step 4: Expand Many-to-Many Associations

"We have three many-to-many associations in our conceptual model, and this is what we need to do with them. Let's start with the one from Member to Committee. When a member joins a committee, there is something created that didn't exist before. Can you think of a *noun*, since it's a *thing*, that would fit here?"

"I'm not sure what you mean." Mike looked puzzled again.

"If you like, think of it as a record of the fact that this member joined up on this committee. What kind of a record would you call that?"

Mike's brow cleared. "Oh, I see. You mean, like a *join*. When she *joins* a committee, the member has a *join* to that committee."

"Yeah," said Nancy, "that would work."

"I think I see what you mean," said June thoughtfully. "But wouldn't something like *Committee Membership* be more appropriate? That's a noun too, isn't it?"

"Good thought, June. So, Mike, what do you think of that one?" Nancy enquired.

Mike nodded. "Yeah, I think so. I wasn't all that happy with join, but it was all I could think of at the time," he said.

"Right," said Nancy, "that's how this process works." Turning, she erased the M:M association between Member and Committee and drew an extra box labeled *"Committee Membership,"* as in Figure 17-33.

"Well," said Nancy, "let's try the Sample Attribute test on it, just like we did in step two, to see if it really is a class that matters to us. Can anyone suggest to me some data items we might need to keep about a *Committee Membership*?"

"I think one of its attributes would be *Date Joined*," said Tim.

"But isn't that just the date the Committee was formed?" asked Peter.

"Not necessarily," said Tim, "*Date Formed* is an item that describes the Committee, so it would be an attribute in the Committee class. This date could be different if he/she joined up later." Nancy mentally noted that Tim had by now become accustomed to the thought processes of the object modeler.

"I see," said Peter, "and it's not something that describes a member, 'cause he could have joined a bunch of committees on different dates. And so if he did that, I suppose he'd have a whole bunch of these Committee Membership things, too. Is that what you meant by 'instances' of a class?"

"Yes, Peter," affirmed Nancy. "And now that brings us to a bit of a complication when we come to the multiplicity. There's a pattern here that always occurs. Let me explain it like this.

"Suppose, as Peter says, a member is on several committees and so has several of these instances of Committee Membership. That means we must show a one-to-many association from *Member* to *Committee Membership*, like this." She drew the association, and the line, that you see in Figure 17-34. "Reading the association, following the arrow, we have 'A Member *has* many Committee Memberships' and 'A Committee Membership *belongs to* only one Member.' OK?"

It was Peter's turn to look puzzled. "But I still don't see what this thing is for. It just doesn't seem to have any purpose," he opined.

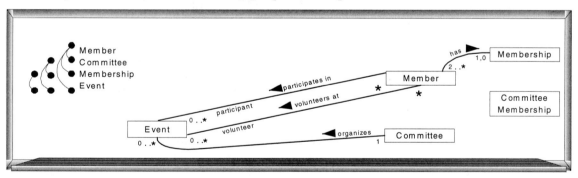

Figure 17-33   Expanding the M:M associations – first pass

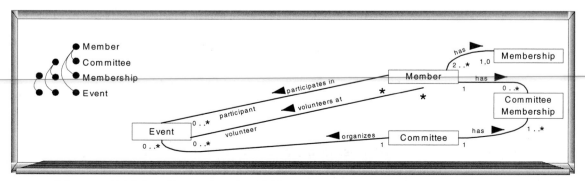

Figure 17-34   Expanding the M:M associations – second pass

"I see," said Peter again, "and on the other side, a Committee would have one of these things for each member who joined it, so that would be one-to-many also."

"Right on!" beamed Nancy, turning to add this to the model, thus completing Figure 17-34. "And the pattern we see here is that *the many-to-many breaks out into a pair of one-to-many, each with the many end of its line against the new class that appears in the middle.* We can just go ahead now and apply that pattern to the other two many-to-many associations we have in the conceptual model.

"It just so happens that they both go from Member to Event, so let's try the *participation* one first. Someone tell me, what is the thing that comes into existence the moment a member *participates in* an event?"

Nancy erased the *participates in* and the *volunteers* lines and replaced them with two new boxes, as in Figure 17-35.

Alnoor looked thoughtful. "It would seem to me," he ventured, "that most of the time this thing you're looking for in the middle is going to be just the noun that comes from that verb. So that would make this one a *Participation*, wouldn't it?"

"Good, you're finding the right patterns here. Yes, that's usually the case." Nancy wrote the class name "Participation" in the upper of the two new boxes. "But look at this other association here. If we apply the same rule, it doesn't quite work. If a member *volunteers* for an event, that would give us a volunteering, which doesn't fit very naturally. But think for a moment. How does he or she actually go about the process of volunteering? What do they have to do to volunteer?"

"They have to *sign up!*" said Diane, with an "aha" expression on her face.

"Yes!" said Nancy," And the noun from that would be ...?"

"Oh, of course, it's a *Sign-Up!*" exclaimed Mike.

"Right," said Nancy, turning to write that one in the lower of the two boxes she had drawn. "Often, the natural name for it is a noun that comes, not from the verb you have, but from an alternative one that says much the same thing. And there will be times when you can't find a natural name for it at all, and then you hyphenate the names of the two classes that gave birth to it. We don't need to do that in this model, but we did a lot of that in your Outhouse model, didn't we, Tim?"

"Yeah, tons of them. This model is way simpler," said Tim.

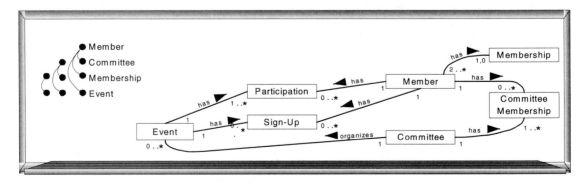

Figure 17-35   "Final" class diagram: expanding the M:M associations

"And now the multiplicity," Nancy continued on. "We follow the rule, and we get a pair of one-to-manies from *Member* to *Participation*, and from *Member* to *Sign-Up*." (Which you can see in Figure 17-35.) "Then we get two more from *Event* to *Participation* and *Sign-Up*. And that's all the many-to-many associations looked after. Now we can go on to the attribute step. That's Step Five."

Step 5: Attributes

"This one should be pretty quick," Nancy began. "We just go around the diagram, and for each class I want you to rattle off as many things as you can think of, that we might need to record about each one. Let's start with Member. What do you need to know about a Member? What do you need to record in the database about a Member?"

"Ah," said Geoff. "That's easy. There's name, address, home phone number, work phone, e-mail address, age, sex, height, weight, date they joined, name of their spouse, names of their kids, name of their boat, length and beam, tonnage, kind of sails, area of the sails, and the number of their berth at the marina."

"Whoa, hold on a minute," Nancy protested. "The first few were fine. Just what we need. But then you went off in two different directions at once. Tim, did you get all those?"

"Ah, what was after 'kind of sails'?"

"Area of sails and berth number," Geoff repeated.

"Okay, said Nancy, standing beside Tim and looking over his shoulder. "Let's look at the first few. Name, address, phone numbers, e-mail, age, sex, height, weight, and date joined, those are all Okay, because they each tell us something about the Member herself, or himself as the case may be. But what about the last few? Length, beam, tonnage, sail type and area? What are they telling us about? What do they describe?"

"Well, not the member, for sure," broke in June, "I'm not telling anyone my 'beam width'!"

"And they don't get to see my 'tonnage' either," said Diane, with a defiant toss of her head.

"No, they're telling us stuff about the *boat!*" said Brent, getting excited again. "They're attributes of a *Boat*. But we don't have a Boat class." He looked a little confused at that.

"That's right," Nancy grinned. "But it looks like we might need one, if all those things Geoff suggested are important enough to keep in the database. Are they?"

"Oh yes," said June, "we're going to need all those alright. We already keep all that stuff in our Members file in the file cabinet."

"Well there we go!" exclaimed Nancy. "This is a class that we missed in our brainstorming. And that's perfectly normal. We always expect to miss some, and then they always turn up later. In this case, we came up with a bunch of attributes and realized we had no class to hang them on. No problem. We just add one more class to our diagram and go back through all the steps from step two on." Nancy placed an additional box on the board, as in Figure 17-36. "So tell me, what *is* a *boat*?"

Peter grinned. "It's defined to be a hole in the water, into which one casts unlimited sums of money," he announced, to a chorus of chuckles and a "C'mon, get serious" from the back of the room.

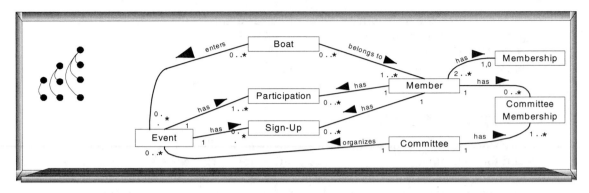

Figure 17-36 Adding the missing class *Boat*

"Okay," he tried again. "How about, 'A watercraft owned by a club member.'"

"Wonderful," said Nancy, looking around at nodding heads. "And how do we tell them apart?"

"Registration number," said a couple of voices at once.

"Good, got that Tim? Okay, now associations. Looking at the diagram on the board here, can you see which other classes Boat might have an association to? What would a boat *do* to any of these other classes?"

"It *belongs to* a member, and it *enters* an event!" Brent proclaimed. Nancy scribbled, and produced most of Figure 17-36.

"Yes, I think that works, said Nancy. "Anything else? No? Okay, multiplicity?"

"They're both many-to-many," said Alnoor. "A Boat can belong to one or more Members, and a Member can own several Boats, that's zero or many. A Boat can enter many Events, and of course an Event can have none, or one, or many Boats. Barbecue events don't have any boats." Nancy was drawing on the board, and it now contained the complete Figure 17-36.

"Good, good, we're flying through this one," said Nancy, pleased. "Now we can expand these two many-to-many associations. If a Member owns a Boat, I think the *thing* that represents that will be called an *Ownership*, won't it?" Heads nodded.

"And when it enters an Event, that will create an *Entry*," said Peter.

"Good. We'll need a box for that," said Nancy, modifying her diagram to look like Figure 17-37. "But there's another little quirk in this one that we haven't seen before. Take a look at the *Entry* and the *Participation* classes. If a Boat enters an Event, it has to have a Member involved, surely? It can't compete in a race by itself!

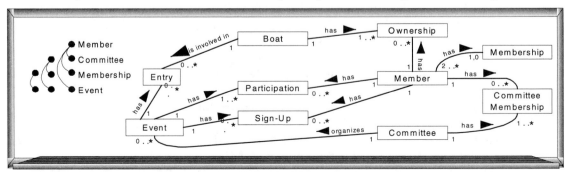

Figure 17-37 Expanding the M:M associations

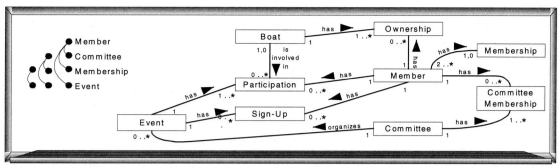

Figure 17-38   Combining the Entry and Participation classes

"Oh, I think I see where you're going with that," said Mike. "That means an Entry can never exist without a Participation."

"Yes, Mike," said Nancy, "and more than that, an *Entry* and a *Participation* are really both the same thing. It'll tie a Member, an Event, and a Boat together. The Boat will be optional, though, because some Events don't need it. So that means 'An Entry *has* zero or one Boats.' Like you said, you don't enter a boat in a barbecue." As she spoke, Nancy turned and erased the *Entry* box from the board, and made the diagram look like Figure 17-38.

The group then turned its attention back to the attributes and pretty soon came up with the list you'll see in Figure 17-48 in the Deliverables section.

"But that last class, *Ownership*, that doesn't have any useful information on it," protested Alnoor. "It just has the identifiers from the two parent classes and no other attributes."

"That's Okay," Nancy reassured him, "it just functions as a cross-reference to show which boats belong to which owners, and that's all it's needed for."

"But wait a minute," said Mike," what about all those *kindsa* Members we had before? What were they now? Ah, yeah, there was *Officer*, and *Sponsor*, and *Volunteer*. What else was there?"

"*Event Chair?*" ventured June. "Wasn't that one of them?"

Tim was consulting his notes. "Yes, and the others were *Nominee* and *Committee Member*," he announced.

"Okay, it's time we looked at those," said Nancy. "First, we'll consider attributes. Are there any attributes that we need to record about, say, a Nominee, that we would not need for other *kindsa* Members?"

"Well, their Status has a value of *Nominated*, doesn't it?" said Peter.

"This is true," said Nancy, "but in that case the attribute is Status, and it's one we already know is present in the Member class. What I'm looking for is some new attribute that we haven't seen yet, that's needed by Nominees, but not by other *kindsa* Members."

"How about 'Date Nominated?' asked Diane.

"That's a new one, alright," said Nancy, "but that's one that all Members will have, because they were all nominated at some stage. So we should add that one to the Member class. Good one, Diane. Tim, you got that?"

Tim nodded, and Nancy went on. "Actually, I think I can see that we're not going to find any. Now, it's not that there's anything wrong with *Nominee*; it certainly is a subclass of Member. It's just that so far it doesn't appear to be a subclass that's important in this database. We can handle it with the Status and Date Nominated attributes. So let's try another one."

A similar discussion around *Sponsor* showed that this also could be handled with an attribute or two, and need not be in the model as a subclass. But Geoff noticed that there was an association between these two *kindsa* Members. "A Sponsor *nominates* a Nominee," he pointed out. Nancy proposed adding this to the model by drawing a M:M loop line from Member to Member, but the meeting decided this didn't really need to go in the database, so she left it out.

"*Volunteer* has a whole bunch," said Mike eagerly. "We like to keep track of the total hours they've worked at events, the number of events, whether they received their fifty-times award and what date, whether they have first-aid training and what level, the same for lifeguard training, and whether they have a working dog. Some of our members have guard dogs and rescue dogs that we use for crowd control and rescue and stuff at the larger events," he explained.

"Okay," said Nancy, "I think that sounds like enough attributes to make this one a worthwhile subclass, just on that basis. Of course, we must bear in mind that some of the other subclasses might still turn out to be important for other reasons. It could be they have distinct associations or different behavior. Anyway, we'll be looking at those shortly."

Some further discussion brought out that *Committee Member* was also a subclass with a number of attributes that didn't apply to other *kindsa* Members. And from the definitions (see Figure 17-22) the group could see that *Event Chair* was a potential subclass of *Committee Member* but didn't have enough unique attributes to make it worth adding to the model at this point. The model now looked like Figure 17-39. "But I suspect we might find later that *Event Chair* has some unique behaviors or associations that might make it an important subclass for us," observed Nancy.

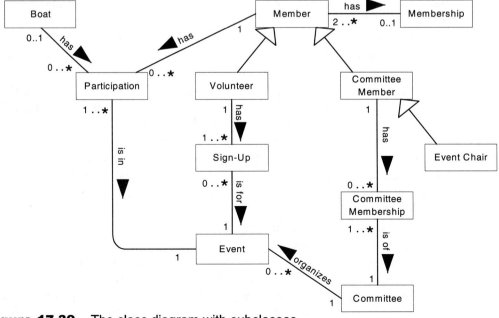

Figure 17-39   The class diagram with subclasses

```
create              attach
nominate            detach
accepted            join committee
rejection           buy boat
register
sign up
```

Figure 17-40   A partial list of operations for the Member class

So the discussion of attributes brought out a whole lot more than just the attributes themselves. And this kind of roundabout, back-and-forth, nonlinear process has to be accepted as normal in this business. Your users, like the RKYC people, are simply not capable of sitting down and producing a nice, ordered list of everything you and I need to know about their business. Expect to loop back often through earlier parts of the Seven Steps, as you discover things you or your users missed earlier. Eventually, your model will converge toward a complete model.

For the "final" list of attributes, you may check Figure 17-49 in the Deliverables section at the end of this chapter. This list is "final" in the sense that this is as far as we'll take it in the analysis phase. New attributes, certain to be discovered as you continue through the OODLC, will be added to the list as they're found.

Step 6: Normalization

"And now, although the list says Step 6 comes next, we're going to skip it for the time being," Nancy intoned, "because it's a technical step that I can do without using up your time. So let's move right on to Step 7."

Step 7: Operations/Behavior

"At this point," Nancy began, cleaning the board vigorously, "we move into something completely different. Up 'til now, we've been looking for *classes*. Once we figured we'd found them all, we said 'What do we need to *know about* these things?' That gave us the attributes. Now, we have to ask, 'What can these things *do*?' Or, in some cases, 'What can this thing have done *to* it?' In other words, we need to look some more at the actions and interactions among these objects, that is, the *operations* that make a business go.

"We'll start by doing it the simple way. That should find the most basic behaviors for us. Then we'll try some more sophisticated methods to dig a little deeper. So, to start with, for each class, I'm going to ask you to tell me everything this kind of object can *do*, that needs to be recorded on the computer. Let's start with *Member*. Someone tell me all the things that can happen to a *Member*."

"Well, I suppose, for a start, he or she can be nominated," said Diane a little cautiously.

"Yes, that's the right place to start," encouraged Nancy, starting a list on the board. "And if you remember, we have a use case that deals with that." Everybody shuffled pages to find it. "Actually, this is the point where we create a record for this person, so I think we should call this operation Create rather than Nominate."

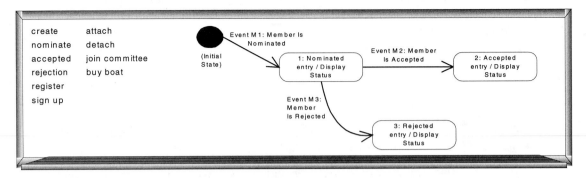

Figure 17-41   Initial statechart diagram for the member class

"But," said June, "What about renominating someone who was rejected before? That would just be a change of the Status attribute, wouldn't it?" So Nancy's list now showed both Create and Nominate. "Okay, what other operations can a member have?"

"Appendectomy?" Peter again, deservedly ignored.

"Well, Members can register to compete in an event, or can sign up to work at one," Geoff spoke up, ignoring Peter. "And they can be attached to a Membership. Sometimes an existing member marries or changes employer, or whatever, and has to be added to a membership or deleted from one."

"I suppose every allowable change of the Status attribute will need an operation," suggested Peter. "That would give us both an Approval operation and a Rejection operation."

"Maybe we should say they're Accepted rather than Approved," suggested June.

"Right," said Nancy, "and they'll do more than just change the Status, but that's the most obvious function of each one. And what else?"

Nancy added several more to her list. The suggestions continued for a while, until the list looked like Figure 17-40.

THE STATECHART DIAGRAM

"But, you know," Nancy said thoughtfully," I think we're missing some. That Status attribute has quite a few values, and I think we should do a life-cycle diagram for the Member class." She began drawing at the right of the board. When she turned to the group, the board looked like Figure 17-41.

"What we're going to do," Nancy began, "is diagram some of the things that can happen to a Member. This won't capture *all* the operations for the Member class, but it'll focus on the Status attribute, and the way a Member changes status, or state, when certain things happen.

"So we have events happening, and each one drives the Member from one state to another. It's like this." She pointed on the board. "The boxes are the states, and the arrows show the transitions between them and the events that cause these transitions."

"I take it you don't mean Events, like races and such," said Geoff.

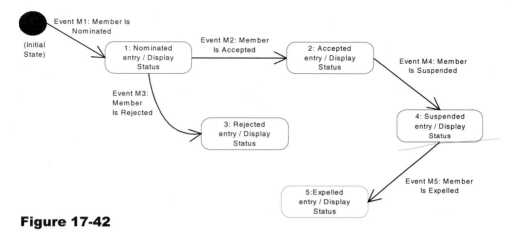

Figure 17-42

"You're right, I don't," said Nancy, "Good point. We need to be clear that these events are happenings that happen to an instance of the Member class, like being nominated, or being accepted into the club, or resigning from it. These are quite distinct from Events with a capital *E,* which are instances of the Event class. Now, let me explain on the diagram."

"Up here you'll see *Event M1: Member is nominated* on this arrow that comes from the big round dot. This kind of arrow indicates that this event causes an instance of Member to be created. And the fact that the arrow ends at the *State 1: Nominated* box tells us that the initial state when this Member instance is created is always the state of *Nominated.*

"Once the Member is in the Nominated state, there are two things that could happen. The Member could receive an '*Event M2: Member is accepted,*' which would move him to the *Accepted* state, which is State 2. Or, he could receive an '*Event M3: Member is rejected,*' which, not surprisingly, would put him in the *Rejected* state, which is state 3."

Nancy was busy tracing the arrows on the diagram as she spoke.

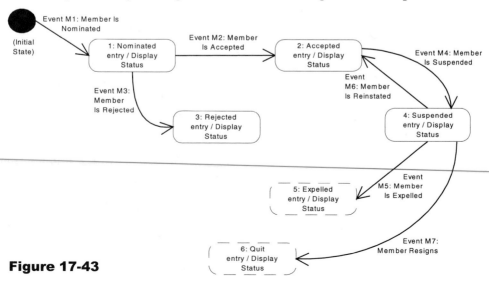

Figure 17-43

"But what happens after that? Well, we have a couple more states that I'm aware of, from the earlier discussions. That would be *Suspended* and *Expelled*." Nancy drew two more boxes and labeled them as in Figure 17-42. "You'll notice I drew the *Expelled* box with dashes. This is my personal convention for what we call an **_archive state_, where we don't expect the Member to do any more.** That is, we don't expect the Member to experience any more state changes. Except perhaps for deletion.

"Normally, there would be no more transitions after that. Once the Member enters this state, the life cycle is effectively over, except for deleting the instance later, that is. But we haven't deleted it yet, so at this point we can't show a transition to a final state, the one with a dot inside a circle."

"So wouldn't we have something similar if someone quit?" asked Diane. "We'd need a dotted box for them, too, wouldn't we?"

"Depends on how you need to handle it," said Nancy. "Would you need to keep their old information around, in an archived form, for occasional reference?"

"Oh, yes, we'd need that. We couldn't just dump all the records," said Peter.

"Okay, then," said Nancy, drawing another dotted box and labeling it *State 6: Quit*. (See FIG 17-43 and 17-44) "So let's go back to State 2, which is your regular member in good standing, once they've been accepted. From here, an *Event M4: Member is suspended* would send them to *State 4: Suspended*." Nancy was adding to the diagram. "But what could happen to them after that?"

June broke a long silence. "Well, if the problem is eventually resolved, I guess they would be reinstated. Otherwise, they might stay suspended for a long time." Nancy added *Event 6: Member is reinstated* to the diagram, as an arrow from State 4 to State 2.

"If the problem wasn't solved, I suppose they might eventually be expelled," mused Brent, and Nancy added an *Event M5* arrow from the *Suspended* box to the *Expelled* box. The board by now looked like Figure 17-43.

"Well, what happens if a member in good standing is expelled?" asked Alnoor. "He would go straight from the 2 box to the 5 box, wouldn't he? But what kind of event would make him do that?"

"That would be the same one, an *Event 5: Member is expelled*," explained Nancy, adding it as she spoke. "The only difference is that he would be in State 2 when he received that event, where the other guy was in State 4."

"You know," said Brent, "Even when someone's been expelled, we can still reinstate them. And the same for people whose nominations were rejected by the membership committee. And these are both the same kind of transaction as the M6 you have up there from box 4 to box 2. All three cases need a recommendation from the membership committee, which has to be approved by the executive of the club. So I think that would give us one M6 event from State 5 to State 2, and another one from *State 3: Rejected* back to *State 1: Nominated*."

"Good," said Nancy, happily adding two more arrows, so she now had Figure 17-44. "You're right on with all that! Now, is there anything else to add?" She looked around the room. "Then let's move on to the second step in building a statechart diagram."

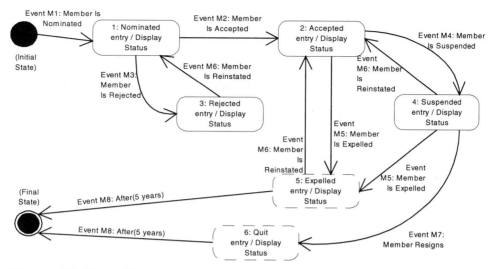

Figure 17-44   The "final" version of the statechart diagram for class Member, not yet quite complete

THE STATE TRANSITION TABLE (STT)

"This is another of those places where we need to verify that we've checked out every possibility," began Nancy, erasing the left side of the board but leaving the diagram. "This time we'll use a table, or call it a *matrix* if you want, with states down the left, and events across the top. Notice the first state is something I've called 'null.' It means that the Member instance doesn't exist yet." What Nancy had drawn was the skeleton for the table you can see in Figure 17-45.

"So the way we read this is to look at the top left cell of the table. Where does the Member go if she receives an *M1: Nominated* event while in the null state?"

"Basically, you mean what happens if she's nominated before she's born, right?" Peter quipped, once again the comic.

"Right. So what state is she born into?"

"Oh, that's State 1," said Mike.

"Correct," said Nancy, "So I write a '1' in that cell to show *State 1* as the *Destination State*. There are actually three things we could write in a cell. There's the *Destination State*, which we use for any valid transition. Then there are events that simply couldn't happen while the Member is in this particular state. Like, could a Member in the null state be receive an *M2: Accepted* event?"

"Whoa, no, that's not possible!" exclaimed Mike. "He can't receive anything at all, because he hasn't been born yet! Except for the one that causes him to be born, that is."

"Perfect! Thank you, Mike," said Nancy, and wrote the word *Impossible* in the cell beside the *1,* (i.e., top row, second column from left).

"Well, actually," said Mike, "The whole rest of that row is impossible. Like I said, a nonexistent member can't receive any event except a nomination."

"Right on, Mike," said Nancy, scribbling *Impossible* in the rest of the row. "And then there's one more possibility. Could it happen that two people who decide to sponsor a new member might both submit a nomination?" A few heads nodded.

Events States	M1 Nominated	M2 Accepted	M3 Rejected	M4 Suspended	M5 Expelled	M6 Reinstated	M7 Resigns	M8 After (5 years)
Null (Initial State)	1	Impossible	Impossible	Impossible	Impossible	Impossible	Impossible	Impossible
1: Nominated	Ignore							
2: Accepted	Impossible							
3: Rejected	Impossible							
4: Suspended	Impossible							
5: Expelled	Impossible							
6: Quit	Impossible							Final State

Figure 17-45   First pass at the state transition table for class Member

"Well, what if the new member is in State 1 and receives *another* event *M1: Nominated*? Shouldn't we just ignore this?" Again, heads nodded, and she carried on, "So we'll write the word *Ignore* in that cell," and she did, second row, column M1. "And since no one can be nominated if they're in any of these other states, that makes the rest of this column *Impossible* also." The table had by now been updated to look like Figure 17-45.

Events States	M1 Nominated	M2 Accepted	M3 Rejected	M4 Suspended	M5 Expelled	M6 Reinstated	M7 Resigns	M8 After (5 years)
Null (Initial State)	1	Impossible	Impossible	Impossible	Impossible	Impossible	Impossible	Ignore
1: Nominated	Ignore	2	Impossible	Impossible	Impossible	Impossible	Ignore	Ignore
2: Accepted	Impossible	Ignore	Impossible	4	5	Impossible		Ignore
3: Rejected	Impossible	Impossible	Ignore	Impossible	Impossible	Impossible	Impossible	Ignore
4: Suspended	Impossible	Impossible	Impossible	Ignore	5	2	6	Ignore
5: Expelled	Impossible	Impossible	Impossible	Impossible	Ignore	2	Ignore	Ignore
6: Quit	Impossible	Impossible	Impossible	Impossible	Impossible	Impossible	Ignore	Final State

Figure 17-46   The almost-complete state transition table for class Member

RKYC Membership System
Class List

Member:	A person who belongs to or used to, or is being or has been considered for, the Royal Korona Yacht Club.
Nominee:	A Member whose status indicates that (s)he is being considered for membership.
Sponsor:	A Member who has recommended a Nominee for membership.
Volunteer:	A Member who has agreed to work on a club project or event.
Officer:	A Member who holds an executive position in the club.
Event Chair:	A Committee Member who is elected or volunteers to be chairperson of the committee for some event.
Committee Member:	A Member who is one of the committee for some club project or event.

Unique Identifier: Member ID

Event:	A party or dinner or other social or fundraising activity, or a race or other competition.
Membership:	An agreement between one or more members as the first party, and the Club as the second party, governing the rights, privileges, and conditions under which they have become members.
Committee:	A group of members with an assigned task, usually to organize some project or Event.

(b)

Left-List

Dues	Invitaion	Clerk	Duplicate	Meeting
Name	Menu	Financial System	Complaint	Fundraiser
Address	Date	Race	Reason	Bingo
Exception	Officer	Error Message	Party	

(c)

Candidate Classes

~~nominee~~	~~invitation~~	~~financial system~~	~~party~~
~~dues~~	~~menu~~	~~race~~	~~meeting~~
~~event~~	~~date~~	~~event chair~~man	~~officer~~
~~name~~	~~exception~~	~~committee~~	~~boat~~
~~address~~	~~clerk~~	~~duplicate~~	~~fundraiser~~
~~membership~~	~~sponsor~~	~~complaint~~	~~bingo~~
~~error message~~	~~volunteer~~	~~reason~~	

Figure 17-47 (a) The final list of class definitions, as typed up by Tim's secretary. (b) Tim's Left-List: These are all the suggested names that were not used for object classes, but almost all of them turned up later somewhere in the project. Some turned out to be attributes, some were inputs and outputs to the system, some were subsumed by other classes, and so on. (c) Tim's candidate list, final version.

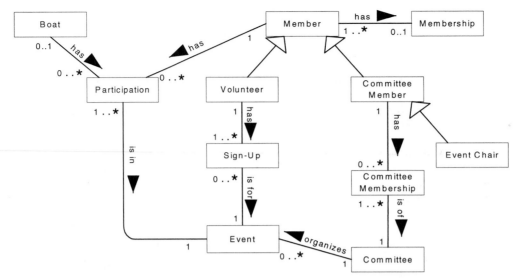

Figure 17-48 The final version of the class diagram, with subclasses. This is the same as Figure 17-39, reproduced here for convenience.

"And," Nancy went on, "we'll do this with every cell in the table. That way, we'll end up checking what happens to a member when they receive every kind of event while in every possible state. The table covers all possible combinations." So for the next little while, they argued and discussed, as the table filled up, until it looked like Figure 17-46. As you've no doubt already noticed, there was one cell left empty, in column M7, third row down.

"We've got an empty cell," observed Mike. "What do you suppose is the significance of that?

Geoff was looking back and forth at the statechart diagram and the STT on the board. "I think we're missing a transition in the statechart diagram," he announced. "What that empty cell is saying is, what happens when a Member in *State 2: Accepted*, or in other words, someone in good standing, experiences an *M7: Resigns* event? In other words, what happens when a normal Member resigns? Well, it seems to me they should go straight to *State 6: Quit*."

"And don't pass *Go*" added Peter, for which he received several pained looks.

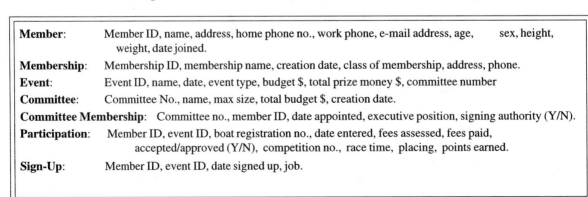

Figure 17-49 The "final" attribute list, as typed up by Tim's secretary.

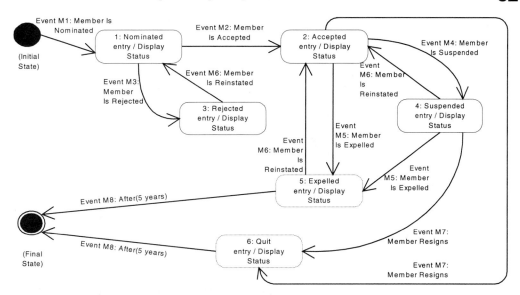

Figure 17-50   The final version of the statechart diagram for class Member

"Very good, Geoff," said Nancy, planting a big *6* in the cell in question. "That's just the kind of error this table is supposed to discover. And what about the statechart diagram?"

Diane jumped in. "We need an arrow from the 2 box to the 6 box, saying *M7: Member resigns*."

"Done!" announced Nancy, putting it in place to make the statechart diagram of Figure 17-50, which you'll find in the Deliverables section.

"But wait," said Alnoor. "Look at the third column, under *Rejected*. We don't have a number anywhere in that column! According to what we have there, a *Rejected* event would be ignored if the Member were in *State 3: Rejected*, and Impossible under any other circumstances! That can't be right, surely?"

"I can see that one," said June. "The second row down should have a *3* in it. If you look on the statechart diagram, you'll see that if some guy has been nominated, then obviously a Rejection will send him to the Rejected state, which is State 3."

"And there's another one, yet," called Tim from the back. "Look at the third column from the right, that's the M6: *Reinstated* column. We said that a rejected member could be reinstated, so the fourth row down, the *Rejected* row, should have a '*1*' in it."

Nancy looked at the board, saw that he was right, and added the '1.' Her STT now matched Figure 17-51, which you'll also find in the Deliverables section of this chapter. "And now," she announced, "The statechart diagram and STT are finished."

"What we'll do now with the statechart diagram is take each event and consider it to be an operation, or behavior, that the Member class is capable of. Just what happens in detail inside each one is something we'll need to sort out later. That can happen in the design phase, after we've finished with the analysis. There's something called an Action that we'll need to add to some of the states and transitions on the statechart diagram. These will show how a Member reacts to each transition, and the things the Member has to do as they enter and leave each state. And we'll use the use cases as further input for that process."

"For now, though, I think it's time we all went home to see if we still have a family!" And the group broke up, amidst a lot of discussion of what had transpired. You, the reader, can see the "final" list of operations in Figure 17-52, in the Deliverables section. This list is "final" in the sense that we don't intend to add any more to it during the analysis phase. More operations can be expected to turn up as we go, however, and we'll add them to the list as we find them.

At the next few meetings, the same procedures were repeated with a number of other classes from the class diagram. Eventually, a fairly detailed model emerged. "The model is not cast in stone," Nancy pointed out. "We can expect to find a few errors as we go, and we'll no doubt discover a few new things that we'll have to add later as we go."

. . . .

DELIVERABLES

In this section, I've gathered the final versions of the diagrams from the Yacht Club project. It's important to note that, since this book doesn't espouse any selected methodology, there may well be differences and omissions compared with the "guru books" and others. It's almost impossible to write a book that's actually methodology-free or methodology-independent, so what I've attempted to give you in this book, is enough to go out and do the work. By now, you're armed with enough skills, knowledge, and understanding to sit down with some users and get started.

If you're in a school or seminar situation, your instructor has probably referred you already to a more advanced book. If you're studying on your own, then I recommend that, either now or shortly, you should follow this up with one or more additional books, specifically those with tried and tested methodologies.

Events States	M1 Nominated	M2 Accepted	M3 Rejected	M4 Suspended	M5 Expelled	M6 Reinstated	M7 Resigns	M8 After (5 years)
Null (Initial State)	1	Impossible	Impossible	Impossible	Impossible	Impossible	Impossible	Ignore
1: Nominated	Ignore	2	3	Impossible	Impossible	Impossible	Ignore	Ignore
2: Accepted	Impossible	Ignore		4	5	Impossible	6	Ignore
3: Rejected	Impossible	Impossible	Ignore	Impossible	Impossible	1	Impossible	Ignore
4: Suspended	Impossible	Impossible	Impossible	Ignore	5	2	6	Ignore
5: Expelled	Impossible	Impossible	Impossible	Impossible	Ignore	2	Ignore	Ignore
6: Quit	Impossible	Impossible	Impossible	Impossible	Impossible	Impossible	Ignore	Final State

Figure 17-51   The completed state transition table for class Member (compare with Figure 17-46)

Operations for class Member		
create	attach	reinstate
nominate	detach	resign
accepted	join committee	update name, etc.
rejection	buy boat	add marina berth
register	suspension	cancel berth
sign up	expelled	

Figure 17-52   The "final" operation list for class member

The advantage to using a "guru methodology" or a purchased methodology is that it has been highly developed and evolved to state of completeness, by many people over time and through numerous projects. In addition, there's a large body of experience out there in that particular methodology, people you can turn to for help. For now, however, here are the diagrams (Figures 17.47 – 17.52) as we have them so far.

FURTHER READING

Now that you've had a whole lot of theory, and in this chapter some exposure to how things are done, you're ready to benefit from exploring the writings of the gurus, particularly those that focus on methodologies.

As I've mentioned before, The Three Amigos (Rumbaugh, Booch and Jacobson) have produced what are so far the definitive books on UML. They are complete, rigorous, and exhaustive, though characteristically somewhat difficult to read and learn from. Watch for my own set of UML "bibles"due out over the 2001 to 2003 timeframe. There will be a *Users Guide* and a *Complete Reference*, both written in *plain English*, with lots of real-world business and e-commerce examples.

In the meantime, you would do well to get copies of Booch et al. (1999), if you find that mine are not yet available.

For a guru methodology, read Jacobson et al. (1999), *The Unified Software Development Process,* which describes a methodology synthesized by The Three Amigos from their earlier ones, predominantly from Jacobson's older *Objectory* methodology.

Wirfs-Brock and others have also written methodology-specific books that would be well worth reading, if you have not already done so.

CHAPTER SUMMARY

For this chapter, the summary has already been looked after in the Deliverables section. The diagrams are shown in the order they were produced, so read carefully through them, looking up any mysteries back in the chapter.

Notice how long it took us to get to the coding! You will recall my comment in Chapter 3 about understanding the problem and *getting it right* before we begin building a solution.

Chapter Glossary

requirements definition The document that spells out what the eventual system must do, the information it must produce, and when and where, without dictating how it will be done.

archive state Where we don't expect the object to experience any more state changes, other than deletion.

What Comes Next

Now it's time to move on into design activities, such as prototyping user interfaces, choosing an ODBMS and designing an object-oriented database, and writing detailed specifications for the methods for all the classes. Finally, after all that, you can start coding!

Please feel free to e-mail me your opinions and your suggestions for future revisions of this book, at flykiw@home.com. Remember that my goal is to enhance people's learning and thus, in some small way, contribute to their productivity, prosperity, and I hope, their happiness. I sincerely hope I've been able to help you in some small way along the path to your goals.

Individual Exercises and Problems

Ex 17.1 On the class diagram in Figure 17-13, add an Event Type class, with subclasses, using an appropriate portion of Figure 17-24. Show with the associations the fact that dinners, since they're always catered, have no need for volunteers. Also show that bingos require an outside contractor and that concerts and art shows are always arranged with a performer, artist, or gallery.

Ex 17.2 Use cases:

(a) For this exercise, you must function both as user and analyst. Find some more use cases to add to Figure 17-13. Add at least one more actor as well.

(b) With one person in your group acting as user, develop three more use cases in full detail.

Ex 17.3 On the statechart diagram: What if a Member was to quit while in State 1, 3, or 5? Modify the statechart diagram to allow for this. Check by modifying the STT.

Ex 17.4 On the statechart diagram: What if a Member has quit already and is in State 6, and we decide to renominate her and put her through the whole acceptance procedure all over again? Modify the statechart diagram and STT to allow this.

Ex 17.5 Now that you've seen my version of a simple membership system, try it yourselves. Go through the analysis process with a club, church, or other group; a student club or association; or just with a few students or friends, if that's all that's available.

Present your results to the class on flip chart or slides and answer the following questions:

(a) How does your model differ from mine?

(b) What additional features or complications have you built into yours? What have you decided to leave out?

(c) For each additional feature, do a rough cost benefit estimation. What is the trade-off between the additional complexity, work, expense, time, and maintenance effort versus the additional benefit and the usefulness of the feature?

PROJECTS AND CASES

P17.1 Build a membership system:

(a) Take the Royal Korona Yacht Club membership system *requirements model* as it is developed in the chapter, along with your results from the exercises above, and from this develop a complete object-oriented design for a generic membership system that could be used by any sports or interest club, church, volunteer organization, or the like.

(b) Now, from your design, build and code this membership system in an object-oriented language. You may be able to get a trial copy of an ODBMS to use with it, but read the rules carefully that come with it, about resale and distribution of the final system. Since this is your design and your system, and not mine, feel free to market it, perhaps as shareware on the Net.

SELF-TEST QUESTIONS

Note: The Appendix has answers to the Self-Test Questions.

Q 17.1 The requirements model consists of four parts

(a) Use cases, interface descriptions, class diagram, and project scope

(b) Project scope, use cases, interface descriptions, and context diagram

(c) Data model, context diagram, class diagram, and project scope

(d) Project scope, use cases, class diagram, and context diagram

(e) Project scope, use cases, interface descriptions, and class diagra

Q 17.2 An actor

(a) Inherits a use case from a subclass and executes it

(b) Executes a use case and then inherits it to achieve a goal of the system

(c) Requests a particular use case by name, and executes it

(d) Interacts with the system by following the steps in a use case script

(e) All of the above

(f) None of the above

Q 17.3 An actor is

(a) A person who may be playing many roles at different times

(b) A function performed by a department

(c) A department

(d) A role played by one or more persons

(e) A role assigned to one or more persons during analysis

(f) All of the above

(g) None of the above

Q 17.4 List the eight factors to consider in preparing for FTS/JAD sessions for analysis, as discussed in the first part of the chapter.

Q 17.5 Explain the importance of the project scope. (State the four points that need to be included in it.)

Q 17.6 Define the following:

(a) Context diagram

(b) External entity

(c) actor

(d) Primary actor

(e) Secondary actor

(f) Use case

Q 17.7 A good use case model

(a) Should completely describe system behavior

(b) Tells us the things the eventual system must be able to do

(c) Models the interactions between the users and the software

(d) Must be developed in conjunction with knowledgeable users

(e) None of the above

(f) All of the above

Q 17.8 List the KRB Seven Steps for building an object class diagram and state the deliverable from each step:

	Step	**Deliverable**
(i)	_____	_____
(ii)	_____	_____
(iii)	_____	_____
(iv)	_____	_____
(v)	_____	_____
(vi)	_____	_____
(vii)	_____	_____

Q 17.9 In brainstorming:
(a) Only good ideas are recorded.

(b) Evaluation of ideas begins immediately and is continued in the next step.

(c) People contribute better when highly stressed and motivated.

(d) You should shut down people with useless or frivolous ideas, so they don't get us off track.

(e) All of the above.

(f) Some of the above.

(g) None of the above.

Q 17.10 A state is
(a) A condition to be satisfied before execution

(b) A condition for an existence criterion

(c) A condition or way of being or existing

(d) A condition to be set before or during a transition.

(e) A condition needed for transitioning

(f) A geographical or jurisdictional area

Q 17.11 Which of the following is not a true statement?

(a) Users will sometimes have different opinions about the definition.

(b) When misunderstandings occur, they can be resolved by referring to the definitions.

(c) We must end up with a clear definition for each class and ensure that everyone understands and accepts it.

(d) Sometimes an identifier and definition are not enough to show that this is a class of interest.

(e) If it's a class, then its instances must carry some data and be capable of some behavior.

(f) The question to ask the users is: "How do we tell one of these from another?"

(g) None of the above.

Q 17.12 An association is

(a) A line on an object class diagram

(b) Represented by the noun that describes the interaction

(c) An interaction between instances of two classes

(d) Often M:M and occasionally 1:M

(e) Often M:M and never 1:M.

(f) Often 1:1 and occasionally 1:M

Q 17.13 Multiplicity

(a) Tells how many behaviors an instance can be involved with

(b) *Isakinda* sin.

(c) Tells how many associations an instance can be involved in

(d) Tells how many users can be involved in the association before it becomes sinful

(e) All of the above

(f) None of the above

Q 17.14 Associations can

(a) Be described by *isa* or *isakinda*

(b) Be described by adjectives

(c) Be based on events

(d) Be described by role names

(e) Have a 1:M component

(f) Be described by verbs

(g) All of the above

(h) Some of the above

(i) None of the above

Q 17.15 Each candidate class must be subjected to three questions, to determine whether it's a class that is important to our project. What are the three questions?

Question 1: _____

Question 2: _____

Question 3: _____

Q 17.16 A transition is

(a) A change in the value of one or more attributes

(b) A change in the way something is

(c) A passage from one state to another

(d) All of the above

(e) Some of the above

(f) None of the above

Q 17.17 An event is

(g) Something that causes a transition

(h) A noteworthy happening

(i) Caused by an important transition

(j) (a) and (b)

(k) (b) and (c)

(l) (a) and (c)

Answers to End-of-Chapter Exercises

Chapter 2

Q 2.1 i, Q 2.2 f

Chapter 3

Q 3.1 f, Q 3.2 a, Q 3.3.d, Q 3.4 e, Q 3.5 e, Q 3.6 d

Q 3.7 A model is a **simplified representation** of a **complex** reality, usually for the purpose of **understanding** that reality, and having all the **features** of that reality necessary for the **current** task or **problem** Modeling is actually a form of **abstraction**

Q 3.8 The **strength** of the object-oriented modeling methods is that objects are one of the **fundamental** ways that humans **organize** their **experience**

Q 3.9 The systems **development** life **cycle** consists of a number of **steps** or **phases**:

Q 3.10 In the **analysis** phase, we study the users' business and their **problems**, to discover what the users **need** the **system** to do It produces a **requirements definition** that spells out what the system must do and the **information** it must produce, without dictating **how**

Q 3.11 In the design phase, we produce a **plan** or **design** showing how the system will do the **functions** identified in **analysis** Here, we consider hardware – software platform, choice of **language**, operating system, and **database management software** (DBMS)

Q 3.12 In the **construction** phase, the **programs** are written and the **databases** are built Then the whole system is **tested** and **debugged**

Q 3.13 The Implementation phase is where the system is **installed**, the users are **trained**, and a **parallel** run is performed

Q 3.14 In the **maintenance** phase, we handle **program bugs**, design errors, and things the users **forgot** **Enhancements** come throughout the life of the system

Q 3.15 Earlier methodologies focused on business **processes** Object modeling first considers the **data** in terms of objects, things people need to **know about** – that is, the **real-world** objects that they need to keep **data** about

Q 3.16 Analysis modeling forces us to **spend time** with the users **up front** There is a need to **identify** the **problem** before we look for a **solution** A brilliant **solution** to the wrong **problem** will not do

Q 3.17 With object-oriented methods, there is much **reuse** of program code The resources spent on **maintenance** are sharply **reduced** by **getting** it **right** the **first** time

Q 3.18 **Functional** decomposition: Breaking a business **process** into **smaller** functions

Q 3.19 **Data** flow diagram: A **process** model diagram showing business **processes** and the **data** that they use and pass among themselves Also shows **data stores** and external **entities**

Chapter 4

Q 4.1 e, Q 4.5 f, Q 4.2 b, Q 4.6 e, Q 4.3 f, Q 4.7 f, Q 4.4.e, Q 4.8 f

Q 4.9 A paradigm **shift** occurs when we adopt a **radically different** way of organizing all or part of our world**view**

Q 4.10 Entity-**relationship** diagrams (ERDs) are **data** models An ERD shows:
- The **entities** (things, **nouns**) in the users' **world** about which they need to store **information**

- The **structure** of the users' data in terms of the **associations** (actions, **verbs**) that link the **entity** types

Q 4.11   Object-oriented model: By taking an **entity** type and adding to it the exclusive **processes** that **manipulate** the data in that entity, we create an object Besides all the benefits of **data** and **process** modeling, object modeling gives us powerful new **features** such as **encapsulation**, inheritance, and **polymorphism**

Q 4.12   Out of the **universe** of all real-world **data**, our system is concerned with a **subset**, the data in the **business area** we're studying The ERD is a tool to **understand** and **document** this data The ERD also is a **template** for designing the **databases**

Q 4.13   An association is a line joining two **entities**; the verb goes **above** or beside the line with an arrowhead, and/or **role** names go **below** the line Entity–verb–entity should make a sentence Multiplicity (cardinality) is shown as **digit** (usually "1") and/or a **star** for many at each end of the **line**

Q 4.14   The Object **Management** Group (OMG) and Object **Data Management** Group (ODMG) are doing valuable work on compatibility **standards**

Q 4.15   Objects are **entities** (things that carry **data**) with **behavior** (**operations**) added These **operations** exclusively **access** and **manipulate** the data **carried** by an object – that is, **no other program code** can touch the data

Q 4.16   The only way that a **program** can read or **change** the **data** carried by an object or **access** it in any way at all, is by invoking one of the **pieces of program code** that the object also carries within itself

Q 4.17   Transient objects are created by OOPLs in **RAM** and **do not survive** beyond the **current session** **Persistent** objects are stored by a **database** (ODBMS) and **do survive** beyond the **current session**

Q 4.18   Because of the **learning** curve for object-oriented **thinking**, as well as new languages and things, the **reuse benefits** only become significant on about the **third** or **fourth** object-oriented project

Q 4.19   There are four styles of models: conceptual, functional, **logical**, and **physical**

Q 4.20   A **conceptual** model is a representation of the users' business in terms of their **conception** of how it operates It's an **overview** of the business operation at a high level of **abstraction**

Q 4.21   A **functional** model shows all parts and aspects of the **users' operation** that they're aware of, including some that are **hidden** from them

Q 4.22   A logical model shows what a system must **do** or have, without regard for **how** it is to be **done**, built, or represented

Q 4.23   A **physical** model is the final **design** document, a **plan** showing **how** things will be **done** or built

Q 4.24   Deliverables from each phase are the **documents** and other products generated during each **phase** and **subphase** of the project and whose production marks the **completion** of the phase

Chapter 5

Q 5.1 b, Q 5.3 d, Q 5.2 c, Q 5.4 a

Q 5.11 Vendor ct; Booking cl; Transaction ev; Product ct; Loan cl; Ownership st; Registration ev; Shoe ct; Withdrawal ev; Department cl

Q 5.12   An object in the real world is a **thing**, and data about it is carried by its corresponding **data object** An object is an **entity** with behavior A **data object** is thus an **abstraction** of the real-world object, carrying the **data** describing it and the program code that is the only **allowable access** to that data

Q 5.13   Entity **objects** are the basic **objects** and classes that we find during **analysis** of the users' business **Interface** objects are used to handle communication between the **system** and the **users** or other systems Control objects are created during Analysis to give us somewhere to put **methods** that don't easily fit into **interface** objects or **entity** objects The **entity/interface**/control split improves maintenance and **stability** by giving greater **encapsulation**

Q 5.14   **Attributes** are the data values carried by objects We gain **stability** when the data is organized around the objects it **truly describes** (normalization)

Q 5.15   Using objects gives **seamless** transitions from one phase of the **ODLC** to the next, with no loss of data owing to changes of **notation** Objects give **traceability**, allowing us to follow a feature from an object in one **phase** of the **ODLC** to the same object in the diagrams from another **phase**

Q 5.16   Identity is the property that says two things are **different**, that they're not **both the same thing** Two things that are identical are not **both the same thing** even if everything about them is the same **Identifiers** such as names, **numbers**, or **OIDs** are used as **evidence** of identity

Q 5.17   By giving an object a piece of **program code** that makes it do something (such as **appear** on the **screen**), we've given it a **behavior** It exhibits that **behavior** in response to a message sent by another object or a **user** The **result** of the **behavior** (the "answer") is returned

Q 5.17   Encapsulation is the forming of a "**crisp**" **boundary** or shell with a "**narrow** interface" to allow communication across the **boundary** Encapsulation reduces **complexity**, and increases system **stability** by reducing the **ripple** effects of changes Encapsulation allows us to use an object by understanding the **published interface** We don't need to know its **inner workings** in order to **use** it effectively

Q 5.18   Encapsulation allows us to make changes **within** the object without affecting any of the **programs** or functions that use it We've **localized** the effects of change Similarly, we can make changes **outside** the object – that is, we can change the **ways** we use it, without needing to change the **object itself**

Q 5.20   Violating **encapsulation** can occasionally be **beneficial** but is **fraught** with **danger**

Q 5.21   At any **moment**, an object exists in a certain **manner** or condition, which we say is its **state** If the object **changes**, we say it has undergone a **transition** into a new **state**

Q 5.22   A class is a **group** of objects with similar **properties** (attributes), common behavior (**operations**), common **associations** to other objects, and common **semantics** (meaning)

Q 5.23   We use classes so that the **internal structure** of the system will closely match the **structure** of the users' **world**

Q 5.24   An instance that belongs to a **subclass** automatically and **simultaneously** belongs also to the superclass An instance of the **subclass** has all the **attributes** and **behaviors** that are defined for that subclass It also **inherits** all the attributes and methods that are defined for the **superclass**

Q 5.25   Part of the definition of object-oriented is that an OOPL or an ODBMS supports classes, **subclasses**, **inheritance**, and **polymorphism**

Q 5.26   The **first** step of object-oriented development is finding the significant **classes** in the **real world**

Q 5.27   **Entity** classes are the ones found in the **real world** and incorporated in the class diagram

Q 5.28   Abstract classes, which have no **direct instances**, are often introduced at design time to exploit **inheritance** and **polymorphism**

Q 5.29   Associations are modeled by **verbs** that express what one kind of object **does** to another kind In UML, an association can also be described by a **role name**

Chapter 6

Q 6.1 d, Q 6.2 f, Q 6.3 c, Q 6.4 External entities

Q 6.5 A use case represents a **script** that 'someone' could follow to **use** the system

Q 6.6. An actor is a person, an organization, or another system that can **initiate and/or follow** a Use Case, thus making use of one or more **features** of the system

Q 6.10   In the object-oriented **design** (**OOD**) phase, we modify the **analysis** models to reflect decisions made about the environment that the system will function in

Q 6.11   The object paradigm has a consistent **notation** for all phases of the OODLC, leading to **smoother** transitions and reduced **information** loss between phases

Q 6.12   Match these definitions Note that some will match more than once, and some are meaningless

(a)	Operational feasibility:	(iii)	Will it do the job being asked for ?
(b)	Management feasibility:		Meaningless!
(c)	Schedule feasibility:	(ii)	Can it be done in the time allowed?
(d)	Economic feasibility:	(i)	Will it pay for itself?
(e)	Technical feasibility	(iv)	Do we have the hardware and software?
		(vi)	Have we the knowledge we need?
(f)	Organizational feasibility	(v)	Will it work in this company?

Q 6.13   Operational and **econom**ic issues often conflict The "**perfect**" system may also be the most **expensive**, and thus it may not be possible to justify it on **economic** grounds

Q 6.14   Opportunity **cost** is the **unrealized** benefit from a project that is **denied**, when choosing to **invest** in one project over another

Q 6.15   The object-oriented development life cycle consists of **OOA**, OOD, **OOP**, object-oriented testing, and **maintenance** The **maintenance** phase is made up of all the previous activities

Q 6.16   All methodologies involve repeated **iteration** through the cycle

Q 6.17   In analysis we model the users' requirements for **what** the system must do A conceptual **analysis** model, consists of these **deliverables**: the requirements model, the **feasibility** analysis, the object model, the statechart diagram model

Q 6.18   The requirements model consists of four closely related **parts**:
- The project **scope** says in general terms what the system will **do**, what **functions** will be part of it, and which users it will **service** It will also state what **will not** be part of the system
- The **context** diagram shows our system as a single box, surrounded by smaller boxes representing **external entities**, which are people, **organizations**, **systems**, and other things **outside** our system that either **provide** data to the system or **draw data** from it
- Jacobson's **Use Case** model describes a case of the usage of the system by an **Actor** Each **use case** represents a **script** that an **Actor** could follow to make use of the system
- There will be **Interface Descriptions** for user interfaces and interfaces to other **systems**

Q 6.19   An **actor** is a person, organization, or another system that can **initiate** an instance of a **use case**, thus making **use** of one or more features of the system

Q 6.20   The object model, or **class** diagram, is sometimes referred to as the **data model** or the **information model** It consists of the **entity** classes – the classes found in the users' **real world**

Q 6.21   The statechart diagram is for examining the **life cycle** of an object to discover what it **does** An object is **created**, goes through the steps of its various **tasks**, and is finally **deleted** It moves from one **state** to another as it lives its **life cycle**

Q 6.22   The **events** that trigger **transitions** from **state** to **state**, along with certain behavior that goes with each state and transition, help us to discover all the operations of a class

Q 6.23   In the design phase, we modify the **analysis** models to reflect **decisions** made about the **environment** that the system will function in This includes **hardware** and **software** decisions, optimization issues such as **response times**, and so on

Q 6.24   The **design** models include a number of new **classes** that don't directly **model** anything from the real world, such as **control objects** Some of these are added for **machine** efficiency, others for programming **simplicity** and **code reuse**

Q 6.25   In the construction phase, we build the **databases** and screens, and write the **program code** The **classes** from **earlier** models stick around, and are **traceable** all the way to the **OOPL** or ODBMS

Q 6.26   The feasibility Study must look at the four **criteria** to decide whether we should **go ahead** and do (or **finish**) the project

Q 6.27   **Operational** feasibility: The first thing we need to check is that if we build the system, will it actually **work in practice**? We must answer these three questions:

- Will it do the **job** being asked for?
- Will it **work** in this **company**?
- Is it **worth** the effort to find a **solution**?

Q 6.28 Technical **feasibility**: Do we have the **hardware**, the software and the **technical know-how** to do it?

Q 6.29 **Schedule feasibility**: Can it be done in the **time** allowed?

Q 6.30 **Economic feasibility**: Will it pay for itself?

Q 6.31 **Economic** feasibility is referred to as the cost–**benefit** analysis, since it must determine whether the **lifetime benefits** from building the system outweigh the **lifetime costs** of the system

Q 6.32   The **bottom line** is that the dollar value of the **annual benefits** from the system (AB = TB + IB) over the **expected** years of **life** of the system (L) must exceed the total of **development costs** (D) plus the annual **operating costs** (AOC) over the expected **lifetime**

$$L * (TB + IB) >= D + L * AOC$$

Q 6.33   **Tangible** benefits (TB) can easily be **quantified**

Q 6.34   **Intangible** benefits (IB) are nebulous and not at all easy to **quantify** Note that AB = TB + IB

Chapter 7

Q 7.1 d, Q 7.2 e

Q 7.3
Attendees:	All levels
Recording analyst:	Knowledgeable filter
User majority:	Avoid 'blinding with science '
Distractions:	None allowed
Background:	Do your homework
Environment:	Your place or neutral
Scheduling:	Sufficient time, in advance
Confirmation:	Day before first meeting

Q 7.4   (i) What the eventual system will do
(ii) What functions will be part of the system
(iii) Which users it will service
(iv) What won't be part of the system

Q 7.5 (a) In the Context Diagram, we show our system as a single box in the center of the page, and we use arrows to show data flowing into and out of it This "black-box" approach allows us to concentrate on the external relationships our system has with the world outside itself Surrounding the box, we show the external entities, and what happens inside the system will be shown with the use cases

Q 7.5 (b), (c): See glossary, Chapter 7.

Q 7.6   To be **successful** in any project, we need to approach the tasks with the **attitude** that we'll do whatever is **necessary** to carry out a successful analysis This includes much **attention** to the **people** side of systems analysis

Q 7.7   The models must reflect the **users' views** and viewpoints and should document the **users' knowledge** of their business, and not what we the analysts **may think**

Q 7.8   You need a **range** of users, covering all **levels** and all parts of the **business** area you're modeling Invite some **management**, as senior as possible, to give **credibility** in the minds of the more junior users

Q 7.9   Designate a person who **understands** the process to be recording **analyst** An **experienced** user is OK Meet at **your** premises, where you **control** the environment, or at **neutral** premises or a **retreat**; all are preferable to meeting at the **users' place**

Q 7.10   Research the **user** group, its structure, **function**, and **reporting relationships**; research its **jargon**, terminology, **abbreviations**, and the like, which you can get from glossaries, **training** documents, introductory **brochures**, and annual **reports**

Q 7.11   State the **business objectives** of this **business** area first, and then check to ensure that the **objectives** of the system harmonize

Q 7.12   The project scope is a **statement** of the system's objectives The project scope is a **statement** of what the project is to **produce** It says in general terms what the **eventual** system will do, and which **users** it will service The project scope must also state what will **not** be part of the system

Q 7.13 The **context** diagram shows how the system relates to the **world** beyond itself It models the **flows** of **data** to and from the **external entities** our system must interact with

Q 7.14 The **objective** of the use case model is to **document** what **functions** the system should offer to the users The purpose is to construct the **developers' view** of what the users want and to provide a starting point for discovering the **object classes** and the **operations** for each **class**

Q 7.15 Check all the ways that all the **actors** interact with the **system** to describe the complete **behavior** of the **system** From this , we'll identify both **classes** and **operations** for the object model

Q 7.16 From our context diagram, we can get a first pass at a list of **actors** Each **external entity** may become an **actor**, although **actors** are more than just this

Q 7.17 Go through the list of **use cases**, and for each one validate the **name** and write a **narrative** description

Q 7.18 The **interfaces** to a system . . main categories: human **interfaces** and **interfaces** to other **systems**

Q 7.19 You may use the use cases for **prototyping**, with dummy **screens** in the correct **sequence**, and later use them for **testing**

Chapter 8

Q 8.1 *Polymorphism* means "occurring in various forms" Polymorphism is the ability to write several versions of a method (function, subroutine) in different classes of a subclass hierarchy, give them all exactly the same name, and rely on the object-oriented environment to establish which version should be executed depending on the class of the target object when the method is invoked

Q 8.3 *Early binding* or *static binding* is when we store the methods as partially compiled object code, which is then linked into the program at compile time Late binding or dynamic binding is when we store the methods as binary executable code in the database, which at run time is executed directly from the database

Q 8.4 *Overriding*: A subclass version of an attribute or operation is said to override the version from the superclass, because it's used in preference to the superclass version for that subclass and its descendants

Resolving polymorphism: Object-oriented compilers are designed so that each object normally has access only to the program code written in that class But if an operation is requested for which there's no method in that class, then in effect the compiler walks up the tree of superclasses until it finds a class that does have a method by that name This is the method (subroutine) that then gets executed.   Q 8.5 b, Q 8.6 d

Q 8.7 A concrete class can have no abstract operations because it would have no program code to execute for those operations when they're invoked on its own direct instances.   Q 8.8.d

Q 8.9 **Polymorphism** means a behavior may be **inherited** unchanged, or it may be **different** between the parent and child classes, and this allows us to **specialize** a behavior for particular subclasses

Q 8.10 A **concrete** class cannot have **abstract** operations, since there is no **program code** to perform these operations on its **direct instances**

Q 8.11 With an object class library, you can change either the **data definitions** or the **methods** by defining a subclass that **inherits** from a class in the library You may extend the library by redefining the **attributes** or **methods** in new subclasses or by adding new ones You don't need the **library source code**

Q 8.12 *Abstract* classes have no **direct instances**, and are often introduced to exploit **inheritance** and **polymorphism**

Q 8.13 Some object-oriented products store the methods as object code, linked at **compile** time This is referred to as **early**, or **static**, binding

Q 8.14 We say a language **supports** a feature if it is **easy** and convenient for programmers to **use** the feature

Chapter 9

Q 9.1 and 9.2

The Seven Steps	Deliverables
Step 1: Candidate classes	List of candidate classes of interest
Step 2: Define classes	List of definitions
Step 3: Establish relationships	Conceptual class model
Step 4: Expand many-to-many	Logical class modelrelationships
Step 5: Attributes	Attribute lists
Step 6: Normalization	"Normalized" class model
Step 7: Operations (behavior)	Operation lists

Q 9.3 d

Q 9.4   Question 1:   Definition," What is a ____?"
Question 2:   Unique Identifier," How do we tell one of these from another?"
Question 3:   Sample Attributes," What might we need to know about one of these?"

Q 9.5 g, Q 9.6 c, Q 9.7 a

Q 9.8 Wait for it! It's *Cardinal Sin*! Yes, believe it or not! Jaime (pronounced "*Hy*'-mee") Cardinal Sin is Philippine-born of Chinese descent, hence the Spanish first name and Chinese family name The Monsignor, who distinguished himself, and indeed became something of a hero, in his opposition to the excesses of the regime of dictator Ferdinand Marcos, revels in puns on his own name and rank He refers to his residence as "The House of Sin" I'm not certain of the *multiplicity* of his family reunions, but I'm sure that the house at those times is definitely Sin-full

Q 9.9   c

Q 9.11   The four methods we mentioned for interviewing users to discover classes:
- Client interviews
- From the requirements model and documentation
- Brainstorming
- The Delphi Method

Q 9.12   Here are some methods for interviewing users to discover classes:
- **interview users** to get the basics, then on your own develop the model Bring the model back to the **users** for **verification, often**
- Scan all your **documentation**, and other **documents** describing users' operation, for **nouns** and list them out
- **Brainstorm** in two **phases, generating** a list of **ideas** and then **evaluating** them
- **Meet with**, or **send** a **memo** to, each participant and get them to write a list of **candidate classes** Then combine the lists and circulate the complete list to all of them for **additions Repeat**

Chapter 10

Q 10.1 c, Q 10.6 e, Q 10.2 d, Q 10.7 d, Q 10.3 a, Q 10.8 a, Q 10.4 , Q 10.9 g (i e , c and e), Q 10.5 f

Q 10.10   At any **moment**, an **object** exists in a certain **state** If anything about the object **changes**, we say it has undergone a **transition** into a new state

Q 10.11   Most objects have a **pattern** of **states** they go through This pattern depends on the **class** of the object; all objects in a **class** have the same **pattern**

Q 10.12   An object moves from one **state** to another in response to an **event**, either from the outside world or from another object within the system

Q 10.13   Not all transitions are **physically** or **legally** possible; only the **permissible** ones are modeled

Q 10.14   An *object life* cycle consists of the various **states** that it may **transition** through, the **permissible** transitions, and the **sequencing** of those as it progresses from **creation** to **disposal** The life cycle includes **actions** that go with each **state** and **transition**

Q 10.15   A state **exists** from one **event**, which caused the **transition** *in*, until another **event** causes a transition **out** of the state Thus, a state has a **duration**

Q 10.16   State transition tables (STTs) can have only these entries:
(a) New state
(b) Impossible
(c) Ignored
(d) Deferred

Chapter 11

Q 11.1 f Q 11.4 e Q 11.2 a Q 11.5 e Q 11.3 e Q 11.6 f

Q 11.7   If a **service** exists, then that implies a **responsibility** to provide that **service** to **someone**

Q 11.8   **Services** are provided by one **object** to another in a   **client–server**   relationship

Q 11.9   A **contract** is "a list of **services** that an **instance** of one **class** can **request** from an **instance** of another **class** "

Q 11.10   A **collaboration** is a request from a **client** to a **server** for a **service** that helps the **client** fulfill one of its own **responsibilities**

Q 11.11   Follow each **use case** through, as the **actor** transacts with the **system** At each step, identify which **classes** are being **queried** or **updated**

Q 11.12   An object that receives **input data** has a responsibility to **validate** the **data**, to report **errors** to the **actor**, and to allow **corrections**

Q 11.13   Each **prompt** represents input, so some **class** has the responsibility of **receiving** and **validating** it

Q 11.14   Many classes will have few **attributes** and **responsibilities** Some will have too many and thus too much **power** and **intelligence**

Q 11.15   Where a few powerful **classes** have large shares of the **attributes** and **intelligence**, they're less **reusable** **Bigger** means less **portable**

Chapter 12

Q 12.1 e Q 12.4 f Q 12.2 d Q 12.5 b Q 12.3 d

Q 12.6   To reduce the **complexity** problem in managing **large projects**, we use **subsystems**, or **packages**, which are a form of **encapsulation**

Q 12.7   A subsystem (or **package**) is a group of **classes, subsystems**, and so on, that have a well-defined, small **interface** to the rest of the **system** and are treated as a **unit**

Q 12.8   Wirfs-Brock defines a subsystem as a "set of **classes** (and possibly other subsystems) **collaborating** to fulfill a set of **responsibilities** "

Q 12.9   The subsystem boundary disappears at **execution** time

Q 12.10   While there is much **interaction** among the classes **within** a **subsystem**, there are **minimal interactions** and **dependencies** across its boundary

Q 12.11   Miller's research says most people can only handle "**Seven, Plus or Minus Two**" pieces of data at a time, and get confused with more than that

Q 12.12   Interactions include:
- Associations
- **Events** from one state machine to another
- Messages passed to an **object**, from an **actor** or from another **object**
- Responsibilities

Q 12.13   Interactions are dependencies, in the sense that a **responsibility** implies that one **class depends** on another to get **something done**

Q 12.14   There are certain points in analysis where you should pause to **divide** your **system** into **subsystems**, although insights may occur any time It saves time and money if we decide **early**
- Before you **begin**
- System **architecture** definition
- The systems **request** document
- Completion of **requirements analysis**
- The **class** diagram
- During behavior analysis
- **Completion** of analysis
- The **design** phase

Q 12.15   Subsystems also improve the **accuracy** of your project **estimates**

Q 12.16   By inspecting the **diagrams**, you can often see which **subsystems** must be developed **before** another One subsystem needs **data** or **services** from another, so must be developed **later**

Q 12.17   Authors have used different names for **subsystems**:
- **subjects** (Coad and Yourdon)
- **domains** (Shlaer and Mellor)
- **subassemblies** (Firesmith)
- **packages** (Jacobson, UML)

Q 12.18   Subsystems are a **vertical** division of a system, and layers are a **horizontal** division of the project (or a part of the system)

Chapter 13

Q 13.1 a, Q 13.4 g, Q 13.2 c, Q 13.5 d, Q 13.3 f,

Q 13.6:   (a) 3,   (b) 1,   (c) 2

P Q 13.7 b, Q 13.12 d, Q 13.8 e, Q 13.13.e, Q 13.9 c, Q 13.14 f, Q 13.10 g, Q 13.15 e, Q 13.11 a, Q 13.16 f

Q 13.17   Your design must be in a **form** such that the **users** can **understand** and **critique** all the **nontechnical** parts

Q 13.18   Both **interobject concurrency**, where different objects are all **working** at the **same time**, and **intraobject** concurrency, with many things happening at once **within** an object are significant

Q 13.19   By reducing **complexity**, more users **understand**; we get better information, cooperation, and user ownership, **critical success factors** for any project

Q 13.20   Plan for **language** and environment purchase, delivery, installation, **testing**, and **training** with or before analysis Allow for **problems** and **delays**

Q 13.21   **Pure** object languages In Smalltalk, **everything** is an object **Java** is totally object-oriented Eiffel is another one The downside is the need for **training** and **experience**

Q 13.22   **Extended** languages Object-oriented features are **added**; examples are Object Pascal and C++ The advantage is an existing **base** of **programmers** The downside is the ability to **violate encapsulation** and to write **old-style** code in the new language

Q 13.23   Compare languages on factors such as strength of **typing**, **execution speed**, and **memory management** Java is fast, **strongly** typed, and does its own automatic **garbage collection**

Q 13.24   Serious **ODBMSs** now have the heavy-duty "**industrial-strength**" features to handle **concurrency**, **transactions**, rollbacks, **distributed objects**, and security for mission-critical applications, as do current **RDBMSs**

Q 13.25   The Object **Management** Group (OMG) has been formed to develop **standards** for **object** request **brokers** (ORBs) An ORB intercepts messages from an object, **translates** them, and **routes** them to the correct **object**, wherever it may be

Q 13.26   The OMG is producing a **standard**, rather than **products** OMG certifies compliance to that **standard**, which describes the **architecture** for the ORB, that is, the **common object request broker architecture** (CORBA)

Q 13.27   With "software **components**," a designer will use as many **off-the-shelf** "parts" as possible

Q 13.28   Repeated reuse reduces the **size** and **complexity** of class libraries, makes **browsing** simpler and more **effective**

Q 13.29   Intelligent **agent** ("software robot"): an intelligent **object**, capable of **independent existence**, designed to perform a certain set of **functions**, and carrying the necessary **data** within itself

Q 13.30   Since design is producing a **plan** for the system, it's also the right time to produce **detailed plans** for testing the system Document and save your **use cases** to be **test cases**

Q 13.31   **Unstructured** testing means trying a few **use cases** and **fixing crashes** or inaccuracies Only a **small** percentage of developers take a **systematic approach** and **test all possibilities**

Q 13.32   Later, in the **coding/construction phase**, you'll **code** a **test suite**, to invoke the unit and run **all** the tests

Q 13.33   Frequent reuse cannot **guarantee** the **entire** class has been exercised When a class is **reused**, you must retest it **completely** Often we find **incompatibilities**, or missing or **inadequate** behavior, in the new environment

Q 13.34 Testing must be **automated** Have a **test suite** in place to run all the tests **automatically**, so that reusers can **retest** the class **completely** Include **predicted** test results and automate **comparisons** of **actual** against **predicted** results The test program must be **updated** every time the class is **modified**

Q 13.35 If not **planned** in design, testing may be **skipped** or neglected under pressure of **meeting deadlines** in later phases Testing must **happen**, even under **deadline pressure**

Q 13.36 Teams who thought they were "**excruciatingly thorough**" exercise only **one third** to **one half** of the statements in a program

Q 13.37 Recommendation: Spend between **5%** and **10%** of the total development cost on all forms of documentation, both the "**external**" and "**internal** "

Chapter 14

Q 14.1 Acronyms Used in This Book Here is a list of acronyms used in this book, in alphabetical order You'll find all the ones from the question here, as well as a few extra

ANSI	American National Standards Institute
BLOB	Binary Large Object
CAD	Computer-Assisted Drafting
CADD	Computer-Assisted Drafting and Design
CAM	Computer-Assisted Manufacturing
CLOS	Common Lisp Object System
CODASYL	Committee for Data Systems Languages
CORBA	Common Object Request Broker Architecture
DCL	Data Control Language
DDL	Data Definition Language
DFD	Data Flow Diagram
DML	Data Management Language
ERD	Entity-Relationship Diagram
GIS	Geographic Information System
IDL	Interactive Development Language
ISO	International Standards Organization
MIS	Management Information Systems
NICE	Nonprofit International Consortium for Eiffel
OCL	Object Control language
ODBMS	Object Database Management System
ODL	Object Definition Language
ODMG	Object Data Management Group
OLE	Object Linking and Embedding
OML	Object Management Language
O-O	Object-Oriented
OOA	Object-Oriented Analysis
OOA&D	Object-Oriented Analysis and Design
OOD	Object-Oriented Design
ODBMS	Object-Oriented Database Management System
OOP	Object-Oriented Programming
OOPL	Object-Oriented Programming Language
OOPS	Object-Oriented Programming System
OOT	Object-Oriented Technology
OQL	Object Query Language
ORB	Object Request Broker
OSQL	Object Structured Query Language
RAM	Random-Access Memory
RDBMS	Relational Database Management System
SQL	Structured Query Language
TLA	Three-Letter Acronym

NICE is the one not used in this chapter

Q 14.2 a

Q 14.3 DML 6 OML 3 DDL 1 ODL 5 DCL 7 OCL 7 SQL 4 OQL 2

Q 14.4 1: SmallTalk is the *GOOD*, 2: C++ is the *BAD*, 3: OOCOBOL is the *UGLY*

Q 14.5 b, Q 14.8 i, Q 14.6 g, Q 14.9 b, Q 14.7 e, Q 14.10 f (i.e., a + b + c)

Q 14.11 A data **definition** language (DDL) is used to **design** and build the database, with syntax to create a **schema**, and to define **integrity** conditions and so on An ODL must also handle **metnods**, complex **attributes**, and subclass relationships, along with **inheritance** and **polymorphism**

Q 14.12 A data management language (DML) is for day-to-day **adding, deleting**, changing, and then **retrieving** the data values in the database

Q 14.13 A *complete* **database language** must have **DDL, DML** and **DCL**, whether it's conventional or object-oriented The object-oriented ones are **ODL, OML**, and **OCL**

Q 14.14 **Garbage collection** involves deleting unwanted **instances** and frees up **RAM** to be **reclaimed** and **reused**

Q 14.15 **Dynamic (late)** binding means **smaller** but perhaps **slower** executables

Q 14.16 ISO/ANSI **Ada** 95 is truly object-oriented, with **dynamic typing** and **abstract** classes, a core language, with standardized **class libraries** (*annexes*), subsystems, and several different models of multiple **inheritance**

Q 14.17 Benchmarks designed for **RDBMSs** are **inadequate** for object-oriented databases Data is **organized differently** and requires different access **Joins** are a bottleneck in RDBMSs and will be in "**extended relational**" ODBMSs

Chapter 15

Q 15.1 d, Q 15.2 b, Q 15.3 g, Q 15.4 c, Q 15.5 f, Q 15.6 d, Q 15.7 d, Q 15.8 e, Q 15.9 e, Q 15.10 h, Q 15.11 f, Q 15.12 d, Q 15.13 h, Q 15.14 b , Q 15.15 a, Q 15.16 e

Q 15.17 The **farther** down this list, the more people **understand** their own **software development processes**

Q 15.18 Do your **investigations** and **decision** making early Get the **training** and **consultants** early

Q 15.19 Choose your **OOPL** and **ODBMS** carefully Make sure their architecture and **features** really do fit your needs

Q 15.20 The first and second projects will cost about **30%** more, the **third** and on will save money

Q 15.21 **Train** for new skills, but have outside **consultants** who are truly experienced in OOT These will guide and **manage** the project, and **nurture** and **mentor** staff Train your staff in **people skills**

Q 15.22 The ideal team size for a **pilot project** is around **seven**

Q 15.23 Some companies have **lost** people who couldn't handle OOT **Careful** choice **minimizes** this loss You need **flexible** and **adaptable** pilot-team members, well supported, including **adequate training**

Q 15.24 Team needs extensive **training**, for **methodology**, OOPL, **ODBMS**, and so on Also, OOA&D **books** and **courses** should be provided **Everybody** needs *this* book

Q 15.25 Mentors **assist** and support Initially, **external consultants**, then **pilot-team** members, **mentor** other developers on early production projects

Q 15.26 Choose **three** pilots The first two will **take longer** with OOT

Q 15.27 Keep a **low profile** Choose a project highly **visible** if **successful**, but play it down if not If not, then keep a **low profile**, learn lots, lick **wounds**, and **try again** Pilots can **fail** Be prepared to **learn** from **failure**

Q 15.28 Pilot should be an **independent** project, not **mission-critical**, so it can't bring down existing systems if it fails Keep it clear of **corporate politics**

Q 15.29 Planning is **critical** for the project and **conversion** plan; have **evaluation criteria** ready in advance

Q 15.30 To interface with **existing systems**, encapsulate the **legacy system** in an object-oriented "**wrapper**" which looks like a regular **object**, gets **messages**, and returns **data** and **behavior** **COBOL** code is inside, **invisible** to the client objects outside

Q 15.31 Later, redevelop the **legacy system** with OOT, with **attributes** to replace fields Write **methods** to replace the legacy COBOL code

Q 15.32 The specs are **rarely right!** Requirements **analysis** is for getting them as **close** as **possible**

Q 15.33 Quality *is* **customer satisfaction**

Q 15.34 Rather than just **meeting specifications**, the product must satisfy the **users' requirements** The specs are an **attempt** to write down requirements, not **actually** the requirements

Q 15.35 QA must work **black-box** or **input–output**, with the workings of the system **encapsulated**, and test by checking each **input** for expected **output** – that is, every **use case** works as intended

Q 15.36 **Designers** do **white-box** testing, where the workings of the system are **visible**

Q 15.37 **High** reuse means each class will be **used** and requires **retesting** every time – that is, each time we **use** it we must **further test** all its **methods**

Q 15.38 Enhanced **traceability** from analysis to **design** to Coding to Implementation means that **corrections** to **requirements** or **design** point directly to the **classes** and the **code** to be **changed**

Q 15.39 The goal of testing is to **find errors**

Chapter 16

Q 16.1 e, Q 16.2 d

Q 16.3: (a) E / I stands for Extrovert / Introvert
(b) N / S stands for Intuitive / Sensing
(c) F / T stands for Feeling / Thinking
(d) P / J stands for Perceiving / Judging

Q 16.4 (a) SJ Organized; administrator/accountant
(b) SP Live-for-the-moment
(c) NF Feeling, creative
(d) NT Scientist

Q 16.5 (a) Leadership I   (f) Mentoring I   (k) Feelings perception check I
(b)   Study skills F   (g) Arbitration I   (l) Communication I
(c) Organizing F   (h) Goal setting F   (m) Decisionmaking F
(d) Scheduling F   (i) Programming T   (n) Object modeling T
(e) Planning F   (j) Reading F   (o) Database design T

Q 16.6 a, Q 16.7 c, Q 16.8 f, Q 16.9 e, Q 16.10 e

Q 16.11 (a) Resistance to the task and to any externally suggested approaches S
(b) Satisfaction at the team's progress: P
(c) Disunity; increased tension and jealousy: S
(d) Insights into personal and group processes: P
(e) Acceptance of membership in the team: N
(f) Better understanding of each other's strengths and weaknesses: P
(g) Lofty, abstract discussions of concepts and issues: F
(h) Sense of team cohesion; common spirit and goals: N
(i) Anticipation: F
(j) Close attachment to the team: P
(k) Complaints about the organization and the task: F
(l) Questioning the wisdom of those who selected the problem and appointed the other team members: S

Q 16.12 No
Q 16.13 It's not like Q 16.12
Q 16.14 Yes

Q 16.15   You get people thinking and talking

Q 16.16   1. Too much writing
                 2. Too much marking
                 3. It takes the students too long to write their answers

Q 16.17   12 and 14 are not open-ended; 13, 15 and 16 are open-ended

Q 16.18 Process improvement skills or **functional** skills are **nontechnical** skills needed to **run** the project   They include project **management** skills; **planning**, **problem-solving**, and **decision**-making skills   They also include the skills that make each **individual** team **member** more productive, such as **reading**, time **management**, and **interpersonal** skills

Q 16.19 The larger the **group**, the more difficult it is to **get along** A larger group is **less likely** to **resolve** their differences They'll have different **personality** styles

Q 16.20 Myers and **Briggs** defined the Four **Temperaments** and further refined them into The **16 Types** They then documented the differing **needs** and **interaction** styles:
    •   **Introvert**   (I)   vs   Extrovert   (E)
    •   Intuitive   (N)   vs   **Sensing**   (S)
    •   **Feeling**   (F)   vs   **Thinking**   (T)
    •   Perceiving   (P)   vs   **Judging**   (J)

Q 16.21 ENFP attracts ISTJ **Opposites attract** and have **complementary** skills

Q 16.22 The Four Temperaments are:

    SJ   **Sensing, Judging**   (**Administrator**)
    SP   **Sensing, Perceiving**   (Live **now!**)
    NF   **Intuitive, Feeling**   (Creative, **feeling**)
    NT   **Intuitive, Thinking**   (**Scientist, logical**)

Q 16.23 SJs (typically **accountants** and **administrators**, etc) like **rules**; NFs (the **feeling**, creative group) want to **change** the **rules** NTs (**scientists**) are very thoughtful, and SPs (**live**-for-the-**moment**) want to do it **now**

Q 16.24   In a team, **differences** will exist and must be **accepted** to **progress** toward the **goals** of the group

Q 16.25   Communication is **sending** and **receiving signals**, and we must agree on the **meanings** of the **signals** Crucial for an OO project is the **definitions** for the **classes**, Step **3** of the **Seven** Steps

Q 16.26   There must be frequent **formal** and **informal** meetings Regularly scheduled **formal meetings** are essential to check where we're up to **Issues** are dealt with before they become **problems**

Q 16.27   A **leader** initiates **discussions**, and **brainstorms** to find solutions; draws information, **opinions**, ideas, suggestions, and **concerns** from members; and shares her own A leader **clarifies** ideas and **points out** issues, interpretations, and **options**; summarizes and **states conclusions** for the team to **adopt** or **reject**; checks for **consensus**; and then moves them toward **action** on the **chosen solution**

Q 16.28   With all the **differences** mentioned, someone on the team must be skilled at **arbitration**, helping people resolve **conflicts** and **disagreements**

Q 16.29   Team members are all there for the same **purpose**, committed to **helping** each other, and together they'll achieve that **goal** **Commitment** to a **common purpose** is what makes them a **team**

Q 16.30   The **best** teams spend a lot of time **identifying** and **clarifying** specific **performance goals**

Q 16.31   Mutual **Accountability** is **trust** built from the **sincere promises** that we make to the other **team members** and to **ourselves**

Q 16.32   A team always goes through **stages** as it forms (the **Stormin' Normin'** model):
    •   **Forming**
    •   **Storming**
    •   **Norming**
    •   **Performing**

Q 16.33   We need to **develop** our listening **skills** (Note: These techniques will only **work** if you **actually use** them)

Q 16.34   No one ever **teaches** us to listen! So, we often end up **answering** the **wrong question** or proposing a **solution** to the wrong **problem**

Q 16.35   **Reflecting** a question back to the **client** in **different words**, we can **clarify** understanding of the question and avoid **wasting time** and effort

Q 16.36   **Reflective** listening can be used for **conflict arbitration** The discussion continues, under your firm **guidance**, with each statement being clarified and understood by the **listener** (**server**) before she responds to it At each step, the **speaker** (client) is in charge of the **loop** and says when the listener (server) is **allowed** to **respond**

Q 16.37   Training is **critical** Team members need training in all the skills for the project It normally takes a **year** to become **proficient** in object-oriented **techniques**

Q 16.38   Especially for the **pilot** project(s) and **early production** projects, begin the change to object-oriented methods by **choosing** the right **people** You want the ones who have already **demonstrated** an ability and a **willingness** to embrace **change** and newness productively

Chapter 17

Q 17.1 b, Q 17.2 d, Q 17.3 d

Q 17.4	Attendees:	All levels
	Recording analyst:	Knowledgeable filter
	User majority:	Avoid "blinding with science"
	Distractions:	None allowed
	Background:	Do your homework
	Environment:	Your place or neutral
	Scheduling:	Sufficient time, in advance
	Confirmation:	Day before first meeting

Q 17.5 (i)   What the eventual system will do
  (ii)   What functions will be part of the system
  (iii)   Which users it will service
  (iv)   What will *not* be part of the system

Q 17.6 (a) In the context diagram, we show our system as a single box in the center of the page, and we use arrows to show data flowing into and out of it This "black-box" approach allows us to concentrate on the external relationships our system has with the world outside itself Surrounding the box, we show the external entities, and what happens inside the system will be shown with the use cases

Q 17.6 (b), (c) See glossary, Chapter 7

Q 17.7 f

Q 17.8 and 17.9 **The Seven Steps**	**Deliverables**
Step 1: Candidate classes	List of candidate classes of interest
Step 2: Define classes	List of definitions
Step 3: Establish relationships	Conceptual class model
Step 4: Expand many-to-many	Logical class modelrelationships
Step 5: Attributes	Attribute lists
Step 6: Normalization	"Normalized" class model
Step 7: Operations (behavior)	Operation lists

Q 17.10 g

Q 17.11   Question 1: Definition, "What is a ?"
      Question 2: Unique identifier, "How do we tell one of these from another?"
      Question 3: Sample attributes, "What might we need to know about one of these?"

Q 17.12 g, Q 17.13 c, Q 17.14 f, Q 17.15 f, Q 17.16 c, Q 17.17.d, Q 17.18 d

Bibliography

· ·

Adams (1989): Douglas Adams (the late). The Hitchhiker's Guide to the Galaxy, (New York, Harmony Books).

Adams (1989): W. Royce Adams. *Developing Reading Versatility*, 5th ed. (New York: Holt, Rinehart & Winston).

Anderson et al. (1989): T. Anderson, A. Berre, M. Moira, H. Porter, and B. Schneider. *The Tektronix HyperModel Benchmark Specification*. Technical Report No. 89 05, Tektronix.

Asimov (1950): Isaac Asimov. *I, Robot*. (New York: Del Rey/Ballantine Books).

Atwood (1994): Thomas Atwood. *ODMG '93 The Object DBMS Standard*. In Proceedings, Object Expo Conference 1994. (New York NY: SIGS Conferences, Inc.).

Barry (1998): Douglas Barry. *ODMG 2.0:A Standard for Object Storage*. In Component Strategies, July 1998. Available at **www.odmg.org** as a white paper.

Bertino and Martino (1993): Elisa Bertino and Lorenzo Martino. *Object-Oriented Database Systems, Concepts, and Architectures*. (Menlo Park, CA: Addison-Wesley).

Binder (1995): Robert V. Binder. Testing Objects: Myth and Reality. *Object Magazine*, May 1995.

Bishop (2001): Judy M. Bishop, *Java Gently: Programming Principles Explained.*(Reading, MA: Addison-Wesley).

Blanchard and Hersey (1982): Ken Blanchard and Paul Hersey. *Management of Organizational Behavior: Utilizing Human Resources*, 4th ed. Englewood Cliffs, NJ: Prentice Hall).

Booch (1994): Grady Booch. *Object-Oriented Analysis and Design with Applications*. (Redwood City, CA: Benjamin/Cummings).

Booch (1996): Grady Booch. *Object Solutions: Managing the Object-Oriented Project*. (Reading, MA: Addison-Wesley).

Booch et al. (1999): Grady Booch, James Rumbaugh and Ivar Jacobson. *The Unified Modeling Language User Guide*. (Reading, MA: Addison-Wesley).

Bouldin (1989): Barbara M. Bouldin. *Agents of Change, Managing the Introduction of Automated Tools*. (Englewood Cliffs, NJ: Yourdon Press/Prentice Hall).

Brockmann (1990): R. John Brockmann. *Writing Better Computer User Documentation,* version 2.0 (i.e., 2nd ed.). (New York: Wiley).

Brown (1998): David Wm Brown. *Surviving the year 2000 Computer Crash*. (Victoria, BC: Trafford Publishing and Flying Kiwi Press)

Budd (1991): Timothy Budd. *An Introduction to Object-Oriented Programming*. (Reading, MA: Addison-Wesley).

Carew et al (1990): Don Carew, Eunice Parisi-Carew, and Ken Blanchard. *Building High-Performance Teams: The Group Development and Situational Leadership II: "A Model for managing groups."* (Escondido, CA: Blanchard Training and Development training booklet) Ph (619)489-5005, Item No. HT-0002-04)

Carmichael (1994): Andy Carmichael, ed. *Object Development Methods*. (New York: Sigs Books).

Cattell et al. (2000): R.G.G. Cattell (Editor), Douglas K. Barry (Editor), Rick Catell (Editor), Mark Berler (Editor), Jeff Eastman (Editor), David Jordan, Craig Russell, Olaf Schadow, Torsten Stanienda, Fernando Velez. *The Object Data Standard: ODMG 3.0* (San Francisco, CA: Morgan Kaufmann)

Cattell et al. (1990): R. Cattell and J. Skeen. *Engineering Database Benchmark*. Technical Report, April 1990. Available from Sun Microsystems, Inc.

Chen (1976): Peter Chen. *The Entity-Relationship Model: Toward a Unified View of Data*. ACM Transactions on Database Systems, vol. 1, no. 1, March 1976.

Chen (1999): Peter P. S. Chen (Editor). *Conceptual Modeling: Current Issues and Future Directions (Lecture Notes in Computer Science, 1565)*, Symposium on Conceptual Modeling (Heidelberg: Springer Verlag)

Chen (1981): Peter Chen. *Entity-Relationship Approach to Logical Database Design*. (E-R Institute).

Coad and Yourdon (1991): Peter Coad and Edward Yourdon. *Object-Oriented Analysis*. (Englewood Cliffs, NJ: Yourdon Press/Prentice Hall).

Codd (1970): Edgar F. Codd. *A Relational Model of Data for Large Shared Databanks*. Communications of the ACM 13, no. 6, June 1970.

Cutler (1993): Wade E. Cutler. *Triple Your Reading Speed* (New York: Prentice Hall).

Daley (1994): Richard Daley. Object-Development Environments. In *Object Development Methods*, ed. Andy Carmichael (see above). (New York: Sigs Books).

Davidson and Rees-Mogg (1993): James Dale Davidson and Lord William Rees-Mogg. *The Great Reckoning*. (New York: Simon and Schuster).

DeMarco (1978): Tom DeMarco. *Structured Analysis and System Specification*. (Englewood Cliffs, NJ: Prentice Hall).

Douglass (1999a): Bruce Powel Douglass. *Doing Hard Time: Developing Real-Time Systems with UML, Objects, Frameworks and Patterns*.(Reading, MA: Addison-Wesley).

Douglass (1999b): Bruce Powel Douglass. *Real-Time UML: Developing Efficient Objects for Embedded Systems*. (The Addison-Wesley Object Technology Series) 2nd ed. (Reading, MA: Addison-Wesley).

Eckel(2000): Bruce Eckel. *Thinking in Java*, (Englewood Cliffs, NJ: Prentice Hall).

Fenker (1984): Richard Fenker. Stop *Studying and Start Learning, or How to Jump-Start Your Brain*. (Fort Worth, TX: Tangram Press).

Firesmith (1993): Donald G. Firesmith. *Object-Oriented Requirements Analysis and Logical Design*. (New York: Wiley).

Fites et al. (1993): Philip Fites, Peter Johnston, and Martin Kratz. *The Computer Virus Crisis*, 2nd ed. (New York: Van Nostrand Reinhold).

Fites (1999): Philip Fites. *Computer Virus*. (DIANE Publishing Co)

Gage (1983): Walter S. Avis, Patrick D. Drysdale, Robert J. Gregg, Victoria E. Neufeldt, and Matthew H. Scargill. *Gage Canadian Dictionary*. (Toronto, ON: Gage Educational Publishing).

Gall (1988): John Gall. *SYSTEMANTICS: The Underground Text of Systems Lore; How Systems Really Work and How They Fail*. (Ann Arbor, MI: General Systemantics Press).

Gane and Sarson (1978): Chris Gane and Trish Sarson. *Structured Systems Analysis: Tools and Techniques*. (Englewood Cliffs, NJ: Prentice Hall).

Harel (1987): David Harel. *Statecharts: A Visual Formalism for Complex Systems*. In Science of Computer Programming, vol. 8.

Humphrey (1989): W. Humphrey. *Managing the Software Development Process*. (Reading, MA: Addison-Wesley).

Jacobson et al. (1992): Ivar Jacobson, Patrik Jonsson, and Gunnar Övergaard. *Object-Oriented Software Engineering, A Use Case Driven Approach*. (Reading, MA: ACM Press/Addison-Wesley).

Jacobson et al. (1999): Ivar Jacobson, Grady Booch and James Rumbaugh. *The Unified Software Development Process*.(Reading, MA: Addison-Wesley).

Katzenbach and Smith (1993): Jon Katzenbach and Douglas Smith. *The Wisdom of Teams*. (Boston: HBS Press).

Keirsey and Bates (1978): David Keirsey and Marilyn Bates. *Please Understand Me, Character and Temperament Types*. (Del Mar, CA: Prometheus Nemesis Book Company/Gnosology Books Ltd, 1984 edition).

Kim (1994): Won Kim. The SQL Legacy. In *Object Magazine*, vol. 4, no. 5, September 1994.

Koontz (1994): Richard W. Koontz. *Lessons from the Experts*, A review of the August 1994 Conference on Object-Oriented Software Development at St Thomas University, St Paul, MN. In Object Magazine, vol. 4, no. 7, November December 1994.

Kriegel and Kriegel (1984): Robert Kriegel and Marilyn Harris Kriegel. *The C Zone, Peak Performance Under Pressure*. (New York: Fawcett Columbine).

LaLonde (1994): Wilf LaLonde. *Discovering Smalltalk*. (Menlo Park, CA: Benjamin/ Cummings).

LaLonde and Pugh (1990): Wilf R. LaLonde and John R. Pugh. *Inside Smalltalk*. (Englewood Cliffs, NJ: Prentice Hall).

Lazarus (1977, 1984): Arnold Lazarus. *In the Mind's Eye; The Power of Imagery for Personal Enrichment*. (New York: Guilford Press).

Lenzi (1994): Marie Lenzi. *Getting the Requirements Right, A Use Case Approach*. In Proceedings, Object Expo 1994 (New York: SIGS Publications).

Lessinger (1991): Jack Lessinger. *Penturbia*. (Seattle, WA: SocioEconomics).

Lilly (1995): Susan Lilly. *The Top Ten Ways to Trash Your OT Training Program*. In Object Magazine, vol. 5, no. 1, March April 1995.

Lorayne (1984): Harry Lorayne. *Page-a-Minute Memory Book*. (New York: Ballantine Books.)

Lorayne (1988): Harry Lorayne. *Memory Makes Money*, (Boston, MA: Little, Brown).

Lorayne and Lucas (1974): Harry Lorayne and Jerry Lucas. *The Memory Book*. (New York: Ballantine Books).

Love (1993): Tom Love. *Object Lessons*. (New York: SIGS Books).

Martin (1977): James Martin. *Computer Data Base Organization*. (Englewood Cliffs, NJ: Prentice Hall).

Martin (1982): James Martin. *Strategic Data Planning Methodologies*. (Englewood Cliffs, NJ: Prentice Hall).

Martin and Finkelstein (1981): James Martin and Clive Finkelstein. *Information Engineering*, 2 vols. (New York: Savant Institute).

Meyer (1988): Bertrand Meyer. *Object-Oriented Software Construction*. (New York: Prentice Hall).

Meyer (1992): Bertrand Meyer. *Eiffel, The Language*. (New York: Prentice Hall).

Miller (1956) George A. Miller. The Magical Number Seven, Plus or Minus Two: Some Limits on Our Capacity for Processing Information. In *Psychological Review*, March 1963.

Miller (1975) George A. Miller. *The Magic Number Seven After Fifteen Years*, In *Studies in Long Term Memory*, ed. A. Kennedy. (New York: Wiley).

Millman (1979): Dan Millman. *The Warrior Athlete*. (Walpole, NH: Stillpoint Publishing).

Modell (1992): Martin E. Modell. *Data Analysis, Data Modeling, and Classification*. (New York: McGraw-Hill).

Moore (1956): E. F. Moore. *Gedanken-Experiments on Sequential Machines*. In Automata Studies. (Princeton, NJ: Princeton University Press).

Myers and Briggs (1962):

Orfali et al. (1994) Robert Orfali, Dan Harkey, and Jeri Edwards. *Essential Client/ Server Survival Guide*. (New York: Wiley).

Oxford (1998): Judy Pearsall (editor) and Patrick Hanks (editor).*The New Oxford Dictionary of English*. (Oxford UK: Oxford University Press).

Oxford (1979): J. Coulson, C. T. Carr, Lucy Hutchinson and Dorothy Eagle. *The Oxford Illustrated Dictionary*. (Oxford, UK: Dorset Press/Marboro Books Corp., by arrangement with Oxford University Press and Clarendon Press).

Peters and Waterman (1982): Thomas J. Peters and Robert H. Waterman. *In Search of Excellence*. (New York: Warner Books, (by arrangement with Harper & Row).

Pirsig (1975): Robert M. Pirsig. Zen and the Art of Motorcycle Maintenance. (New York: Random House/Bantam/Dell)

Pohl (1993): Ira Pohl. *Object-Oriented Programming Using C++*. (Redwood City, CA: Benjamin/ Cummings).

Random House Webster (1998):*Unabridged Dictionary*, (New York NY: Random House).

Reich (1991): Robert Reich. *The Work of Nations*. (New York: Vintage Books/ Random House).

Riehle (1995): Richard Riehle. *Ada 95, the New Object-Oriented Standard*. In Object Magazine, vol. 5, no. 2, May 1995.

Rotzell and Loomis (1994): Katy Rotzell and Mary Loomis. *Benchmarking an ODBMS*. In *Focus on ODBMS*, selected articles from Journal of Object-Oriented Programming. (New York: SIGS Publications).

Rumbaugh (1994): James Rumbaugh. *Object-Oriented Modeling and Design*. In Proceedings, Object Expo 1994. (New York: SIGS Publications).

Rumbaugh et al. (1991): James Rumbaugh, Michael Blaha, William Premerlani, Frederick Eddy, and William Lorenson. *Object-Oriented Modeling and Design*. (Englewood Cliffs, NJ: Prentice Hall).

Sanders (1995): G. Lawrence Sanders. *Data Modeling*. (Danvers, MA: Boyd & Fraser).

Scharenberg and Dunsmore (1991): M. E. Scharenberg and H. E. Dunsmore. *Evolution of Classes and Objects During Object-Oriented Design and Programming*. In Journal of Object-Oriented Programming, January 1991, pg 3. Quoted in Jacobson et al. (1992).

Schildt (1994): Herbert Schildt. *C++ from the Ground Up*. (Berkeley, CA: Osborne McGraw-Hill).

Scholtes (1988): Peter Scholtes. *The Team Handbook*. (Madison WI: Joiner and Associates).

Shepherd (1990): John C. Shepherd. *Database Management: Theory and Application*. (Boston, MA: Irwin).

Shlaer and Mellor (1988): Sally Shlaer and Stephen J. Mellor. *Object-Oriented Systems Analysis, Modeling the World in Data*. (Englewood Cliffs, NJ: Yourdon Press/Prentice Hall).

Shlaer and Mellor (1992): Sally Shlaer and Stephen J. Mellor. *Object Lifecycles, Modeling the World in States*. (Englewood Cliffs, NJ: Yourdon Press/Prentice Hall).

Sutherland (1995): Jeff Sutherland. Smalltalk, C++ and OO COBOL: The Good, the Bad, and the Ugly. In *Object Magazine*, vol. 5, no. 2, May 1995.

Swan (1998): Tom Swan. *Tom Swan's Mastering Borland C++ 5*, (Indianapolis, IN: SAMS/Macmillan).

Taylor (1997): David A. Taylor. *Object-Oriented Technology, A Manager's Guide*. (Reading, MA: Addison-Wesley).

Taylor (1995): David A. Taylor. *Business Engineering with Object Technology*. (New York: Wiley).

Taylor (1992): David A. Taylor. *Object-Oriented Information Systems, Planning and Implementation*. (New York: Wiley).

Taylor (1995): David A. Taylor. Missing the Message. In *Object Magazine*, vol. 5, no. 2, May 1995.

Voss (1991): Greg Voss. *Object-Oriented Programming, An Introduction*. (Berkeley, CA: Osborne McGraw-Hill).

Wang and Wang (1994): Barbara Lin Wang and Jin Wang. Is a Deep Hierarchy Considered Harmful? In *Object Magazine*, vol. 4, no. 7, November December 1994.

Weber (1982): Richard C. Weber. The Group: A Cycle from Birth to Death. In *Reading Book for Human Relations,* ed. Lawrence C. Porter and Bernard Mohr. (Alexandria, VA: NTL Institute).

Webster (1975): *Webster's New Collegiate Dictionary*. (Springfield, MA: G & C Merriam Company). [See also *Random House Webster* (1998.)]

Whitten et al. (1989): Jeffrey L. Whitten, Lonnie D. Bentley, and Victor M. Barlow. *Systems Analysis and Design Methods*, 2nd ed. (Boston: Irwin).

Whitten et al. (1994): Jeffrey L. Whitten, Lonnie D. Bentley, and Victor M. Barlow. *Systems Analysis and Design Methods*, 3rd ed. Boston: Irwin).

Whitten et al. (2000): Jeffrey L. Whitten, Lonnie D. Bentley, and Kevin C. Dittman. *Systems Analysis and Design Methods*, 5th ed. Berkeley, CA: McGraw Hill).

Wiener (1995): Richard Wiener. *Software Development Using Eiffel*. (Englewood Cliffs, NJ: Prentice Hall).

Wirfs-Brock et al. (1990): Rebecca Wirfs-Brock, Brian Wilkerson, and Lauren Wiener. *Designing Object-Oriented Software*. (Englewood Cliffs, NJ: Prentice Hall).

Yourdon and Constantine (1976): Edward Yourdon and Larry Constantine. *Structured Design*. (Englewood Cliffs, NJ: Prentice-Hall).